Wanderlust

Hiking on Legendary Trails

gestalten

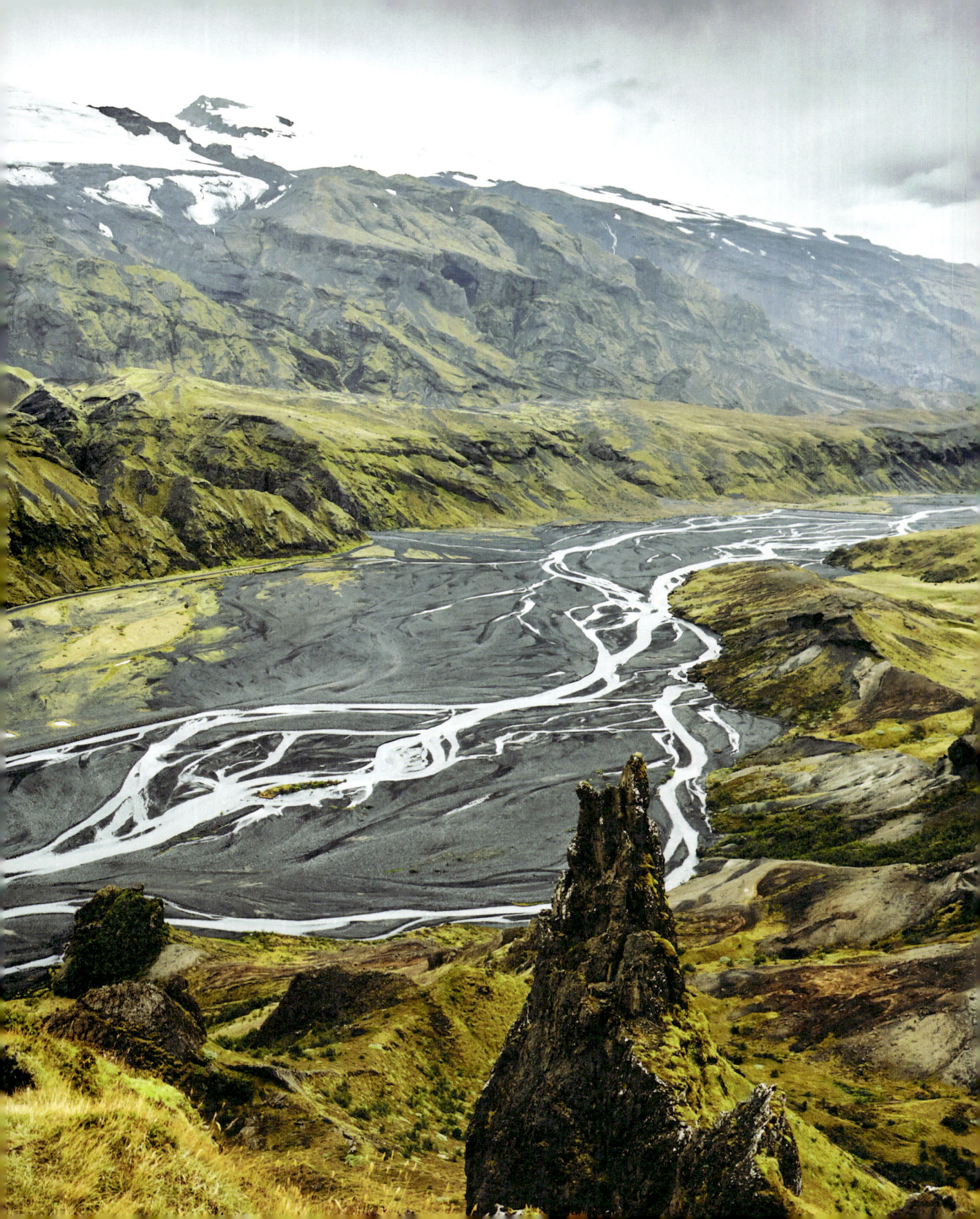

FOREWORD

"The earth is many planets," John Updike once wrote, "that intersect only at moments." I recalled this line the first time I wandered through the pages of the remarkable book you hold in your hands. Because if we could walk this planet's full breadth, we would immediately be struck by how drastically one part differs from the next, each made up of unique ecosystems, topographies, cultures, and histories. This is in large part a function of life itself, with its endless evolutionary lust for experimentation and diversification. Compared to a still-born planet like Mars, where red deserts stretch from pole to pole, the variation we find on earth is one of pure fantasia, from the xeric expanses of Jordan's Wadi Rum to the floral riot of Hawaii's Na Pali Coast. On certain mountains you can even experience this diversity all in one place. Climbing from the humid jungles at the base of Mount Kilimanjaro to its famously (albeit vanishingly) snowy crest, you pass through at least five distinct ecosystems—walking, as it were, from the equator to the poles.

Stitching this many-faced planet together are myriad paths that guide us across landscapes and across continents, rendering them cohesive and comprehensible. The editors of this volume have selected a vast array of different trails to match the dazzling range of landscapes and cultures they traverse. Flipping from one page to the next, the reader is reminded of the true capaciousness of the word "path." You find modern hiking paths, of course, but also an ancient indigenous trade route; a goat trail; a mule path; a camel path; a frozen river (in Ladakh); an unfrozen river (in Utah); *via ferratas*, or "iron roads," made up of metal rungs bolted into cliffsides; pilgrimage routes dedicated to a Nordic saint, a Hebrew prophet, and a Tibetan Buddha; and, in the Canadian Rockies, a nascent but sprawling hiking path made up of dirt roads, old trails, and, at times, nothing at all. These paths span from the wettest to the driest locales on earth, from sub-sea-level salt pans to high Himalayan peaks, from wild forests to bustling villages and ghost towns. Gathered together, these trails testify to our species's deep need to explore, and to the paths' elegant capacity to preserve and communicate our explorations.

I have been lucky enough to hike on or near a good number of the trails featured here—in Canada, New Zealand, Tanzania, Australia, Iceland, Morocco, Peru, and along the entirety of the Appalachian Trail—and I can vouch that they are all as awe-inducing as they appear in these pages. But this book is not meant to be used as a practical hiking guide. (For one thing, it is much too bulky to take along in your backpack.) Instead, I prefer to think of it as a compendium of dream walks, some to be walked in our waking lives, and others to be walked only in the imagination. For me, the true beauty of trails is that they do not only exist in the world's most spectacularly scenic places, the places fit for large-format glossy books of photography; they exist everywhere. So even if you cannot afford to travel to Mount Sinai or the tip of the Troll's Tongue, I hope these pages inspire you to find a trail closer to home. Because, when seen in the right way, every trail is grand, beautiful, and even exotic in its own regard, even the squiggly little footpath leading through that patch of woods behind your house, or that gravel bike path cutting through the park at the end of your subway line. There are many different planets to explore right here on earth, and often they are closer than we think. May this book help you go out and find them. ⸻

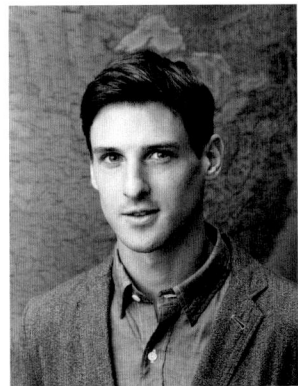

ROBERT MOOR

Robert Moor is the award-winning author of *On Trails: An Exploration*. The recipient of the Middlebury Fellowship in Environmental Journalism has written for numerous publications, including *The New York Times*, *New York Magazine*, *Harper's*, and *GQ*.

ON TRAIL MAGIC, THRU-HIKERS AND ALPENGLOW

The Allure of Hiking

In a world where discontinuity prevails, the experience of walking a trail offers a sense of orientation. To follow a trail makes things simpler—it reduces the contingency of the world surrounding us to the task of navigating a path. There is a clear start as much as there is a clear goal to head towards. In a world full of uncertainties, this sort of predetermined trajectory provides one with a soothing sense of linearity. Then there is the existential aspect inherent to walking. Lost in between perplexing flight schedules and tiring traffic jams, the technological effort we have put into making distances shrink becomes, at times, more of a burden than a feeling of progress. What can be more liberating and empowering in those moments than to simply walk? The pace of walking mysteriously resonates in our brains. Taking step after step curbs the trains of thought in our heads and calms down our restless stream of consciousness. While our transportation system has reached a degree of complexity where the individual traveler is highly dependent on processes they neither understand nor act upon, walking remains one of a few means of movement where one feels empowered, because every decision—and literally every step—taken has a direct impact on the further course of one's own journey.

Hiking has not always been in vogue. Before the age of romanticism, it hardly appealed to anyone of a certain standing to venture out into the wild or to walk for the sake of walking. Those who did so were considered to be vagabonds and lost souls, and it was not until industrialization had transformed big parts of the Western world that perspectives concerning this began to change. The so-called wilderness that was meant to be conquered suddenly became a source of inspiration for painters (Malerweg, p. 8), and society slowly started to perceive it as something that would need to be protected rather than tamed. The conservation movement that originated in Europe in the seventeenth century and gained momentum in the United States in the nineteenth century resulted from precisely this paradigm shift. Fierce political debates—led by Theodore Roosevelt—and philosophical elaborations (as in Henry David Thoreau's *Walden*) stood at the beginning of a fundamental shift that would later serve as a precondition for the emergence of recreational hiking trails. The creation of the Appalachian Trail (p. 244)—the longest hiking-only path in the world—has its roots

in these endeavors to preserve nature, and one of the world's most scenic and renowned trails was named in honor of the Scottish naturalist and preservationist John Muir (p. 180).

Trails and Their Evolution

Although the word "trail" suggests some sort of continuity or stability, the nature of most trails is anything but static. There exist various reasons as to why a trail was created in the first place. Yet, shaped by forces of nature or culture, a trail's original use is often transformed over time. As the decades and centuries pass by, its course as much as its purpose are altered, and sometimes its origins persist only in the narratives that are passed down from generation to generation. This was exactly what happened to the most prominent trade route of the old world: with its origins in pre-historic times, the Silk Road was a network of trade routes that spanned Asia, running from China to Europe. Besides the precious fabric that lent the route its name, paper, gunpowder, and spices were traded between Rome and Constantinople, Damascus and Samarkand. Subsisting throughout the golden ages of several great empires, and fostering the exchange of art, religion, and technology between the different cultures, the route was ultimately silenced once the Ottomans had conquered the Byzantine Empire in the fifteenth century. Nowadays, the former route network has been rendered unrecognizable, as some of the sections have been transformed into modern highways and others have perished in the aftermath of natural disasters or war. Yet, a railroad linking China, Kazakhstan, Mongolia, and Russia is often referred to as the New Silk Road, and plans have been ushered in to expand this connection in order to reestablish the ancient link between Asia and Europe.

While the Silk Road might be emblematic of the various reincarnations a trail can live through, other examples that have gone through puzzling transformations are abundant. Former strategic paths from times of conflict have been turned into scenic hiking destinations (Alta Via 1, p. 16); narrow roads serving as the only connection between a far-flung village and the rest of civilization have been bridged by modern highways; coastal paths that were created to spot smugglers now invite strolls along the seashore (South West Coast Path, p. 24); high-altitude passes that were once the preferred routes for transporting goods are today sought-after holiday locations. The imprint contemporary tourism has had on the evolution of these centuries-old connections is undeniable, and often there is a certain irony to it: some routes that were once established out of necessity or for trade have now become desirable destinations for adventurers from across the globe (Chadar Trek, p. 102). Other routes known as paths for pilgrimages are now major tourist attractions. Most trails now frequented by sightseers very often have roots that stretch back to commercial or religious uses.

Yet, as much as there are different types of trails, there are also different types of hikers, each with their own set of reasons as to why they decide to venture out. Some of them want to escape the concrete walls they find themselves surrounded by in their cities; others strive to break down the walls in their heads. For the former group, it is mostly sufficient to embark on a micro-adventure that will take them to a near or far corner of the world that will allow for a change of scenery. For the latter, it is more of an existential question, and goes beyond outdoor exploration and enjoyment. These individuals seek various ways to reconnect with themselves, and hope to be able to do so through reestablishing the connection with the environment surrounding them—and what better way to do so than to absorb it through walking?

A Thru-hiker's Fate

It is for a reason that traditional pilgrimage paths such as the Camino de Santiago have gained popularity among urban dwellers who, prior to embarking on the trail, had not shown much of an interest in religion. Having run up against frontiers of different kinds in their lives, they decide to leave everything behind for weeks, months, or sometimes even years to follow a path and to rewire their thinking while walking. Yet, it is less out of a desire to run away or to erase what is left behind and more in the hope of gaining a new perspective on life. The paths they decide to follow are not necessarily pilgrimage routes. Long-distance walking seems to be therapeutic and enlightening in itself, and thus, following the footsteps of St. Olav Ways (p. 58) or spending months on the Appalachian or the Pacific Crest Trail can have a similar effect on one's psyche. While shorter treks often promise enchanting scenery and rewards after each challenging section, long-distance hikes are tests of endurance. The so-called thru-hikers who attempt to follow colossal trails spanning several thousands of miles stand apart from regular hikers and could be seen as modern-day pilgrims. For them, the spiritual value of a trail does not depend on the trail's sacred destination, but consists in the experience of walking itself. Ready to give up the comforts of modern life, they are willing to spend days without proper food or steady shelter; exposed to the forces of nature at all times and forced to overcome their physical limits day after day, they could easily be called fatalists. Yet, their strong sense of determination and the willingness to overcome any hurdle—be it of a physical or psychological, or an external or internal nature—reveal the more noble drives behind their trips. Many of them report that the hardest part of their journeys began once they had returned from the trail to their regular lives. The shift in perspectives comes at a price, and the revaluation of all one's prior values is a drastic yet liberating process. The lessons learned on the trail unfold their full potential only once we find ourselves going back to normal.

Whether through long-distance wandering or micro-adventures, experiencing the allure of hiking does not have to mean trekking for thousands of miles. However, once you are hooked, there is no guarantee that you won't be willing to go further and further. ——————

WRITER'S NOTE

Over the past quarter of a century, my hiking journeys have taken me from Tibet to Tasmania and from the Alps to the Appalachians. Of the many lessons I have learnt during my time out in the wilderness, one of the biggest has been that when it comes to experiencing the wonders of terra firma—I mean really experiencing them from the inside out, rather than from the outside in—there is simply no better way to do so than on foot, with everything you need in the world on your back.

Whether it be through far-flung deserts, luxuriant forests or majestic alpine terrain, when we choose to walk rather than fly or drive, something wonderful happens: our awareness and appreciation of the natural world begins to grow. It can be the faint sound of a gently meandering stream, the distinct smell of decaying leaves on a crisp autumn morning, or even a bowl of cereal that never tasted better than when eaten on a mountaintop at sunrise. By immersing our senses in nature, our smiles grow wider and our thoughts become clearer—regenerative benefits that have long been recognized by many peoples and cultures around the world, including the Japanese, who advocate *shinrin-yoku* (forest bathing) for its physical, mental, and emotional benefits.

Whatever your hiking dreams and goals may be, my hope is that this book will help supply the inspiration and information necessary for you to plan and realize your journeys. Happy trekking, and I look forward to meeting at least a few of you out on the trail! ——————

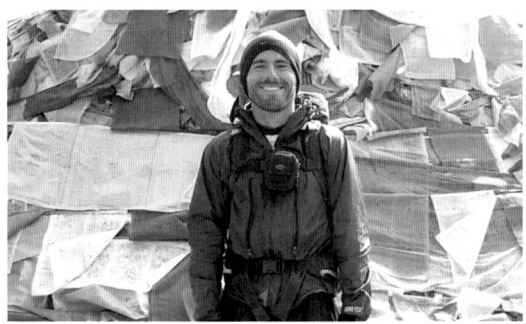

CAM HONAN
Described by Backpacker Magazine as the "most travelled hiker on earth", over the last quarter of a century Cam Honan has trekked more than 90,000 km (55,000 mi.). He has hiked in over 50 countries across six continents, and documents his travels on his blog, The Hiking Life.

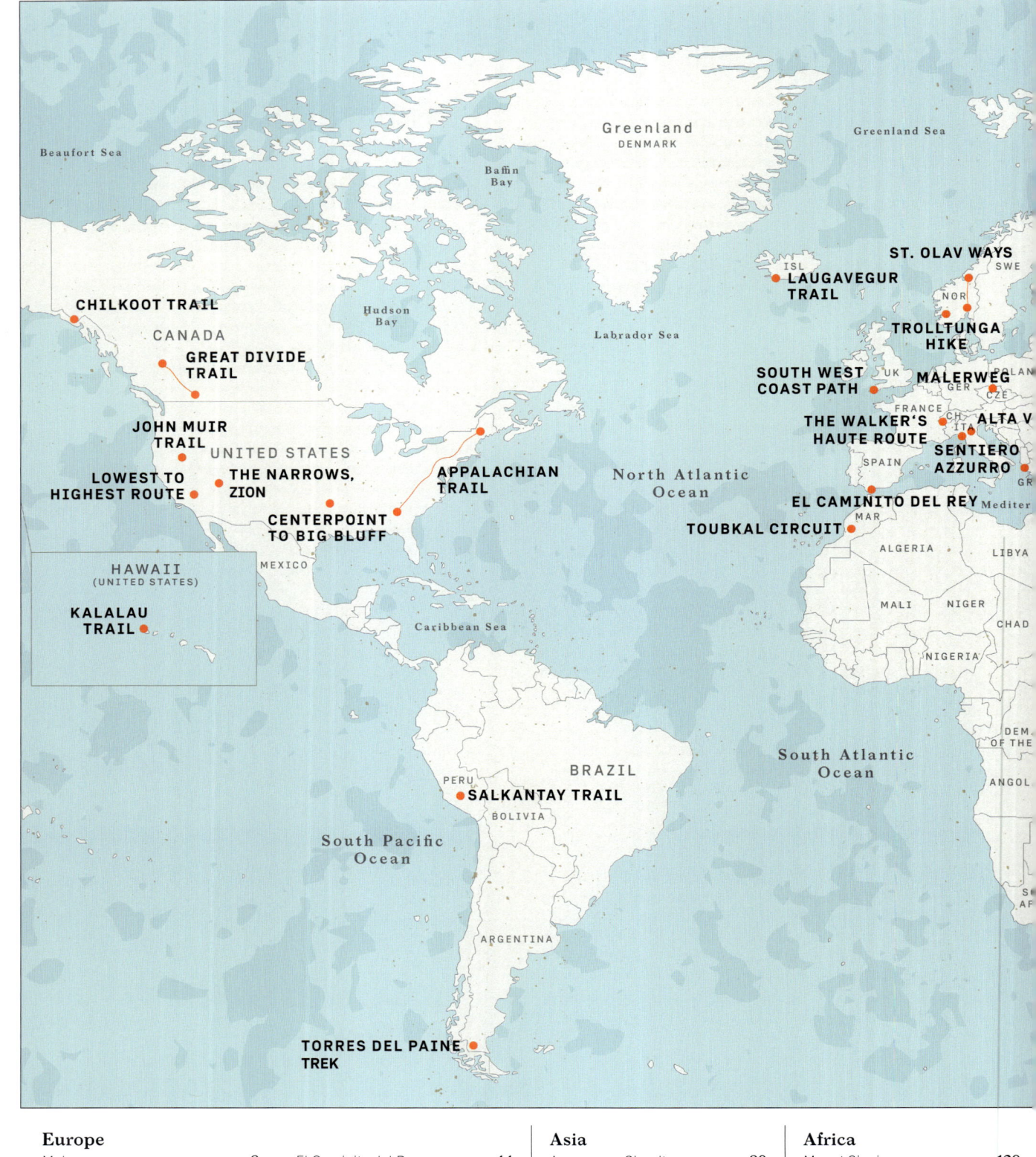

Beaufort Sea

Greenland
DENMARK

Greenland Sea

Baffin
Bay

ST. OLAV WAYS

ISL

SWE

CHILKOOT TRAIL

Hudson
Bay

Labrador Sea

**LAUGAVEGUR
TRAIL**

NOR

CANADA

**GREAT DIVIDE
TRAIL**

**TROLLTUNGA
HIKE**

**SOUTH WEST
COAST PATH**

UK

MALERWEG

POLAN

**JOHN MUIR
TRAIL**

UNITED STATES

North Atlantic
Ocean

FRANCE

GER

CZE

**THE WALKER'S
HAUTE ROUTE**

CH

ITA

ALTA V

**LOWEST TO
HIGHEST ROUTE**

**THE NARROWS,
ZION**

**APPALACHIAN
TRAIL**

SPAIN

**SENTIERO
AZZURRO**

GR

**CENTERPOINT
TO BIG BLUFF**

EL CAMINITO DEL REY

Mediter

MEXICO

TOUBKAL CIRCUIT

MAR

ALGERIA

LIBYA

HAWAII
(UNITED STATES)

Caribbean Sea

MALI

NIGER

CHAD

**KALALAU
TRAIL**

NIGERIA

BRAZIL

South Atlantic
Ocean

DEM.
OF THE

PERU

SALKANTAY TRAIL

ANGOL

BOLIVIA

South Pacific
Ocean

S

AF

ARGENTINA

**TORRES DEL PAINE
TREK**

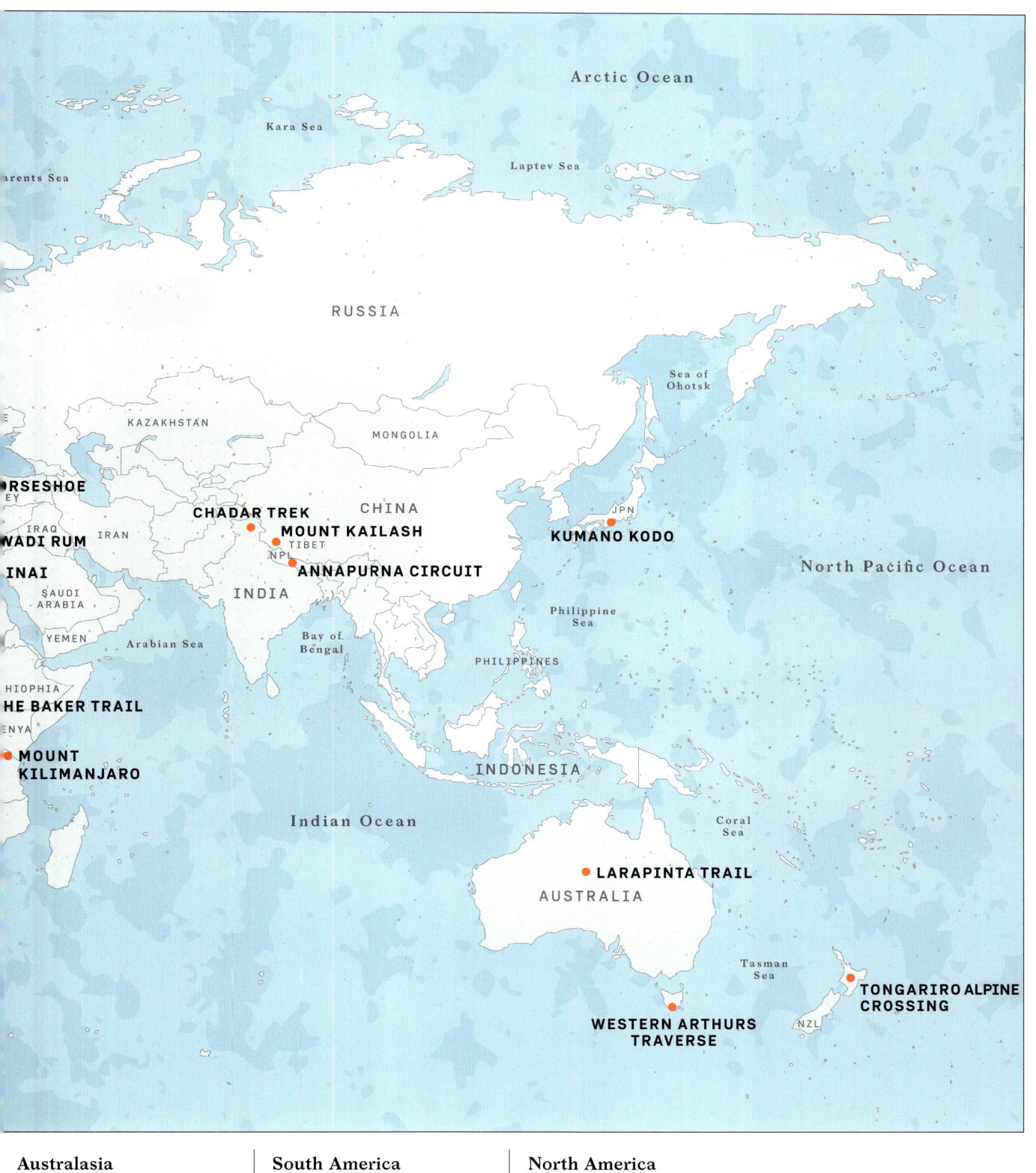

Arctic Ocean

Kara Sea

Laptev Sea

arents Sea

RUSSIA

Sea of
Ohotsk

KAZAKHSTAN

MONGOLIA

JPN

RSESHOE
EY

CHADAR TREK

CHINA

KUMANO KODO

North Pacific Ocean

IRAQ
WADI RUM

IRAN

MOUNT KAILASH

TIBET

INAI

NPL

ANNAPURNA CIRCUIT

ŞAUDI
ARABIA

INDIA

YEMEN

Arabian Sea

Bay of.
Bengal

Philippine
Sea

HIOPHIA

Bay of.
Bengal

PHILIPPINES

HE BAKER TRAIL

ENYA

MOUNT
KILIMANJARO

Indian Ocean

INDONESIA

Coral
Sea

LARAPINTA TRAIL

AUSTRALIA

Tasman
Sea

TONGARIRO ALPINE
CROSSING

WESTERN ARTHURS
TRAVERSE

NZL

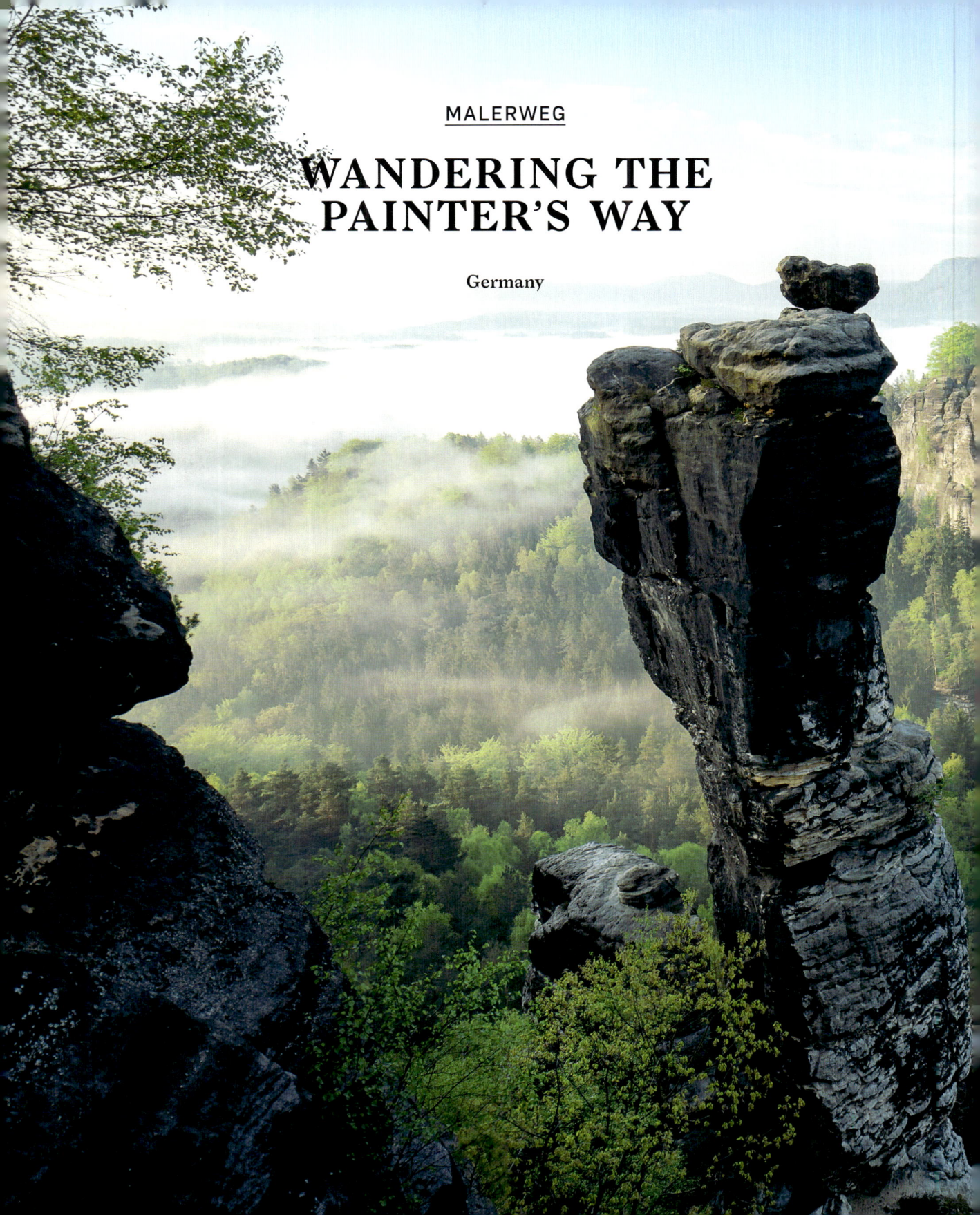

MALERWEG

WANDERING THE PAINTER'S WAY

Germany

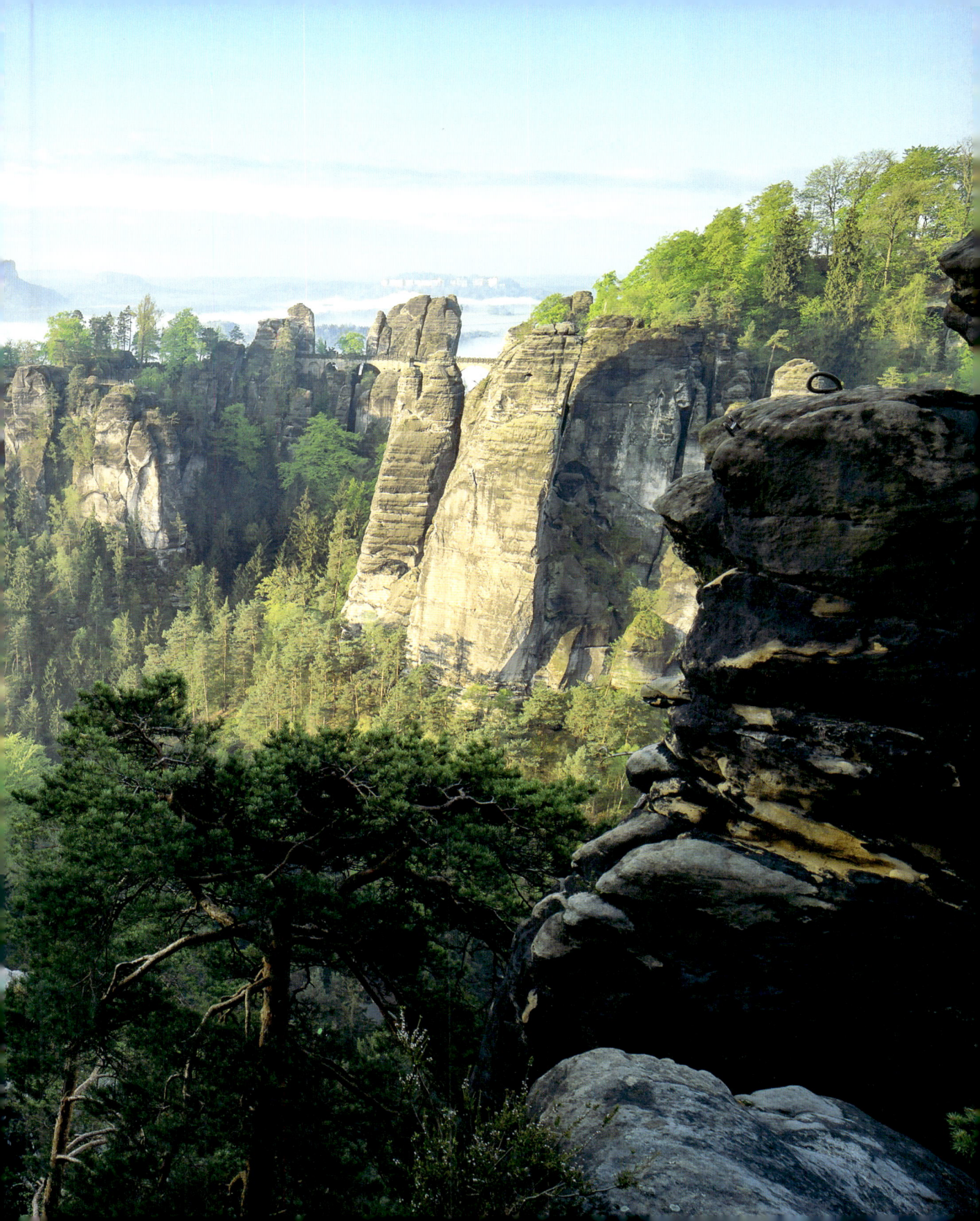

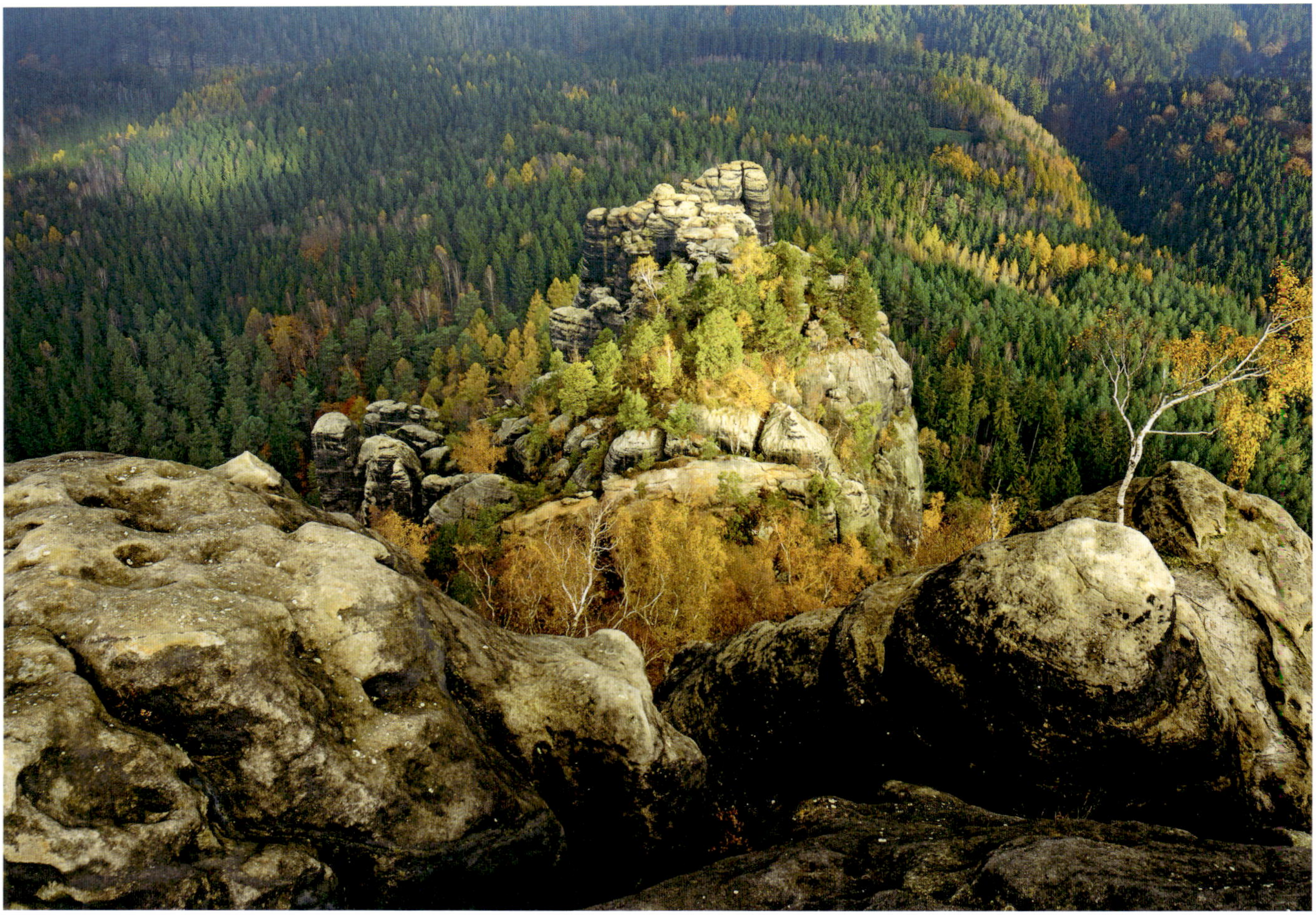

↑ Fall colors on top of the sandstone mountains.
↗ The Bastei Bridge traverses rounded peaks.
↘ Steep pathways lead hikers up the peaks.

The rocky landscapes, which have, over millennia, been chiseled into other-worldly forms by the elements, boast a memorable collection of dramatic spires, grand mesas, and precipitous cliffs.

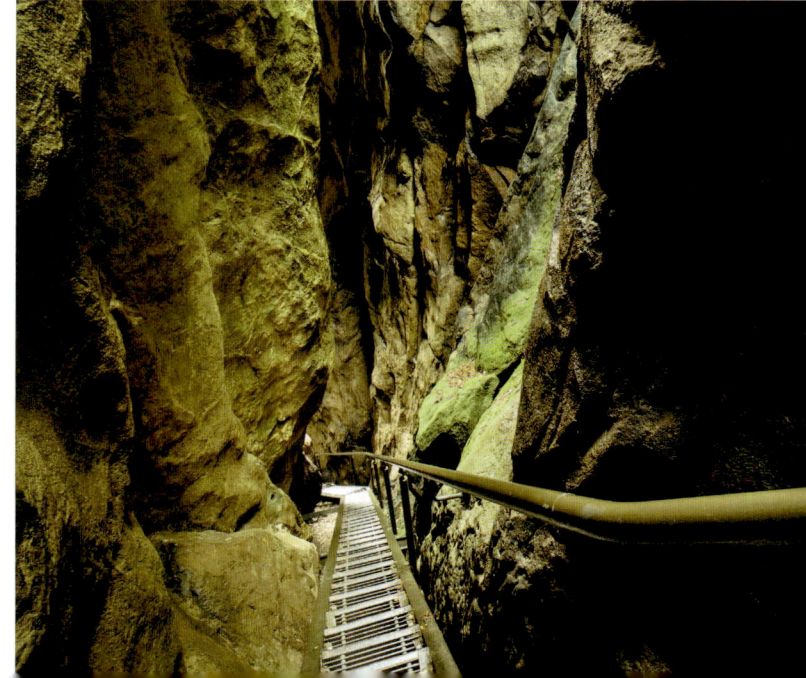

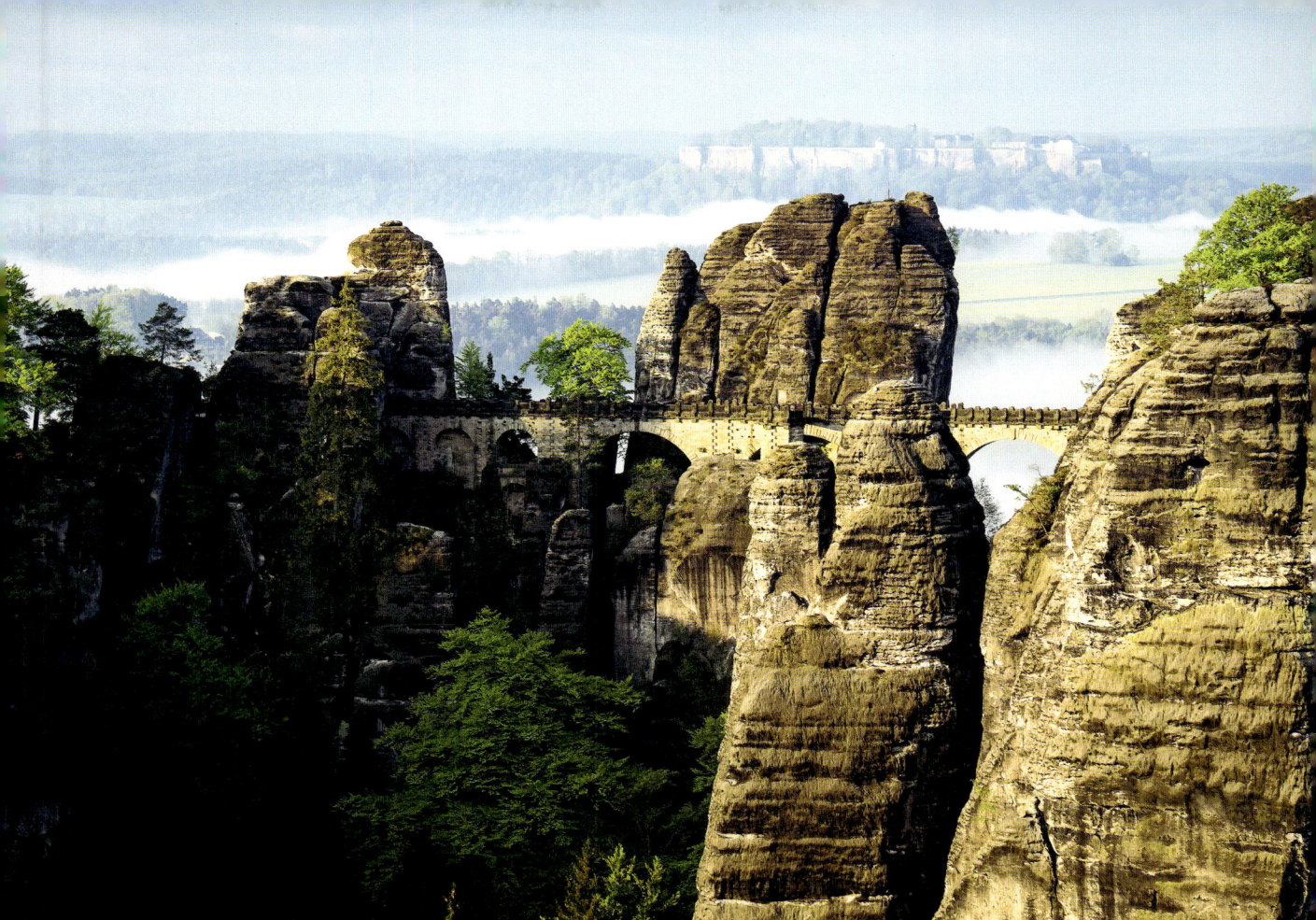

The Malerweg (in English the "Painter's Way") is a 112 km (70 mi.) pathway situated in Saxon Switzerland. Often referred to as Germany's most beautiful hiking trail, it follows a sinuous route through surreal sandstone rock formations along either side of the Elbe River. Peaks and valleys, caves and ravines, and all manner of dreamlike forms come together here to make up a bizarre landscape.

Established in 2006, the Malerweg is a modern-day incarnation of a trail made famous by Romantic-era artists. From the eighteenth century onwards. painters including Johann Alexander Thiele and Caspar David Friedrich began to be drawn to the region's picturesque landscapes and rugged beauty. Their sojourns inspired many memorable works, most notably Friedrich's masterpiece, *Wanderer above the Sea of Fog* (c. 1818). Saxon Switzerland, the area's name, is thought to have originated from Swiss painters Adrian Zingg and Anton Graff, who were part of the Dresden Art Academy and visited the nearby region.

Today the Malerweg continues to attract both artists and hikers alike, and places captured by the artists are signposted on the route. Consisting of eight stages ranging between 11 and 17 km (6.8 and 10.5 mi.) in length, the almost circular route is well marked and easy to follow throughout its course. Nonetheless, it contains a number of steep, challenging sections, some of which involve stairs and ladders. A reasonable level of fitness is recommended, but thanks to the relatively short distance and accessibility of each of the stages, this is a trail that is open to hikers of all levels of fitness and experience.

From a scenery perspective, the Malerweg is a nature lover's delight. The rocky landscapes, which have, over millennia, been chiseled into otherworldly forms by the elements, boast a memorable collection of dramatic spires, grand mesas, and precipitous cliffs. Originally an inland sea 90 million years ago →

ABOUT THE TRAIL

→ DISTANCE 112 km (70 mi.)
→ DURATION 8 days
→ LEVEL Easy

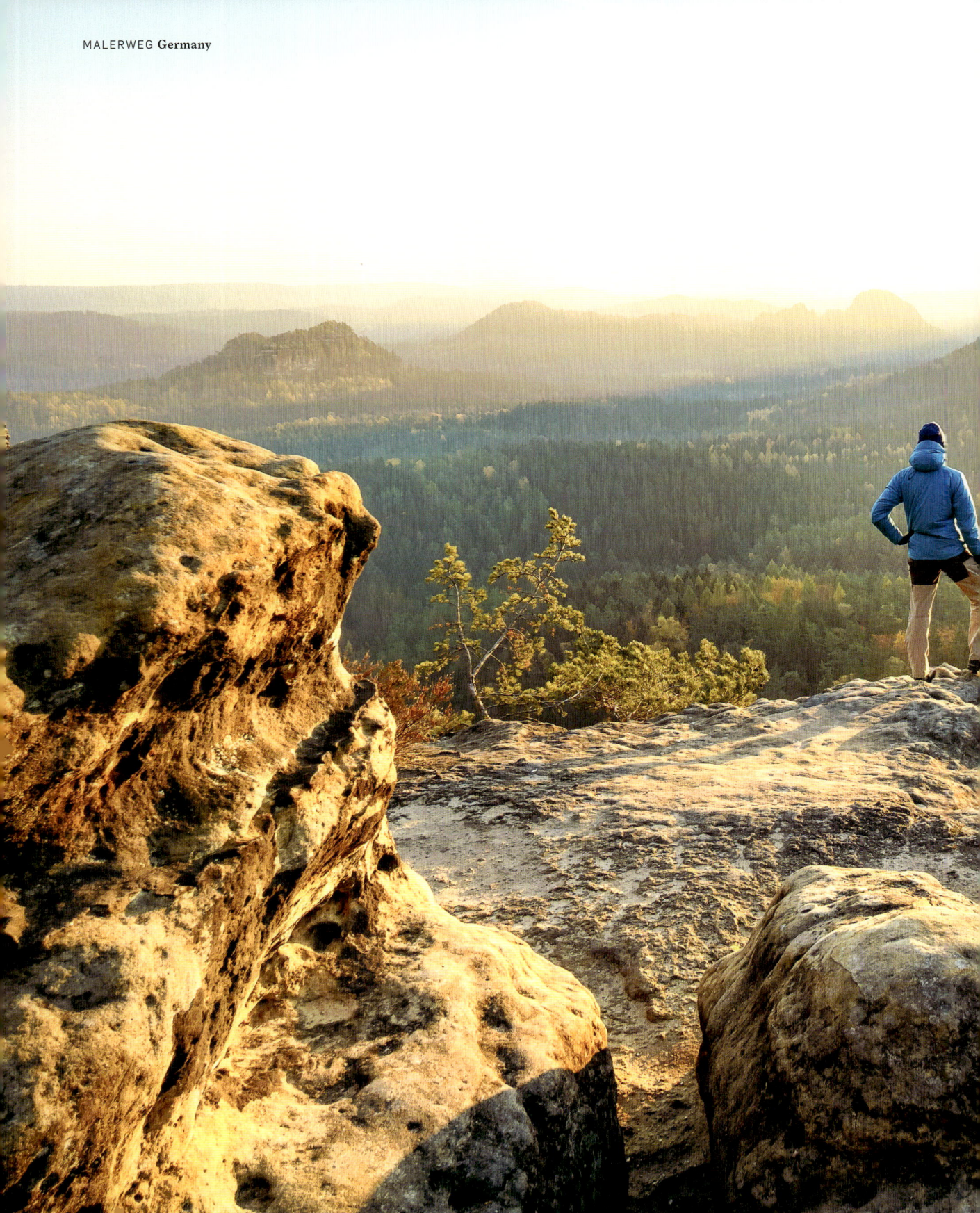

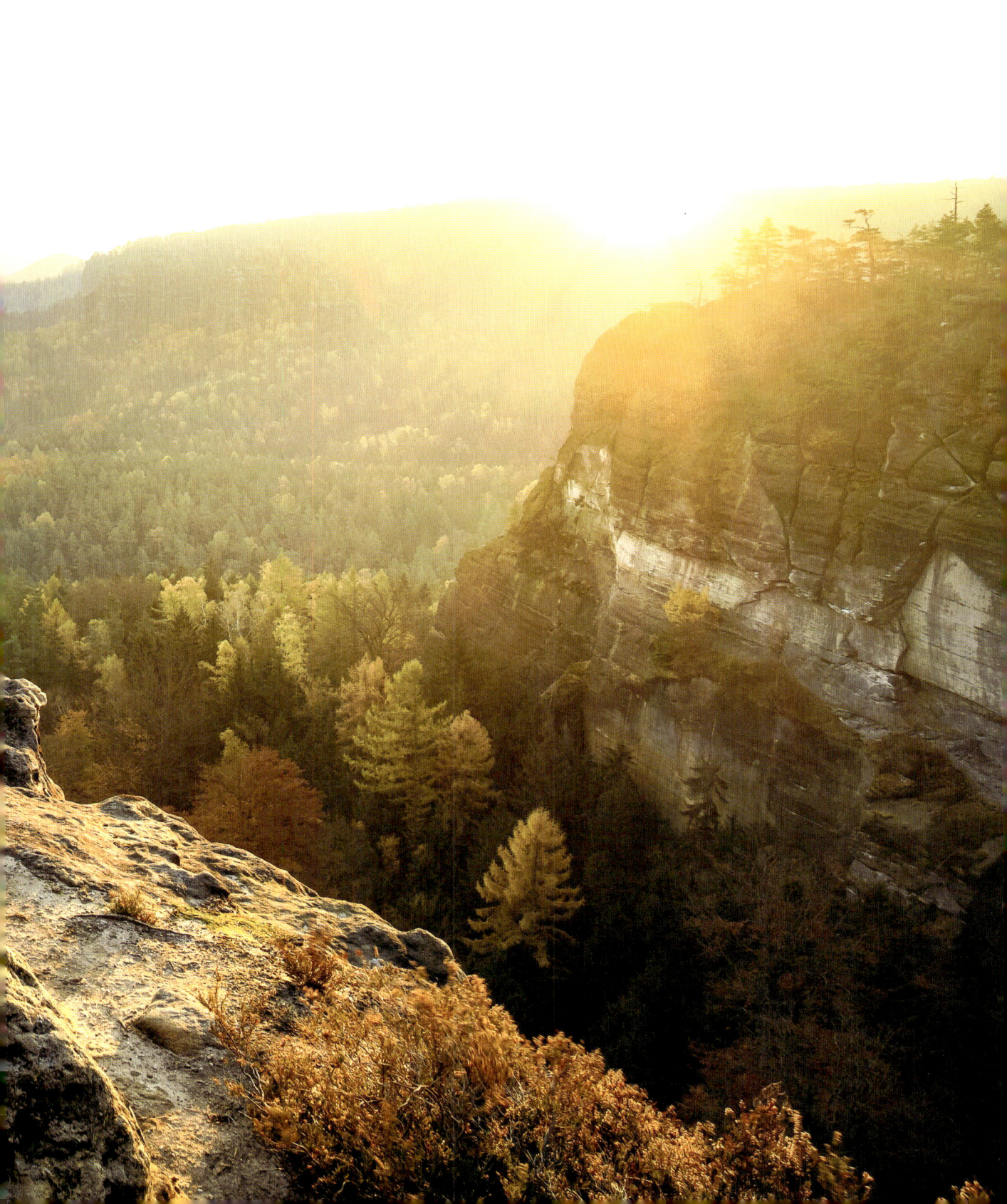

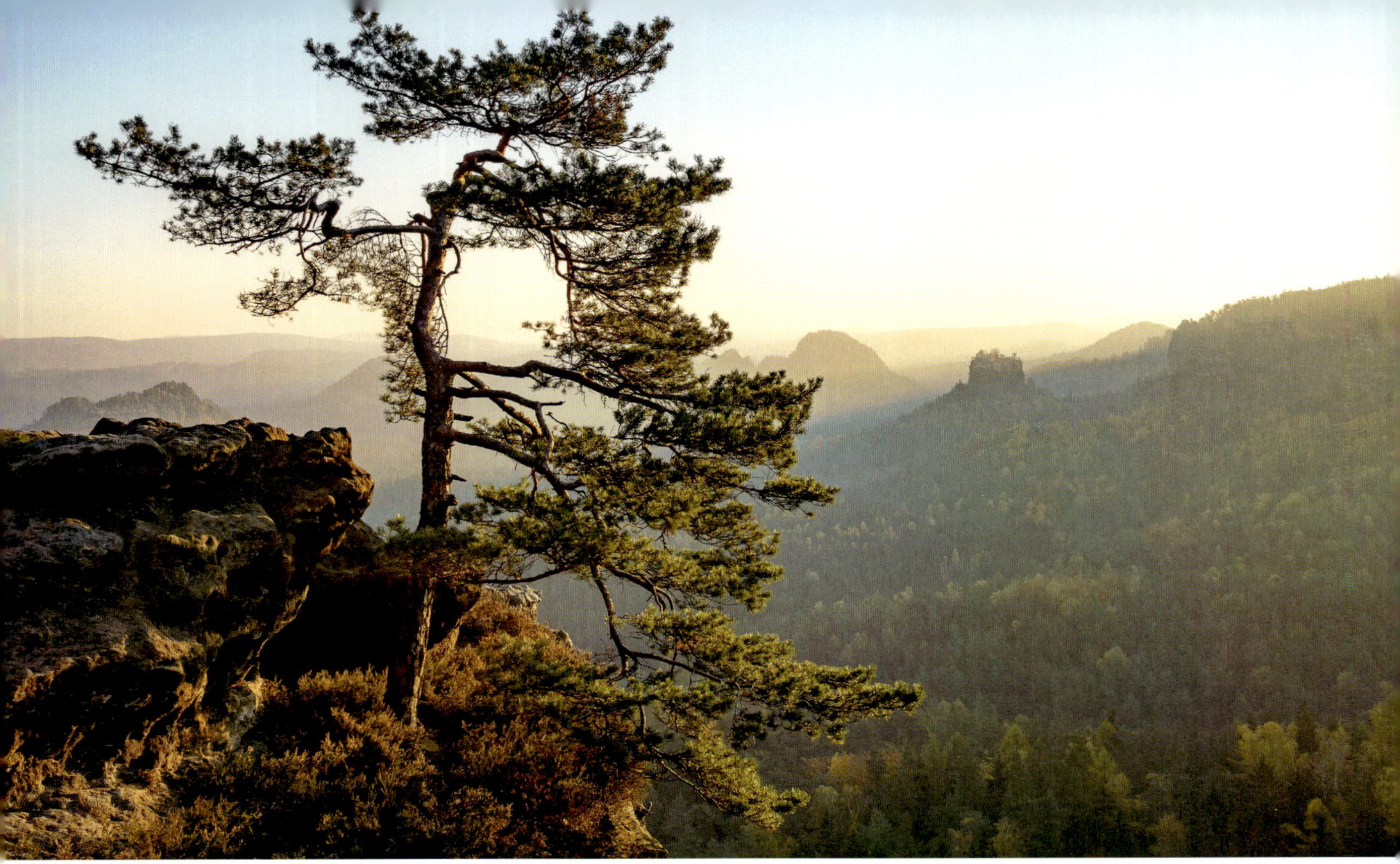

during the Cretaceous period, the area was gradually formed after the water retreated. The basalt peaks that stand among the predominantly sandstone ones were created by volcanic activity.

Through the rocks meanders the serpentine Elbe River, and many points along the trail provide views over the picturesque waterway. One of the most well known of these is the Bastei Bridge (itself a highlight on the route), from which visitors can enjoy panoramic vistas of the river, the distinctive silhouette of the Lilienstein mesa, and the 750-year-old Königstein Fortress.

Along the route there are many villages and towns. The area is well outfitted for tourists and there are numerous establishments offering a wide array of Saxon cuisine, including hearty fare such as stews and soups, cakes, pastries, and freshwater fish—which are, naturally, well complemented by the regional beer.

The Malerweg encapsulates a captivating combination of nature, history, and culture. The sublime and beautiful qualities sought by painters, musicians, and countless others since the eighteenth century can still be seen along this accessible trail, which is one of the most highly regarded long-distance hikes in Europe.

The Malerweg follows a sinuous route through surreal sandstone rock formations along either side of the Elbe River.

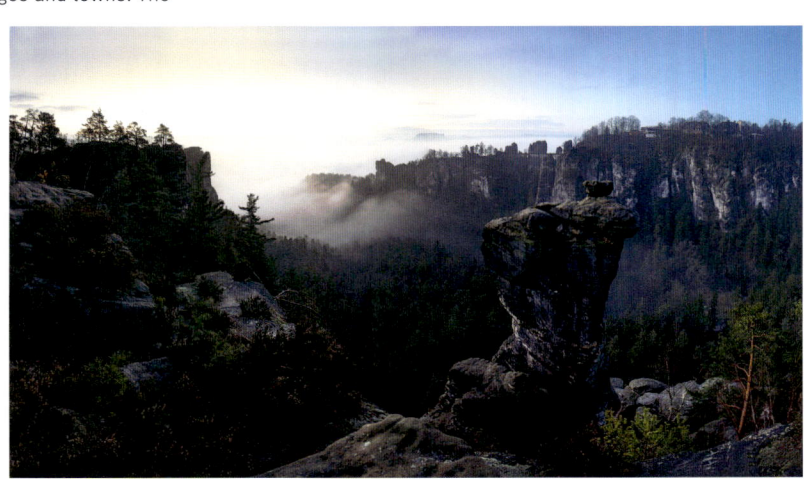

GOOD TO KNOW

START/FINISH
🚩 Liebethal
🚩 Pirna

SEASON
Year round

CONDITIONS
A well maintained trail, which can be hiked independently or with a guide.

ACCOMMODATION
Campsites, hostels, B&Bs, hotels.

LANDSCAPE
Schrammsteine, Bastei, Lilienstein, panoramic views over the Elbe River, pine and beech forests.

HIGHLIGHTS
Bastei Bridge, Königstein Fortress, locations from famous paintings of the Romantic period.

TIP
To avoid the crowds, hike outside of the summer months. Autumn is particularly beautiful, with the forests turning a spectacular kaleidoscope of yellow, orange, red, brown, and green.

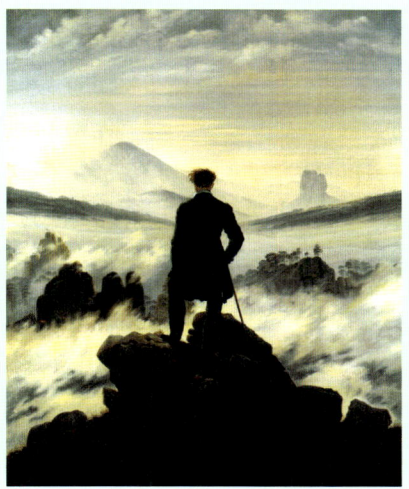

BACKGROUND

THE PAINTER'S WAY One of the central figures of the Romantic movement in the nineteenth century, the German painter Caspar David Friedrich dealt with subjects such as solitude and eternity in his symbolic landscape paintings. In general, Romantic artists saw nature as a powerful and unknowable force and an alternative to the scientific thought of the Enlightenment. Landscapes such as those in Saxon Switzerland—Friedrich lived in Dresden and hiked in the terrain covered by the Malerweg—provided inspiration for works including *Rocky Landscape in the Elbe Sandstone Mountains* (1822–3) and *Wanderer above the Sea of Fog* (c. 1818), which depict impressive and seemingly far off rock formations.

FLORA & FAUNA

CROSSING BORDERS Saxon Switzerland is close to the Czech border and hiking trails in Bohemian Switzerland are similarly stunning. Visitors can see Pravčická brána, which spans 26.5 m (87 ft.) and is Europe's largest natural sandstone arch, and rare wildlife including lynx and garden dormice.

HELPFUL HINTS

HEARTY FARE Saxon cuisine can be sampled along the Malerweg and includes specialties such as Fettbemme (pork dripping with bread) and Leipziger Allerlei (mixed vegetables, including carrots, peas, mushrooms, asparagus, and crayfish). Some famous beer brands from the area include Radeberger and Wernesgrüner.

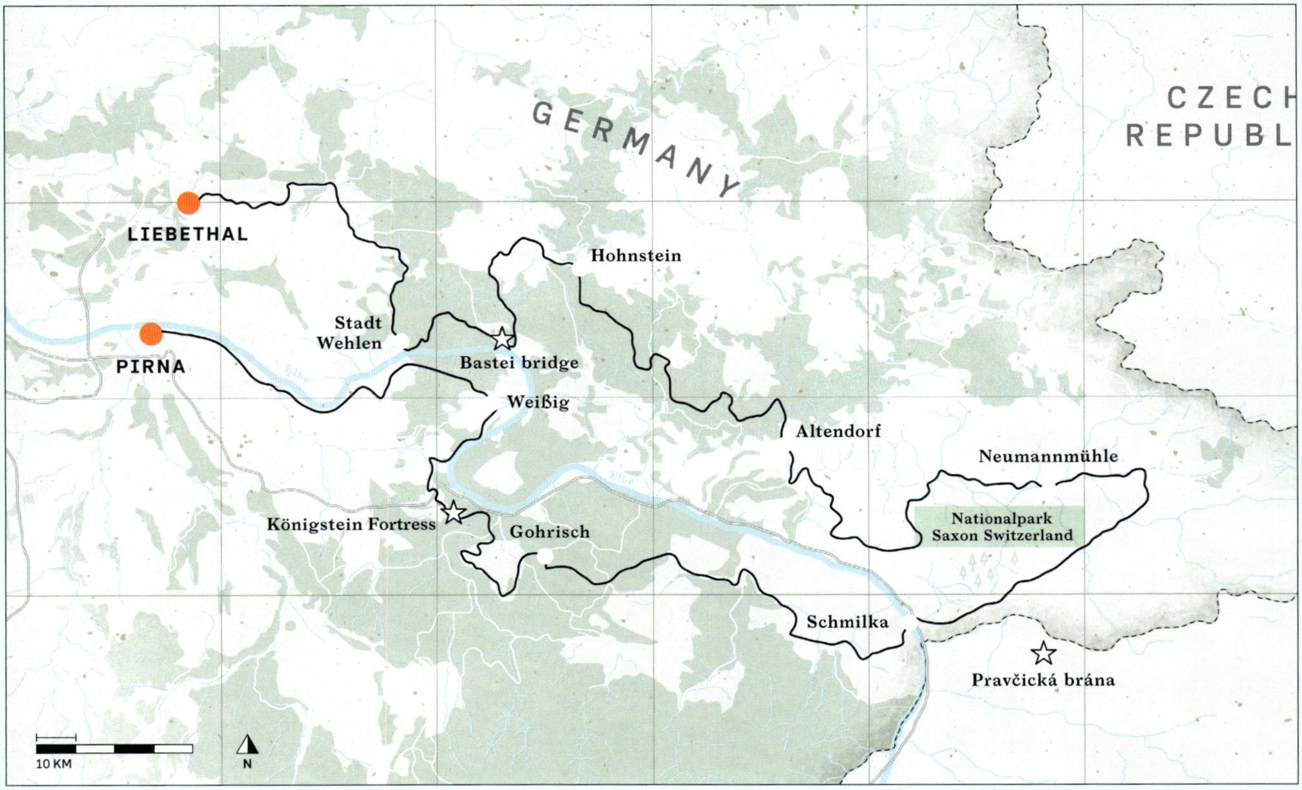

GERMANY

CZECH REPUBL

LIEBETHAL

Hohnstein

PIRNA

Stadt Wehlen

☆ Bastei bridge

Weißig

Altendorf

Neumannmühle

Königstein Fortress ☆

Gohrisch

Nationalpark Saxon Switzerland

Schmilka

☆ Pravčická brána

10 KM

N

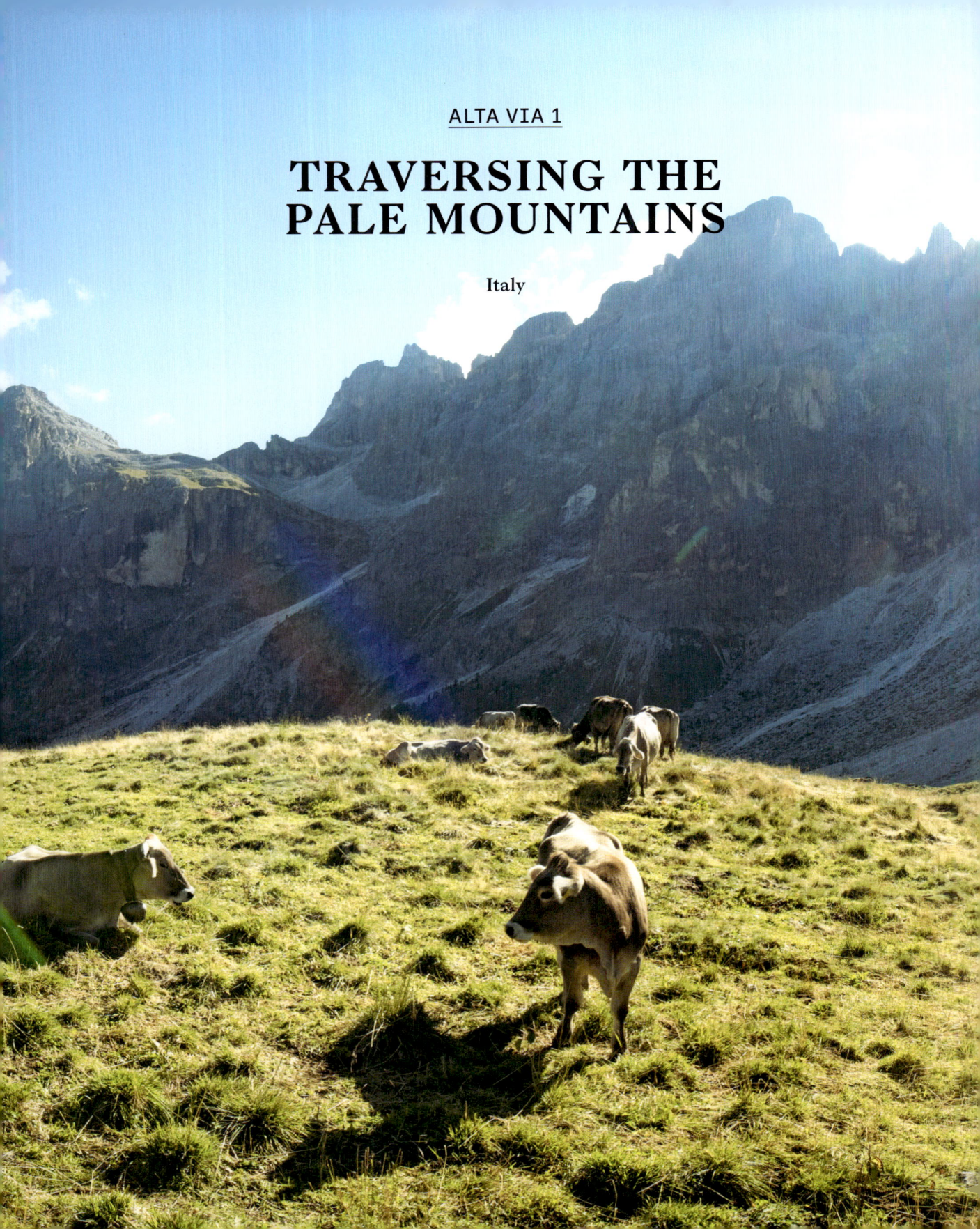

ALTA VIA 1

TRAVERSING THE PALE MOUNTAINS

Italy

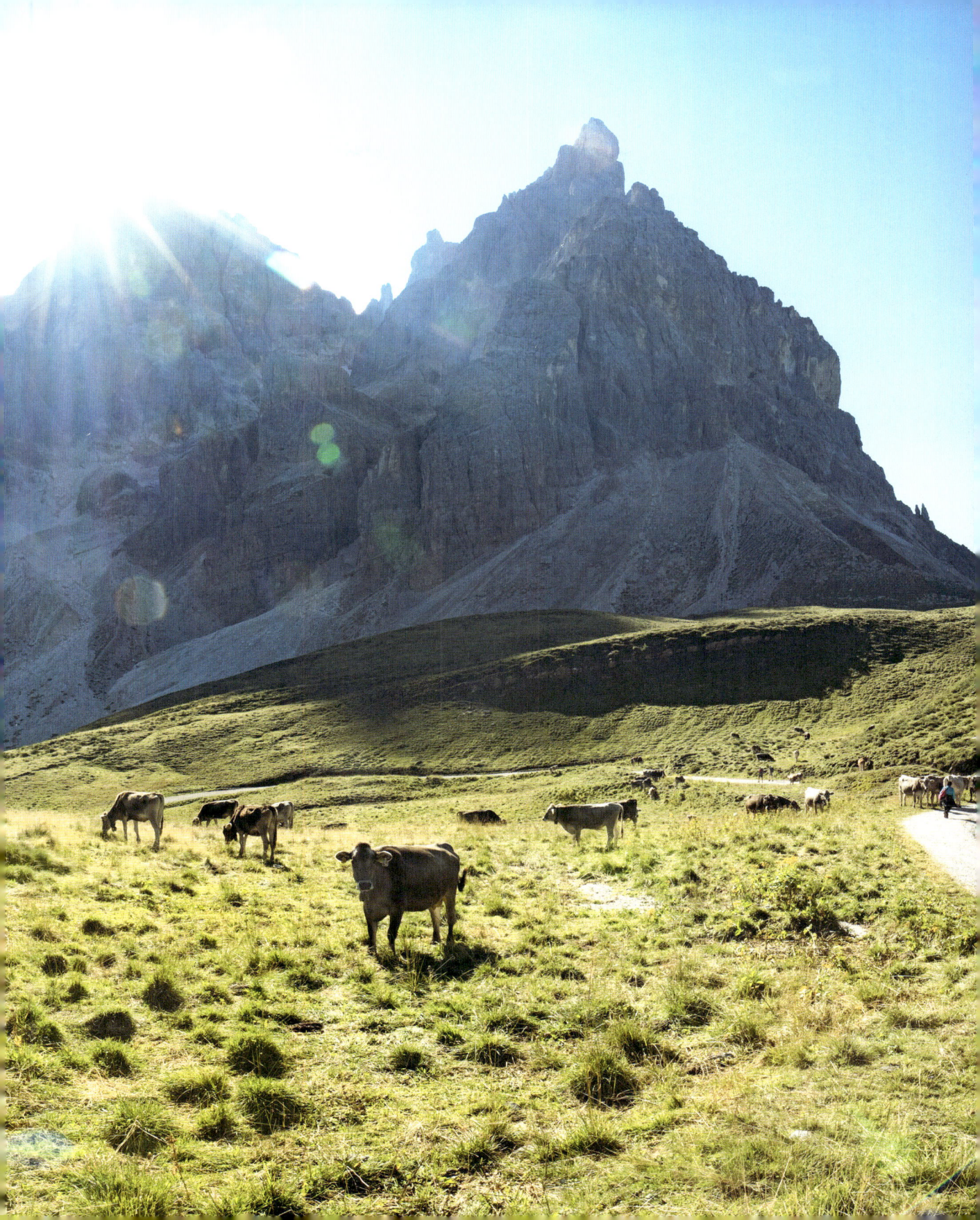

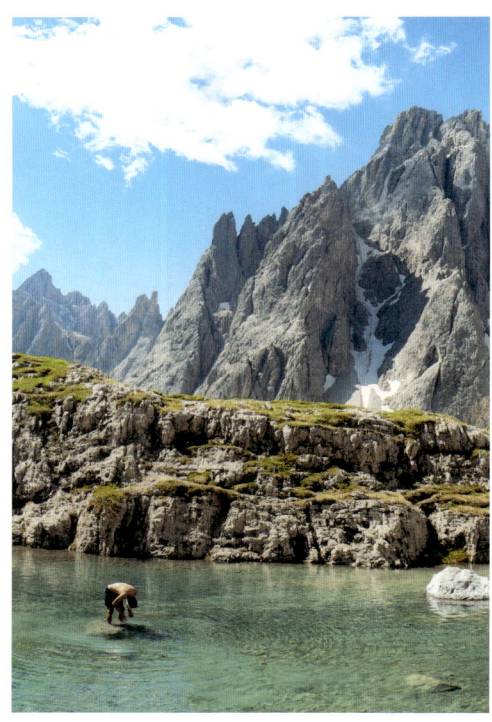

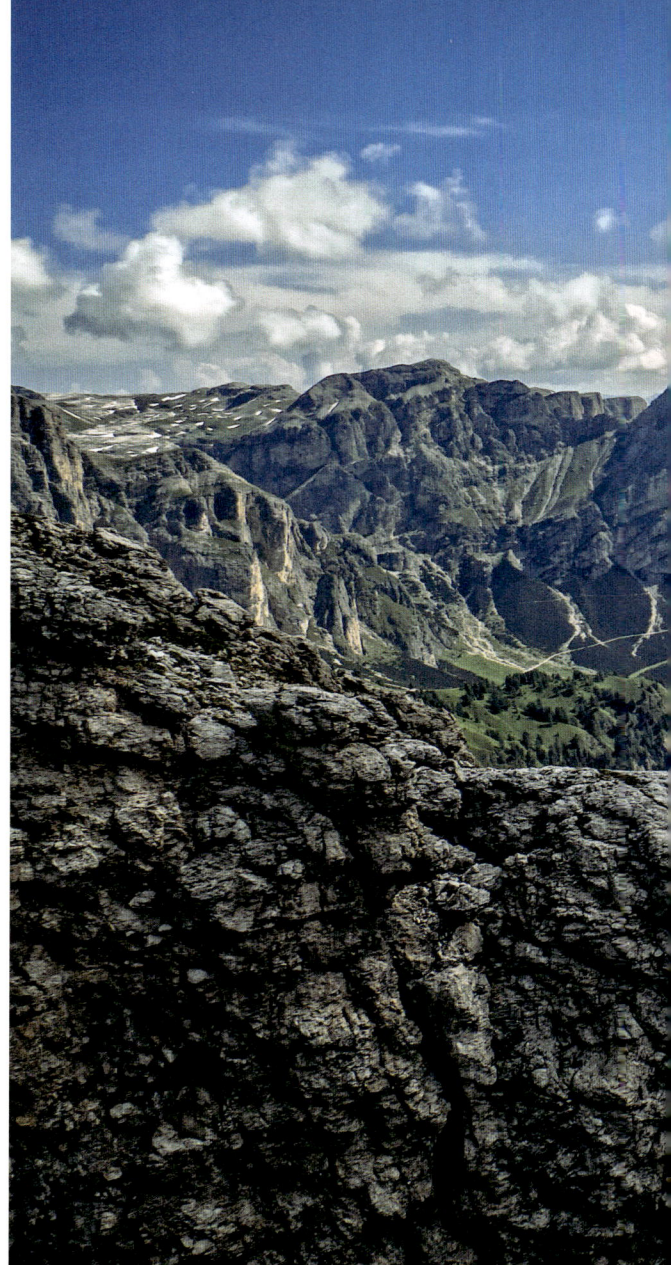

A dramatic combination of serrated limestone peaks, sheer cliffs, shimmering alpine lakes, and deep, narrow valleys, the Dolomites are listed as a World Heritage site by UNESCO for good reason. Situated in northeastern Italy, the mountain range, which includes 18 pinnacles that rise above 3,000 m (9,483 ft.), has long been a magnet for geologists, travelers, and outdoor enthusiasts from around the globe.

From a hiker's perspective, the excellent network of pathways that crisscrosses the Dolomites is ideal. The most famous of these is the Alta Via 1. Stretching some 120 km (75 mi.), the trail is a journey through fine Alpine landscapes from beginning to end. There is a total of 6,665 m (21,867 ft.) elevation gain throughout, meaning the hike is demanding in sections; however, the route is well signed and maintained, and in fine weather stays within the capabilities of most hikers.

Unlike the region's *via ferrata* routes, the Alta Via 1 does not include any technical sections that require specialized gear.

ABOUT THE TRAIL

→ <u>DISTANCE</u> Approx. 120 km (75 mi.)
→ <u>DURATION</u> 10 days
→ <u>LEVEL</u> Moderate to Difficult

The *via ferratas*, or "iron roads," are protected climbing paths made up of cables, ladders, and metal rungs attached to rock walls. The Alta Via 1 passes some of these precarious pathways, which vary in length and difficulty and feature breathtaking views, so those with the requisite skills, equipment, and head for heights can try them out. Mountaineering experience is not strictly necessary, but travelers who climb the routes do so at their own risk.

The *via ferratas* are more than an exhilarating way to experience the Dolomites' magnificent landscapes; they also re-

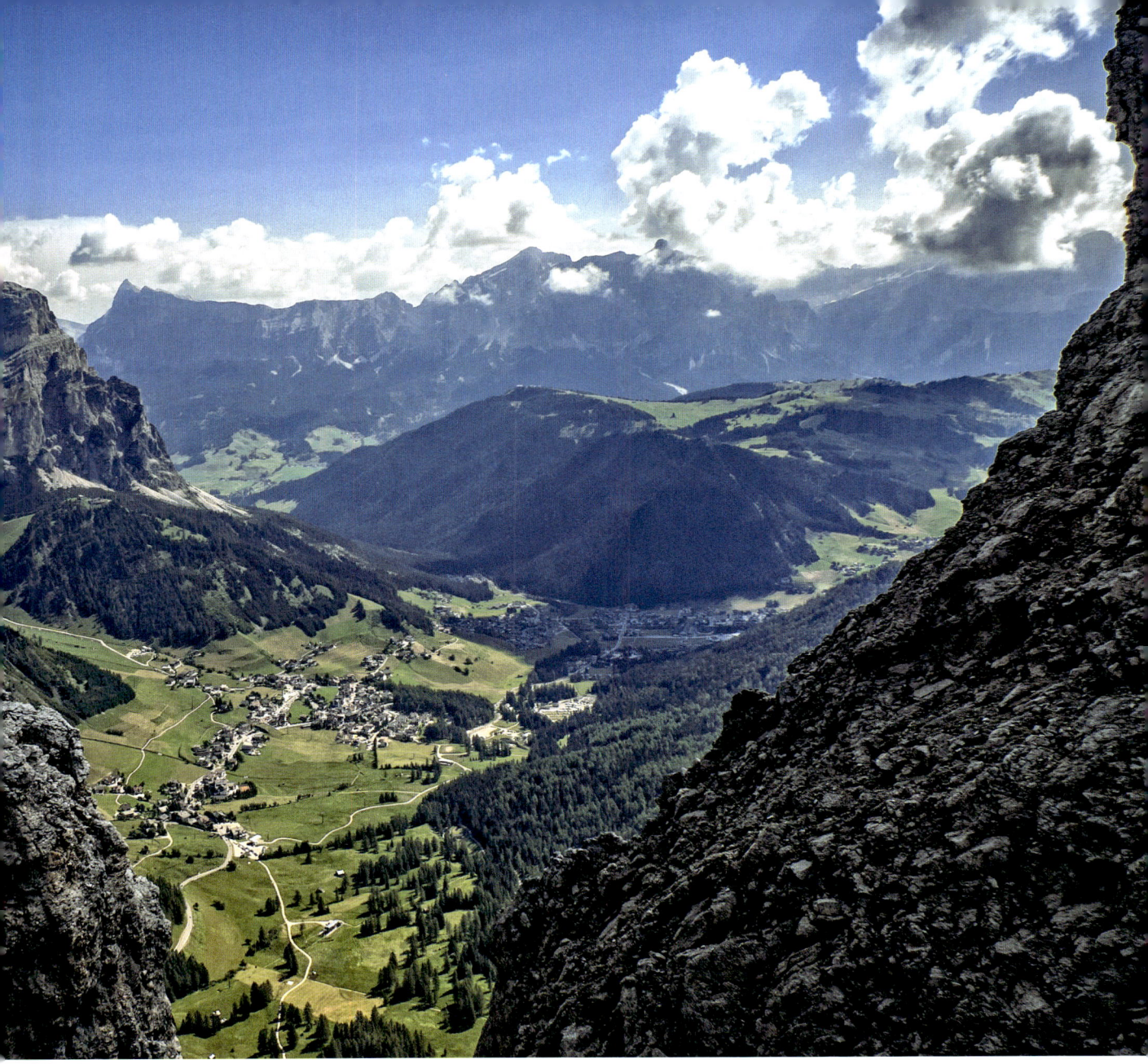

present a visual reminder of the area's bloody history. Mainly constructed during the First World War, when the peaks were the scene of ferocious battles between Italian and Austro-Hungarian forces, the network was devised as a means of allowing troops quicker and safer access to the front line. The Alta Via 1 weaves past open-air war museums at Mount Lagazuoi and Cinque Torri (five towers). The first is the Alta Via 1's highest point and the site of a restored First World War tunnel, which can be explored with a torch. At the second scenic location, hikers can witness an extensive system of

trenches first hand. In both places, the juxtaposition between somber history and natural beauty is affecting.

One of the things that distinguish the Alta Via 1 from many other great long-distance walks is that there is no need to carry a shelter or much in the way of provisions. While following the Via's remarkable progress, hikers can stay at the welcoming refugios (huts), which are dotted at regular intervals along the trail. These atmospheric mountain huts represent an integral part of any walking experience in the Dolomites. Whether it →

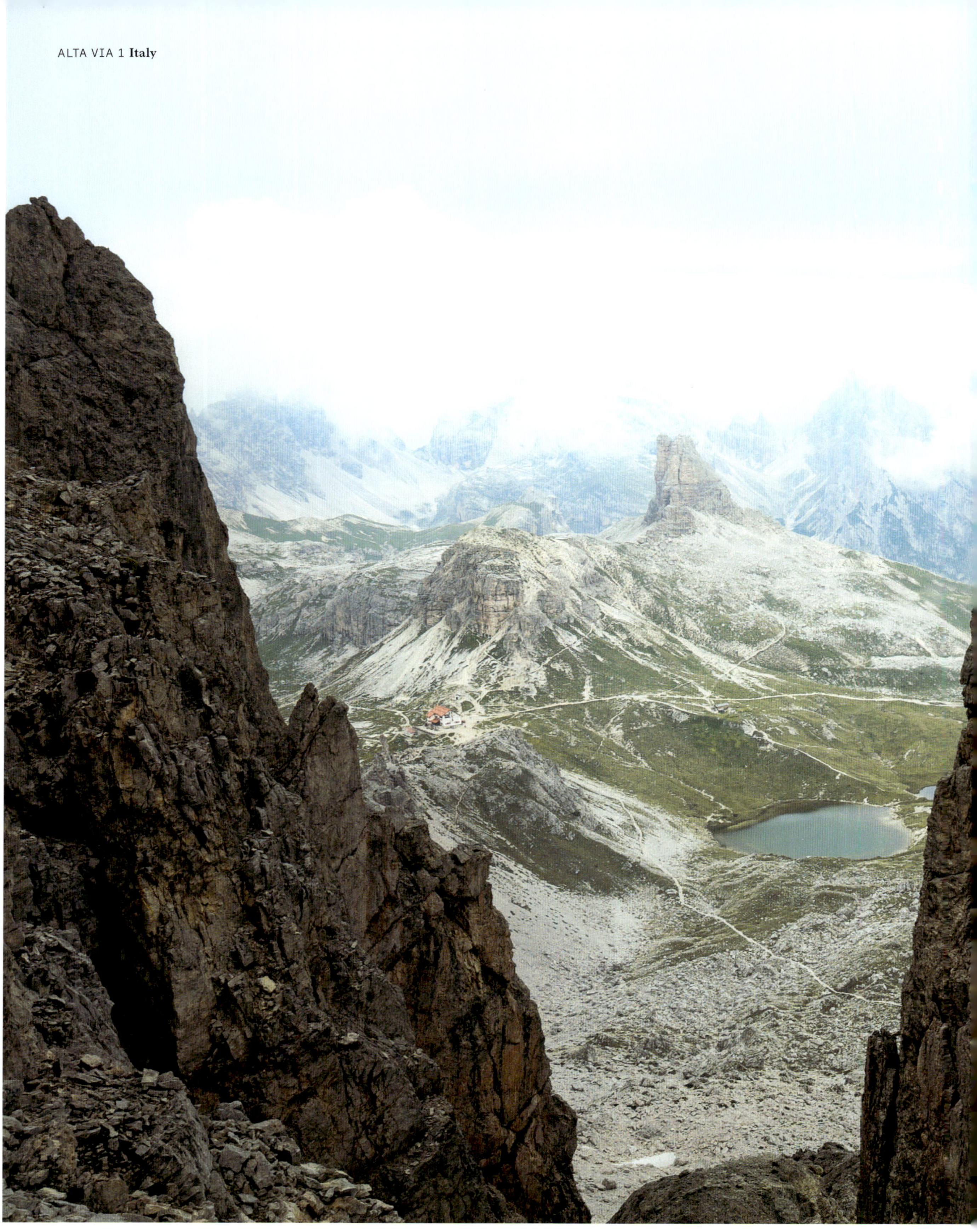

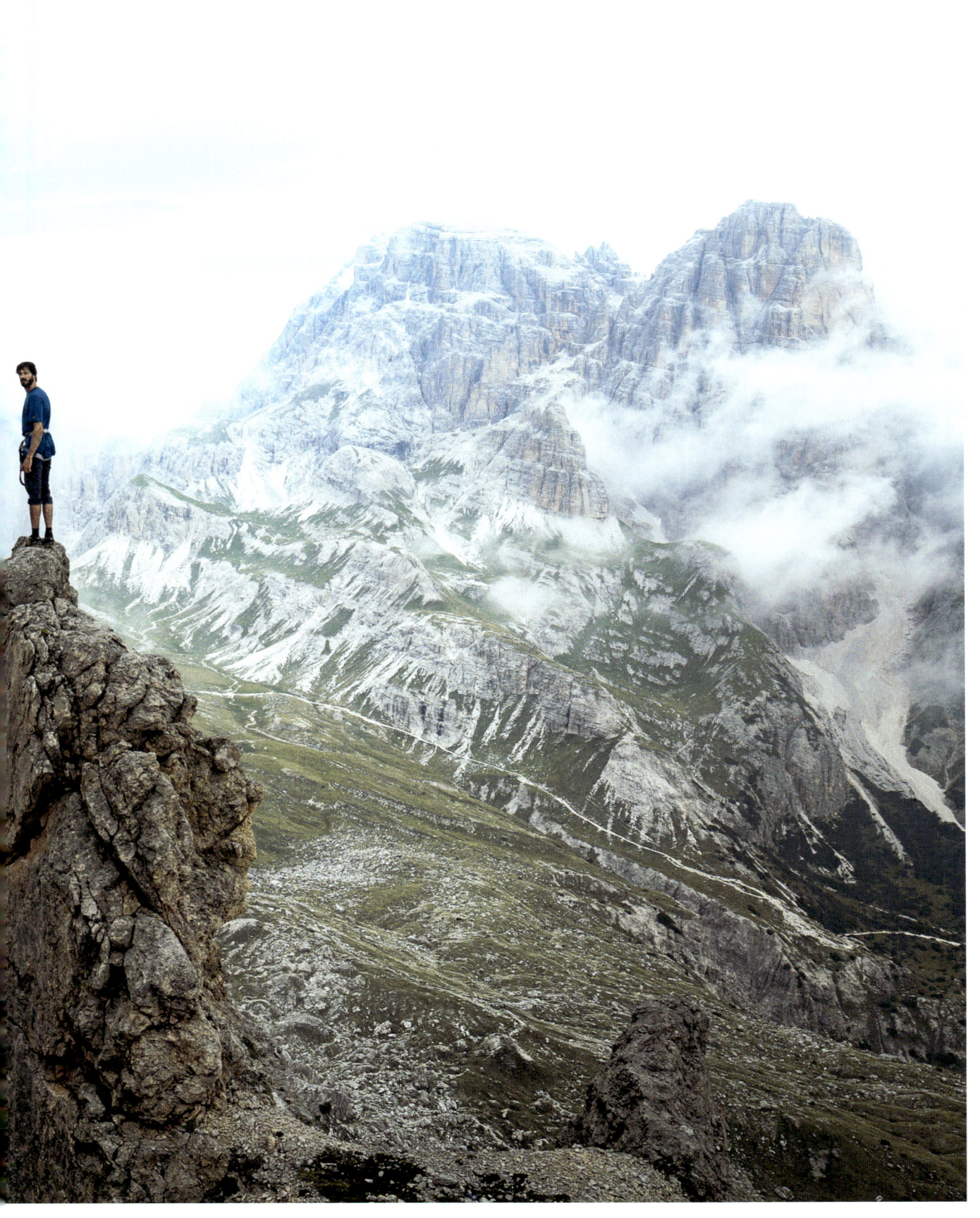

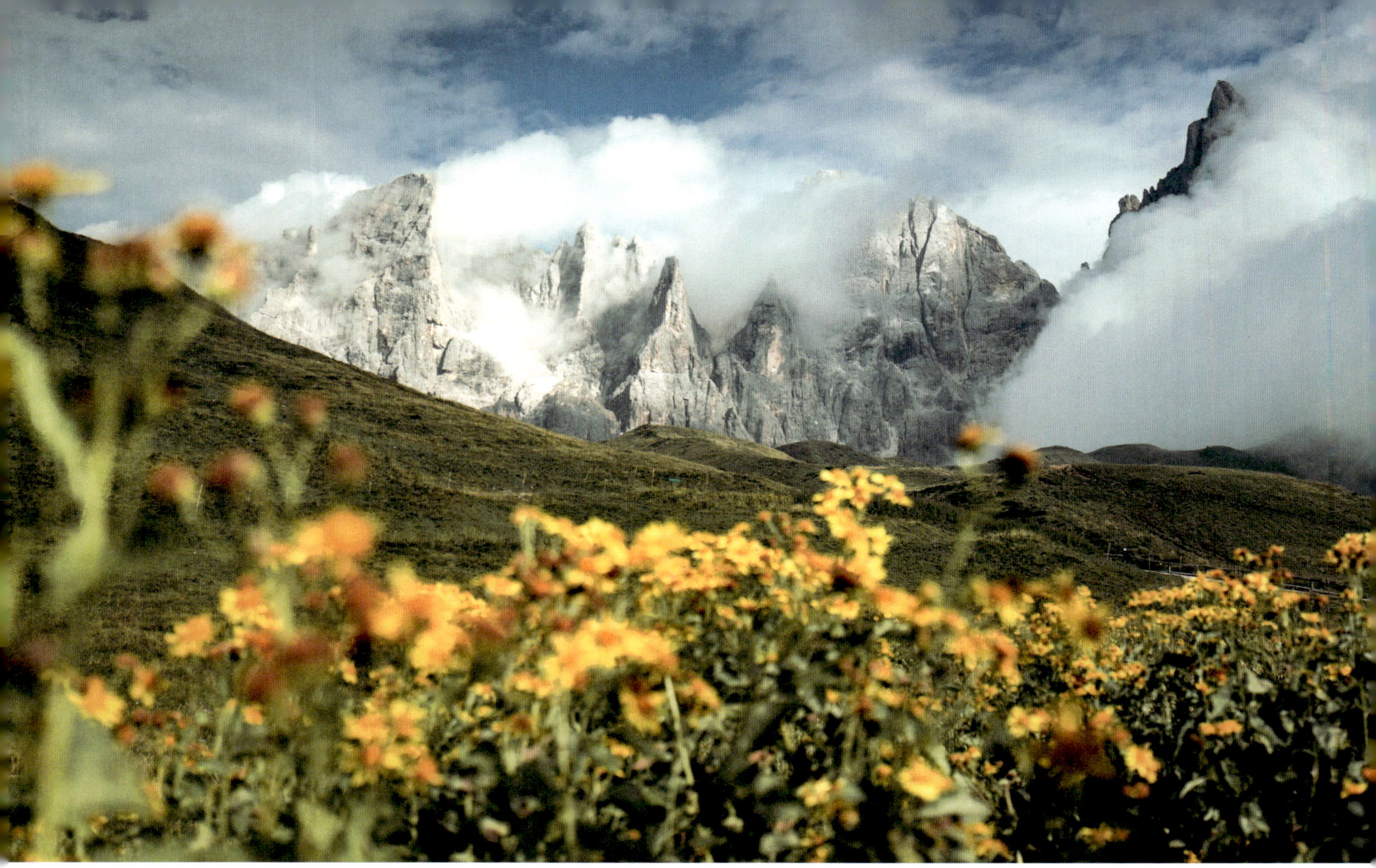

↑ The pale mountains partially enveloped in cloud.
↘ Three peaks in South Tyrol: the Tre Cime di Lavaredo.

is for breakfast, lunch, or dinner, hikers congregate in the communal dining rooms and share stories over hearty home-cooked meals (or their own food, if they prefer) and a glass of wine or two. Thanks to the services on offer at the refugios, aspirants are able to carry significantly lighter packs on the Alta Via 1—a much-appreciated boon during the hike's many steep climbs and descents.

Although the huts are comforting and the history compelling, it is, of course, the mountains that are the main draw of the region. These sculptural rock pinnacles and spires come to life at sunrise and sunset, as the pale dolostone peaks light up with an ethereal salmon-colored glow. The Italians refer to this as enrosadira (alpenglow), and, when experienced in the Dolomites while hiking the Alta Via 1, the vivid rose-tinted scene is captivating and idyllic. ⟶

Situated in northeastern Italy, the mountain range, which includes 18 pinnacles that rise above 3,000 m (9,483 ft.), has long been a magnet for geologists, travelers, and outdoor enthusiasts from around the globe.

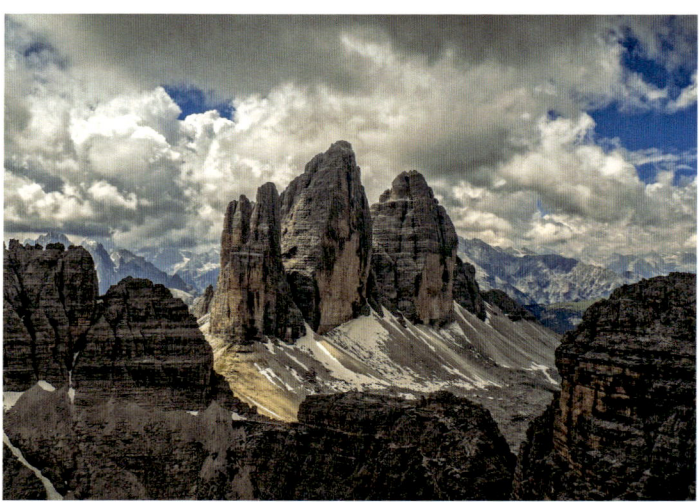

GOOD TO KNOW

START/FINISH
Dobbiaco, South Tyrol
Belluno, Veneto

SEASON
July to September

CONDITIONS
Even in summer, inclement winter conditions can strike. Snow, wet weather, and bad visibility can mean that hikers may have to rely on a compass or GPS for navigation.

LOWEST/HIGHEST POINT
389 m (1,276 ft.)/2,752m (9,029 ft.)

ACCOMMODATION
No camping is permitted on the Alta Via 1. Hikers stay in refugios (huts), which should be booked in advance.

HIGHLIGHTS
Pragser Wildsee, open-air First World War museums, views of the Civetta, Pelmo, and Tofane peaks, and *enrosadira* (alpenglow).

TIP
Afternoon storms are not uncommon during the summer months. It is best to make early starts and get the lion's share of the hiking done during the morning hours.

BACKGROUND

AN OUTSTANDING TRIO By venturing further into the Trentino-Alto Adige region—or Südtirol, as it is known by its German-speaking residents, or South Tyrol in English—hikers can experience one of the best-known sites of the Dolomites: the Tre Cime di Lavaredo, or the Drei Zinnen as they are known in German. This trio of limestone peaks now sits on the border between two Italian provinces, one of which speaks Italian and the other German. The reason for this is that place was once in Austria. In Italian, the three mounts are named the Cima Piccola, Cima Grande, and Cima Ovest: the small peak, the big peak, and the western peak. The German name Zinnen roughly translates as "battlement," emphasizing the peaks' distinctive form. With multiple trails catering to different abilities and sites such as abandoned First World War bunkers, the area allows for varied hiking adventures.

FLORA & FAUNA

SET IN STONE Formed from what was a wide tropical sea during the Triassic period (over 250 million years ago), the Dolomites today contain marine fossils. The mountains are made from dolomite, a pale, limestone-like stone that is named after the eighteenth-century French naturalist Déodat de Dolomieu.

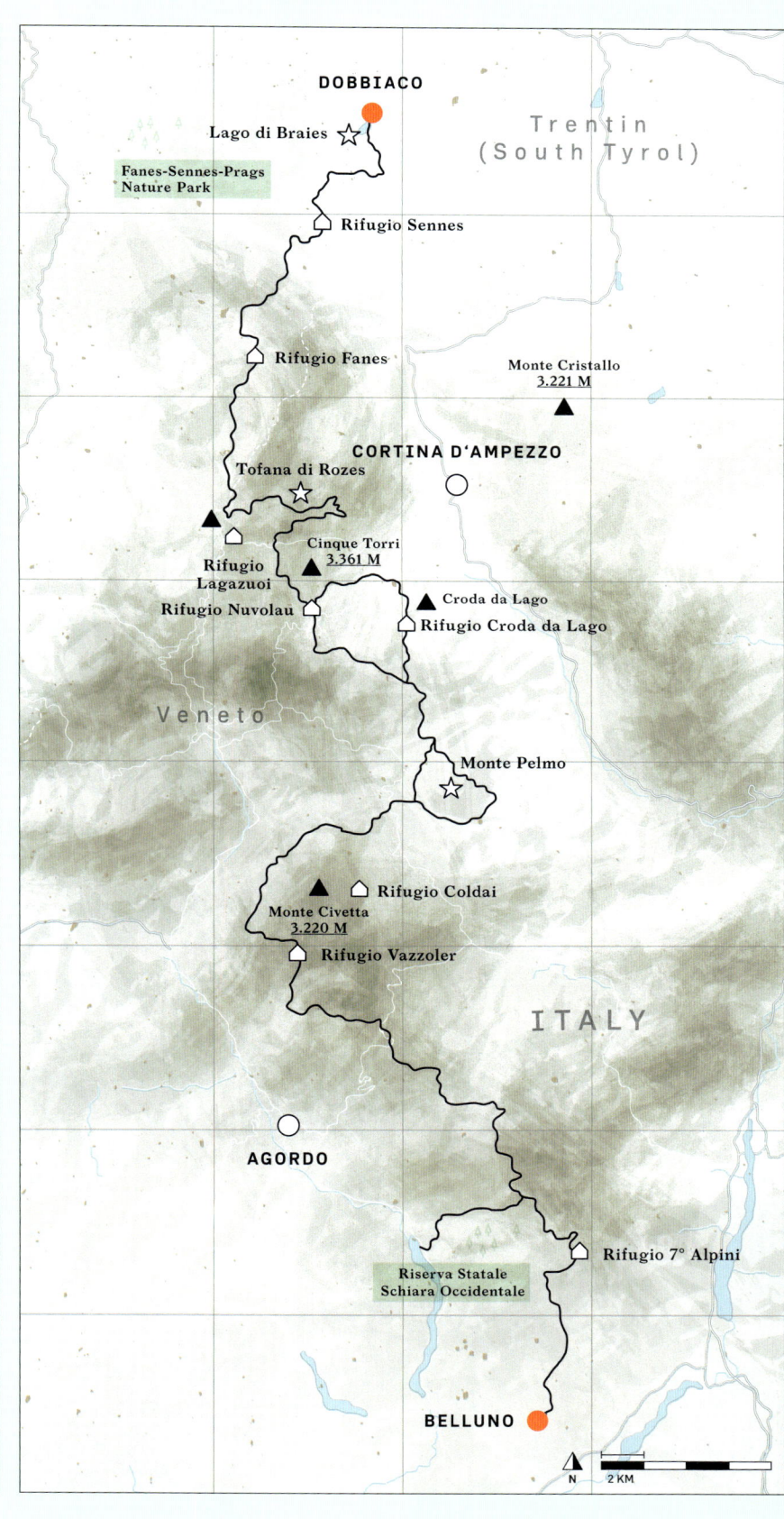

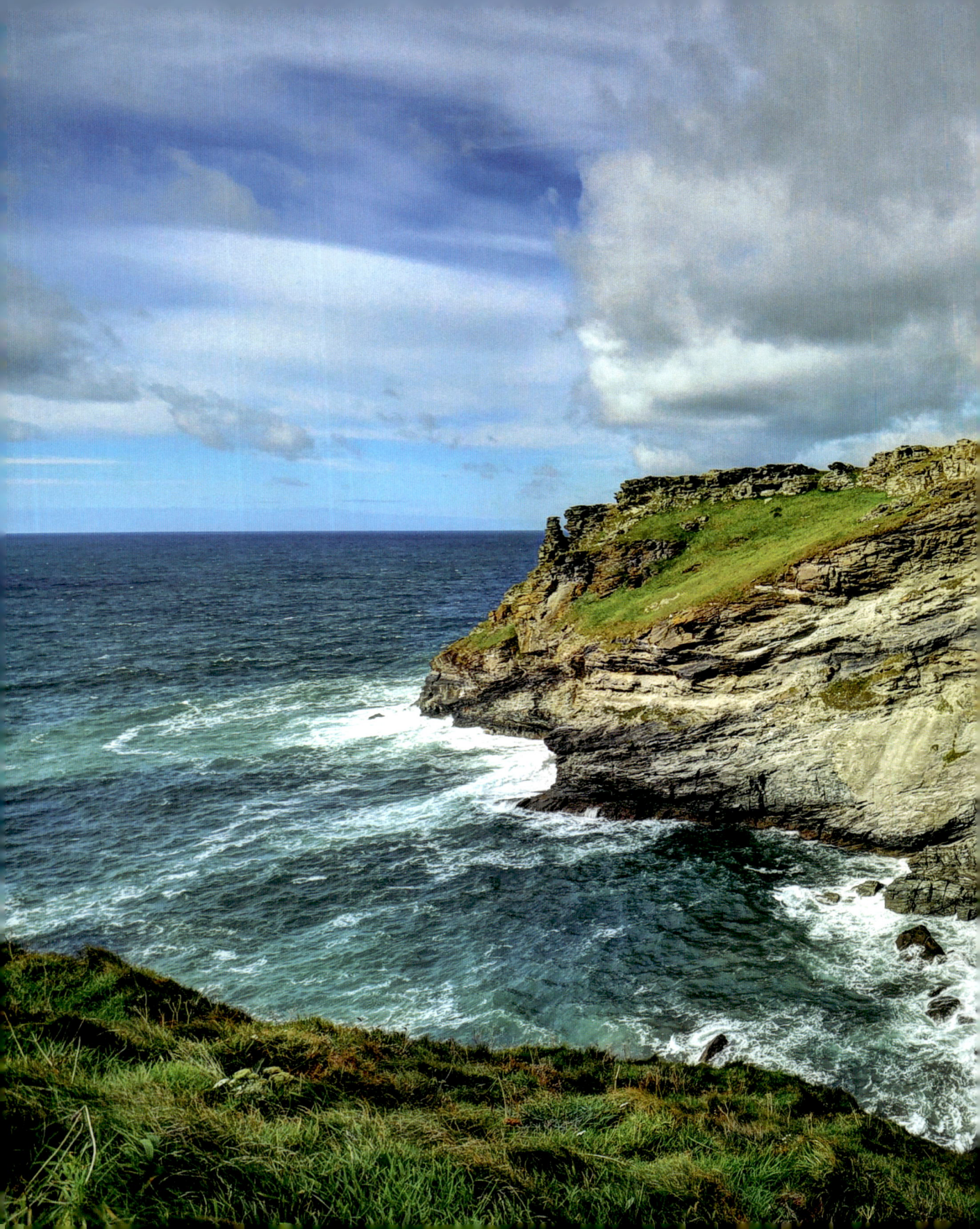

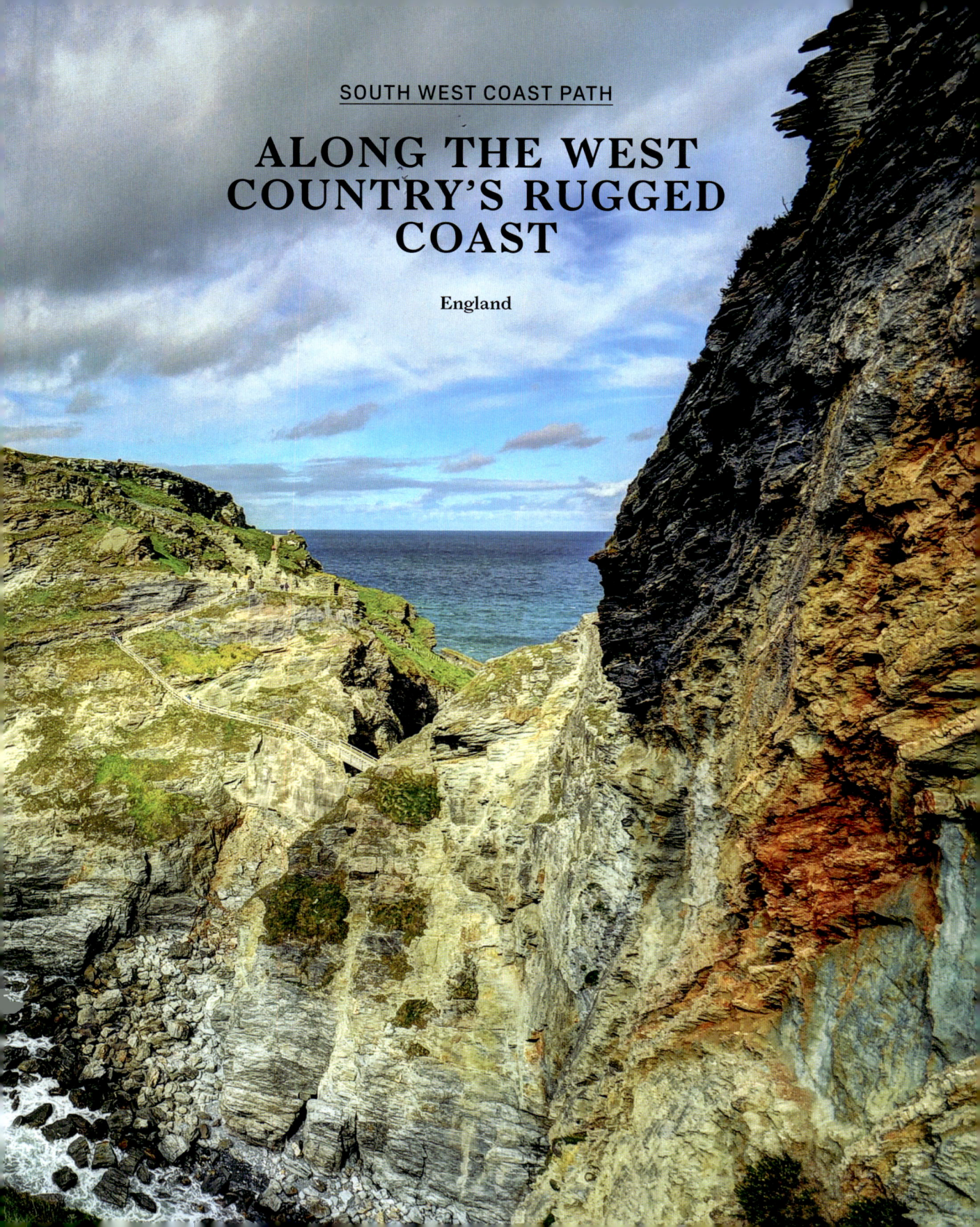

ALONG THE WEST COUNTRY'S RUGGED COAST

England

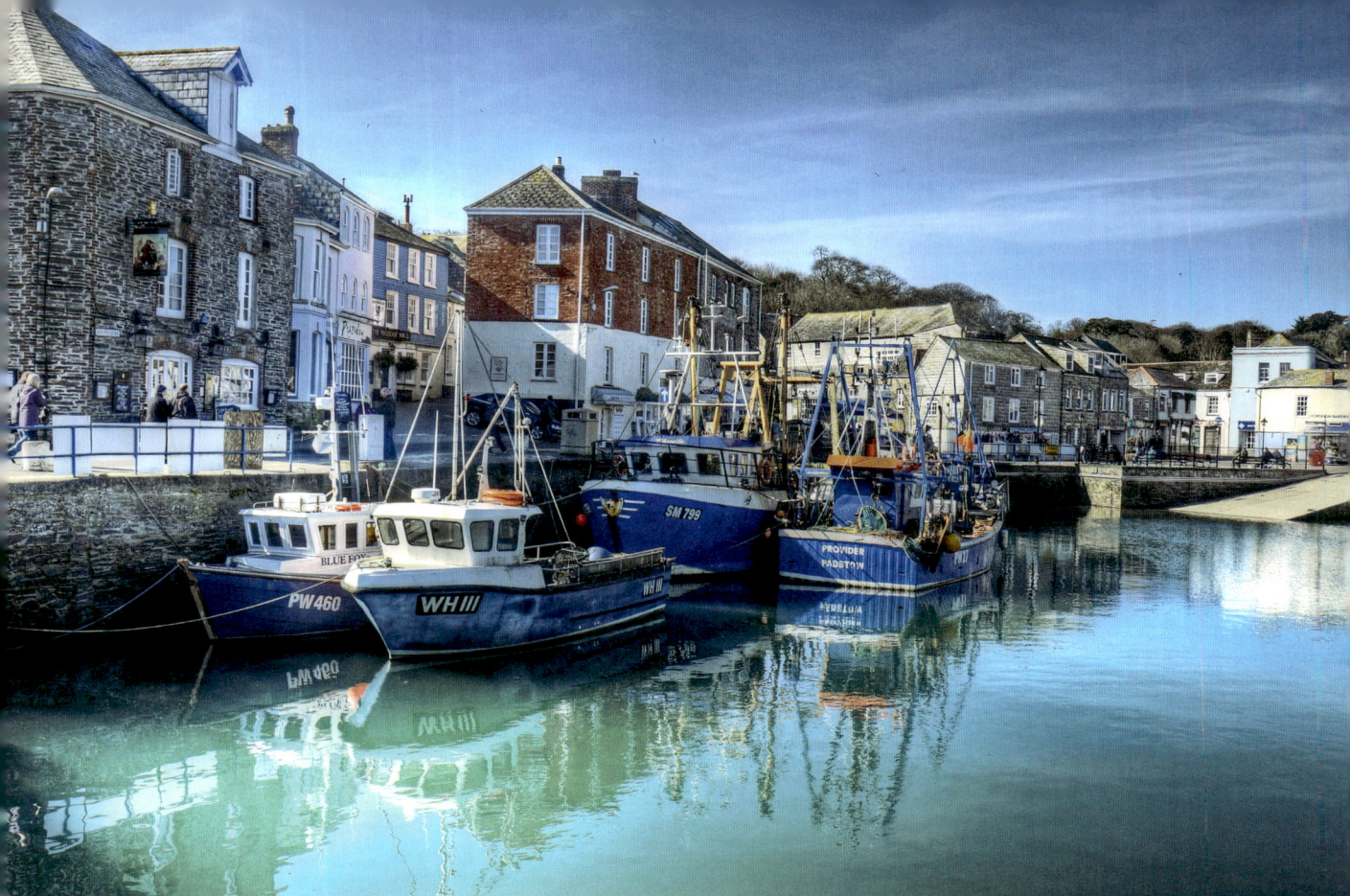

Snaking around bays, passing into small coves and along windblown clifftop paths, the South West Coast Path provides pristine views out over the sea and across the rugged coastline of southwest England. And so it should, given that a large portion of it follows the route patrolled by the coastguard or customs officers when looking out for ships in trouble or smugglers bringing in contraband. These officials walked the paths right up until 1913. Fishermen also used them to check the conditions of the sea and spy shoals of fish.

Today the South West Coast Path is a well-signposted route for walkers of any ability. With day hikes and longer routes, the path has parts that are a manageable start for beginners, as well as stretches that are a satisfying challenge for more experienced hikers. Fast walkers can complete the whole path in around four weeks, though this can rise to seven or eight if exploring the

towns and other pleasant diversions the four counties have to offer in more depth. Routes range from a gentle stroll over the sandy dunes near the River Camel in Cornwall to a challenging trek in the quarry-scarred landscape around Swanage, which crosses often-muddy fields and climbs steep inclines.

The extensive path spans counties: it begins in Somerset, runs through North Devon, around the whole coast of Cornwall, along the south coast of Devon, and ends in Dorset. In over 1,000 km (621 mi.), it takes in ancient geological features and a range of flora and fauna while immersing travelers in the history of the region. Natural rock formations on a grand scale can be found—the arch at Blackchurch Rock is just one—as can traces of a man-made history, such as Second World War defenses. Buildings from the region's mining heritage are set in rugged landscape. And contemporary life in cites, villages, towns, and hamlets can also be experienced.

The exposed rocks on the Jurassic Coast in East Devon and Dorset illustrate 185 million years of earth's history. Hikers can take a "Walk through Time" on this 153 km (95 mi.) stretch of coast, which is England's only natural World Heritage site, and hunt for their own pieces of history—fossils—at Charmouth. Also

ABOUT THE TRAIL

→ <u>DISTANCE</u> 1,014 km (630 mi.)
→ <u>DURATION</u> 1 month
→ <u>LEVEL</u> Moderate

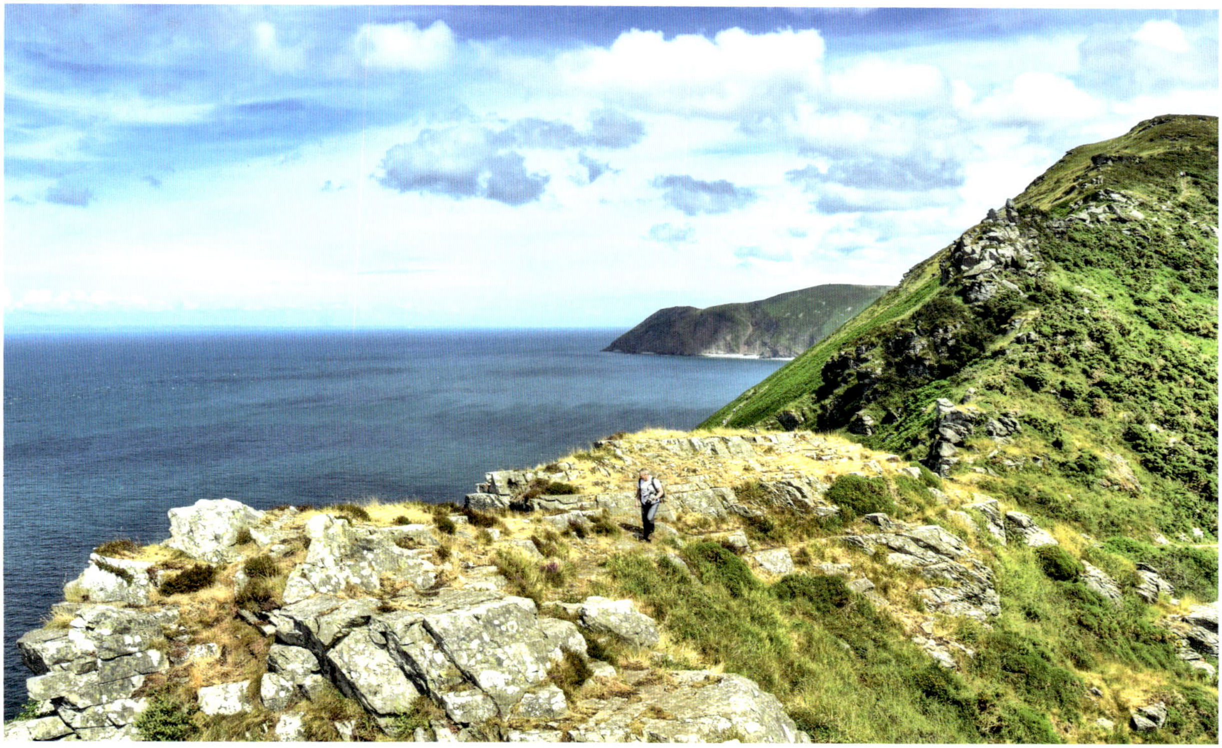

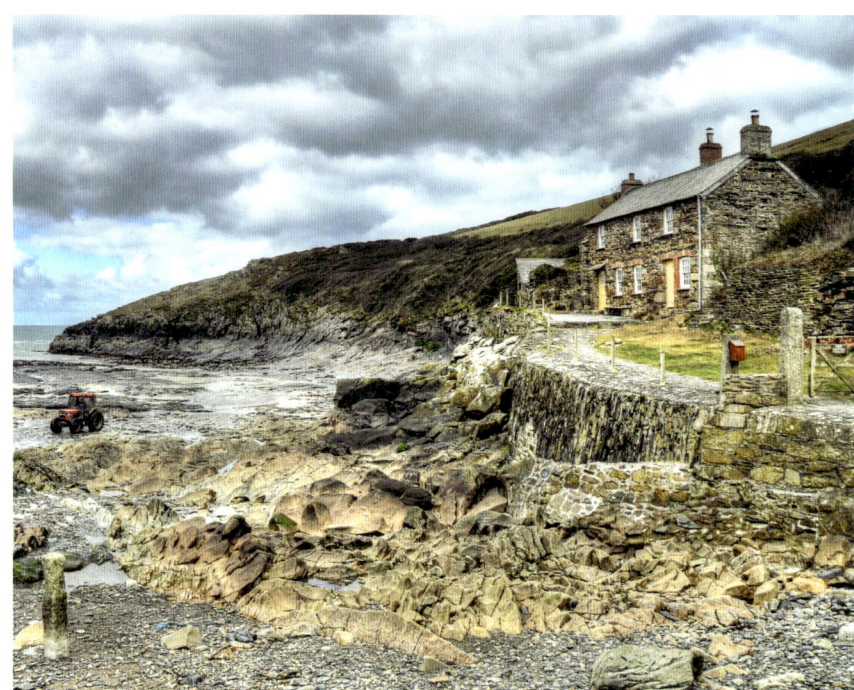

← Padstow Harbour in North Cornwall.
↑ The path following the Exmoor coast near Lynton in North Devon.
↓ Port Quin, a hamlet on the North Cornwall coast.

in the protected area are the Durdle Door, a limestone arch with an iconic form, and horse-shoe-shaped Lulworth Cove—both trail highlights with distinctive curved forms. Not far away is the Isle of Portland, a peninsula joined to the mainland by a shingle ridge (Chesil Beach), which hikers can walk around in a 21 km (13 mi.) loop, traveling along old quarry paths and visiting hidden coves.

The selection of animal and plant life in the route's national parks is particular to this part of the United Kingdom. The harsh landscape of Dartmoor National Park is a habitat for threatened species such as the blue ground beetle and the horseshoe bat. Exmoor—a site with the highest sea cliffs in mainland Britain—is home to the rare heath fritillary butterfly and two species of whitebeam tree that are only found in the reserve.

Industry sits alongside nature at many points along the path. On one 4.8 km (3 mi.) stretch named the Levant, Botallack and the Crowns walk, hikers will view a landscape studded with engine houses and chimneys—structures from the heyday →

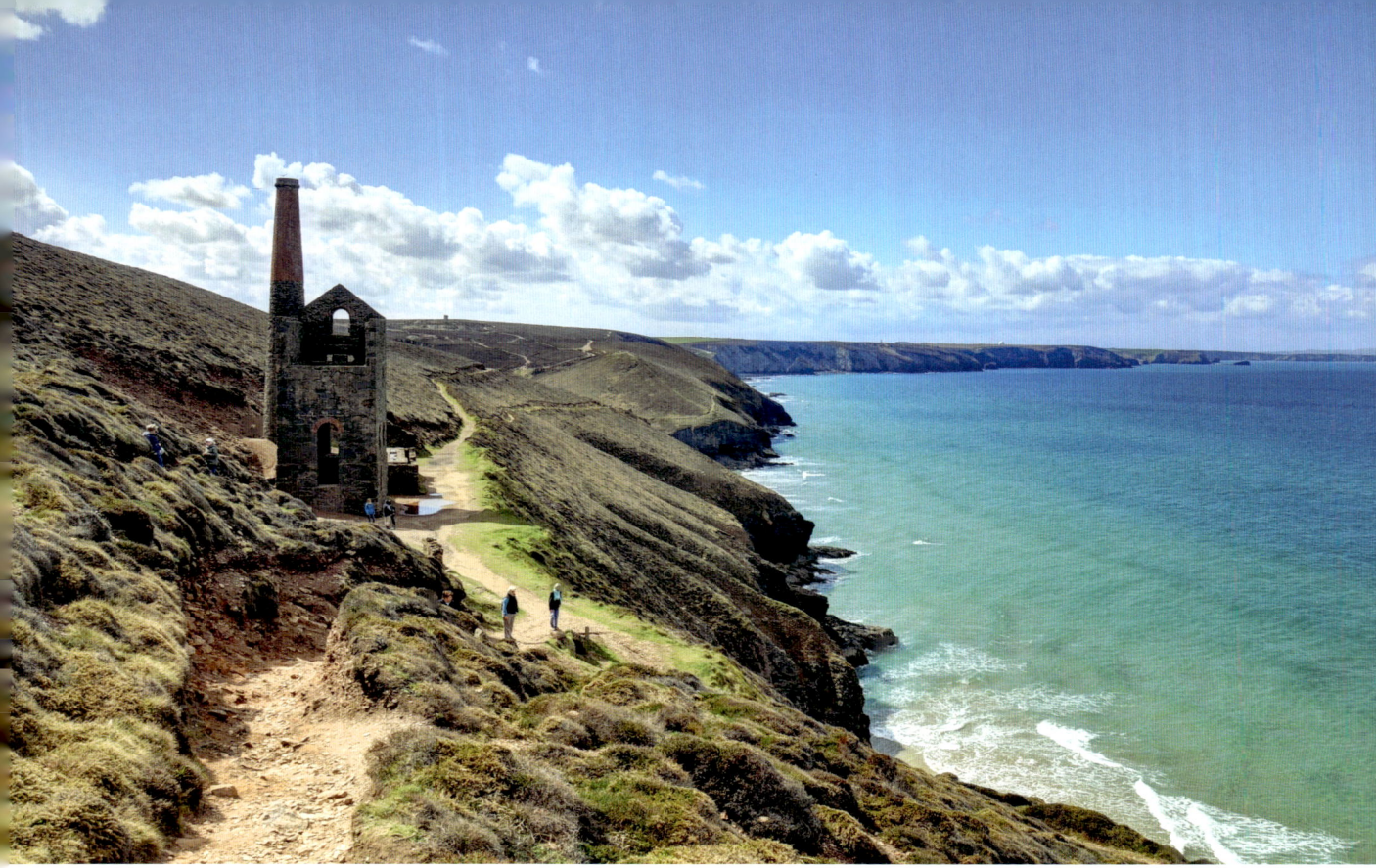

↑ Former tin-mine engine house near Chapel Porth in North Cornwall.

of mining. Set near the base of cliffs, the Crowns engine houses at Botallack cut striking figures. Levant Mine was one of the most successful mines in Cornwall, and copper, tin, and arsenic were extracted there; today its 1860s steam-powered beam engine can still be seen.

Overlooked by mining buildings and cliffs covered by heathland that is painted yellow and purple by gorse and heather from late summer, Chapel Porth is a beach of note on a trail that includes a plethora of sandy stretches. This National Trust site is home to birds such as rock pipits, and there are small caves that can be visited at low tide.

The show of color continues on the Lizard peninsula, an area featuring the southernmost point on mainland Britain, Lizard Point. In the region, hikers will notice serpentine, deep-green rock with lines of red and white running through it. In the 1800s, the stone was polished and was used for diverse purposes, including for fireplaces. On the strenuous 16.7 km (10.4 mi.) walk from the Lizard to Coverack, there are also stiles made from the rock. Walkers should be careful, though—these look attractive but are very slippery when wet.

Towns on the route have characteristics as varied as the path's natural aspects: St Ives, which was once home to painters such as Barbara Hepworth and Ben Nicholson, remains a

In over 1,000 km (621 mi.), it takes in ancient geological features and a range of flora and fauna while immersing travelers in the history of the region.

destination for art enthusiasts today; Padstow, a working fishing port, has become renowned for its food culture; and Exeter, a large city, is the home of a fine Gothic cathedral. Planning in a few extra days to explore towns and villages in more detail is highly recommended.

The South West Coast Path gives walkers of any ability a taste of England's history, nature, and geology, and shows how all three are intertwined. Whether rock pooling at the edges of long expanses of sand, marveling at red-and-white striped lighthouses on rocky outcrops, or trekking rugged coastline and gorse-lined tracks, hikers of all abilities will find one or more activity to suit on this diverse trail. ─────

GOOD TO KNOW

START/FINISH
Minehead, Somerset
Poole, Dorset

SEASON
Year-round

ACCOMMODATION
Holiday cottages, hotels, hostels, B&Bs, campsites.

HIGHLIGHTS
Durdle Door rock arch, Isle of Portland, Chapel Porth Beach, Jurassic Coast, and the Cornish Mining World Heritage sites.

TIP
As the path crosses estuaries, rivers, and streams, travelers should check ferry schedules or tide tables for the relevant areas before setting off. Services and tide levels can vary with the season or time of day.

BACKGROUND

DIGGING DEEPER Cornwall has a long mining heritage. The geological and geomorphological processes that created the county's landscape mean that there is a rich selection of minerals. In days past, miners recognized where mineralization occurred through indicators such as plant species and the hardness or tone of rocks (for example, greens marked secondary copper minerals or reds iron). Tin and copper were the main targets for miners, though other substances such as zinc and arsenic were also sought after. Though the mining industry has for the most part died out today, there are World Heritage sites throughout the region tracing their history between 1700 and 1914. Visitors can see the distinctively shaped stone buildings and tour sites such as Geevor Tin Mine, where an extensive selection of machinery is on show.

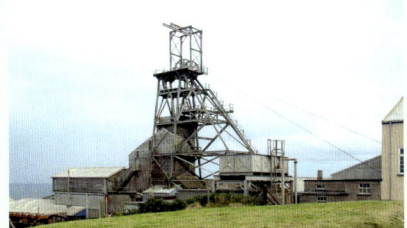

HELPFUL HINTS

SUSTENANCE Cream teas (tea with scones, clotted cream, and jam), fish and chips, and seafood are all culinary highlights of the West Country. Tired hikers might also find solace by making stops in pubs to sample locally brewed ales and the cider the region is renowned for.

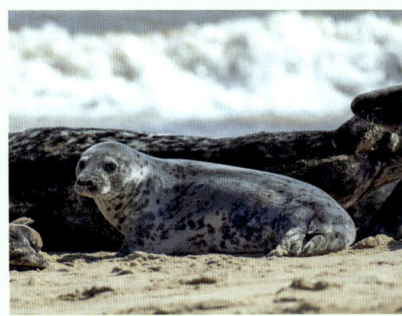

FLORA & FAUNA

SEA VIEWS Gazing out over the ocean waves, visitors might see grey seals or dolphins. In the summer, basking sharks can sometimes also be spotted off the headlands of West Cornwall.

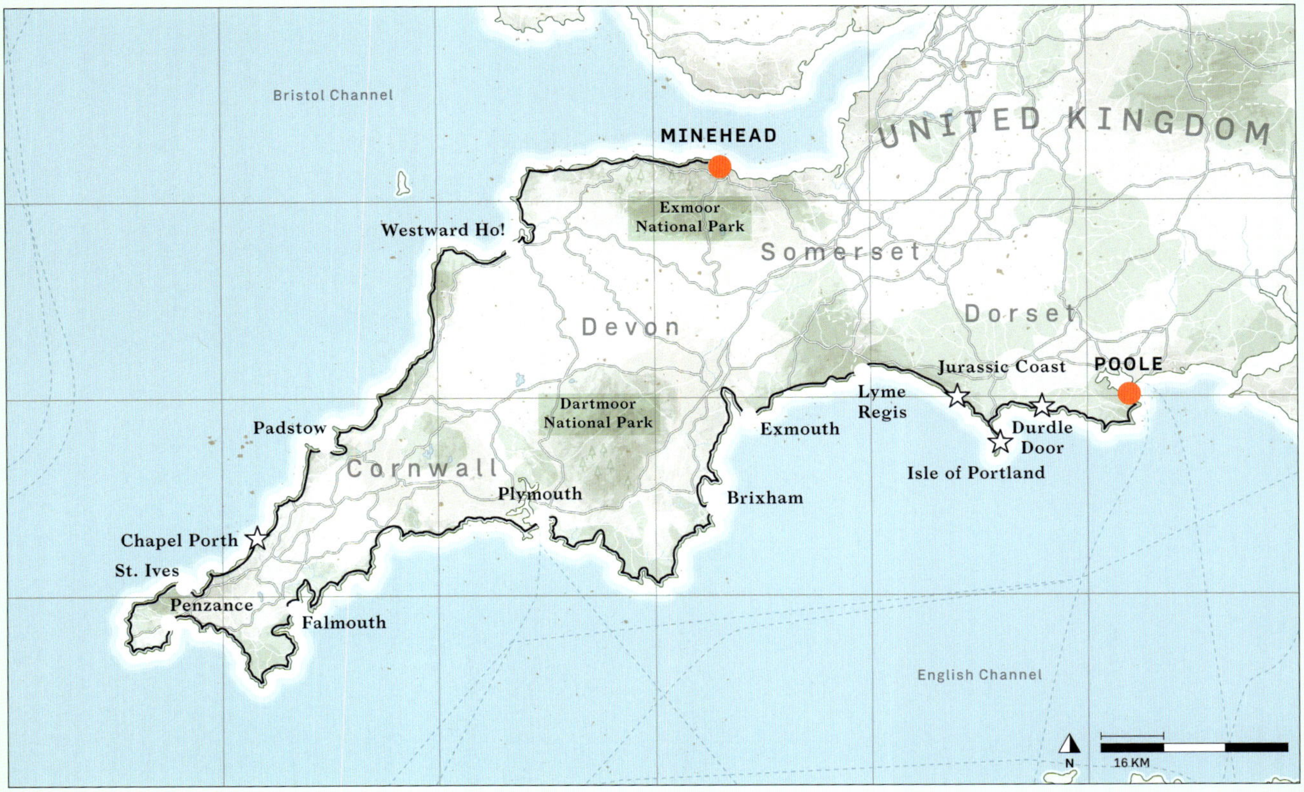

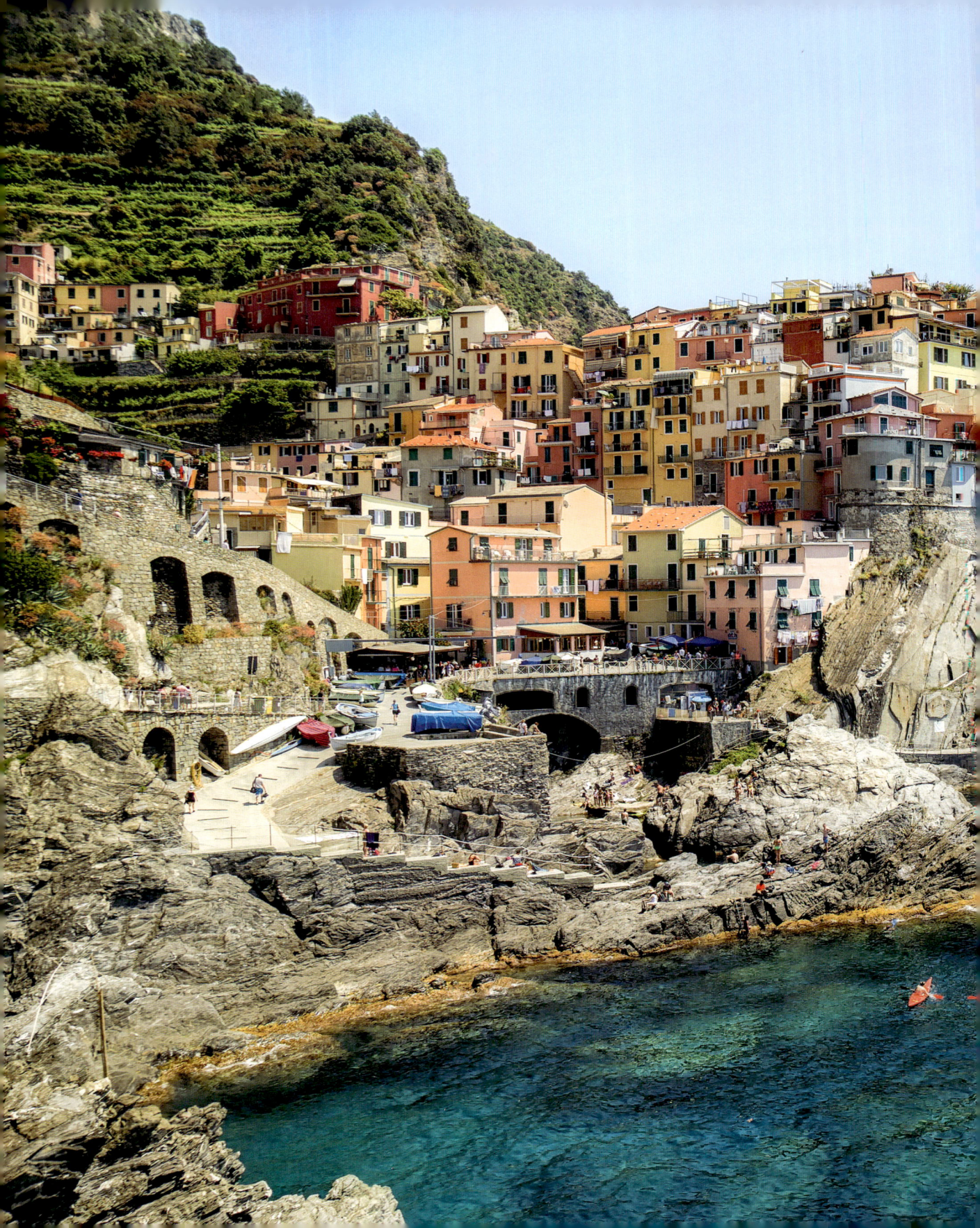

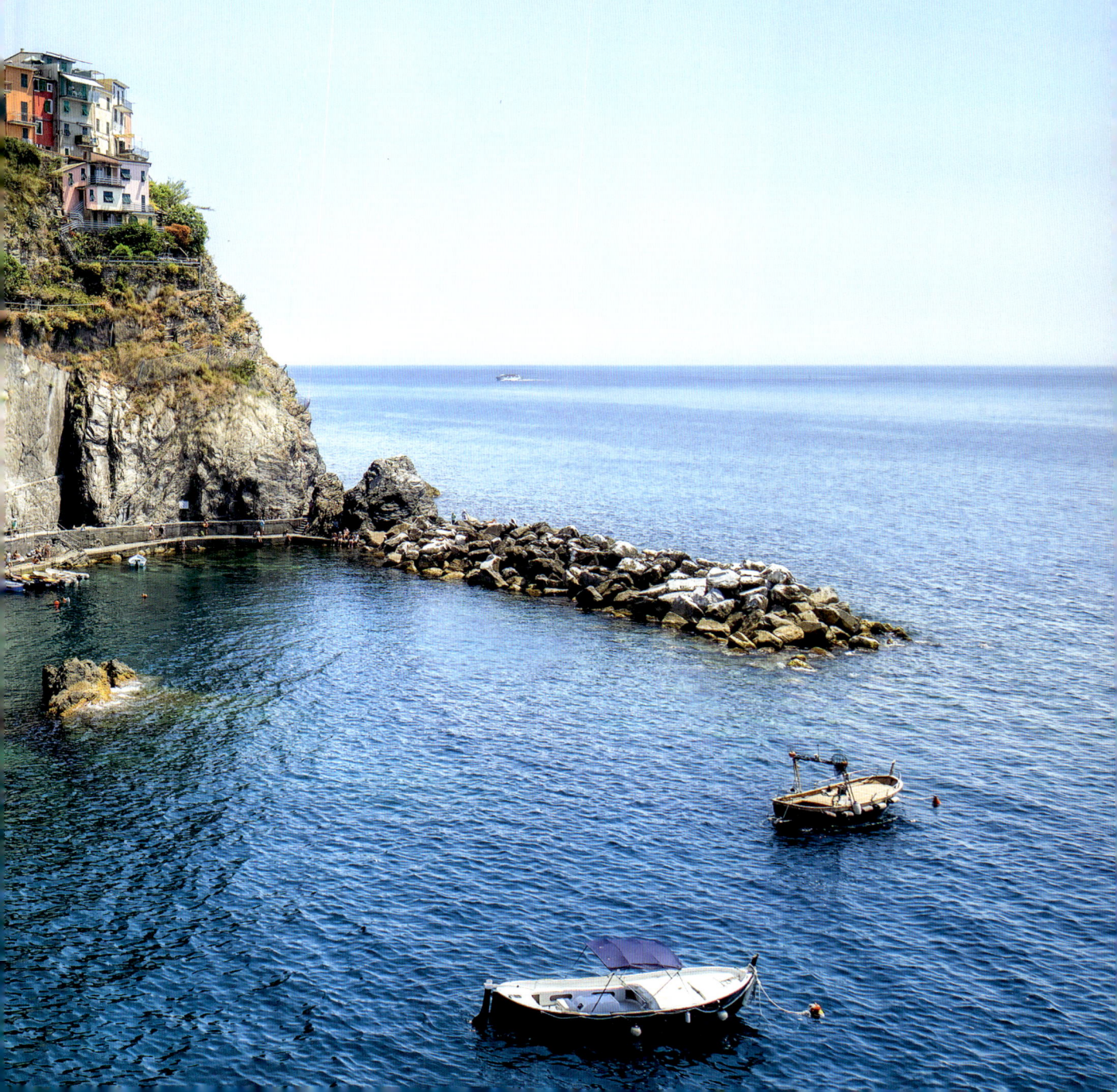

ALONG THE CINQUE TERRE COAST

Italy

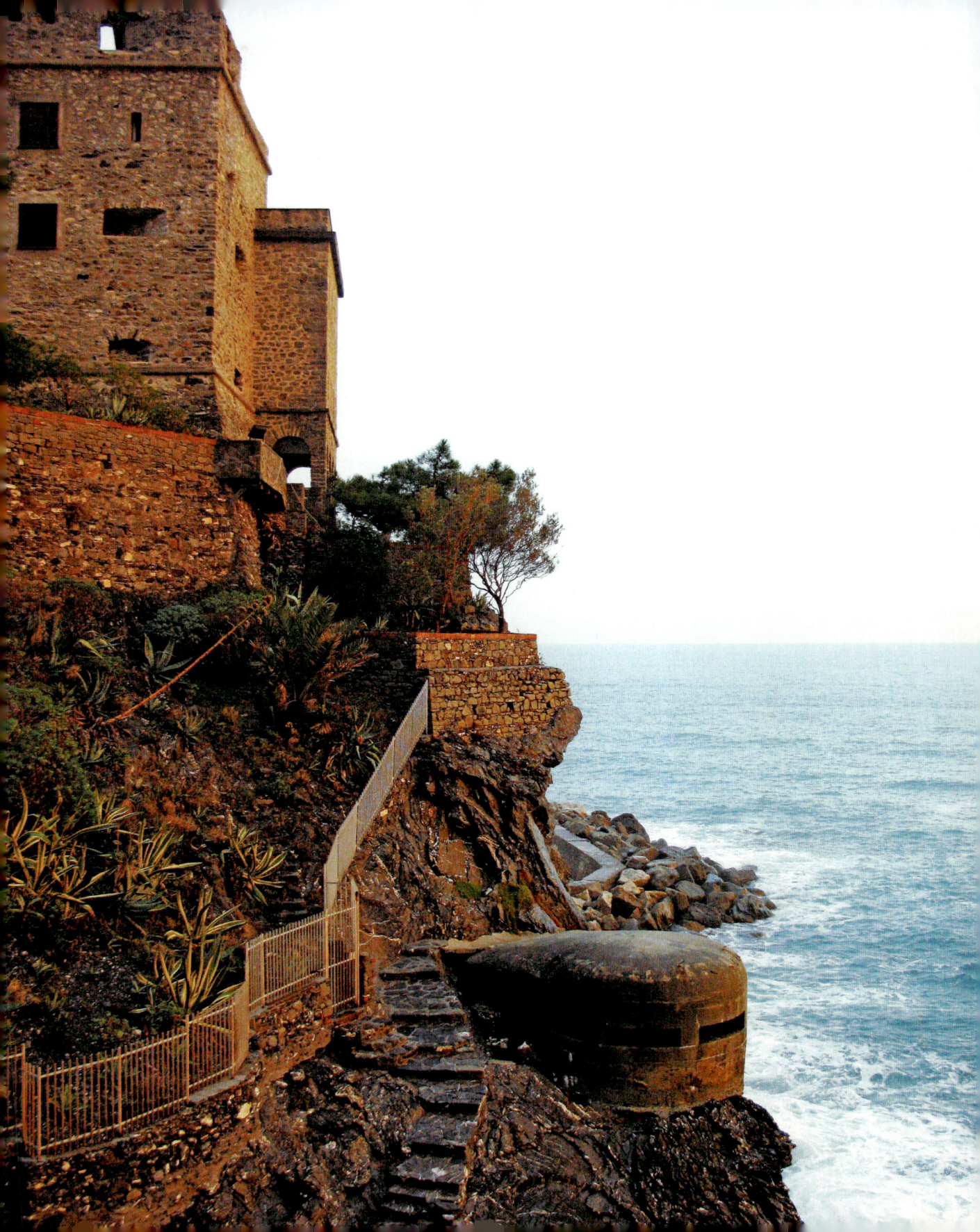

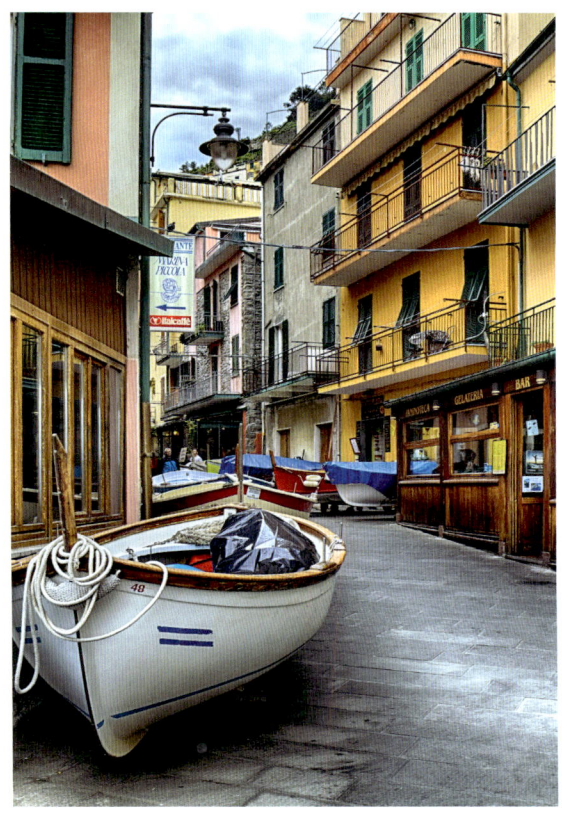

Walking the Cinque Terre coastline affords hikers views of some stunning coastal scenery—pastel-colored buildings that appear stacked against each other on steep slopes, aromatic lemon groves, and vineyards on chiseled inclines.

the course—particularly during the 600-step section between Monterosso and Vernazza. But there are multiple places to rest and catch one's breath along the way, and the next restaurant or village is never far away.

Scenically and geographically speaking, the Sentiero Azzurro is a tour de force from its beginning at the the village of Monterosso to its end at Riomaggiore, a charming settlement spanning a seaside valley. The views overlooking the Ligurian Sea are sublime, and the centuries-old villages with their cobblestone streets, churches, and soft-toned domiciles retain a sense of magic, despite the fact that the area has long been a mecca for tourists. If selecting just one standout feature, it would be hard to go past the fairy-tale-like seaside village of Vernazza, with its natural harbor, narrow lanes, and quaint character. →

↖↓ Colorful houses and seaside village life.
← Natural and man-made forms on the Cinque Terre coast.

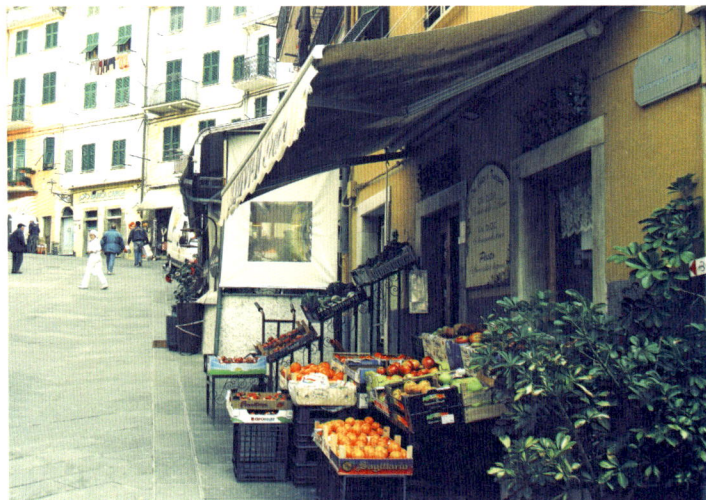

The Sentiero Azzurro (Blue Path) may be the world's longest short walk. Measuring only 11.3 km (7 mi.) in length, this classic pathway through the five villages of Cinque Terre can take anywhere between three hours and three days to complete. The reasons for this considerable discrepancy are motivation and appetite, not fitness and hiking experience. Because of the plethora of culinary options available, the Sentiero Azzurro is one hike where walkers will probably have gained rather than lost weight by the time they have finished.

Linking together a quintet of medieval villages—Monterosso, Vernazza, Manarola, Corniglia, and Riomaggiore—along Italy's rugged Ligurian coast, the Sentiero is accessible to hikers of all ages and ability levels. All that is really needed to complete the walk is comfortable footwear and an empty stomach. However, hikers sometimes do have to walk up and down throughout

---

ABOUT THE TRAIL

→ DISTANCE 11.3 km (7 mi.)
→ DURATION 3 hours to 3 days
→ LEVEL Easy

Hikers with the time and inclination should consider combining the Sentiero Azzurro with the Sentiero Rosso (Red Path). Going from south to north, this longer and more strenuous pathway begins in the seaside town of Porto Venere. From there, walkers can follow the trail northwest along the coast until they reach the Colle del Telegrafo restaurant. At this point they can descend to the picturesque village of Riomaggiore to link up with the Sentiero Azzurro.

Walking the Cinque Terre coastline affords hikers views of some stunning coastal scenery—pastel-colored buildings that appear stacked against each other on steep slopes, aromatic lemon groves, and vineyards on chiseled inclines. This, combined with excellent restaurants, wonderful architecture, and hundreds of years of history, makes the Sentiero Azzurro trail an ideal way to soak in the atmosphere of Cinque Terre, a gem of the Mediterranean.

Because of the plethora of culinary options available, the Sentiero Azzurro is one hike where walkers will probably have gained rather than lost weight by the time they have finished.

↓ Ocean views, centuries-old architecture, and stunning coastline.

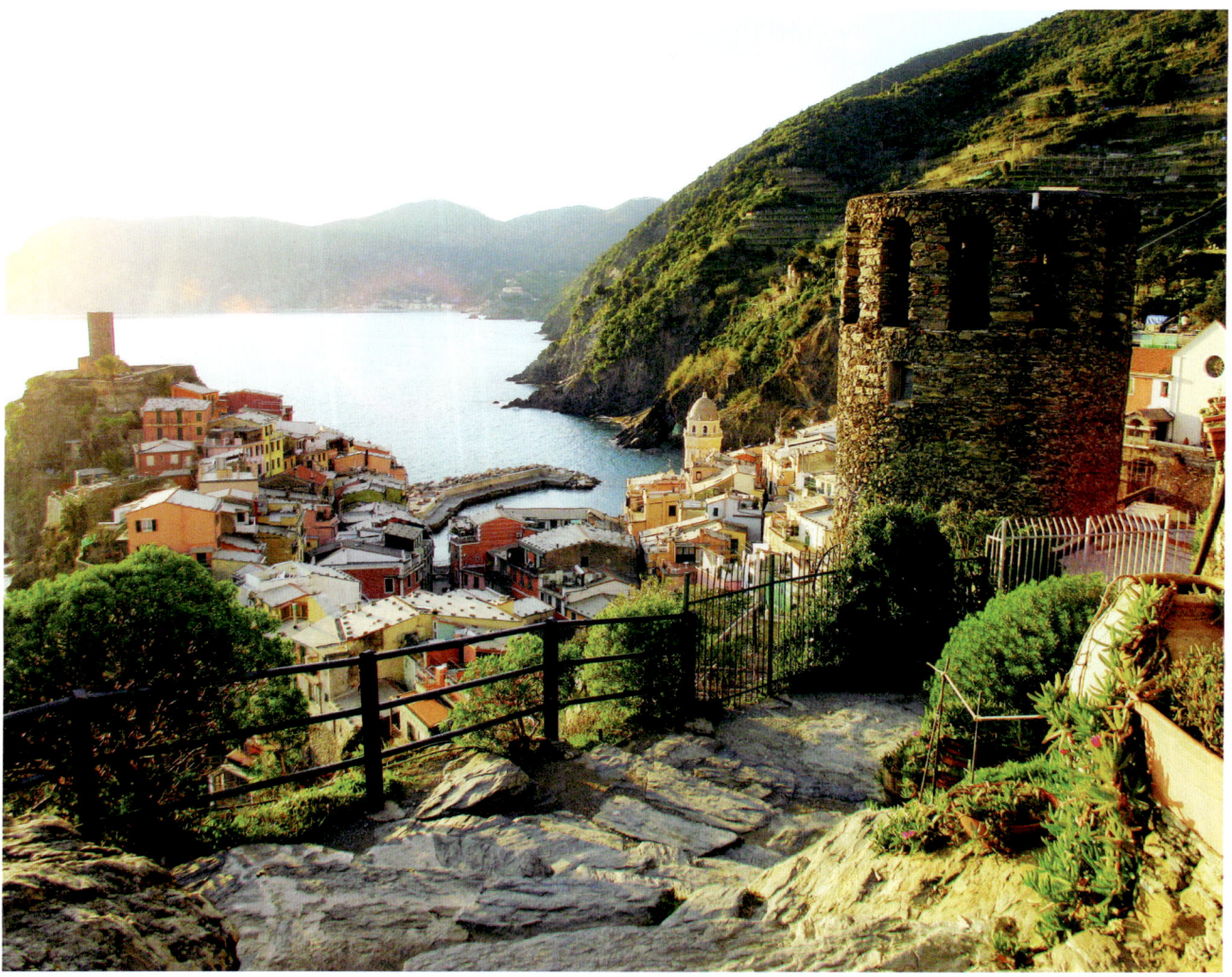

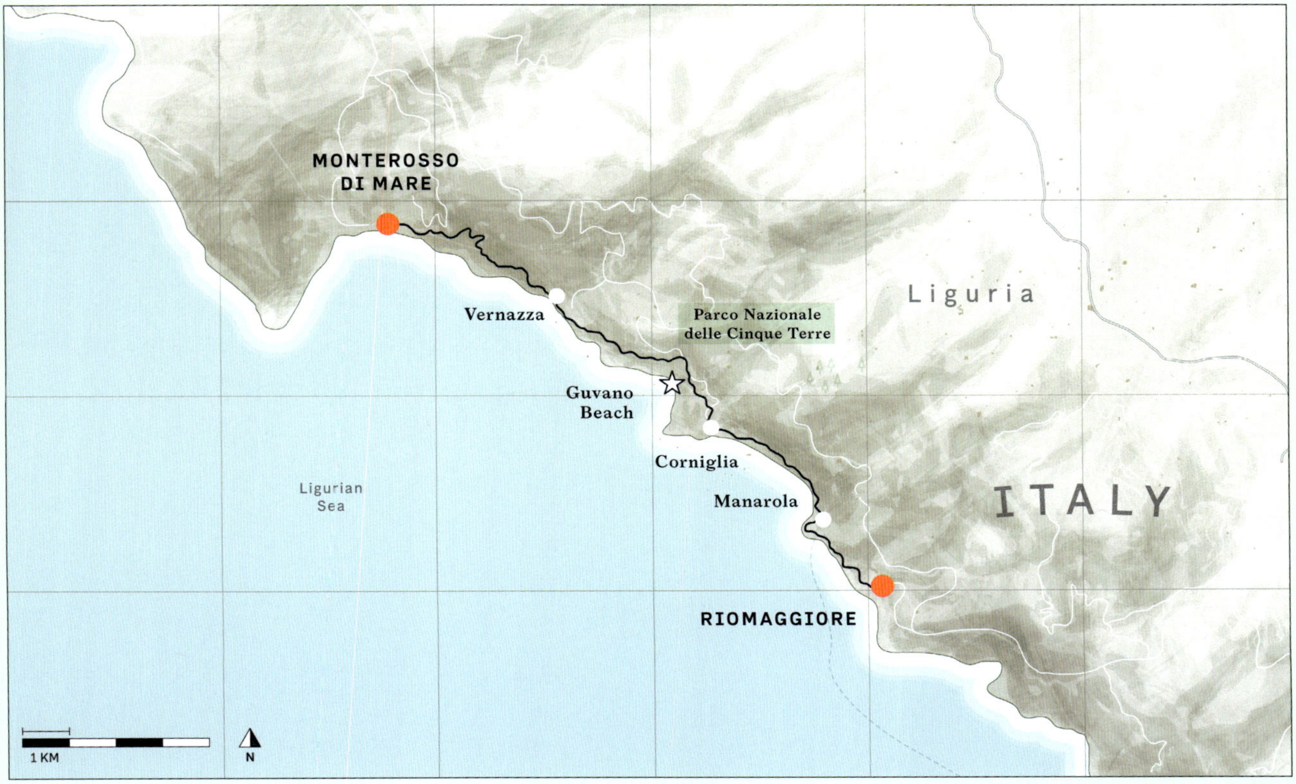

Map

MONTEROSSO
DI MARE

Vernazza

Parco Nazionale
delle Cinque Terre

Liguria

Guvano
Beach

Corniglia

ITALY

Manarola

Ligurian
Sea

RIOMAGGIORE

1 KM

N

GOOD TO KNOW

START/FINISH
Monterosso
Riomaggiore

SEASON
Year-round

CONDITIONS
Due to landslides, certain sections of the
trail may occasionally be closed. This should
be checked in advance.

ACCOMMODATION
A variety of options are available in all five
villages. Monterosso is the largest and
has the widest range of choices. Corniglia
and Manarola are the smallest, and have
the fewest.

SIDETRIP
The Sentiero Azzurro (Blue Path) can be
linked up with the Sentiero Rosso
(Red Path) via the Colle del Telegrafo.

TIP
To avoid some of the crowds, hikers should
consider visiting the Cinque Terre in winter.
There are fewer people, it is not that cold,
and the accommodation is considerably
cheaper.

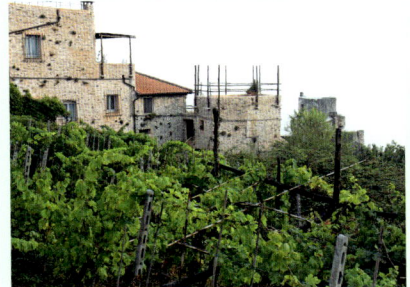

HELPFUL HINTS

LA DOLCE VITA Pesto, an Italian delicacy
that most will already know, originated
from the Liguria region, and so is worth
sampling in generous quantities. A lesser-
known specialty is Sciacchetrà, a sweet wine
produced from grapes grown in the Cinque
Terre hills and made according to traditional
methods, where grapes are dried into raisins
and then fermented.

FLORA & FAUNA

WILD SNACKING The trails in Cinque
Terre National Park contain an abundance
of culinary delights—wild garlic, rosemary,
thyme, figs, and wild asparagus.

BACKGROUND

THE HISTORY Dating back to the twelfth
and thirteenth centuries, the Sentiero Azzurro is an old mule path that until 1874 was
the only functional way to travel between the
five fishing villages it links together. Today
the Cinque Terre—the name for Monterosso,
Vernazza, Manarola, Corniglia, Riomaggiore, which lie in a string along the coast—is
listed by UNESCO for its scenic and cultural
importance.

The two oldest of the villages are
Monterosso and Riomaggiore. The first was
established in 643 AD, and Greek settlers
are said to have founded the second in the
eighth century. A lot of the architecture
in the settlements today is said to date from
the late High Middle Ages; castle remains
and parish churches are among the note-
worthy sites.

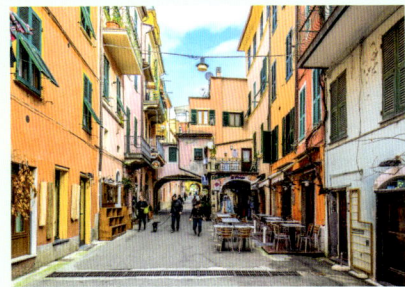

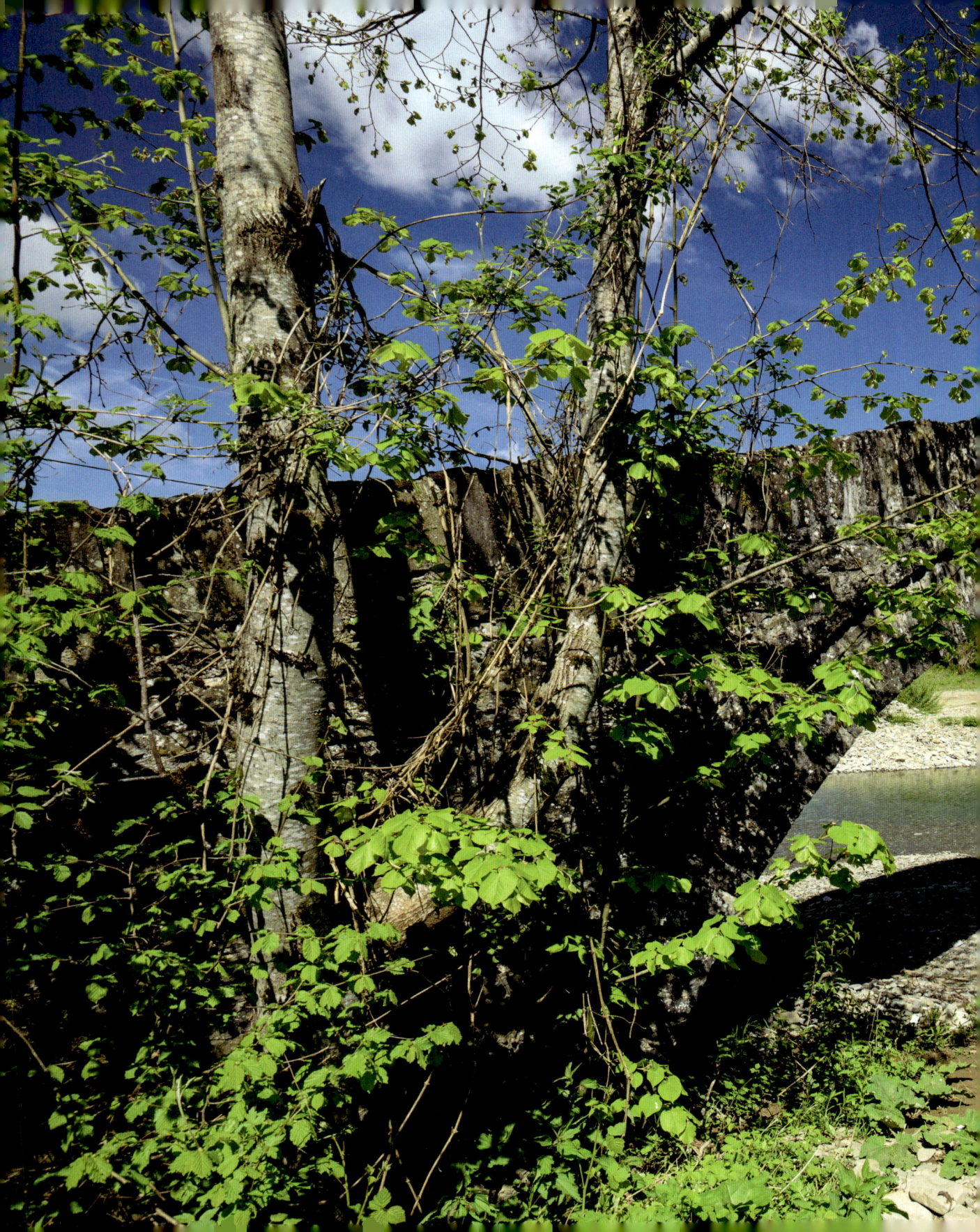

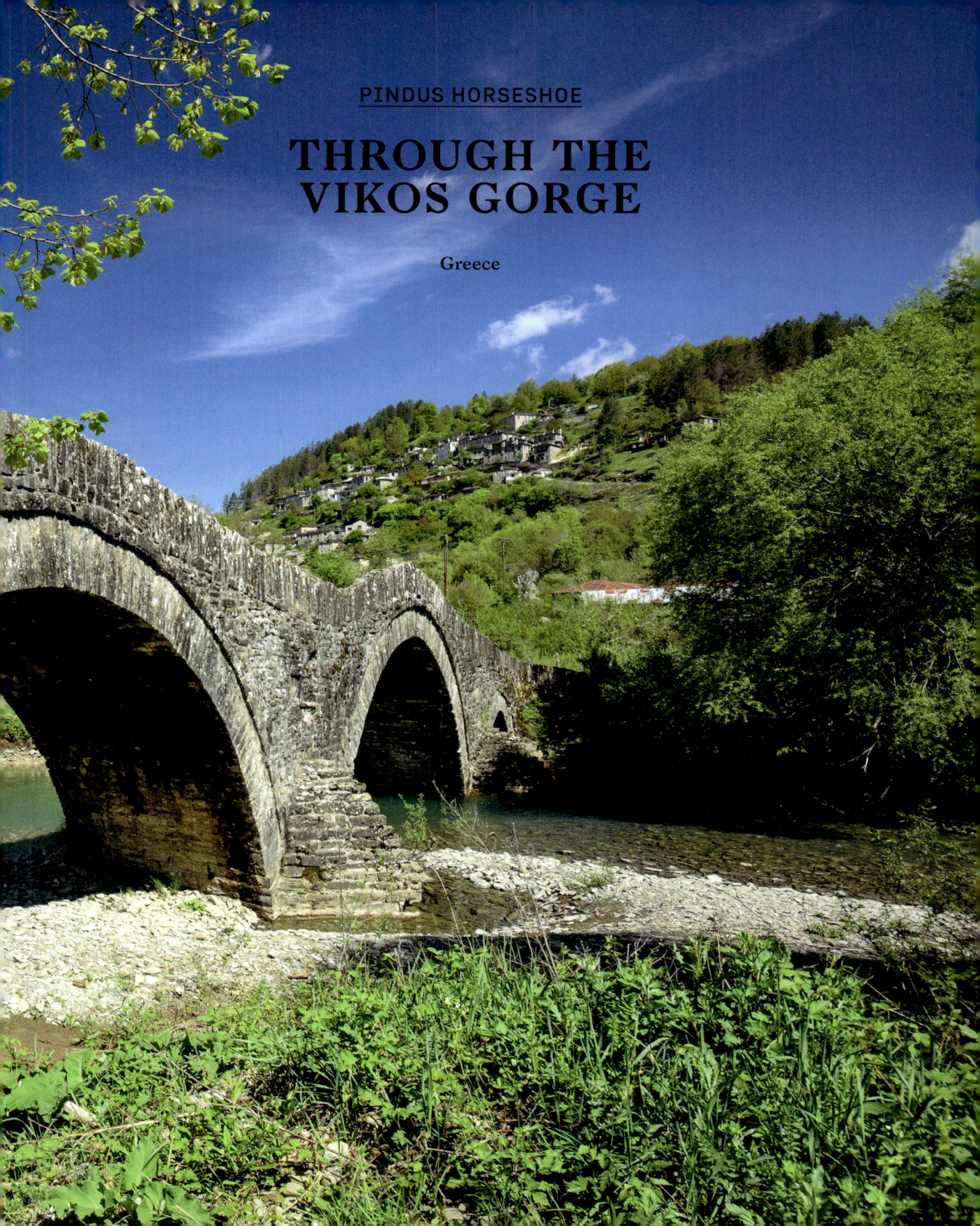

THROUGH THE VIKOS GORGE

Greece

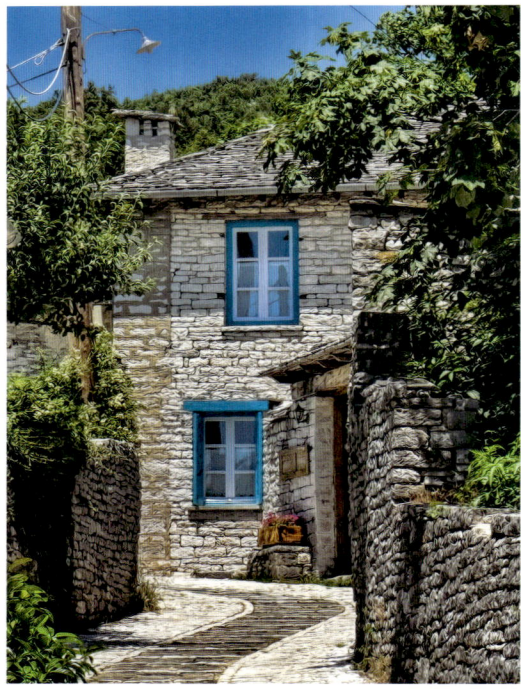

↑ In the village of Monodendri.

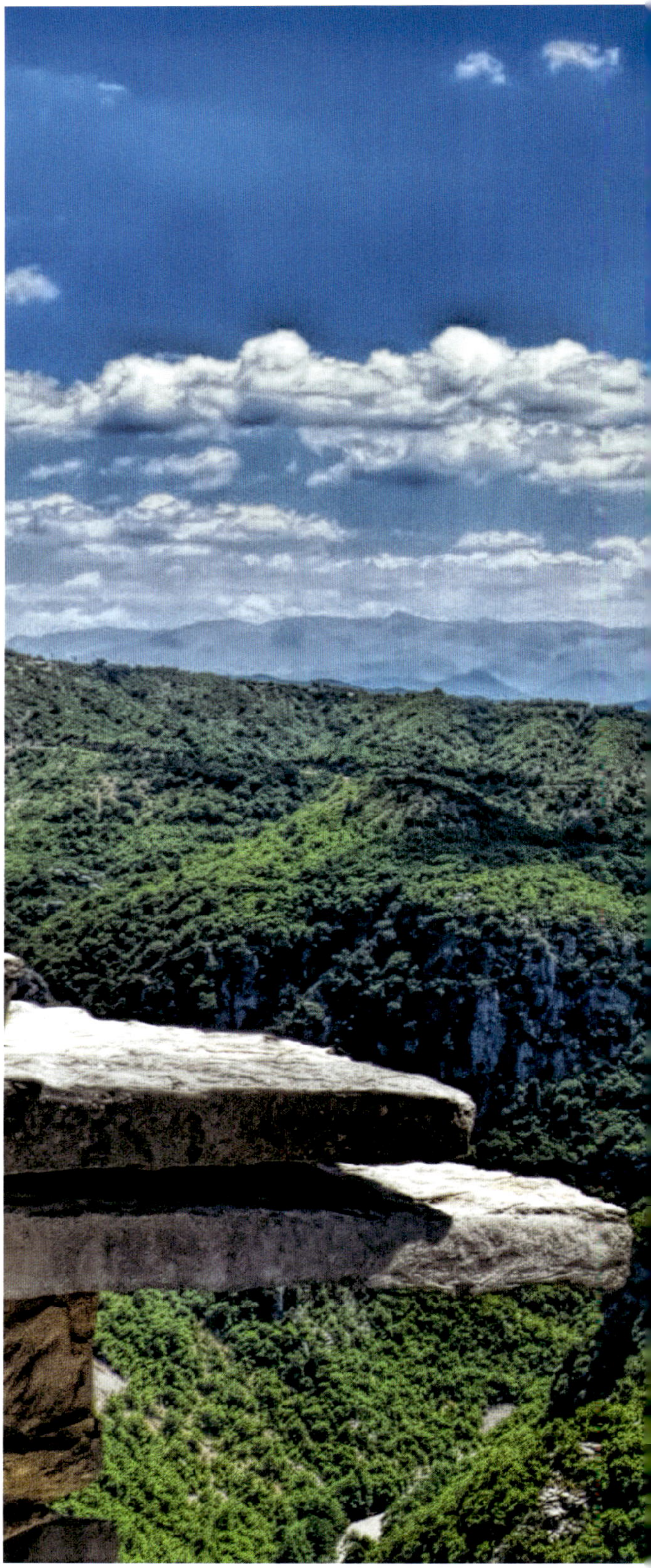

The Pindus Mountains of northwestern Greece are one of the hiking world's best-kept secrets. Alpine lakes and jagged limestone mountains combine with centuries-old stone villages and rainbow-shaped bridges to provide visitors with a singular combination of natural and historical elements. A diverse array of flora and fauna—from tiny, scuttling lizards to huge brown bears, and from conifers to pine forests—along with tavernas serving traditional Greek specialties—potent, locally made ouzo, honey-soaked baklava—also make for a trip to remember.

The Pindus Horseshoe begins in the village of Monodendri, which is situated near the rim of the spectacular Vikos Gorge. With a depth that ranges between 450 and 1,600 m (1,476 and 5,249 ft.), the Vikos is entered into the *Guinness Book of Records* as the world's deepest gorge. The trail descends to the floor of the ravine, passing through a diverse forest of oak, beech, maple, and birch trees. Winding its way up the gorge, →

ABOUT THE TRAIL

→ <u>DISTANCE</u> 58 km (36 mi.) (including ascent of Astraka Peak)

→ <u>DURATION</u> 4 to 5 days

→ <u>LEVEL</u> Moderate

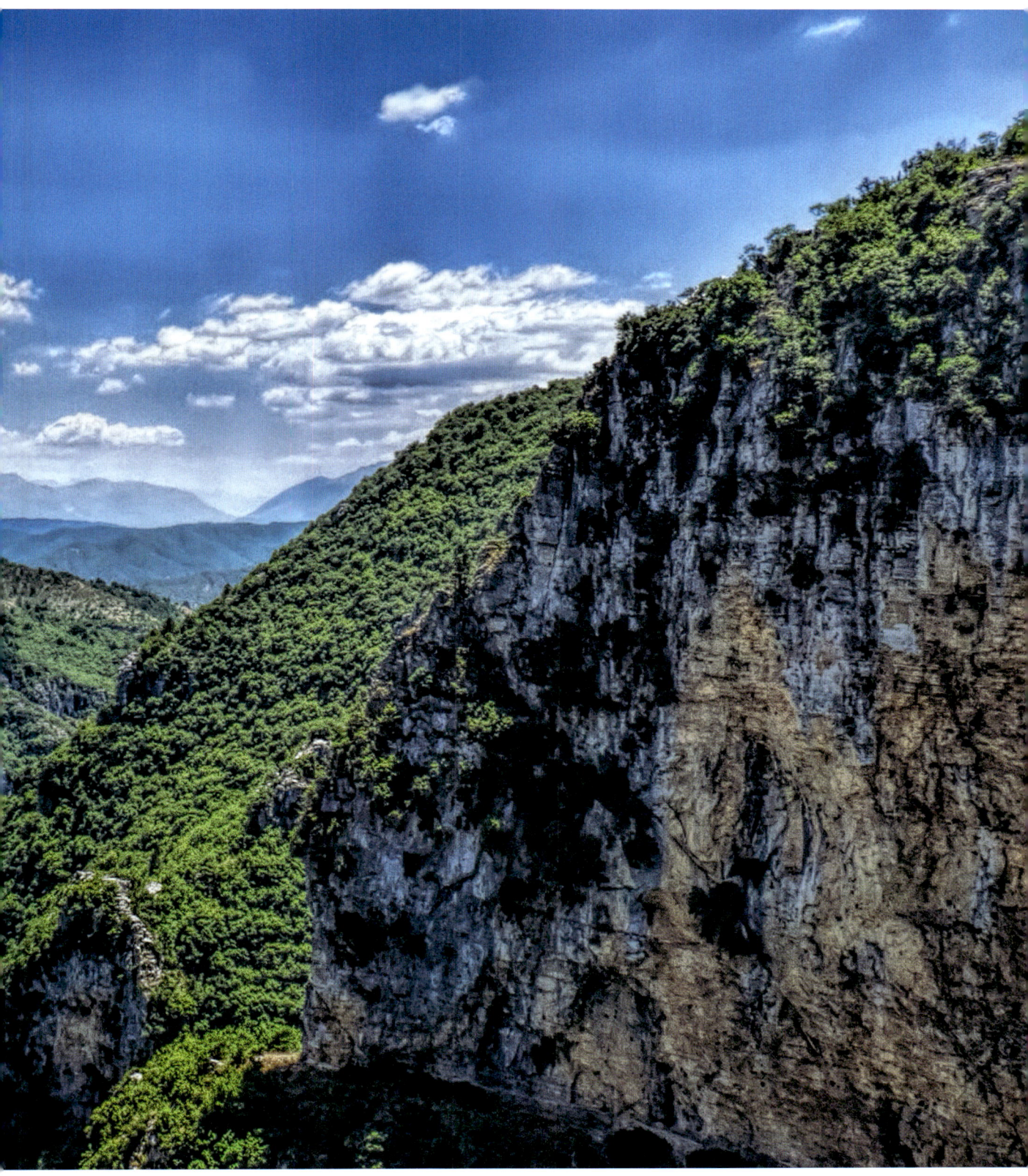

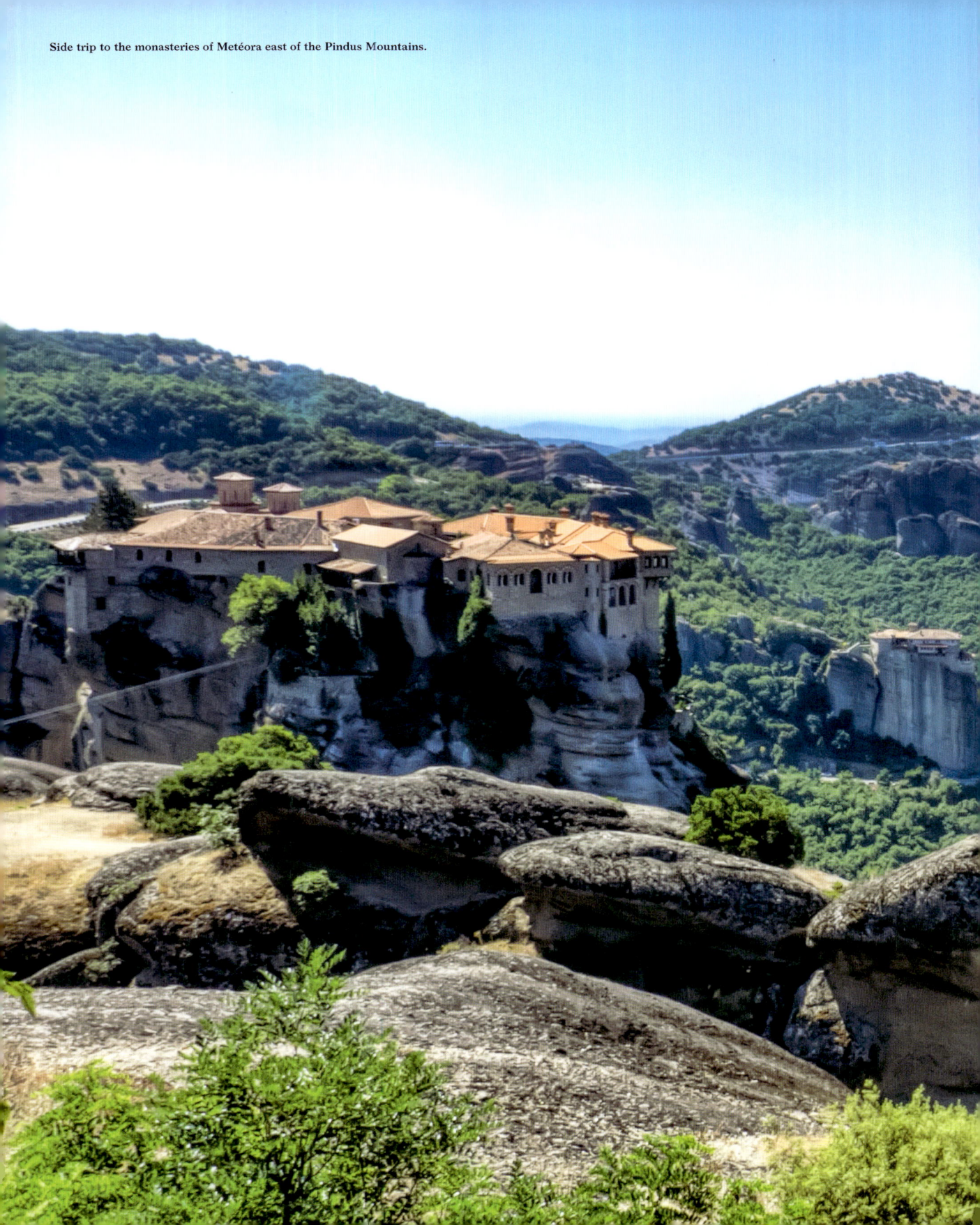

Side trip to the monasteries of Metéora east of the Pindus Mountains.

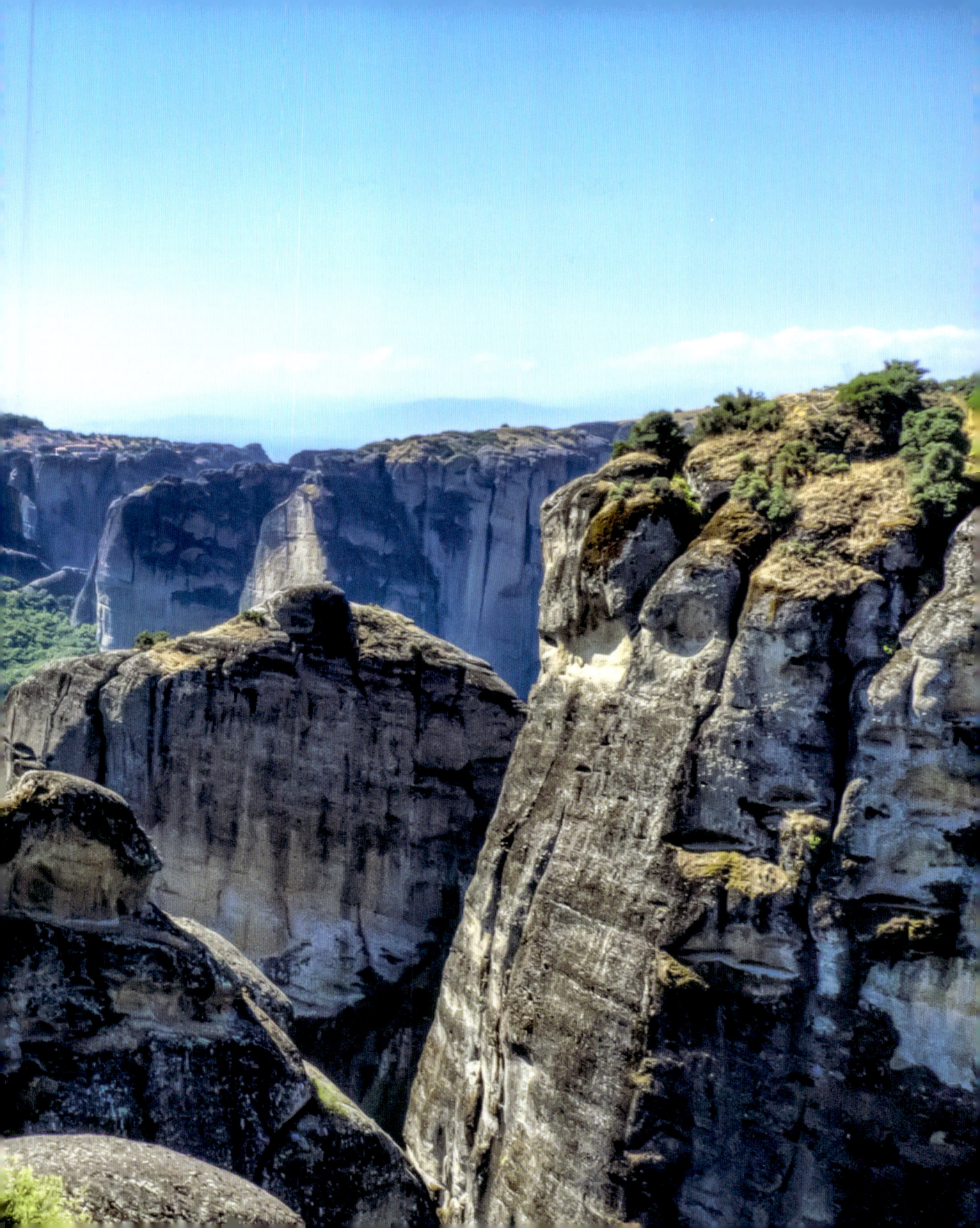

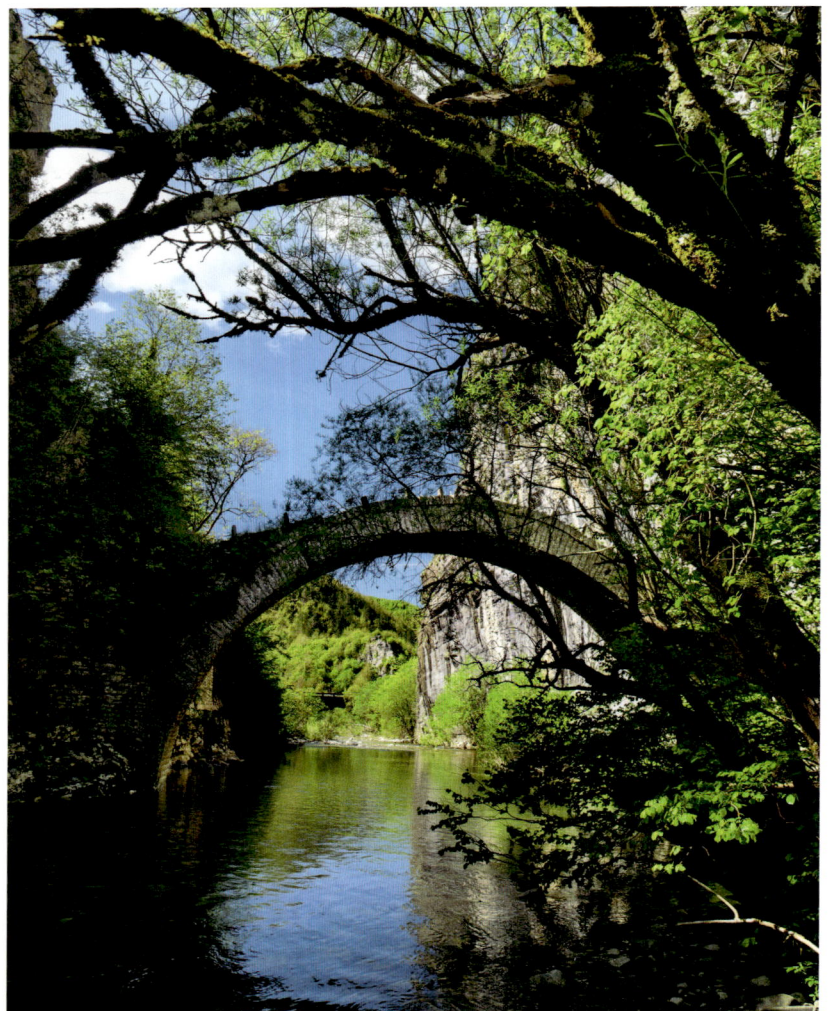

↑ The bridge of Lazaridis or Kontodimos (c. 1753) near the village of Kipi.

Looking like something out of Rivendell in Tolkien's *The Lord of the Rings*, these striking overpasses date back to the eighteenth and nineteenth centuries.

it periodically emerges to open spaces, where the imposing cliffs and peaks that line its sinuous course come into full view. With luck, walkers may even spot some of the wildlife for which the Pindus Mountains are famous, including brown bears, wolves, lynx, and wild horses.

After around 20 km (12 mi.), the trail ascends from the gorge to arrive at the picturesque village of Mikro Papigo. Nestled in the shadows of towering Mount Tymfi, this age-old settlement is enchanting, with its winding cobble-stoned streets, the beautiful church of Taxiarches, atmospheric plazas, and seemingly everything made of stone. Hikers might want to stay, relax, and spend a couple of days drinking in the atmosphere (and perhaps even an ouzo or two).

Apart from the villages, the architectural highlights of any visit to the Pindus region are the Zagori bridges. Looking like something out of Rivendell in Tolkien's *The Lord of the Rings*,

these striking overpasses date back to the eighteenth and nineteenth centuries. Altogether there are 92 of these stone arched bridges in Zagoria, many of which have been named after those who built them. The most famous ones include the Kokori, Missios, and Kalogeriko bridges. For many years, these, along with the extensive system of cobblestone pathways, represented the sole means by which some of the more remote Zagori villages could be accessed.

The multitude of paths and bridges in the Pindus Mountains act as segues into the region's varied natural landscapes. Foremost among these is the area around Astraka Peak and Dragon Lake. As with other similarly named bodies of water throughout Greece, Dragon Lake was named after the small lizards that live in it. The views from the top of Astraka are breathtaking, as is the ascent. Situated at the base of the mountain is the Astraka Col Refuge. This hut is the only one of its kind on the Pindus Horseshoe, and makes for a great overnighting option. It has plenty of room, serves hearty meals, and often boasts an international cast of lodgers.

After leaving Astraka, hikers continue south over a high, grassy plateau, which during May and June is laden with wildflowers. In the summer months, local shepherds often use this area to graze their flocks. Once again the views are impressive. Eventually the route reaches the ancient stone villages of Tsepelovo and Vradeto, marking the end of the journey.

The Pindus mountain range is a hard-to-reach place that possesses a timeless quality. A particular fusion of ancient culture and architecture, together with some of the most strikingly beautiful landscapes in Europe, makes the region one to linger in and explore, and there is no better way to do so than on foot, hiking the Pindus Horseshoe. ───

GOOD TO KNOW

START/FINISH
📍 Monodendri
📍 Vradeto

SEASON
May to October

ACCOMMODATION
Accommodation is available in the ancient stone villages of Mikro Papigo and Tsepelovo. There is also a mountain hut at Astraka Col. Although officially illegal, wild camping is possible along the route so long as discretion and Leave No Trace principles are practiced.

HIGHLIGHTS
Vikos Gorge, Mikro Papigo village, Dragon Lake, Zagori bridges.

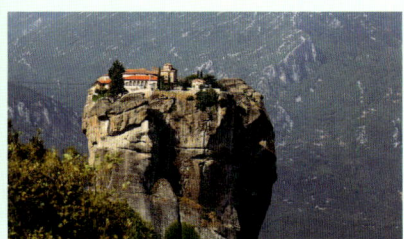

BACKGROUND

ON HIGHER GROUND For those traveling in northern Greece, Metéora is a site of interest, and is situated only a few hours drive from the Pindus Mountains. Meteora is an awe-inspiring collection of predominantly sandstone monoliths with centuries-old monasteries perched on top of them. The oldest of these constructions dates from the fifteenth century, though monks settled on the towering rocks from the eleventh century onwards. Originally there were 24 monasteries, but today only six remain. These holy buildings, which appear to almost grow out of the rock, can today be reached by various means (roads, bridges, cable cars, or on foot) but formerly the only way up was by climbing steep rocks. Today, walkers can follow the old monks' trails (monopatia); one of these passes Agia Triada, or the Monastery of the Holy Trinity, a site featured in the 1981 James Bond film *For Your Eyes Only*.

HELPFUL HINTS

SIDE TRIP Before setting out from Monodendri, a visit to Agias Paraskevis monastery, which was founded in 1413, is worthwhile. It is just 15 minutes walk away, and the views over the Vikos Gorge are well worth the effort.

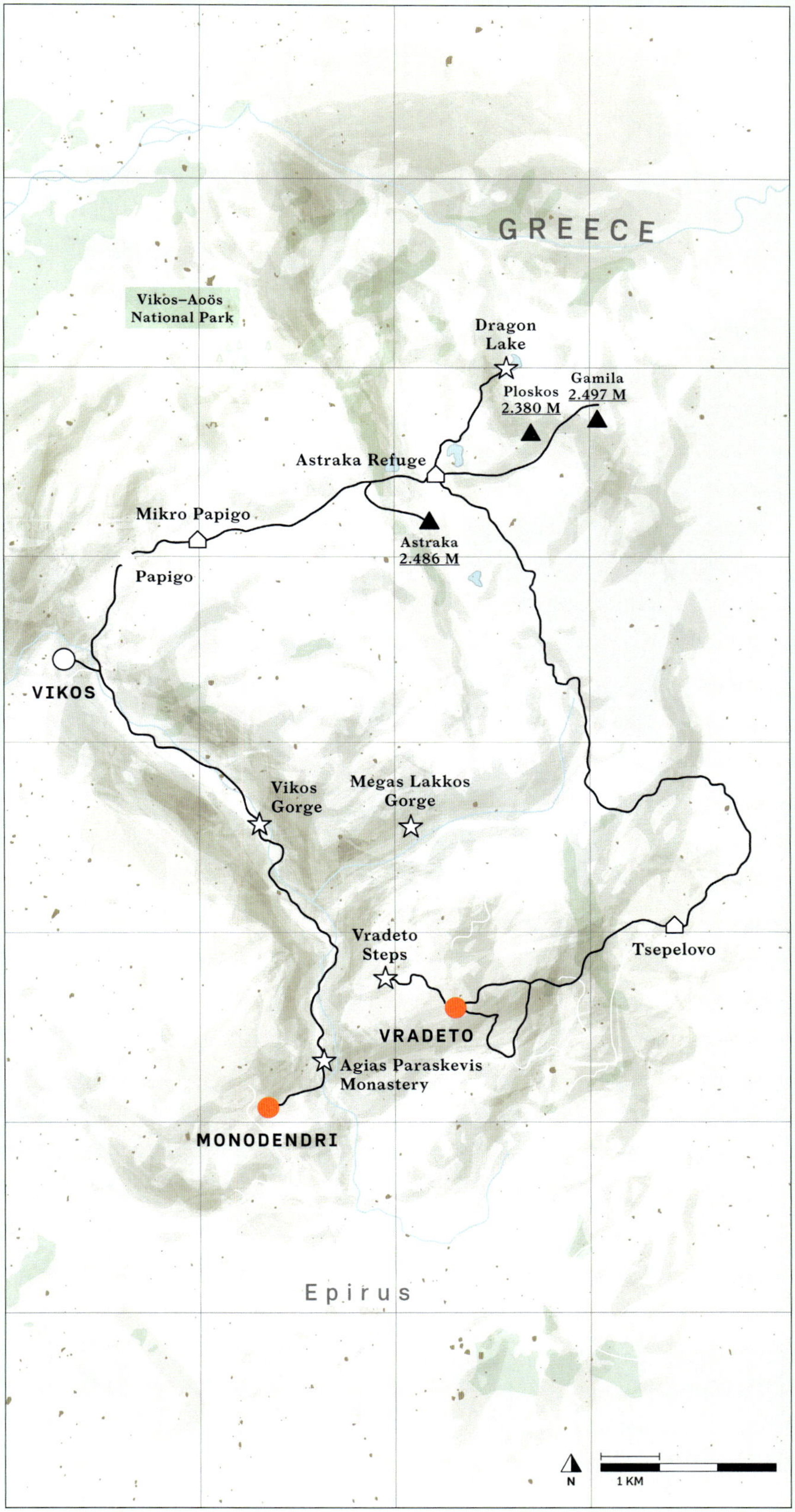

GREECE

Vikos–Aoös National Park

Dragon Lake

Gamila 2.497 M

Ploskos 2.380 M

Astraka Refuge

Mikro Papigo

Astraka 2.486 M

Papigo

VIKOS

Vikos Gorge

Megas Lakkos Gorge

Vradeto Steps

Tsepelovo

VRADETO

Agias Paraskevis Monastery

MONODENDRI

Epirus

N   1 KM

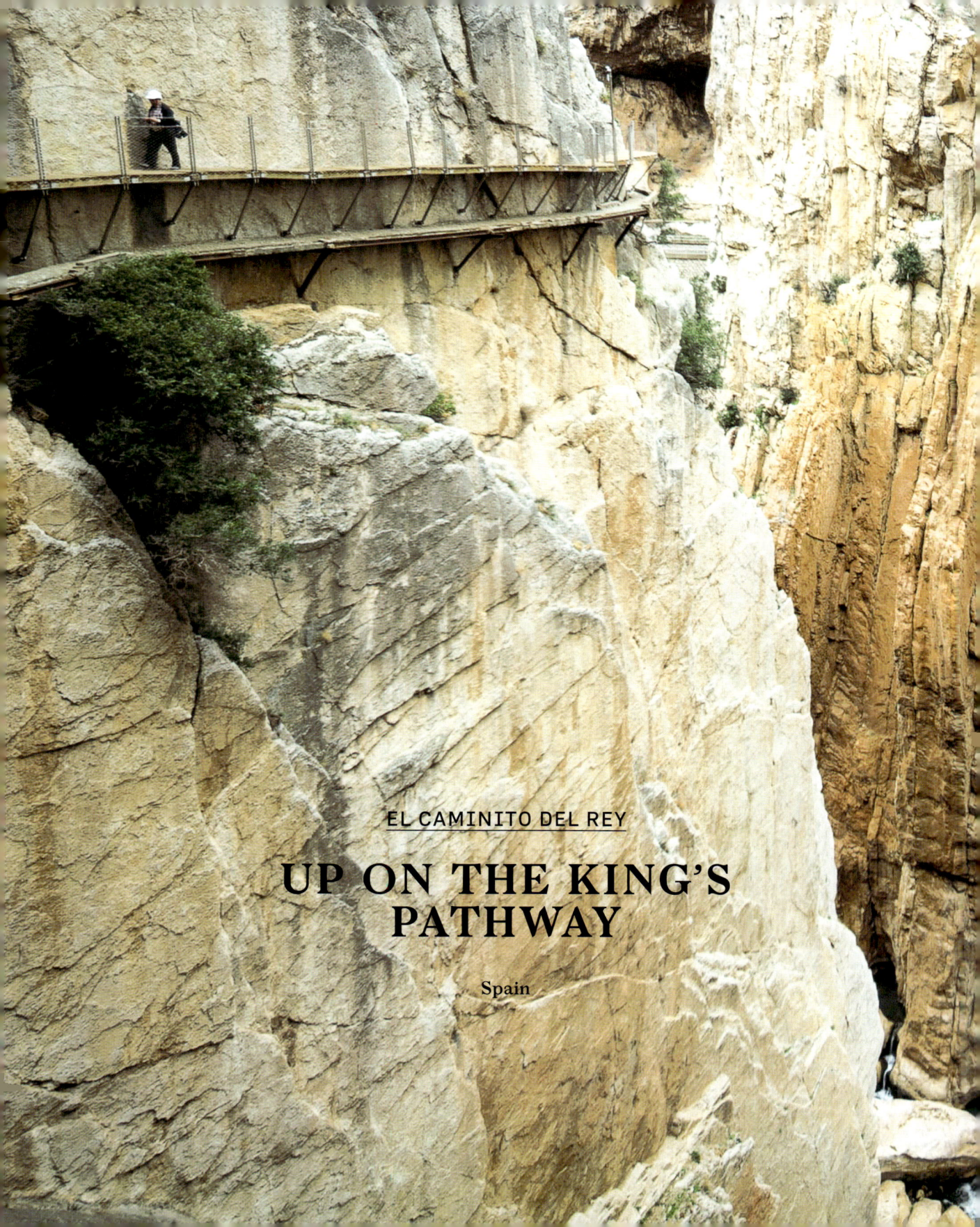

EL CAMINITO DEL REY

UP ON THE KING'S PATHWAY

Spain

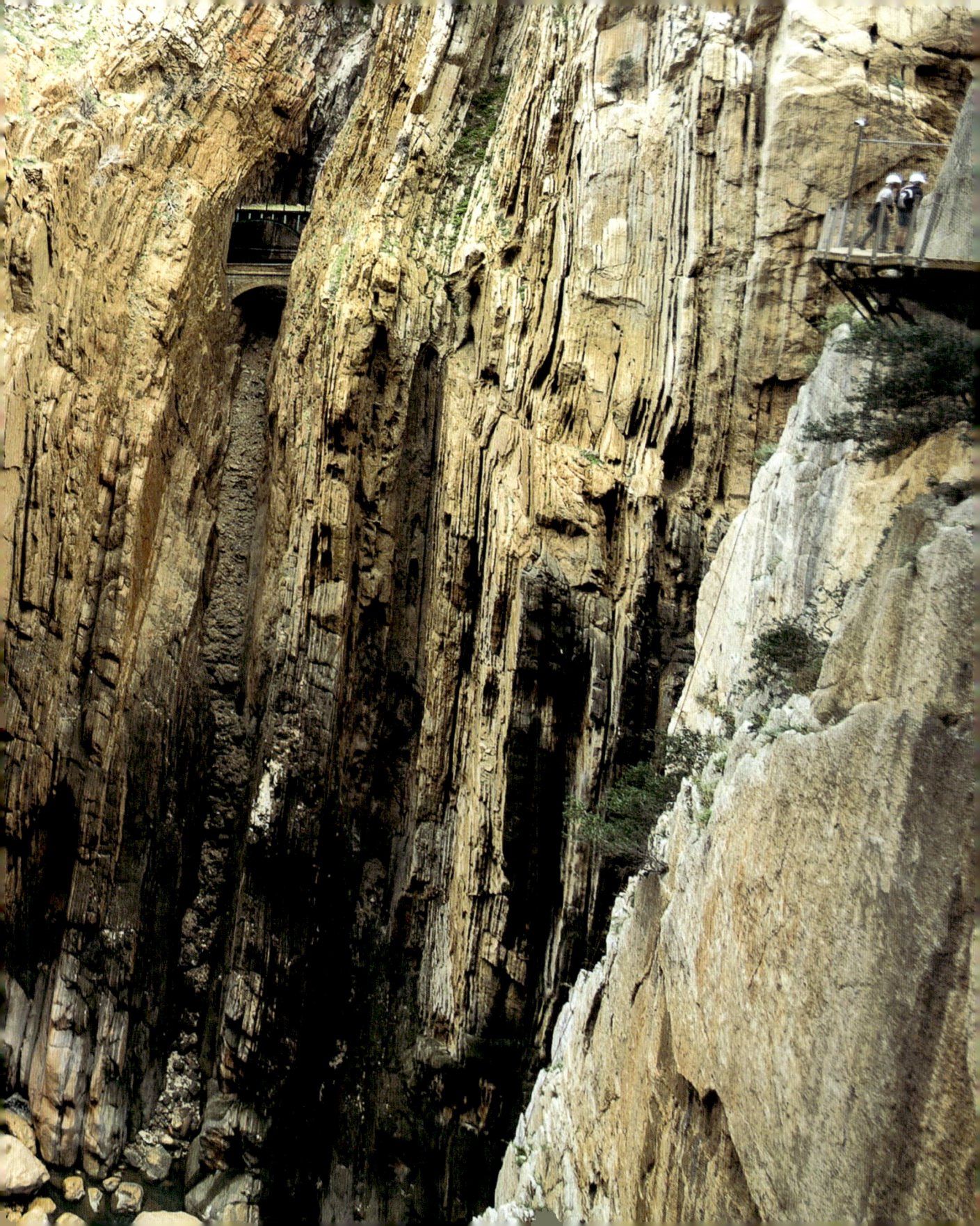

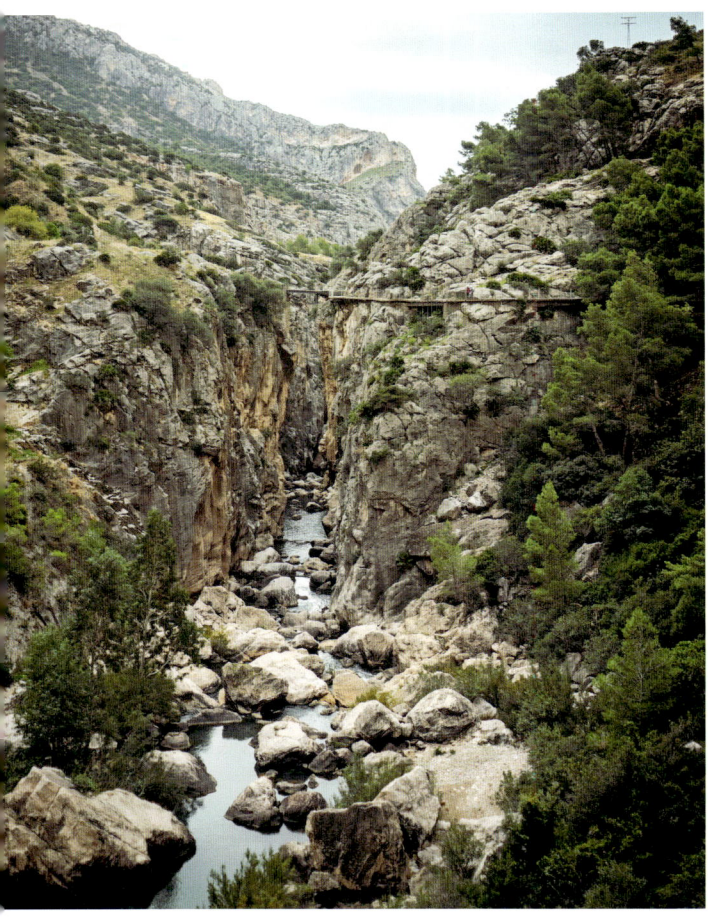

Built in the early 1900s to provide workers passage between the two power stations situated at either end of the gorge, it received its current name when King Alfonso XIII walked its length in 1921.

version sported handrails and reinforced wooden boards, replacing the dilapidated concrete of old (which had included multiple gaping holes), thereby providing a much more visitor-friendly experience.

Despite the overhaul, parts of the original walkway remain, acting as a tangible reminder of the architectural marvel's history. Built in the early 1900s to provide workers passage between the two power stations situated at either end of the gorge, it received its current name when King Alfonso XIII walked its length in 1921, on his way to inaugurating the Conde del Guadalhorce dam. →

→ A precarious crossing on the old path.
↓ The cliff-hugging new and old paths from afar.

F or many years the infamous El Caminito del Rey ("the king's little pathway" in English) was known as one of the world's scariest hikes. It was a decrepit aerial walkway attached to the sheer walls of El Chorro gorge in Malaga, southern Spain. Perched some 105 m (344 ft.) above the Guadalhorce river, it attracted thrill seekers from around the world, some of whom died in making the attempt to negotiate its perilous path. In 2000, it was closed due to the advanced state of disrepair; however, in subsequent years, a steady stream of daredevils continued to chance their luck.

The narrative of El Caminito took a new turn in March 2015, when, after four years of renovations and repairs, it was officially reopened to the public. The new and considerably safer

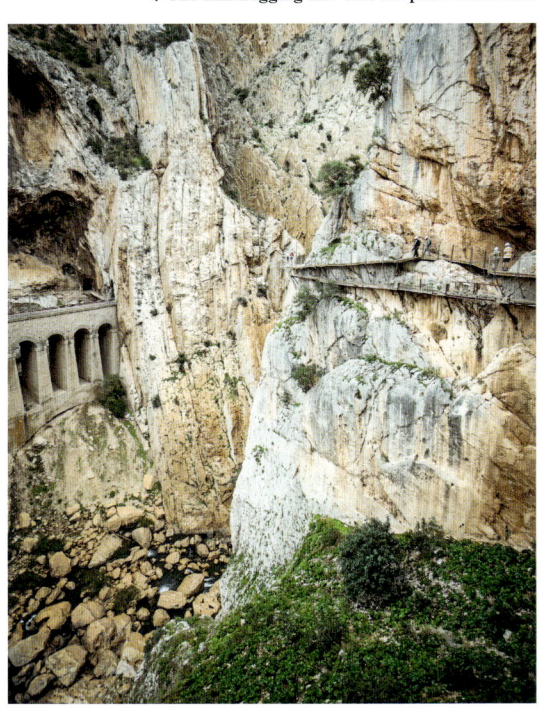

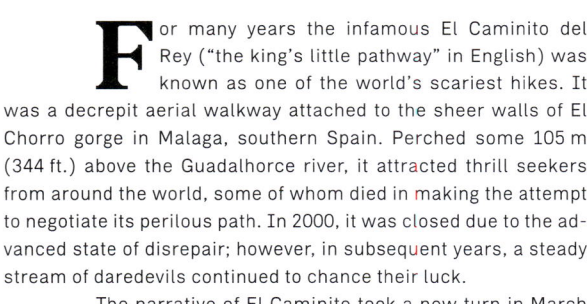

ABOUT THE TRAIL

→ DISTANCE 7.7 km (4.8 mi.)
→ DURATION 3 to 4 hours
→ LEVEL Easy

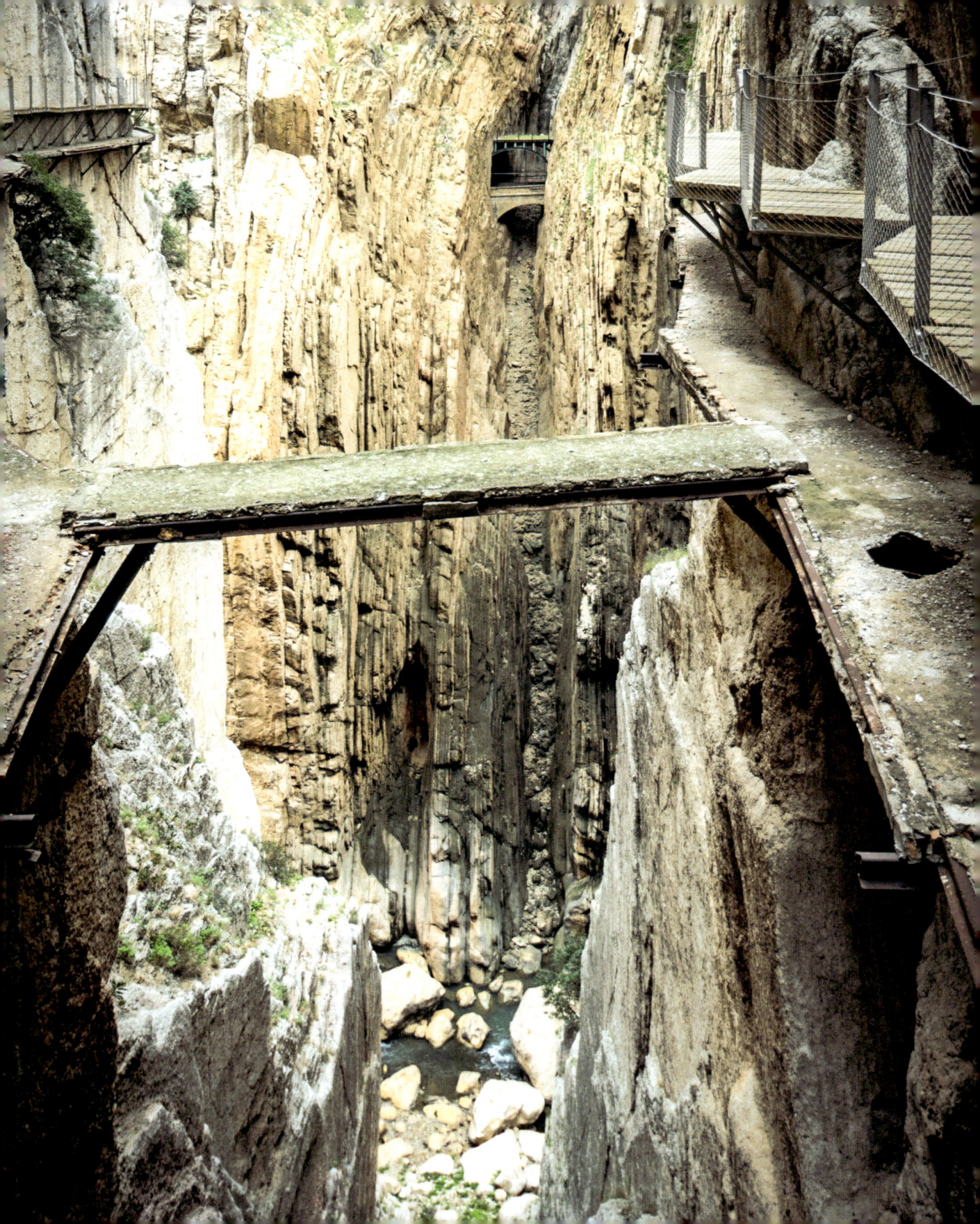

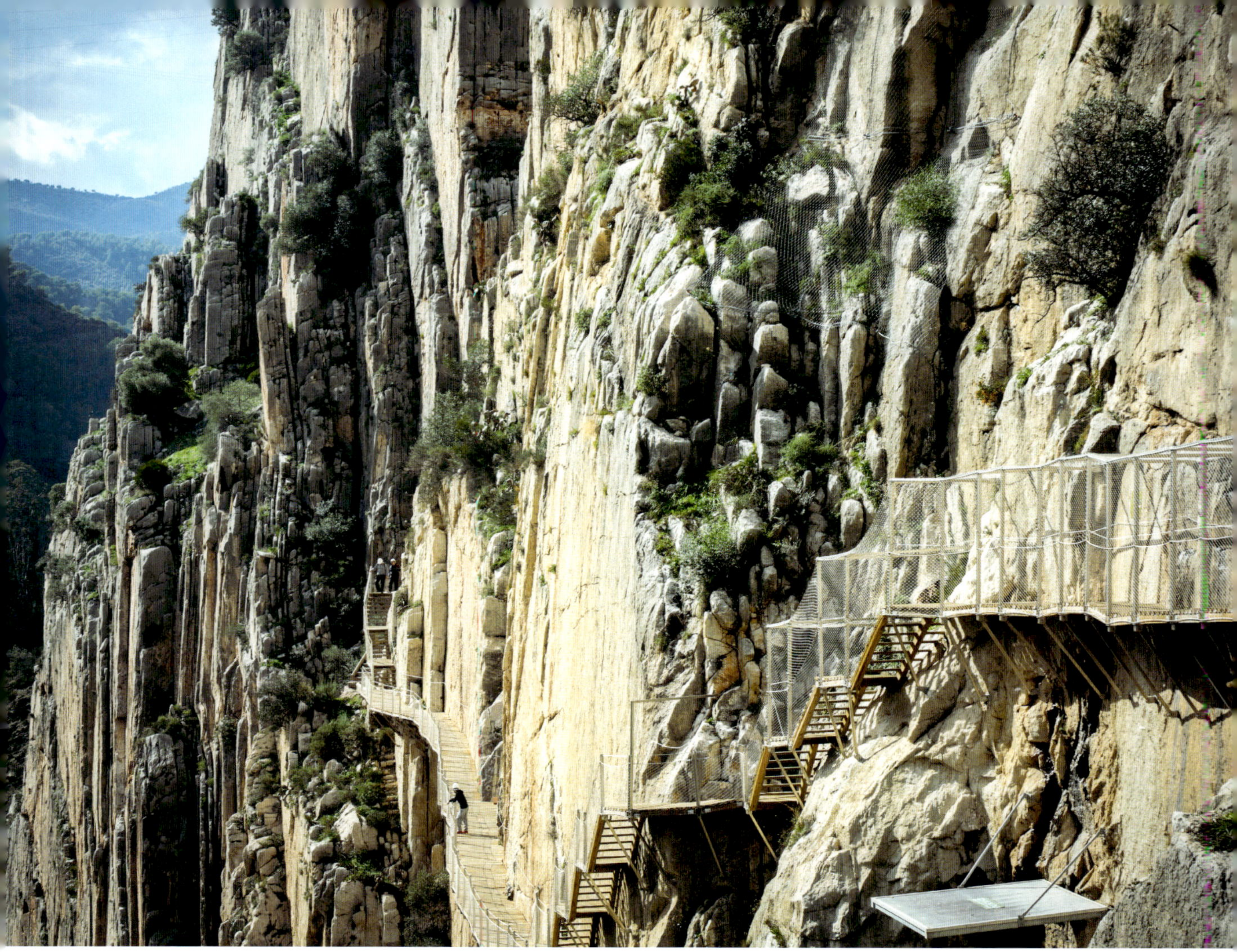

↑↓ Steps on the boardwalk path snake across the rock face.

In the following decades, El Caminito fell into disrepair due to lack of maintenance. However, despite its increasingly poor state, its fame continued to grow, and in 2011 the regional government of Andalusia decided to begin the restoration process. It turned out to be a good decision, both fiscally and from a safety perspective. Since it reopened in 2015, the elevated pathway has become a great draw for tourists.

　　　　While walking El Caminito del Rey may not be the tense, sweat-inducing experience of days past, the views of the 400 m (1,312 ft.) deep gorge remain as magnificent as in the past, and thanks to the renovations, it is now a pathway that can be enjoyed by people of all ages and fitness levels. No special skills or equipment are necessary to complete the hike, but the path is narrow—it does not go beyond 1 m (just over 3 ft.) wide—and cliff-hugging characteristics mean that it is not the best route for walkers who suffer from vertigo.

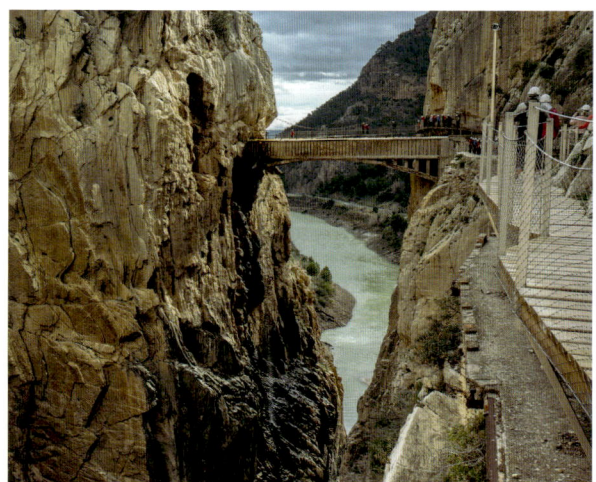

GOOD TO KNOW

START/FINISH
📍 Ardales
📍 El Chorro

SEASON
Year-round

CONDITIONS
Can be closed due to heavy rain and/or high winds. Check the forecast in advance.

HIGHLIGHTS
The 2.9 km (1.8 mi.) boardwalk section through El Chorro gorge.

TIP
Permits are required, so organize one in advance.

HELPFUL HINTS

A RELAXED END Regular buses shuttle walkers between the end point and the start, traveling over 10 km (6 mi.)—something that will be particularly appreciated by those who are feeling a little queasy from looking down into the depths of the gorge.

BACKGROUND

AN ELECTRIFYING HISTORY Industrial electricity arrived in Spain in the 1870s, and hydroelectric power stations began to appear in the early twentieth century.

Named after King Alfonso XIII, who walked it when he opened a dam in May 1921, the Caminito del Rey was built for a not-so-regal purpose: it allowed workers to access two hydroelectric power stations with supplies and equipment. The precarious pathway, which had no safety rails, was constructed between 1901 and 1905 and led to the waterfalls where the plants were located—Chorro Falls and Gaitanejo Falls.

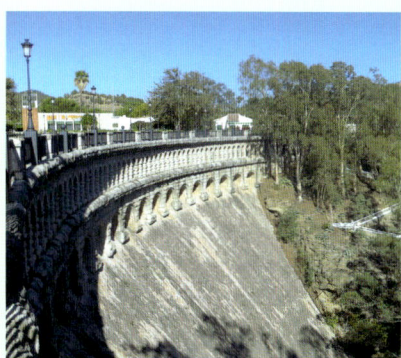

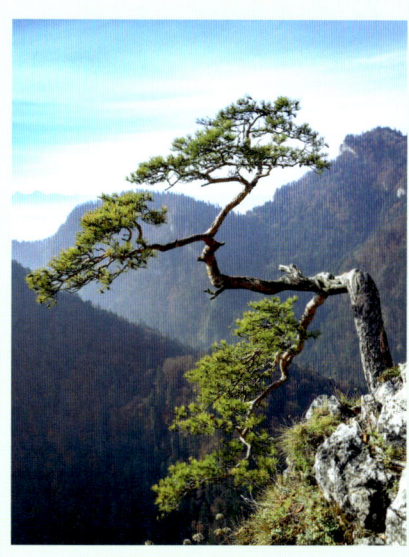

FLORA & FAUNA

ON THIN SOIL The trees that grow around the El Caminito include Aleppo and stone pines. While not exactly pretty, the Aleppo pine, which grows on steep slopes and flourishes in a thin layer of soil, creates a distinctive atmosphere when its richly colored needles are seen against sheer limestone walls.

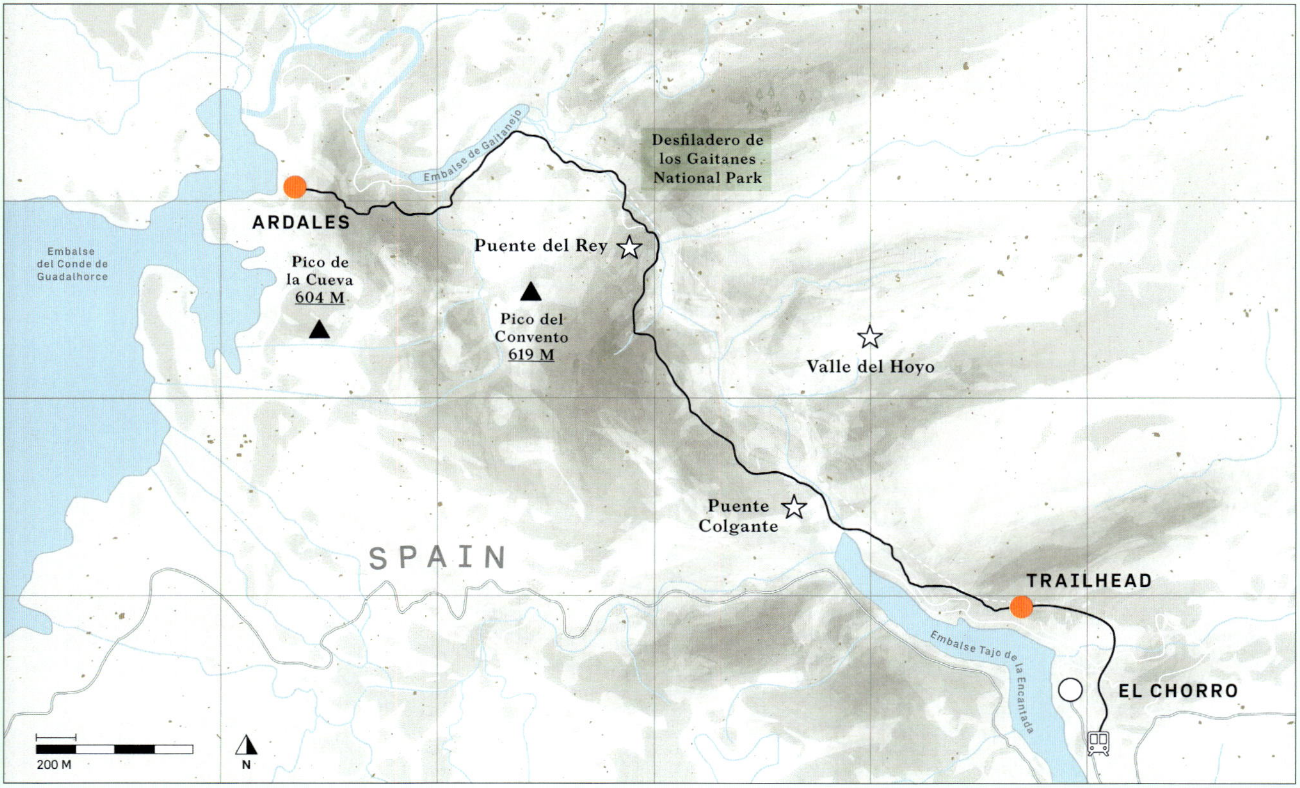

Map:

Embalse del Conde de Guadalhorce

ARDALES

Embalse de Gaitanejo

Desfiladero de los Gaitanes National Park

Pico de la Cueva 604 M

Puente del Rey ☆

Pico del Convento 619 M

Valle del Hoyo ☆

SPAIN

Puente Colgante ☆

TRAILHEAD

Embalse Tajo de la Encantada

EL CHORRO

200 M

N

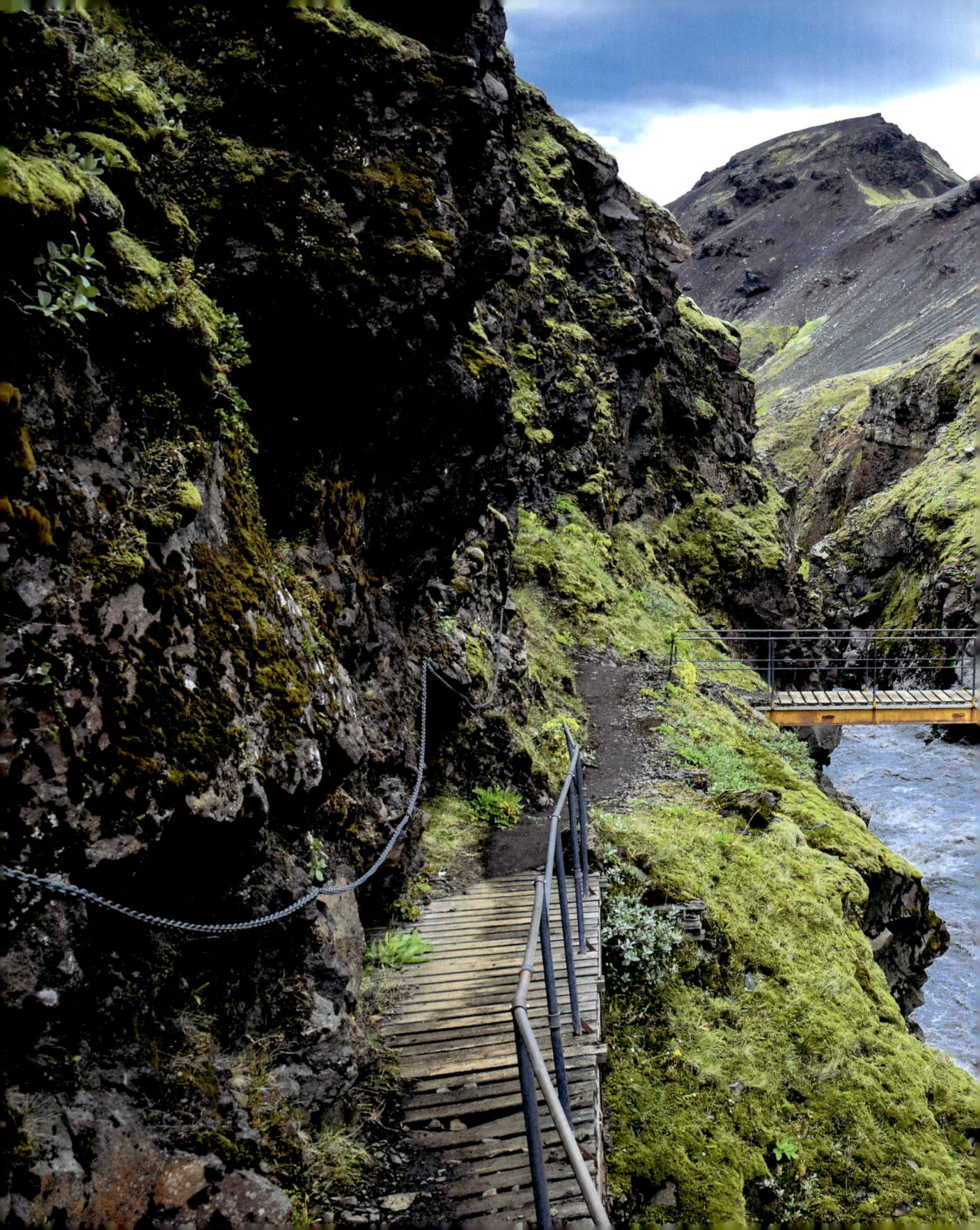

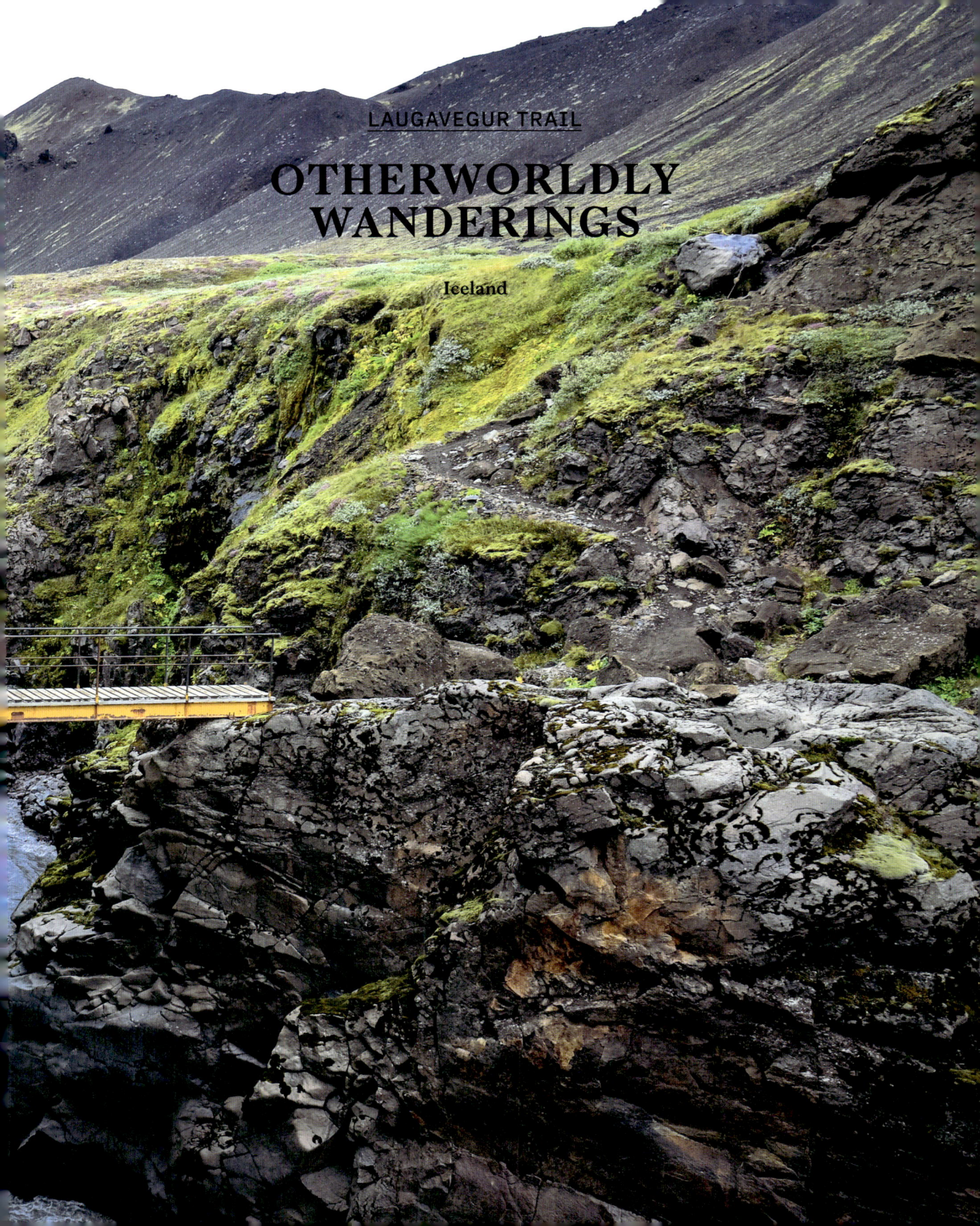

LAUGAVEGUR TRAIL

OTHERWORLDLY
WANDERINGS

Iceland

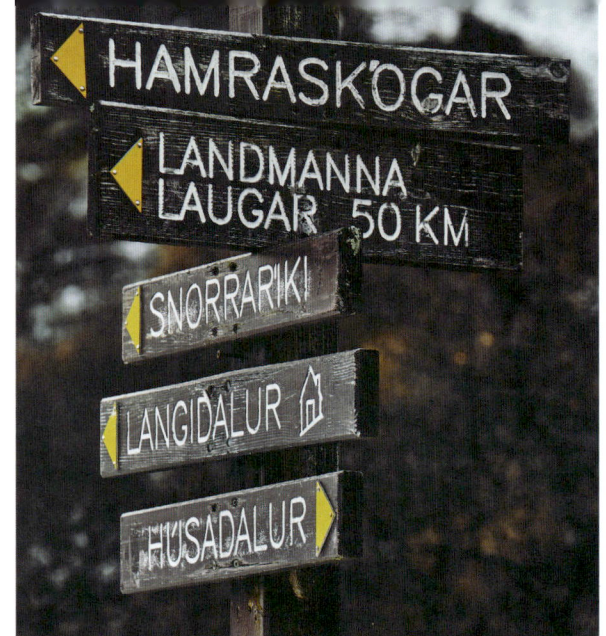

W hen it comes to natural wonders, Iceland sets the bar very high. It is home to around 130 active volcanoes and is one of the finest places to witness the northern lights. But even in a land that contains an abundance of extraordinary features, the Laugavegur stands out.

Stretching between Landmannalaugar and Thórsmörk, this renowned trail takes in lava fields, multicolored rhyolite mountains, black-sand deserts, steaming vents, and glaciers—not to mention the soothing multi-temperature natural springs. The diversity is astonishing.

Though the trek is undoubtedly one of Iceland's finest, walking the Laugavegur between its traditional northern and southern termini is the hiking equivalent of watching two thirds of a classic movie. There are a lot of great things to see, but at the end of the experience there will still be something missing. In this case, it is a 24-km (15-mi.) stretch of spectacular trail known as the Fimmvörðuháls. This particular section, which runs between Thórsmörk and the seaside hamlet of Skógar, boasts one of the finest collections of waterfalls anywhere on the planet—the highlight of which is the mighty Skógafoss. Plunging some 60 m (197 ft.) over coastal cliffs, Skógafoss regularly produces some of the most memorable double rainbows imaginable. And according to a Viking legend dating back to 900 AD, there is even a treasure chest of gold buried behind its thunderous curtain of water.

The trail is well marked with wooden marking posts. In fine conditions, it is straightforward to follow, but the weather →

ABOUT THE TRAIL

→ <u>DISTANCE</u> 78 km (48.5 mi.)
→ <u>DURATION</u> 4 to 5 days
→ <u>LEVEL</u> Moderate

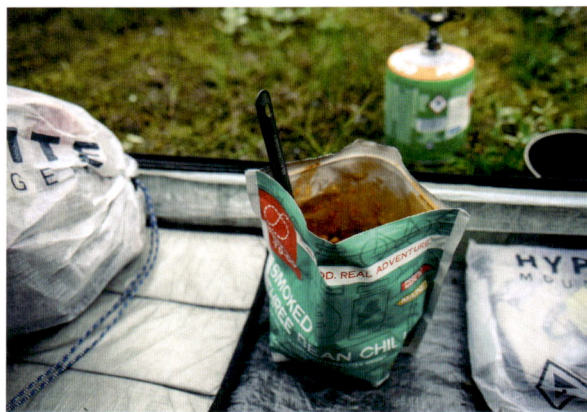

→ One of the many waterfalls on the Laugavegur Trail.
↙ Setting up camp in stark surroundings.

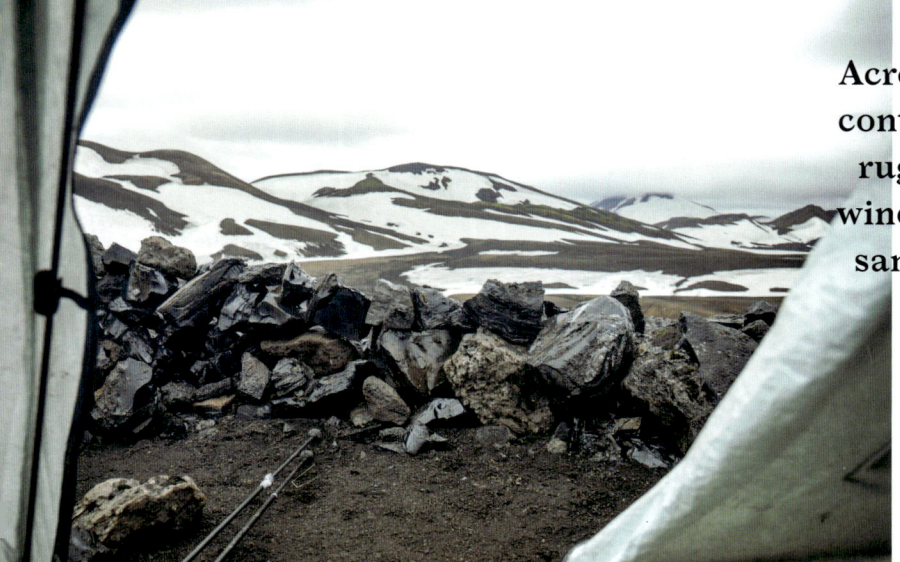

Across the trail's length, the contrasts are mesmerizing— rugged coast gives way to windswept highlands; black-sand deserts yield to vivid moonscapes.

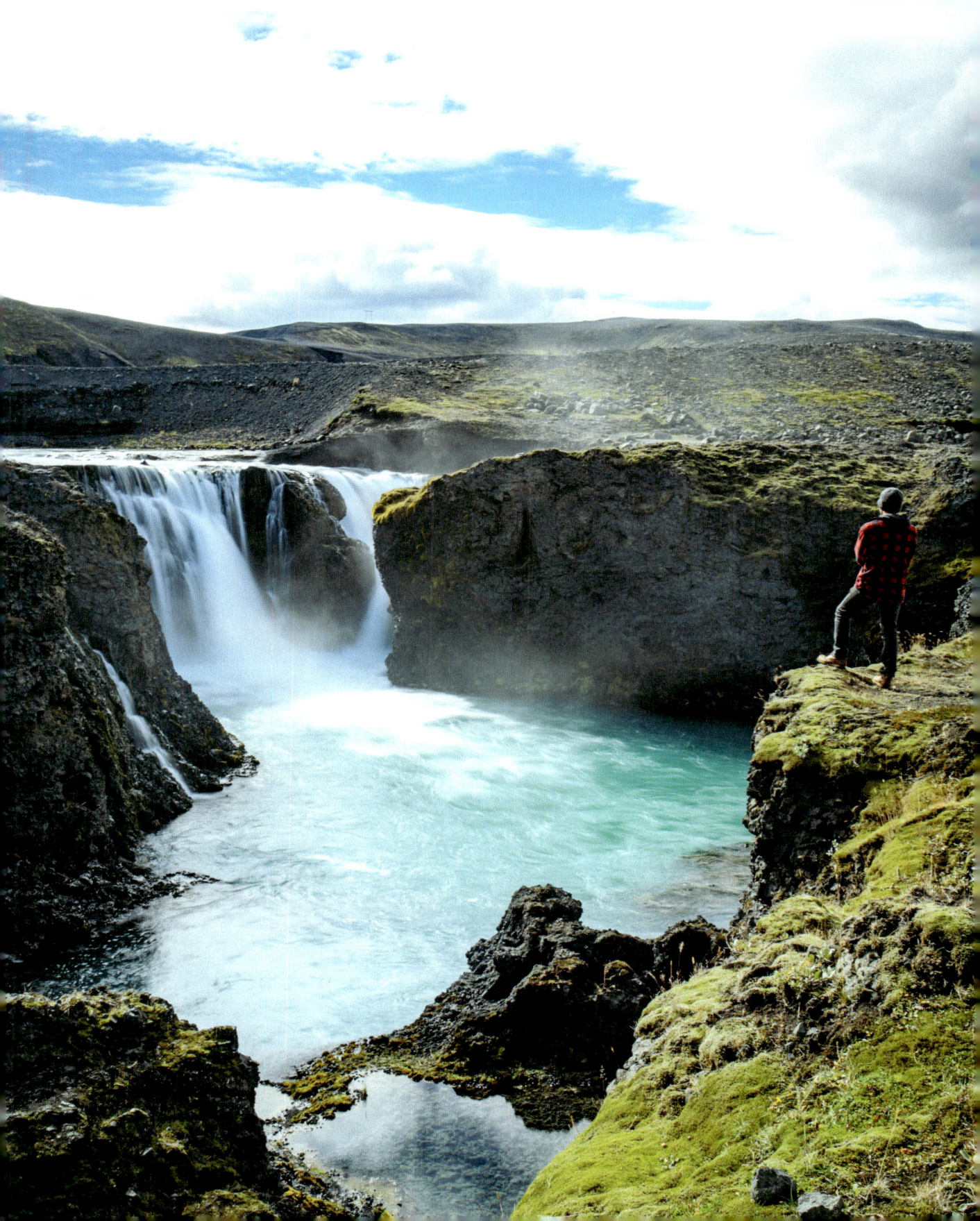

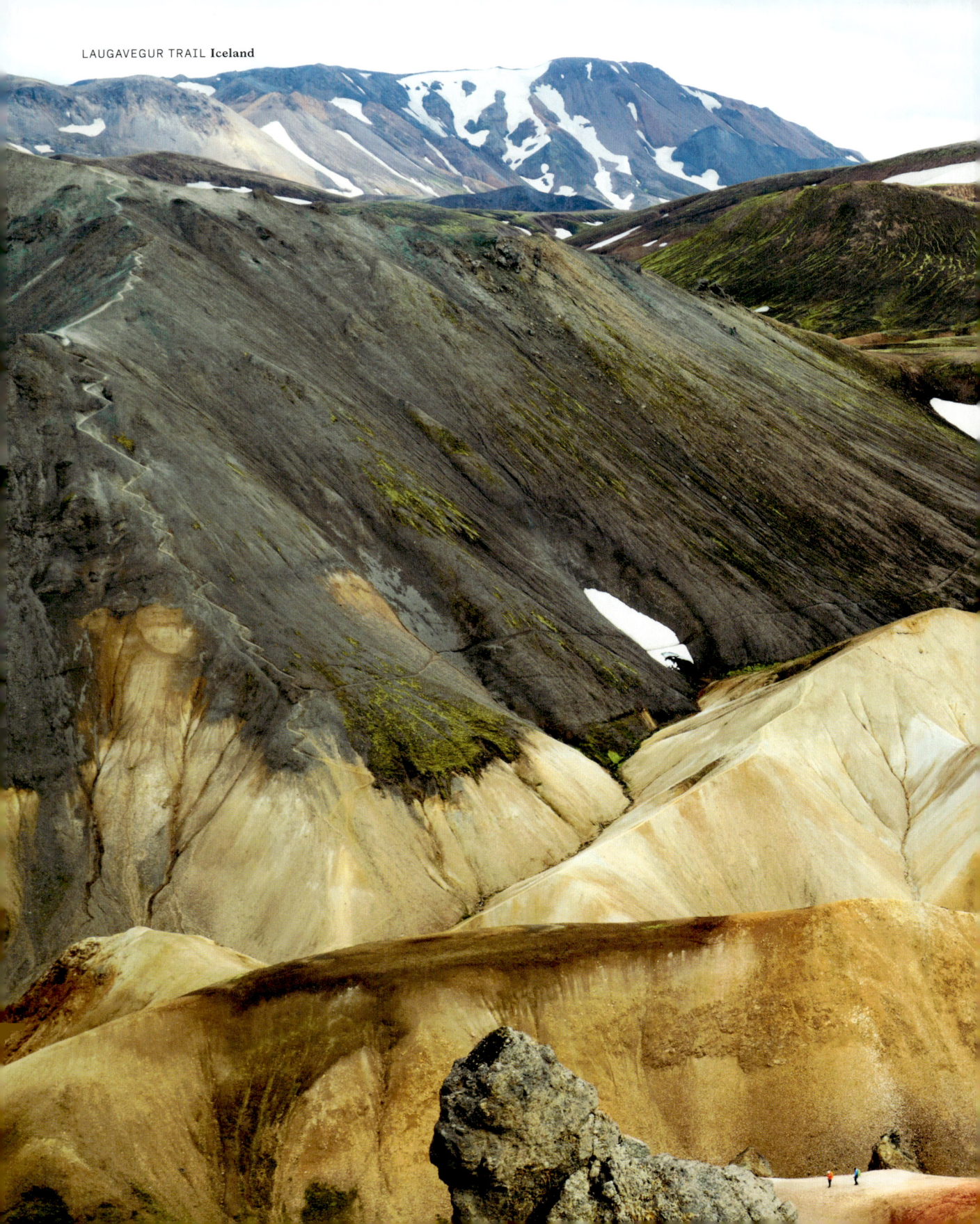

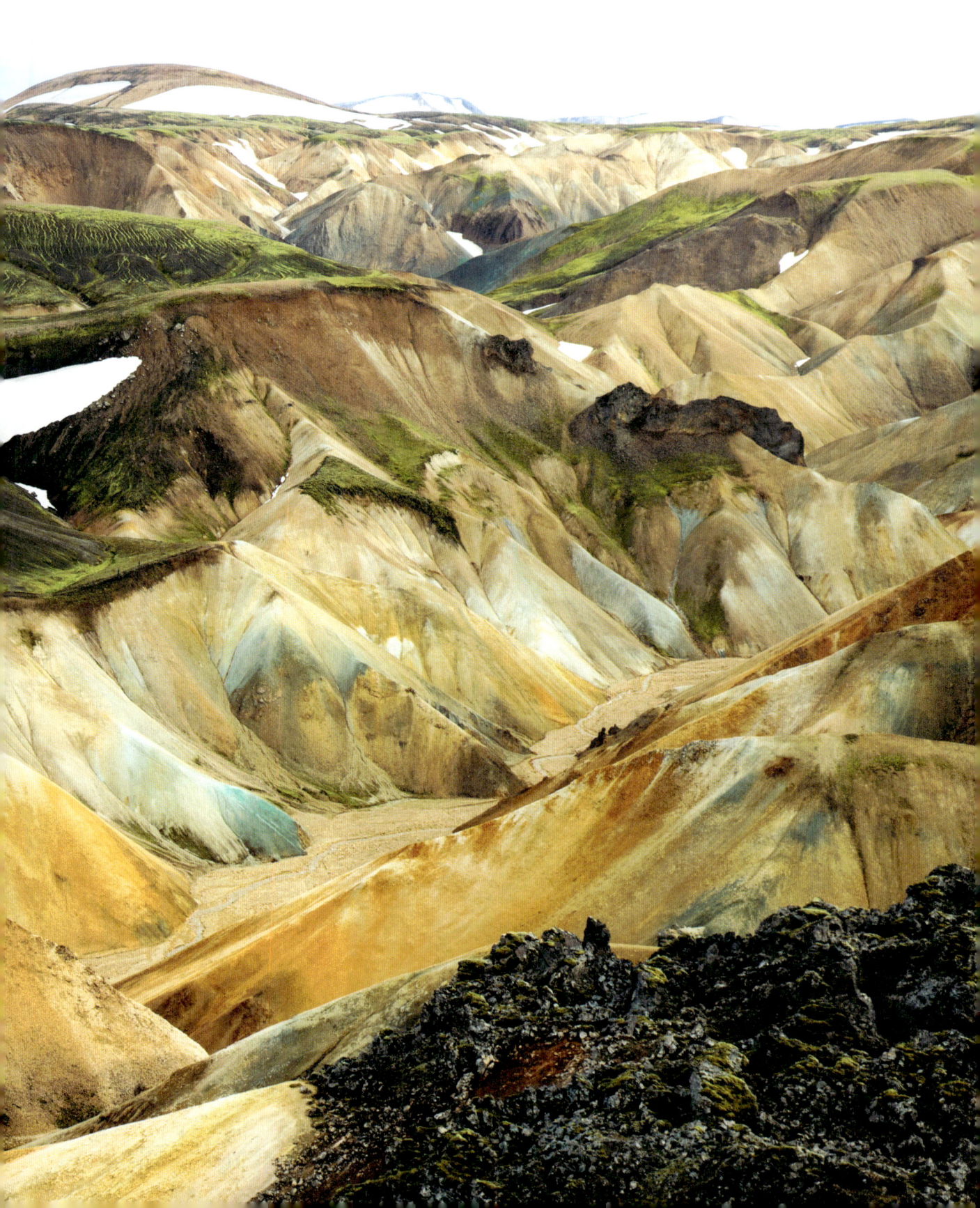

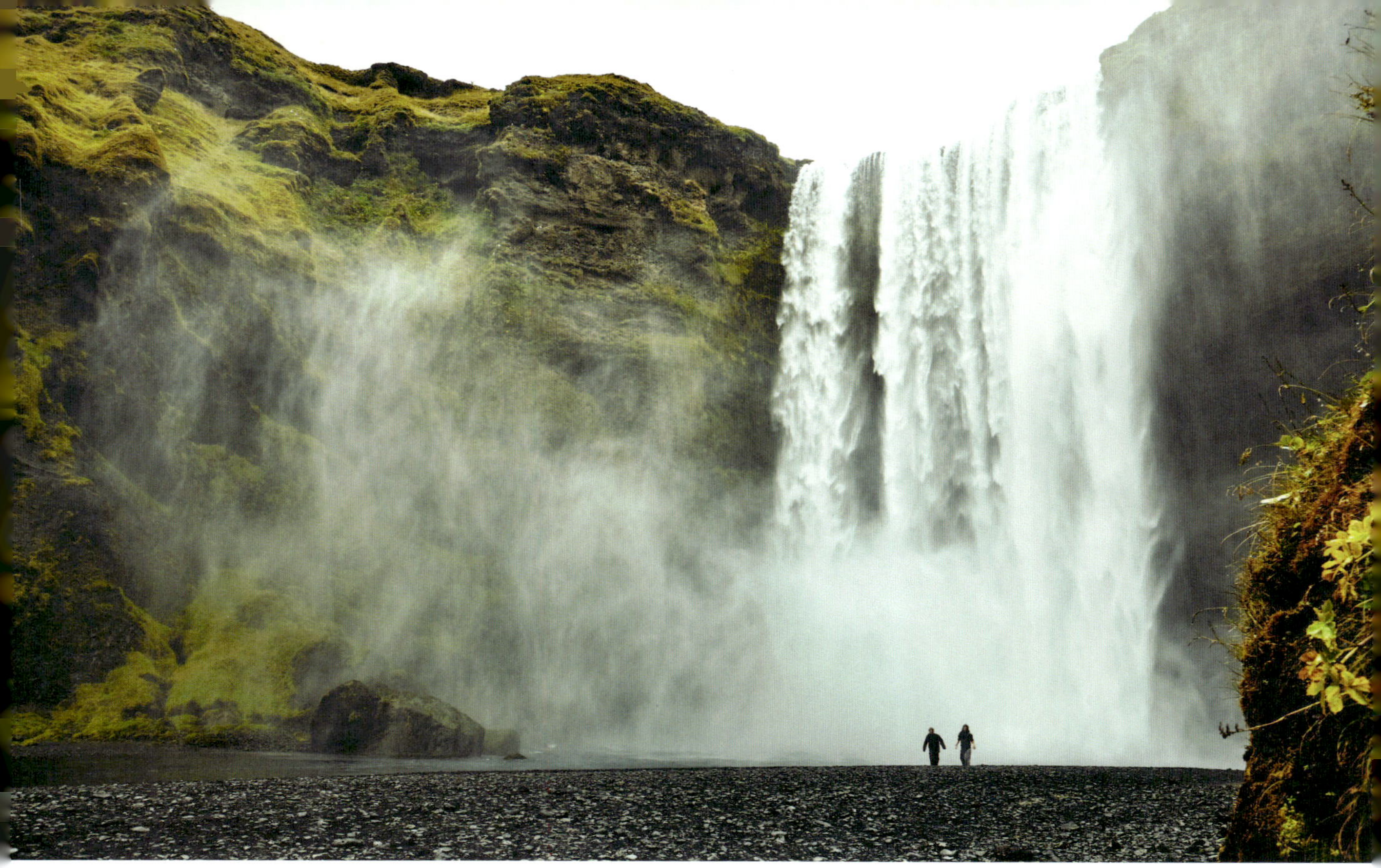

in this part of the north Atlantic is notoriously unpredictable: rain, snow, and high winds are possible year round. This variable, coupled with the exposed nature of the terrain (Iceland has very few trees), means that hikers must bring good rain gear, a solid shelter, and a map and compass (or GPS) irrespective of the forecast. An ironic sense of humor may also come in handy after multiple rainy days. For those without a storm-worthy tent or wanting a little more comfort, there is indoor accommodation in six cozy backcountry huts at intervals along the trail.

Iceland's landscape is a draw for many. As the country is situated on both the Mid-Atlantic Ridge (a seam in the earth's surface that separates the North American and Eurasian tectonic plates) and the Icelandic Plume (a geological hotspot that was responsible for forming the island), it is a hub of geothermal activity, containing volcanoes, geysers, hot springs, mud pots, and fumaroles.

Traversing the Laugavegur is almost like walking through a 78 km (49 mi.) long postcard. Across its length, the contrasts are mesmerizing—rugged coast gives way to windswept highlands; black-sand deserts yield to vivid moonscapes. For those who have chosen to trek northbound, the reward for four or five days of exertion comes in the form of a dip in Landmannalaugar's warm waters. Set among surreal many-hued hills on the edge of a giant lava field, the geothermal springs provide a suitable (and relaxing) finale to a hike through the land of fire and ice. ⎯⎯⎯⎯→

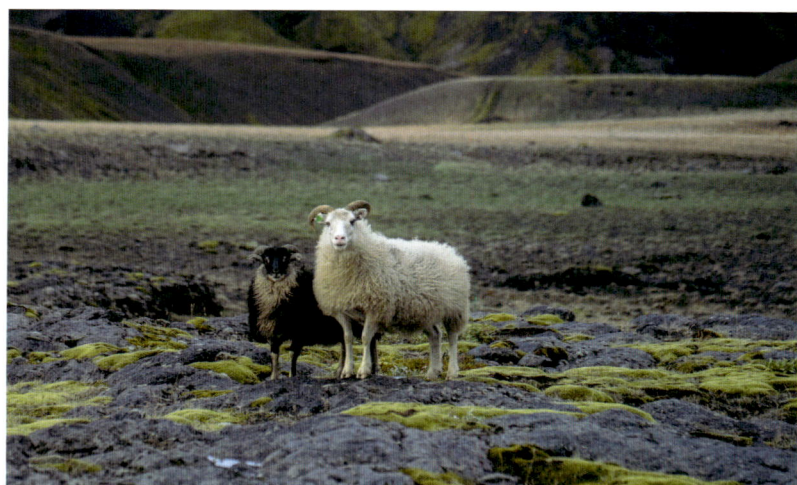

↑ The crashing waters of Skógafoss.
← Some inhabitants of the otherworldly landscape.

GOOD TO KNOW

START/FINISH
🏁 Landmannalaugar
🏁 Skógar or Thórsmörk

SEASON
June to August

CONDITIONS
Weather conditions can vary from the beginning of the trail to the end: snow, fog, and storms are all possible.

LOWEST/HIGHEST POINT
600 m (1,969 ft.)/1,100 m (3,609 ft.)

ACCOMMODATION
Huts or camping. If choosing the former, bookings should be made in advance; if selecting the latter, shelters should be able to withstand extreme weather conditions.

TIP
Weather- and terrain-wise it does not make much difference which direction the Laugavegur is walked. However, if heading northwards the finish is at Landmanna-laugar, where a celebratory post-hike soak in the multi-temperature thermal waters is very welcome.

BACKGROUND

LANDMANNALAUGAR A bizarre highland landscape with volcanic craters, steaming lava fields, and pink, orange, and grey tones in its jagged rhyolite peaks, Landmannalaugar is a dynamic place to pass through. The area, located between a glacial river and a rough lava flow created in 1477, was traditionally used as pasture for sheep, but today is a draw for hikers, tourists, and those wanting to unwind. Visitors can watch the tones of the mountains change with the sun, soak in the geothermal hot springs, stay overnight in the huts or designated campsites, and fish for quarry such as Arctic char and brown trout.

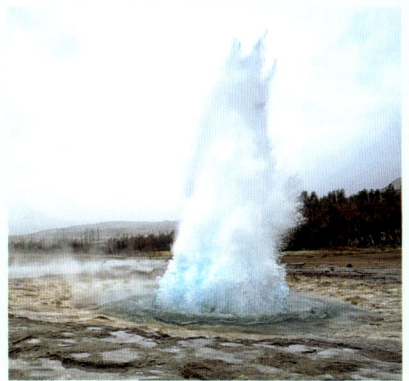

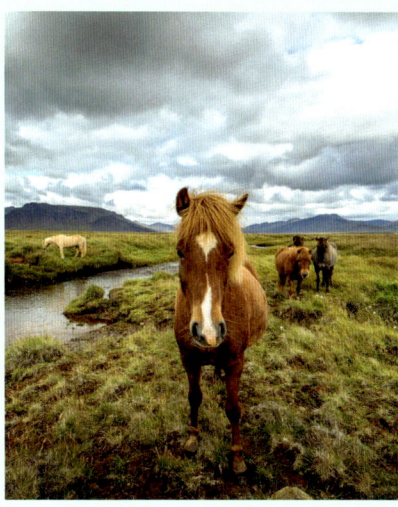

FLORA & FAUNA

EQUINE COMPANIONS Animals are thin on the ground on the Laugavegur trek. One that does sometimes appear is the Icelandic horse. The creatures, which were originally brought from Norway in the ninth and tenth centuries by Norse settlers, are typically short (1.4 m [4.6 ft.] tall on average), stocky, and characterized by their thick manes and tails.

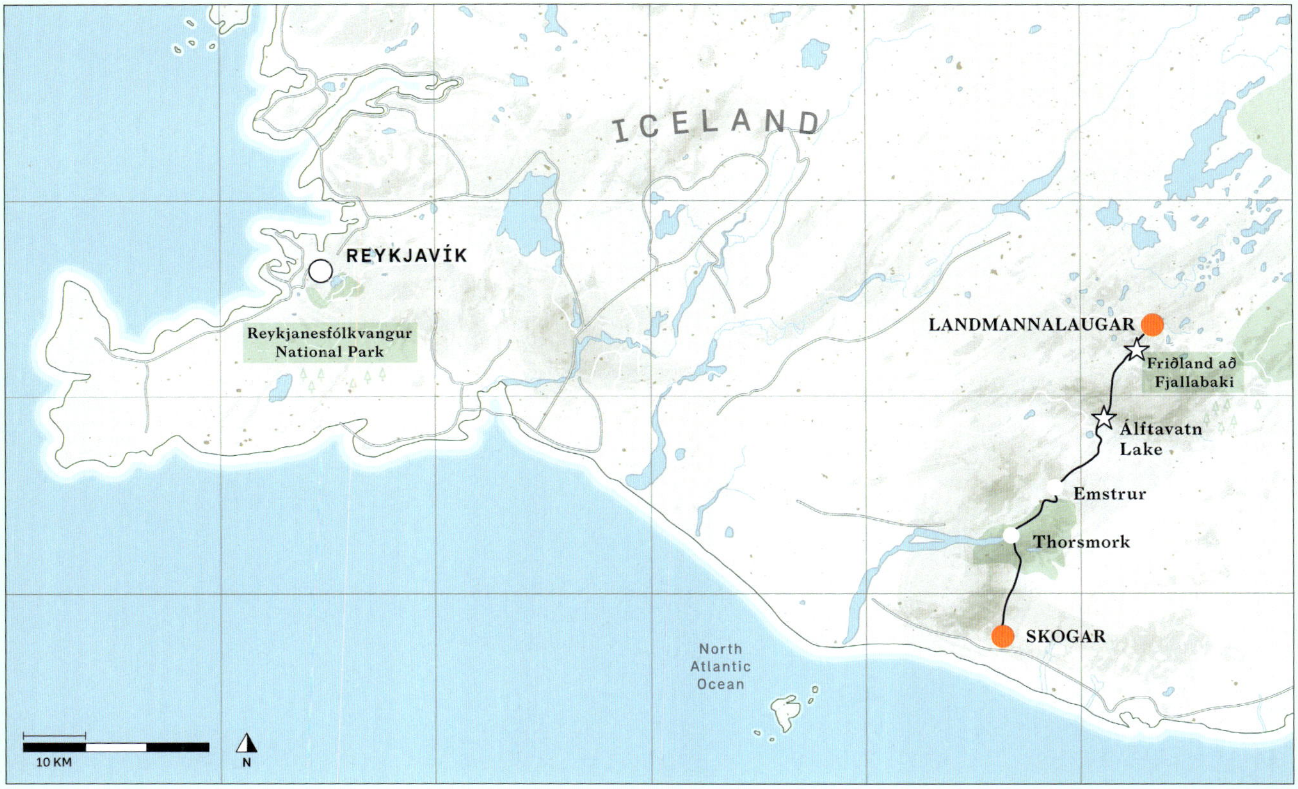

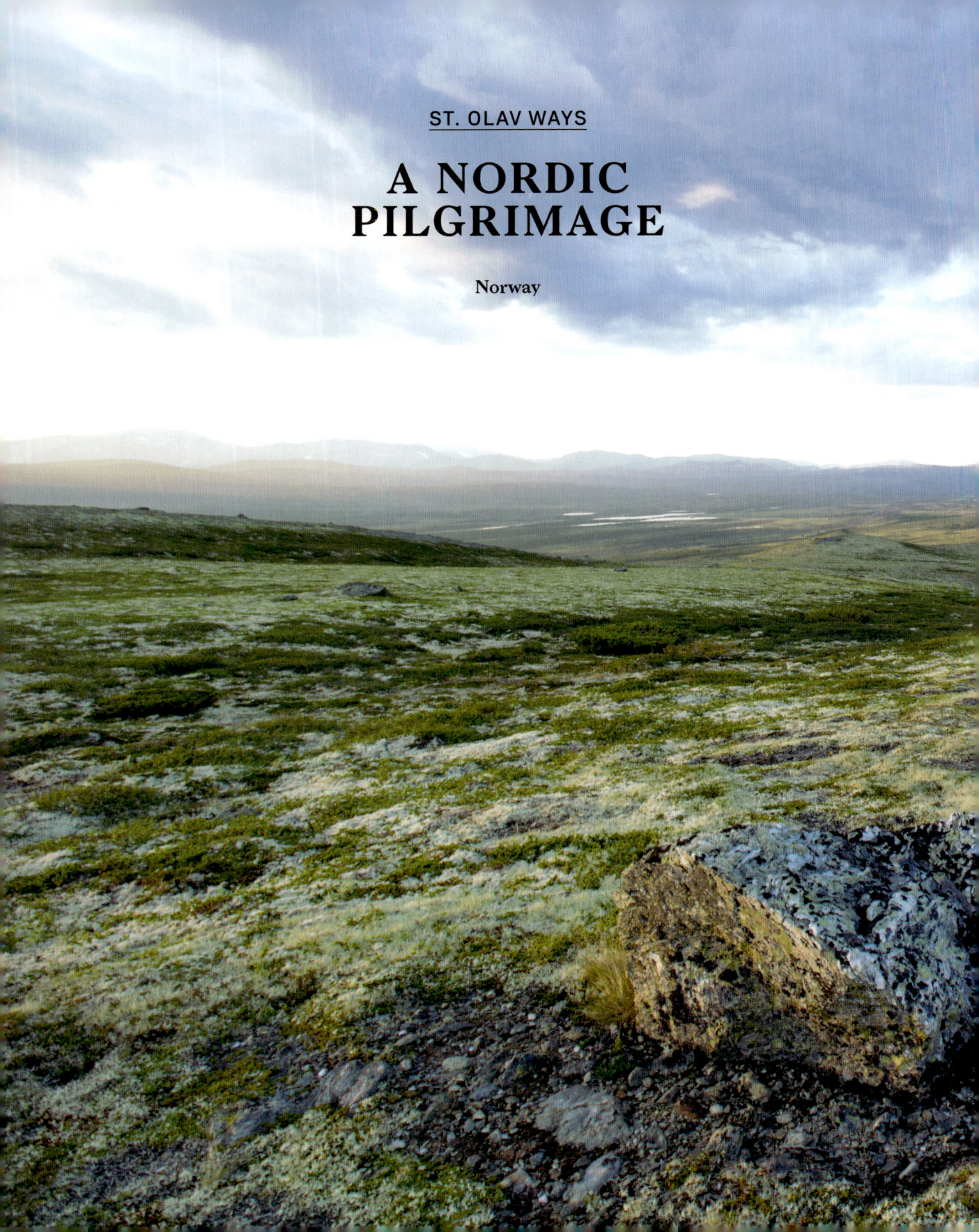

A NORDIC PILGRIMAGE

Norway

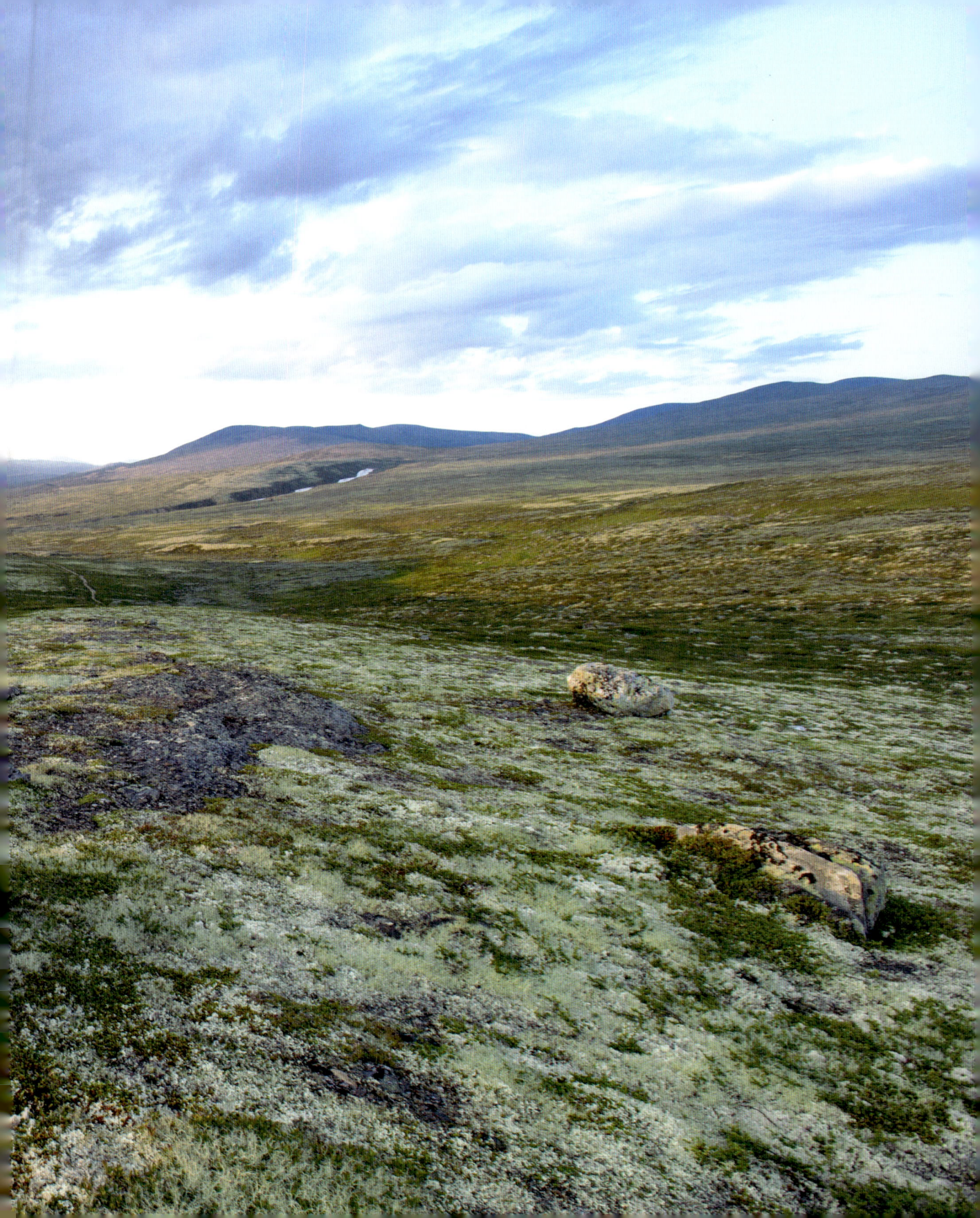

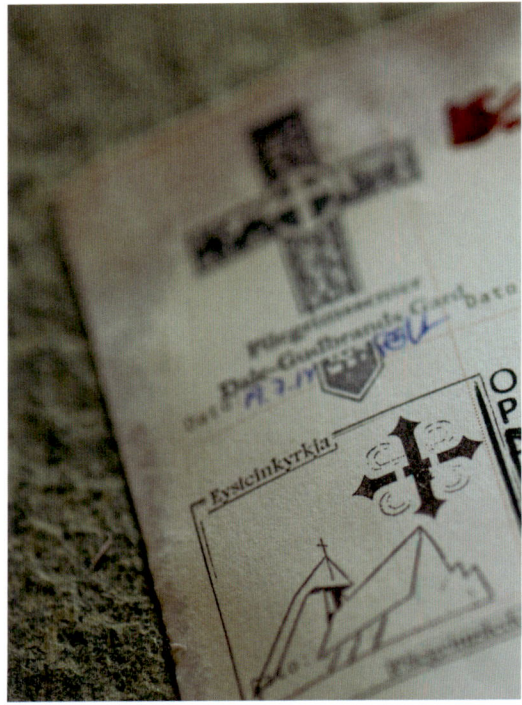

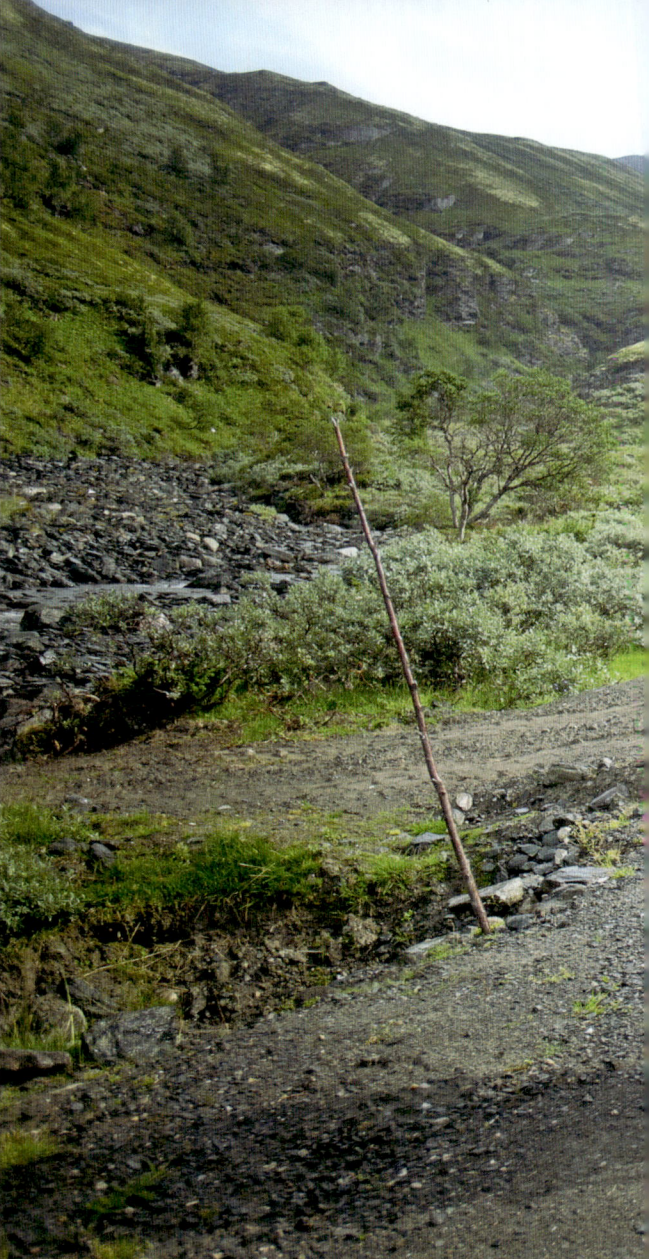

The St. Olav Ways are ancient pilgrimage pathways in Scandinavia. The series of walks is
named after Norway's patron saint, King Olav
II, who was influential in the country's conversion to Christianity
in the eleventh century. The routes begin in different places, but
all finish at the same location: Olav's tomb at Nidaros Cathedral
in Trondheim.

Of the various St. Olav Ways, the most well known is the
Gudbrandsdalen Path. Stretching some 643 km (400 mi.) north
from Oslo, this particular route has been extensively signposted
since the mid-1990s. From its beginning in the suburbs of the capital, it passes through small towns, agricultural lands, and remote
wilderness areas as it winds its way towards Trondheim. En route
there are plenty of accommodation options for hikers, ranging
from hotels to guesthouses to huts. However, thanks to Norway's
Allemannsretten or "freedom to roam" laws, wild camping is possible along most of the way, and is the most budget-friendly choice
in what can be a very expensive country.

ABOUT THE TRAIL

→ <u>DISTANCE</u> 643 km (400 mi.)

→ <u>DURATION</u> 25 to 35 days

→ <u>LEVEL</u> Easy to Moderate

Throughout its course, the Gudbrandsdalen Path provides pilgrims with a memorable combination of cultural and natural elements. Hikers pass by a myriad of important historical sites
such as the medieval ruins of Hamar and Olav's birthplace in
Bønsnes. However, more than any other man-made feature, it
is the churches that provide the biggest reminder of Olav's role
in the Christianization of Norway. From the Sister Churches of
Granavollen to the striking stave church in Ringebu, the distances between one house of worship and the next are not too long.

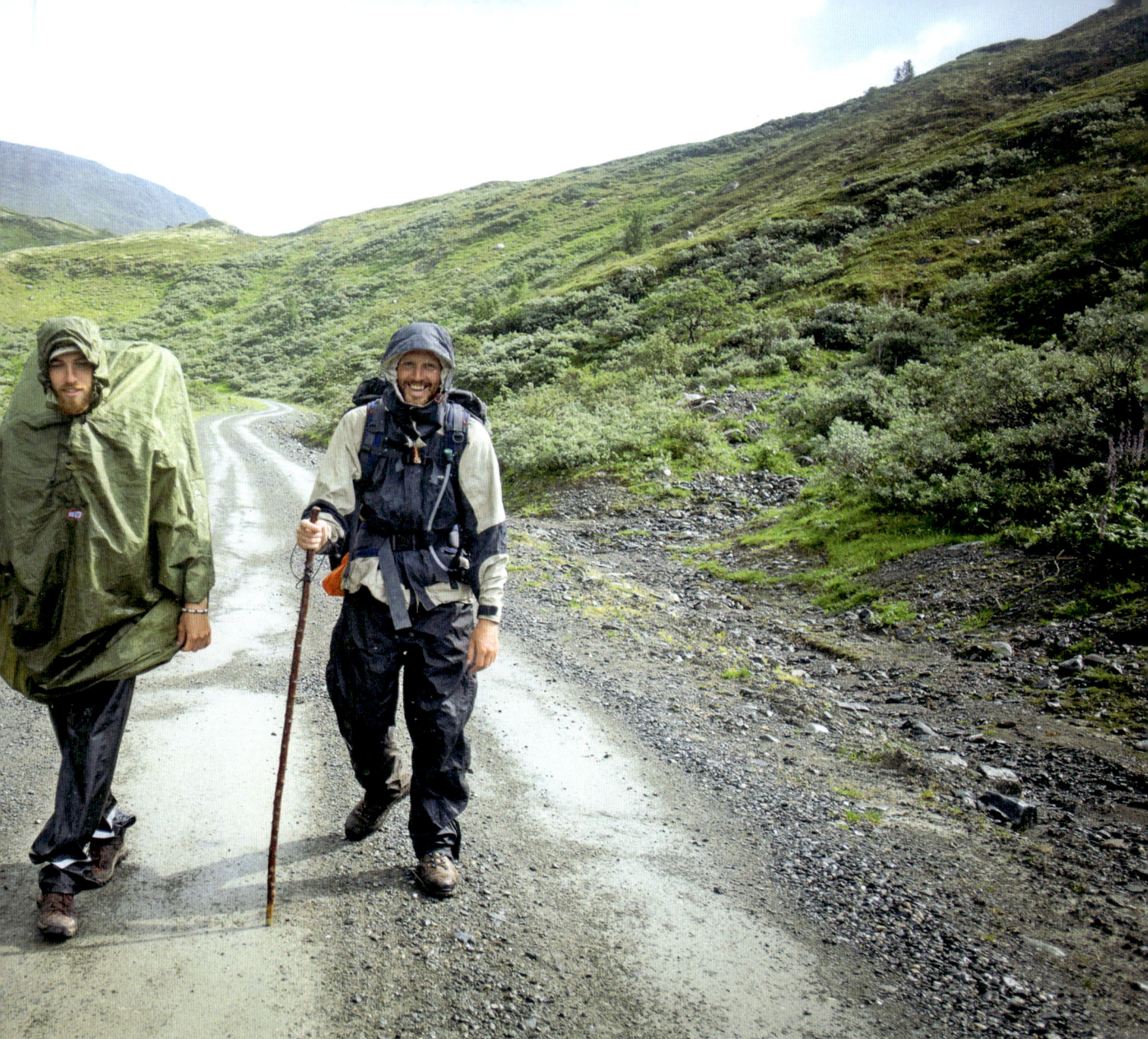

↖ Stamps for "Pilgrim Passports" are collected at churches and lodgings.
↑ Wet weather strikes en route to Trondheim.

Indeed, there's a good reason why pilgrims of centuries past believed that walking the St. Olav Way would cleanse them of all their sins—they had clergymen reminding them the whole way from Oslo to Trondheim.

The main thing that sets the St. Olav Ways apart from other famous pilgrimage routes such as the Camino de Santiago is that hikers pass through fewer towns and more wilderness areas. It could even be said that the St. Olav Ways are Norway's version of Spain's famed Camino—only with far fewer people,

St. Olav's Feast, also known as Olsok, is celebrated every year on July 29 in Scandinavia.

colder weather, and, perhaps, prettier scenery. Principal among the natural highlights of the St. Olav Ways are Lake Mjøsa (Norway's longest lake at over 100 km [62 mi.]), Gudbrandsdal Valley, and the rugged Dovre Mountains. The latter represent the wildest and most remote section of the entire journey. On the 53 km (33 mi.) stretch of trail between Dovre and Kongsvold, hikers encounter snowcapped peaks, alpine →

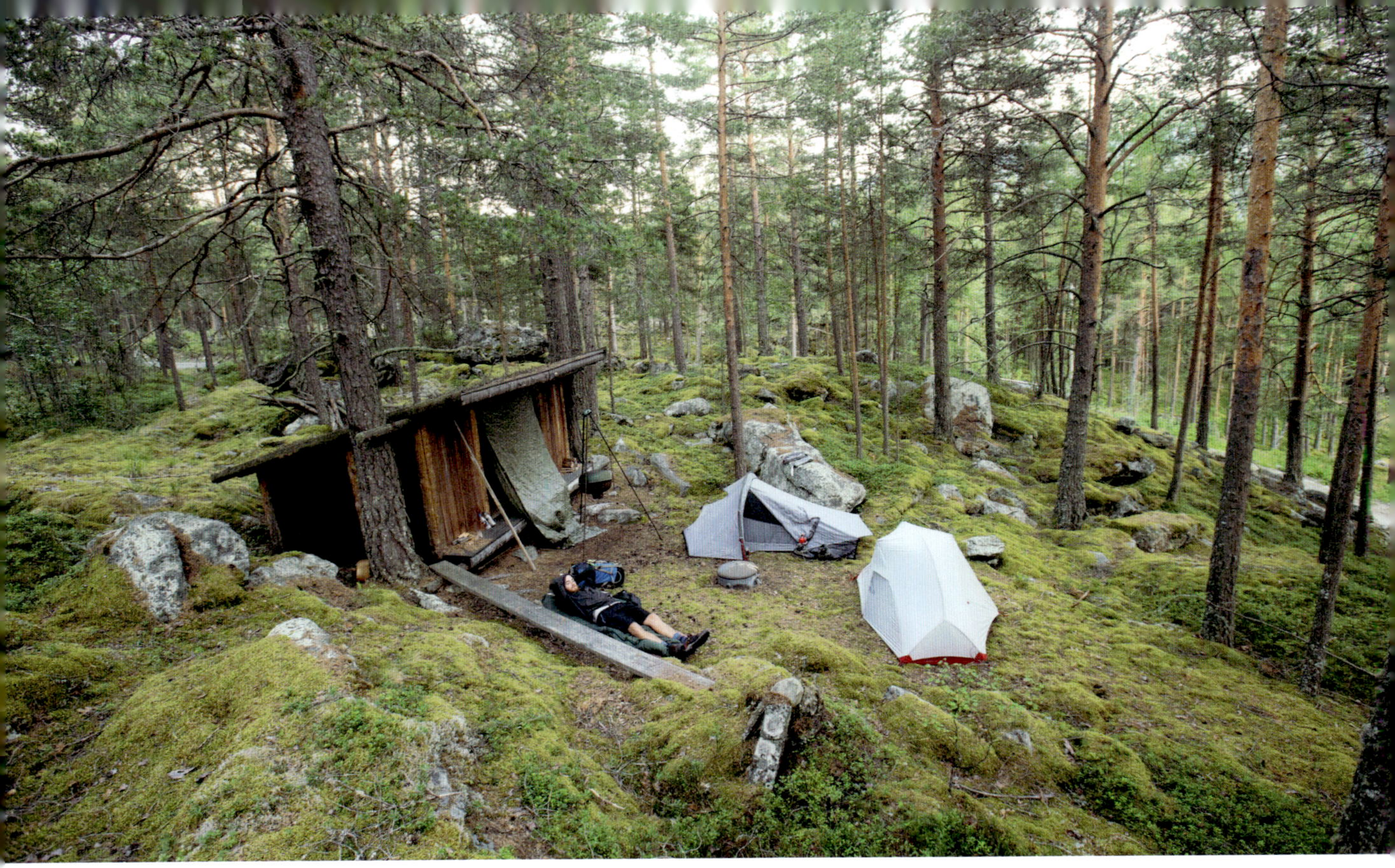

↑ Camping at a Gapahuk shelter outside Oppdal in the Dovre region.
↘ Ringebu Stave Church, Gudbrandsdalen, built around 1220.

Over the course of the hike, travelers pass through not only the country's geographical center but also its cultural and spiritual heart.

tundra, and lonely windswept valleys. In addition, the Dovre range is home to a diverse variety of fauna, including musk oxen, golden eagles, and wild reindeer. Because of the exposed nature of much of this stretch, this segment can also be the most challenging from a meteorological perspective. It is advisable to double check the weather forecast before setting out from Dovre and to carry good rain gear in case of inclement weather.

The Nidaros Cathedral—a stone and stained-glass construction that dates from medieval times and used to be the location of coronations and burials of Norwegian royalty—is the end of the journey for modern-day St. Olav pilgrims. Over the course of the hike, travelers pass through not only the country's geographical center but also its cultural and spiritual heart—the natural wonders, the churches, the village hospitality, the archeological remnants of an ancient past. The Gudbrandsdalen Path is as much a journey into Norway's national consciousness as it is a beautiful walk from Oslo to Trondheim. ————

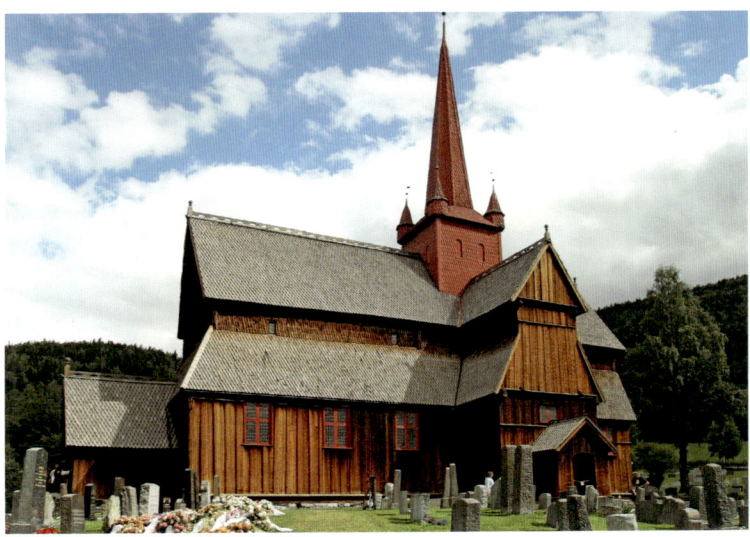

GOOD TO KNOW

START/FINISH
🏳 Gamlebyen, Oslo
🏳 Nidaros Cathedral, Trondheim

SEASON
June to September

CONDITIONS
Often referred to as Scandinavia's answer to the Camino, St. Olav Ways is a well-maintained and simple-to-follow trail.

ACCOMMODATION
Guesthouses, hotels, hostels, farms, cabins, church community centers, camping.

LANDSCAPE
Distinctive rock formations, alpine tundra, waterfalls, caves, Norway's longest lake (Mjøsa).

TIP
For those who are short of time, a combination of the upper Gudbrandsdal Valley and the traverse of the Dovre Mountains offers some of the wildest and most scenic hiking. The 141 km (87.6 mi.) section between Hundorp and Kongsvold can usually be covered in five to seven days.

BACKGROUND

WHO WAS ST. OLAV? Olav Haraldsson, a Viking king of Norway, lived from 995 to 1030, and reined from 1015 to 1028. He died in battle in 1031 and was canonized the year after. Soon after that, pilgrimages began to his tomb in Nidaros Cathedral in Trondheim (a city formerly known as Nidaros). Into the eleventh century and onwards, pilgrims were arriving from the Nordic countries and British Isles and eventually beyond, with the St. Olav tradition burgeoning in Northern Europe and adherents found as far afield as Russia. In the period before the Reformation, around 340 Olav churches and chapels are known to have existed, and 288 of that number were in countries outside Norway.

HELPFUL HINTS

JOTUNHEIMEN A short and very worthwhile side trip for St. Olav Ways' pilgrims is to Jotunheimen National Park. Containing the country's highest mountains and many of its most beautiful lakes, Jotunheimen provides many walking opportunities. The most famous is a 15 km (9.3 mi.) day hike along Besseggen Ridge, and the highlight of the walk is the 1 km (1.6 mi.) stretch where hikers experience the iconic view over Gjende Lake and Bessvatnet Lake.

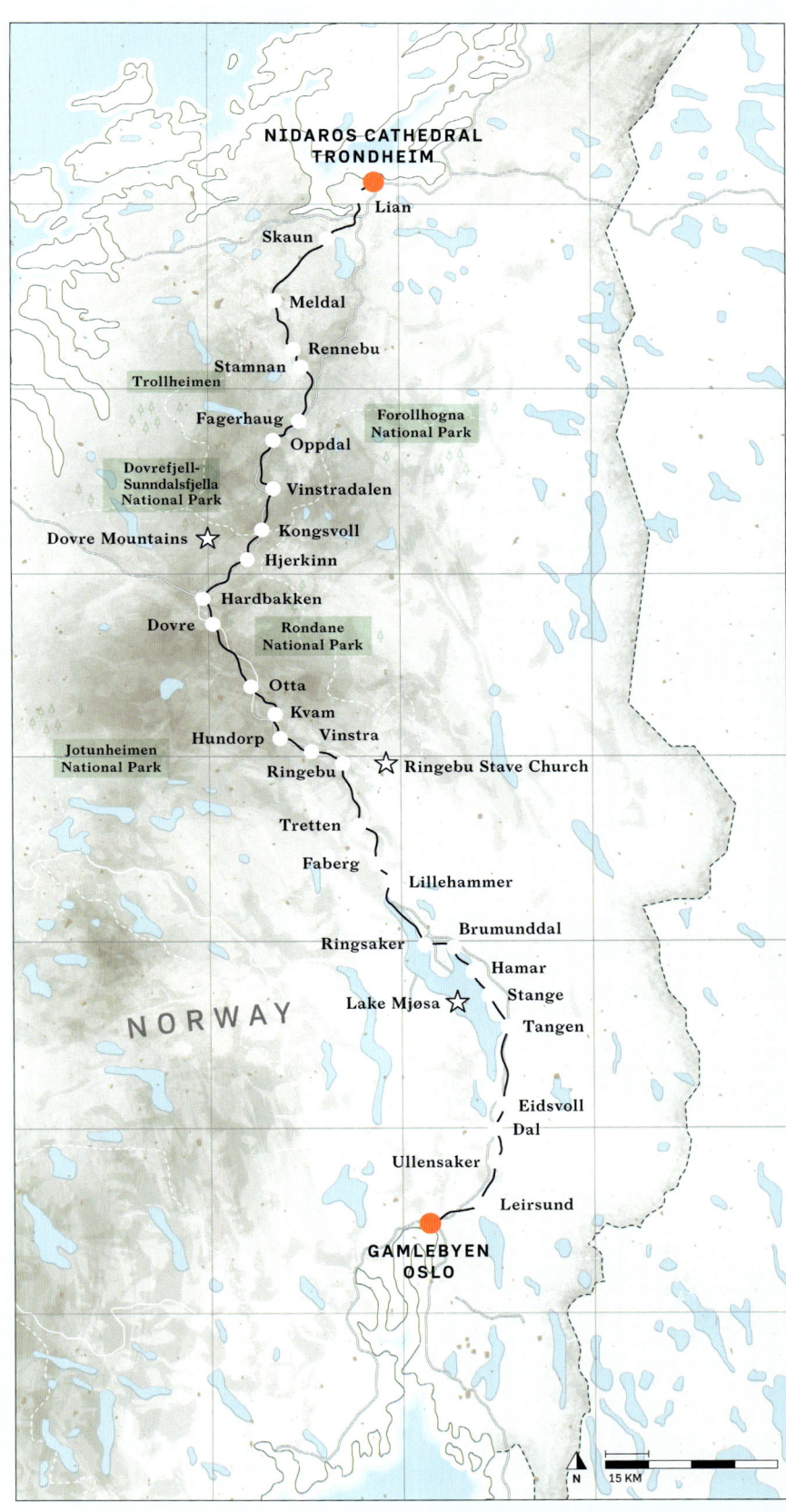

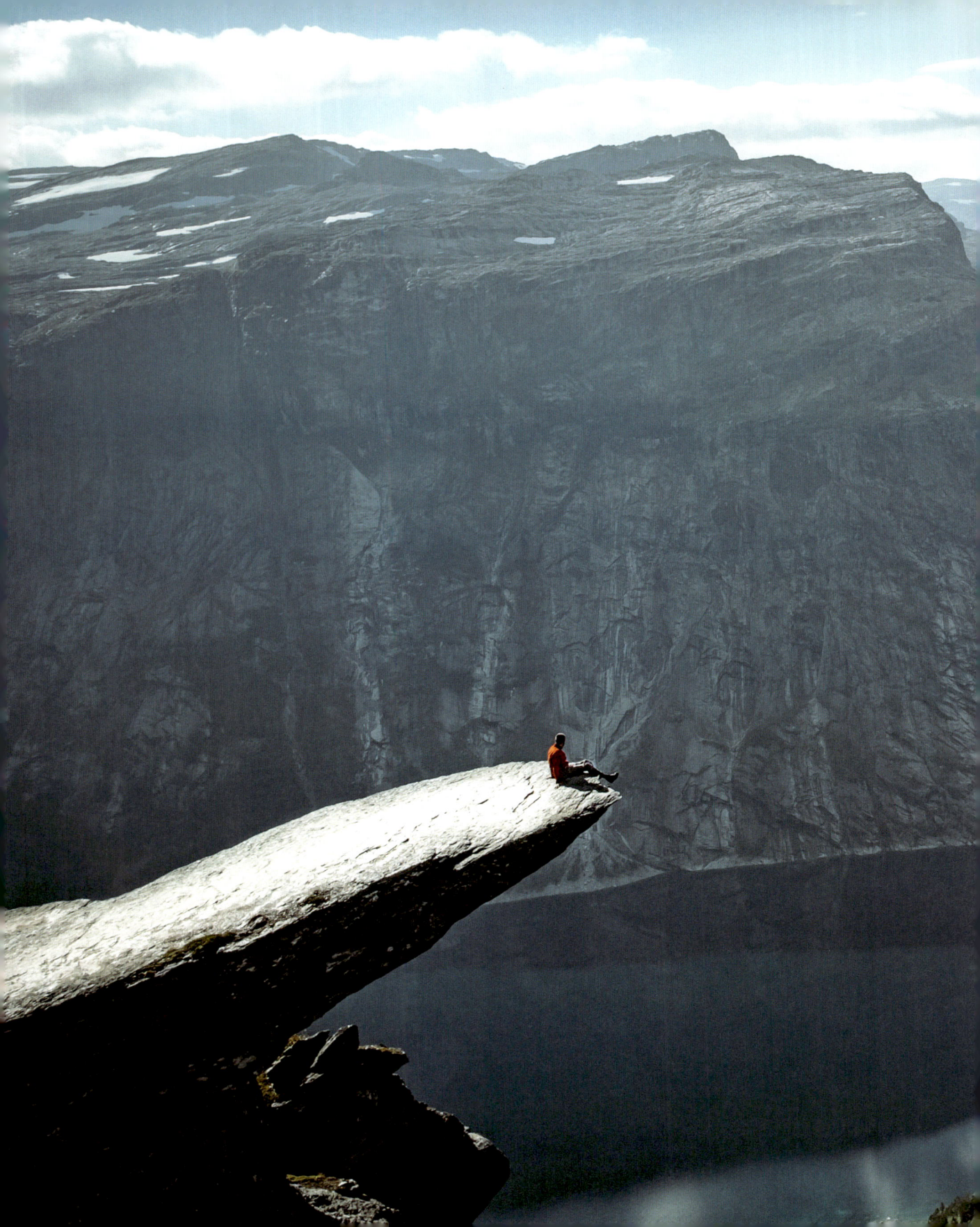

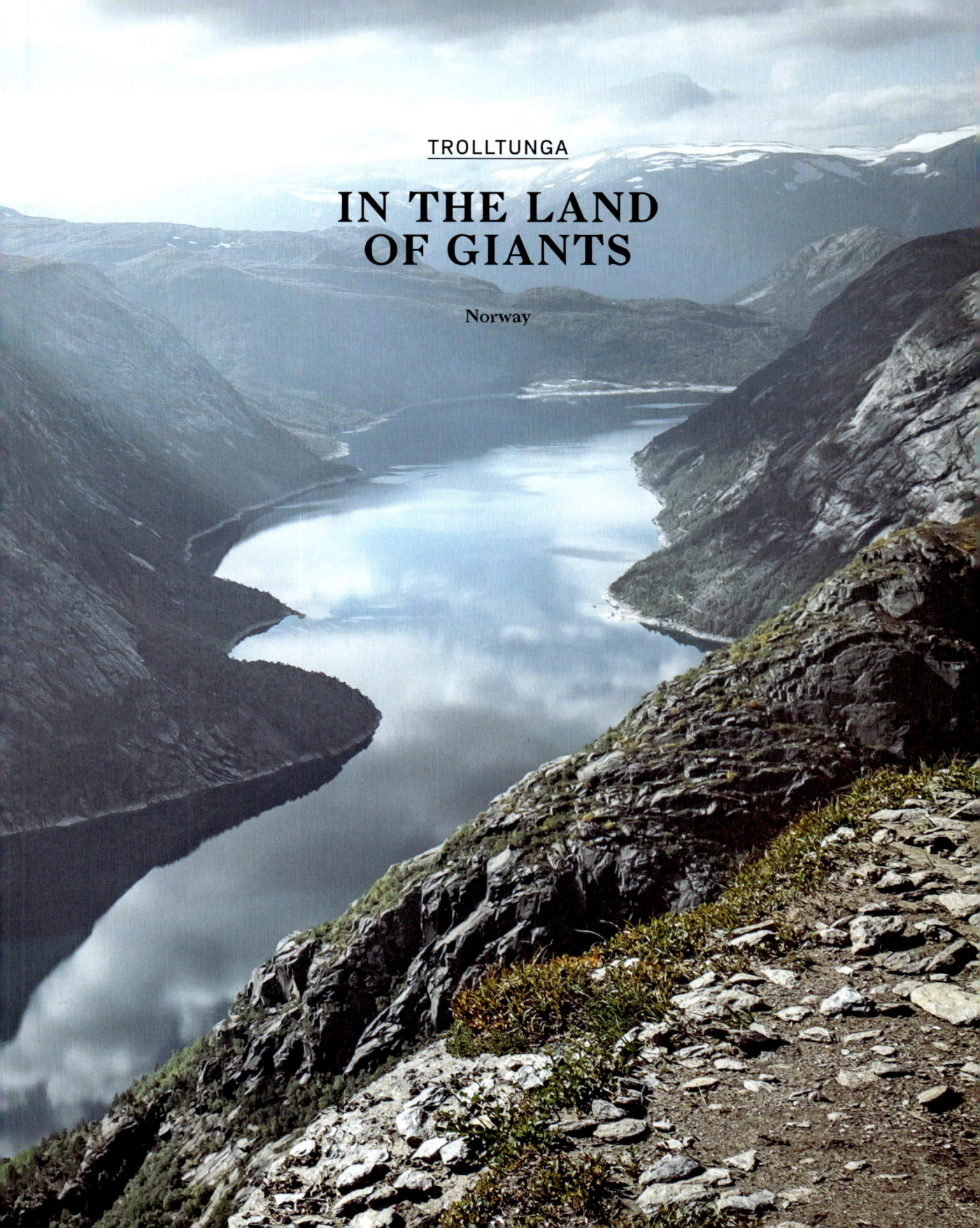

TROLLTUNGA

IN THE LAND
OF GIANTS

Norway

The moose may be Norway's national animal, but its most notorious mythological creature must surely be the troll. Huge and strong, they are said to dwell in rocky surroundings and seek to avoid the sunlight, as it would turn them back to the stones from which they originate. This may have been just what happened to the doomed creature whose tongue has become one of the most popular hiking destinations in Norway.

Situated only a few hours away from Bergen, the Troll's Tongue—or Trolltunga in Norwegian—is a peculiar stone formation that sticks out horizontally from a cliff and hovers about 700 m (2,300 ft.) above Ringedalsvatnet lake. The projection was formed about 10,000 years ago, during the Precambrian era, when a giant glacier broke off angular stone blocks from the cliff as its water froze in the mountain's chasms.

To sit at the tip of the tongue is probably the moment that hikers long for the most. Yet, to get there, they have to traverse an exposed muddy and rocky terrain, as well as snowfields

ABOUT THE TRAIL

→ <u>DISTANCE</u> 23 km (14 mi.)
→ <u>DURATION</u> 10 to 12 hours
→ <u>LEVEL</u> Moderate

Walkers are cast into a vast translucent space, with the stone platform the only remaining touch point with the solid world.

that linger into the summer months. As is regularly the case in mountain regions, the weather can be volatile, necessitating that hikers carry clothes to cover a wide range of climatic scenarios, ranging from stifling heat to heavy rain and even the occasional snow shower.

The hike starts at the main car park in Skjeggedal and takes aspirants directly to the steep and mucky stone stairs that mark both the beginning of the hike and one of its most challenging sections. Climbing these steps, one can see the remnants of a funicular tourists used to take in order to avoid this tiring ascent. After the operating company stopped the service, the tracks of the funicular were still used by hikers to climb the mountain. The construction was then completely abandoned and gradually started to deteriorate. →

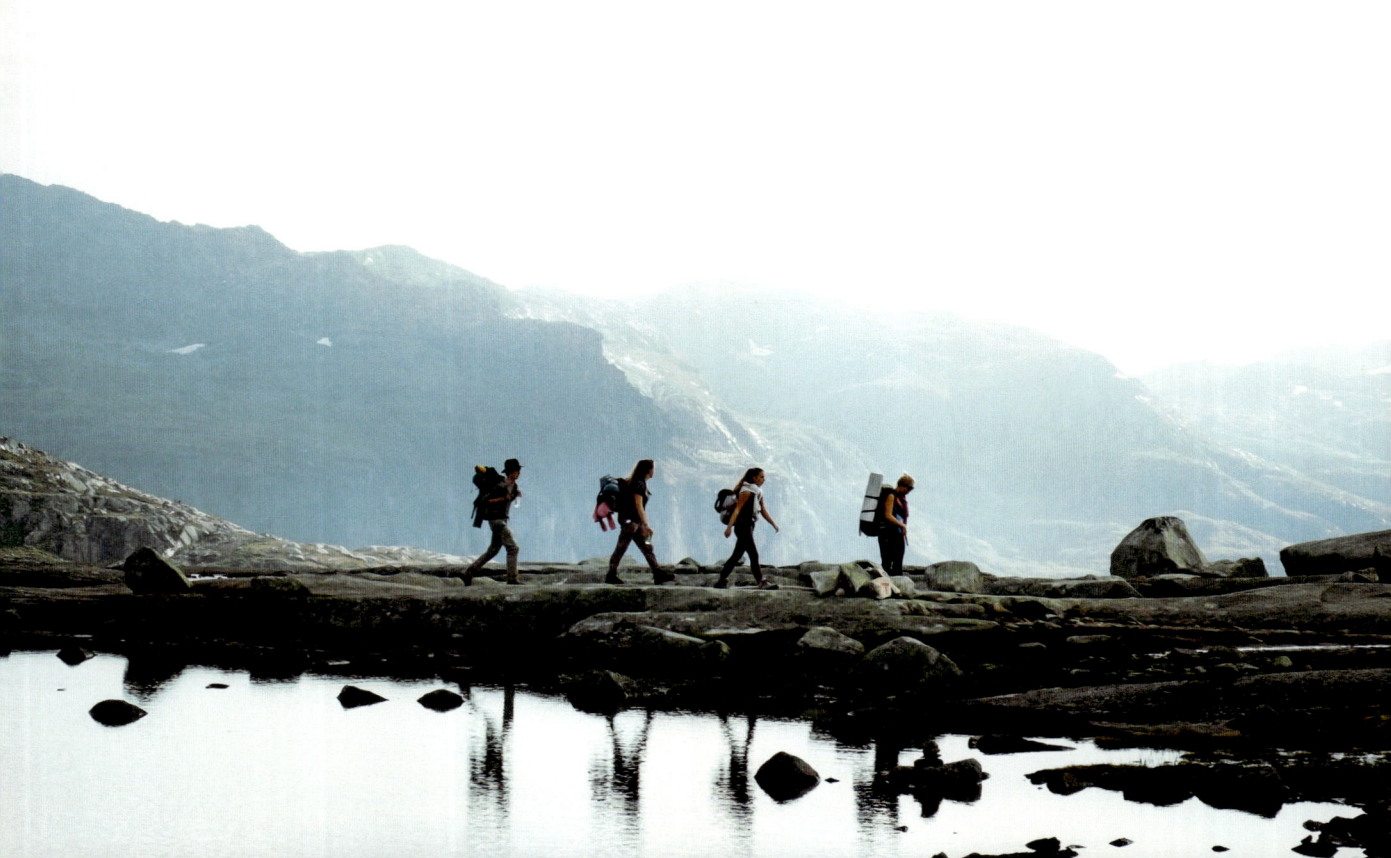

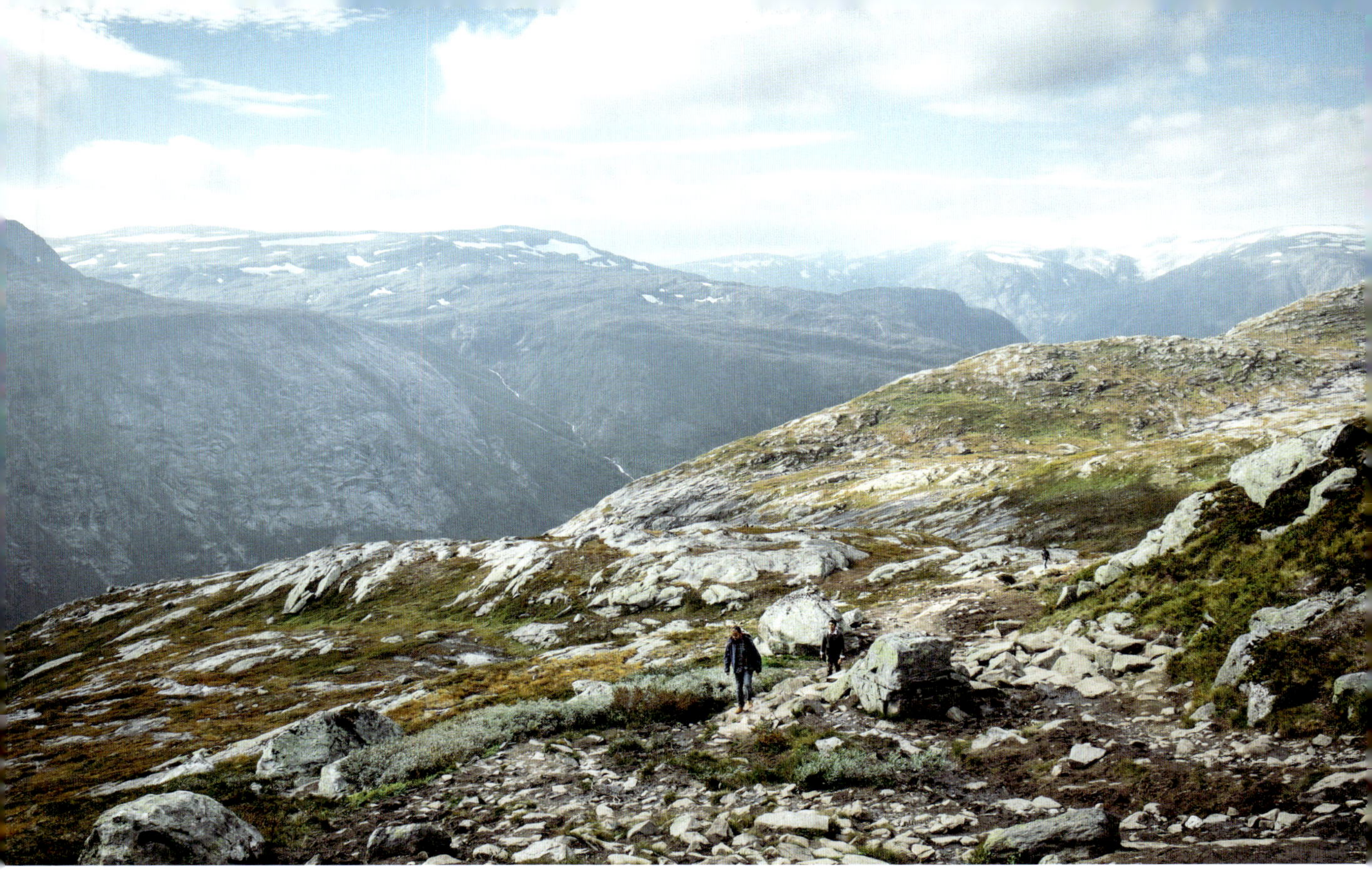

↑ Above Ringedalsvatnet lake.
↓ Occasional stretches of flat rocks make for easy walking.

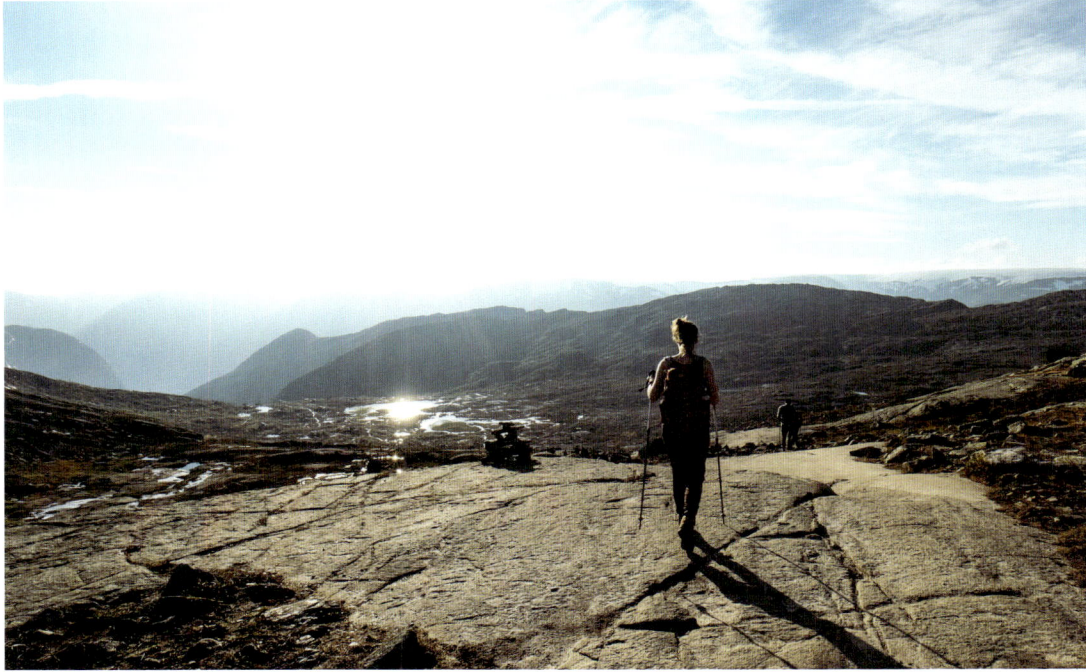

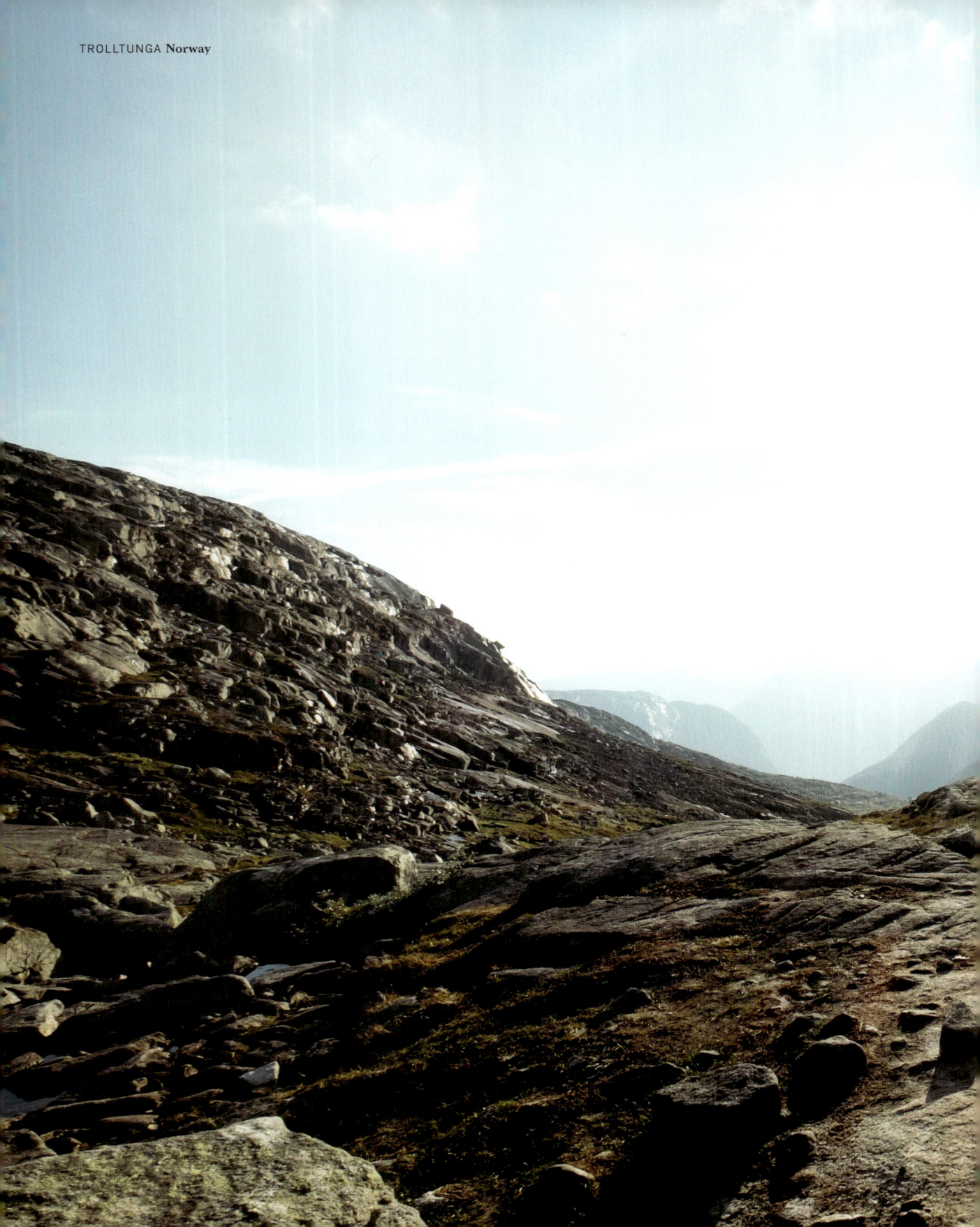

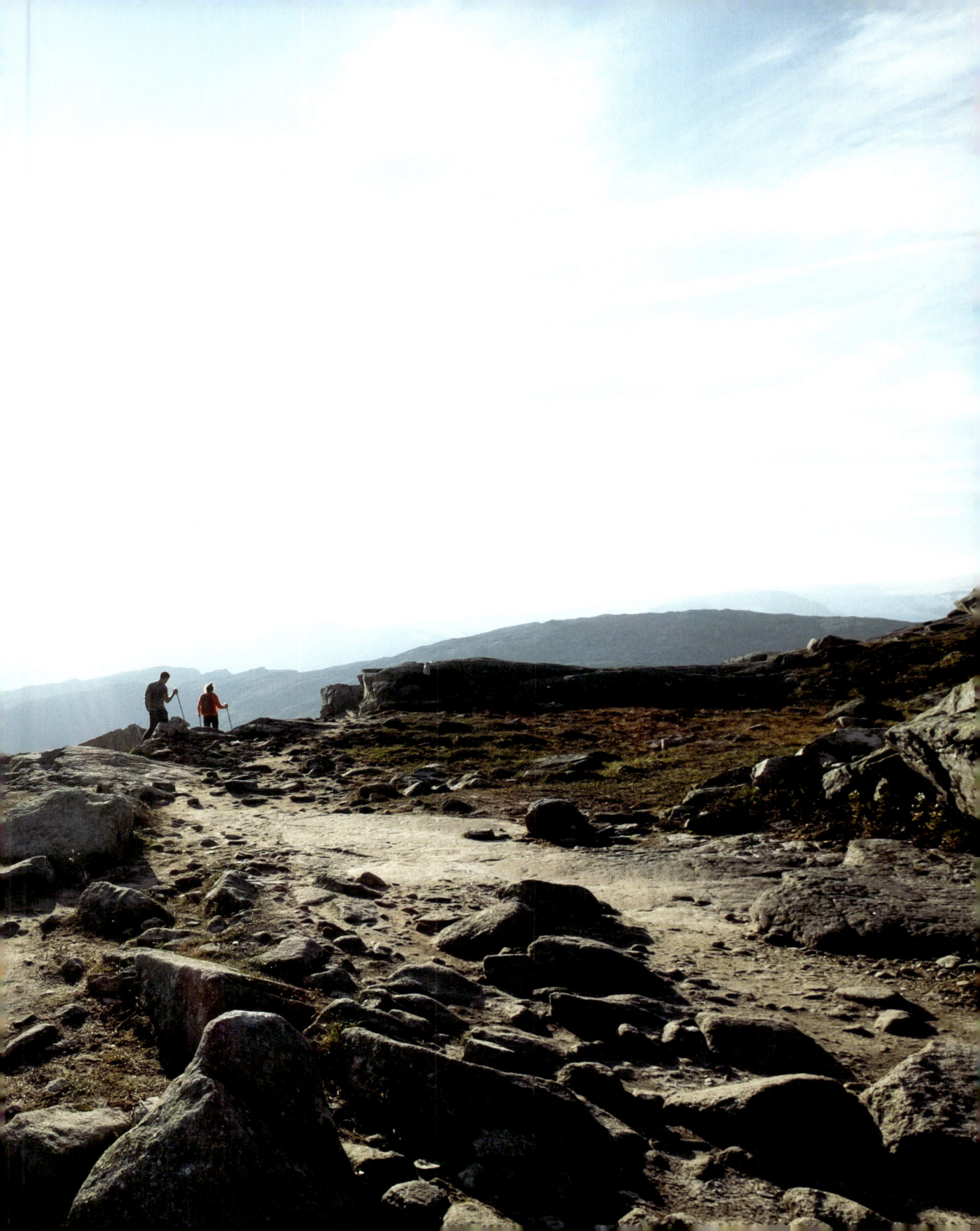

Following this initial climb, there is another strenuous ascent to accomplish before reaching the first viewpoint over the waters of Ringedalsvatnet. The trail is well signposted, and where there are no other indicators designating the path, cairns provide sufficient guidance. Despite the demanding first section and the mud holes along the way, the hike to Trolltunga is a rewarding one. Every couple of miles there is a scenic spot that invites walkers to take a break and have a snack while enjoying the vistas. Crystal clear glacier water that is suitable for drinking is abundant all along the way, and just at the point where tired trekkers might feel like giving up, the Trolltunga itself comes into view.

Even from afar, the sight of the narrow rock passage jutting out over blue waters is enough to make one forget the initial struggles and boggy inclines along the way. Yet, the hike would not be complete without taking the time to appreciate the area and then making the approach out onto the legendary giant's tongue. Although the spot seems somewhat angst-inducing from far off, it is actually quite safe—so long as walkers watch their step and treat the rocky giant with the necessary respect.

As much for urban dwellers who are used to rather limited horizons as it is for outdoor experts who are familiar with all kinds of breathtaking vistas, standing on the tip of Trolltunga is an impressive experience. Walkers are cast into a vast translucent space, with the stone platform the only remaining touch point with the solid world. Surrounded by nothing more than thin air and steady wind currents, they stand above the seemingly endless gorge that is lined with a lake. Instead of providing some sense of orientation, the water mirrors the surroundings and doubles the space. The location is a world of its own, and rather than feeling triumph when standing at the very top, one is inclined to feel a sense of humbleness and gratitude for having been granted a glance into this awe-inspiring realm of giants. ——————

Even from afar, the sight of the narrow rock passage jutting out over blue waters is enough to make one forget the initial struggles and boggy inclines along the way.

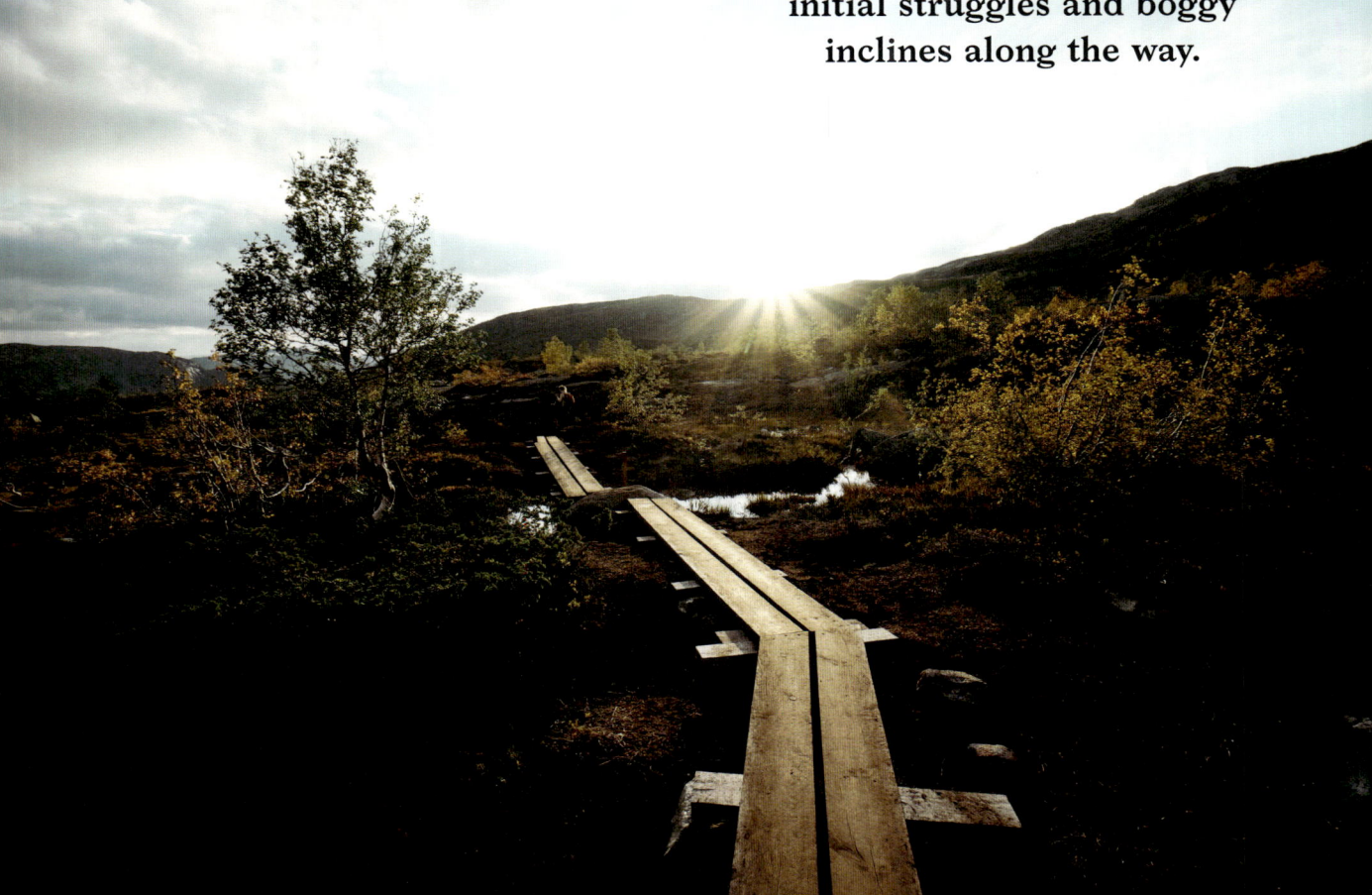

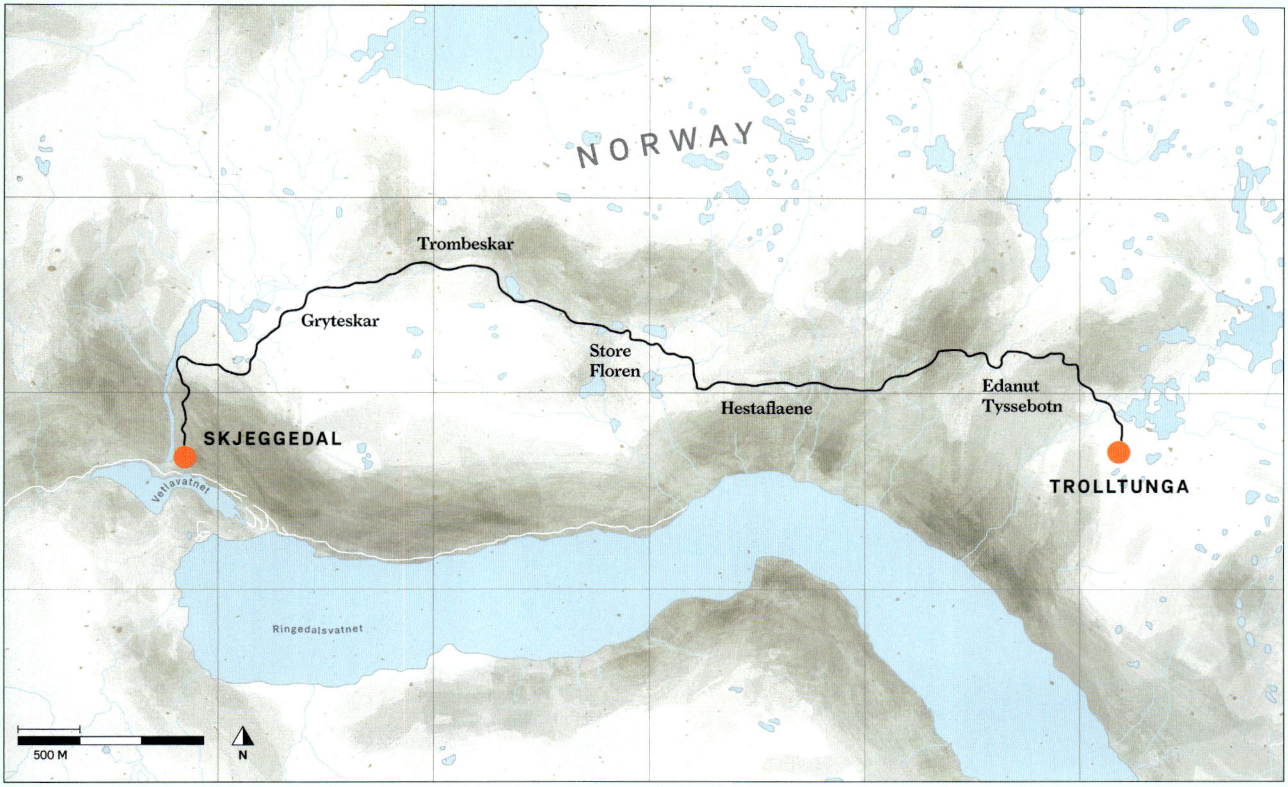

Map labels:

NORWAY

Trombeskar
Gryteskar
Store
Floren
Hestaflaene
Edanut
Tyssebotn

SKJEGGEDAL
Vetlavatnet
Ringedalsvatnet

TROLLTUNGA

500 M
N

GOOD TO KNOW

START/FINISH
Out-and-back from Skjeggedal

SEASON
Mid-June to mid-September

CONDITIONS
The trail is well marked and easy to follow. The real challenges are the weather conditions, which tend to be quite volatile. Hikers should be prepared for hot, cold, and rainy weather.

LOWEST/HIGHEST POINT
450 m (1,476 ft.)/1,100 m (3,609 ft.)

LANDSCAPE
Norway is famous for its unique rock formations. Those who cannot see enough of the giants' features can also hike Preikestolen, the preacher's cliff, or even Kjeragbolten, a stone mysteriously wedged between two rocks.

TIP
Norway is far north on the globe, which means daylight is short from September onwards and nights are very cold. It is therefore recommended to start the hike at 8 a.m. at the latest. During the summer months, travelers can camp on top of Trolltunga.

FLORA & FAUNA

PLANTLIKE ORGANISMS On the ascent to Trolltunga, lichen-covered rocks make up the main feature of the landscape. These composite organisms—made up of a fungus and either an alga or a cyanobacterium—are not considered plants because they do not have roots that absorb water and nutrients; instead they thrive through the symbiotic relationship they enter with the surface on which they grow. Lichens live for long periods and grow quite slowly. To reproduce, it is thought that parts of the organism break off and then grow nearby. They are an important food source for insects and bigger animals such as reindeer.

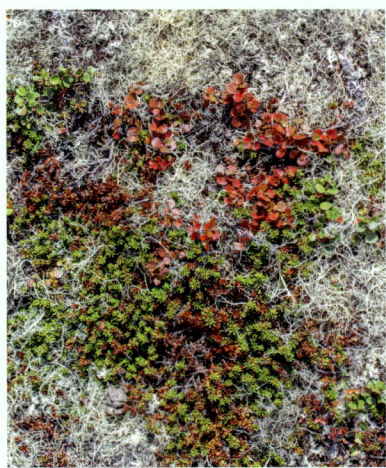

HELPFUL HINTS

LOOK UP To experience Trolltunga from below, take a kayak tour through Eidfjord. Tours can be arranged from Øvre Eidfjord, a small town that is centrally located between Hardangervidda National Park and the Trolltunga hiking area. Once there, travelers can also visit Vøringsfossen, one of the most famous and majestic waterfalls in Norway.

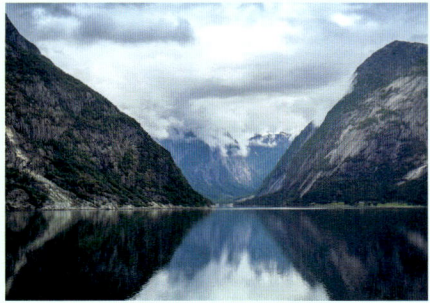

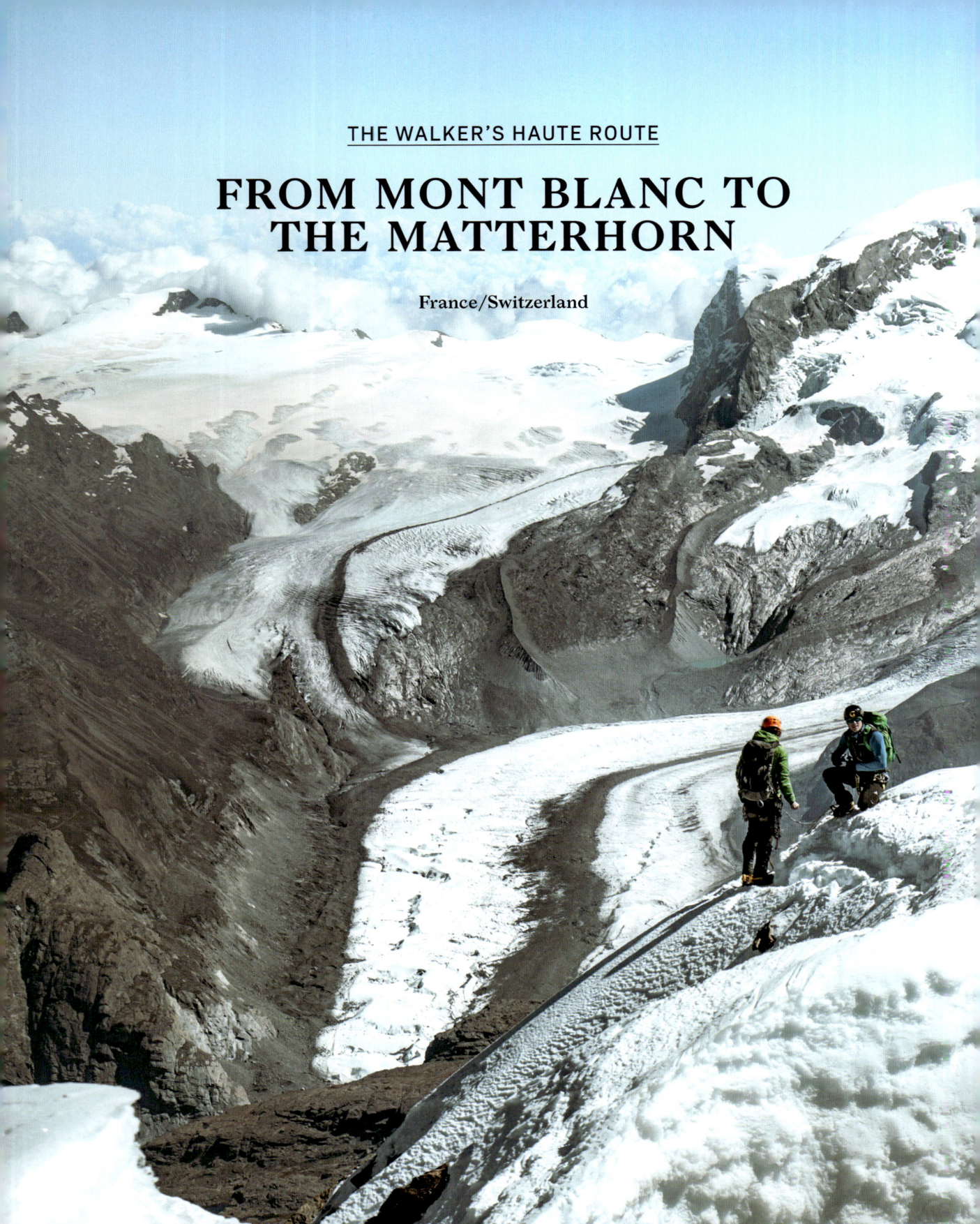

THE WALKER'S HAUTE ROUTE

FROM MONT BLANC TO THE MATTERHORN

France/Switzerland

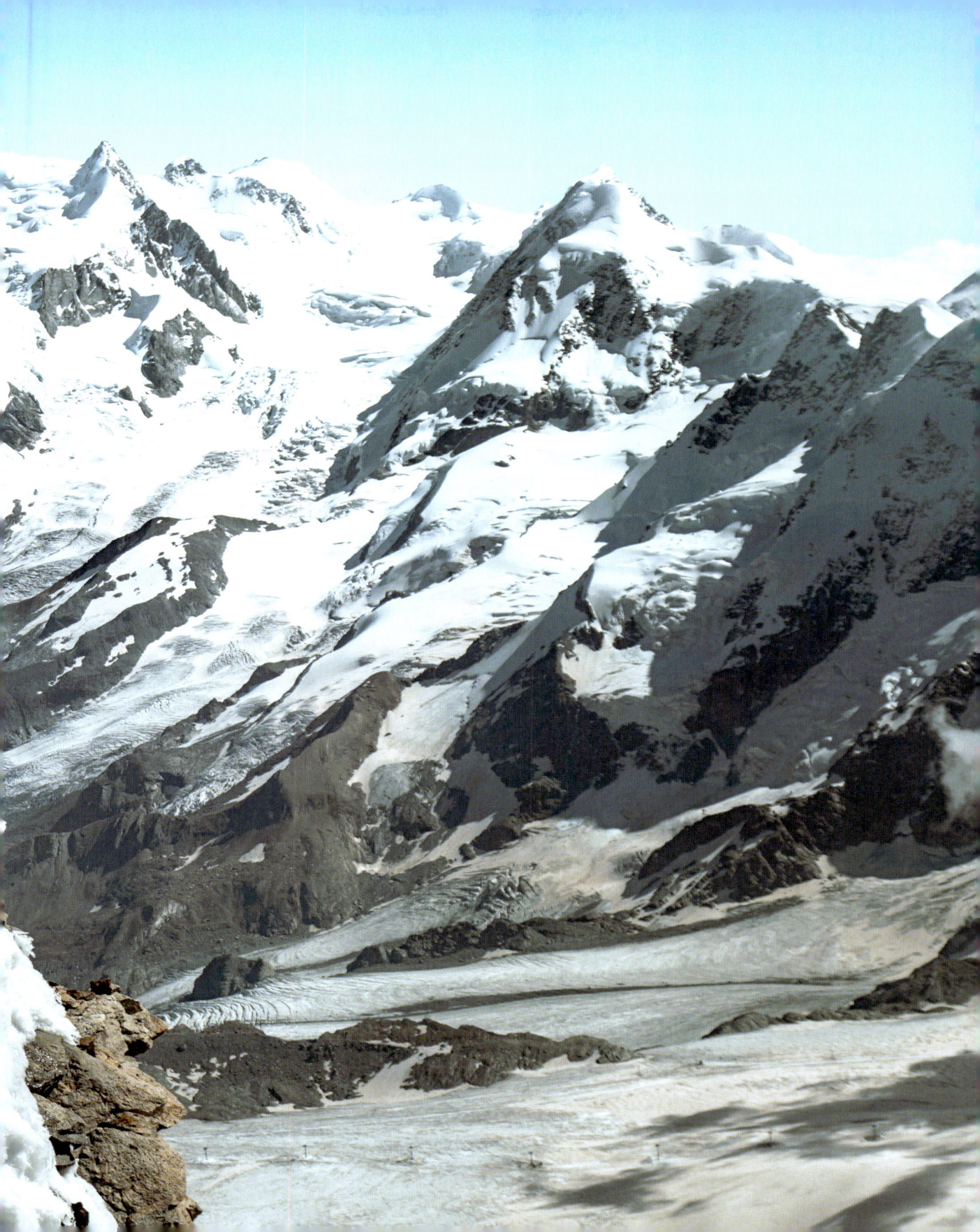

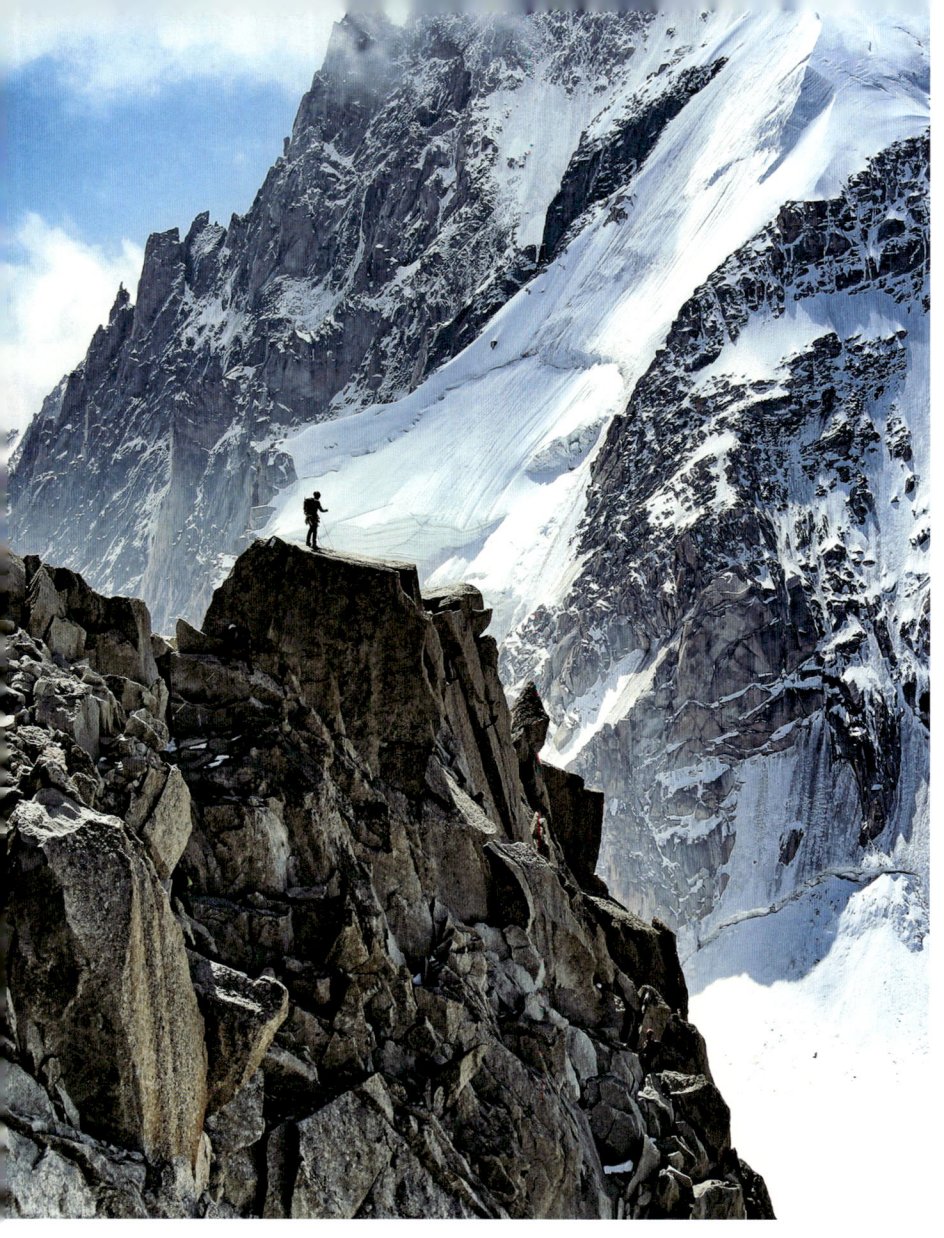

Squeezed in between glaciers and mountain peaks, the route's alpine huts are atmospheric refuges that boast hearty food, spirit-rousing wine, and, more often than not, an international cast of diners.

R ising majestically over Chamonix in eastern France, Mont Blanc is the highest mountain in Western Europe and overlooks what has come to be known as one of the best mountaineering centers in the world. Approximately 70 km (43.5 mi.) west of there as the crow flies lies the Matterhorn, a pyramid-shaped peak that has been a holy grail for climbers since the nineteenth century. Linking these two iconic mountains together is the Haute Route, a sinuous Alpine pathway that passes through glacier-sculpted valleys, flower-laden meadows, and enchanting villages.

The idea for a high-level route between Chamonix and Zermatt—resort towns that nestle below their respective peaks—was first conceived by the British Alpine Club in the 1860s. In its current incarnation the path is renowned as both a hiking trail in the summer and a cross-country skiing route in the winter, the routes of which vary slightly. Winding through isolated hamlets, traversing icy streams, and passing magnificent glaciers, aromatic forests, and sparkling waterfalls, the route is a varied one.

The Walker's Haute Route is a marked trail that crosses 11 mountain passes for an accumulative elevation gain of over 12,000 m (39,370 ft.). Traversing some of the highest and finest alpine terrain and passing several 4,000 m (13,123 ft.) peaks, this trail can hardly be described as a walk in the park. Yet, each pass

---

ABOUT THE TRAIL

→ <u>DISTANCE</u> 180 km (112 mi.)

→ <u>DURATION</u> 9 to 12 days

→ <u>LEVEL</u> Moderate to Difficult

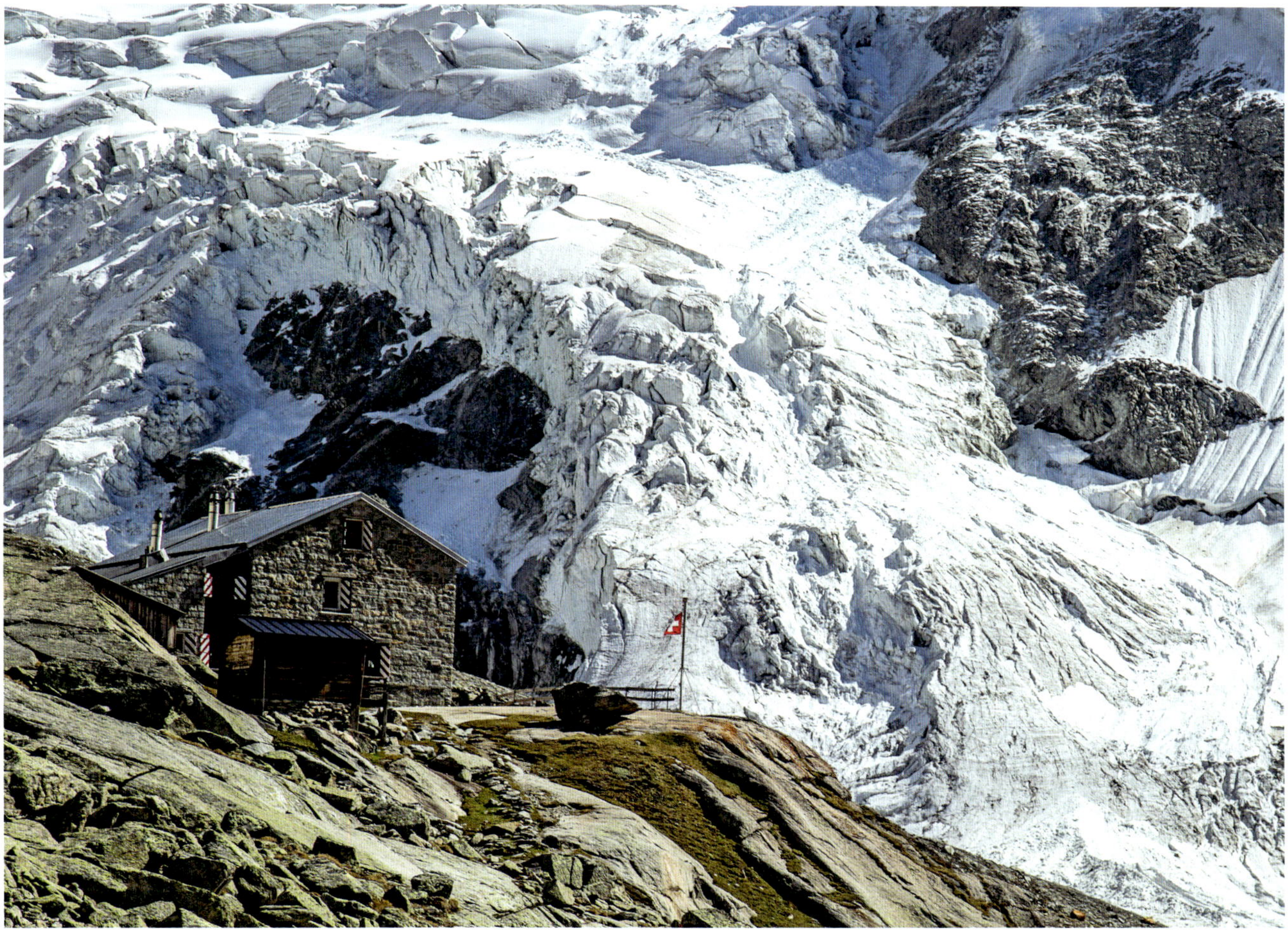

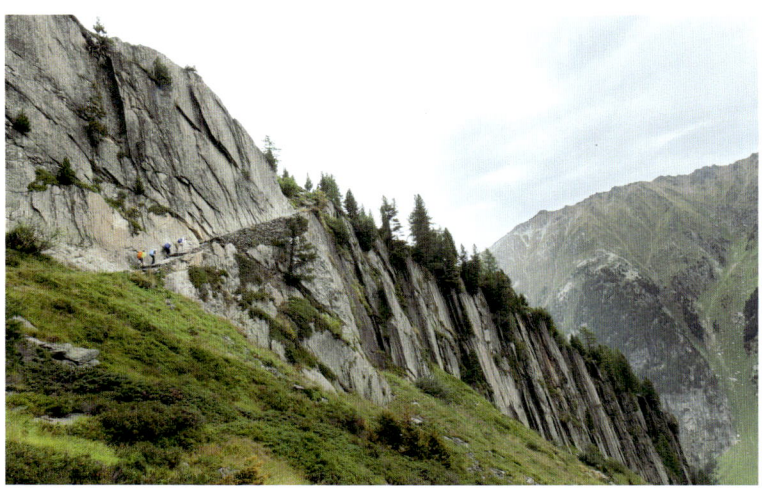

↑ **The refuge du Grand Mountet Hut.**
← **On the Aiguille du Midi.**

climbed promises adequate compensation in the form of pristine views. At some of them one can let the gaze wander across lush green valleys; at others one finds oneself elevated above age-old glacier fields.

Many of the standout features of this particular hike are found on alternate stages rather than the standard path. Two such examples are the section between the Col de Balme pass and the Chalet du Glacier and when crossing the Fenêtre d'Arpette. The second path takes the hiker over a challenging rocky pass with spectacular views of the undulations of the Trient Glacier. After reaching the scenic high point, the route descends steeply over boulders and scree into the forests and open meadows of the Arpette valley. In fine conditions, this 14 km (8.7 mi.) alternate stage is not to be missed.

Squeezed in between glaciers and mountain peaks, the route's alpine huts are atmospheric refuges that boast hearty food, spirit-rousing wine, and, more often than not, an international cast of diners. The social elements—sitting down and enjoying a meal and conversation with other trekkers—also play a part in this hike.   →

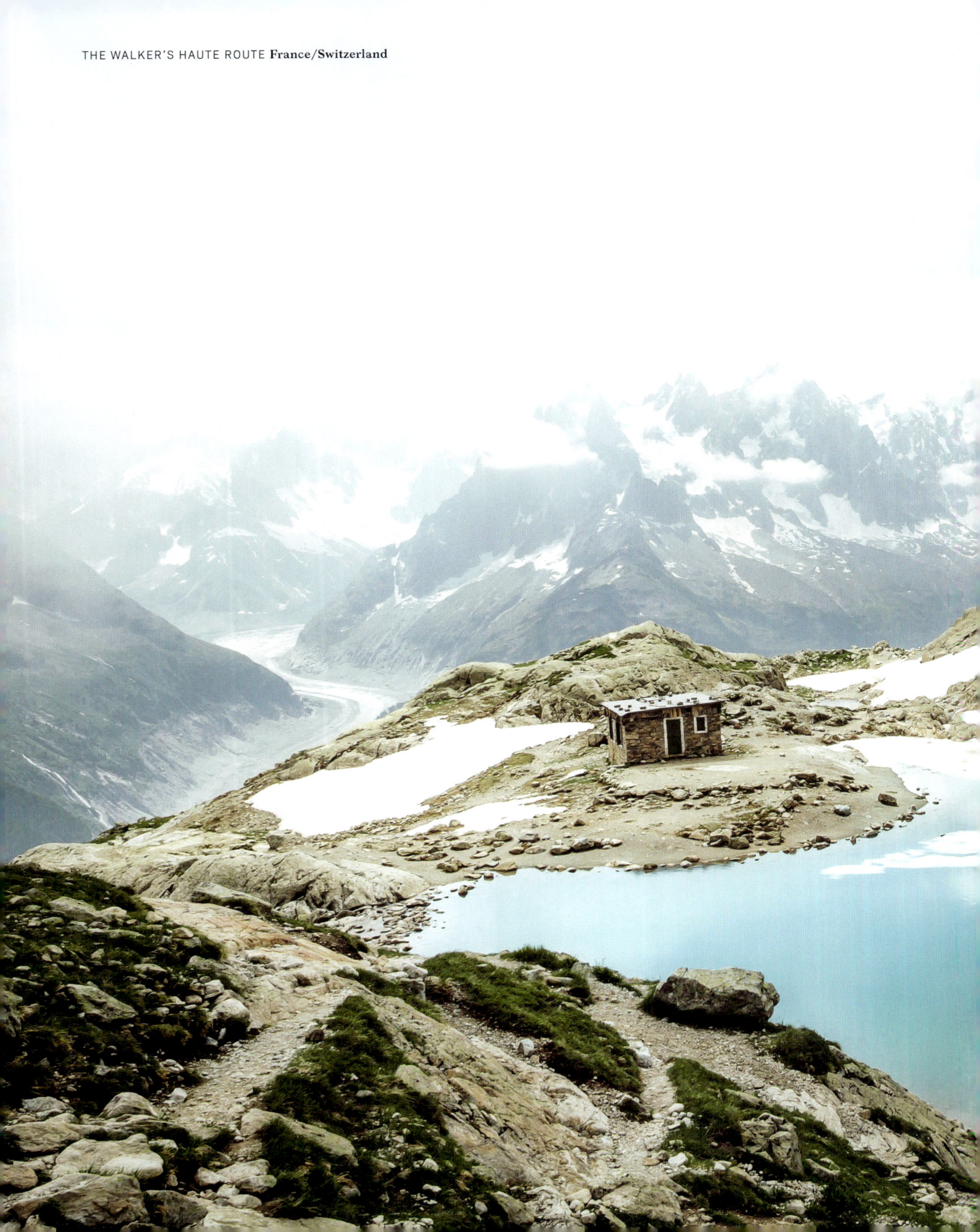

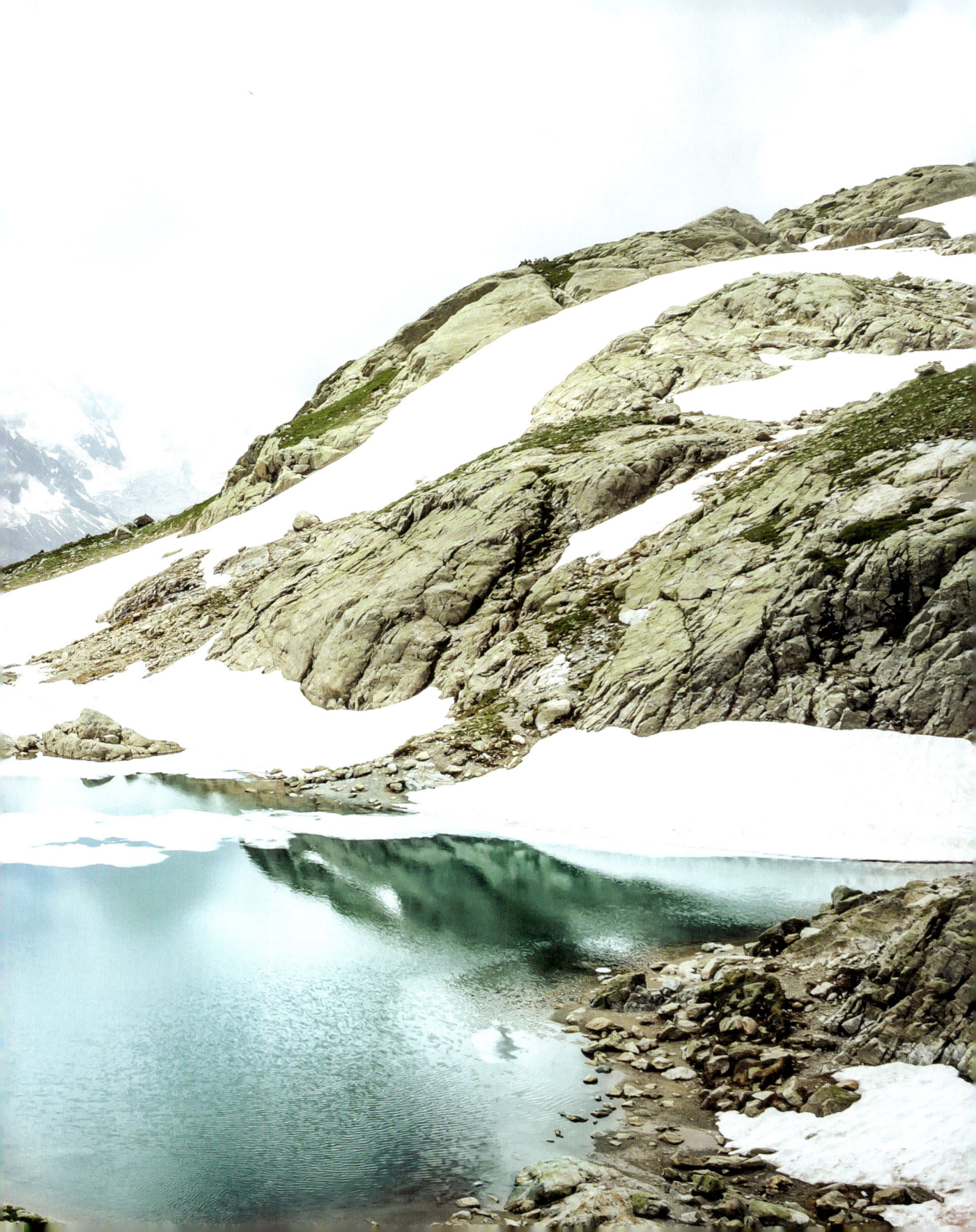

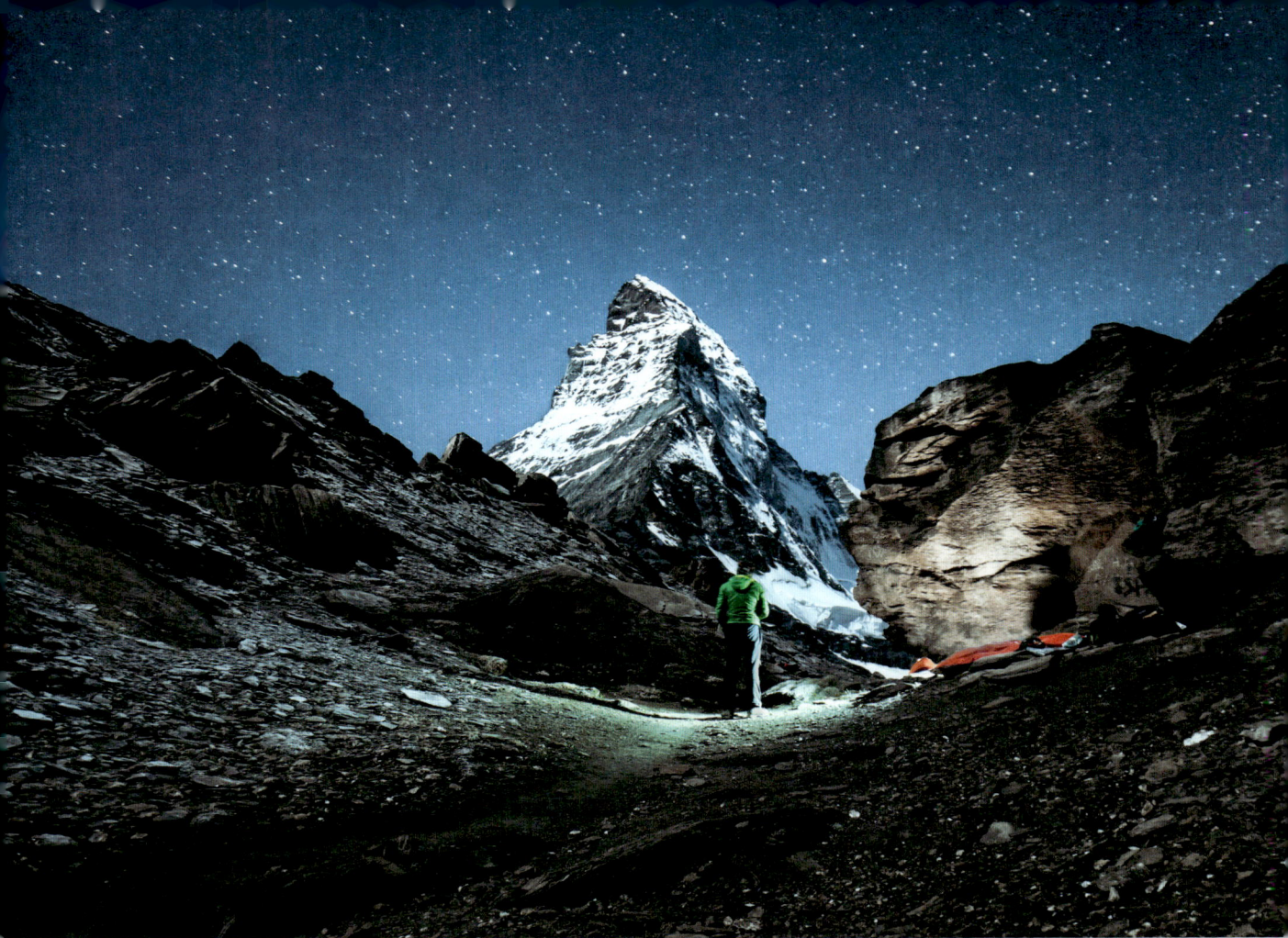

↑ Matterhorn views under the stars.

Though staying at least one or two nights in the huts is recommended, travelers looking for a little more solitude than indoor accommodation options provide should consider taking along a tent. Wild camping is possible in the higher, undeveloped areas. In addition to being more affordable, this strategy has some other great benefits: the sunrises and sunsets. Instead of viewing these from the balcony of a mountain hut, there is the opportunity to take in the wonders of both dawn and dusk from a higher, less-crowded perch in the company of snowcapped peaks, exquisite tarns (small mountain lakes or pools), and perhaps the odd marmot trying to steal your supplies.

The varied scenery, the welcoming huts, the diverse cultures, the regional food and wine that one would expect from two countries famed for their fine tastes, and of course the imposing peaks found on this famous route all mean that the Walker's Haute Route captures the essence of this part of the Alps in just 180 km (112 mi.) of hiking. It is therefore no surprise that when hikers talk about Europe's finest long-distance trails, this famed route is one of the first names mentioned.

Winding through isolated hamlets, traversing icy streams, and passing glaciers, aromatic forests, and sparkling waterfalls, the route is a varied one.

START/FINISH
🚩 Chamonix, France
🚩 Zermatt, Switzerland

SEASON
Mid-June to late September

LOWEST/HIGHEST POINT
1,000 m (3,281 ft.)/2,987 m (9,800 ft.)

ACCOMMODATION
Huts, B&Bs, hostels. Wild camping is also possible in some of the higher areas as long as discretion is practiced and Leave No Trace principles are followed.

HIGHLIGHTS
Stretches from the Col de Balme pass to the Chalet du Glacier, and from the Cabane de Prafleuri to the village of Arolla. Also crossing the Fenêtre d'Arpette, and the Europaweg.

TIP
Mountain huts are often full during July and August, so booking ahead is advised.

BACKGROUND

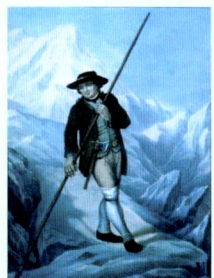

LOFTY FACTS
Mont Blanc's name translates as White Mountain. This stems from the fact that glaciers cover around 100 km² (40 mi.²) of its surface. The 4,807 m (15,771 ft.) Alpine peak lies on the French-Italian border and is the highest mountain in Europe. The first to scale it were Michel-Gabriel Paccard, a doctor from Chamonix, and Jacques Balmat, his porter, in 1786. The year afterwards the scientist Horace-Bénédict de Saussure, who had previously offered prize money for the first person to reach the summit, also made the climb.

The Matterhorn's name comes from the German words *matte*, meaning "meadow," and *horn*, meaning "peak." Situated on the Swiss-Italian border, the 4,478 m (14,692 ft.) high peak is pyramid shaped and has one face pointing in each of the cardinal directions. The first team to reach the summit did so in 1865, led by the British artist Edward Whymper, but the trip finished in disaster as only three of the seven climbers survived the descent. A sad end to a historic trip.

FLORA & FAUNA

RODENT SIGHTINGS
Although more commonly associated with North America, marmots can also be found in high regions of the Alps. The thick-furred rodents hibernate through the winter, but may be spotted as they occasionally venture out of their burrows on milder days.

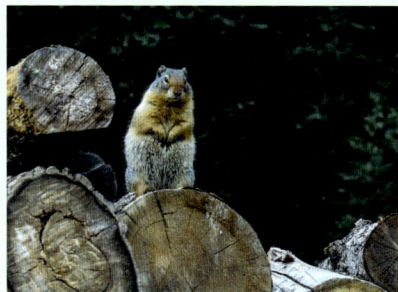

HELPFUL HINTS

MOUNTAIN HUTS
There are many scenically situated *refuges* (mountain huts) on the Haute Route; however, the standout in terms of location is arguably the Refuge des Grands Mulets, which features an impressive view over the Glacier des Bossons.

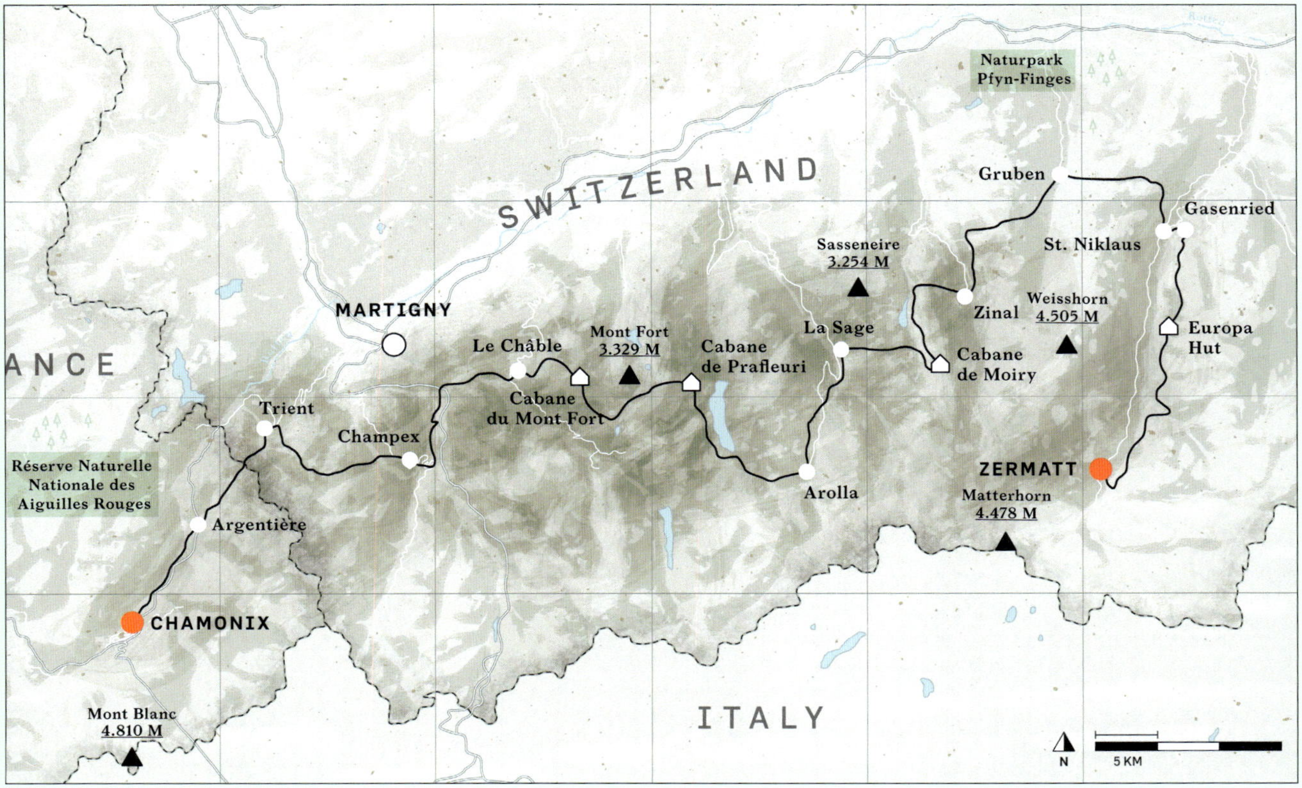

Map

Naturpark Pfyn-Finges

SWITZERLAND

Gruben
Gasenried
Sasseneire 3,254 M
St. Niklaus
Zinal
Weisshorn 4,505 M
La Sage
Cabane de Moiry
Europa Hut
MARTIGNY
Le Châble
Mont Fort 3,329 M
Cabane de Prafleuri
Cabane du Mont Fort
Trient
Champex
ZERMATT
Matterhorn 4,478 M
Arolla
FRANCE
Réserve Naturelle Nationale des Aiguilles Rouges
Argentière
CHAMONIX
Mont Blanc 4,810 M
ITALY

N
5 KM

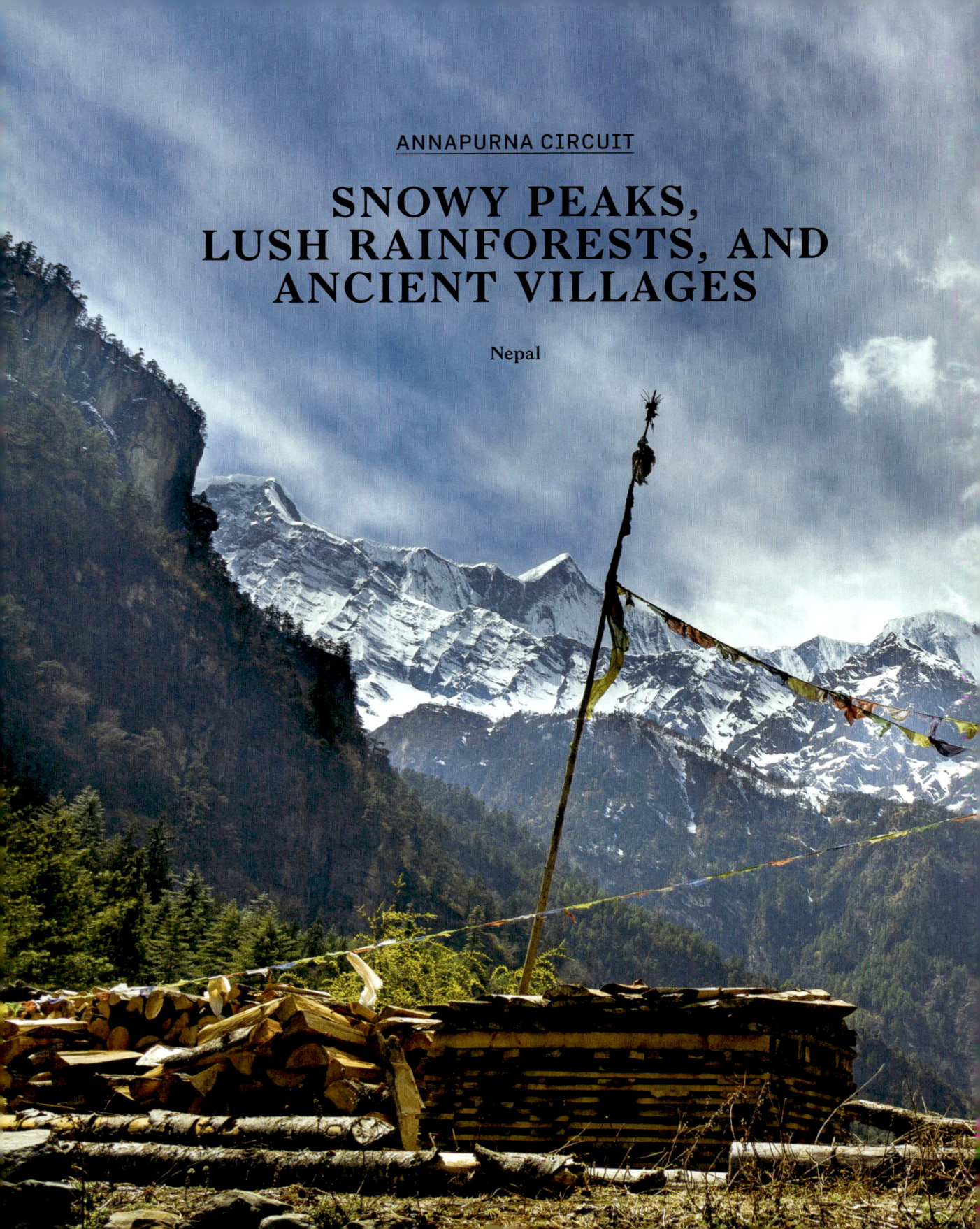

ANNAPURNA CIRCUIT

SNOWY PEAKS, LUSH RAINFORESTS, AND ANCIENT VILLAGES

Nepal

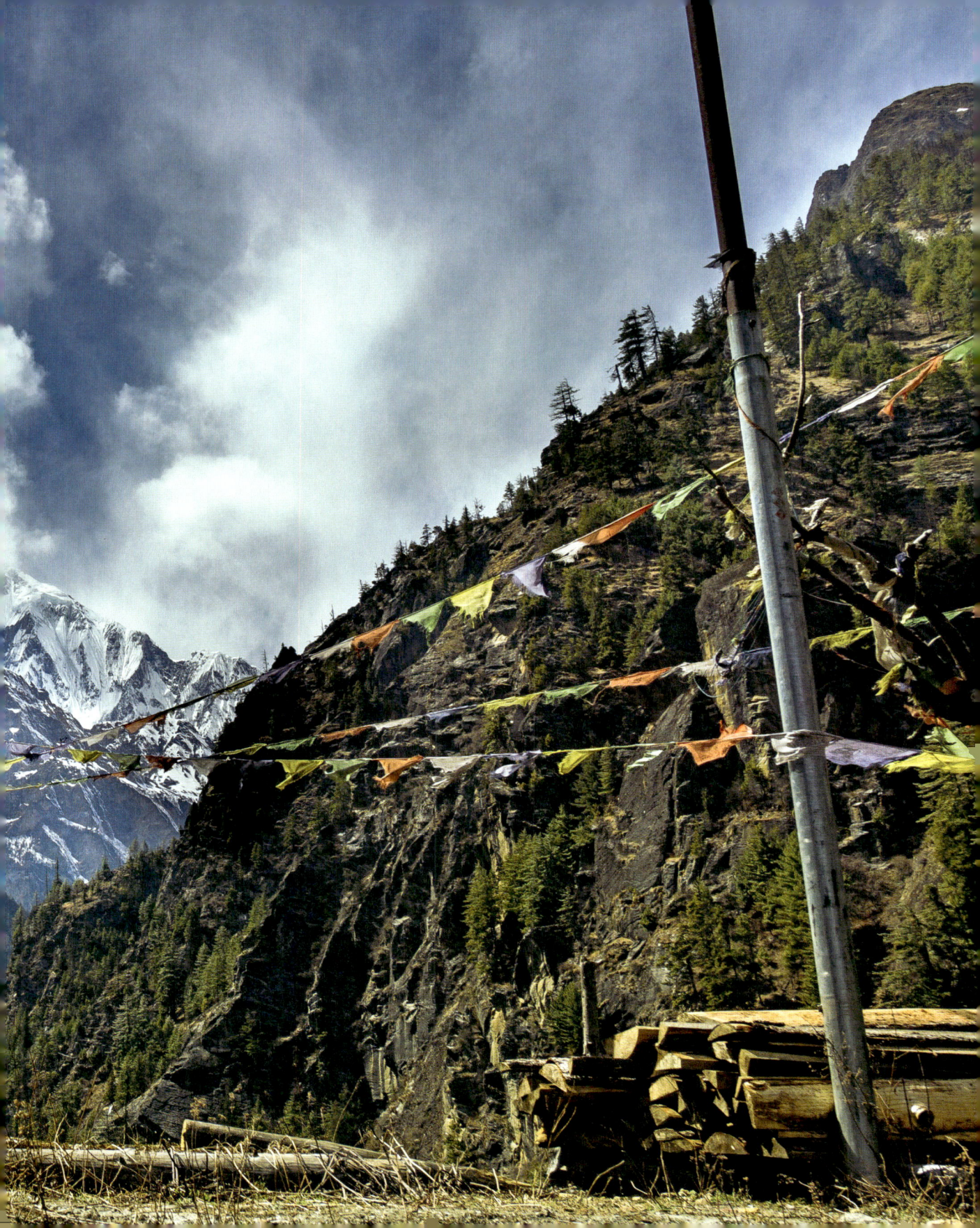

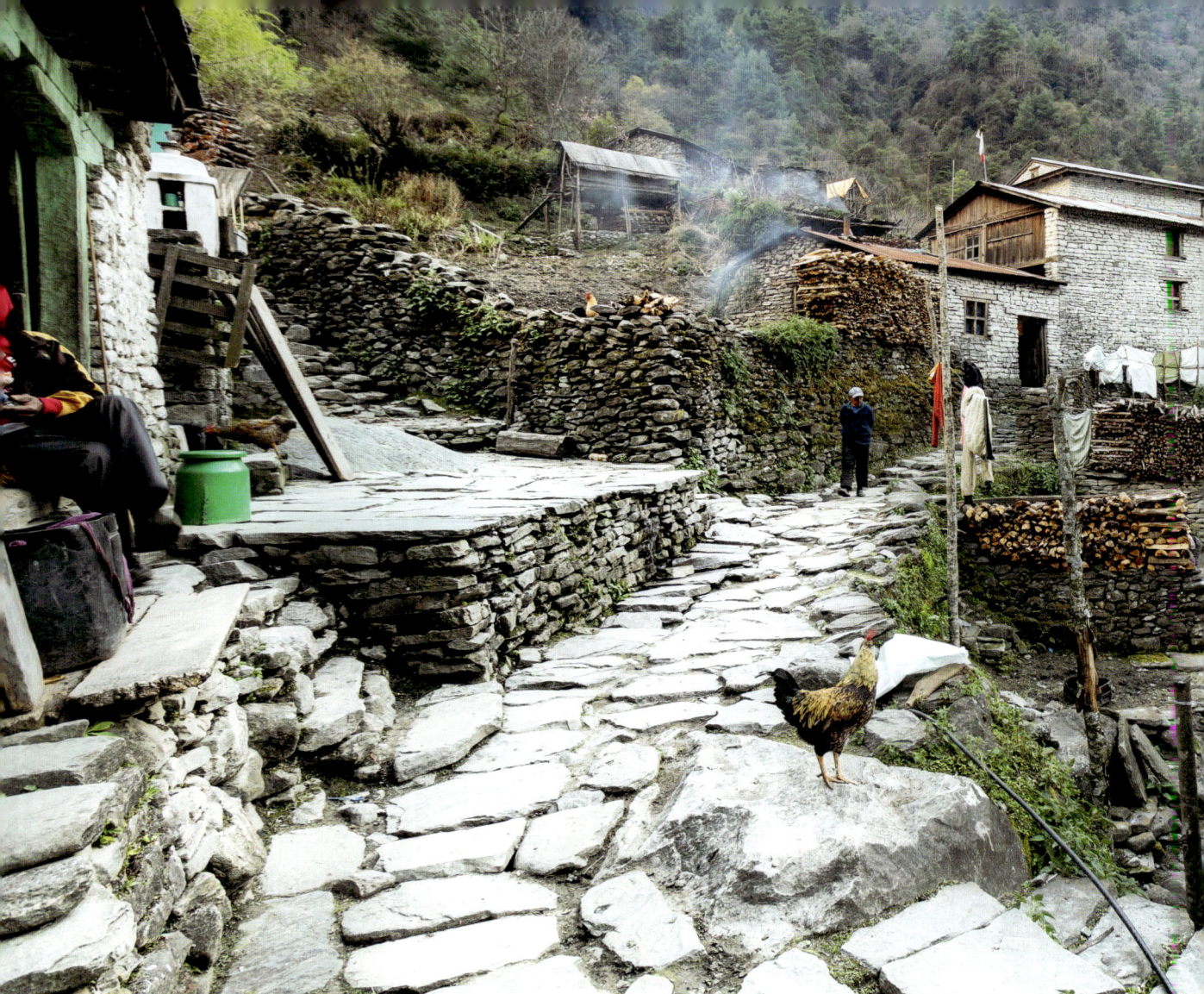

The Annapurna Massif is a 48 km (30 mi) long series of towering peaks situated in central Nepal. Nestled between two of the country's major river systems, it is an area that contains centuries-old villages, a diverse range of ecosystems, and, of course, some of the highest mountains on earth—including the mighty Annapurna I, which stands at a dizzying 8091 m (26,545 ft). It also boasts a hiking trail that since it was first open to foreigners in 1977, has become universally recognized as one of the world's finest long-distance treks.

The Annapurna Circuit takes walkers on a journey of anywhere from 160 to 230 km (99 to 143 mi.) around the massif. Depending on route choices, the trek typically requires anywhere between 13 and 17 days to complete, and is traditionally done in an anti-clockwise direction in order to allow aspirants the chance to acclimatize gradually. The ecological diversity encountered along the trek is incredible—something that is not surprising for a hike with an altitude range of more than 4,500 m (14,764 ft.). Beginning in sub-tropical rainforest, it weaves through terraced farmland, pine and rhododendron forests, dramatic gorges, rocky waterfalls, and over formidably high plateaus.

ABOUT THE TRAIL

→ <u>DISTANCE</u> 160 to 230 km (99 to 143 mi.), depending on route
→ <u>DURATION</u> 13 to 17 days
→ <u>LEVEL</u> Moderate to Difficult

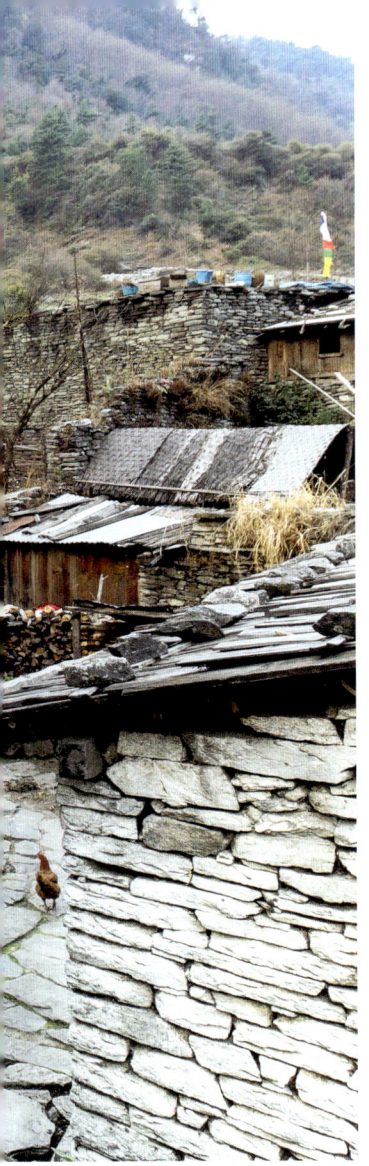

Beginning in sub-tropical rainforest, the trek weaves through terraced farmland, pine and rhododendron forests, dramatic gorges, rocky waterfalls, and over formidably high plateaus and swaying suspension bridges.

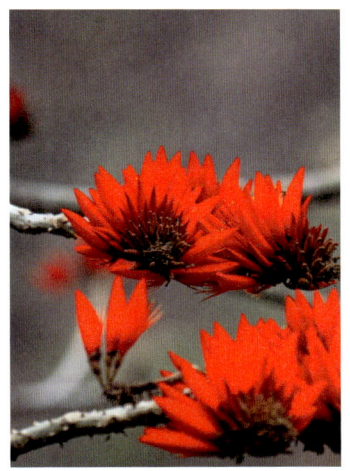

← Village life in the Annapurna Range.
↓↗ Mountain flora and fauna.

Though hikers must be wary of the conditions—these can include sudden, violent storms and in the past trekkers have had to be rescued from the 5,416 m (17,769 ft.) high Thorung La Pass—the Annapurna Circuit is achievable for most individuals with a reasonable amount of fitness and experience. It is signposted throughout, and although most people do it as part of an organized group, tackling the circuit independently is possible. With villages and teahouses at intervals along the trail, travelers are able to carry fewer provisions: shelters can be left at home, and there is no need to lug around more than half a day's food at a time.

Over the course of two to three weeks, it is common to run into fellow hikers at teahouses and villages along the circuit. Over ginger-and-lemon tea, or daal bhaat (lentils and rice), hikers can swap tales of past and present, just as Nepalese traders did in centuries past, when the circuit's pathways represented the region's only means of access to the outside world. English is widely spoken in the villages along the circuit; however, as a gesture of respect, it is recommended that hikers learn at least the common courtesy phrases in Nepalese.

For those with the time, fitness, and inclination, there are various side-trip options available while hiking the Annapurna. The most notable one is to Tilicho Lake, which is a two-day →

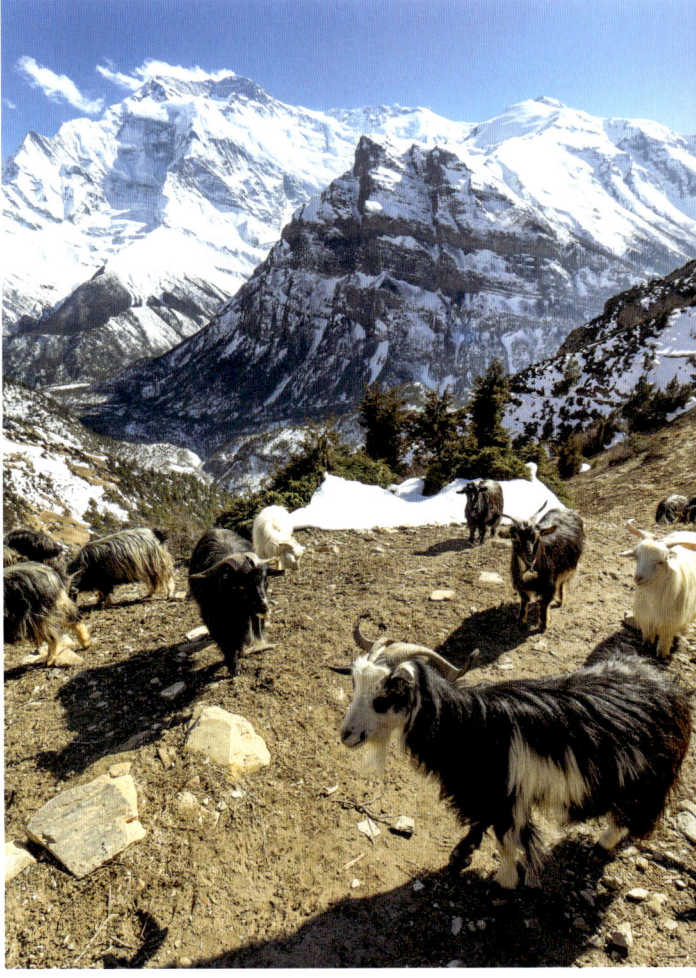

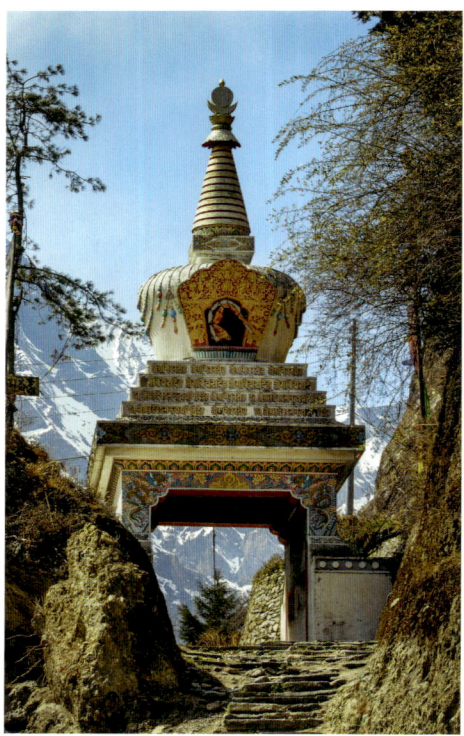

→ **A suspension bridge on the way from Besisahar to Bahundanda.**

out-and-back excursion from the village of Manang. Tilicho is situated at 4920m (16,142 ft), and is one of the world's highest lakes. Between September and May it is usually frozen solid; however, during the warmer months of the year, its turquoise-colored waters often sport mini icebergs that have calved off from the adjacent glacier. Even on a hike as highlight-filled as the Annapurna Circuit, the side trip makes an indelible impression.

Over past decades, one of the biggest challenges facing the Annapurna region has been navigating the inevitable march of development. Case in point is the road construction that has occurred on both sides of the massif. On the one hand, locals have wanted the roads for many years because it means easier access to markets for their goods and medical assistance for their families. On the other hand, trekking tourism is a big part of the area's economy, and more roads could potentially mean fewer adventure-seeking foreigners—not many people want to walk on a road.

Fortunately, alternatives to the busy road sections exist in the form of the New Annapurna Trekking Trails (NATT). In recent years, the government has worked along with the Annapurna Conservation Area Project to establish and promote these →

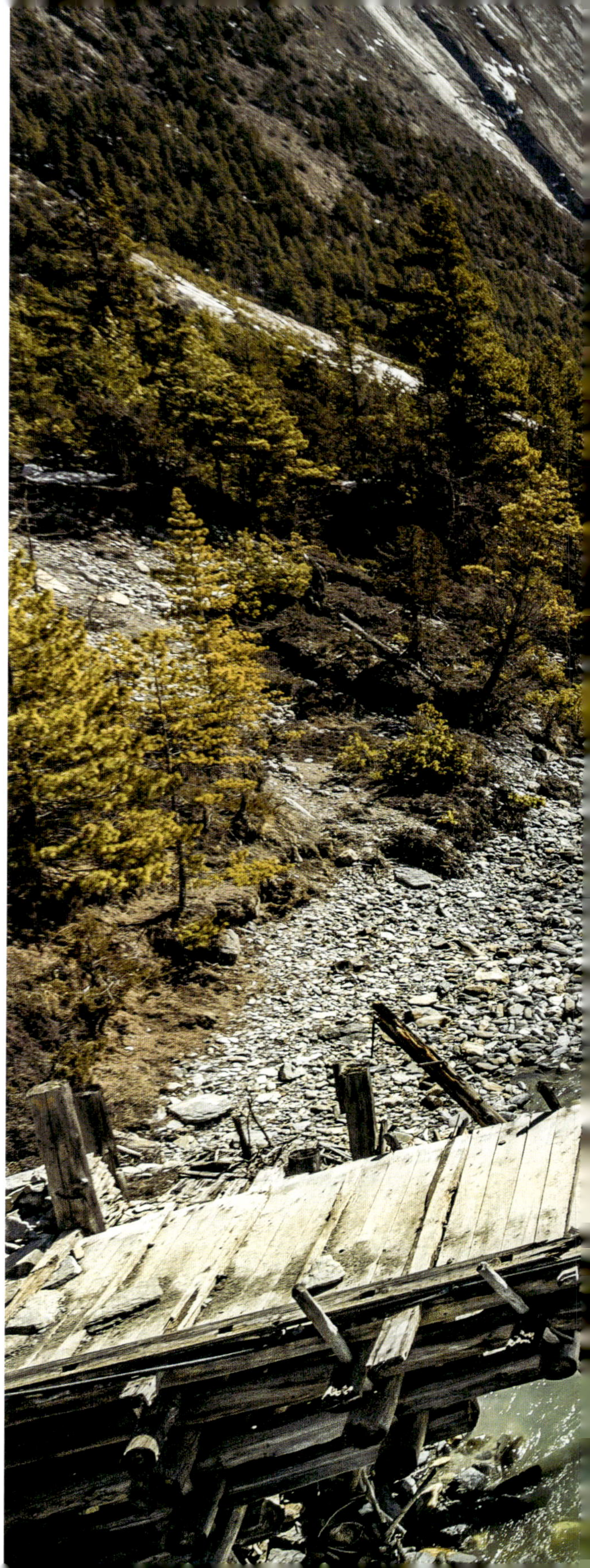

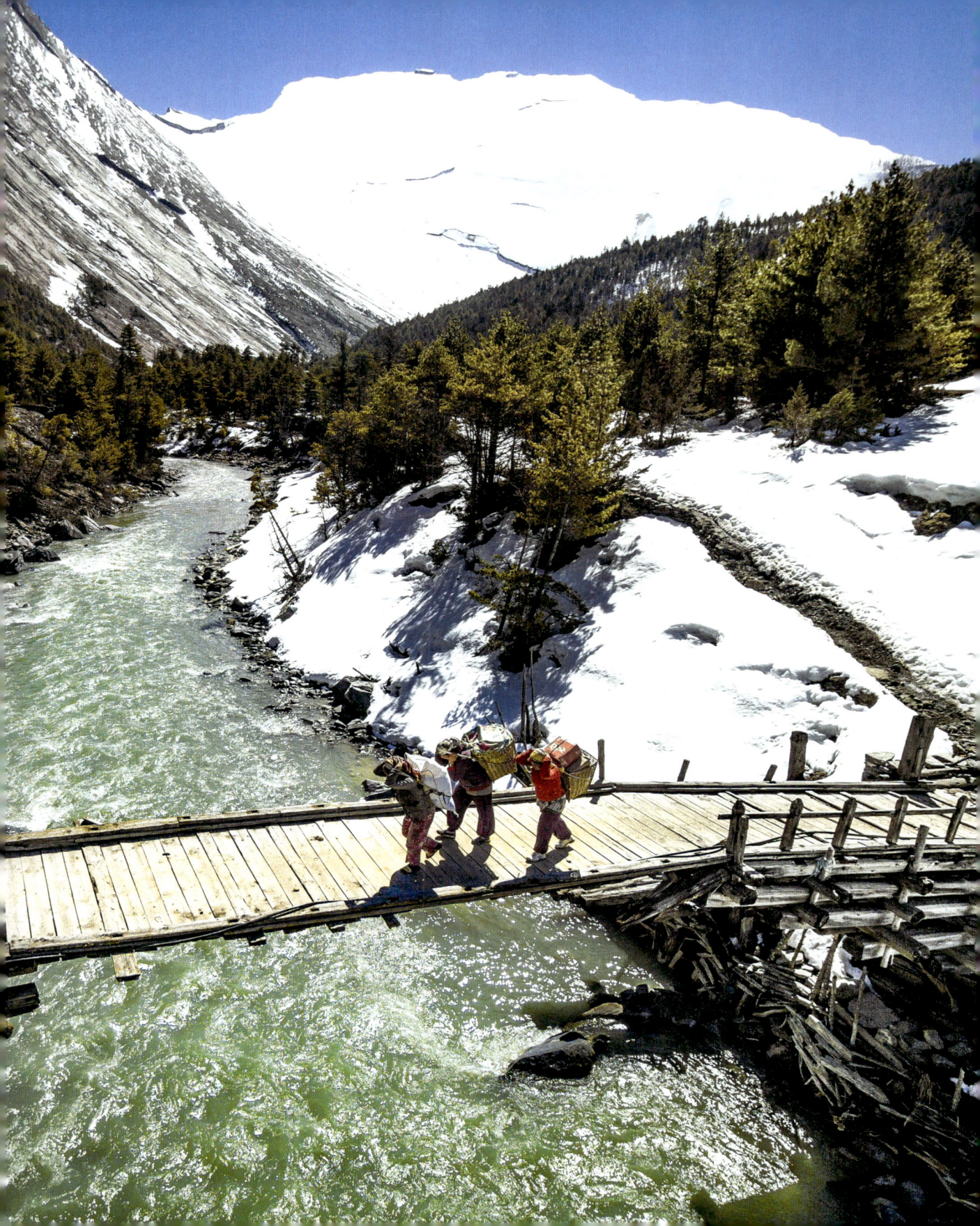

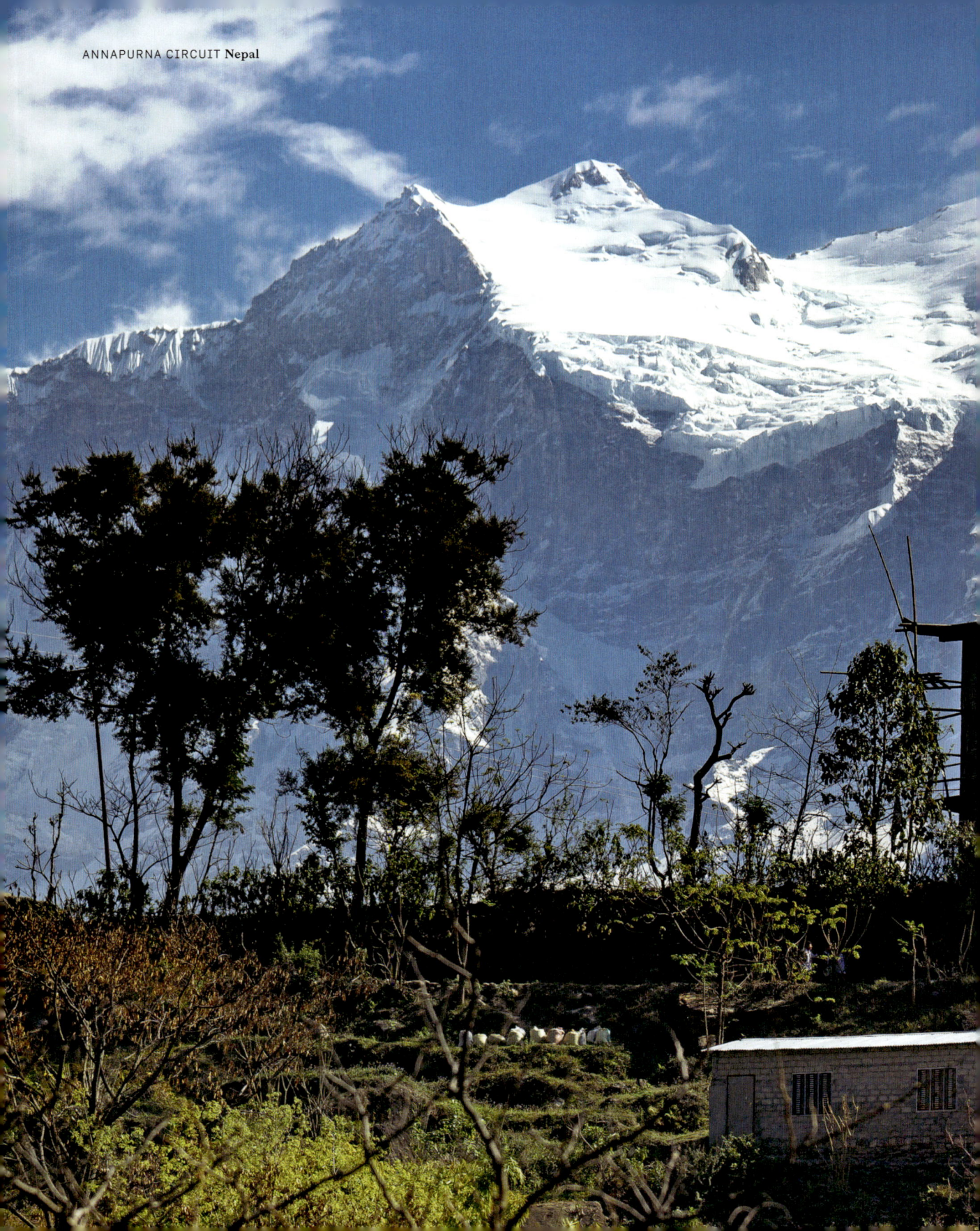

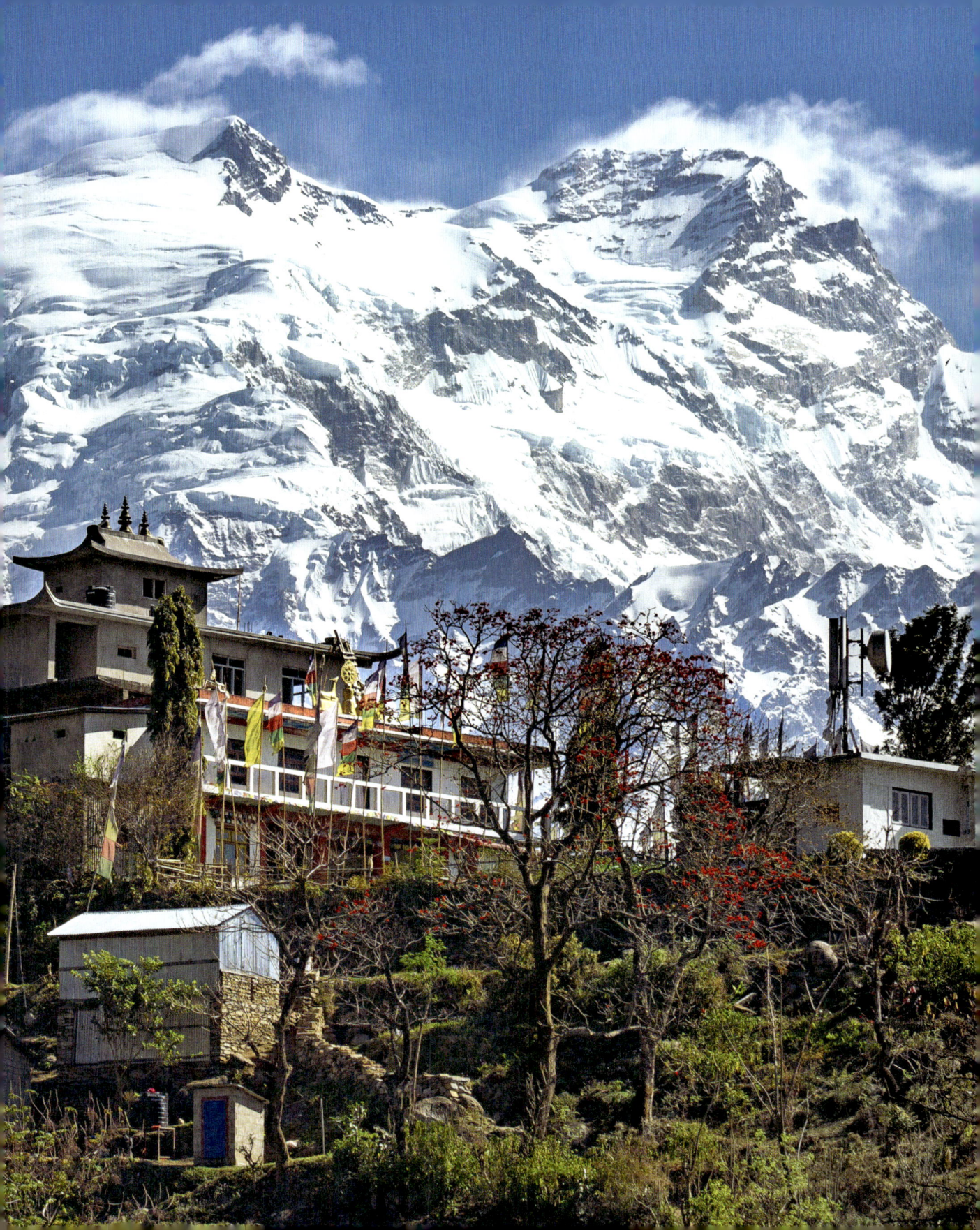

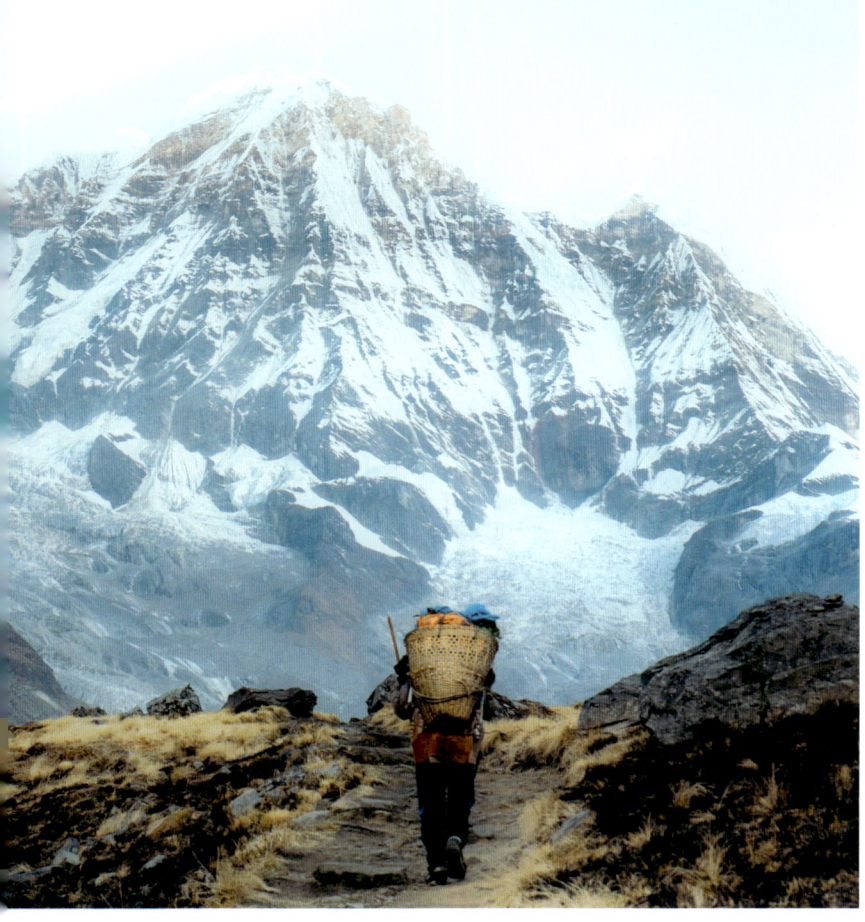

Nestled between two of Nepal's major river systems, the Annapurna Massif is an area that contains centuries-old villages, a diverse range of ecosystems, and some of the highest mountains on earth.

↑ A heavily laden porter hikes the Annapurna.
↓ Ending the day at a traditional teahouse.

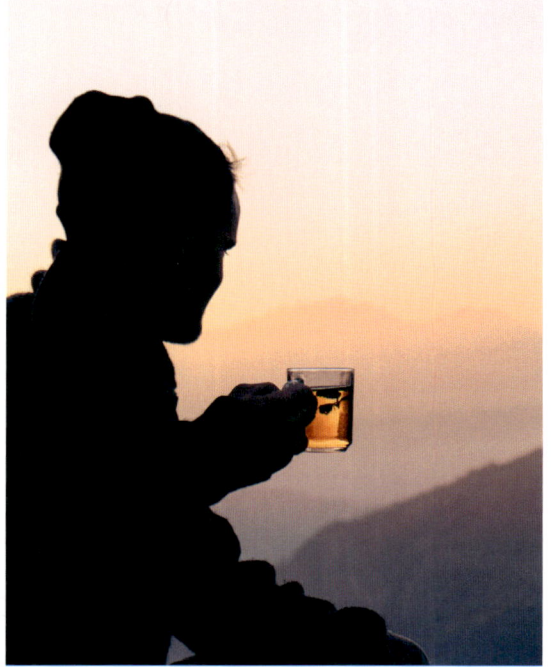

trails, and they represent a real boon for hikers looking to experience the Annapurna region as it once was. Of the alternate routes that currently exist, a particularly special option is the stretch between Upper Pisang and Manang. This segment adds on an extra day to the standard circuit; however, the views are among the best of the entire trail. Additionally, this affords the hiker the opportunity to visit the ancient villages of Ghyaru and Ngawal, with their holy stupas, temples, and mani walls (stone surfaces inscribed with Lamaist prayers).

Dirt roads and its ever-increasing popularity notwithstanding, the Annapurna Circuit is still one of the world's great long-distance hikes. It may not offer much in the way of solitude, but it does allow for natural and cultural discoveries, and it can be done in as much or little luxury as is desired. By taking the alternate routes and side trips and embracing the aspects of "teahouse" trekking, a multi-week ramble around the Annapurna Massif remains a rich experience. The mountains are as beautiful as ever, the Nepalese as welcoming, and the ubiquitous daal bhat and chai never tasted better. ———————————

GOOD TO KNOW

START/FINISH

⚑ Besisahar
⚑ Multiple options including Jomson, Tatopani, Beni, and Birethanti

SEASON

April to May, October to November

CONDITIONS

October and November offer the best weather; however, they are also when the trail is at its most crowded.

LOWEST/HIGHEST POINT

760 m (2,493 ft.)/5,416 m (17,769 ft.)

ACCOMMODATION

Leave the tent at home and enjoy the hospitality, delicious food, and occasional hot shower on offer at the teahouses. Good spots to stay include Ghyaru and Kagbeni.

HIGHLIGHTS

Alternate route between Upper Pisang and Manang, side trip to Lake Tilicho, Thorung La Pass, and the town of Kagbeni.

TIP

Permits are required, so pick one up in advance in either Kathmandu or Pokhara.

BACKGROUND

UPS AND DOWNS Nepal is the country with the greatest variation in altitude in the world, and Annapurna I is the tenth highest mountain on earth. Therefore, hikers must be aware of the risks of walking the Annapurna Circuit and leave time to acclimatize. The air is drier and thinner at high altitude, and due to cooler temperatures many hikers make the mistake of not drinking enough water. Walkers should aim for at least three liters per day, beginning when they arrive in Nepal. As the initial symptoms of acute mountain sickness (AMS) are similar to those of dehydration, people often assume they have AMS when in actual fact they are dehydrated. Either way, drinking water is best. Walkers should limit their intake of alcohol and caffeine, as these increase dehydration—this particularly holds true during the first few days of a hike.

HELPFUL HINTS

SIDE TRIPS For those with the time, fitness, and inclination, there are some beautiful trips off the standard circuit. Two of the most notable are Tilicho Lake and the Dhaulagiri Icefall, a glacier on the south slope of the Annapurna Range. The hiking is challenging, but the scenery is outstanding.

FLORA & FAUNA

COLORFUL COMPANIONS Rhododendrons are common in Nepal at altitudes of between 3,048 and 3,658 m (10,000 and 12,000 ft.). They can typically be seen flowering in March and April, and the Annapurna Circuit takes walkers through vividly colored forests of the country's national flower.

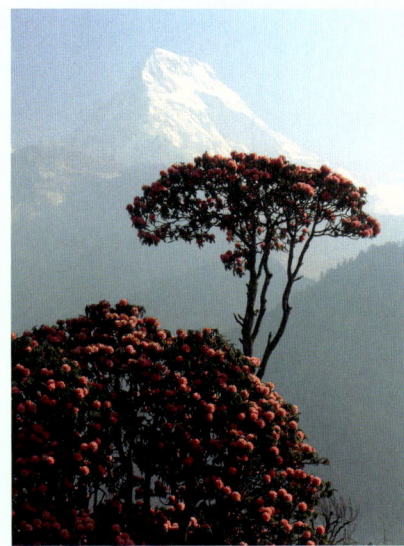

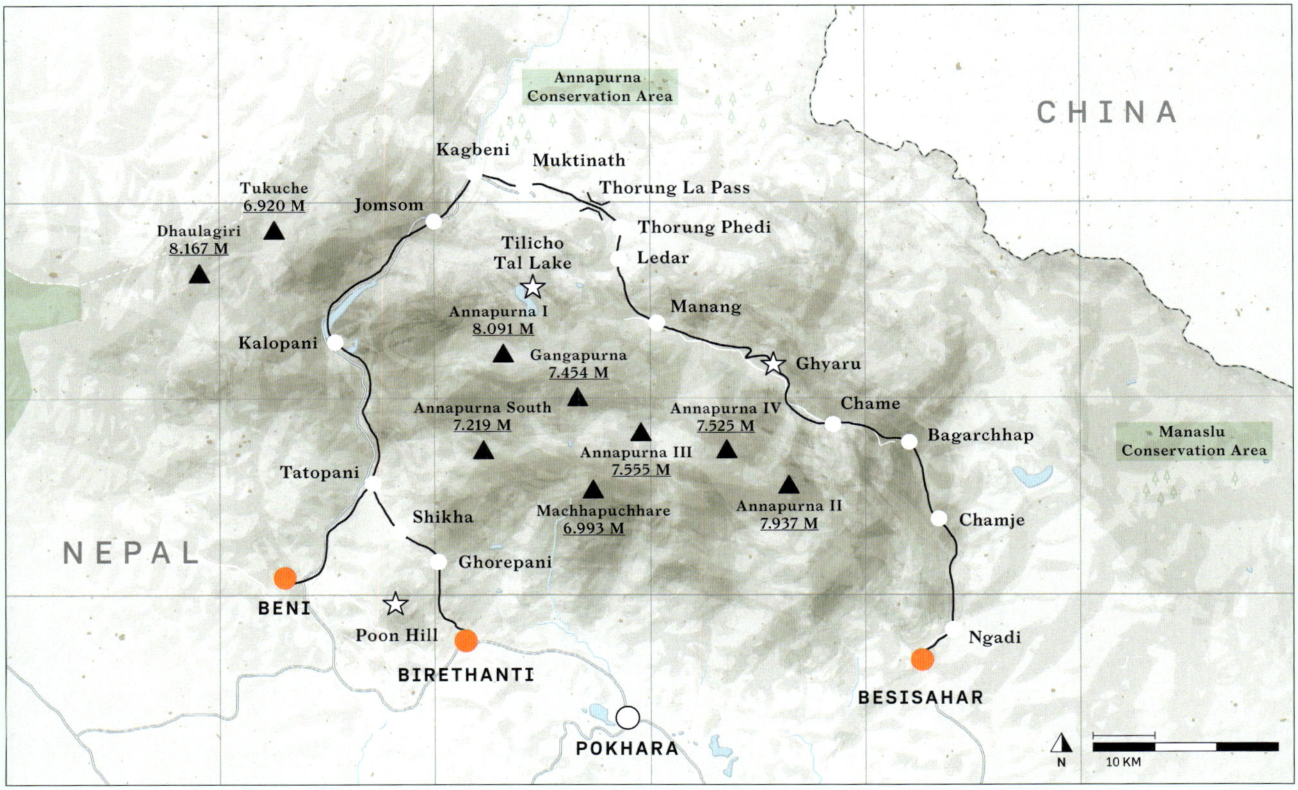

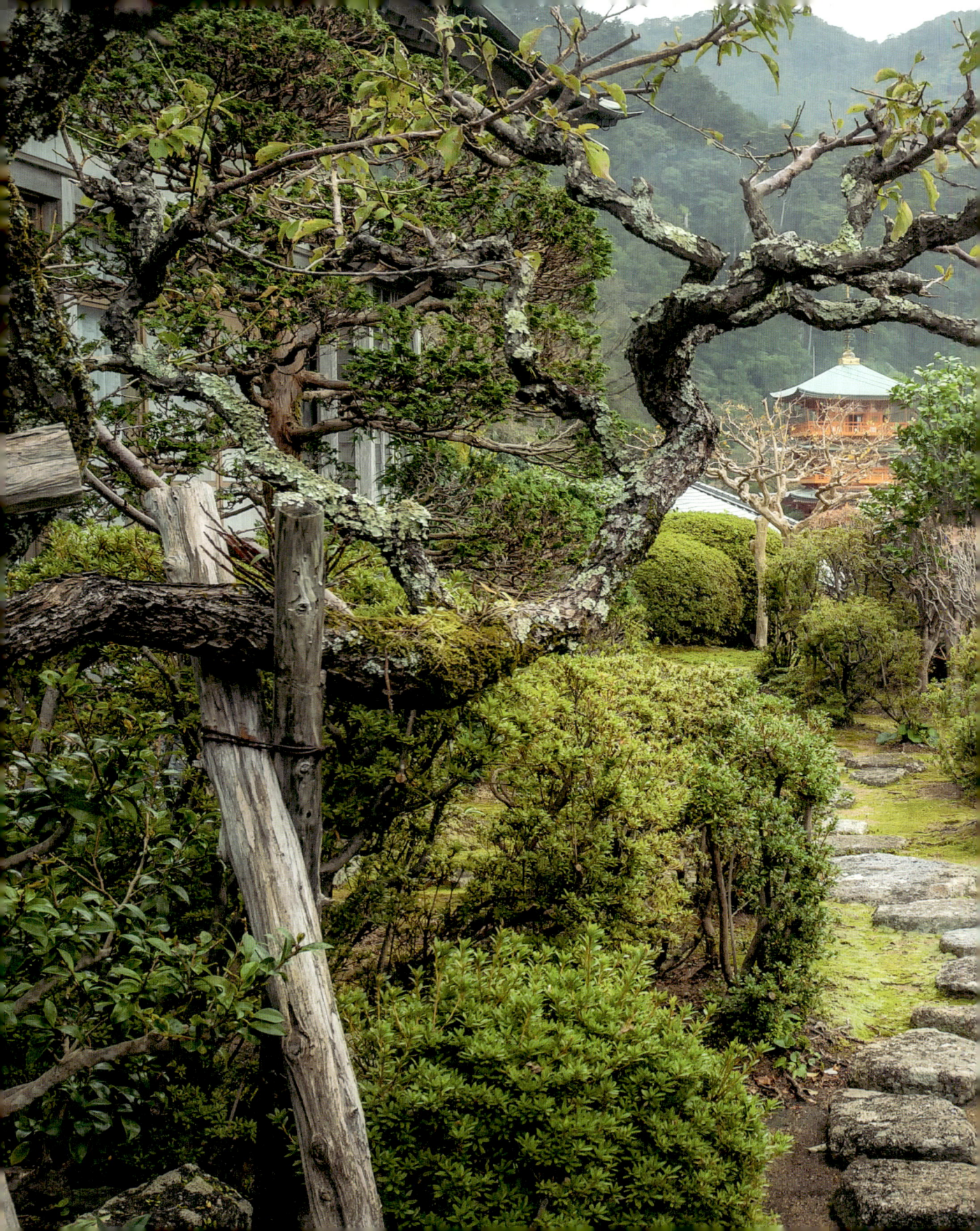

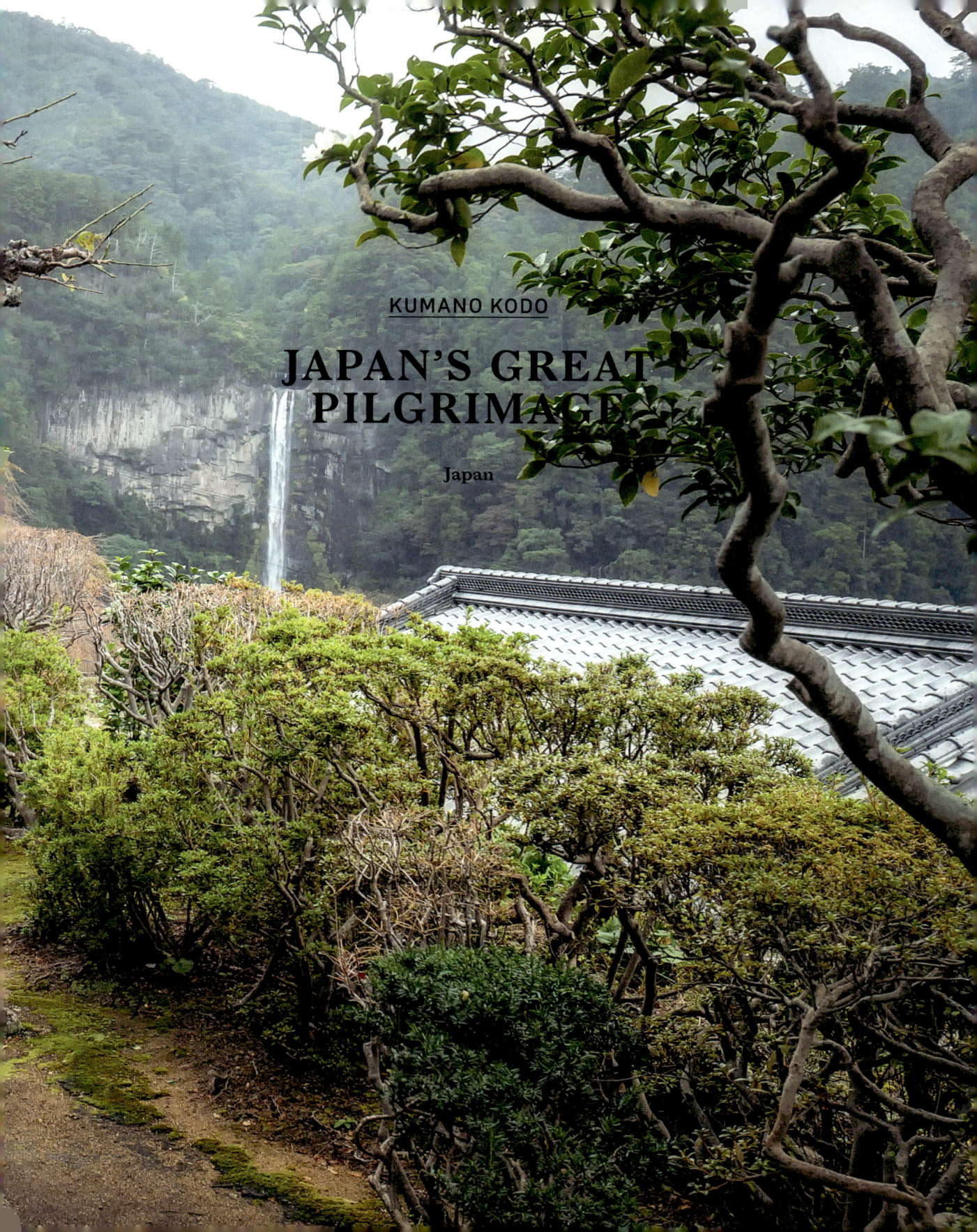

KUMANO KODO

JAPAN'S GREAT PILGRIMAGE

Japan

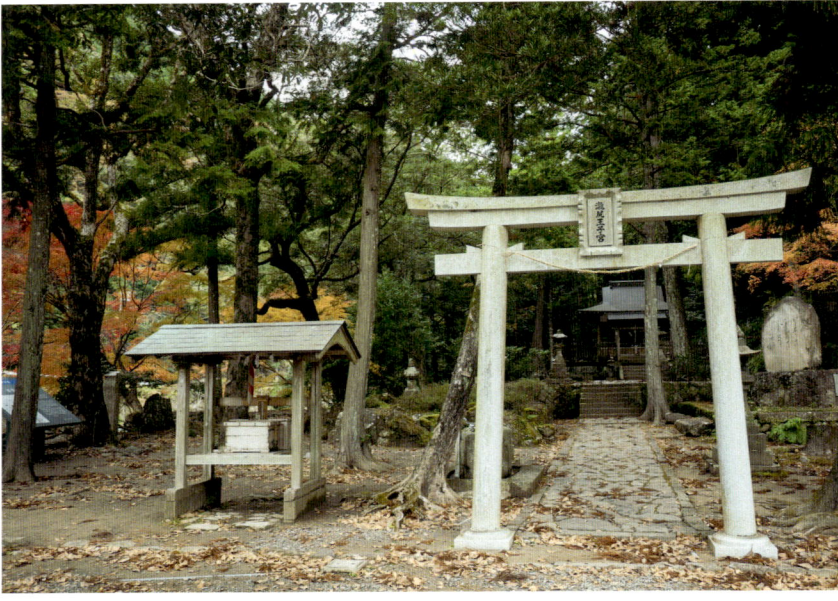

↑ Takijiri-Oji, the shrine at the beginning of the Kumano Kodo.

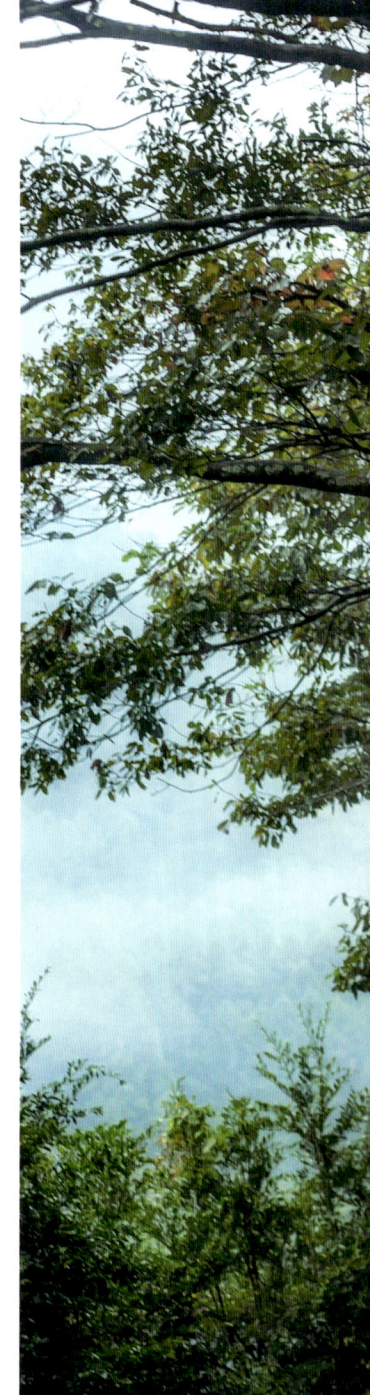

hinrin-yoku is Japanese for "forest bathing." It is the act of immersing all of one's senses in a natural environment with the goal of improving physical, mental, and spiritual well-being. The term was officially coined in the 1980s by the Japanese Ministry of Agriculture, Forestry, and Fisheries, but the Japanese have had strong connections to nature for centuries, with Shinto beliefs and practices drawing their deities from the natural world. The set of ancient pilgrimage routes known as Kumano Kodo bathes walkers in tree-filled landscapes (among other picturesque scenery) while leading them through holy sites of the Shinto and Buddhist religions.

Since the early tenth century, pilgrims have traveled to the remote and mountainous Kii Peninsula with the intent of walking to the Kumano Sanzan, or Three Grand Shrines of Kumano (Hongu Taisha, Hayatama Taisha, and Nachi Taisha), the spiritual heart of Japan. Of the network of pathways that lead to the trio of sacred sites, the oldest and most frequently used is known as the Nakahechi, or Imperial Route.

Named for the emperors and nobles that first journeyed on it more than 1,000 years ago, the modern incarnation of the Nakahechi begins in Takijiri-Oji. Set among forested hills at the confluence of two rivers, Takijiri is the first of many Oji subsidiary shrines visited by pilgrims during their journey to Kumano. It represents an appropriate starting point for a route that fuses natural, cultural, and spiritual elements. Seamlessly moving between verdant valleys and isolated mountain villages, mist-laden forests and sacred ancient temples, the Imperial Route affords pilgrims an insight into a region steeped in history and legend.

Although many people choose to do the Kumano Kodo as part of an organized tour, there are no issues with walking the trail independently. The way is clearly signposted in both Japanese and English, and though the terrain is roller-coaster-like in character, the hike is achievable by walkers with a reasonable level of experience and fitness. Because of the high amount of precipitation in the Kii Peninsula (one of the wettest regions in

ABOUT THE TRAIL

→ <u>DISTANCE</u> 70 km (43 mi.)
→ <u>DURATION</u> 5 days
→ <u>LEVEL</u> Easy to Moderate

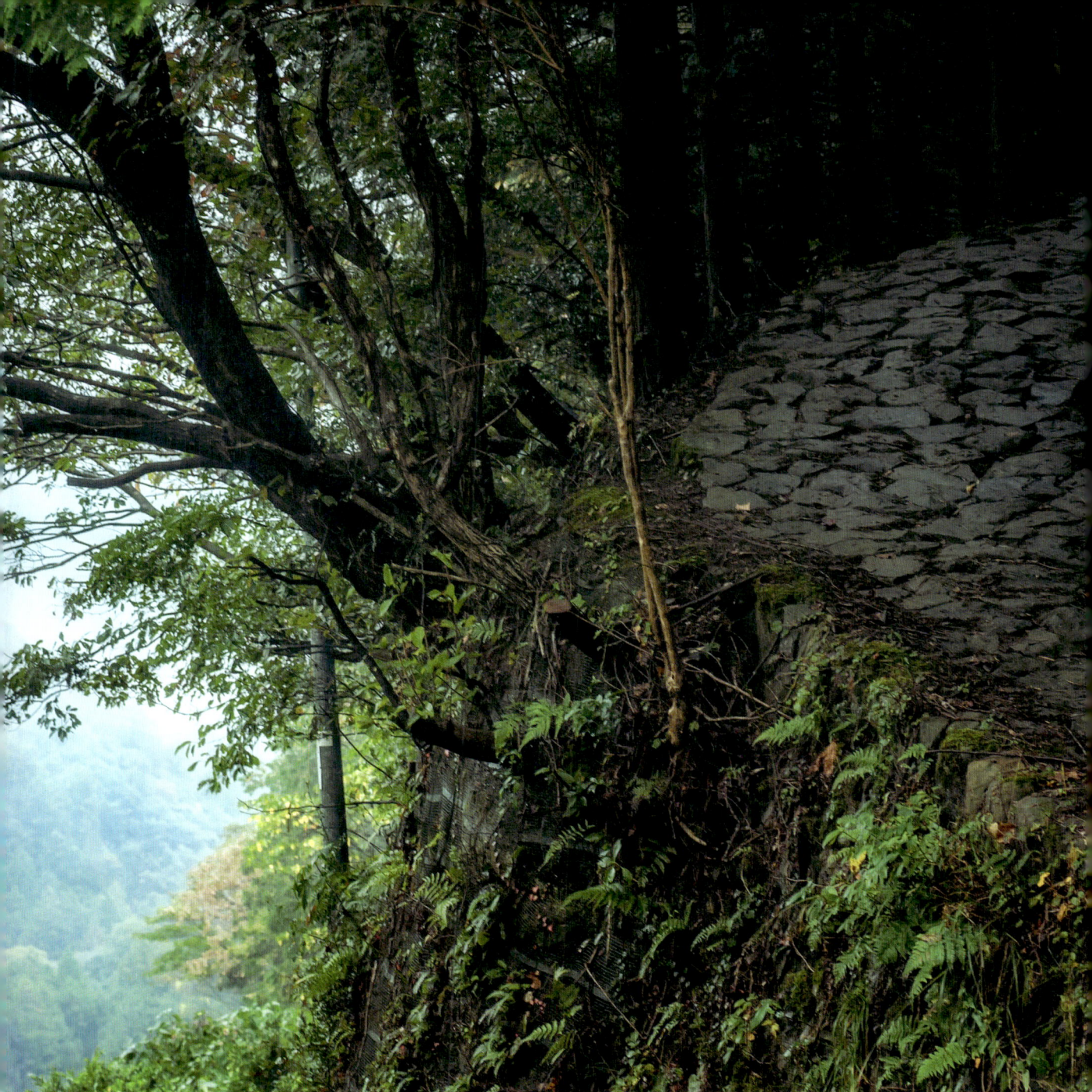

mainland Japan), the steeper sections of path can often be slippery and muddy. In these conditions, footwear with good traction and a lightweight umbrella are strongly recommended irrespective of the season.

One of the highlights of the trail is Yunomine Onsen. First discovered around 1,800 years ago, it is one of Japan's oldest hot springs, and has been an integral part of the Kumano Kodo since the pilgrimage's origin more than 1,000 years ago. Yunomine, a small cluster of traditional inns (*ryokan*), is renowned for the healing qualities of its thermal pools, and pilgrims have traditionally performed water purification rituals there in preparation for visiting Hongu Taisha, one of the three grand →

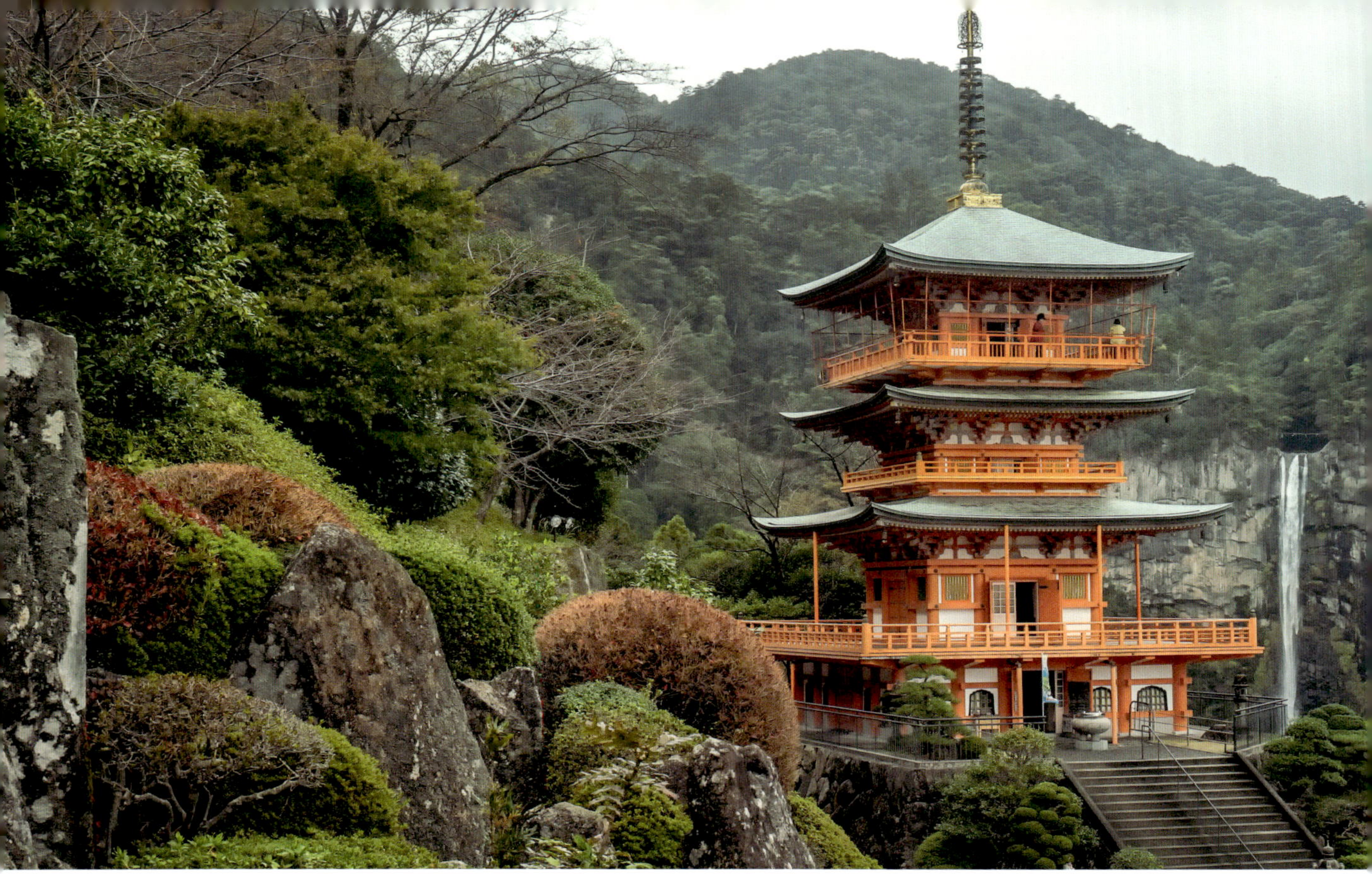

↑ Kumano Nachi Taisha next to Nachi Falls.

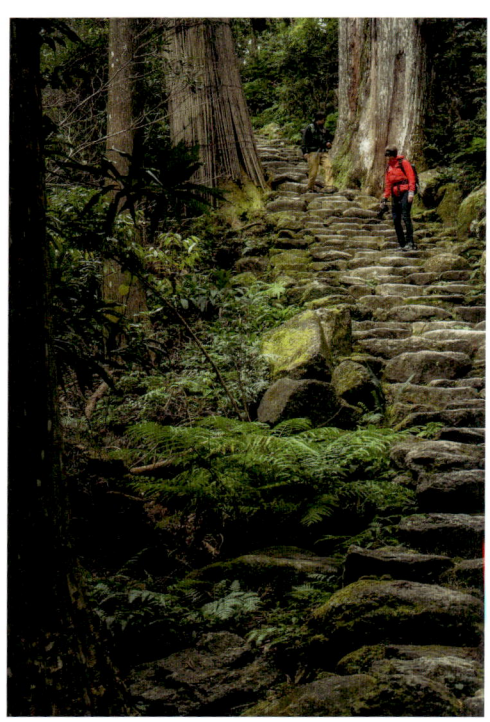

shrines. In a country in which hot springs (*onsen*) form an important part of the culture, Yunomine holds a special place because of its spiritual significance. Those walking the Nakahechi Route might choose to linger here for multiple days to enjoy the therapeutic benefits of the soothing waters.

The path reaches its dramatic conclusion at Nachi Taisha, the last of the three grand shrines. Situated beside the rushing waters of Nachi Falls, Japan's tallest waterfall, the vibrantly-colored shrine is a fitting finale for a journey that encapsulates the healing and enlightening qualities of the spiritual and natural worlds. ——————————————————————————

Seamlessly moving between verdant valleys and isolated mountain villages, mist-laden forests and sacred ancient temples, the Imperial Route affords pilgrims an insight into a region steeped in history and legend.

GOOD TO KNOW

START/FINISH
⚑ Takijiri-Oji
⚑ Nachi Taisha

SEASON
Year-round

CONDITIONS
These can vary greatly depending on the season. The Kii Peninsula is one of the wettest regions in Japan; hiking poles and footwear with good traction can help in negotiating some of the trail's steep and muddy stretches.

ACCOMMODATION
There are places to stay in the villages along the route. Because of the limited options in some of the smaller villages, it is better to avoid hiking during weekends and Japanese national holidays.

HIGHLIGHTS
Yunomine Onsen (hot spring), traditional guesthouses (*ryokan*), regional cuisine, Three Grand Shrines, Nachi Falls (Japan's tallest waterfall).

BACKGROUND

SACRED LANDSCAPE Shinto—the beliefs and practices of Japan's indigenous people—reveres nature. Unlike many other religions, Shinto has no icons or holy texts. Deities are taken from nature and include rocks, sun, wind, and trees. Buddhism was introduced to Japan from China and the Korean Peninsula, and the Kumano area was used for ascetic training in the sixth century. The two religions mixed and the Kumano Kodo trails show the blend of the two religions.

The three main shrines—Kumano Hongu Taisha, Kumano Hayatama Taisha and Kumano Nachi Taisha—are accompanied by a multitude of smaller ones that are collectively called the Kyujukyu Oji, which means "ninety-nine Oji." Though ninety-nine is not exact, there are many shrines. The five Oji that are the most important are Fujishiro, Kirime, Inabane, Takijiri, and Hosshinmon.

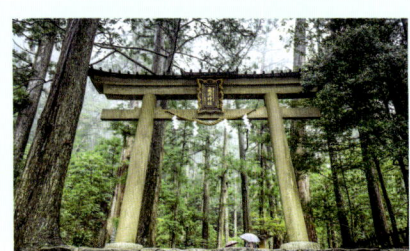

FLORA & FAUNA

AROMATIC WOODS Mikan orange, cedar, and cypress are just some of the tree types on the route, where tea bushes abound. Visits are recommended in spring when the cherry blossoms are in full bloom, or in the fall when there is a kaleidoscope of autumnal hues.

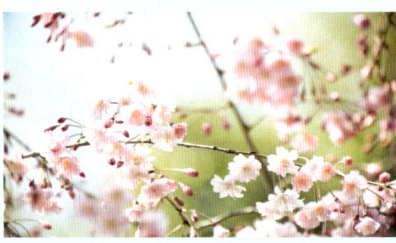

HELPFUL HINTS

REFRESHMENTS The route is studded with places for walkers to eat and drink. There are booths that operate on a trust system (customers leave the requested amount in a collection box), as well as restaurants in towns and villages. Fish dishes are worth sampling. Fresh trout—often accompanied by wild mushrooms, sweet potatoes, and a variety of other locally grown vegetables—is often served at both breakfast and dinner.

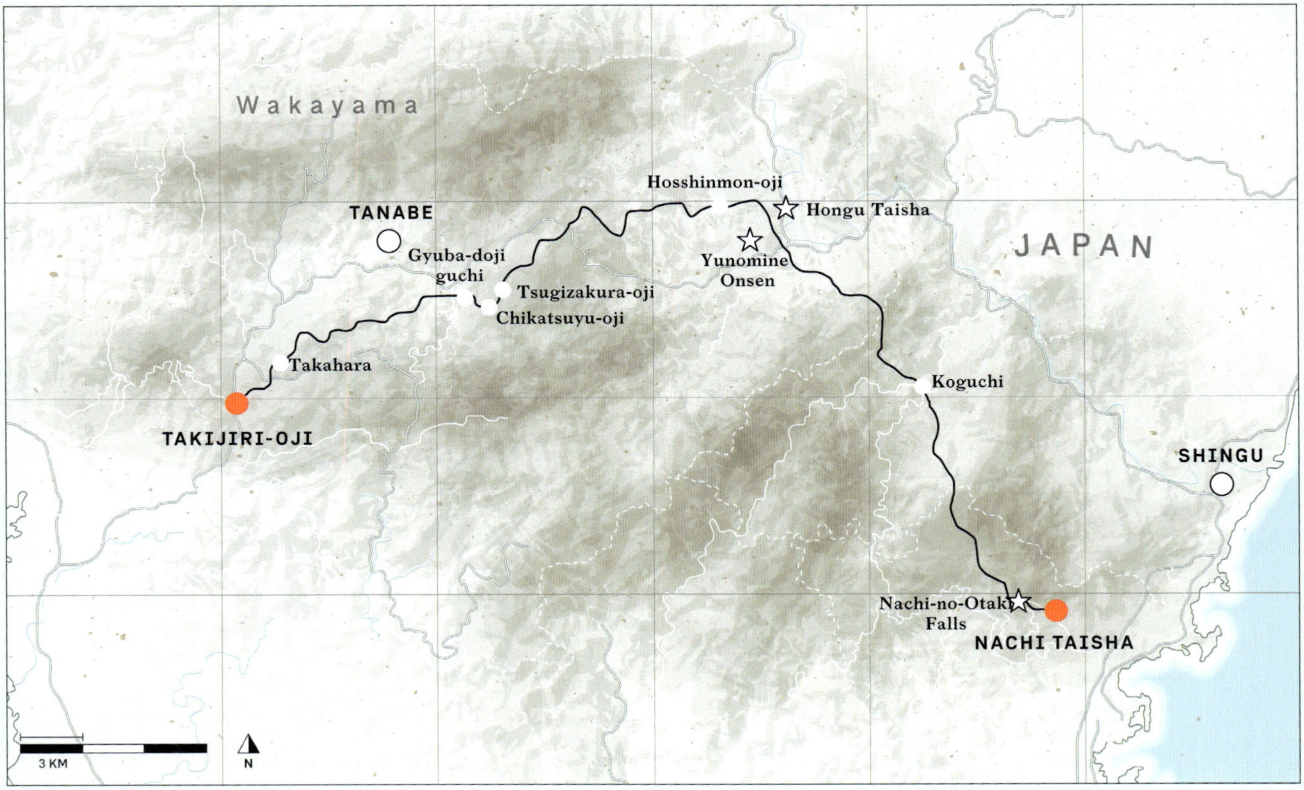

Wakayama

TANABE

Gyuba-doji guchi

Tsugizakura-oji

Chikatsuyu-oji

Hosshinmon-oji

☆ Hongu Taisha

☆ Yunomine Onsen

JAPAN

Takahara

Koguchi

TAKIJIRI-OJI

SHINGU

Nachi-no-Otaki Falls

☆ NACHI TAISHA

3 KM

N

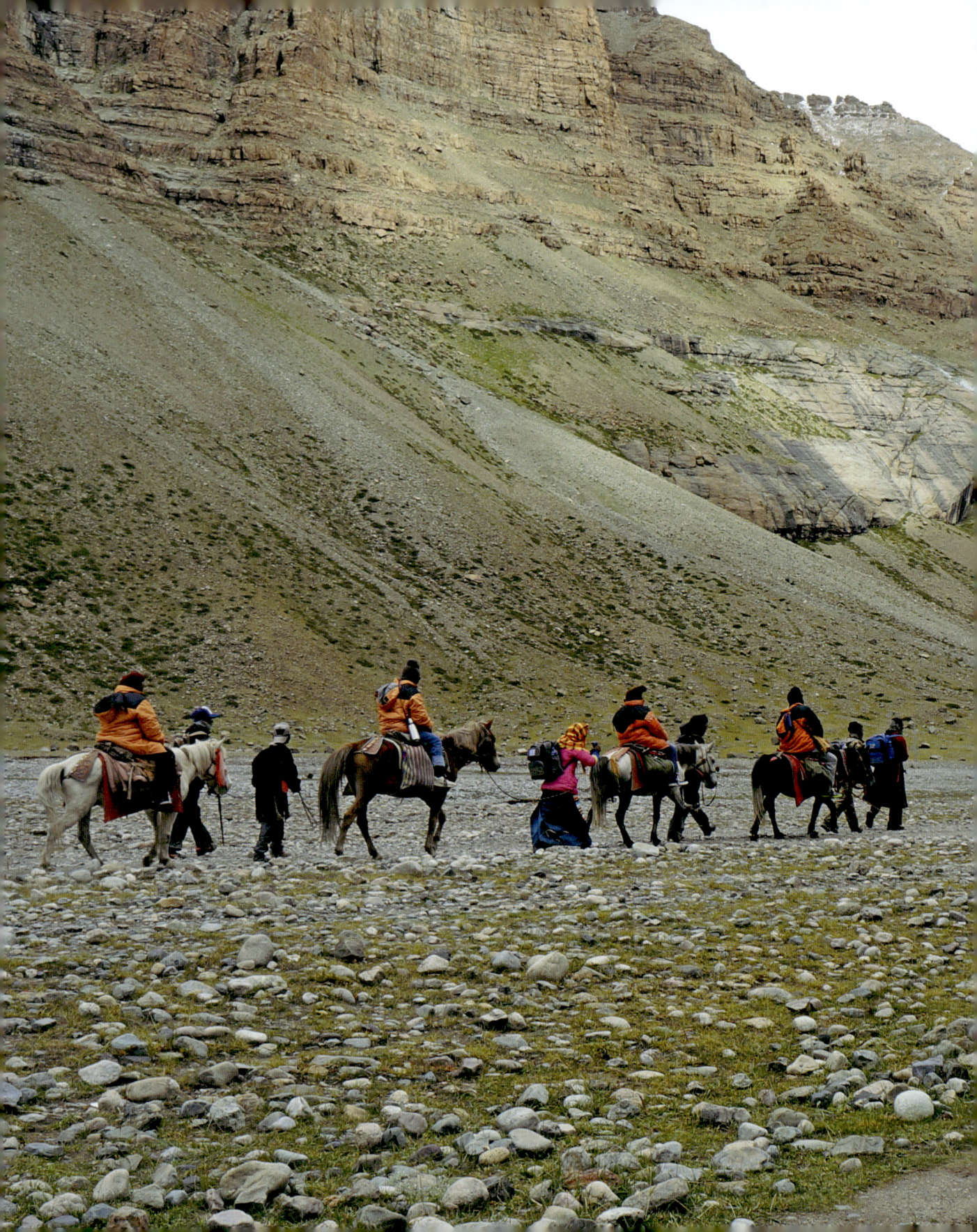

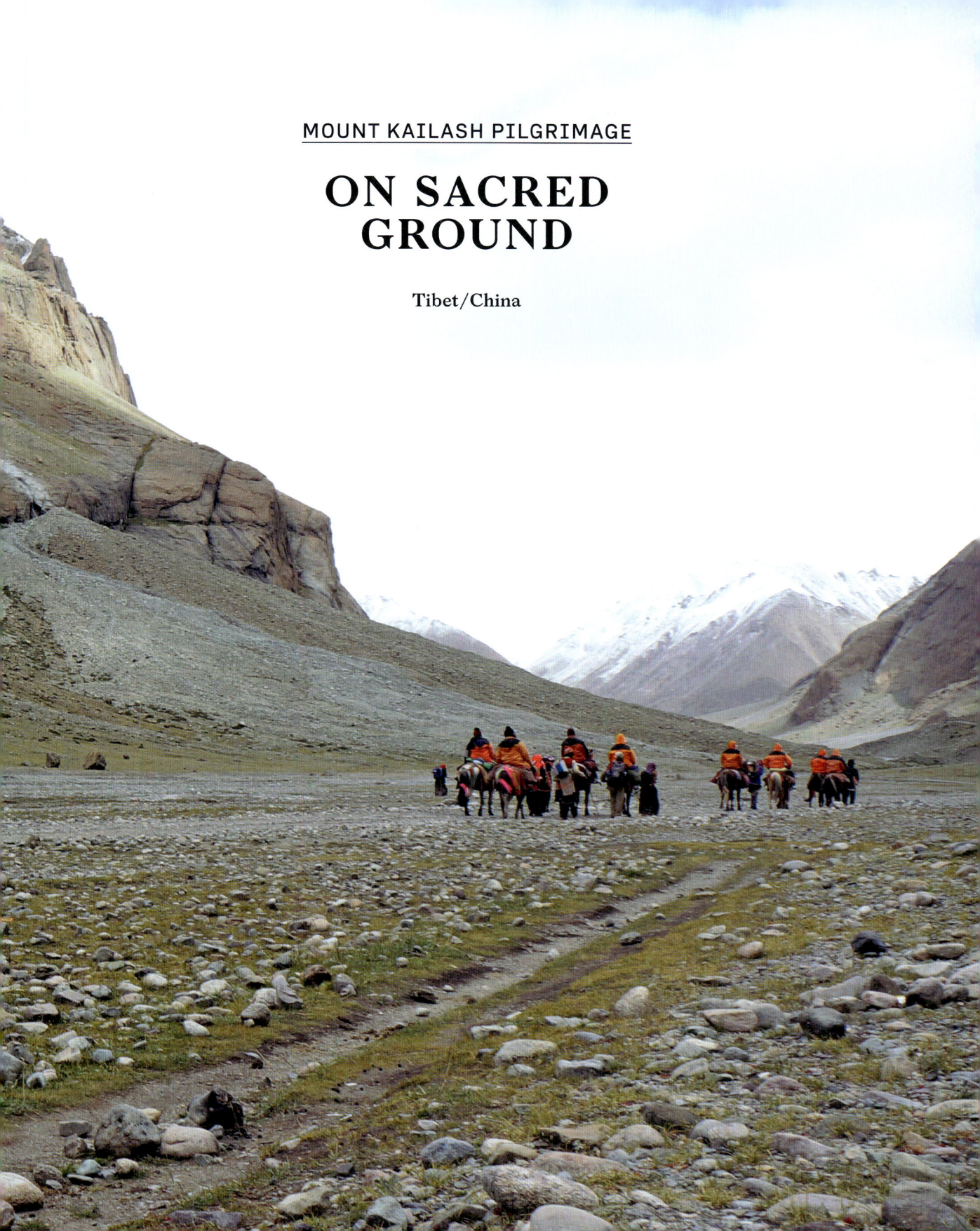

MOUNT KAILASH PILGRIMAGE

ON SACRED GROUND

Tibet/China

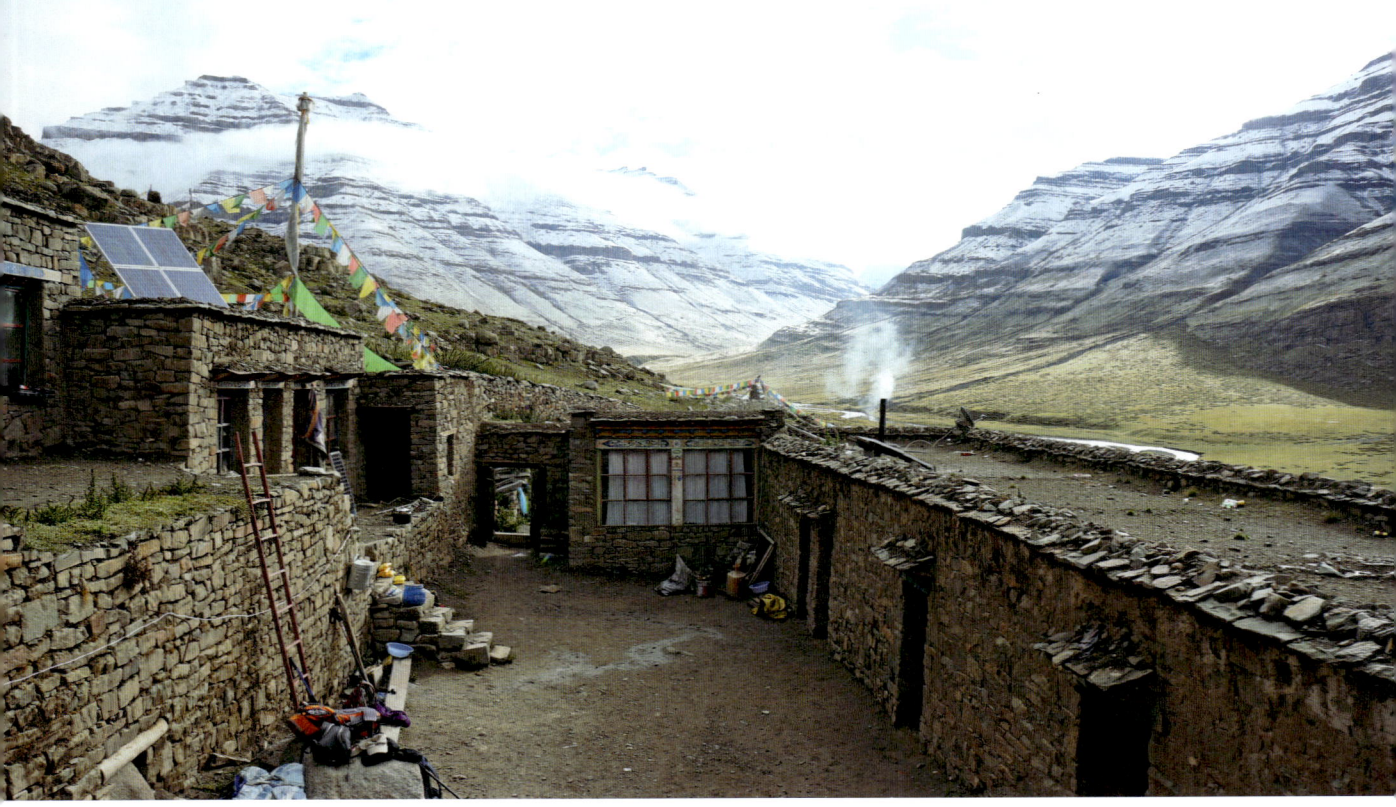

Mount Kailash stands at 6,638 m (21,778 ft.) above sea level. Compared to many of its Himalayan neighbors, it is not particularly high. In terms of cultural and spiritual significance, though, the mountain stands incredibly tall.

Located in the far reaches of western Tibet, Mount Kailash represents an important pilgrimage site for Hindus, Buddhists, and members of the Bon and Jain faiths. Lying near the source of four great rivers (Indus, Sutlej, Brahmaputra, and Karnali), Kailash is deemed sacred in Hinduism; it is considered to be the heart of the world, and Lord Shiva, one god in their holy trinity, is said to live on its snowcapped summit. Buddhists also believe that Kailash is the spiritual center of the universe, as well as being the home of Buddha Demchok, who symbolizes supreme bliss.

For centuries, pilgrims have been drawn to this remote corner of Tibet, with the goal of completing a circumambulation of Mount Kailash. In Tibetan this is called a *kora*; for Hindus it

ABOUT THE TRAIL

→ <u>DISTANCE</u> 52 km (32 mi.)
→ <u>DURATION</u> 2 to 3 days
→ <u>LEVEL</u> Moderate

The time needed to complete a circuit of the sacred mountain can vary considerably. Tibetans traditionally do the hike in one very long day, while foreigners usually take a more sedate three or four days.

is known as parikrama. Circuits are supposed to lighten karma and lead towards nirvana, known to Hindus as moksha. A single circuit is said to absolve the sins of a lifetime for Buddhists. For those looking for a little more karmic insurance, it is believed that 108 circuits will lead to nirvana and freedom from reincarnation. Because of its sacred qualities, the mountain has never been summited.

Buddhist and Hindu pilgrims traditionally walk the 52 km (32 mi.) trek in a clockwise direction, whereas adherents

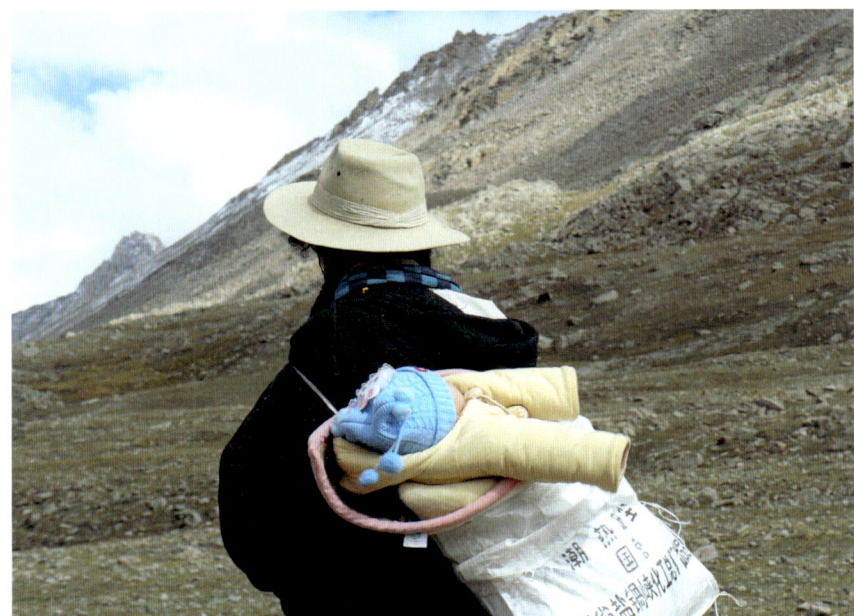

of Bon and Jainism hike in a counterclockwise direction. The time needed to complete a circuit of the sacred mountain can vary considerably. Tibetans traditionally do the hike in one very long day, while foreigners usually take a more sedate three or four days. Some devout aspirants even choose to circumnavigate Kailash doing full-body prostrations—an arduous journey that can take up to two weeks or more.

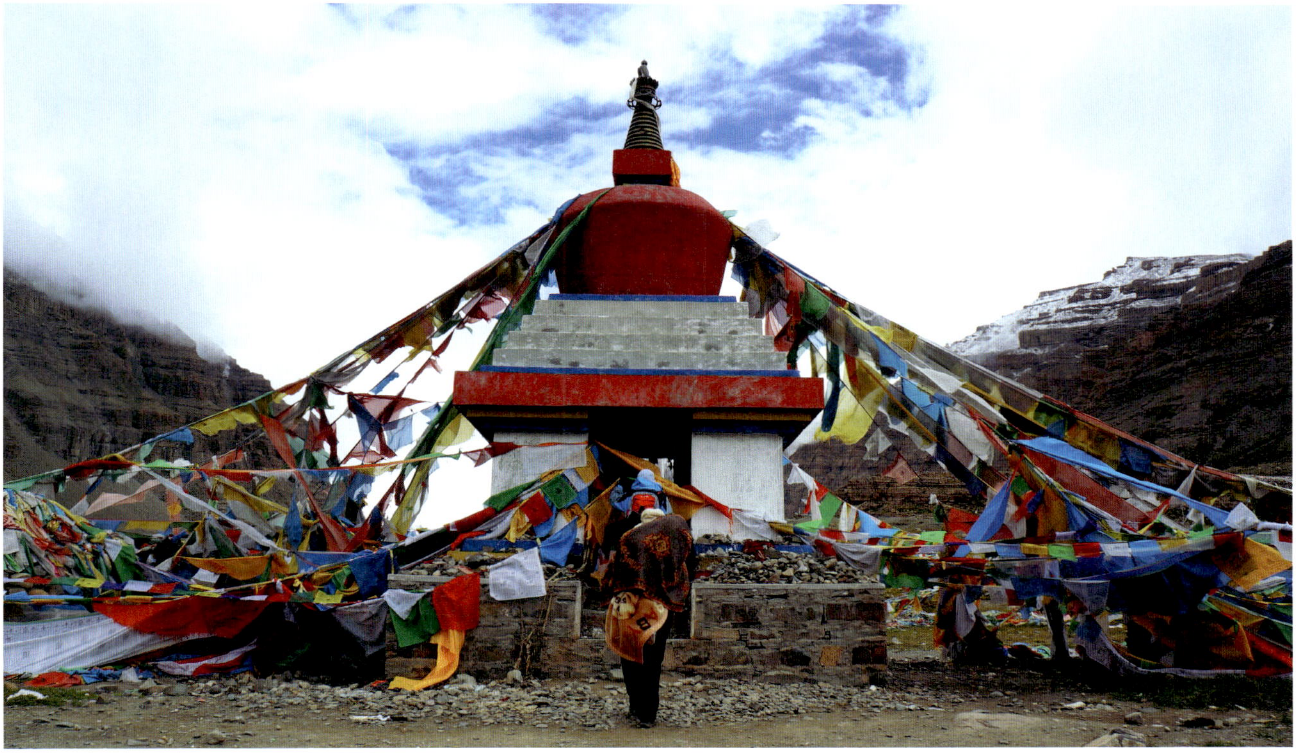

Navigationally and logistically, the Kailash circumnavigation is not difficult. The path is well worn, camping options are plentiful, and, during the main pilgrimage season, there are even large tents set up for selling provisions. Despite all of this, any trail that goes up and over an often-snowbound 5,630 m (18,471 ft.) high pass (Drolma La) will never be considered easy. Before attempting a trek around Kailash, hikers should be well prepared in regards to fitness, equipment, and acclimatization. Although there are impressive valleys, rivers, and rock formations along the route, it is the mountain itself →

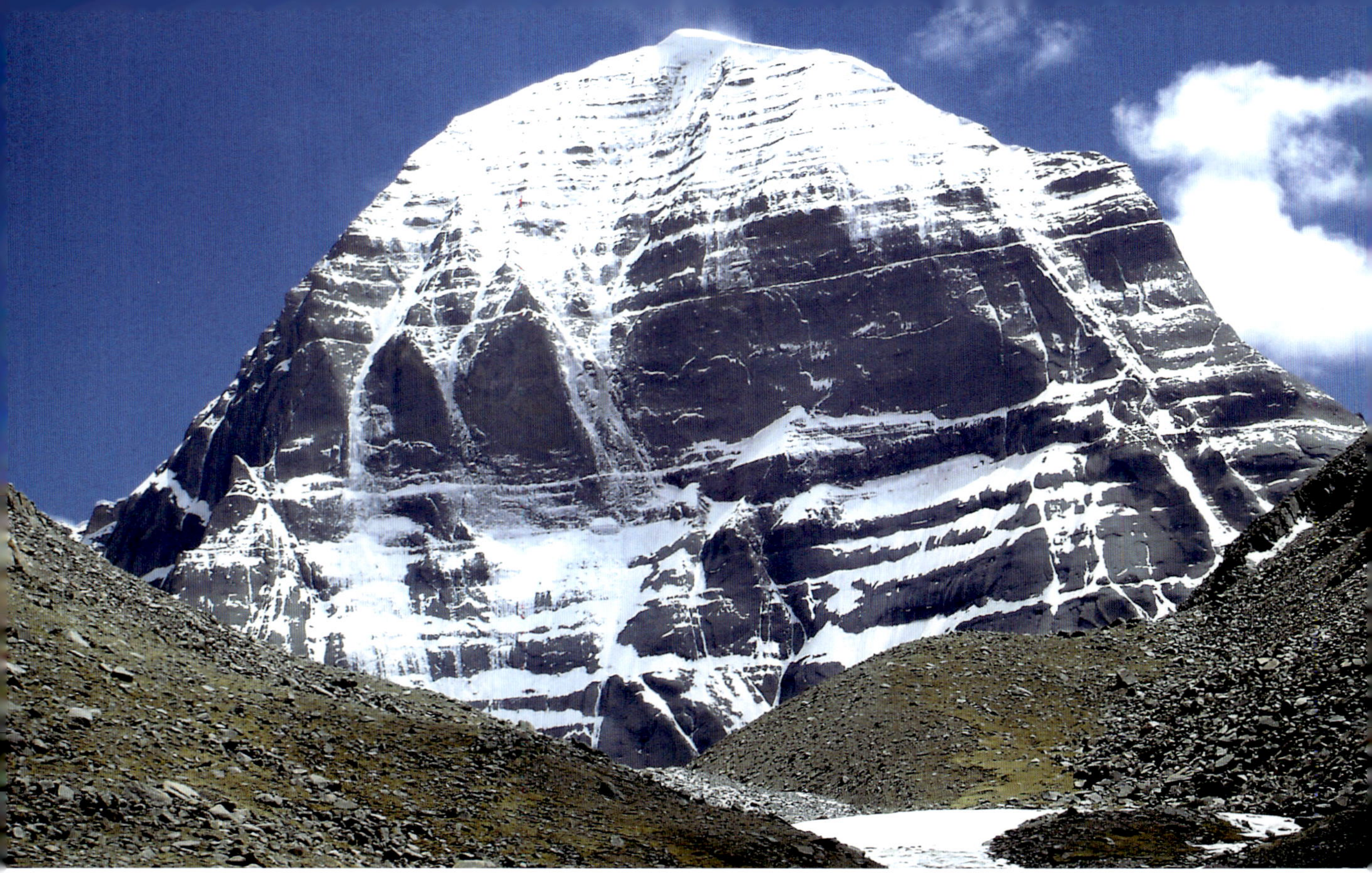

↑ The north face of Mount Kailash.

Compared to many of its Himalayan neighbors, Mount Kailash is not particularly high. In terms of cultural and spiritual significance, though, the mountain stands incredibly tall.

that is the star attraction. Kailash's snowcapped dome, with its diamond-like shape, is a stirring sight to behold, and hikers are treated to outstanding views of the peak throughout much of the trail. One of the best vantage points is on a highly recommended side trip to Gangjam Chu Valley. Beginning at Drira Phug monastery, this strenuous out-and-back excursion takes between four and six hours to complete, and affords walkers the opportunity to get close to Gangjam glacier and Kailash's sheer north face.

Mount Kailash brings together people of different beliefs, cultures, and origins. It connects diverse individuals through the ancient bond of pilgrimage. And perhaps therein lies another significance of the mountain: the sense of camaraderie it inspires among pilgrims. This remote mountain in the west of Tibet is a beacon of shared faith, and a walk around its circumference represents the realization of many collective goals and dreams. ─────────

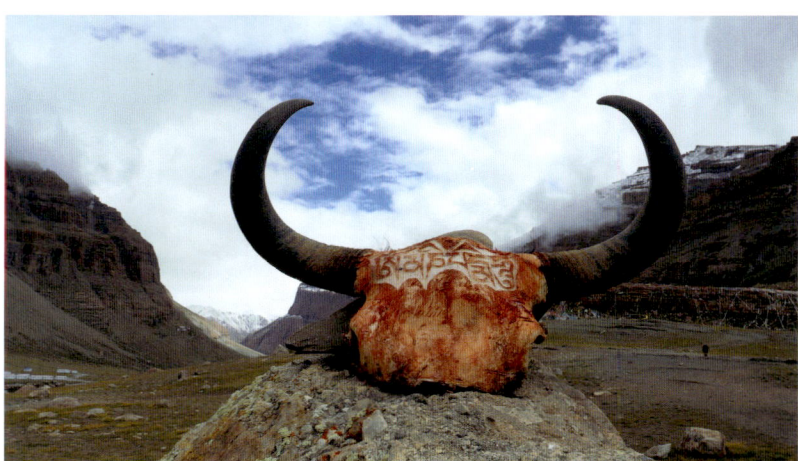

GOOD TO KNOW

START/FINISH

🚩 Round trip from Darchen

SEASON

May to October

CONDITIONS

During trekking season, daytime temperatures are usually around 13–19°C (55–66°F), with nighttime temperatures often dropping below freezing. Snow is possible at any time of year.

LOWEST/HIGHEST POINT

4,675 m (15,338 ft.)/5,630 m (18,471 ft.)

ACCOMMODATION

Camping is possible all along the route. Indoor accommodation is available at the monastery guesthouses.

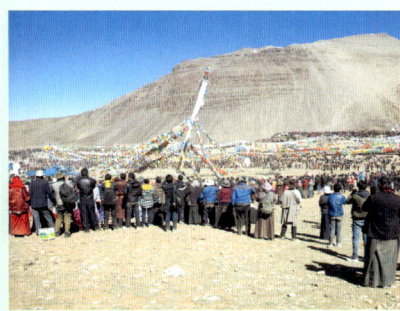

BACKGROUND

RELIGIOUS FESTIVITIES Saga Dawa is one of Tibet's most important religious festivals. It is celebrated annually on the full moon day of the fourth Tibetan lunar month (in either May or June), in honor of the birth, enlightenment, and death of Buddha. Many pilgrims time their visit to Kailash to coincide with the Saga Dawa celebrations, the highlight of which is the raising of the Tarboche Flagpole. Each year the old pole is replaced by a new one, and how straight the pole stands once it is erected is said to be a harbinger of the country's fortunes for the coming year. Completely vertical is ideal; leaning too much to either side does not bode so well.

HELPFUL HINTS

HOLY LAKES Manasarovar and Rakshastal are both situated close to Kailash. The first contains freshwater, and is considered sacred by both Hindus and Buddhists, with the former believing that bathing there is redemptive. The second body of water is saline in character and is known as the Lake of Demons.

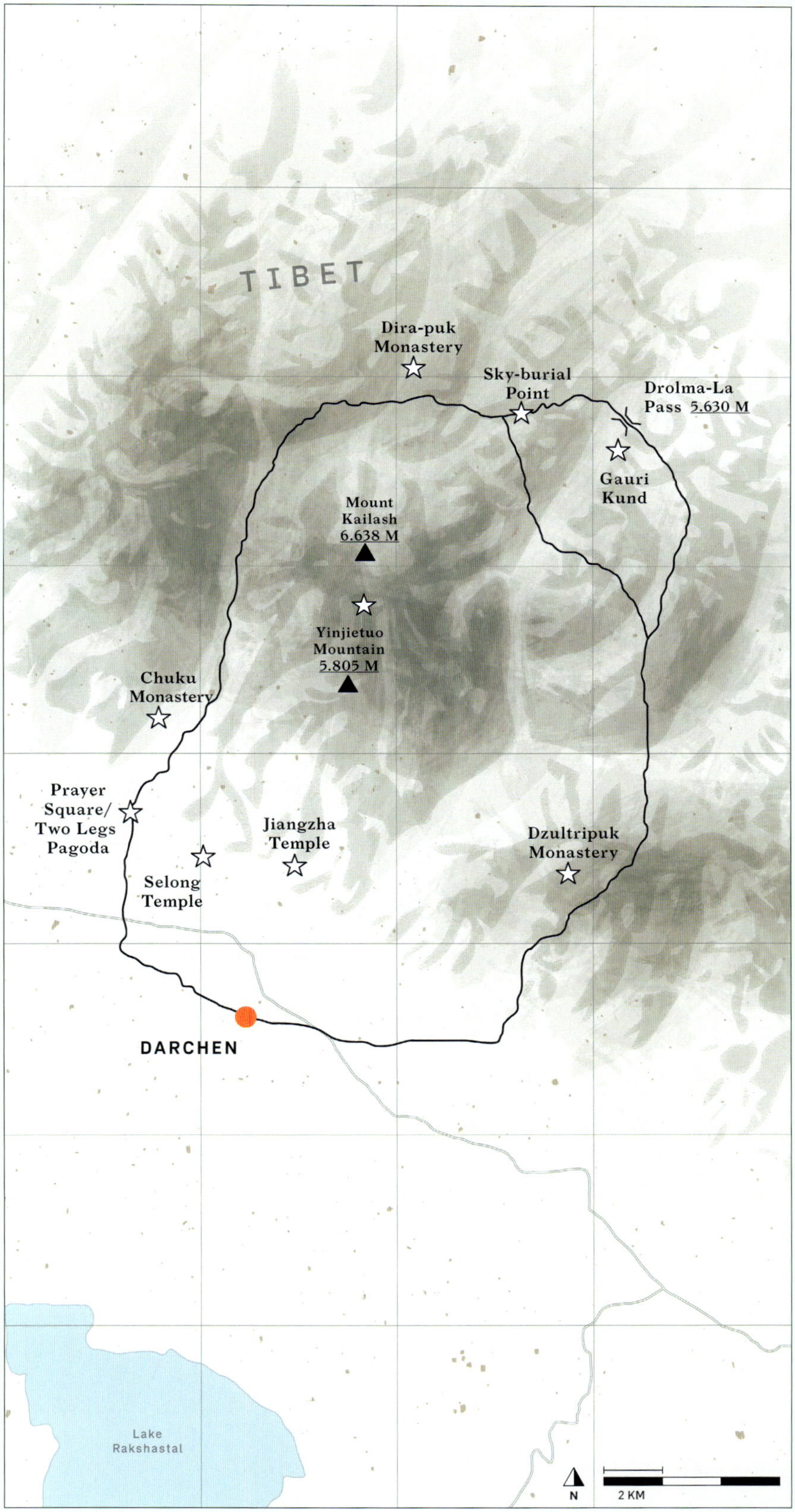

TIBET

Dira-puk Monastery ☆

Sky-burial Point ☆

Drolma-La Pass 5.630 M

Gauri Kund ☆

Mount Kailash 6.638 M ▲

Yinjietuo Mountain 5.805 M ▲ ☆

Chuku Monastery ☆

Prayer Square/ Two Legs Pagoda ☆

Jiangzha Temple ☆

Dzultripuk Monastery ☆

Selong Temple ☆

🔴 DARCHEN

Lake Rakshastal

N   2 KM

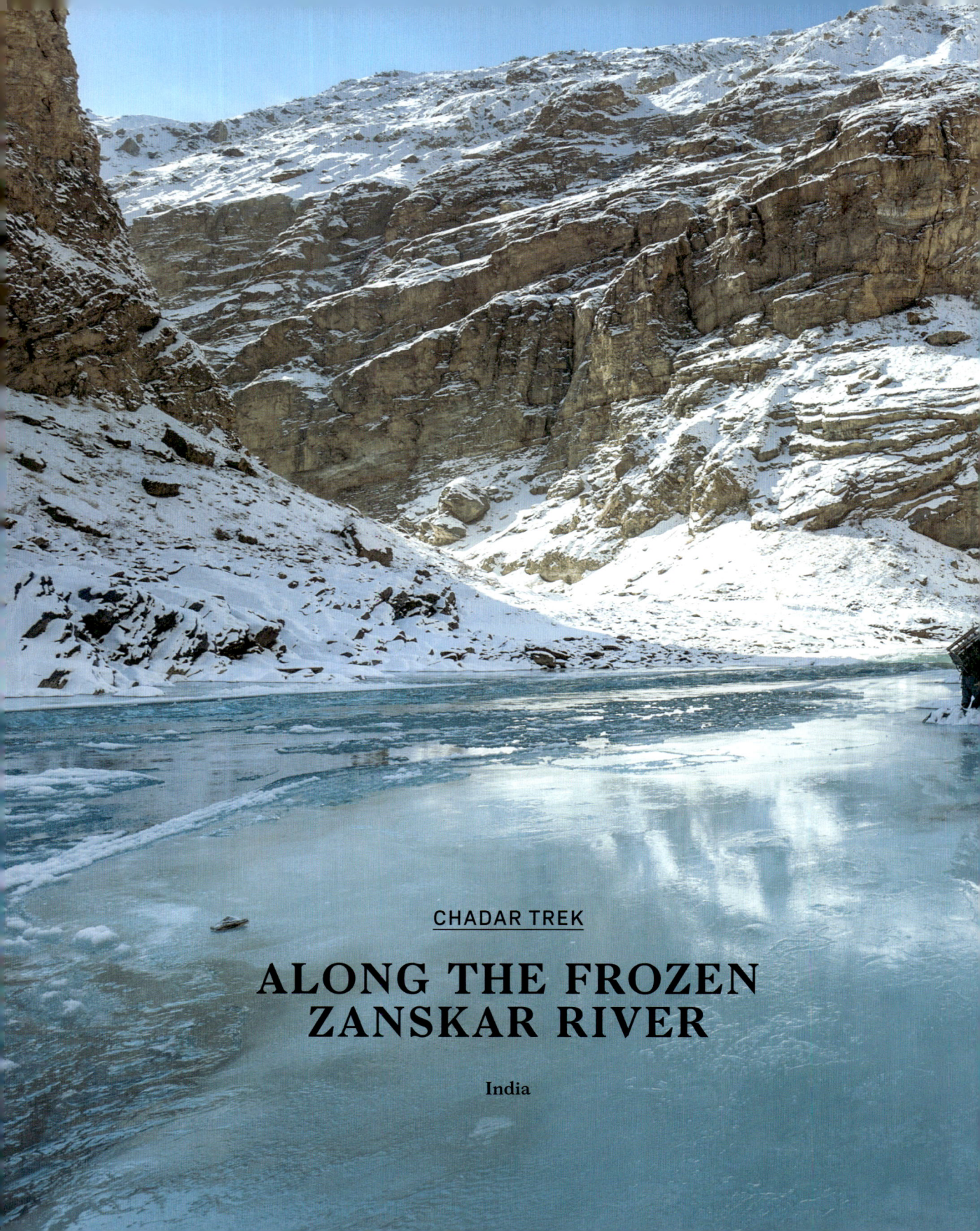

ALONG THE FROZEN ZANSKAR RIVER

India

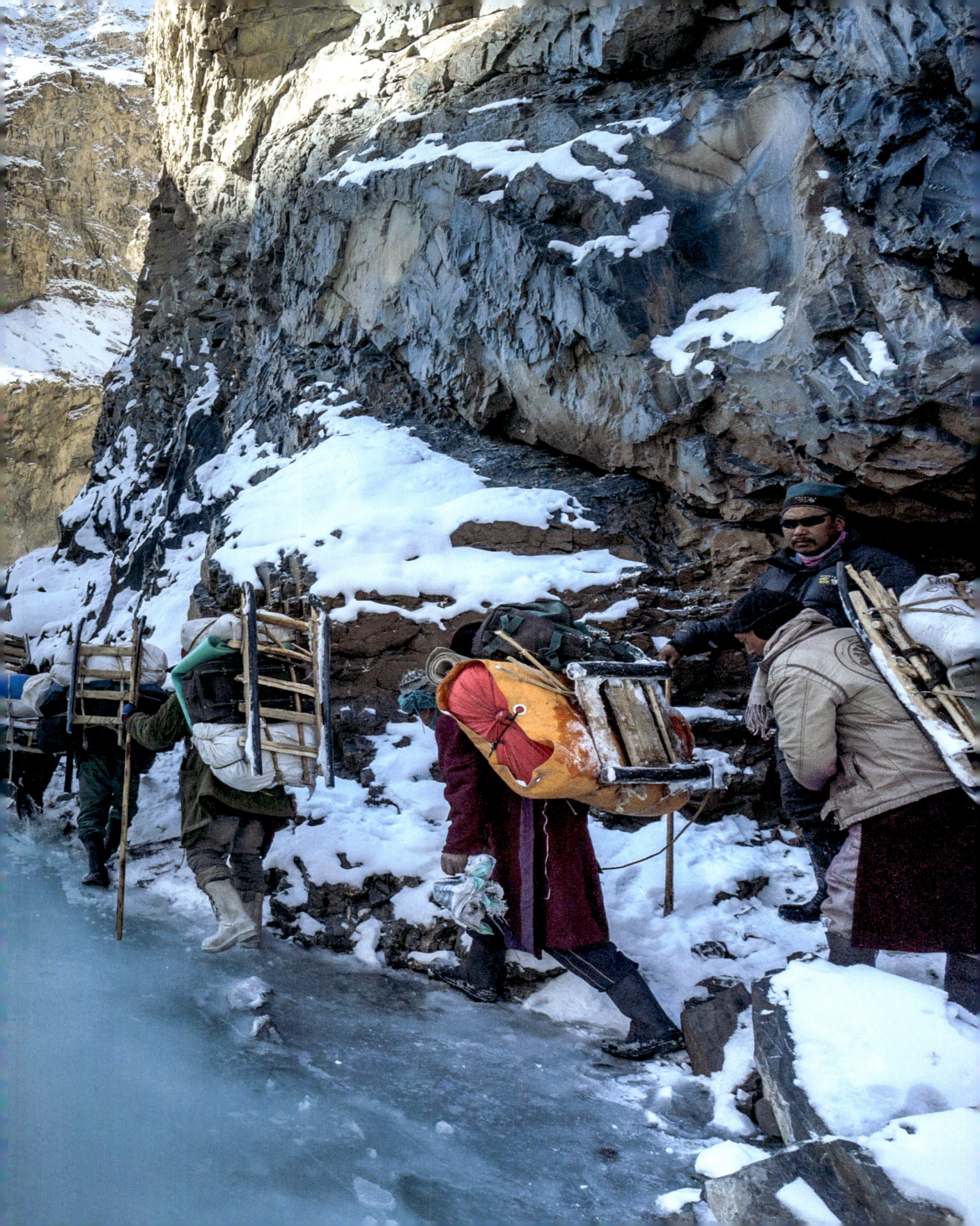

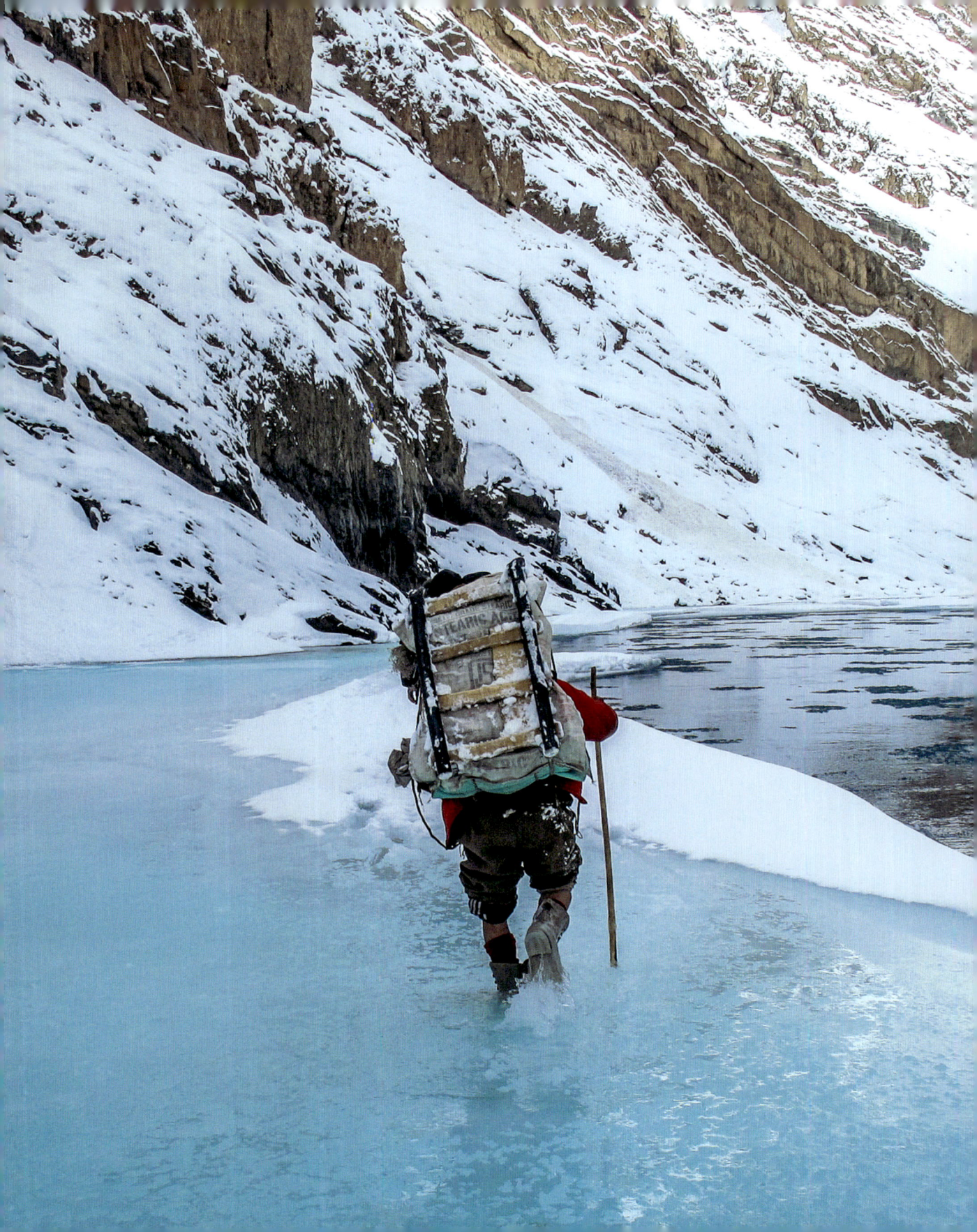

I magine hiking over 100 km (62 mi.) along a most-ly frozen river in a remote and mountainous region of northern India. Just inches underneath the ice the water flows fast. Now picture a spectacularly deep and sinuous gorge with dizzying 600 m (1970 ft.) high walls and an array of towering waterfalls frozen in their tracks. Finally, throw in unpredictable ice thicknesses, bone chilling winter temperatures (between 5°C and -35°C [23°F and -31°F]), and ancient riverside caves. That is the Chadar Trek in a nutshell.

The route follows the course of the Zanskar River Gorge and takes place in Ladakh, which translates to "Land of the High Passes" in English. Situated in the state of Jammu and Kashmir and renowned for its moonscape terrain and ancient monasteries, this remote and rugged high altitude region shares its border with Tibet to the east, Pakistan to the west, and the Himalaya to the south.

Chadar is the Hindi word for "sheet," and it is used by the local residents, the Ladakhis, to describe the layer of ice that covers the Zanskar River during the winter. For centuries, this seasonally frozen highway has represented the lone means by which local residents could travel from the remote Zanskar Valley to the regional capital of Leh during the coldest months of the year.

← A porter helps carry a trekker's load.
↓ Sliding packs over the ice surface.

Chadar is the Hindi word for "sheet," and it is used by the local residents, the Ladakhis, to describe the layer of ice that covers the Zanskar River during the winter.

The Chadar has a two-month hiking season of January and February. The trek cannot be done independently, and because of the relatively small weather window, reservations should be made well in advance. The beginning of the trail is at Chilling, which is a 64 km (40 mi.) drive from Leh. Most parties take six to eight days to complete the out-and-back journey, which should be made →

ABOUT THE TRAIL

→ <u>DISTANCE</u> 105 km (93 mi.)
→ <u>DURATION</u> 6 to 9 days
→ <u>LEVEL</u> Difficult

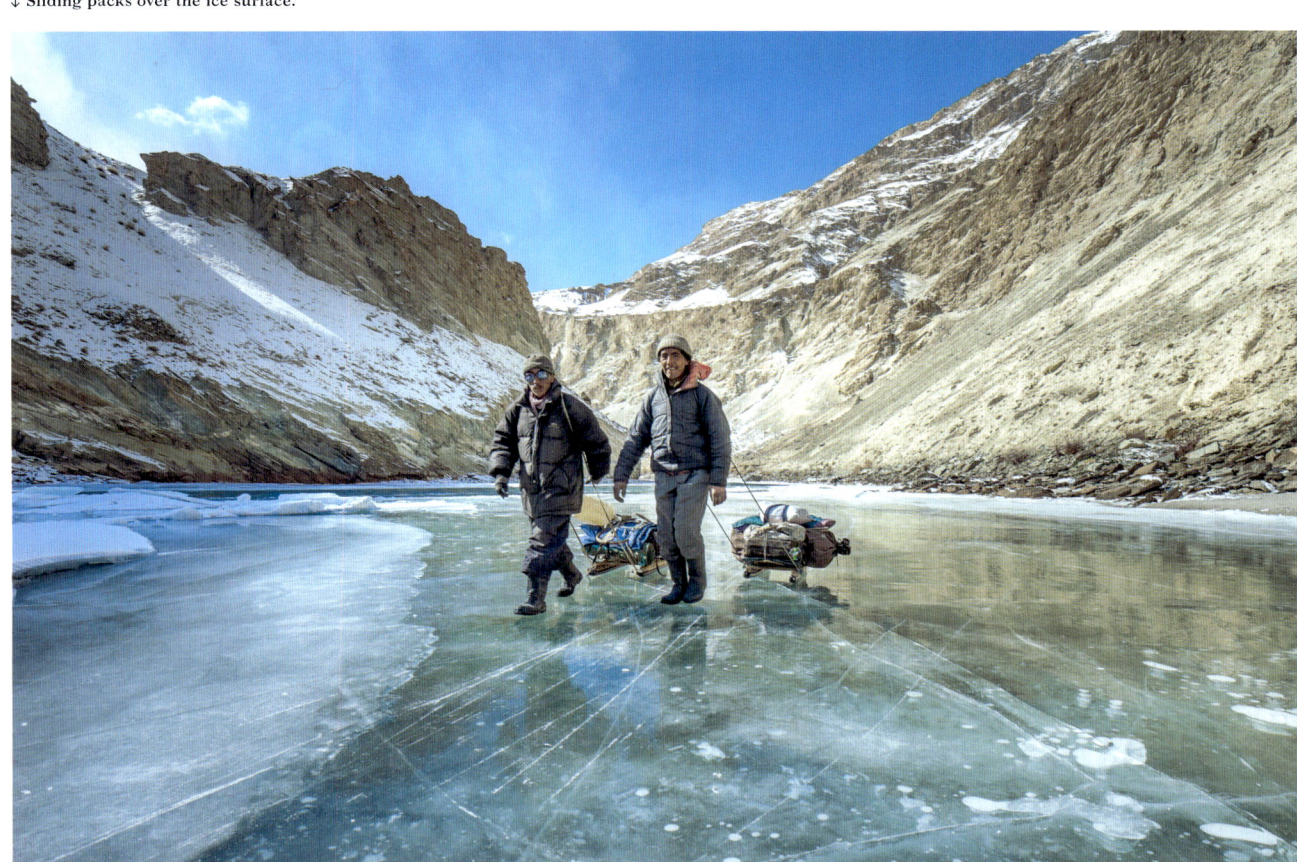

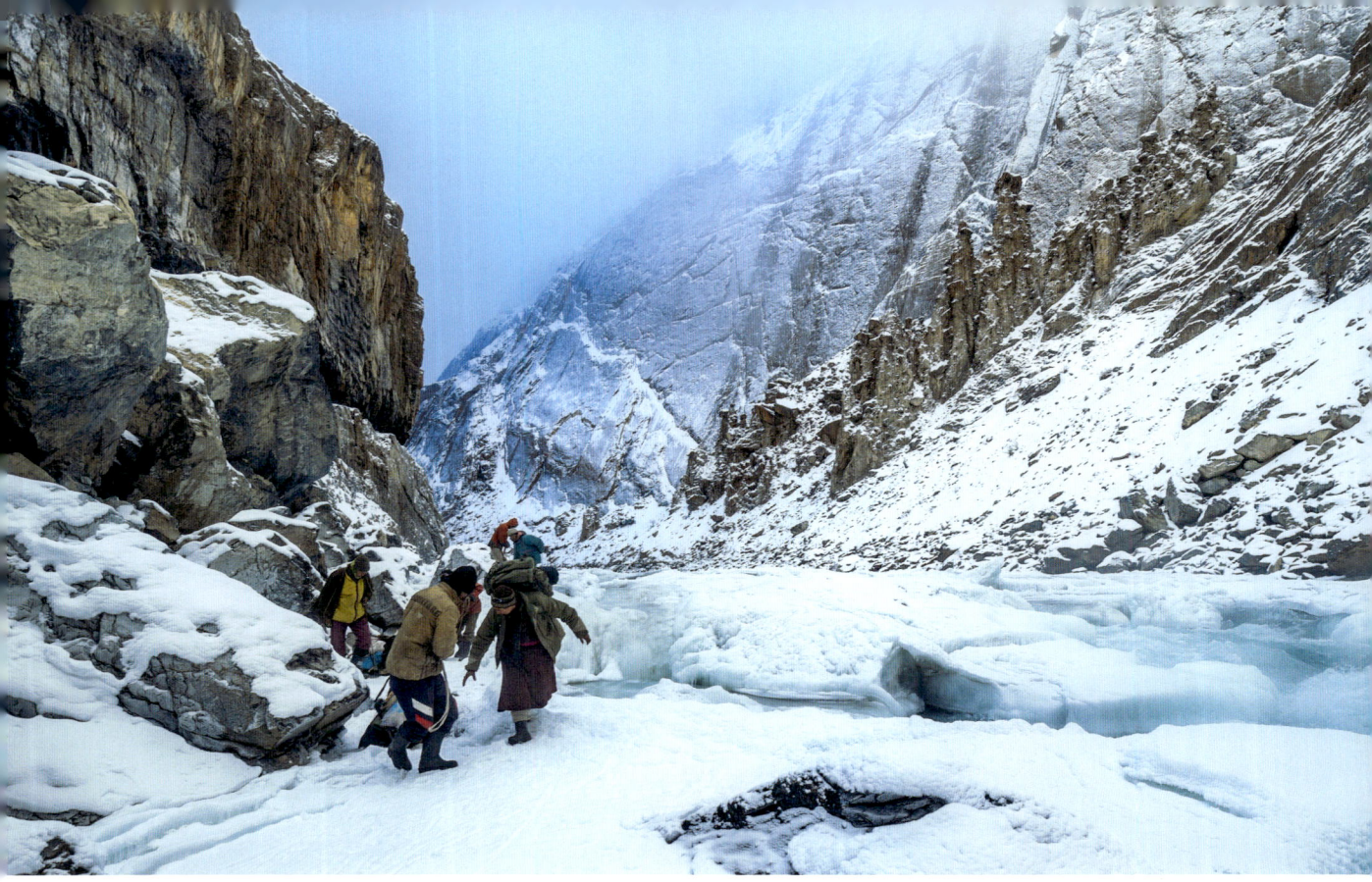

↑ Fresh fallen snow makes the path less slippery, but not necessarily easier to walk on.

with a reputable operator. When not slowed down by foreign tourists, nimble-footed locals traditionally make the trip in less than half that time.

Because of the extreme environmental conditions, hikers need to be especially well prepared before beginning the Chadar Trek. Although it is possible to pick up clothing and equipment at the market in Leh, it is advisable to bring as much gear as possible from home in order to be assured of both quality and correct sizing. As for acclimatization, intrepid visitors should plan on spending at least two (or preferably three) days in Leh becoming accustomed to the altitude before setting out. This is not a trip that should be undertaken straight after stepping off the plane from New Delhi.

A good level of pre-trip conditioning will stand Chadar trekkers in good stead. Hiking 11–15 km (6.8–9.3 mi.) each day in temperatures as low as -10°C (14°F), hiking on ce with varying thicknesses, and spending the nights in caves and at other makeshift campsites is sure to take its toll. The inhospitable environment is a physical challenge, but the vertiginous landscape makes this an experience that is unmatched by any other.

The region has a fragile ecosystem, and in the face of inevitable modern developments, such as the construction of an all-season road into Zanskar and an increasing number of visitors completing the hike, the challenge for locals is to find a balance between change, tradition, and sustainable environmental management. This appears to be possible as the incredible resourcefulness of the Ladakis, honed from centuries of surviving and thriving in one of the world's harshest environments, is almost as legendary as the fabled frozen river over which they have traveled for so many generations. ——————

When not slowed down by foreign tourists, nimble-footed locals traditionally make the trip in less than half the time visitors take.

BACKGROUND

RIVER ROUTE Once part of the Silk Road, the Zanskar River was formerly an important pathway for the locals who live in the villages along it. During the two months of the year when all other routes were impassable, the Chadar route was used for trade—locals transported Zanskari butter to Leh, for instance—and today it is still used by Ladakhis for goods or going to work or school.

One saying the Ladakhi people have about their region is, "The land is so barren and the passes so high that only our fiercest enemies or our best friends would want to visit us." To ask for safe passage on the treacherous stretch of river, they hang prayer flags or leave out traditional ceremonial scarves or juniper incense.

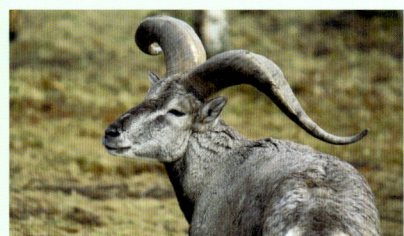

FLORA & FAUNA

THE BHARAL Lucky hikers might spot a bharal or blue sheep along the Chadar Trek's route. The animal is typically found on the high mountain slopes of the Himalaya, and, contrary to its name, is more closely related to a goat than a sheep.

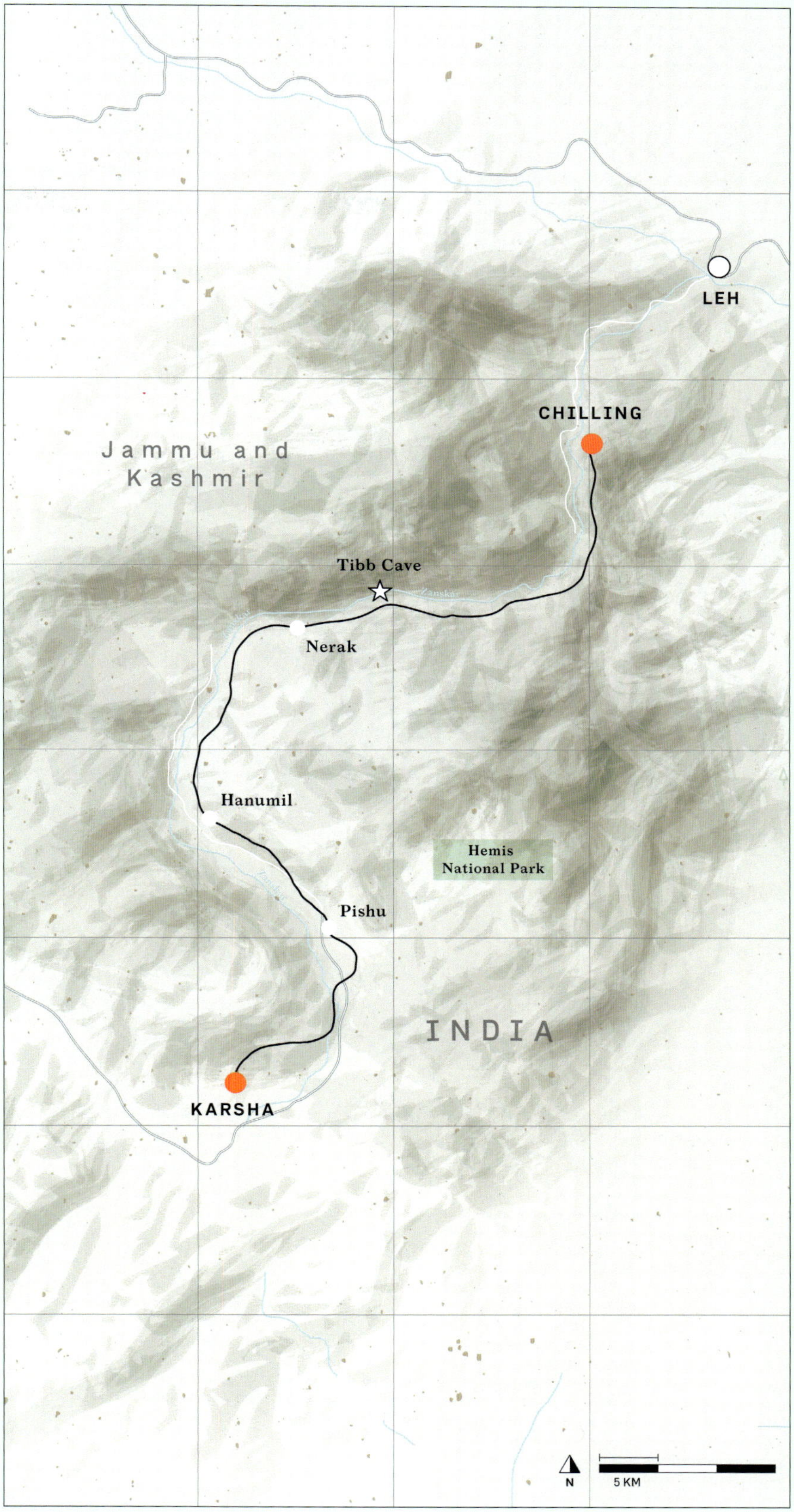

LEH

CHILLING

Jammu and Kashmir

Tibb Cave

Nerak

Hanumil

Hemis National Park

Pishu

INDIA

KARSHA

N

5 KM

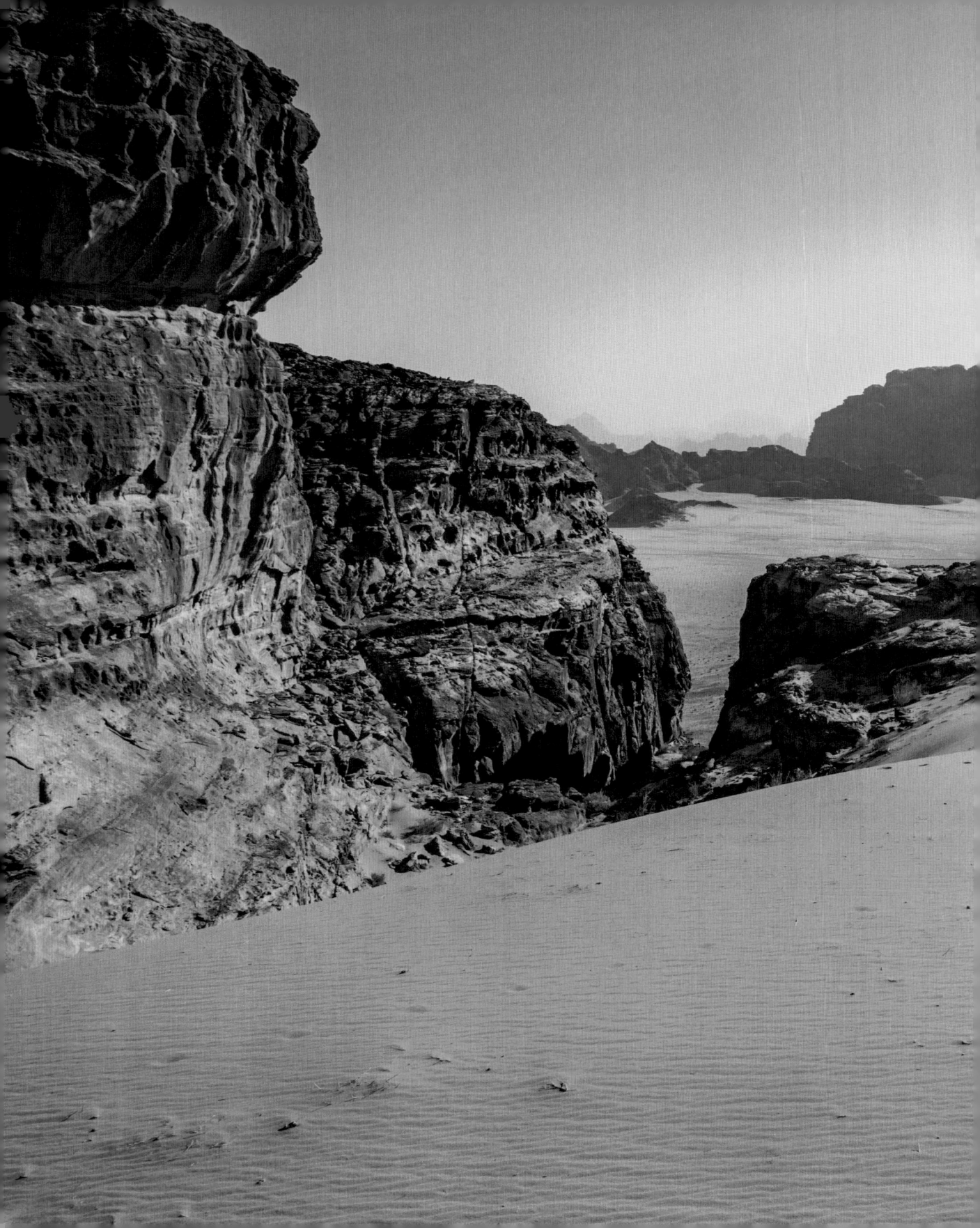

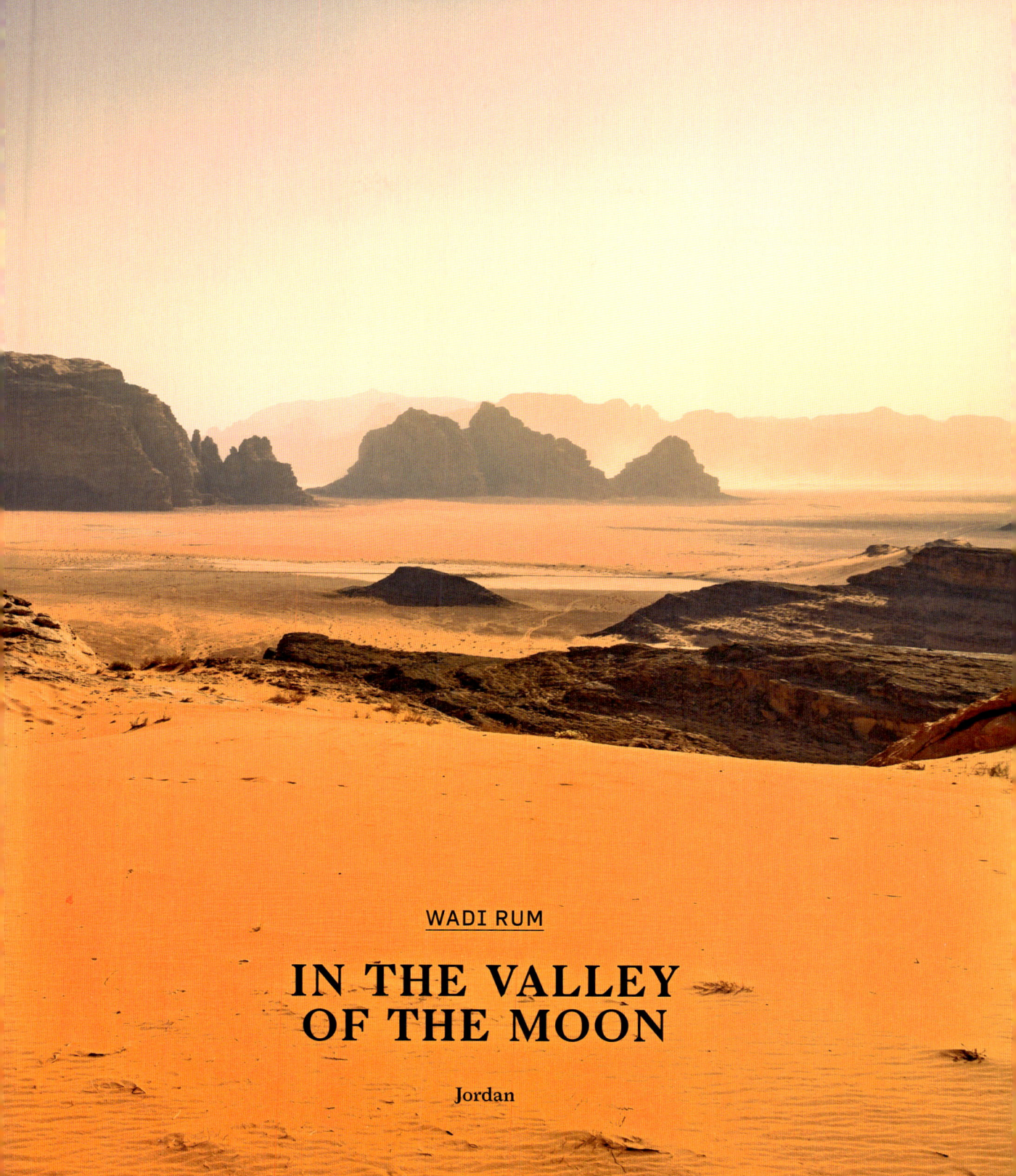

WADI RUM

IN THE VALLEY
OF THE MOON

Jordan

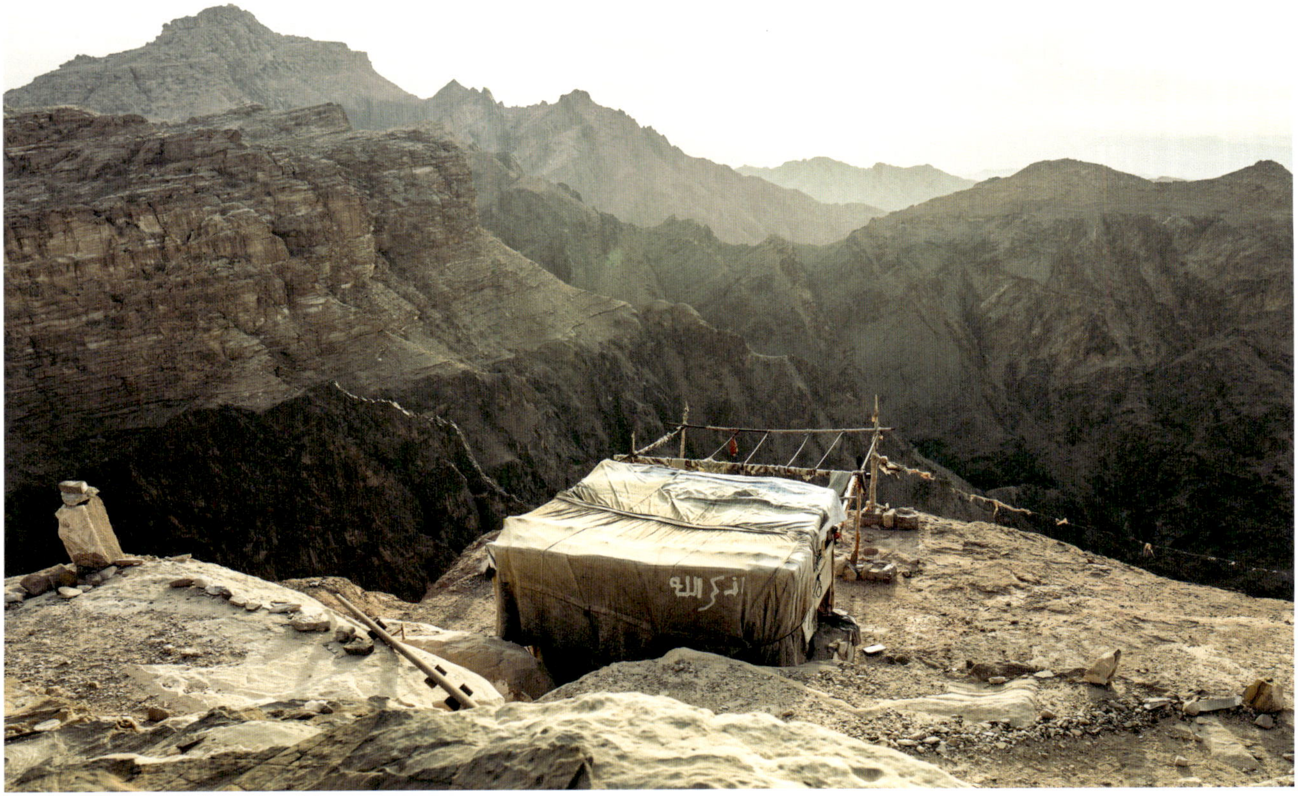

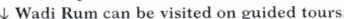

→ Side trip to the Wadi Hasa Canyon north of Wadi Rum (see also pp. 112-113).
↓ Wadi Rum can be visited on guided tours.

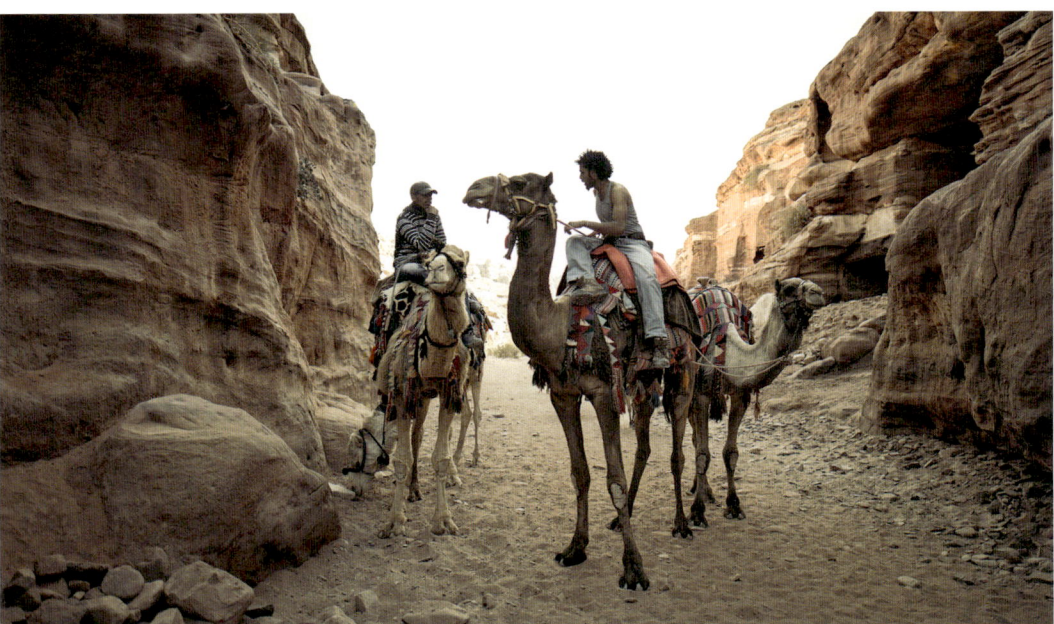

A part of the earth that resembles the surface of Mars, and one where other planets can be seen in their blazing glory, Wadi Rum is almost part of another world.

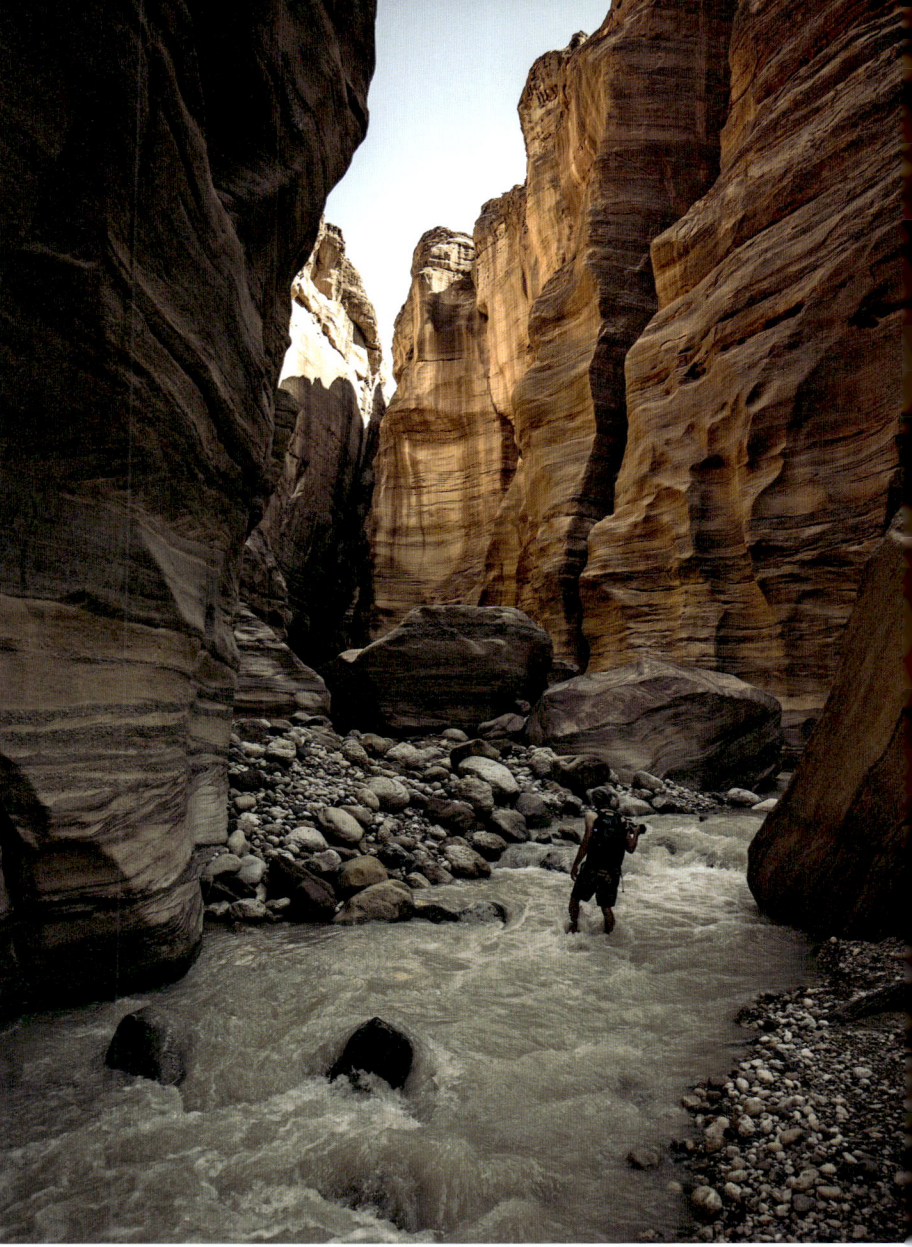

Dusty, red, blisteringly hot on summer days, and dotted with ancient carvings, Wadi Rum is an otherworldy desert. Situated in southern Jordan, this "Valley of the Moon" is actually a series of valleys that run down to Saudi Arabia and is home to gorges, arches, pillars, flaming sands, and even some timid desert wildlife. The area's natural wonders, along with its many ancient petroglyphs (rock carvings) and inscriptions, led to it being designated a UNESCO protected site in 2005, and it has long been a destination of interest for adventurers, travelers, and even Hollywood filmmakers.

The beauty of its landscapes and its archeological history are not the principal reasons that most westerners have heard of Wadi Rum. Outside of the Middle East, the area is primarily known for its association with T.E. Lawrence, the British soldier and writer who became known as Lawrence of Arabia. The famed scholar and tactician passed through Wadi Rum on multiple occasions during the Arab Revolt of 1917–18 and later detailed his wartime activities in his 1926 book the *Seven Pillars of Wisdom*. With tourism being the main source of income for the local economy, many of Wadi Rum's outstanding natural features have been renamed for Lawrence or his book. However, whether or not he actually visited some of these sites is a matter of conjecture.

The movie version of *Lawrence of Arabia* was filmed in Wadi Rum in the early 1960s (though on release the film was banned in Jordan for its inaccurate depiction of the local culture),

and numerous movies and television series have followed. These include Ridley Scott's blockbuster *The Martian* (2015), where the area doubled for the surface of Mars. The canyons, caverns, and sand bear an uncanny resemblance to the red planet. Only, in this location, there is life to speak of. Though it only camels and the →

ABOUT THE TRAIL

→ <u>DISTANCE</u> Various
→ <u>DURATION</u> 4 to 5 days
→ <u>LEVEL</u> Easy to Moderate

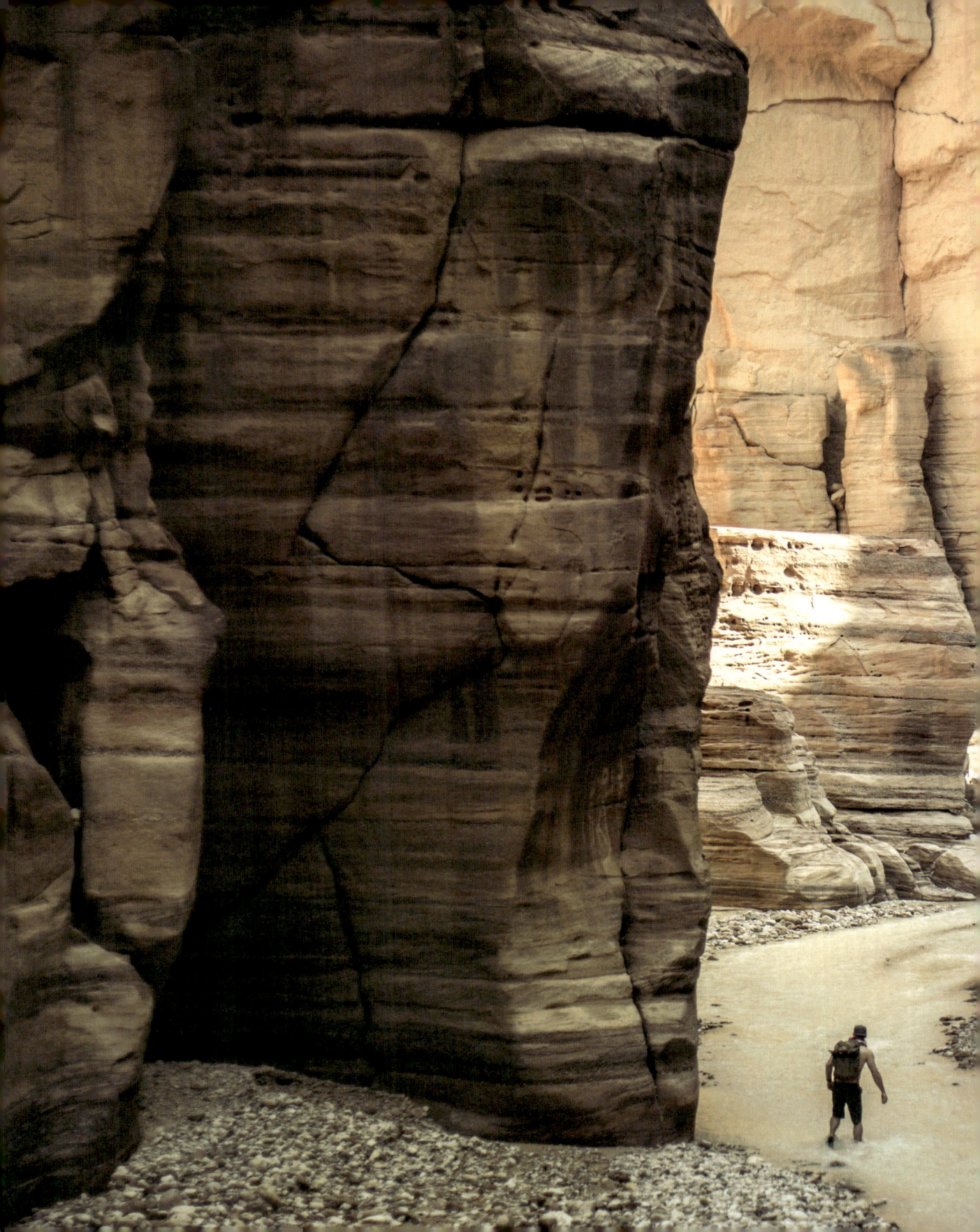

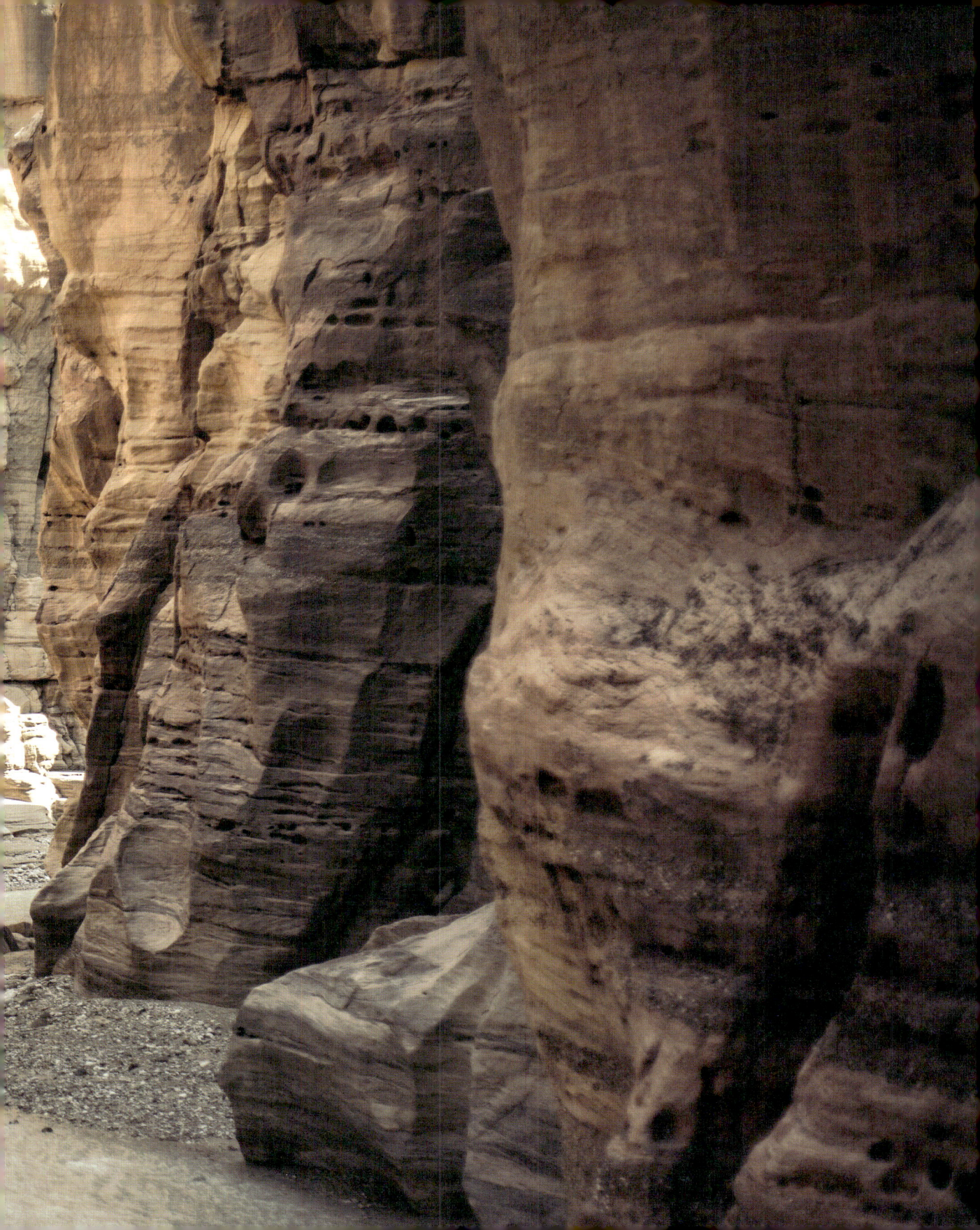

occasional bird that are usually sighted, ibex and mountain goats live in the landscape, reclusive desert foxes and sand cats emerge at night, and vultures and buzzards occasionally glide overhead.

From a hiking perspective, there is no one long trek that stands out in the Wadi Rum region. Instead, hikers can string together a series of satisfying shorter walks, all of which can depart from the Wadi Rum visitors' center. Some of the notable sites to journey to include Burrah Canyon with its imposing, rounded sandstone walls; Khazali Canyon, which features some of the area's finest petroglyphs; and the Burdah Rock Bridge, a natural arch in red sandstone that reaches around 300 m (984 ft.) above the desert floor.

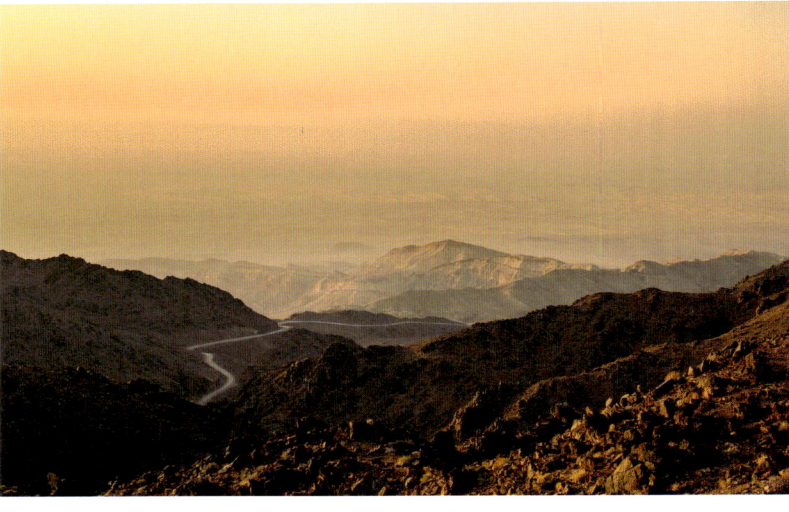

→ **Camping under bright stars.**
↓ **On one of Wadi Rum's rock bridges.**

Visitors have the choice of experiencing the area independently or as part of a tour with the local Bedouin guides, who are usually part of the Zalabia tribe. The vast majority (probably 90 percent) opt for the latter; however, for those that have experience hiking in arid environments and feel comfortable with the occasional rock scramble, going independently could be a good choice. A compass or GPS and a reliable guidebook are essentials. Other recommended items include a wide-brimmed hat, a water carrier with a four liter or more capacity, and a warm sleeping bag for any overnight stays. For those planning to do multi-day hikes without guides, it is best to leave an itinerary at the Rum village visitors' center for safety. →

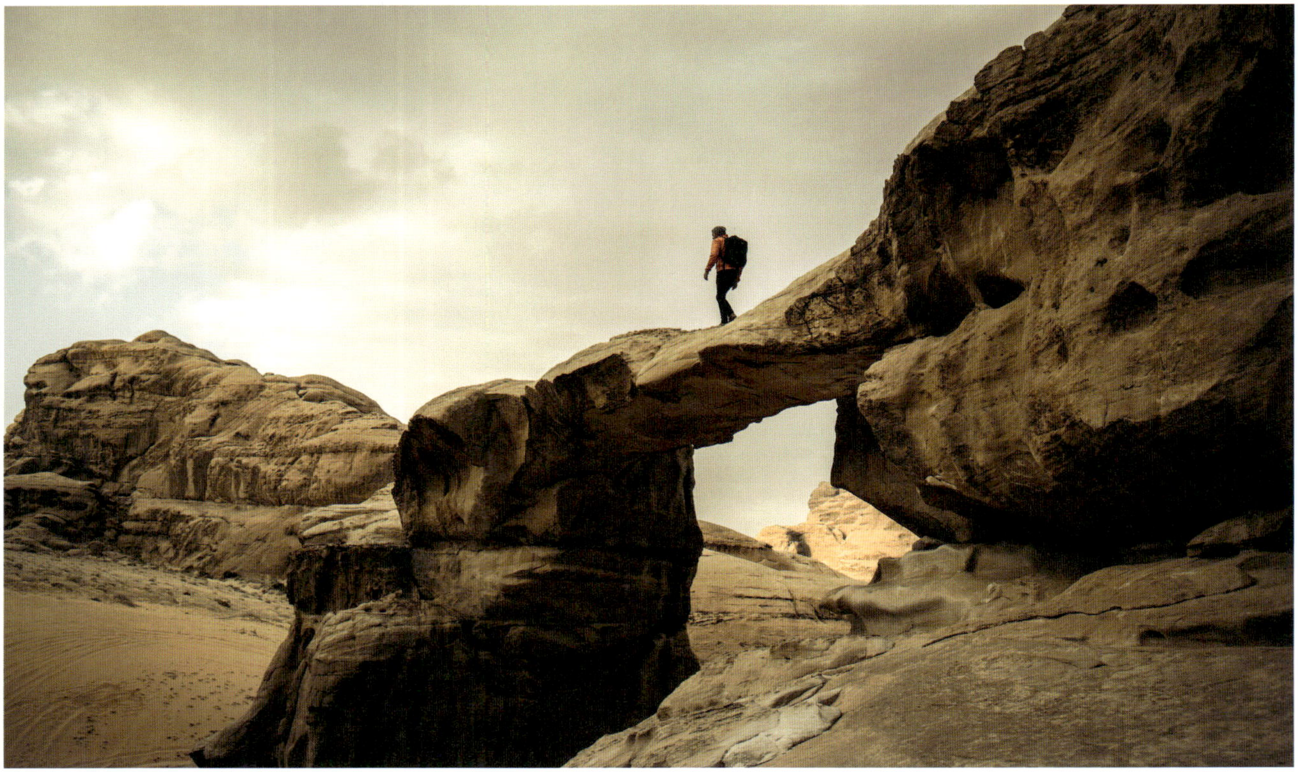

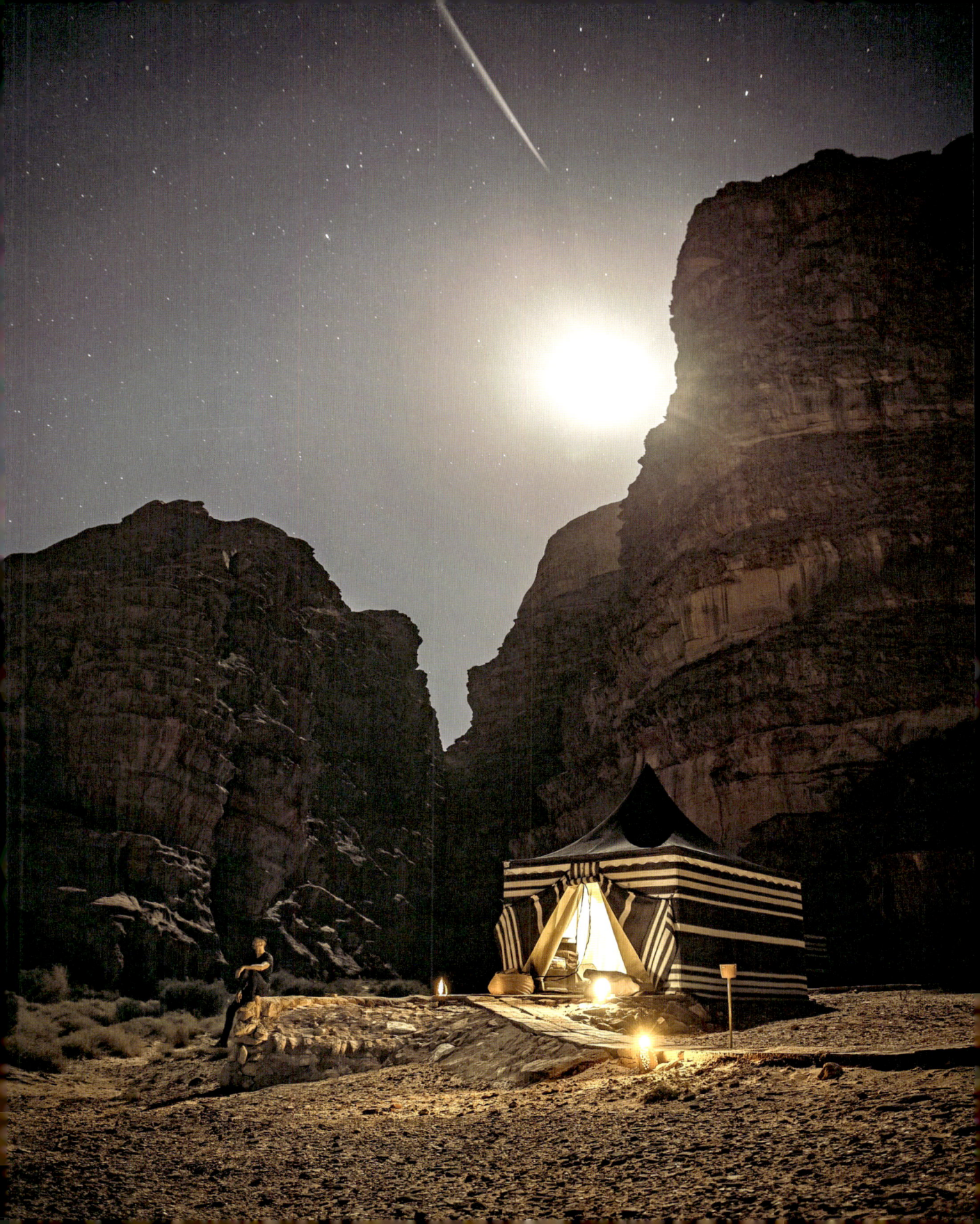

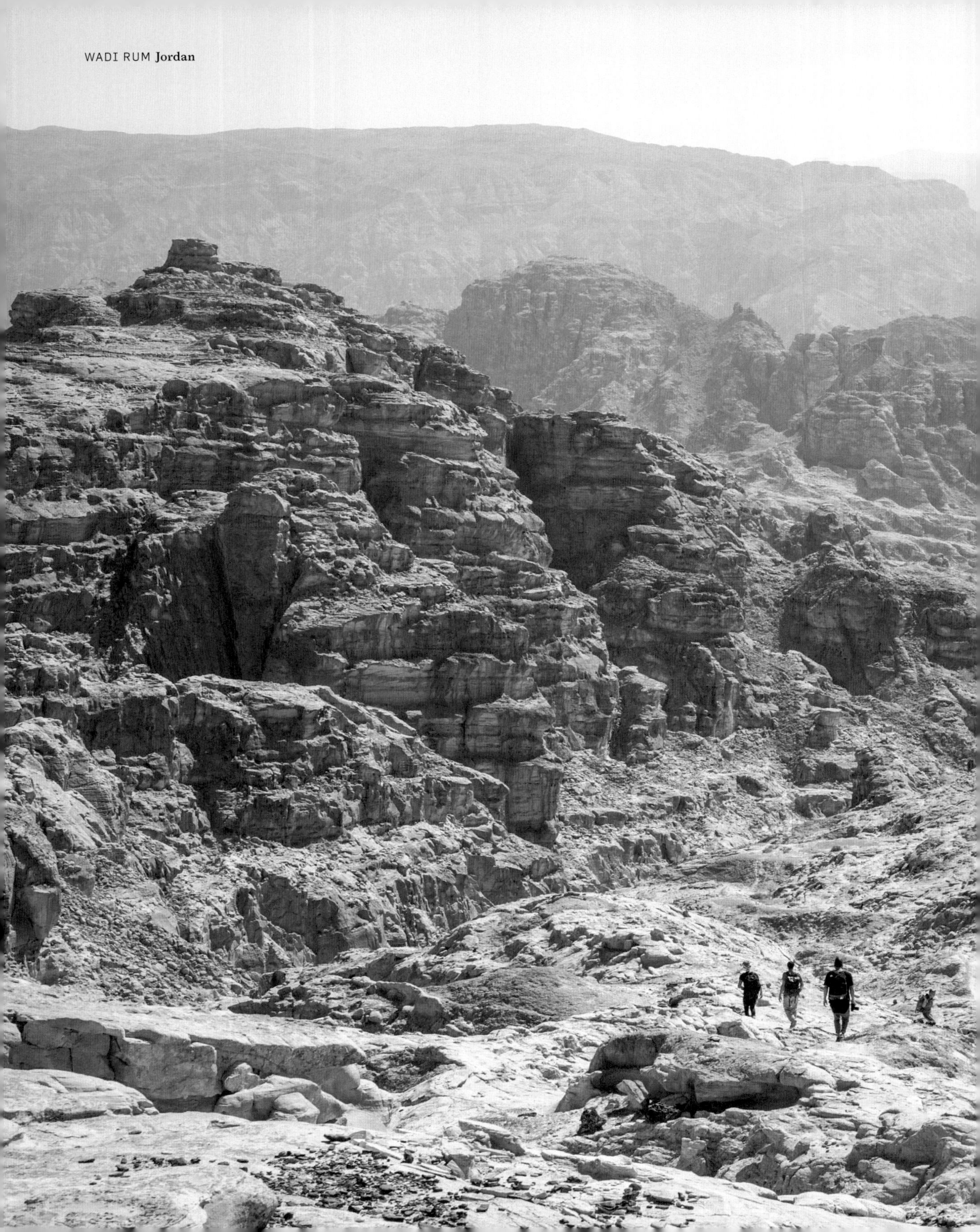

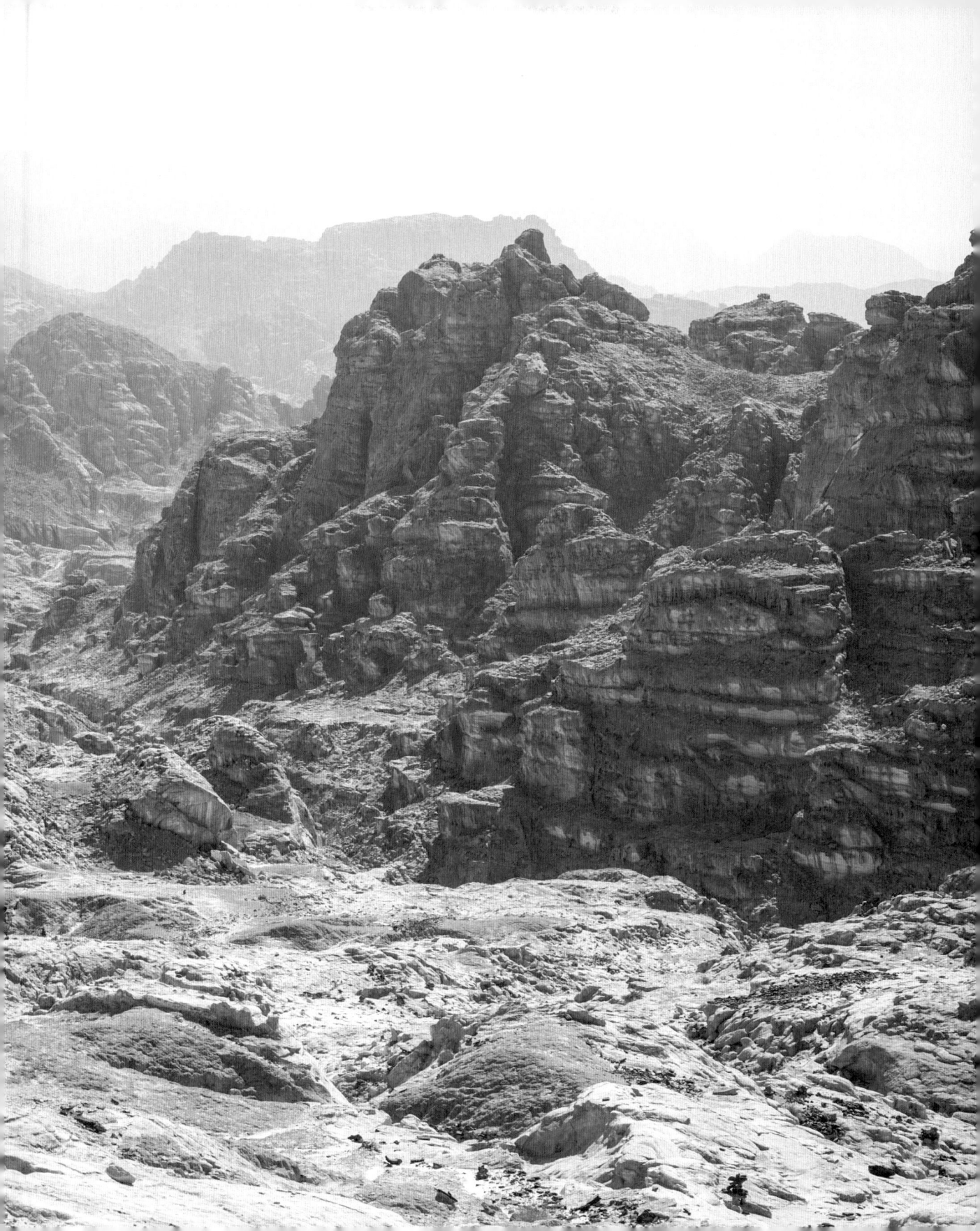

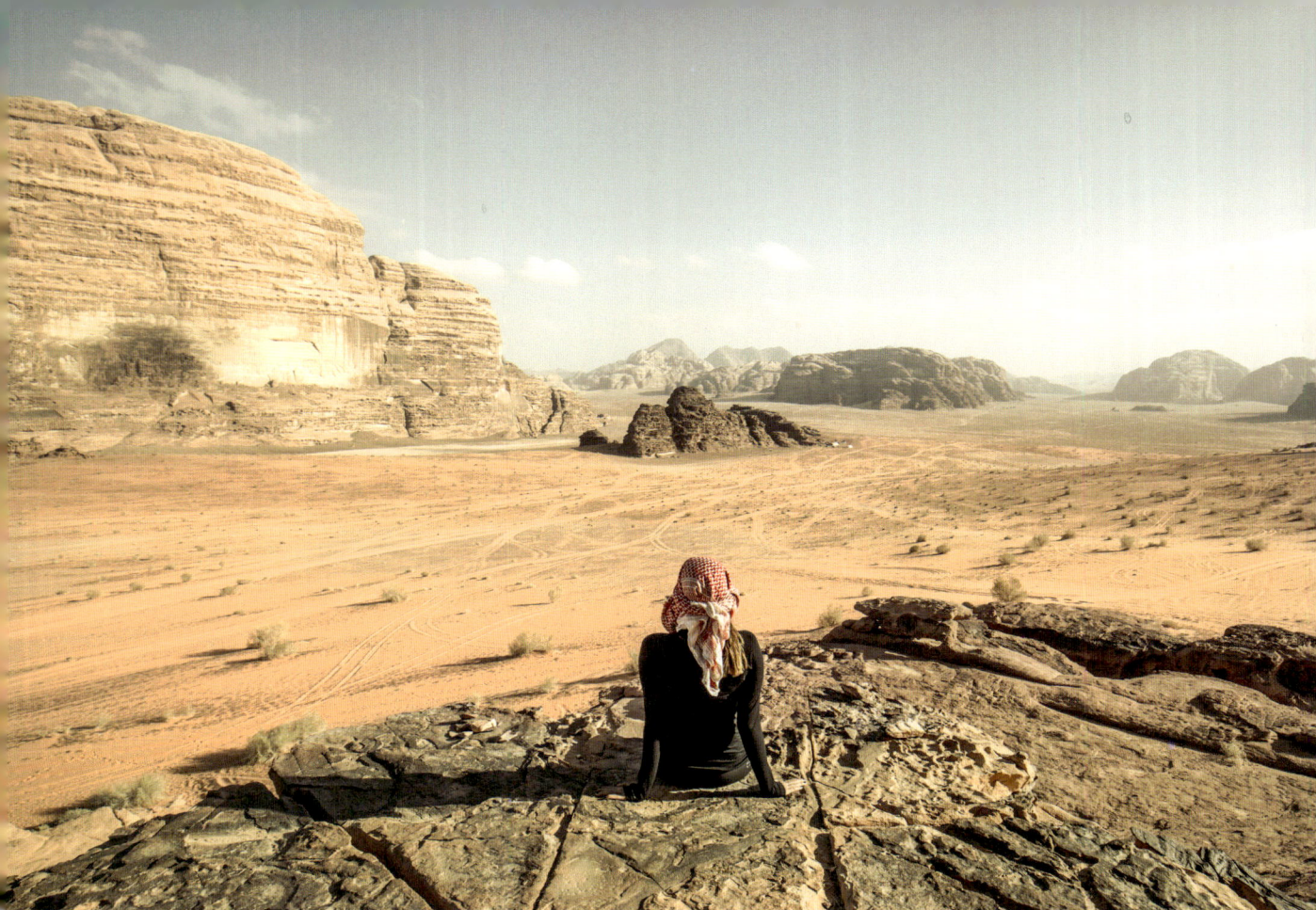

↑ Admiring the traces in the red-toned sand.

One excursion where a guide is highly recommended is the ascent to the summit of Jebel Um Adaami. Jordan's highest peak, which stands at 1,832 m (6,010 ft.) above sea level, is situated in the far reaches of the Wadi Rum protected area (about 40 km [25 mi.] from the village). The climb is not technically difficult, and the views from the summit over Wadi Rum to the north and Saudi Arabia to the south are some of the best in the region.

Whichever form of travel is preferred—be it on two legs, four legs (by camel or horse), or four wheels—travelers should be sure to sleep under the stars at least once during their stay. Gazing up at the night sky in the chilly desert, they can watch shooting stars tracing paths across the dark heavens. The same principle holds true for the sunrises and sunsets—visitors should see as many as possible. In the early morning and late afternoon, the desert valleys light up in a kaleidoscope of red, orange, and crimson. It is at these atmospheric times that Lawrence's description of Wadi Rum as "vast, echoing and God-like" resonates most deeply. A part of the earth that resembles the surface of Mars, and one where other planets can be seen in their blazing glory, Wadi Rum is almost part of another world. ———————

Situated in southern Jordan, this "Valley of the Moon" is actually a series of valleys that run down to Saudi Arabia and is home to gorges, arches, pillars, flaming sands, and even some timid desert wildlife.

START/FINISH
Series of short walks all easily accessed from the visitors' center in Rum village.

SEASON
Early spring and late autumn

CONDITIONS
Warm days and cool nights during trekking season.

ACCOMMODATION
Indoor accommodation is available at Wadi Rum village. Camping is possible in the desert; this can be done either independently or in Bedouin-style tents with organized groups.

TIP
Two handy books on hikes and scrambles are *Treks and Climbs in Wadi Rum, Jordan* by Tony Howard and *Hiking in Jordan* by Gregory F. Maassen and Chris Grant.

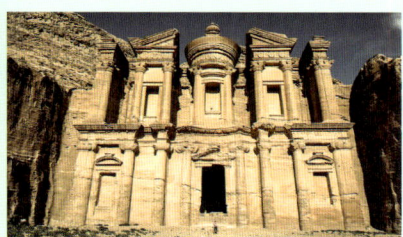

BACKGROUND

MARKINGS AND TRACES Occupied by humans for at least 12,000 years, Wadi Rum still bears the remains of ancient civilizations. Petroglyphs—pictorial communications carved into rock—mark boulders, cliffs, and stone surfaces in the area. These inscriptions portray both humans and animals and seem to provide evidence of animal husbandry and agriculture in the varied landscape in times from the Neolithic period to the days of the Nabataean people.

The Nabataeans—an Arabic-speaking nomad people who settled in southern Jordan in the fourth century BC—had their capital in Petra, which lies around 100 km (62 mi.) north of Rum village. Wadi Rum formed part of their trading route. Along with their engravings, the ruins of a temple can be seen in the area.

FLORA & FAUNA

SOUNDS OF THE WILD The desert is not as barren as it seems. Around sunset or in the evenings, reclusive fennecs (desert foxes) sometimes emerge from their burrows. The diminutive animals, which are on average just 36–41 cm (14–16 in.) in length, are incredibly shy, and on rare occasions visitors may hear their screeching calls.

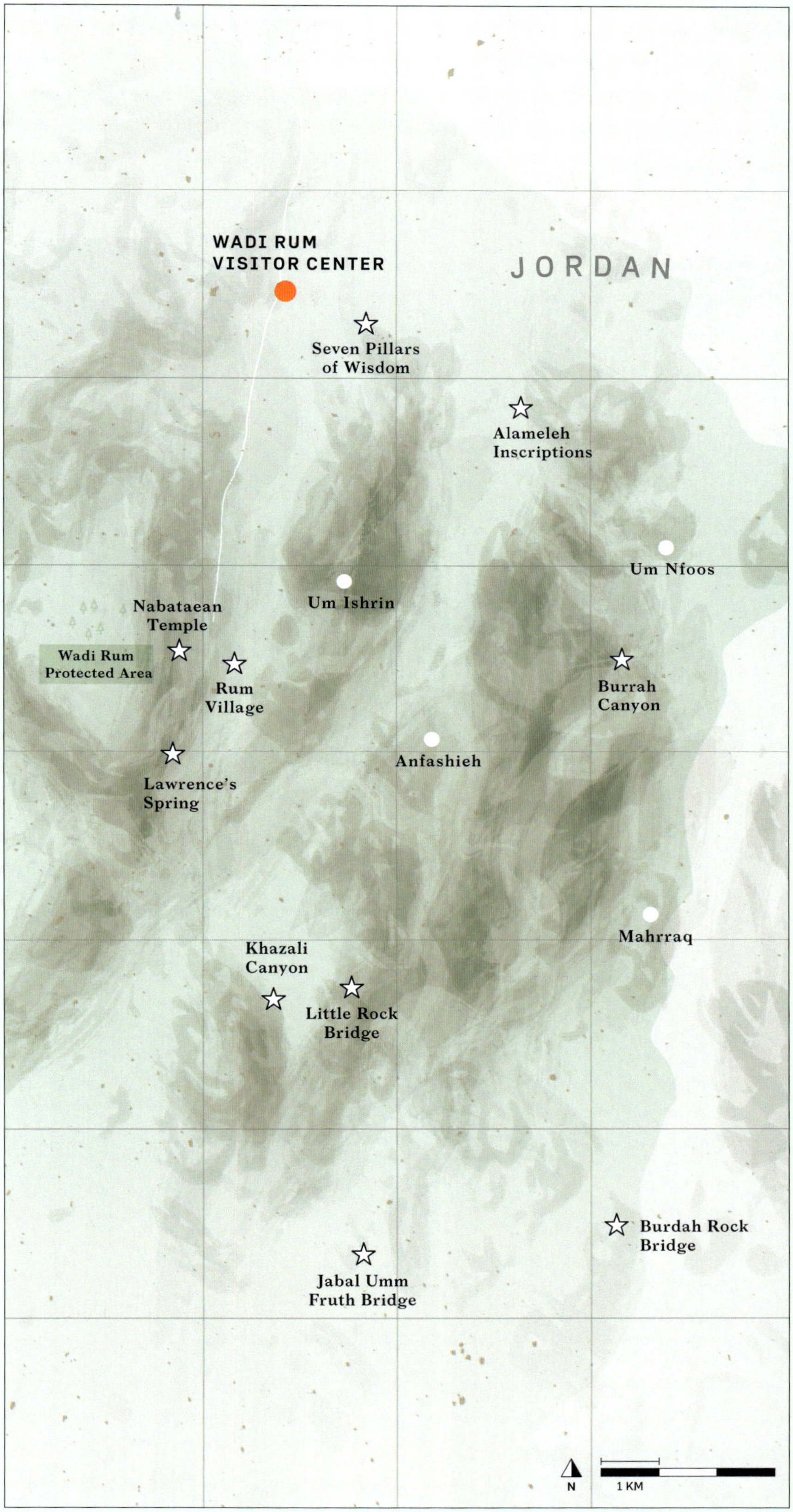

WADI RUM
VISITOR CENTER

JORDAN

☆ Seven Pillars
of Wisdom

☆ Alameleh
Inscriptions

● Um Nfoos

● Um Ishrin

Nabataean
Temple

☆ Burrah
Canyon

Wadi Rum
Protected Area

☆ Rum
Village

● Anfashieh

☆ Lawrence's
Spring

● Mahrraq

Khazali
Canyon

☆ Little Rock
Bridge

☆ Burdah Rock
Bridge

☆ Jabal Umm
Fruth Bridge

N

1 KM

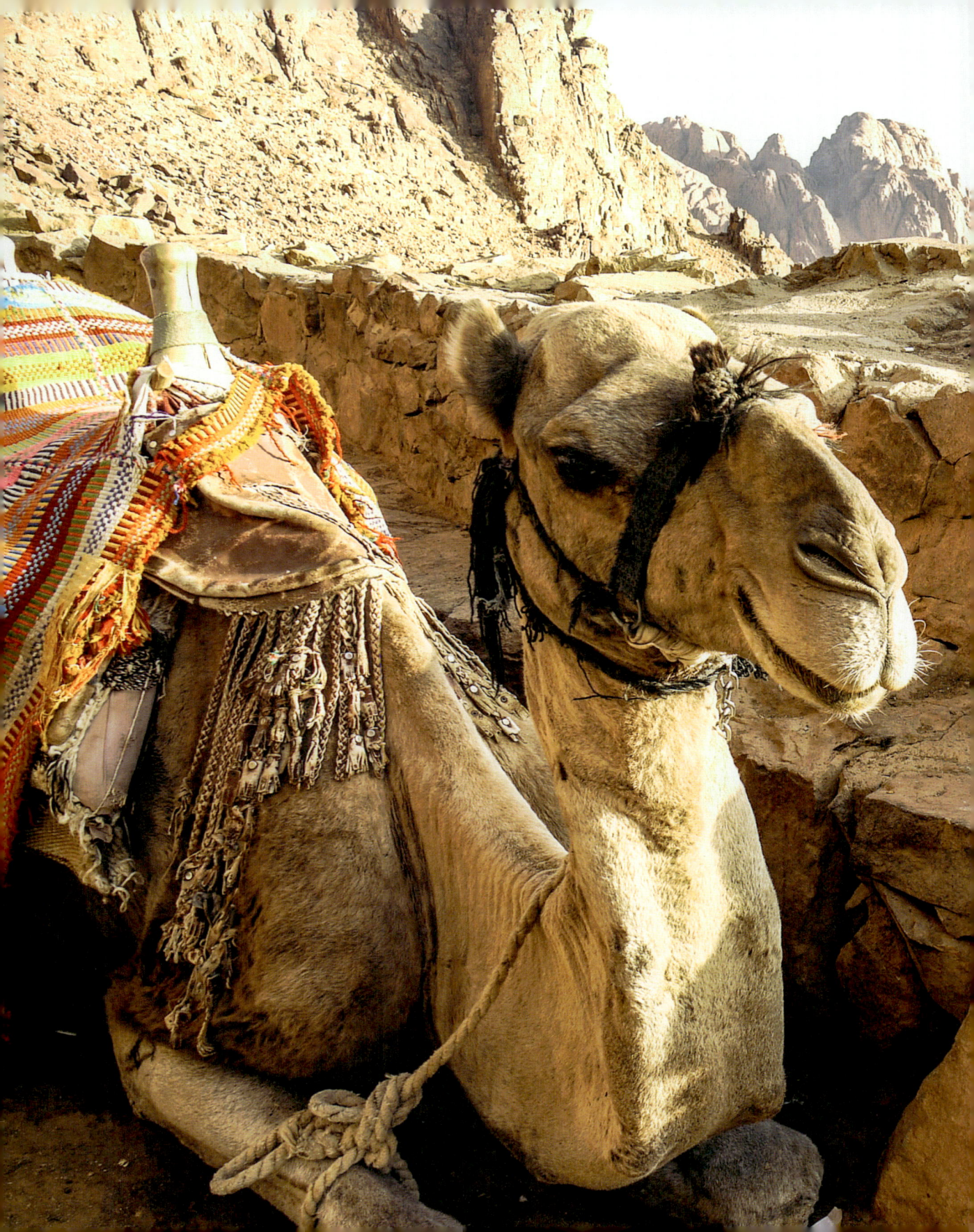

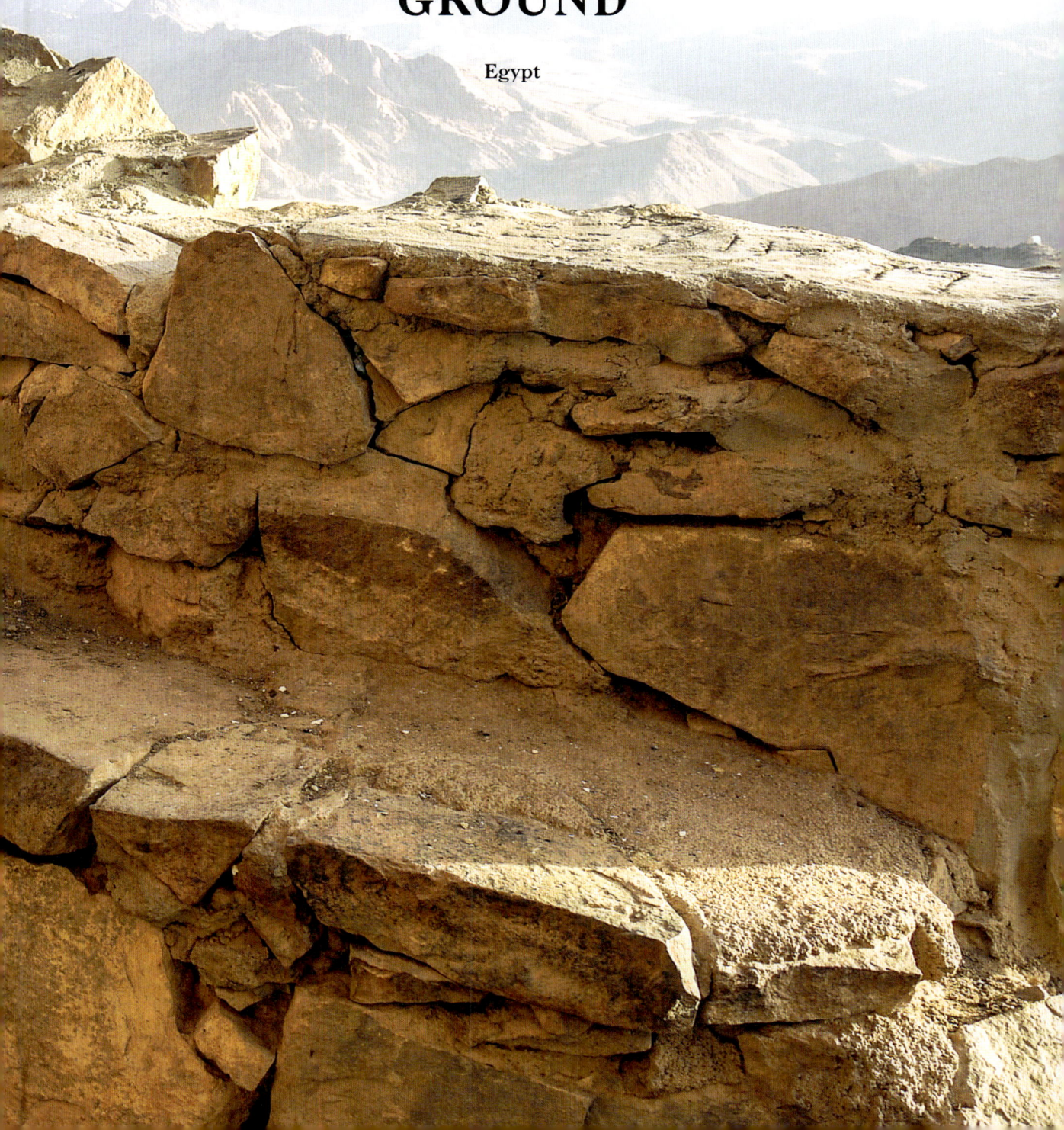

MOUNT SINAI

SCALING HOLY GROUND

Egypt

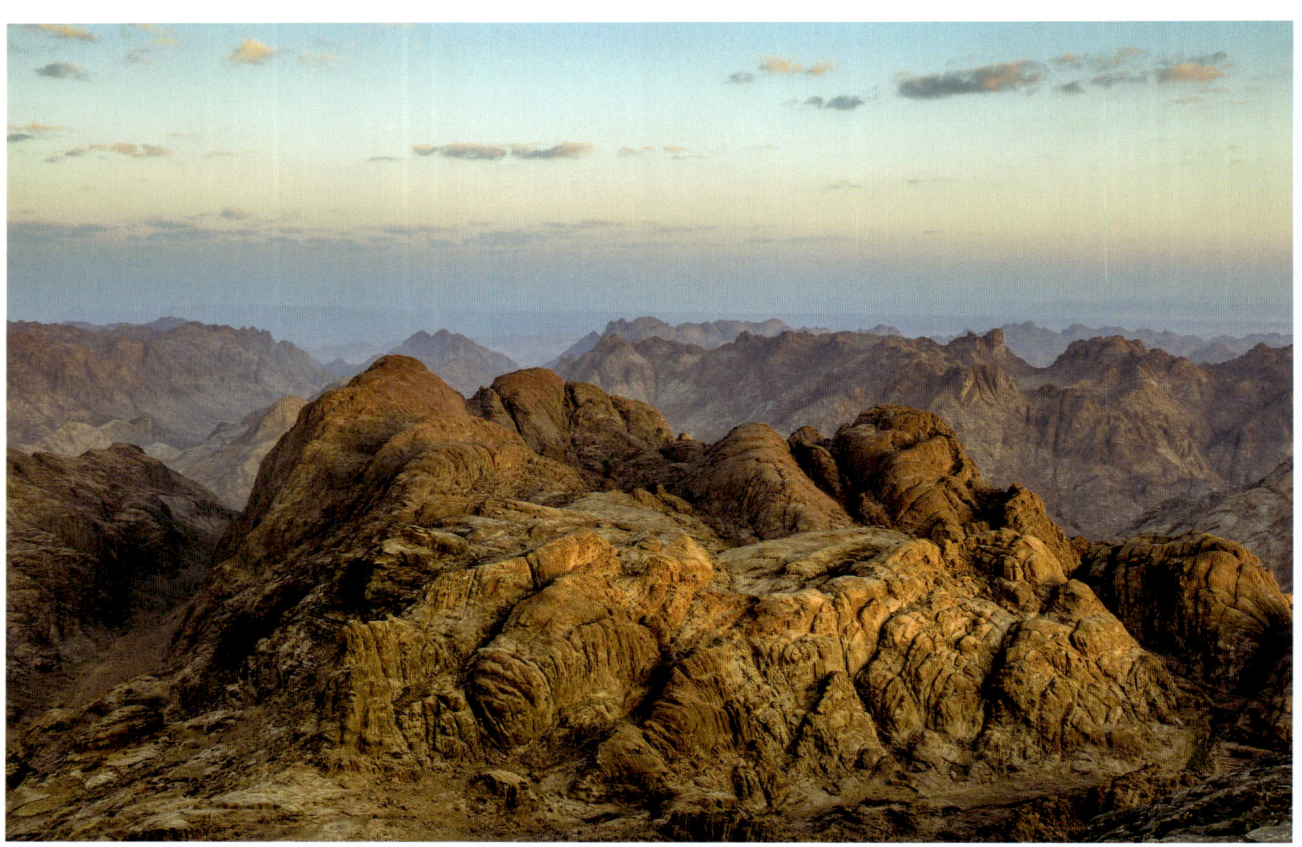

According to the Old Testament, the summit of Mount Sinai (2,285 m [7,497 ft.]) in Egypt is the place where Moses received the Ten Commandments from God. Considered sacred by Christians, Jews, and Muslims alike, the holy mountain has, over centuries, become a popular pilgrimage site, and it now attracts tens of thousands of tourists per year.

Most of these visitors follow in past pilgrims' footsteps by climbing to the top of the fabled peak. This must be done with the help of a guide. Guides are usually from one of the Bedouin tribes in the region—the Sinai Peninsula is a mix of territories belonging to this nomadic people—and local tribespeople know their own terrain best.

Aspirants have two route options at their disposal: the Camel Path, which is wide, gradual, and long, and the Steps of Penitence path, which is shorter, more challenging, and consists of some 3,750 steps. As its name suggests, the former route can

---

ABOUT THE TRAIL

→ <u>DISTANCE</u> 7 km (4.2 mi.)
→ <u>DURATION</u> 4 to 6 hours
→ <u>LEVEL</u> Easy to Moderate

While taking in Mother Nature's twice-daily sky show and listening to pilgrims belt out a chorus or three of "Kumbaya," it is hard not to feel moved.

be ascended on a camel—that is until the last 750 steps, which have to be scaled on foot.

Most visitors opt for the easier Camel Path, but those who are relatively fit should consider taking the Steps of Penitence. There are far fewer people and no camels, and when hiking in the daytime the walk represents the more scenic of the two options. Those with suitably robust knees can try descending via the Steps. The views over Saint Catherine's Monastery and the surrounding valley are spectacular.

The vast majority of walkers make the climb pre-dawn in order to avoid the heat of the day. This is definitely the better option for the summer months, when temperatures can be →

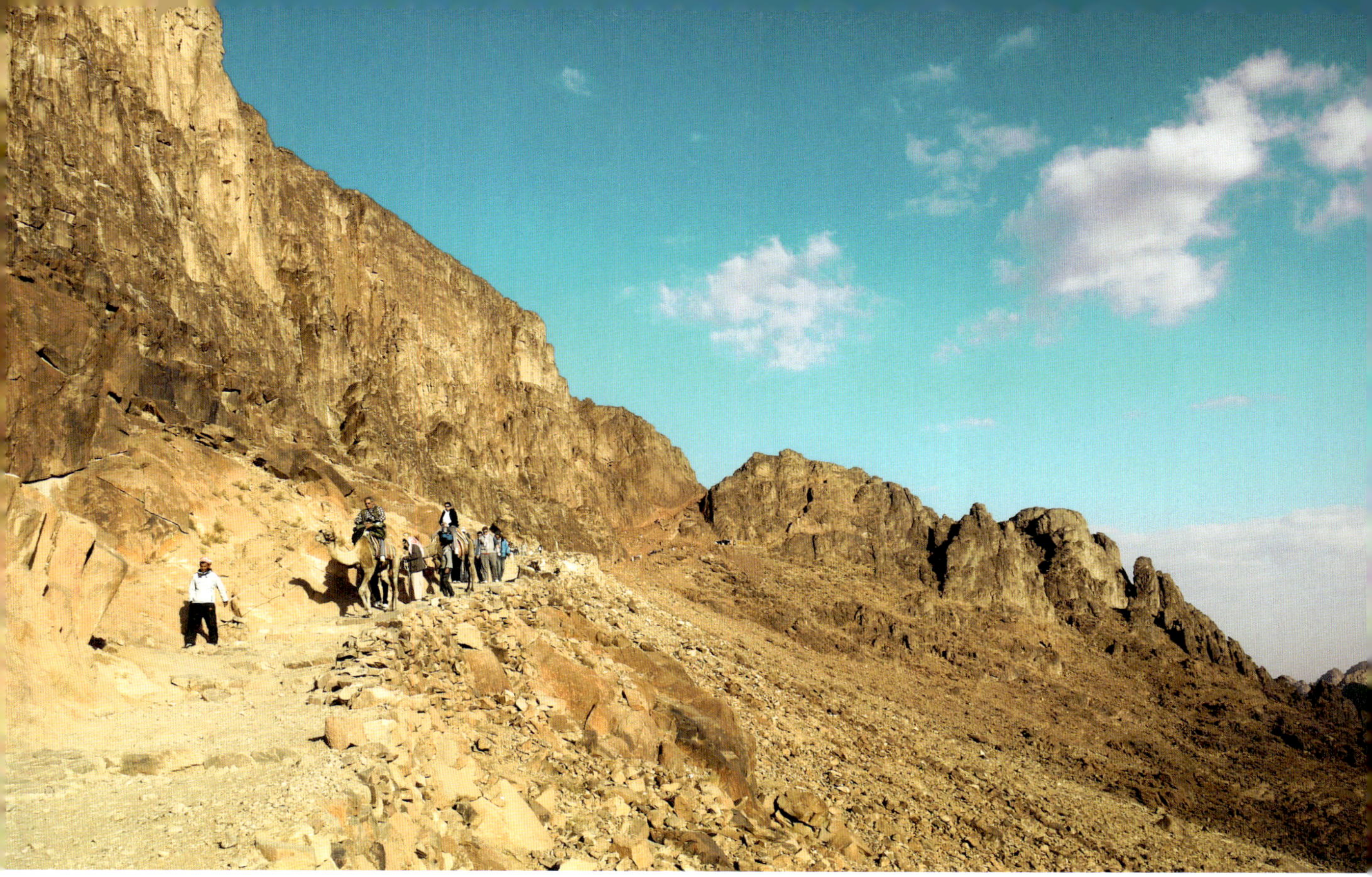

← Close to sunrise on Mount Sinai.
↑ On the Camel Path.
↓ A stop for snacks en route.

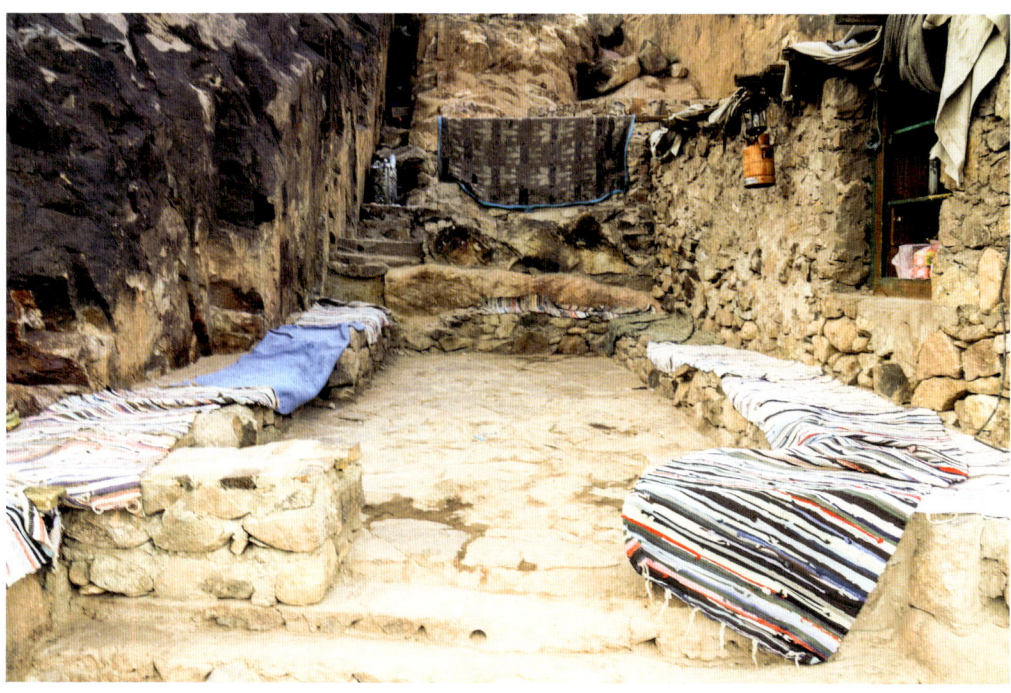

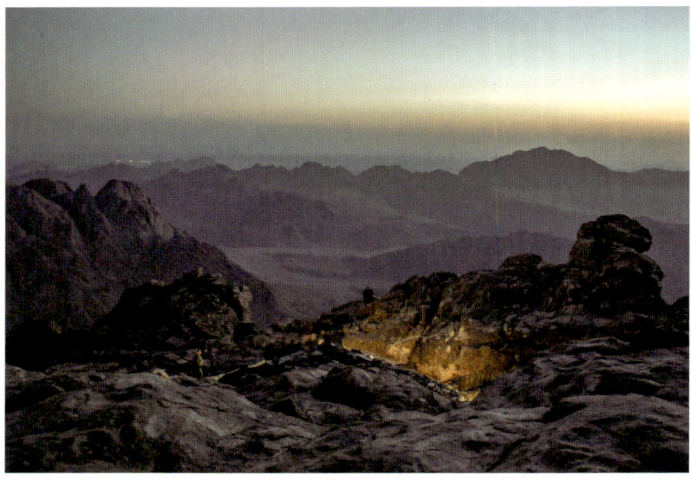

scorching. As individuals ascend, the velvety black in the sky will fade into light, and bright tones will slowly appear as the sun rises. Those who are hiking during the cooler months of the year and wish to avoid some of the crowds (there can sometimes be hundreds of people on the summit at sunrise) should go in the afternoon.

Whichever path or time of day visitors scale the mountain, they can take solace in the fact that there are teahouses along the way for relaxation and refreshment. These way stations are particularly welcome during the chilly pre-dawn hours. A good tip for morning hikers is to grab a hot beverage and maybe even a cup of noodles at one of the last teahouses (situated at Elijah's Hollow) before ascending the final 750 steps to the summit.

The bright shades of sunrise and sunset seen from the top of the peak make the climb well worthwhile. While taking in Mother Nature's twice-daily sky show and listening to pilgrims belt out a chorus or three of "Kumbaya," it is hard not to feel moved. Irrespective of religious beliefs, the palpable combination of faith and enthusiasm, together with the beauty of a crimson-orange horizon, make surmounting Mount Sinai an unforgettable experience.

At the end of a Mount Sinai pilgrimage, a closer look inside Saint Catherine's Monastery's high red walls is recommended. Situated at the foot of the mountain, Saint Catherine's is a Greek Orthodox monastery built in the sixth century and is said to be on the site where God spoke to Moses through a burning bush. It is one of the world's oldest active Christian monasteries, and in 2002 was declared a UNESCO World Heritage Site. ———————

↗ Colors change minute by minute as the sun comes up.
↓ Awaiting sunrise in cosy surroundings.

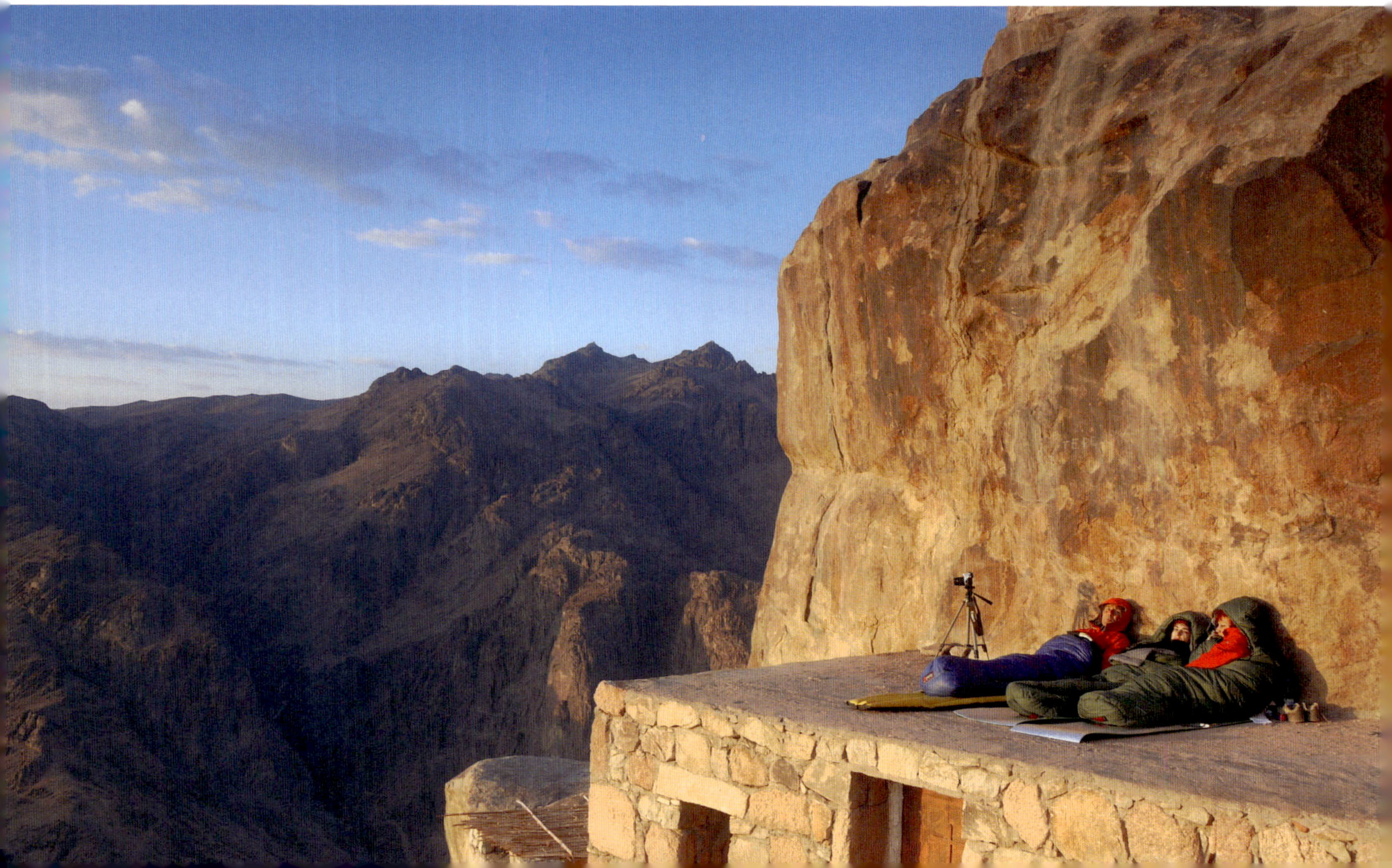

GOOD TO KNOW

START/FINISH
📍 Round trip from Saint Catherine's Monastery

SEASON
Year round

LOWEST/HIGHEST POINT
1,586 m (5,203 ft.)/2,285 m (7,497 ft.)

HIGHLIGHTS
Sunrise or sunset at the summit, views from the Steps of Penitence route, Saint Catherine's Monastery.

TIP
It is obligatory to make the trip with a guide. One can be arranged through most guesthouses or hotels in the region.

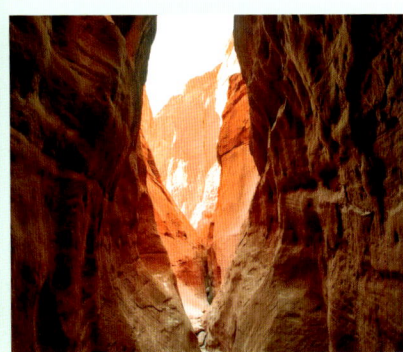

BACKGROUND

ON THE SINAI PENINSULA Around Mount Sinai there are many other destinations of geographical, cultural, or religious interest. At 2.629 m (8,625 ft.) high Mount Catherine ranks as Egypt's tallest peak. The ascent is challenging; however, the 360-degree panorama from the top more than compensates for the effort. A short drive away is the Coloured Canyon (pictured above) with its 40 m (131 ft.) high multi-hued sandstone walls. As with Sinai and Catherine, visitors are required to be accompanied by a local guide. Finally, for those with more time and energy, the 200 km (124 mi.) long Sinai Trail takes hikers on a sinuous route from the Gulf of Aqaba to the summit of Mount Catherine.

FLORA & FAUNA

HOOFED HELPERS For those unable or unwilling to make the whole journey on foot, it is possible to take a camel ride up to Elijah's Basin (750 steps below the summit). Tours with the animals can be organized with local Bedouin guides.

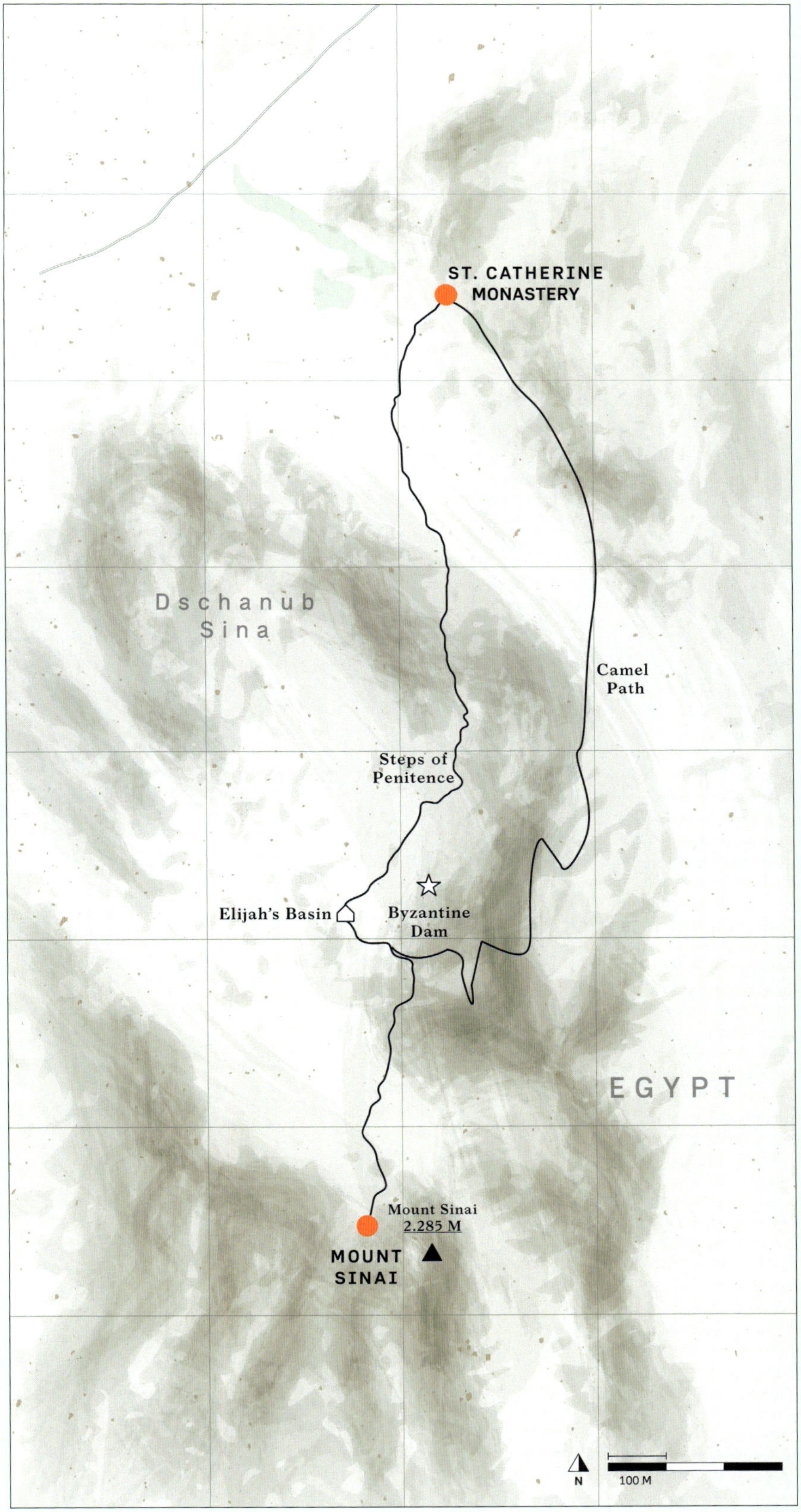

ST. CATHERINE
MONASTERY

Dschanub
Sina

Camel
Path

Steps of
Penitence

Elijah's Basin

Byzantine
Dam

EGYPT

Mount Sinai
2.285 M

MOUNT
SINAI

N

100 M

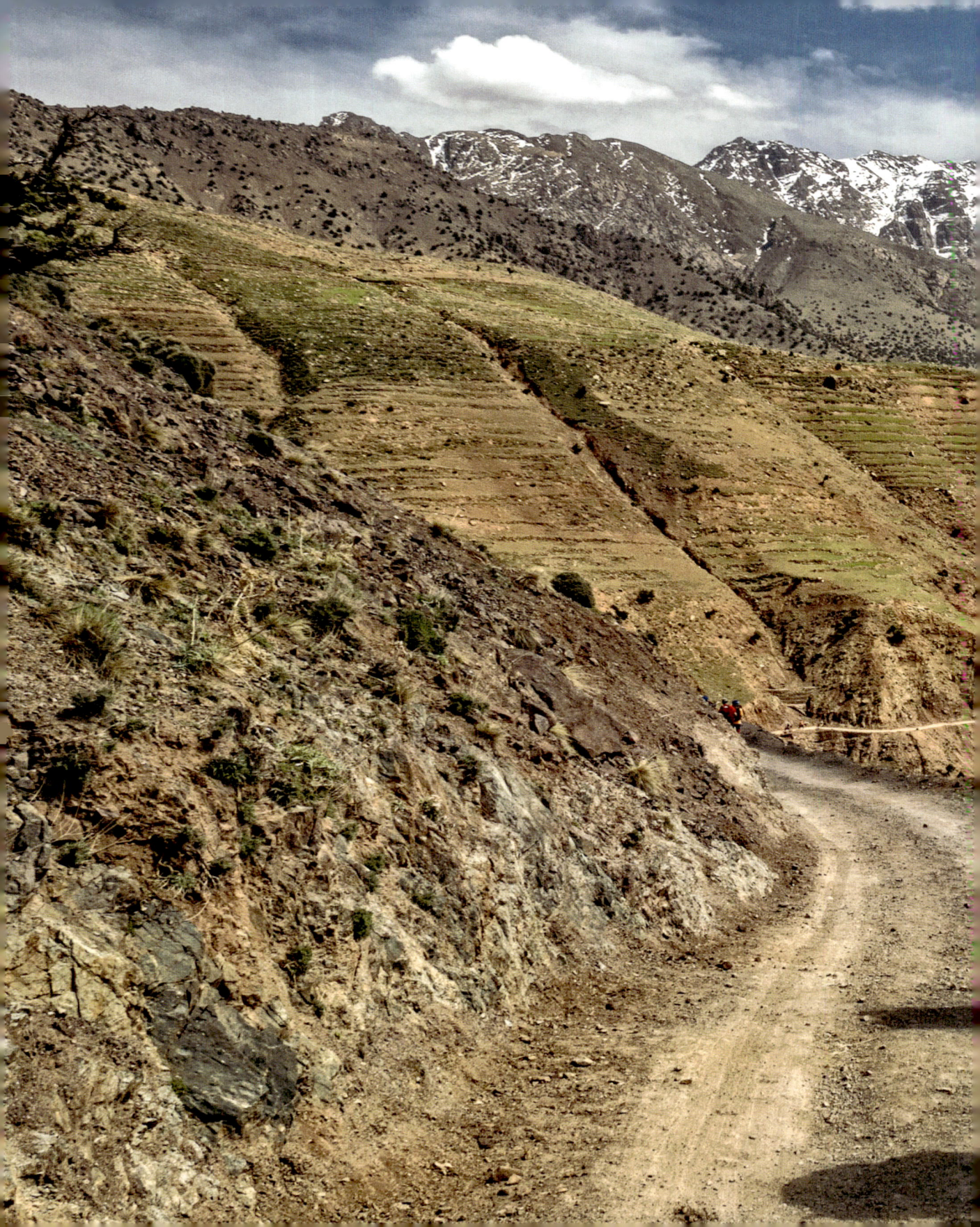

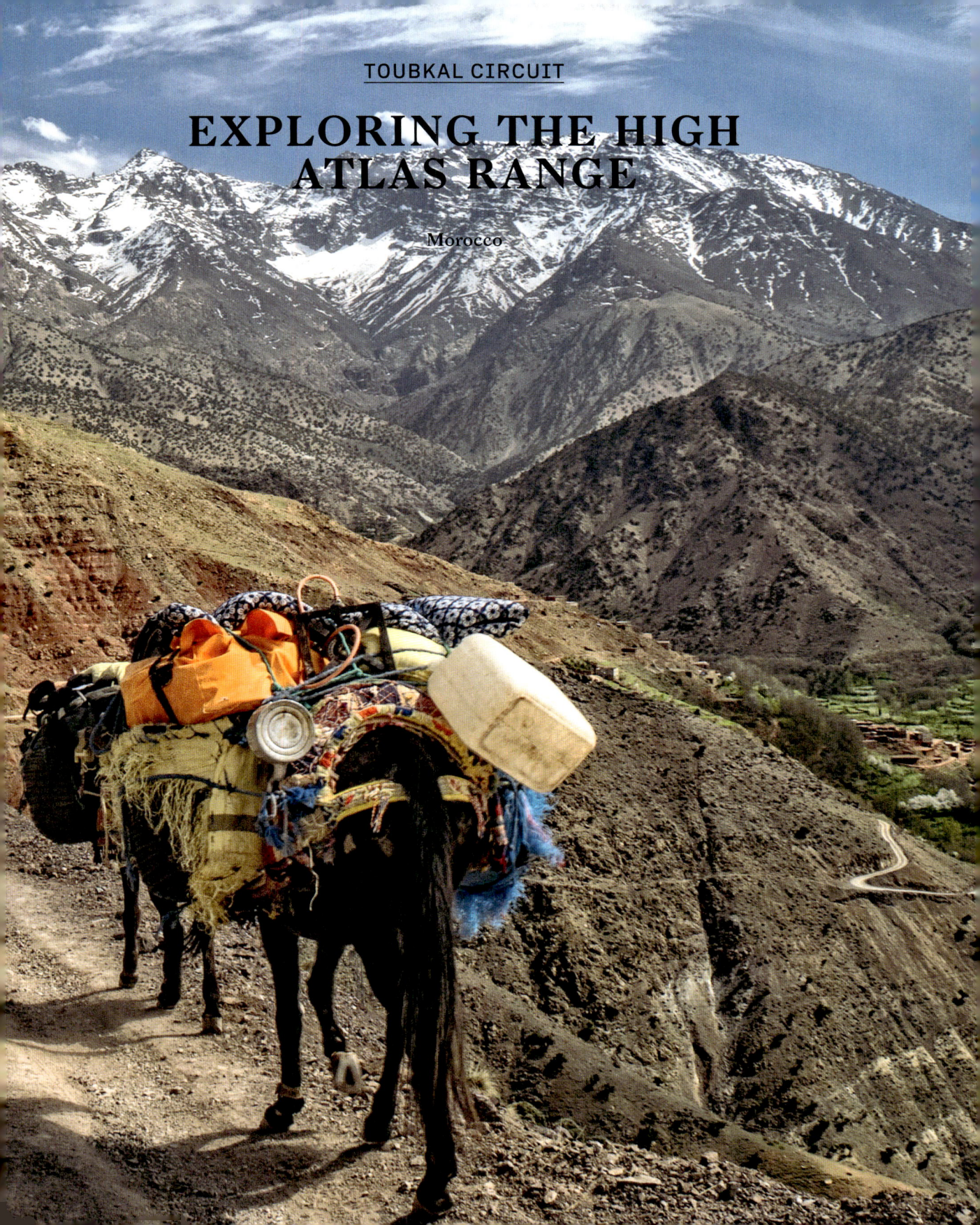

EXPLORING THE HIGH ATLAS RANGE

Morocco

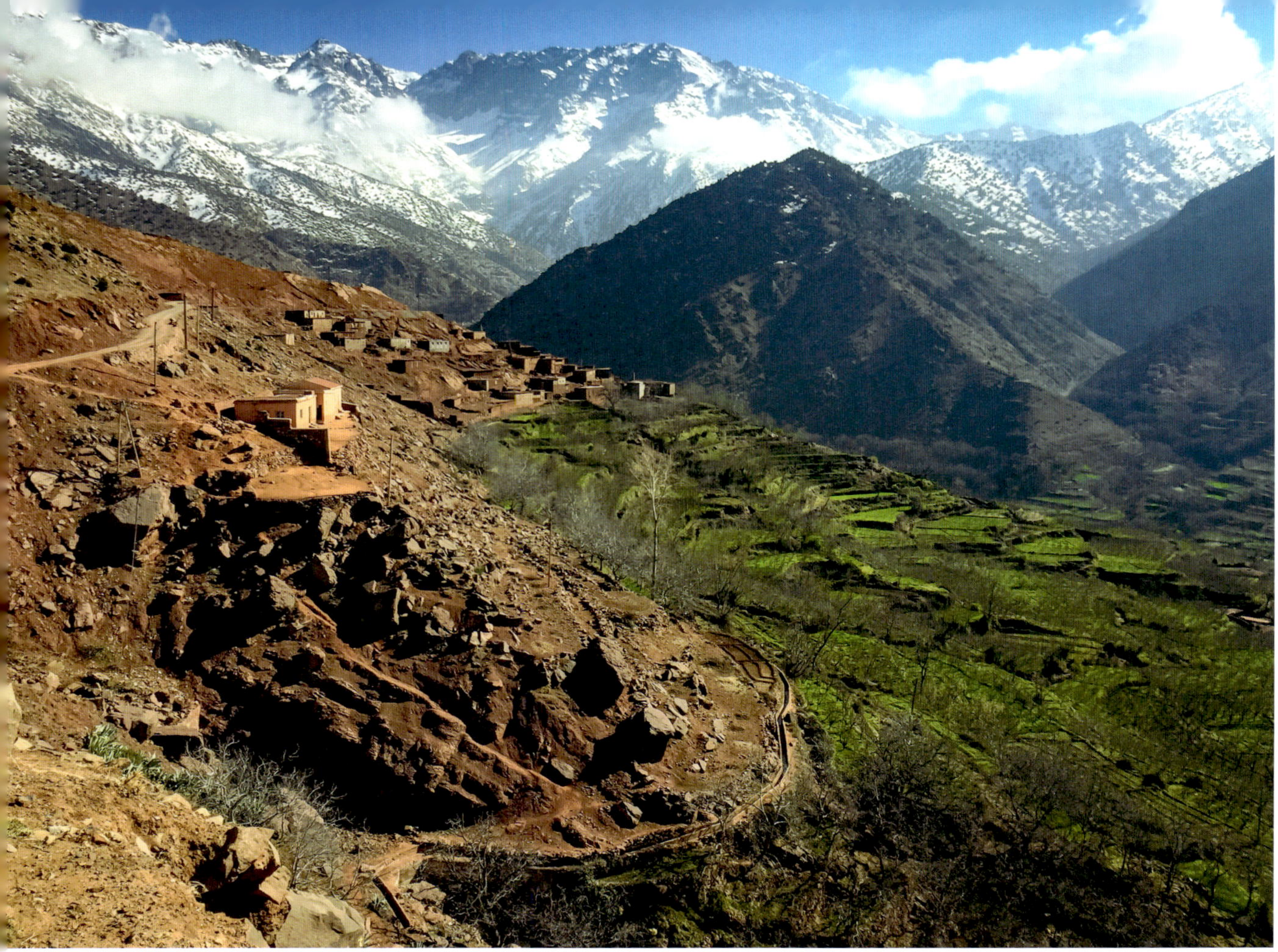

The High Atlas mountains stretch diagonally across Morocco, from the Atlantic Ocean in the west to the border with Algeria in the east. As the name suggests, they contain the Atlas range's tallest peaks. In recognition of their imposing nature, they are referred to by the Berbers—the region's native inhabitants—as Idraren Draren or "Mountains of Mountains."

The High Atlas region represents some of the best trekking on the African continent. Walking the same trails that locals have trodden for millennia, hikers are treated to a memorable combination of hidden passes, oasis-like valleys, snowcapped peaks, and panoramic ridges. Studded throughout these impressive natural wonders are the ancient villages of the Berbers themselves. With their mud-brick houses and terraced fields, these hamlets and the welcoming people who inhabit them are as much a part of trekking in the High Atlas mountains as the majestic landscapes.

ABOUT THE TRAIL

→ DISTANCE 60 km, or 72 km if ascending Jbel Toubkal (37 or 45 mi.)
→ DURATION 5 to 6 days
→ LEVEL Moderate to Difficult

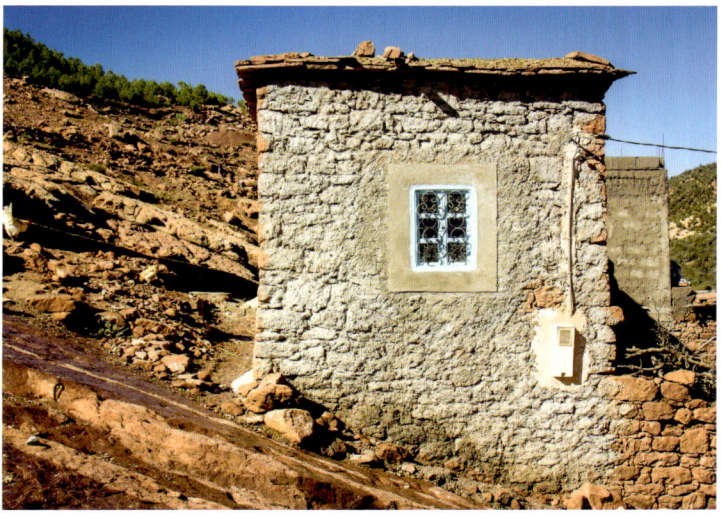

The Toubkal Circuit begins and ends in the picturesque village of Imlil. During its 60-km (37-mi.) course, it circumnavigates the Toubkal Massif by way of a series of interconnected valleys and mountain passes. The way is not always clear, and for those that choose to hike independently, good navigation skills are required. Climbs are often rocky and long, and outside of the often scorching summer months, the higher sections are regularly covered in snow. The adjoining valleys range in character from lush and cultivated to barren and windswept. One of the standout natural features is the beautiful Lake Ifni, an emerald-colored jewel situated just west of the village of Amsouzert.

Aside from the impressive landscapes, one of the highlights of hiking in the Atlas Mountains is experiencing the Berber culture. The several ancient villages the Toubkal Circuit passes through provide the trekker with a fascinating insight into the local way of life. Mud-brick dwellings that sometimes look as though they might extrude from the sloping topography, children splashing around in a river, a local shepherd wandering through the main street with his flock in tow: in many ways it feels like not much has changed over the centuries. While sipping on multiple cups of mint tea and taking all of this in, it is hard not to be enamored by the Berber's traditional existence.

Walking the same trails that locals have trodden for millennia, hikers are treated to a memorable combination of hidden passes, oasis-like valleys, snowcapped peaks, and panoramic ridges.

During the circuit there are multiple side-trip options for those with the time and energy. The most notable are excursions to the summits of Agounss n'Tiniline and Jbel Toubkal. The latter peak is the highest mountain in Northern Africa, standing some 4,167 m (13,671 ft.) above sea level. The trail to the top is non-technical, easy to follow, and, unlike the rest of the Toubkal Circuit, remains a popular option with hikers all year round. →

← Berber village on the slopes of the Atlas Mountains.
↓ Under a starry canopy.

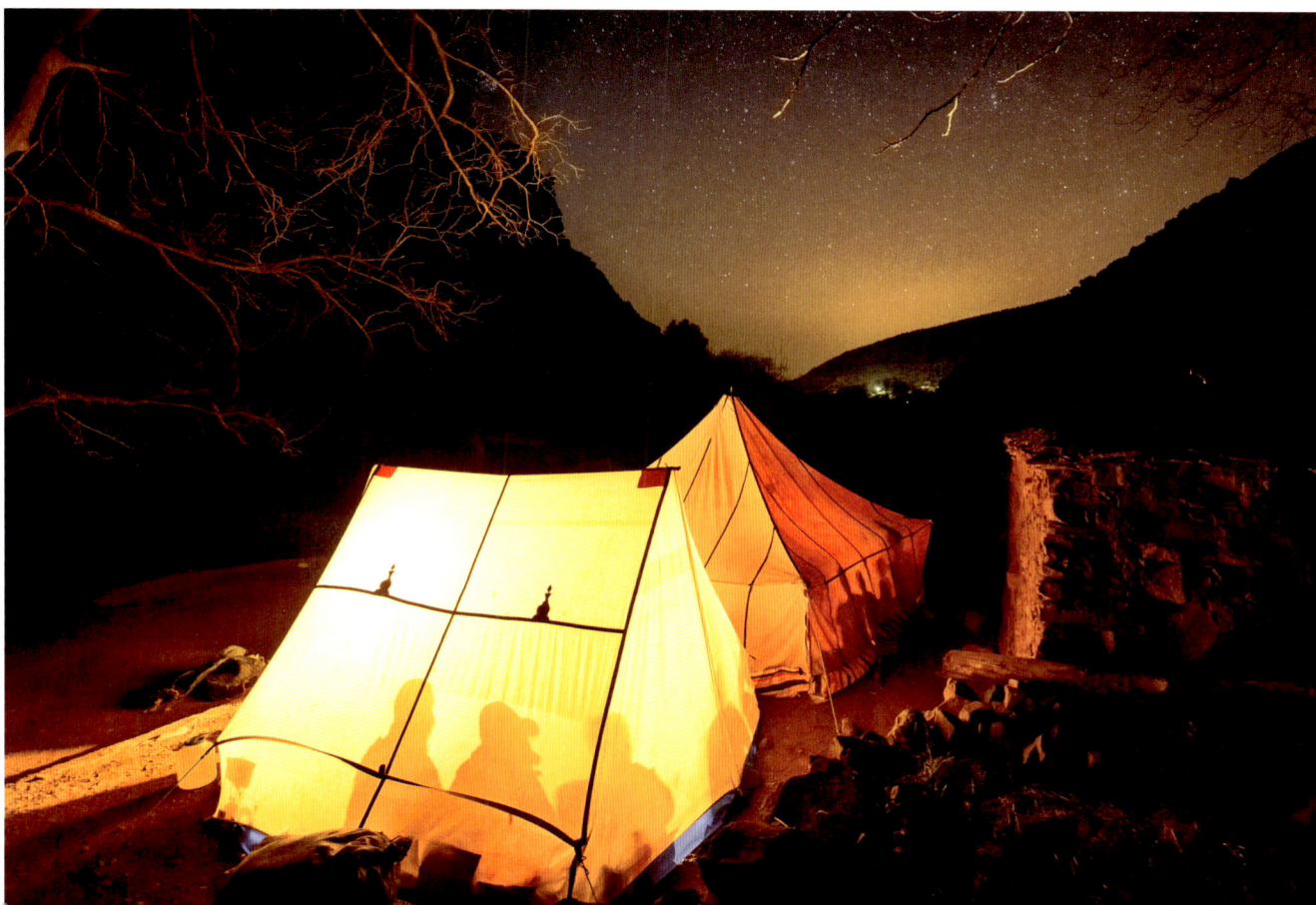

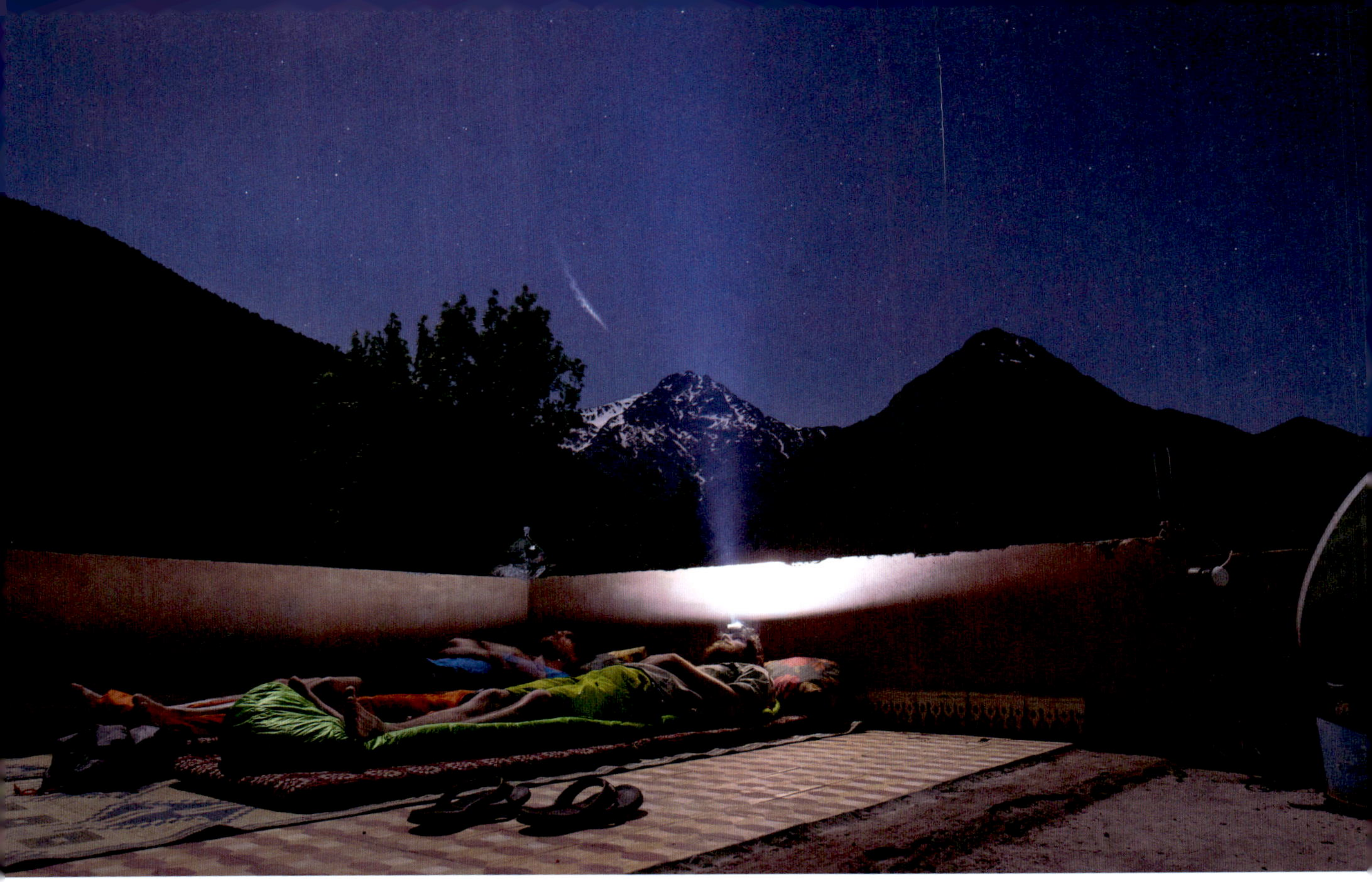

↑ Comet spotting in a Berber village.
↘ Mint tea and hospitality.

The Toubkal Circuit offers hikers an insider's view into a unique culture. This, alongside incredible, rugged scenery, some equally great cuisine—hikers should try as many tajines as they can—and the legendary hospitality of the local population, makes it easy to understand why many visitors keep returning to the High Atlas. The place may only be a short drive away from the hustle and bustle of Marrakesh, but when walking the ancient pathways of the Berbers over stony terrain, it is difficult not to feel like one has been transported back to a simpler time and place—one in which the primary mode of transport is still by foot, and people nod and say hello as you pass them by.

Climbs are often rocky and long, and outside of the often scorching summer months, the higher sections are regularly covered in snow.

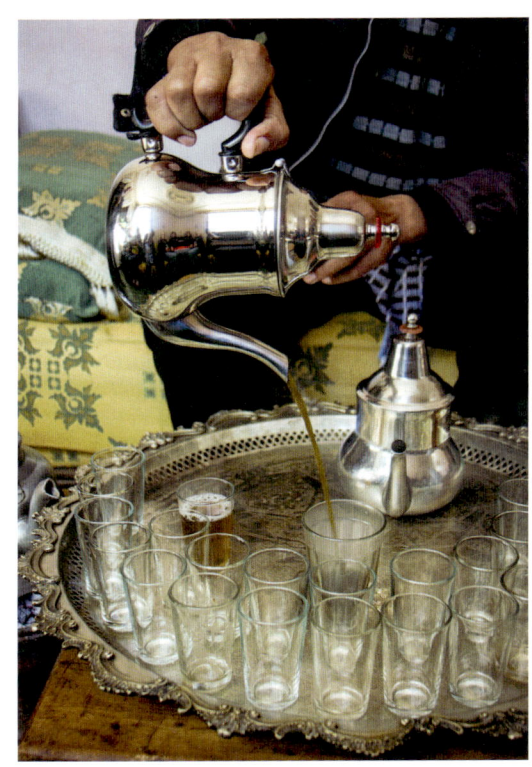

GOOD TO KNOW

START/FINISH
📍 Round trip from Imlil

SEASON
Late spring and early autumn

LOWEST/HIGHEST POINT
1,740 m (5,708 ft.)/4,167 m (13,671 ft.)

ACCOMMODATION
Camping, staying at Gîtes d'Etapes (rest houses) in the villages, or a combination of both. There is also a large mountain hut at the base of Jbel Toubkal that sleeps 80 people.

TIP
Summer, despite the heat and lack of water, is peak season and is often inundated with foreign trekking groups. It is better to avoid going then if possible.

BACKGROUND

TRADITIONAL CULTURE For the Berber people in the High Atlas villages, preserving traditions is very important. Their remote villages, which are situated in a barren environment and are often fortified, have helped them retain their time-honored cultures and languages. As a sign of both courtesy and respect, it is suggested that foreigners dress modestly (pants rather than shorts, no sleeveless tops) and make an effort to learn some basic Berber phrases. This is particularly helpful when hiking independently. Locals will be far more likely to offer assistance to hikers who they see are making an effort to adapt.

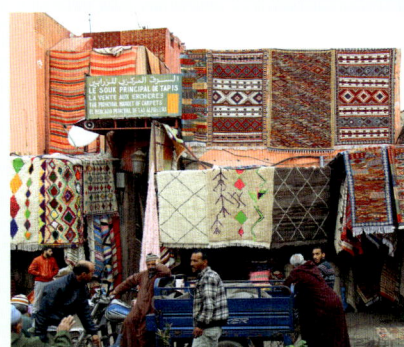

FLORA & FAUNA

JUNIPER TREES Vegetation is sparse on the dry slopes of the Atlas Mountains. Stands of junipers can be found on the lower slopes of Jbel Toubkal. The evergreen trees or shrubs thrive in shallow soil, have aromatic wood, and bear flavorsome berries.

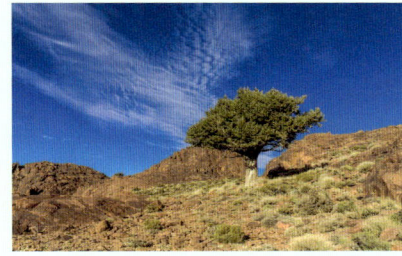

HELPFUL HINTS

GUIDED OR INDEPENDENT? Most people hike the Toubkal Circuit with a guide or as part of an organized group. However, for those with reasonable navigation skills and good equipment, there are no issues with doing the trek independently. If choosing the latter option, eating at the villages along the way can save some pack weight. The food is very tasty and reasonably priced.

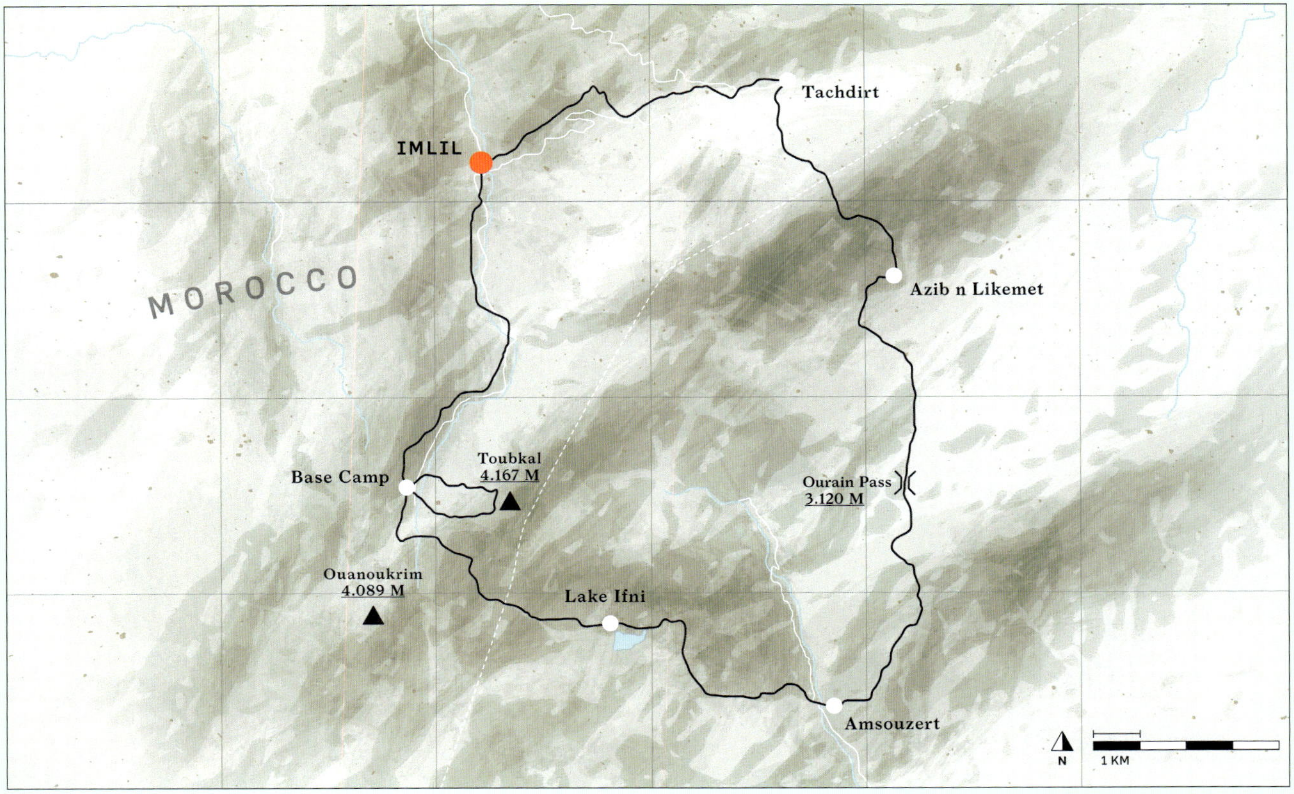

MOROCCO

IMLIL

Tachdirt

Azib n Likemet

Base Camp

Toubkal
4,167 M

Ourain Pass
3,120 M

Ouanoukrim
4,089 M

Lake Ifni

Amsouzert

N

1 KM

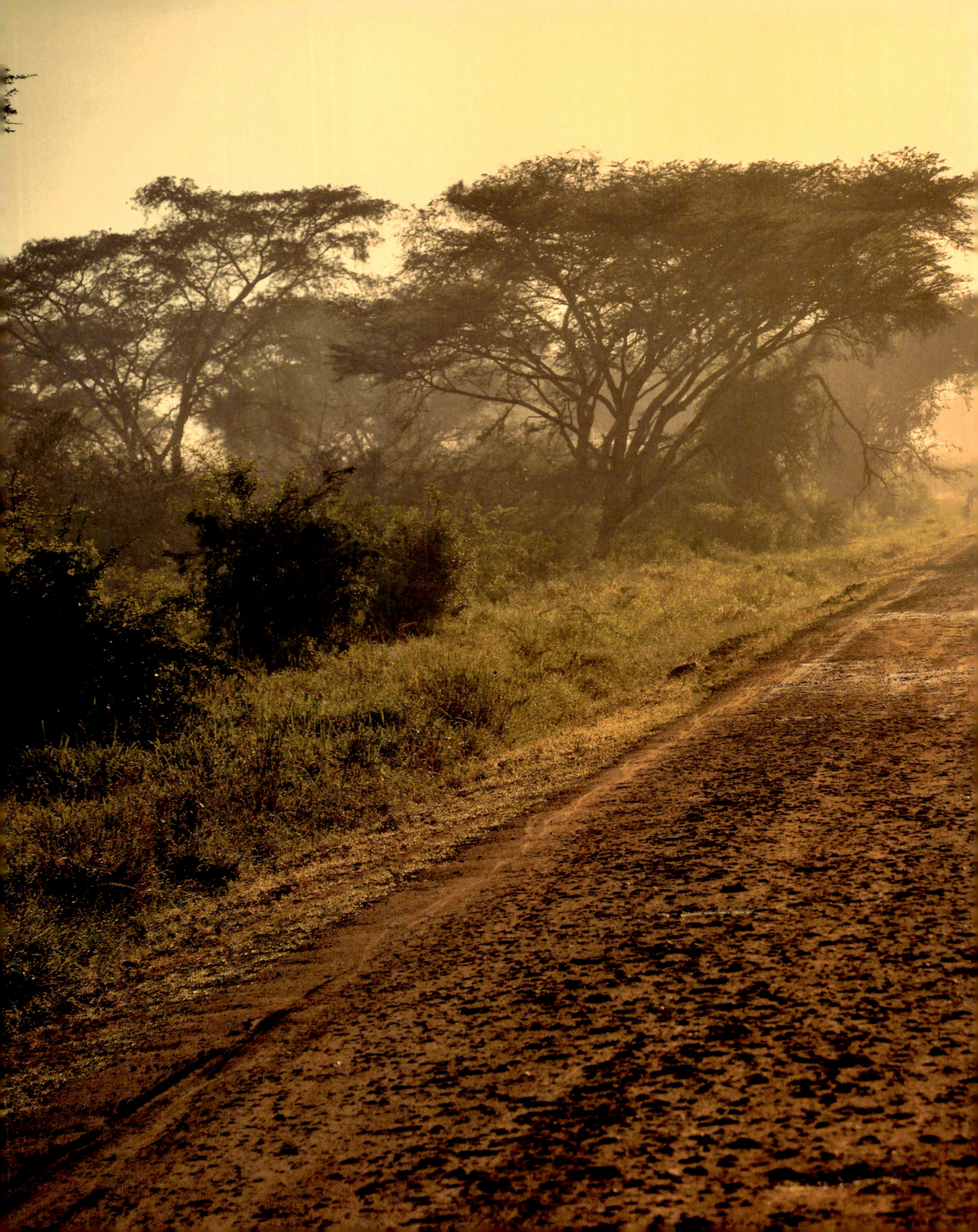

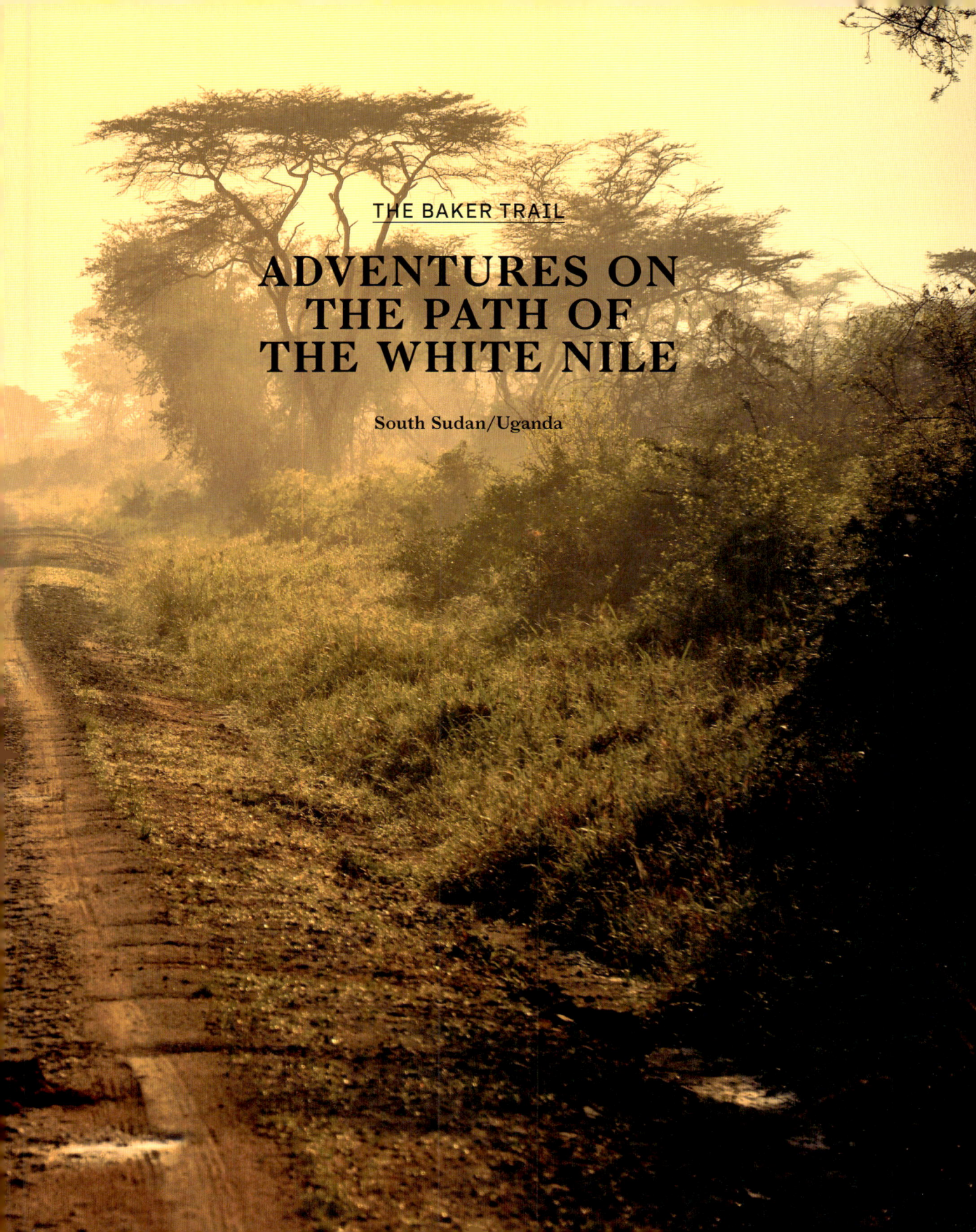

THE BAKER TRAIL

ADVENTURES ON
THE PATH OF
THE WHITE NILE

South Sudan/Uganda

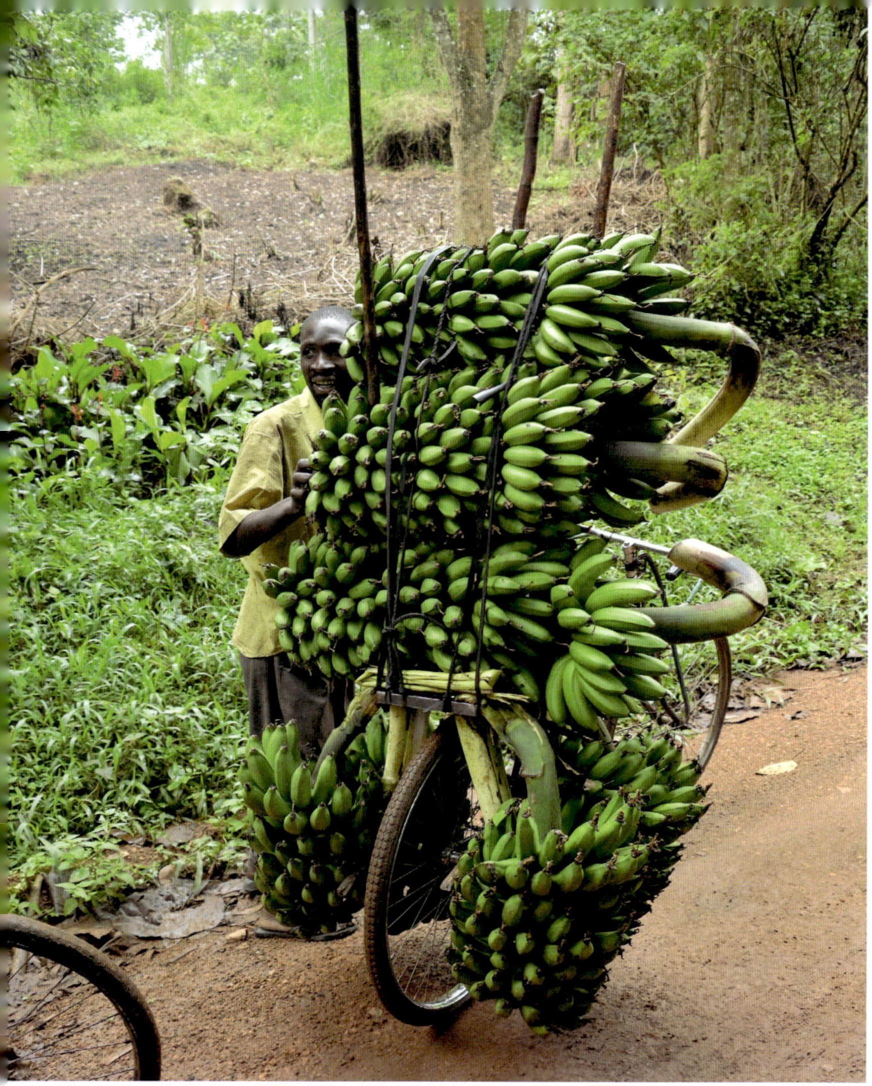

as some years before Sir Samuel had rescued the 17-year-old Florence from a slave market in the Ottoman Empire.

The modern-day trail retraces the footsteps of the couple's African expeditions, and was the brainchild of explorer and anthropologist Julian Monroe Fisher. Working in cooperation with both Ugandan and South Sudanese government agencies, Fisher established the walk with the aim of shining a positive spotlight on a long-troubled region, or to use his own words: "Expressing to the world that northern Uganda and South Sudan are open for business."

Beginning near Juba, the capital of South Sudan, the Baker Trail follows Sir Samuel and Lady Florence's routes along the White Nile (one of the Nile's tributaries) into Uganda. On the way it passes through villages rarely visited by westerners; historical sites such as Fort Patiko, the remains of a fort set up by the Bakers in 1872; and arguably the high point of the trail, the magnificent Murchison Falls National Park.

Spanning almost 4,000 km², Murchison is Uganda's largest park and boasts an incredible array of fauna and flora. Hippos, lions, giraffes, chimpanzees, and Uganda's biggest population of crocodiles all populate the area. In total there are some 76 types of mammals and more than 450 species of birds. The park is named after Murchison Falls, the towering cascade of roaring water which is situated on the White Nile between Lake Kyoga and Lake Albert, and which was named by Baker for the British geologist Sir Roderick Murchison. The waterfall's violent force is gathered as the river rapids narrow to a width of 6 m (20 ft.), before the water plunges dramatically over a three-tiered falls into a foaming whirlpool below. →

→ The thundering waters of Murchison Falls, Uganda.
↓ Lush vegetation around the Nile.

E stablished in 2014, the Baker Historical Trail stretches some 805 km (500 mi.) between the young nation of South Sudan, which only gained independence in 2011, and Uganda. The trail is named after Sir Samuel and Lady Florence Baker, a venturesome couple who conducted two expeditions into Central Africa in the 1860s and 1870s.

The Bakers' trips were both exploratory—in the 1860s they searched for the source of the River Nile as part of one of the great scientific quests of the time—and altruistic in nature—in the 1870s they were commissioned by the Viceroy of Egypt to help expand exploration and to work against the slave trade in the region. The latter issue was very close to both of their hearts,

ABOUT THE TRAIL

→ DISTANCE 805 km (500 mi.)
→ DURATION 30 to 40 days
→ LEVEL Moderate to Difficult

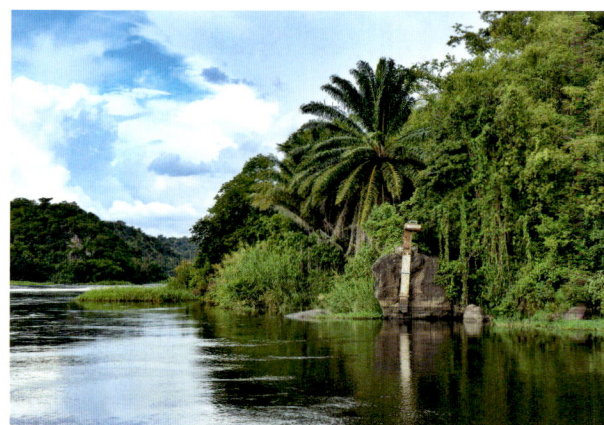

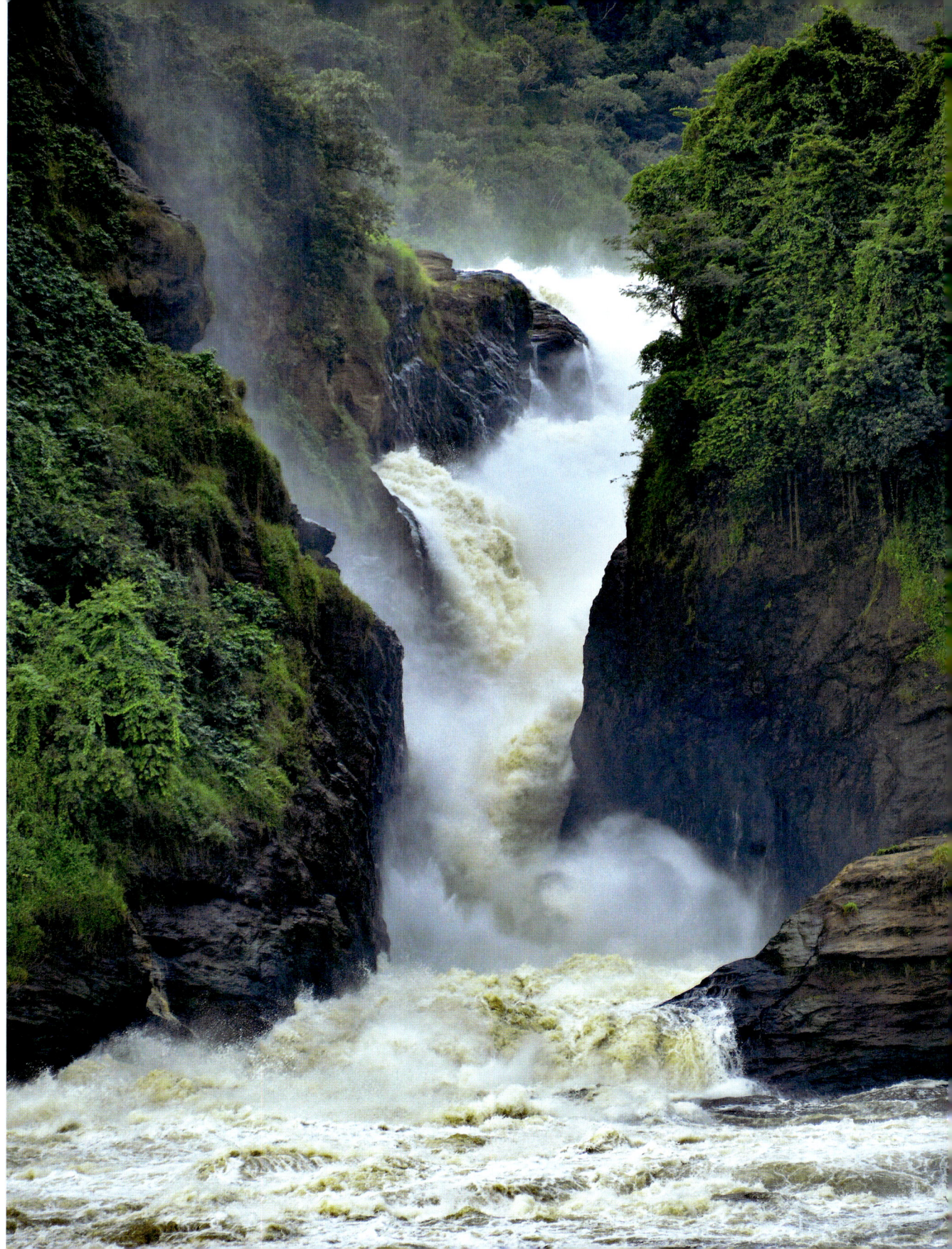

Throughout its path, the Baker Historical Trail connects 15 separate locations used by the husband and wife for camping during their expeditions. Each of these spots is marked by a sign providing meticulously researched information about the Bakers' trips. The hike's southern terminus is Baker's View. In 1864, this was the place where Sir Samuel and Lady Florence became the first westerners to lay eyes upon Lake Albert; Samuel subsequently named it in honor of Queen Victoria's deceased husband. The expanse of water that supplies the White Nile makes the ideal finishing point to a trek through a region once explored by a pair of courageous adventurers looking for the source of the longest river in the world.

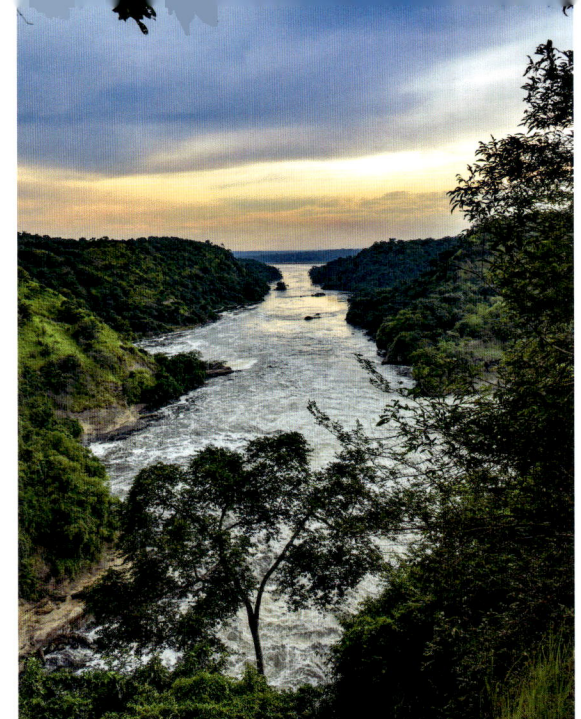

↑ Looking over the Nile from top of Murchison Falls.
↓ Life on the road in Uganda.

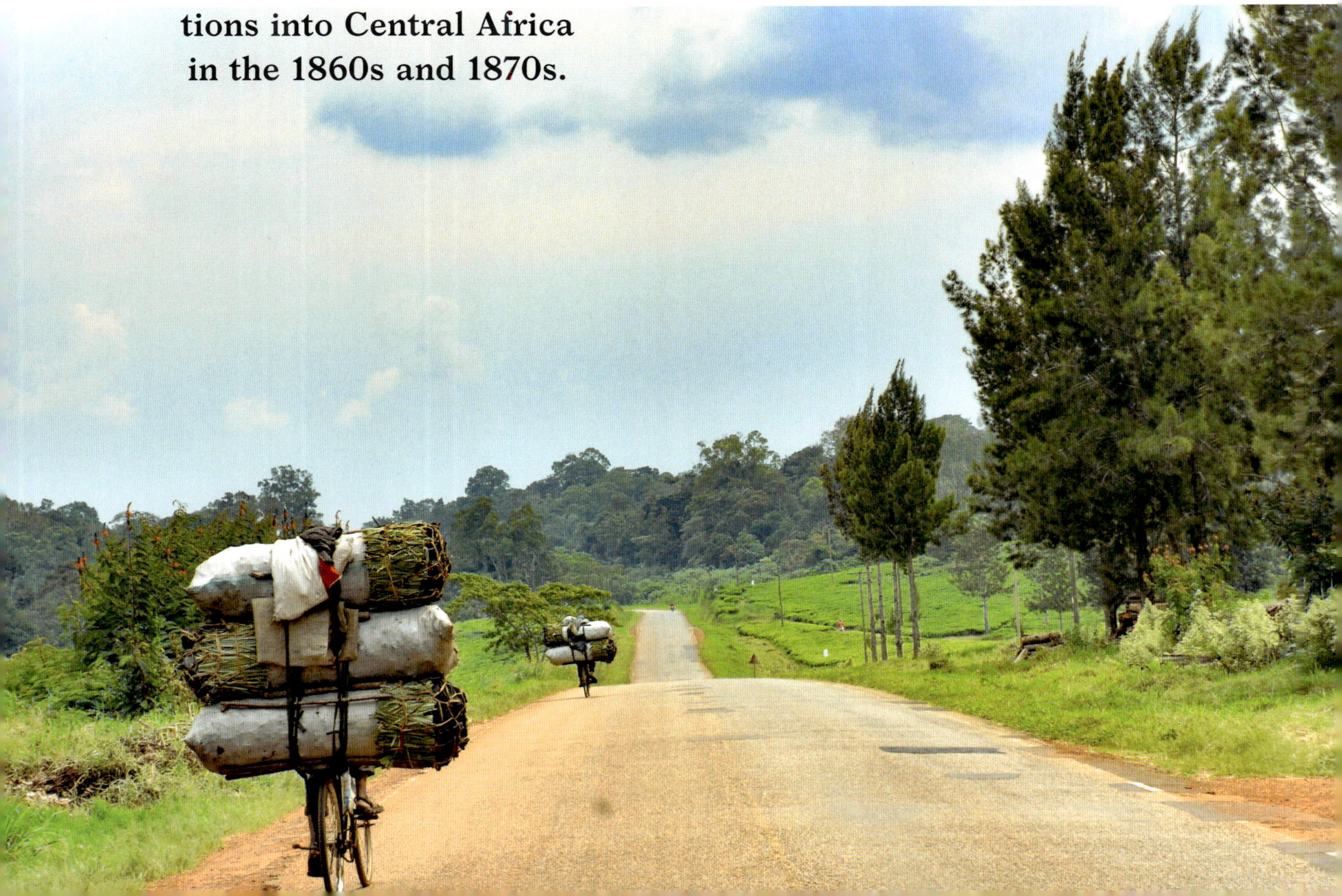

The trail is named after Sir Samuel and Lady Florence Baker, a venturesome couple who conducted two expeditions into Central Africa in the 1860s and 1870s.

GOOD TO KNOW

START/FINISH
📍 Gondokoro, South Sudan
📍 Lake Albert, Uganda

SEASON
January and February, and from June to September

TIP
The majority of the trail is situated in Uganda, which is considered to be relatively safe for hikers and offers plenty of scope for exploration. However, South Sudan has been politically unstable, so it is best to check before traveling.

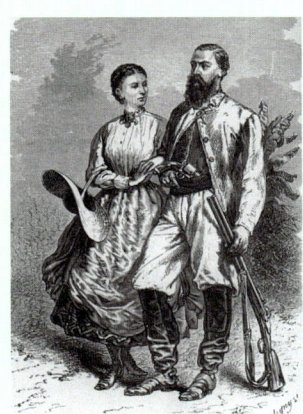

BACKGROUND

THE BAKERS Sir Samuel White Baker was a wealthy English explorer who lived from 1821 to 1893. After residing in diverse places including Mauritius and Ceylon (now Sri Lanka) and journeying through the Middle East, Baker traveled to Africa with Florence von Szasz in 1861. Von Szasz, who was born in Eastern Europe in 1841, was saved from an Ottoman slave market by Baker in 1859. The couple's journey to the Sudan-Ethiopia border was made to investigate the tributaries of the Nile River, and in 1863 they searched for the source of the waterway. They were married in Britain in 1865. A later trip to Africa in the early 1870s was focused on abolishing the Nile slave trade.

FLORA & FAUNA

WILDLIFE A diverse range of wildlife visits the waters near the bottom of Murchison Falls: white hippos, buffaloes, giraffes, elephants, crocodiles, and many others. Despite the killing of lots of animals from the 1960s onwards, the numbers are today recovering—though they are not what they once were.

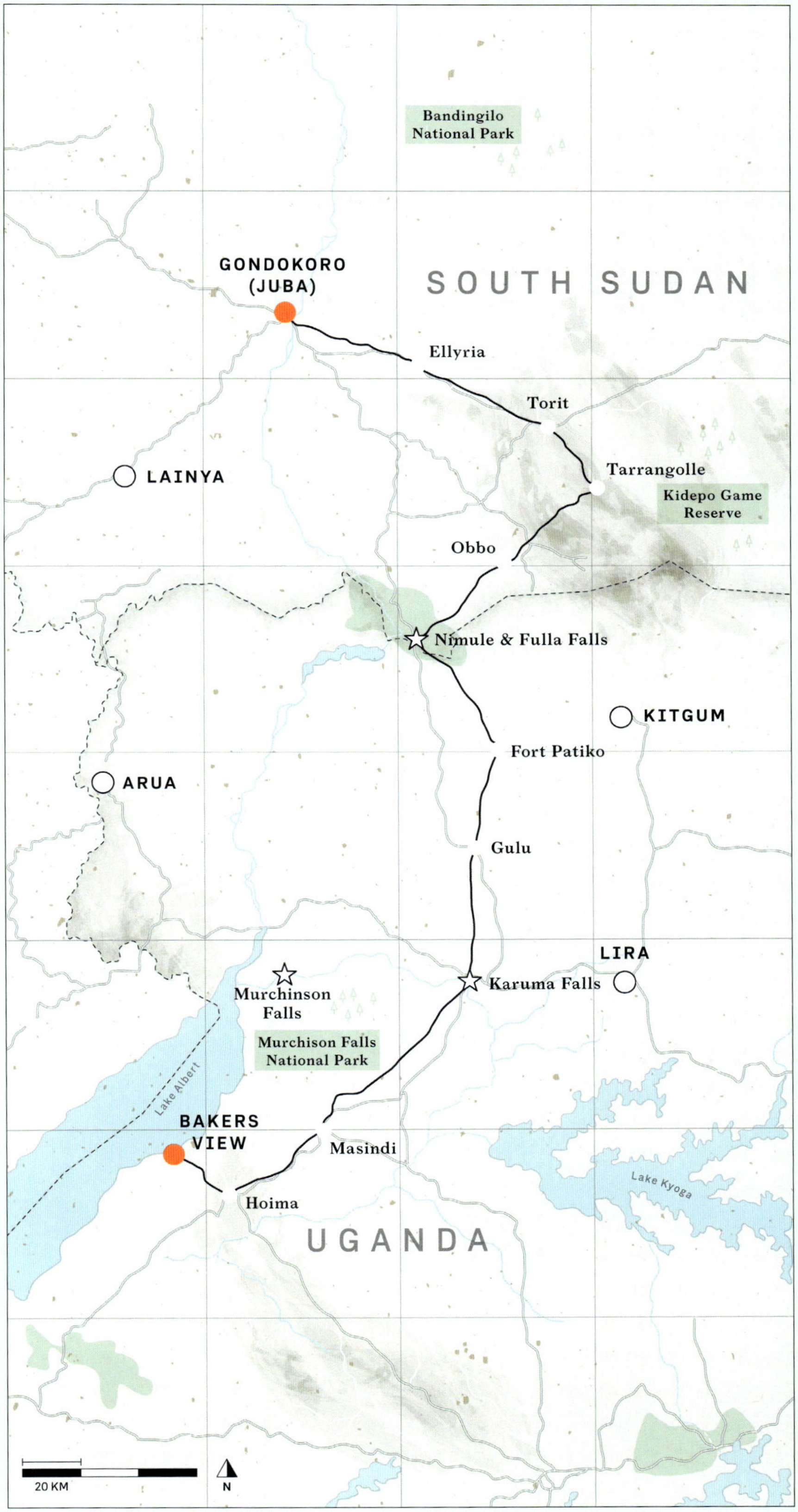

SOUTH SUDAN

Bandingilo National Park

GONDOKORO (JUBA)

Ellyria

Torit

Tarrangolle

Kidepo Game Reserve

LAINYA

Obbo

Nimule & Fulla Falls

KITGUM

Fort Patiko

ARUA

Gulu

LIRA

Karuma Falls

Murchinson Falls

Murchison Falls National Park

BAKERS VIEW

Masindi

Lake Kyoga

Hoima

Lake Albert

UGANDA

20 KM

N

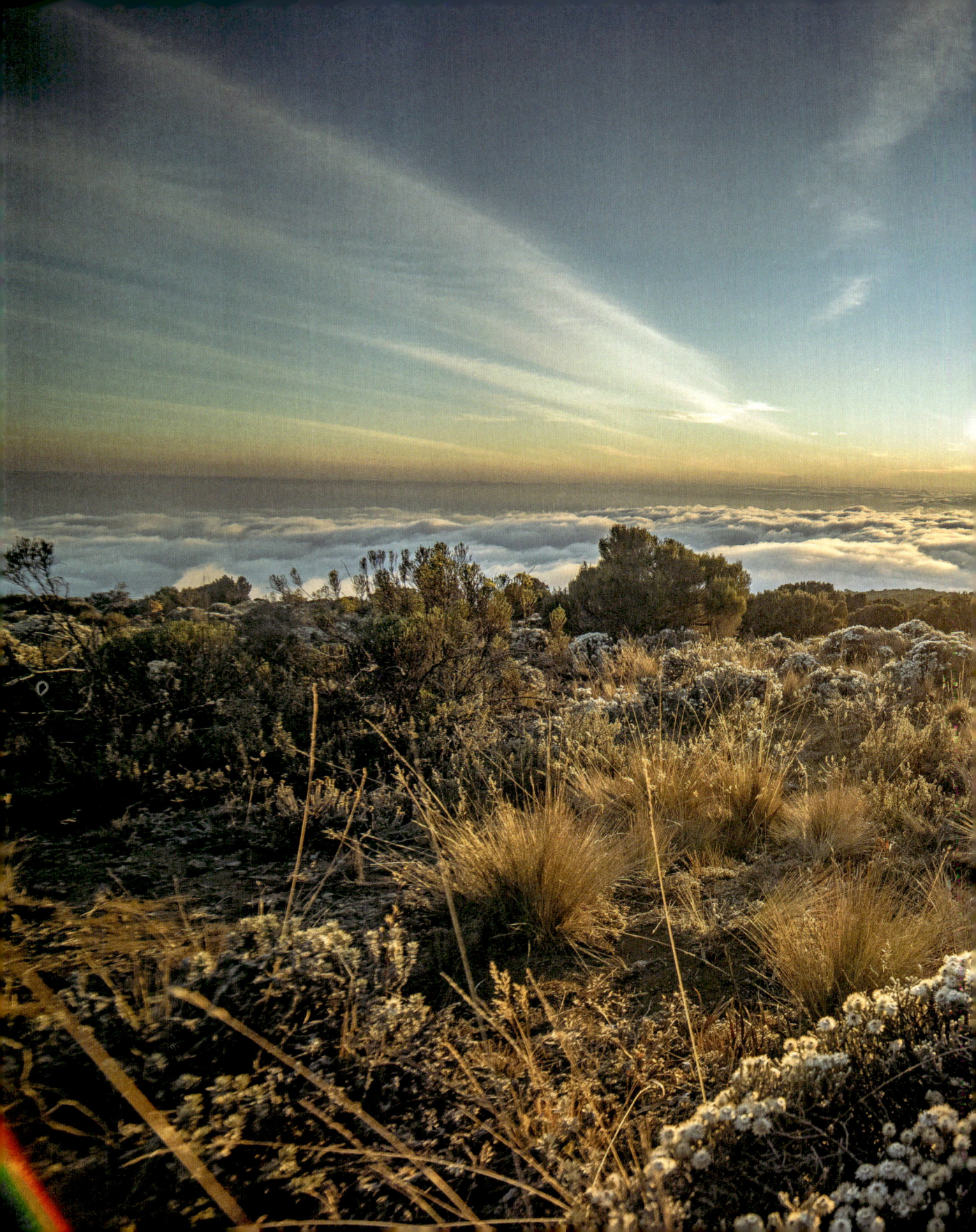

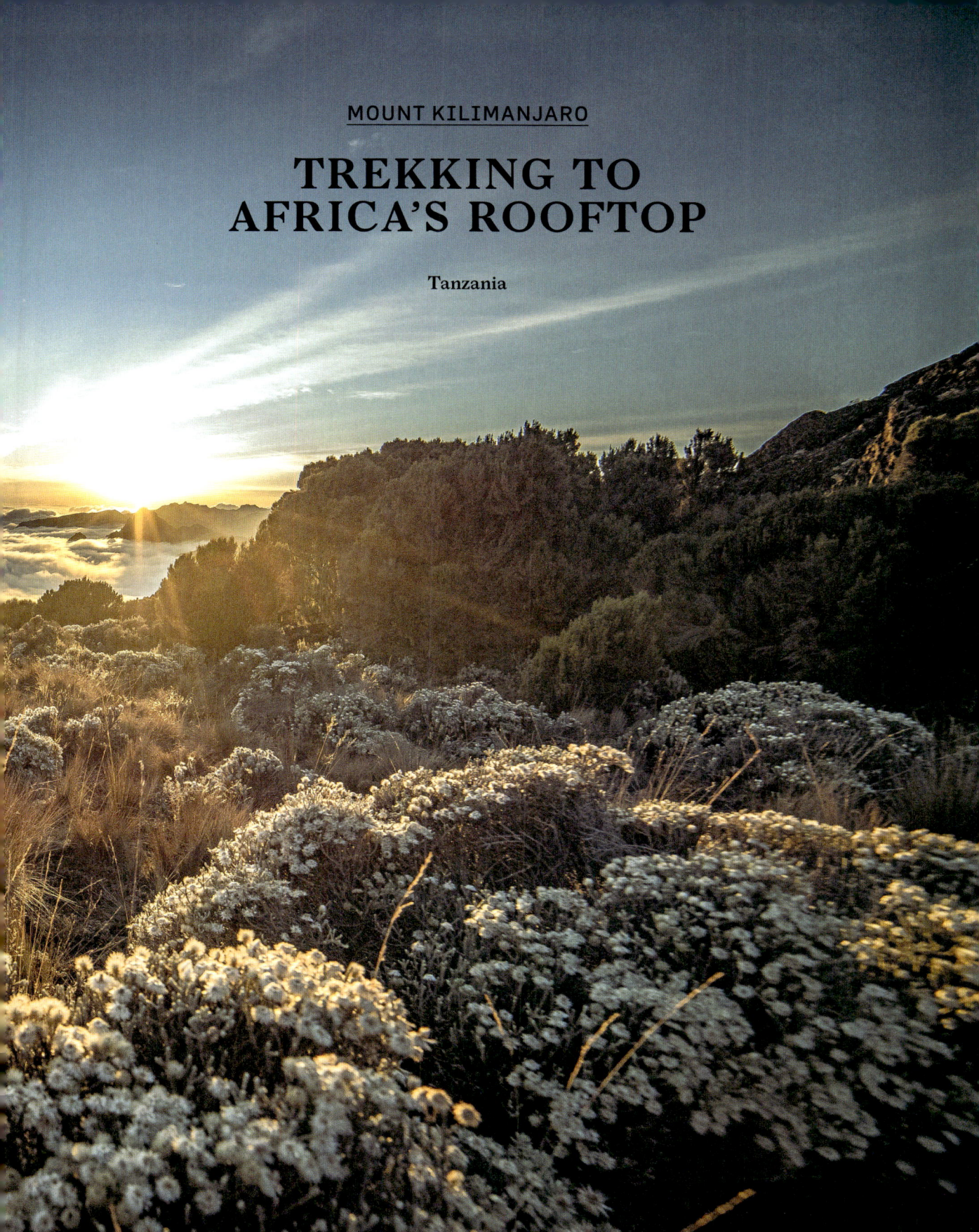

MOUNT KILIMANJARO

TREKKING TO AFRICA'S ROOFTOP

Tanzania

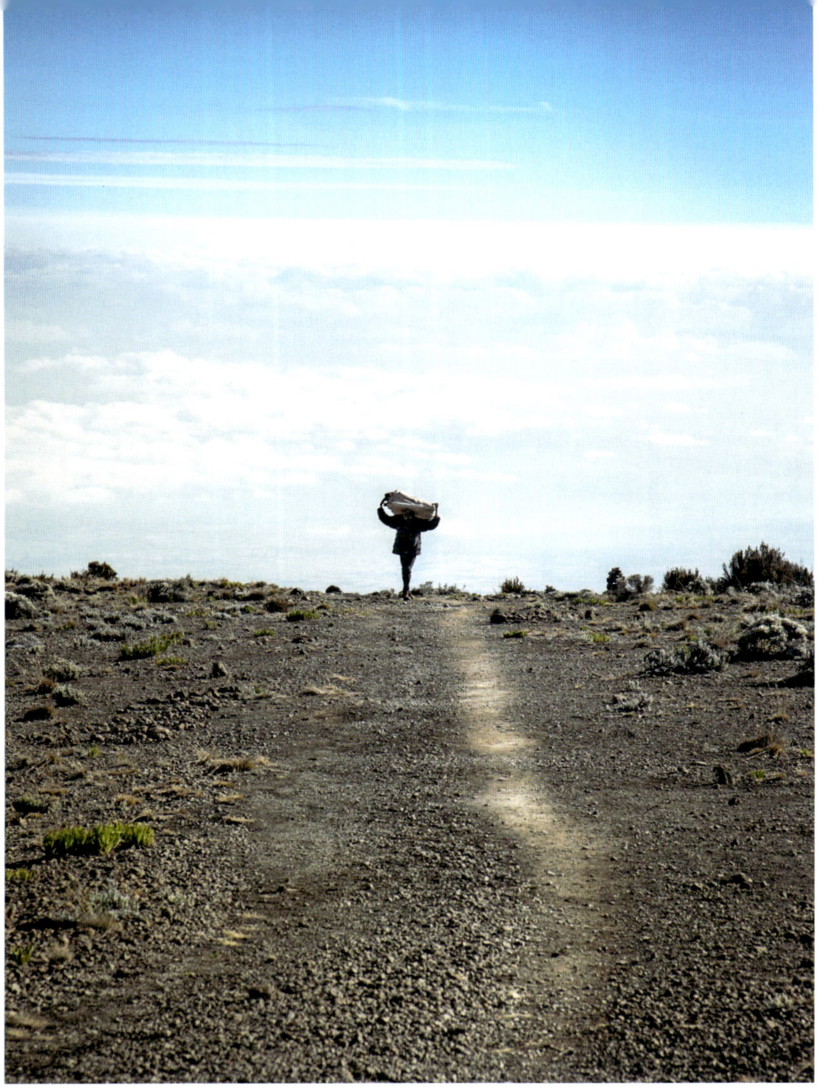

Mount Kilimanjaro has long been wrapped in myths and legends, and climbing to its tri-coned summit is a bucket-list experience for many trekkers around the globe.

vary considerably in regards to scenery, difficulty, length, traffic, cost, and remoteness. One option that provides an appealing balance between the many variables is the Lemosho Route. Beginning at Londorossi Gate on the western side of the mountain, the Lemosho is a relatively new and uncrowded route that has a high summit-success rate. It is one of the more expensive options; however, the combination of beautiful scenery and an acclimatization-friendly gradient makes it the route of choice for many Kilimanjaro veterans. After reaching the top—Uhuru Peak on Kibo—the descent is via the Mweka Route. This scree-laden, rocky path is the shortest to and from the summit, but is today only used on the descent from the cratered dome.

Whichever trail walkers choose, perhaps the main constant on a Kilimanjaro trek is that of change. During the course of an ascent, hikers pass through distinct climatic zones that provide an incredible array of flora. The Lemosho Route begins in the lush greenery of the rainforest, where birdlife is abundant and black-and-white colobus monkeys can often be spotted. →

Made up of three inactive volcanoes (Mawenzi, Kibo, and Shira), and with an icy crown that towers over the sunburnt savannah, Mount Kilimanjaro has a distinctive shape. The highest peak in Africa stands at 5,895 m (19,340 ft.) and is situated in northeast Tanzania, roughly 300 km (186 mi.) south of the equator. It has long been wrapped in myths and legends, and climbing to its tri-coned summit is a bucket-list experience for many trekkers around the globe.

Ascending Kilimanjaro does not require any special equipment or technical skills, but aspirants should have a high level of fitness and determination mixed in with a solid acclimatization approach. There are several routes to the summit that can

↗ Celebrating at the summit of Kibo.
→ Stargazing at Barranco Camp with Kilimanjaro's peak just behind.
↓ En route to Shira Camp.

ABOUT THE TRAIL

→ <u>DISTANCE</u> 70 km (44 mi.)
→ <u>DURATION</u> 7 to 8 days
→ <u>LEVEL</u> Moderate to Difficult

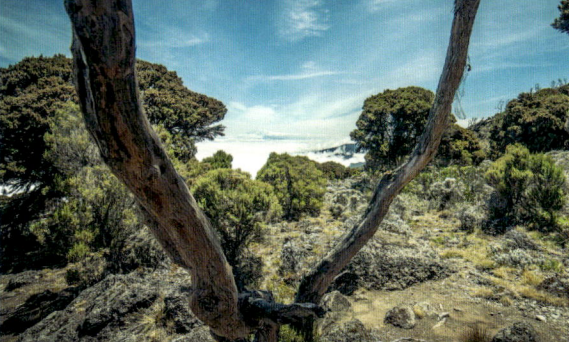

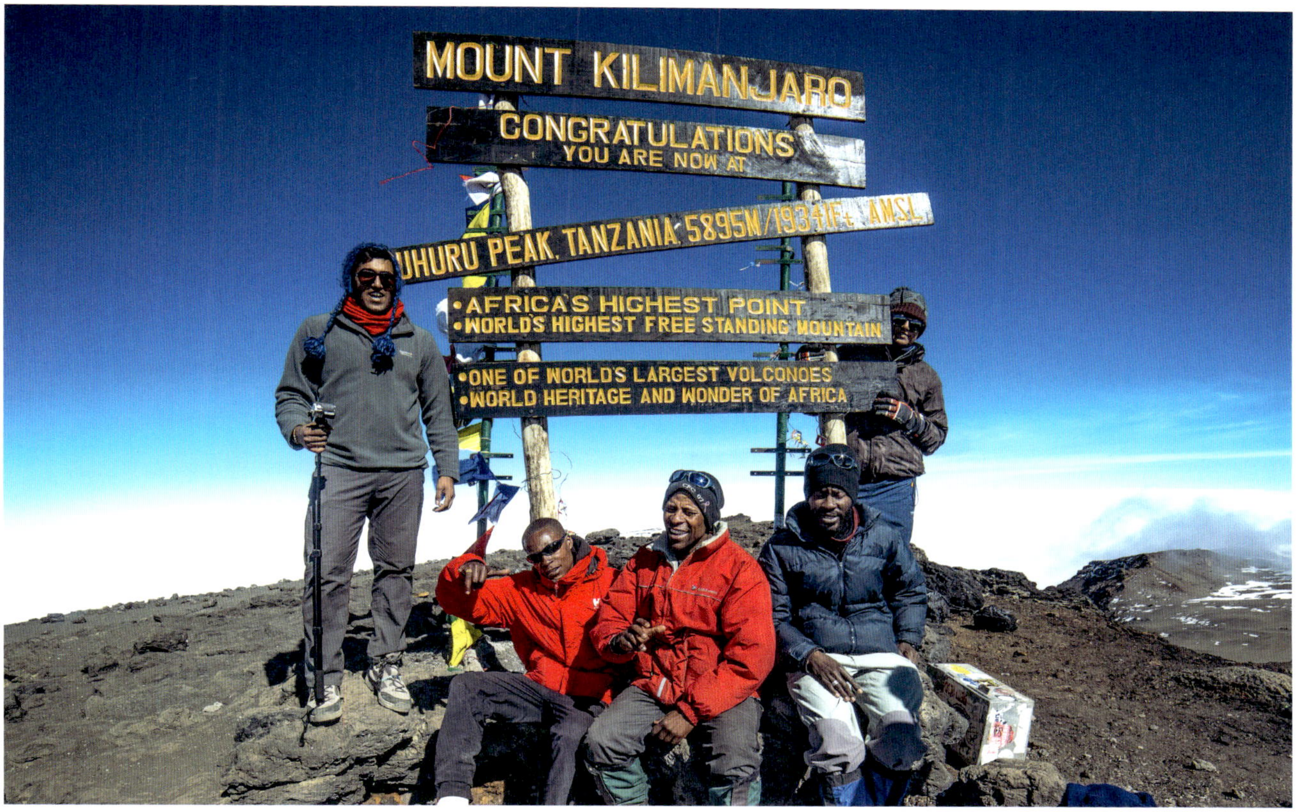
MOUNT KILIMANJARO
CONGRATULATIONS
YOU ARE NOW AT
UHURU PEAK, TANZANIA 5895M/19341Ft. AMSL
• AFRICA'S HIGHEST POINT
• WORLDS HIGHEST FREE STANDING MOUNTAIN
• ONE OF WORLD'S LARGEST VOLCANOES
• WORLD HERITAGE AND WONDER OF AFRICA

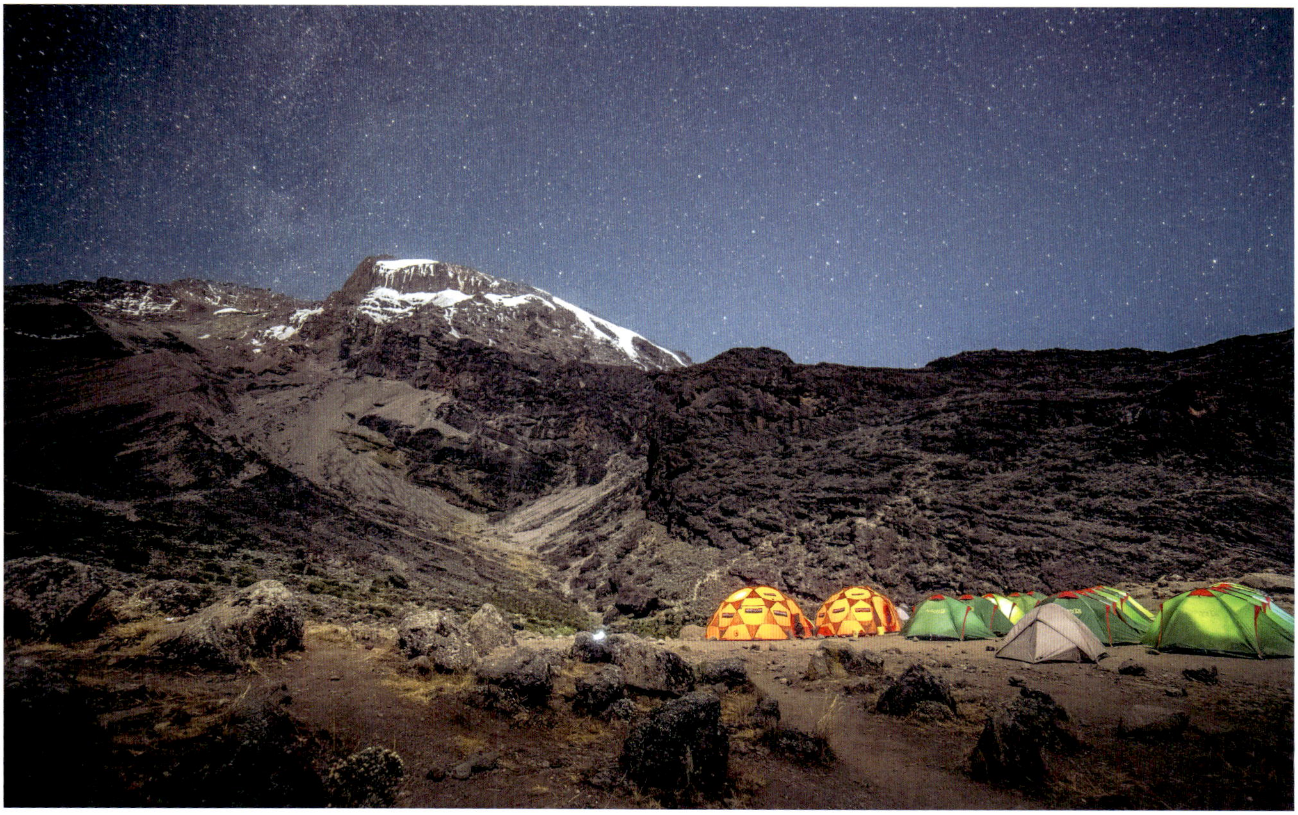

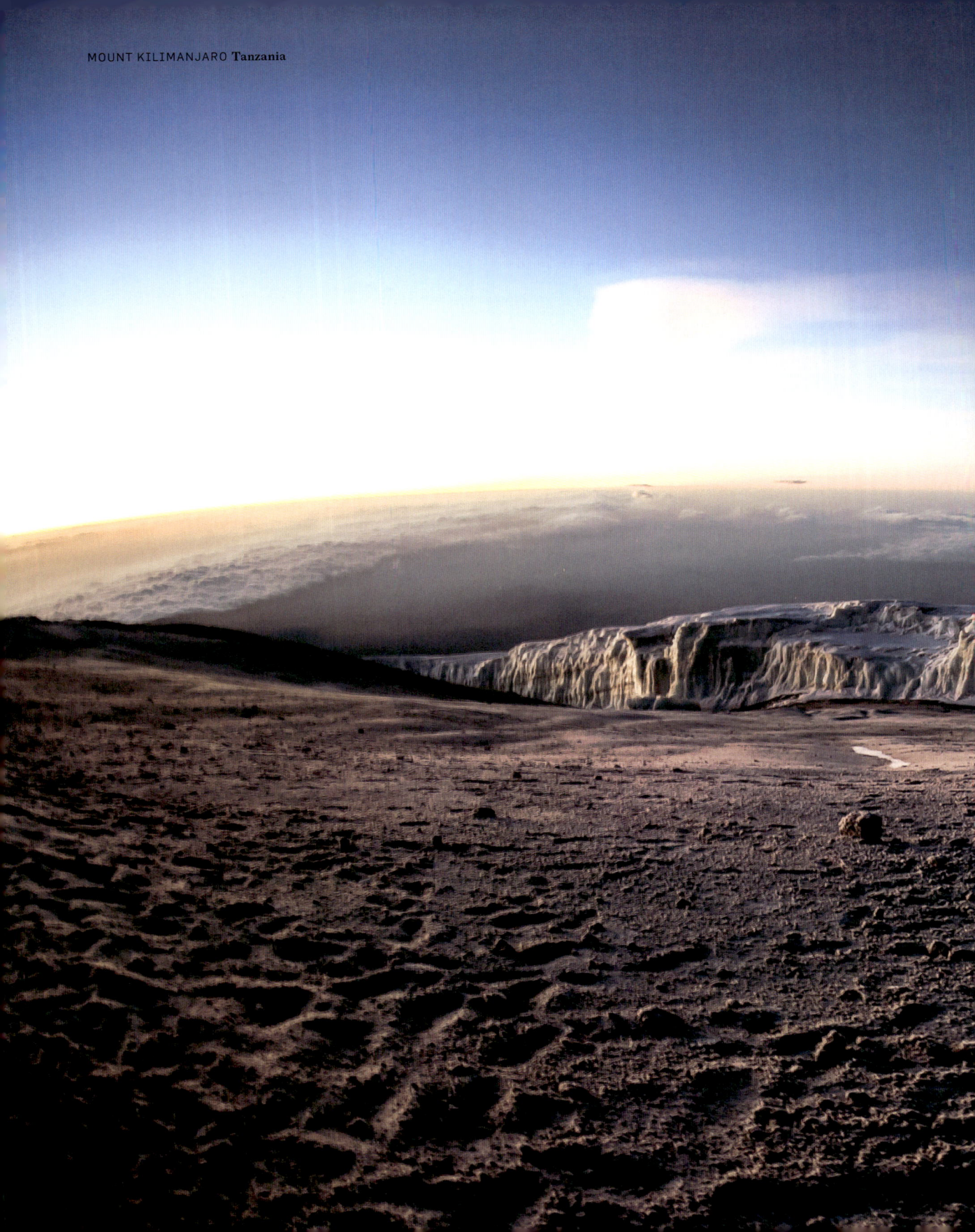

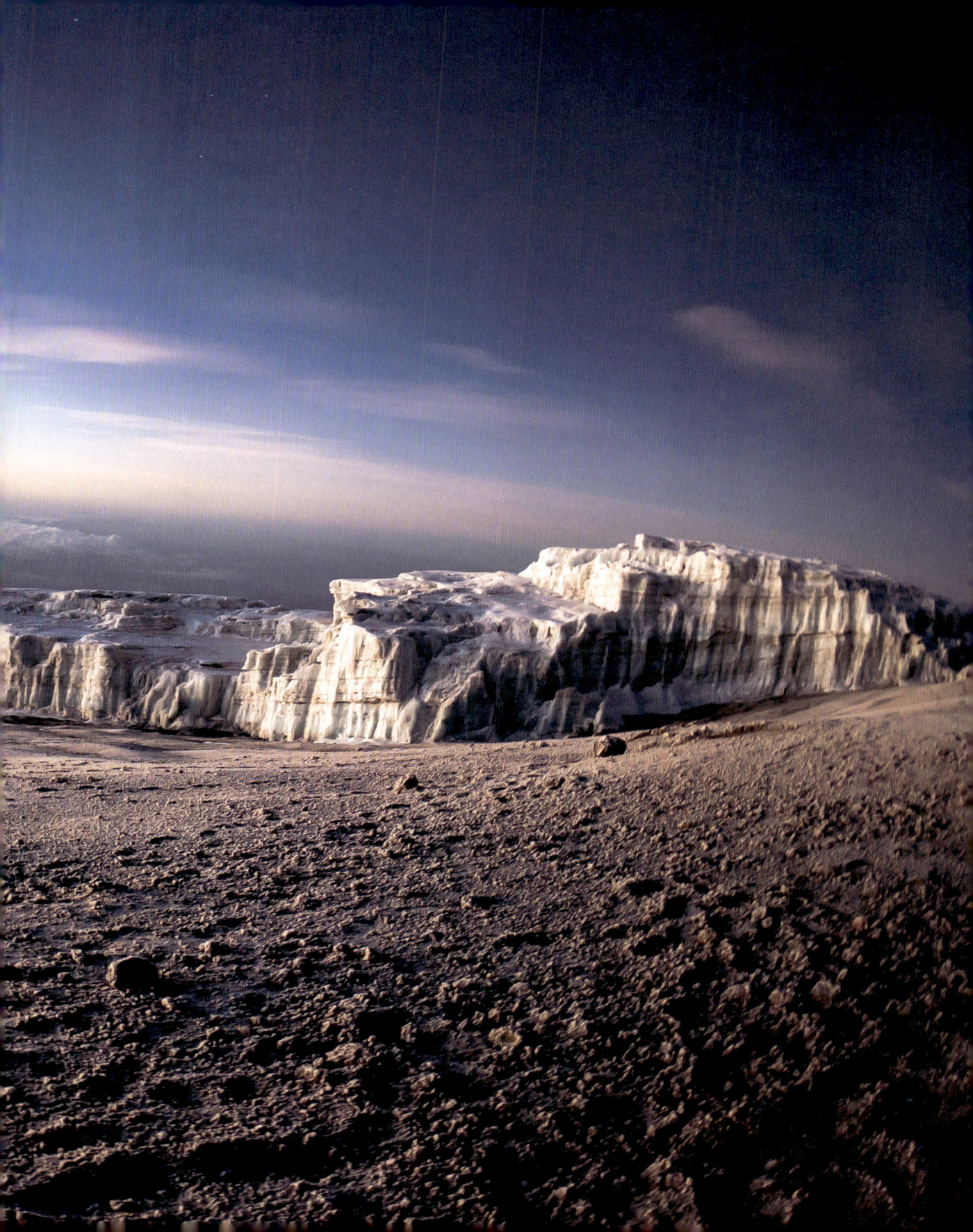

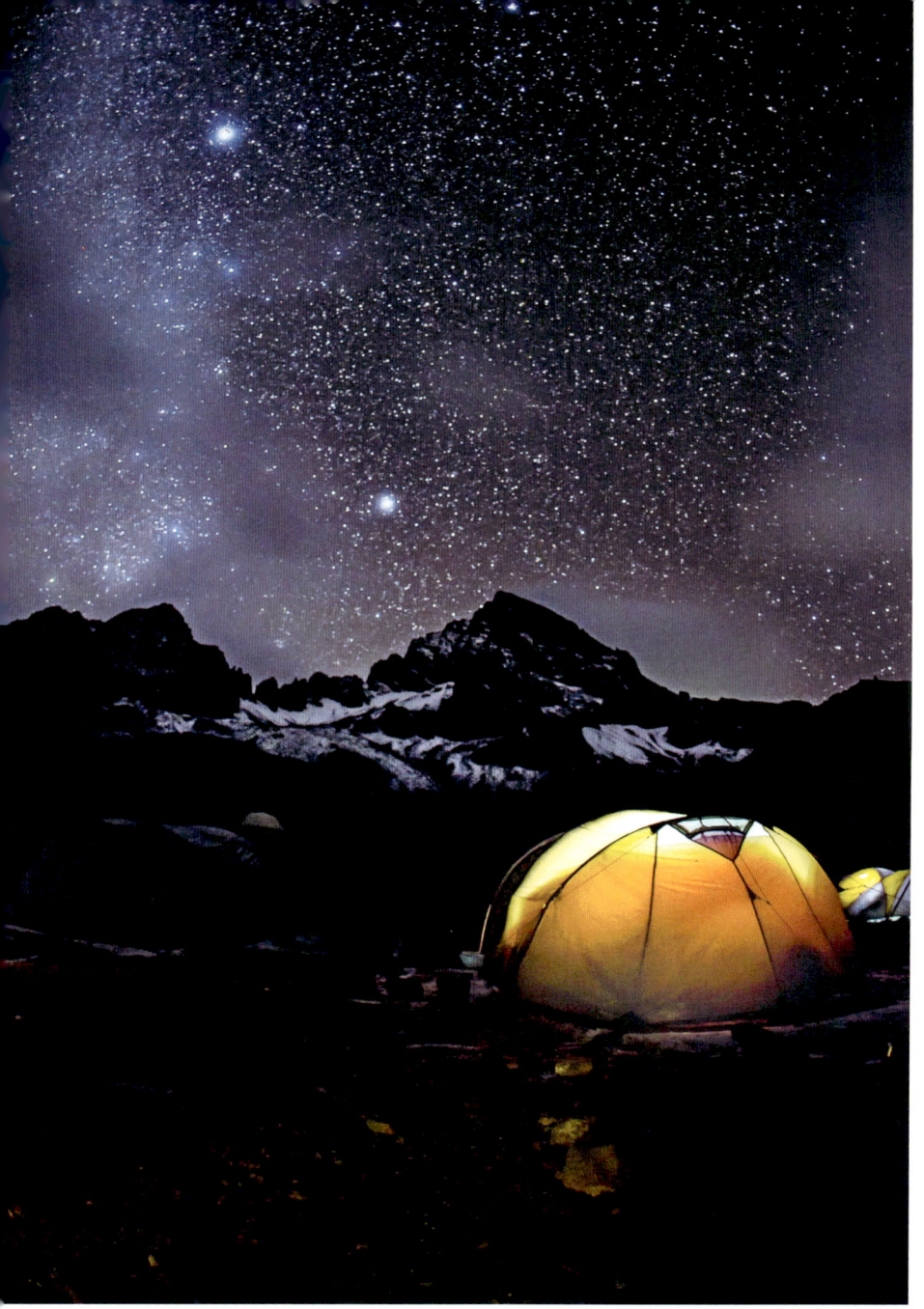

From the lush vegetation and warm climes at the outset to the cold, desolate summit is a long way.

lush vegetation and warm climes at the outset to the cold, desolate summit is a long way.

In order to manage this lengthy and varied ascent, pace and acclimatization are key. Climbing too high too quickly is a recipe for altitude sickness. When choosing an agency, travelers will find it pays to go with one that has a high success rate for reaching the summit and that provides its clients plenty of time—at least seven days—to get used to the altitude. Short, fast, and cheap is not a good combination when it comes to Kilimanjaro. On the trail, hikers should drink lots of water and not worry if others are moving faster than they are. It is best to always think tortoise rather than hare—or pole, pole (slowly, slowly), as the local guides put it—and to remember that altitude sickness is far easier to prevent than it is to cure.

Although there are never any guarantees when it comes to high-altitude trekking, with the proper preparation the chances of making it to the summit in good shape are better than average. Once hikers are there—hopefully in time to catch the sun coming up—individuals can take a moment or two to look back over their journey. By any criteria, attaining the crest of the world's tallest freestanding mountain is a mammoth achievement. And while soaking in dawn's first light and gazing out at the plains below, individuals should not be surprised if they break out into a big grin and start to laugh. The rooftop of Africa tends to have that effect on people—that, or maybe it is mountain madness setting in due to the altitude. ————————

Next is the heather zone, a more open space that is drier than the forest, and where lichen drapes down from trees. Then there is the open moorland, which contains the giant groundsel, a tree-like plant from the same family as the common weed ragwort and giant lobelia. At the next level, the alpine desert, is a rocky and barren moonscape. Mosses and lichens can live up to about 4,570 m (15,000 ft.), but the arctic zone at the peak is a stark, white, and windswept area at freezing temperatures. From the

GOOD TO KNOW

START/FINISH
📍 Londorossi Gate (western side)
📍 Mweka Gate

SEASON
Year-round

CONDITIONS
Inclement weather is possible at any time of year. The best chance of fine conditions is during the "dry" seasons of mid-December to late February, and July to the end of October.

LOWEST/HIGHEST POINT
2,100 m (6,900 ft.)/5,895 m (19,341 ft.)

REGULATIONS
It is not possible to climb Kilimanjaro independently. Since 1991 it has been obligatory to go with an agency. These companies will handle all permits and logistics for the trek.

HIGHLIGHTS
The diverse ecosystems encountered along the route and sunrise at the summit.

TIP
Though it is possible to rent gear for the ascent, hikers are often better off bringing all essential items from home to be assured of quality and the correct fit.

BACKGROUND

MOUNTAIN LIFE A national park since 1973 and a UNESCO World Heritage Site—in the area from 1,829 m (6,000 ft.) to the summit—since the 1980s, Mount Kilimanjaro is today a protected location. Though it was first "discovered" in the West after being seen by German missionaries in the late 1840s, its lower slopes have been inhabited for over 2,000 years. On the south and east slopes, the Chaga people grow bananas on smaller farms or home gardens. In these areas, coffee and millet are cultivated and cattle are also raised. Tourism is a thriving industry, and with at least six main routes running up the mountain, there is something to suit hikers with varying abilities, budgets, and desires throughout the seasons. Each path showcases a slightly different side of the multifaceted mountain and must be walked with a skilled guide.

HELPFUL HINTS

MAKE INFORMED CHOICES The route and trekking companies that walkers choose will have a major impact on their experience. Everyone should do thorough research, consider what they want to gain from the climb, and remember that if a price seems too good to be true, it often is.

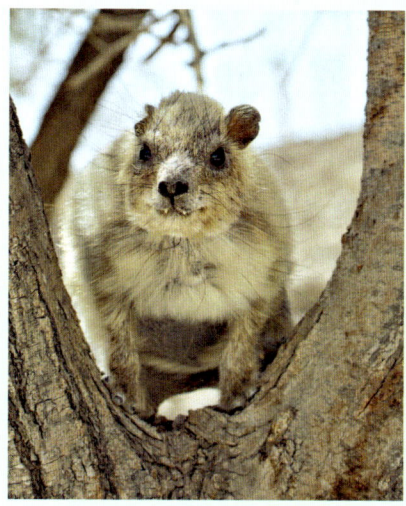

FLORA & FAUNA

TREE DWELLERS The eastern tree hyrax inhabits the forested parts of the southern and northern slopes of Kilimanjaro up to altitudes of around 3,000 m (9,843 ft.). The dark brown mammal with a yellow-orange underbelly is arboreal, so visitors are more likely to see signs of the creatures (deposits at the tree bases) rather than the animals themselves.

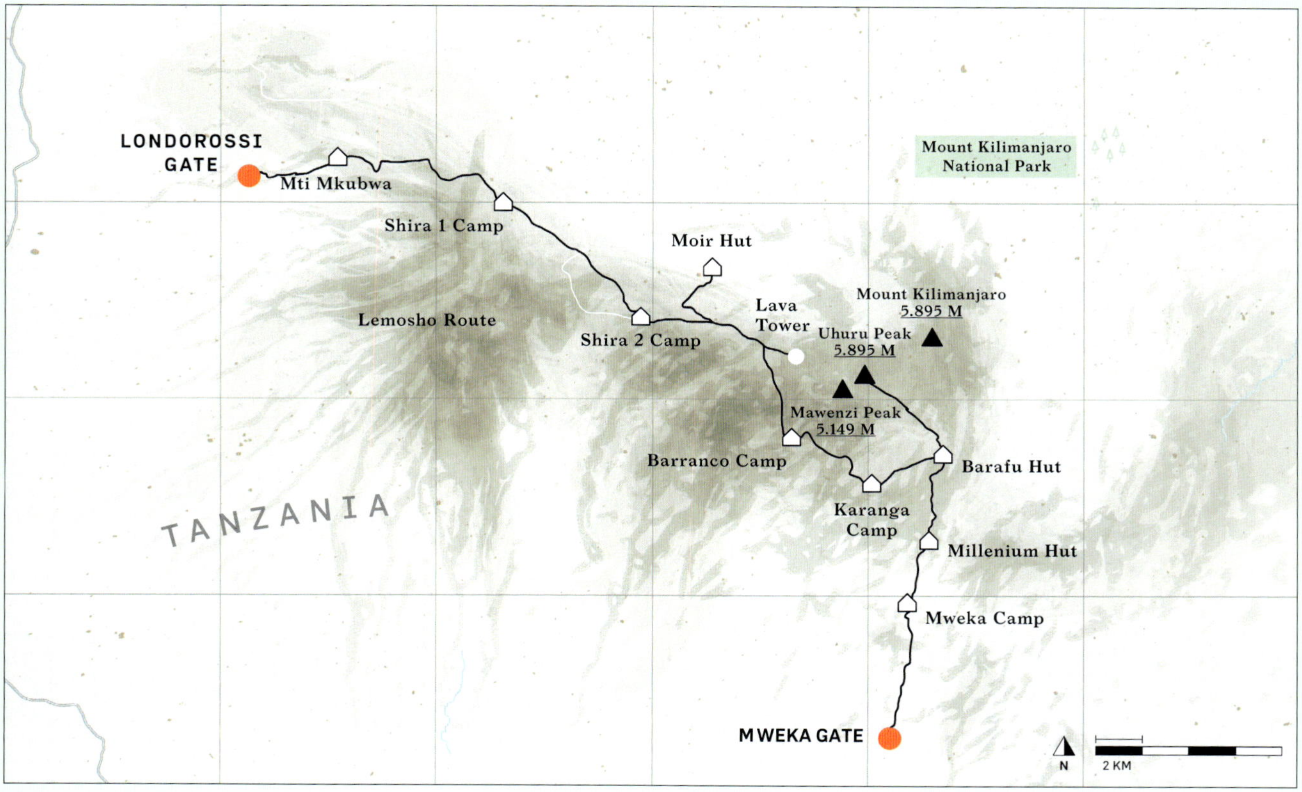

LONDOROSSI GATE

Mti Mkubwa

Shira 1 Camp

Moir Hut

Lemosho Route

Mount Kilimanjaro National Park

Shira 2 Camp

Lava Tower

Mount Kilimanjaro 5,895 M

Uhuru Peak 5,895 M

Mawenzi Peak 5,149 M

Barranco Camp

Barafu Hut

Karanga Camp

Millenium Hut

TANZANIA

Mweka Camp

MWEKA GATE

N

2 KM

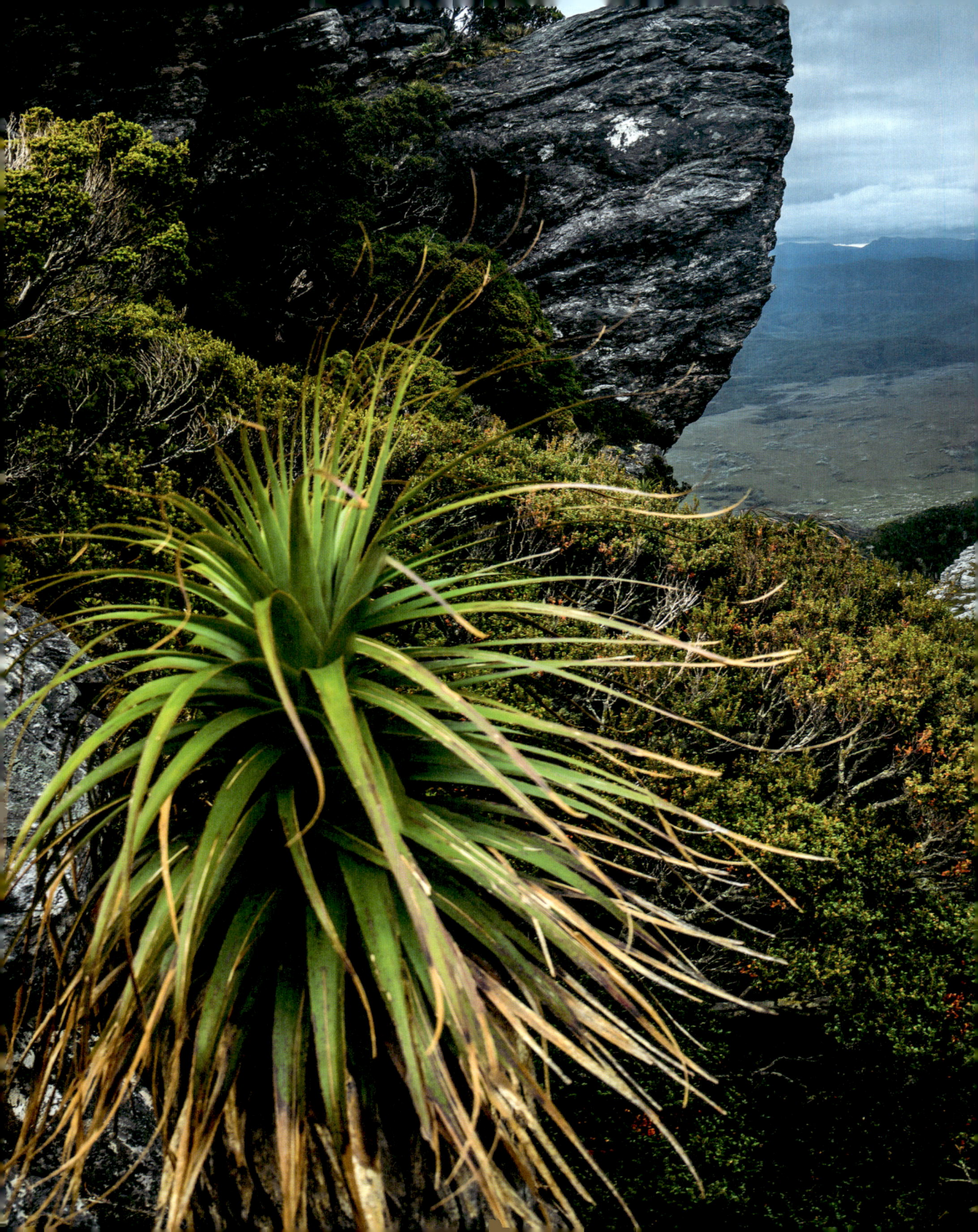

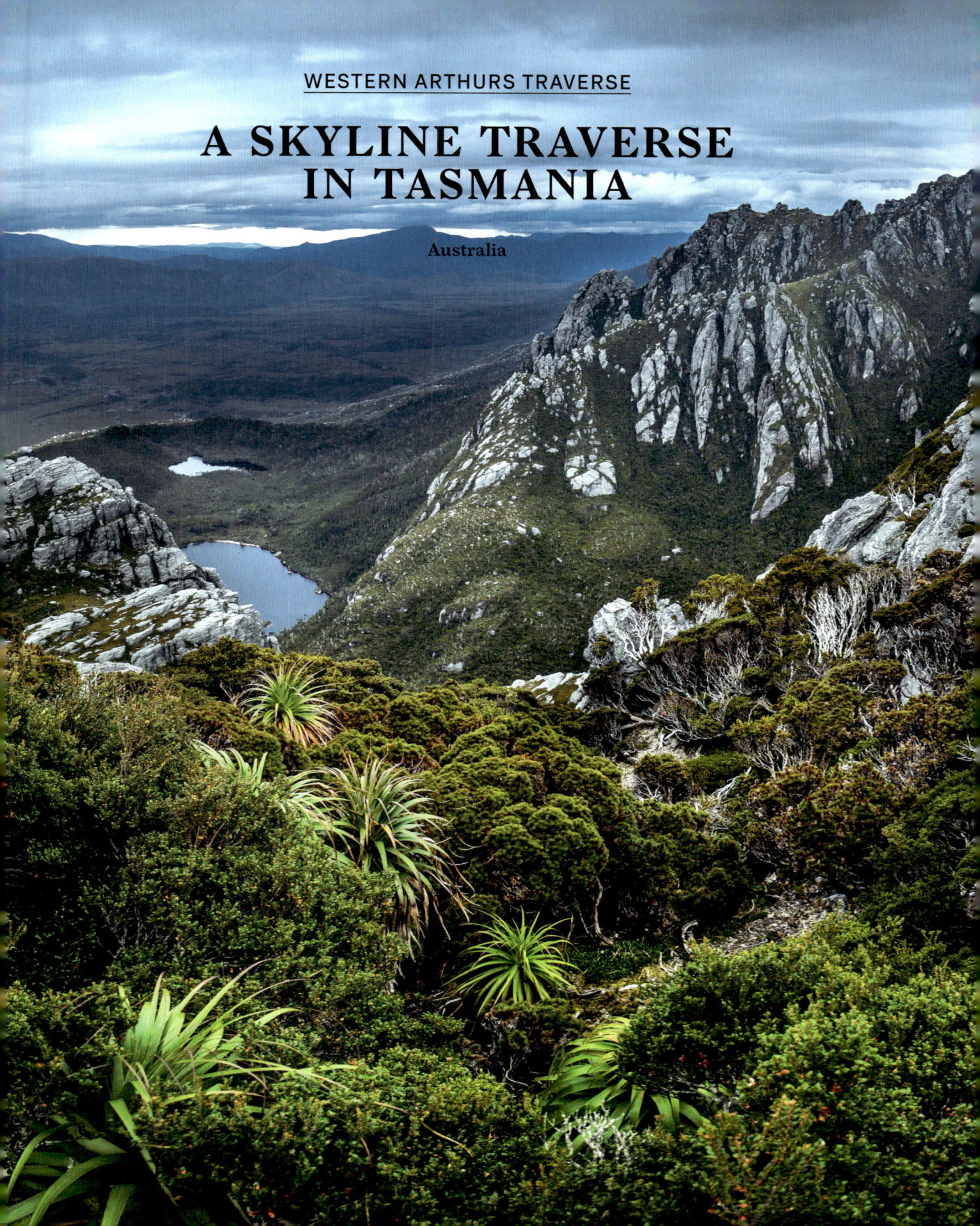

A SKYLINE TRAVERSE
IN TASMANIA

Australia

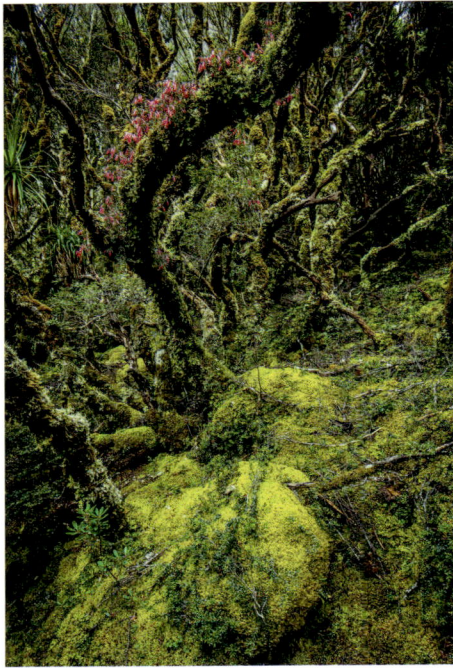

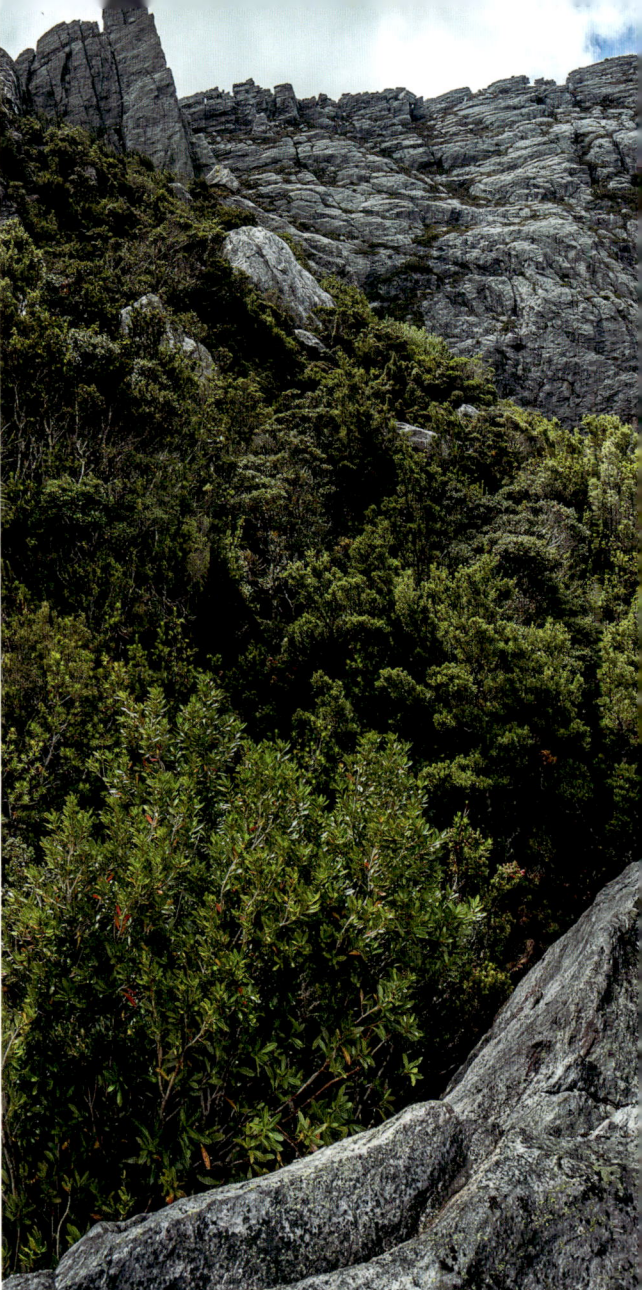

When most hikers think of walking in Tasmania, the first name that comes to mind is the Overland Track. This is a 65-km (40-mi.) five- or six-day hike through the state's beautiful Cradle Mountain-Lake St Clair National Park on a path that is well maintained, easily accessed by public transport, and within the capabilities of most hikers. However, the most spectacular mountain scenery on the island of Tasmania (and perhaps even in Australia) cannot be found on the Overland Track. To experience that, one has to venture down to the remote and rugged Arthur Range, situated in the state's Southwest National Park.

A relatively short and compact mountain chain, the Arthurs boast an impressive collection of jagged quartzite peaks, hanging valleys, glacier-carved lakes, and moraines (masses of rock debris left by glaciers). Approached from the north, the range rises dramatically out of the mud-laden buttongrass plains. Its serrated profile and sheer rock walls have given many a hiker pause for thought—with this generally running something along the lines of, "What have I gotten myself in for?"

ABOUT THE TRAIL

→ <u>DISTANCE</u> 75 km (47 mi.)
→ <u>DURATION</u> 8 to 10 days
→ <u>LEVEL</u> Very Difficult

The Western Arthurs Traverse is a hike of extreme contrasts. The opening and final segments are flat, boggy, and for the most part relatively easy. The middle section, which crosses the mountains' dramatic skyline, is rocky, precipitous, and anything but a walk in the park. During this section, the distances covered are relatively short, however, and due to the arduous nature of the terrain, the going is invariably slow (1 to 1.5 km [0.6 to 0.9 mi.] per hour). There are steep gullies, windswept ridges, and a

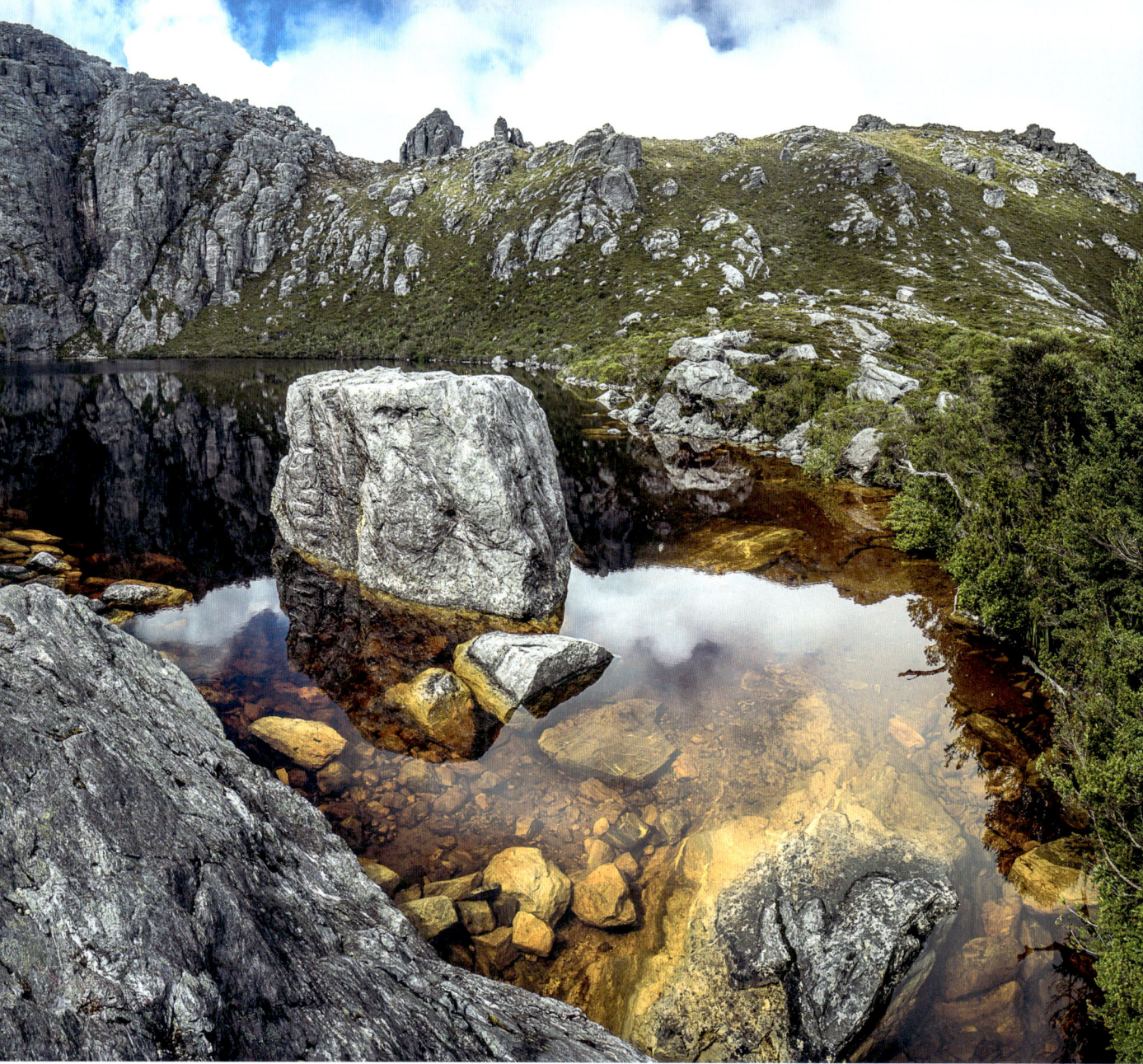

↖ Plant life in the subalpine rainforest.
↑ Surveying Square Lake's calm waters.

myriad of slippery down-climbs, meaning that this is certainly not a trail for vertigo sufferers.

Hiking in Tasmania's southwest wilderness cannot be described without making special mention of the weather. The Arthur Range plays host to some extremely wild, wet, and unpredictable conditions that commonly change multiple times over the course of a single day. Thanks in no small part to the Roaring Forties—gale-force westerly winds found in the Southern Hemisphere, typically between latitudes 40° and 50° south—backcountry trips in the Arthurs are a barometrical roll of the dice at any time of year. This, combined with the exposed nature of the ridge sections, means that the Western Arthurs Traverse is a trek that should only be attempted by experienced hikers who are equipped with gear that is made to withstand extreme conditions. The challenging nature of hiking in the Western Arthurs is somewhat mitigated by the regular campsites situated along its course: →

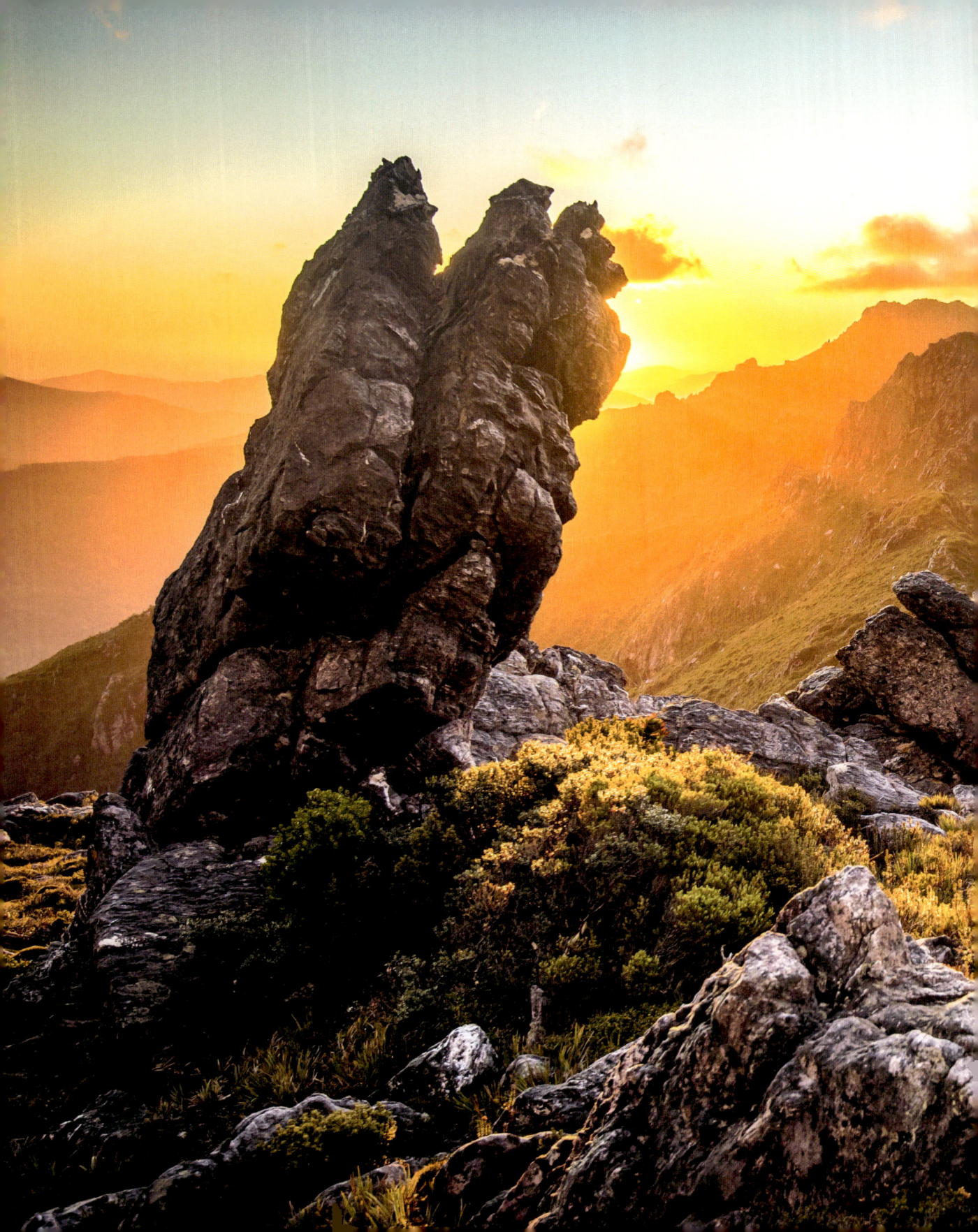

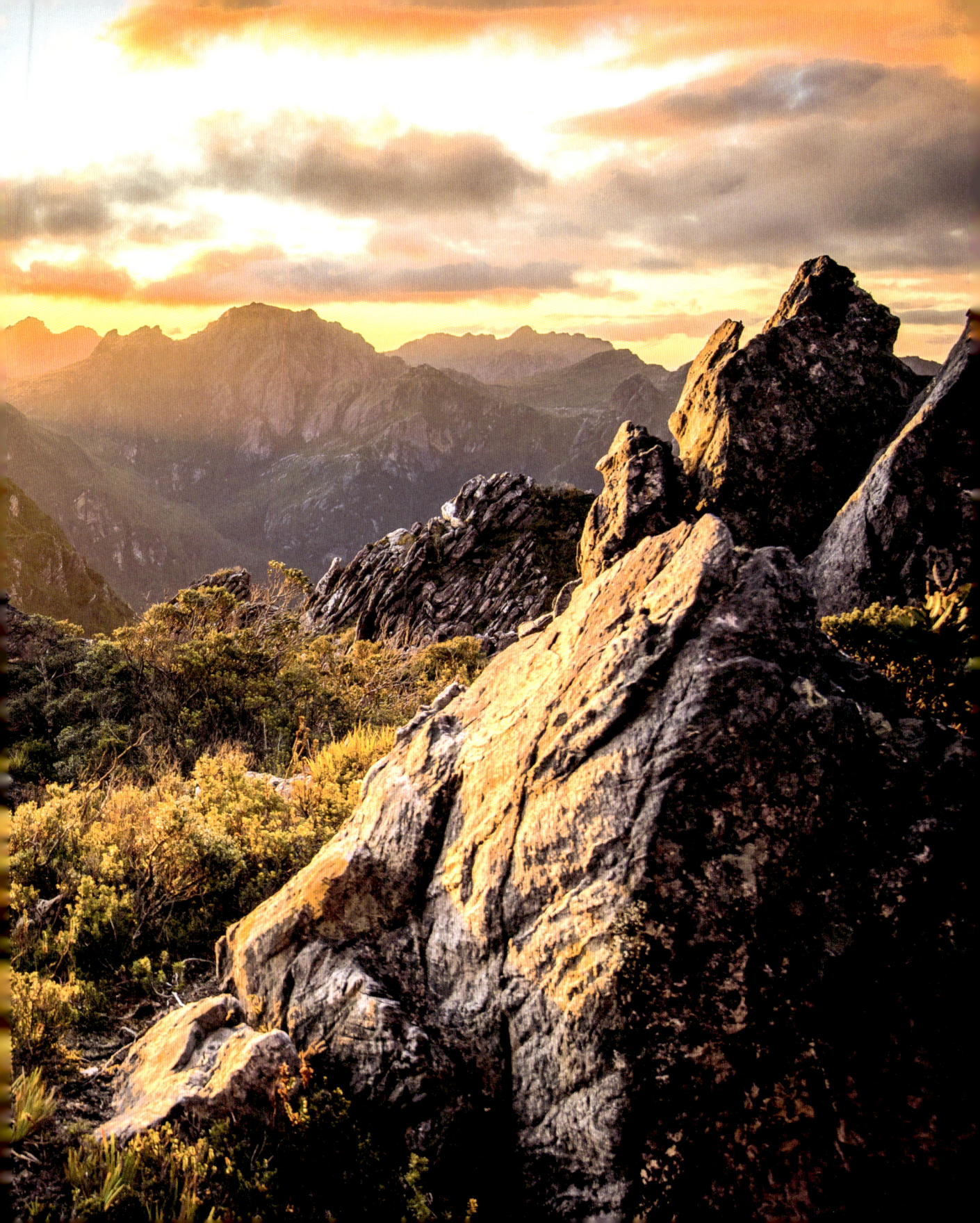

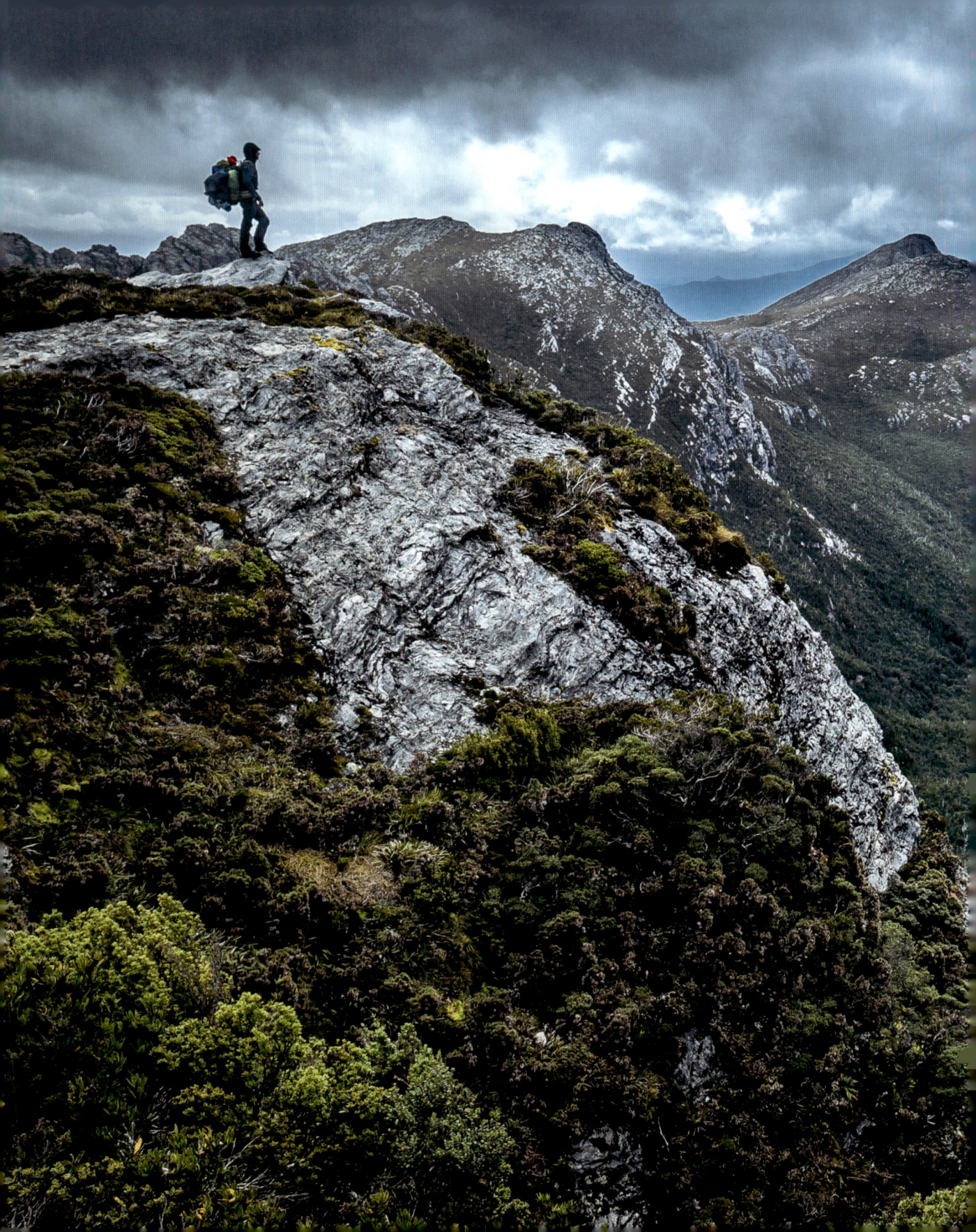

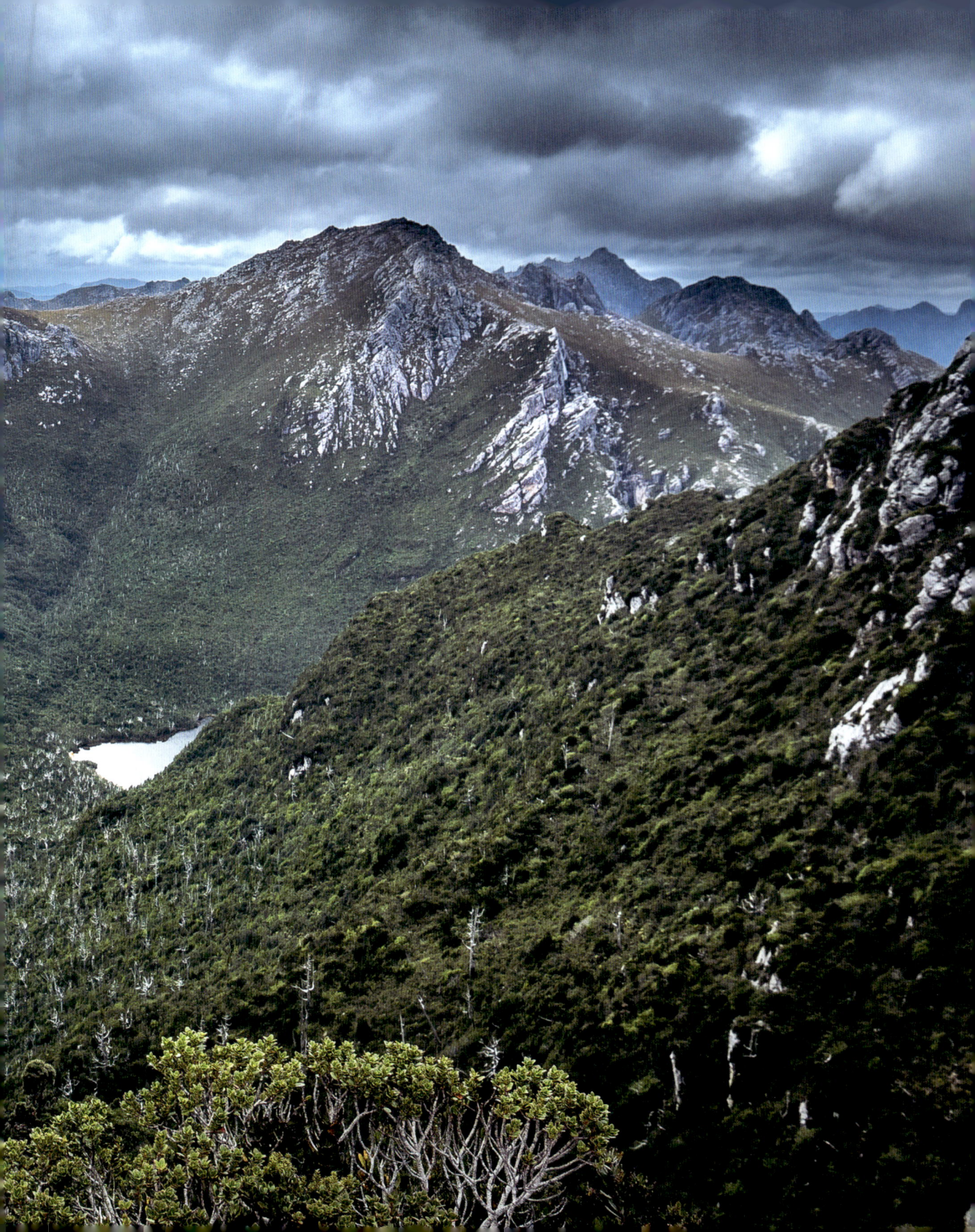

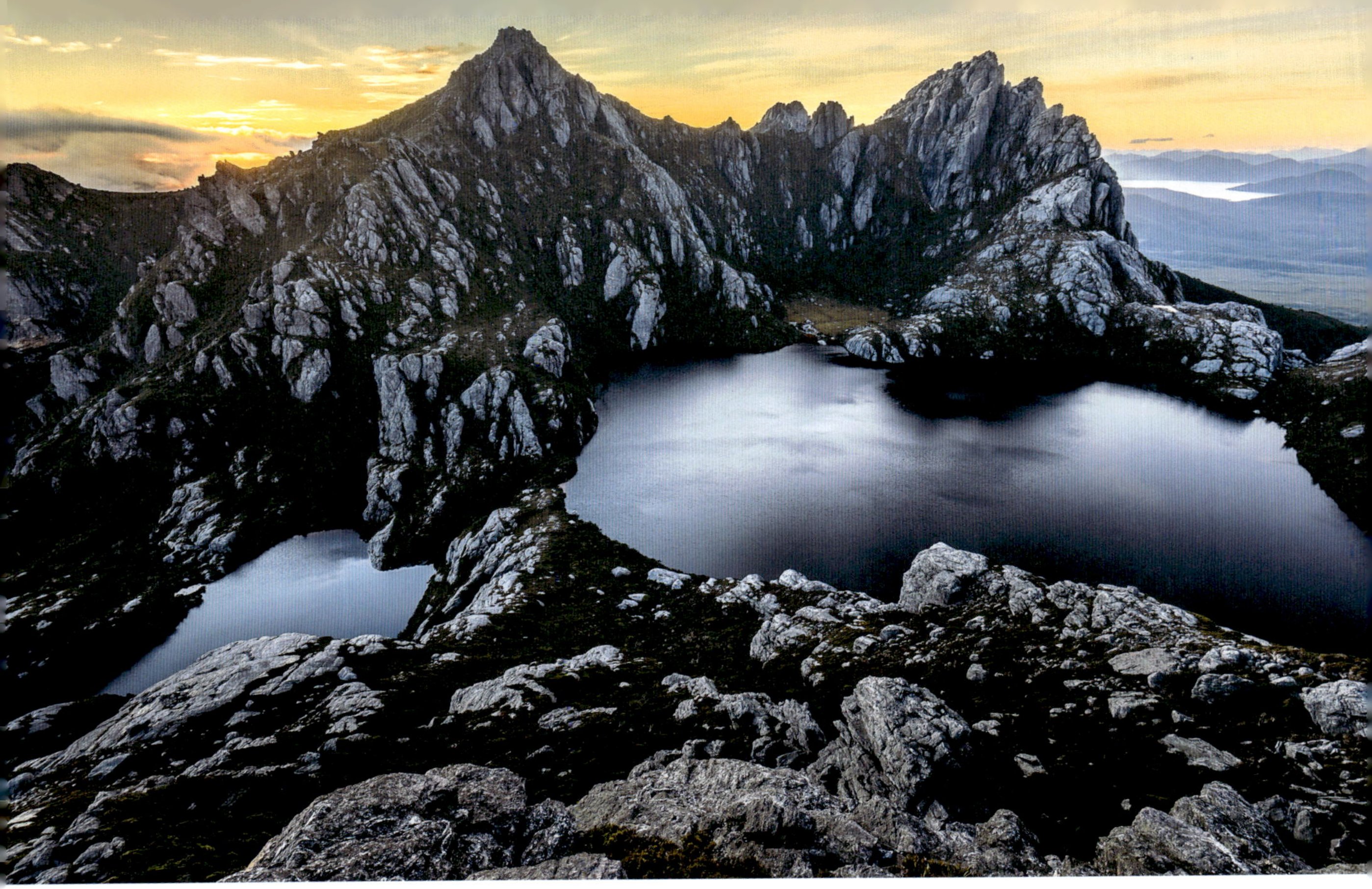

↑ Looking out over Lake Oberon.
↘ Temporary base amongst the quartzite peaks.

If the weather takes a turn for the worse and/or energy levels are low, then one never has to go too far before they can choose to call it a day. As well as timber platforms, the main camping areas sport modular toilets that can be flown out by helicopter when full. Neither of these features is aesthetically pleasing; however, both play an important role in helping to minimize the damage to the Arthurs' fragile alpine environment. No small matter, considering the increase in hiking numbers in recent years.

Hiking in the Arthur Range is an exercise in patience, perseverance, and meteorological faith—and one best attempted in February and March. Those afforded an extended stretch of fine conditions will consider themselves very fortunate to witness some of the finest mountain scenery on the planet. But those unlucky enough to experience a big storm front rumbling through, with only horizontal rain and thick fog for three straight days, must simply shrug their shoulders, have an ironic chuckle, and try to remember that Mother Nature does not have a copy of their hiking itinerary. ─────

Hiking in the Arthur Range is an exercise in patience, perseverance, and meteorological faith.

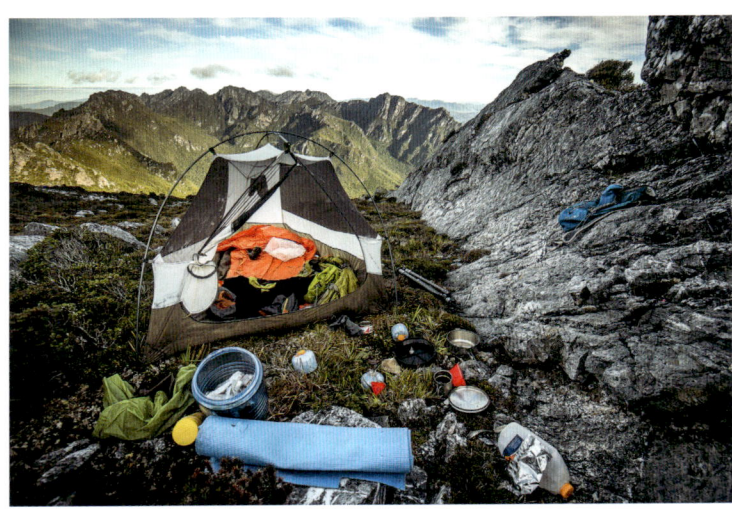

GOOD TO KNOW

START/FINISH
⚑ Round trip from the northern Port Davey Track trailhead

SEASON
December to March

CONDITIONS
The climate is unstable: inclement conditions are the norm and snow, high winds, and heavy rain are possible at any time of year. Due to the exposed nature of much of the route, this is a trek that should only be attempted by experienced hikers.

ACCOMMODATION
Camping only. In the more fragile alpine areas, tents can be pitched on wooden platforms.

HIGHLIGHTS
Lake Oberon, Lake Uranus, Beggary Bumps, side trips to the summits of Mount Hayes and Dorado Peak.

TIP
The trek is usually done in a counterclockwise direction in order to go with rather than against the prevailing winds when walking in the Arthur Range.

BACKGROUND

ALTERNATIVE ROUTES This is a trek for experienced hikers only. For travelers who are hiking in Tasmania for the first time, trails such as the South Coast or the Overland Track may be better options.

The Arthur Range is split into two main sections: the Western and Eastern. Hikes on both parts can be combined to create a full-length 68-km (42-mi.) A-to-B traverse; this takes most hikers between 12 and 16 days. This trip begins at Scotts Peak Dam and finishes at the Farmhouse Creek trailhead, which is southwest of the town of Geeveston.

A shorter and more popular alternative to the full Western Arthurs Traverse is to descend from the range via Kappa Moraine. This cuts off two or three days from the overall time.

HELPFUL HINTS

SHED THE POUNDS Keep pack weight as low as possible. With all the scrambling, mud-slogging, and steep, slippery terrain that needs to be negotiated, excessively heavy backpacks are a burden.

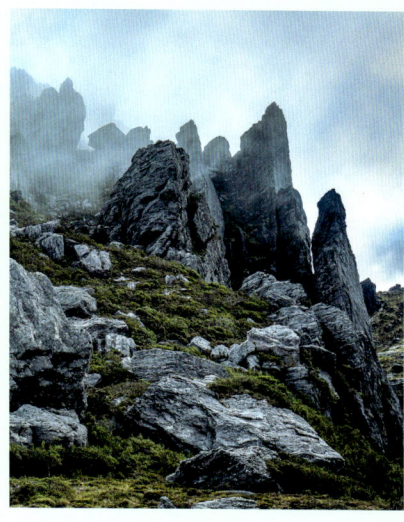

FLORA & FAUNA

QUARTZITE PEAKS The Arthurs are mainly made up of quartzite, a metamorphic rock. The stuff of the mountains was, over a billion year ago, the sand and silt on an ocean floor. Grains of sand were first converted into sandstone and then recrystallized into the rock one sees today.

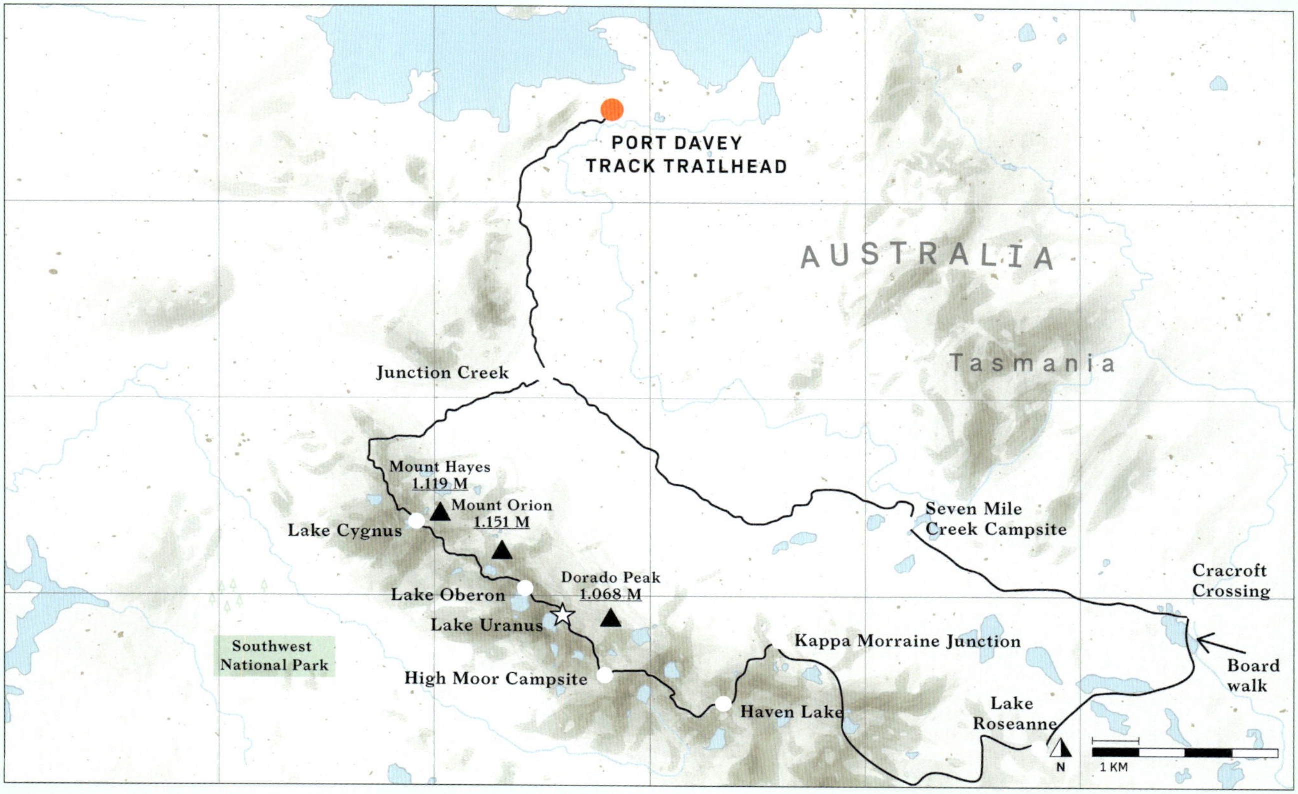

PORT DAVEY
TRACK TRAILHEAD

AUSTRALIA

Tasmania

Junction Creek

Mount Hayes
1,119 M

Mount Orion
1,151 M

Lake Cygnus

Seven Mile
Creek Campsite

Cracroft
Crossing

Lake Oberon

Dorado Peak
1,068 M

Lake Uranus

Southwest
National Park

Kappa Morraine Junction

High Moor Campsite

Board
walk

Haven Lake

Lake
Roseanne

N   1 KM

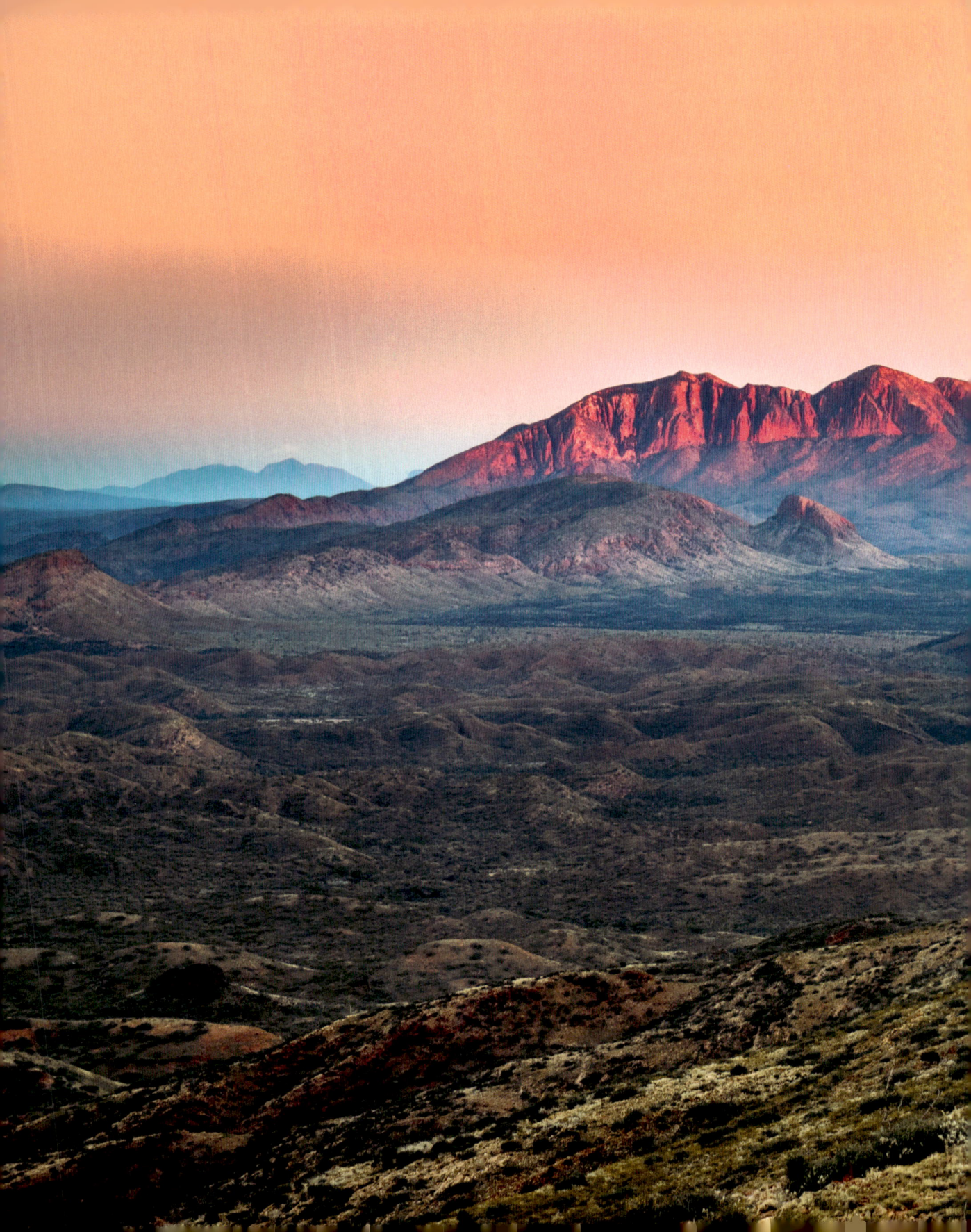

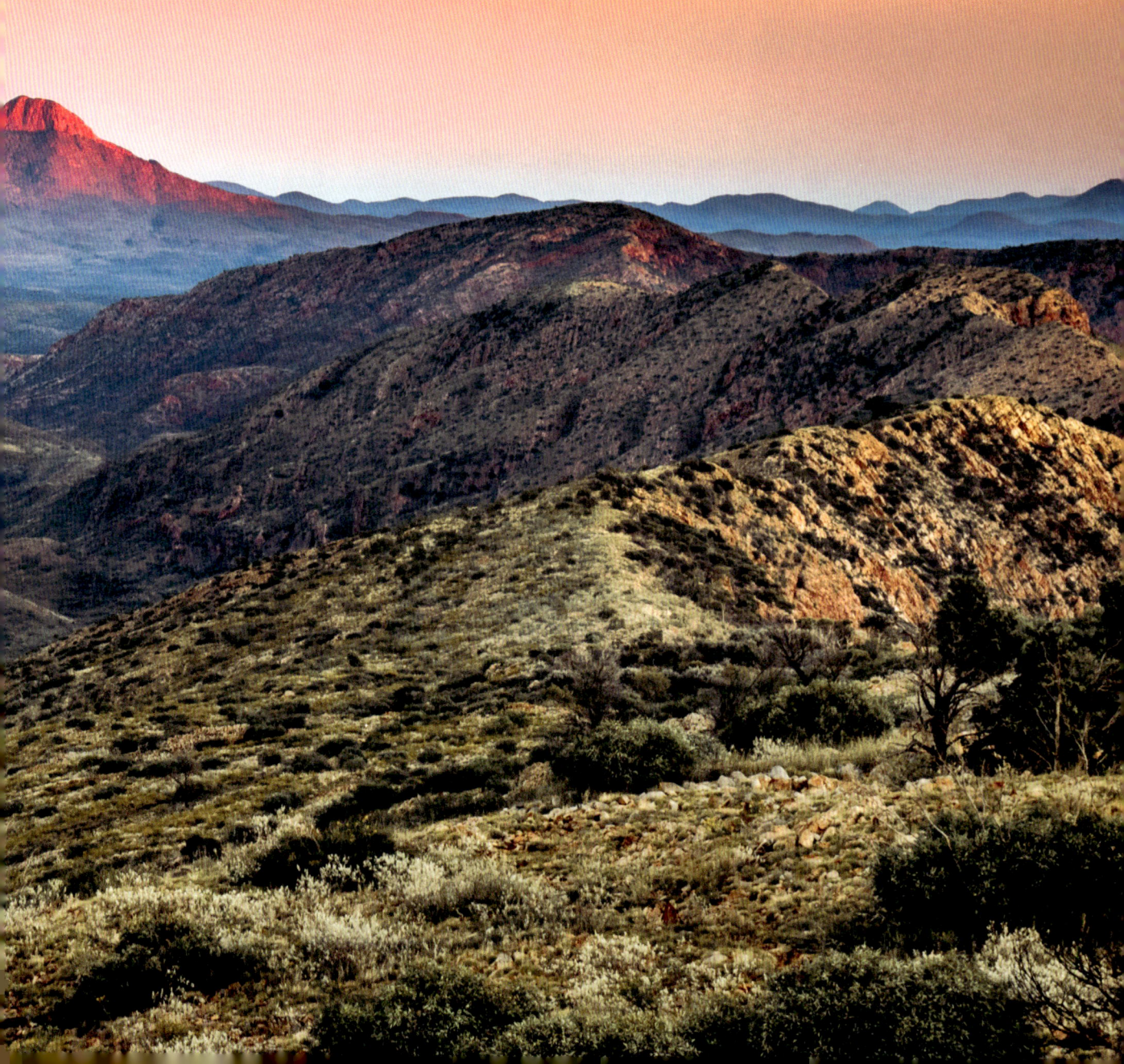

THROUGH AUSTRALIA'S RED CENTRE

Australia

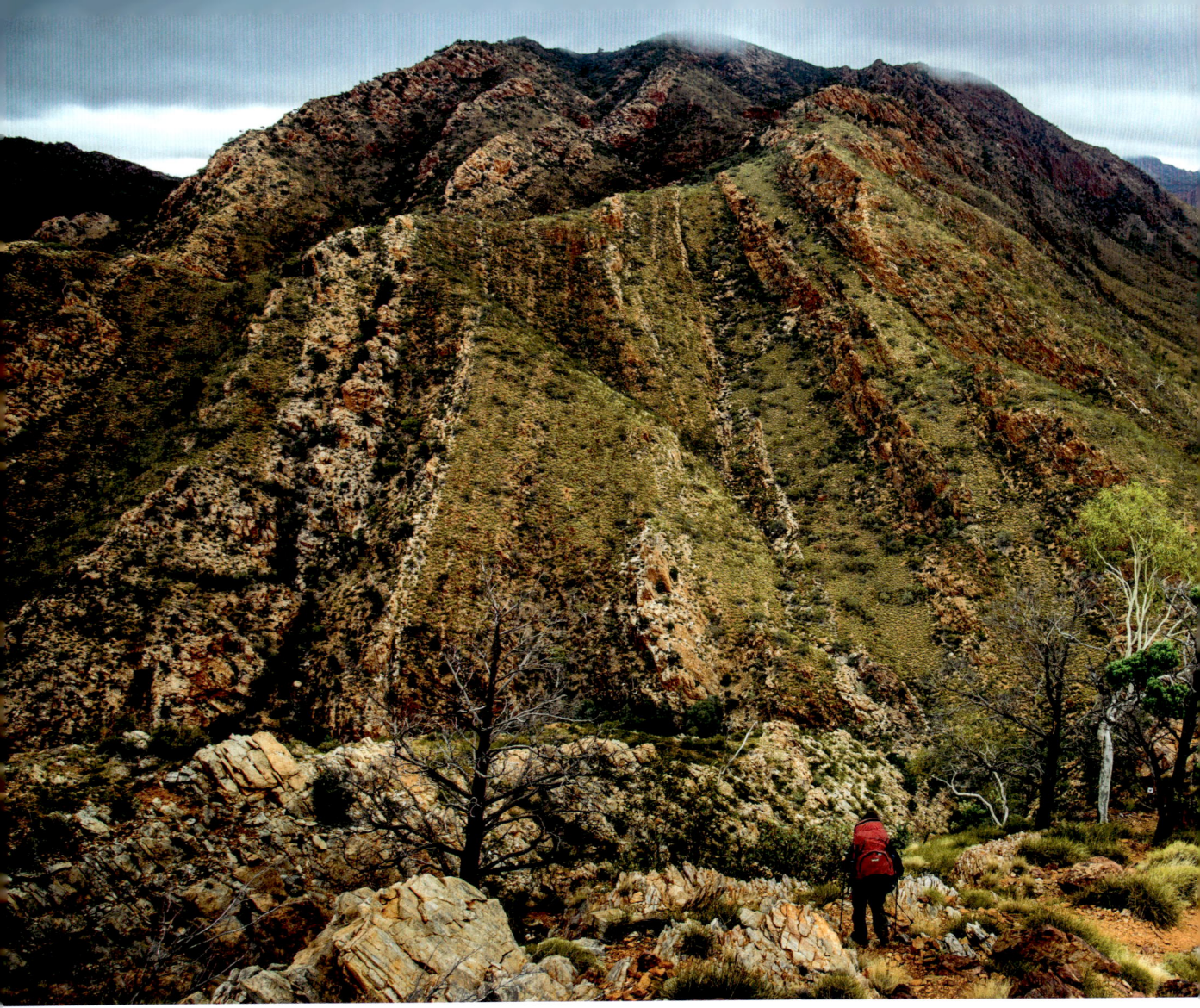

ustralia's Outback is not all barren desert. Smack bang in the middle of the Red Centre are the spectacular MacDonnell Ranges. Named after Sir Richard MacDonnell (the governor of South Australia at the time) by John McDouall Stuart, whose 1860 expedition reached the mountain chain in April of that year, the range boasts dramatic gorges, serene waterholes, and a fascinating geological history.

ABOUT THE TRAIL

→ <u>DISTANCE</u> 223 km (138.6 mi.)
→ <u>DURATION</u> 10 to 14 days
→ <u>LEVEL</u> Moderate

These towering ridges are the location of one of Australia's premier long-distance hikes: the Larapinta Trail. In the language of the Arrernte people lhere-pirnte means "salty river" and is the traditional name for the Finke River, which is one of the oldest watercourses on earth.

Stretching some 223 km (138.6 mi.) from Redbank Gorge to Telegraph Station (situated on the outskirts of the town of Alice Springs), the Larapinta is a 12-stage trek through the western section of the MacDonnell Ranges. Formed some 300 to 350 million years ago, the MacDonnells is one of the oldest mountain chains on the planet. Shaped by a combination of folding, faulting, and erosion, the peaks rise up dramatically from the arid plains that surround them in the form of quartzite and

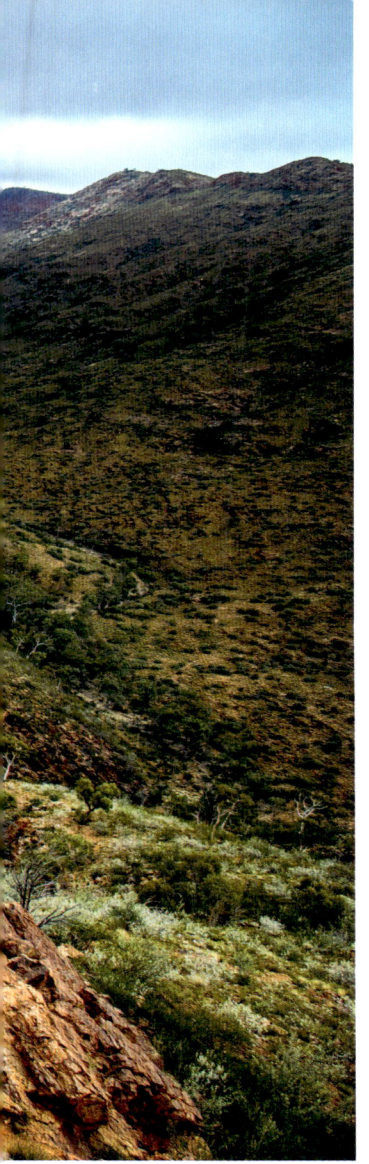

There is something magical about swimming in this emerald-colored waterhole, which was shaped by surges of floodwater over the course of thousands of years and lies in the middle of the Australian Outback.

sandstone ridges. The juxtaposition of flat desert and long rocky ridgelines colored in varied tones is one of the most striking aspects of the entire hike.

One of the trail's many standout natural features is Standley Chasm, an impressive gorge with deep red walls that are up to 80 m (260 ft.) high, located in a reserve owned and operated by Aboriginal family members whose ancestors have lived in the area for thousands of years. Here, sunlight only reaches the ground at noon, yet the slot gorge is at its most dramatic in the afternoon of a sunny day, when the reflections of the sun project a range of coppery tones onto the majestic ochre walls that stretch towards the blue of the sky. Absorbing the intensity of colors in this confined space, one begins to understand why it was ochre that Aborigines used for body decoration and to paint their caves.

Another not-to-be-missed experience is going for a dip at Ellery Creek Big Hole. There is something magical about swimming in this emerald-colored waterhole, which was shaped by surges of floodwater over the course of thousands of years. Partially ringed by a ribbon of golden sand, the refreshingly cool water is nigh on impossible to resist after a long day on the trail. Another notable waterhole is at Simpsons Gap, a place that is rich in Aboriginal history and where it is said that several dreaming trails and stories are supposed to have crossed.

By no means is it just the landscapes and swimming opportunities that make the Larapinta Trail such a unique wilderness experience. The region also boasts a diverse array of flora and fauna. →

← The descent to Fringe Lily Creek.
↓ Cooling waters at Redbank Gorge.

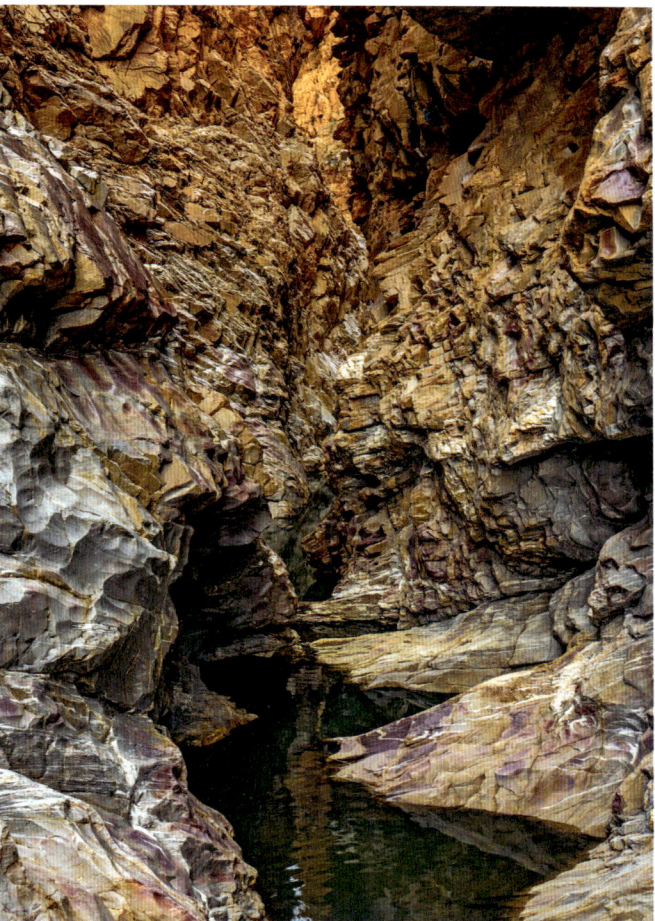

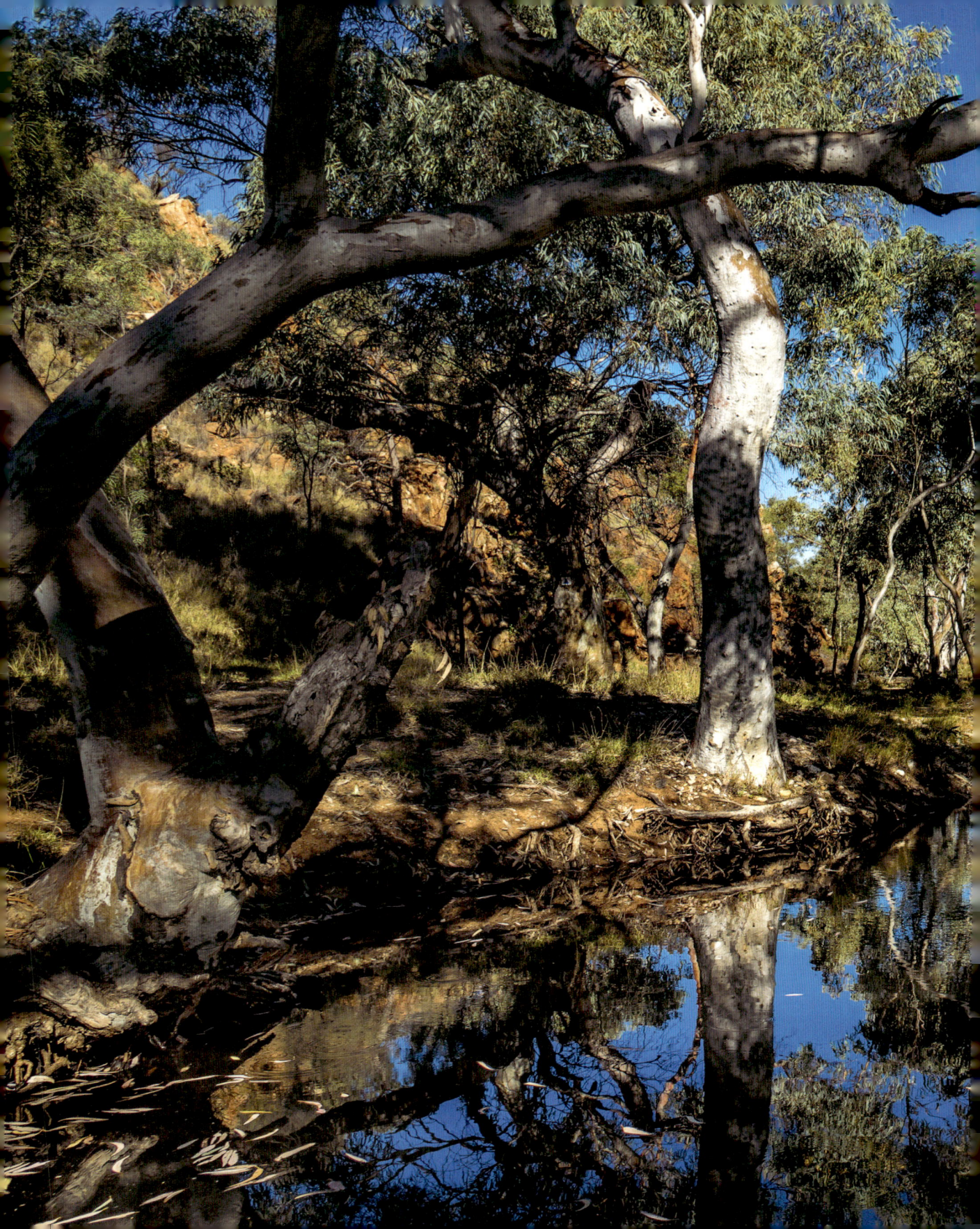

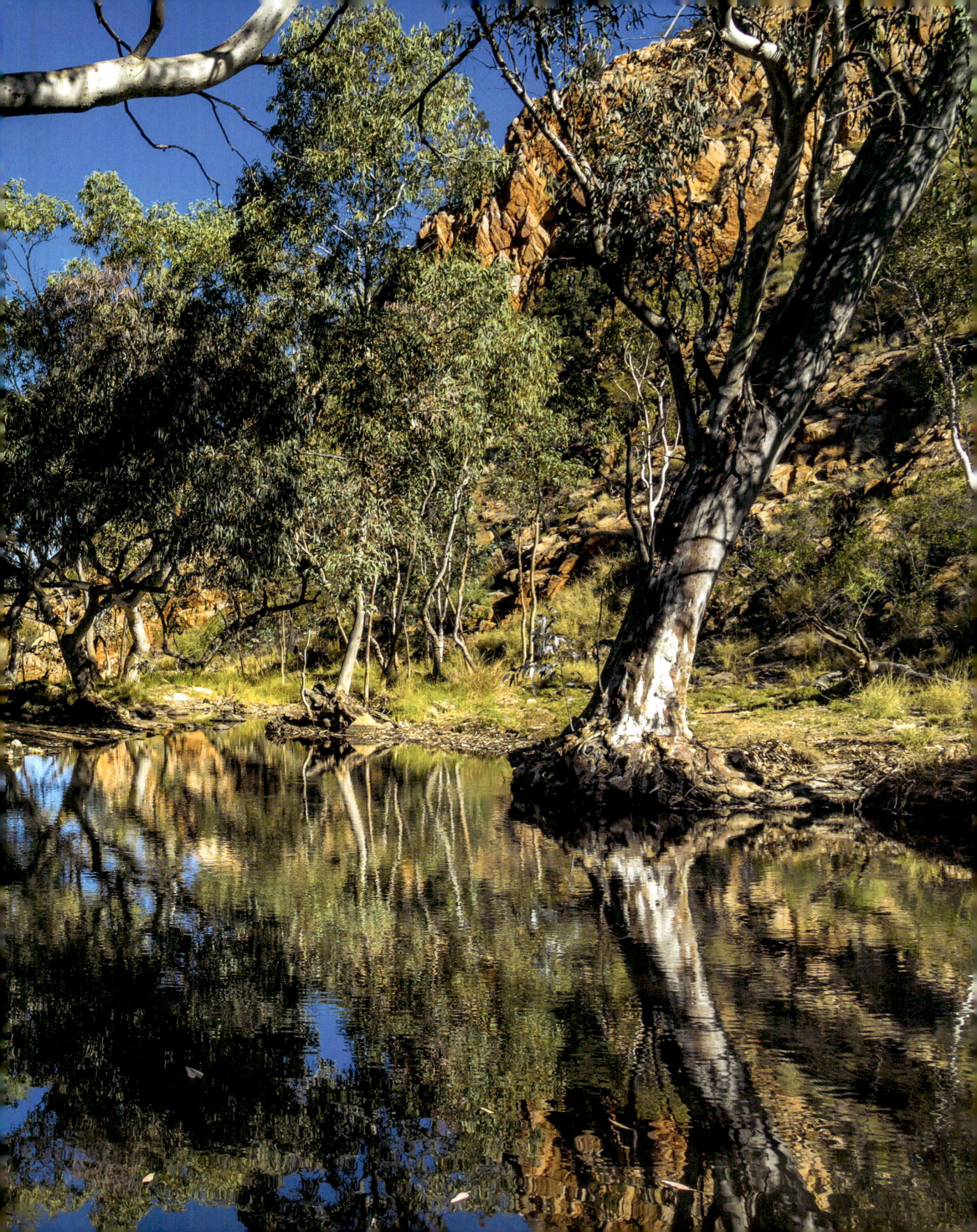

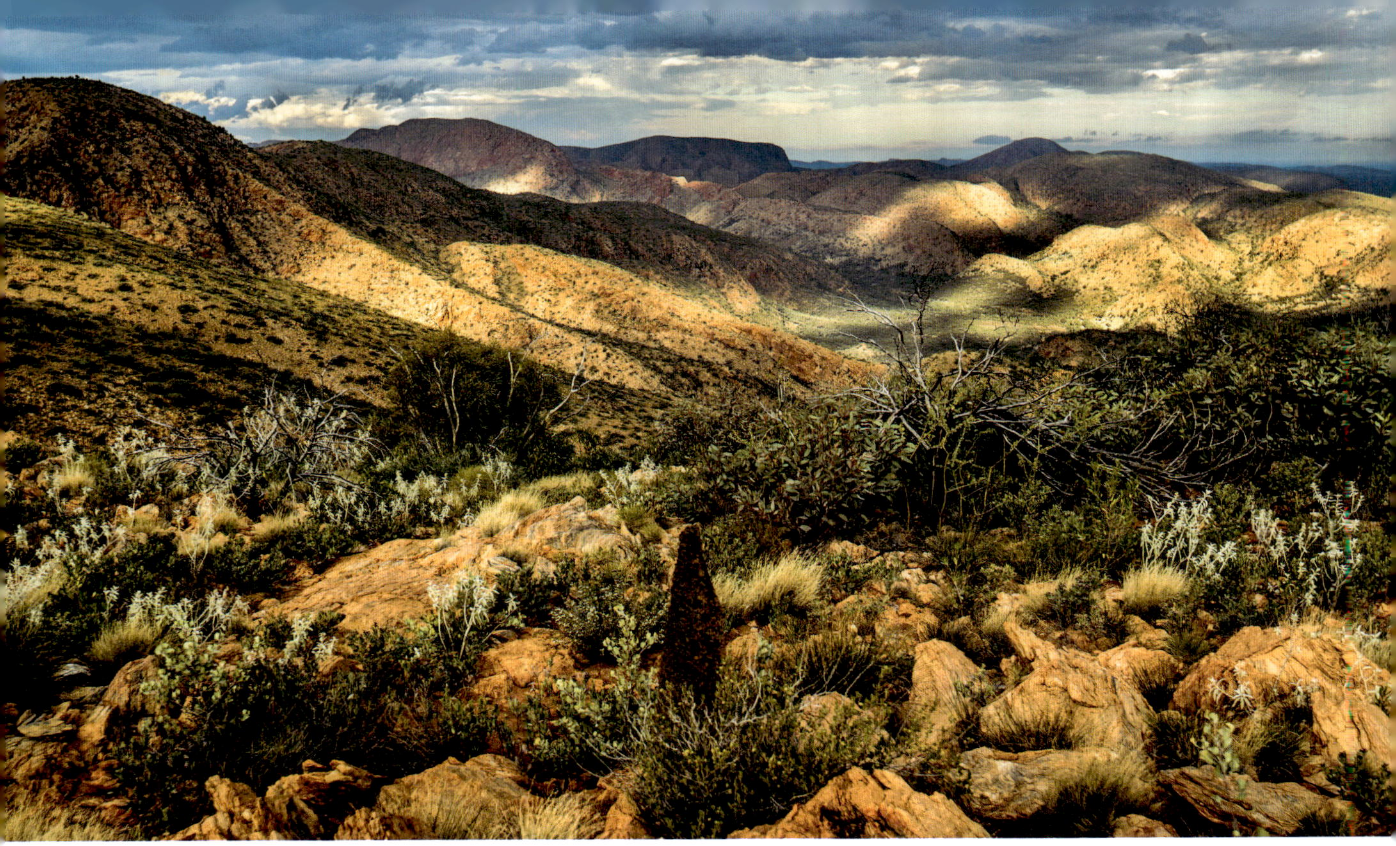

↑ The undulating landscape of Razorback Ridge.
↓ Shady waterhole at Serpentine Gorge.

Hikers may encounter dingoes, kangaroos, wallabies, and a myriad of birds and reptiles during their walk. Particular care should be taken when hiking through the occasional brushy section of trail. King brown, or mulga, snakes are fairly common; however, the only time they are likely to be a problem is if they are stepped on. It is therefore handy to have a trekking pole or a sturdy stick in order to push back vegetation to ensure your way is clear. The species is the second most venomous in the world and must be watched out for when walking through overgrown sections.

Since its completion in 2002, the Larapinta Trail has quickly become a draw not only for Australian bushwalkers but, increasingly, for international hikers as well. The well-marked route provides an opportunity to admire a rough and inhospitable yet strikingly beautiful region. Trekking along its scenic ridges, gazing out upon the sun-beaten landscapes below, the heart of the arid Outback is at one's feet. ⸻

The juxtaposition of flat desert and long rocky ridgelines colored in varied tones is one of the most striking aspects of the entire hike.

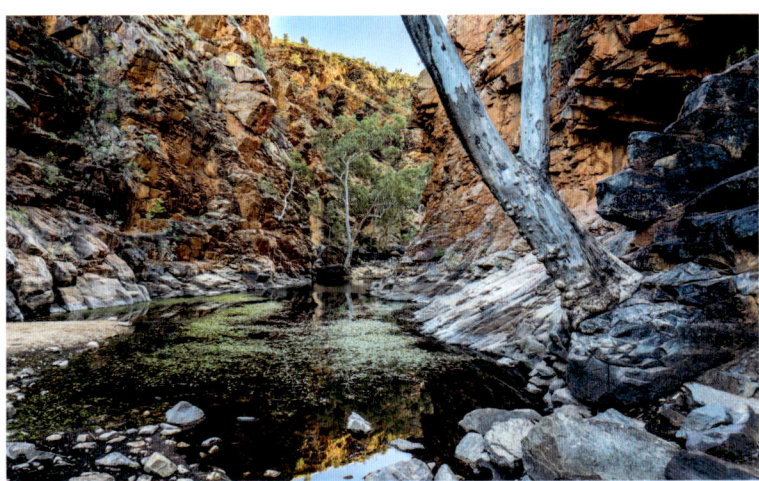

GOOD TO KNOW

START/FINISH
📍 Redbank Gorge
📍 Alice Springs Telegraph Station

SEASON
April to September

CONDITIONS
The intense heat makes it inadvisable to complete this trail during the summer.

LOWEST/HIGHEST POINT
611 m (2005 ft.)/1379 m (4524 ft.)

WILDLIFE
Dingoes, king brown snakes, wallabies.

SUPPLIES
There are three points to leave resupply boxes: Ellery Creek, Serpentine Gorge, Ormiston Gorge. Supplemental provisions are available at Standley Chasm and Ormiston Gorge.

TIP
The Red Centre can be hot irrespective of the season, and there is little in the way of shade for most of the Larapinta Trail. Therefore it is recommended that hikers carry a light-weight trekking umbrella, and try to do the majority of their walking during the cooler hours of early morning and late afternoon.

BACKGROUND

THE RED CENTRE A vast and rugged region that contains the MacDonnell Ranges, Watarrka National Park, and sacred Aboriginal sites including Uluru and Kata Tjuta (formerly known as Ayers Rock and Mount Olga), the Red Centre holds more than just geographical interest. The Uluru-Kata Tjuta National Park is the ancestral home of the Anangu people and in 1987 was listed as a UNESCO World Heritage Site for both its natural and cultural importance. Though climbing Uluru is not advised because of the rock's sacred nature, adventurous hikers can explore the park and trek the 10.6-km (6.6-mi.) loop around the red monolith or watch as the colors fade and alter as the sun rises or sets over it.

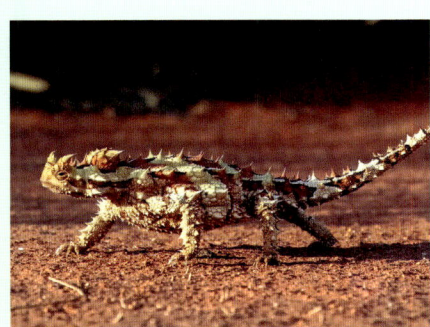

FLORA & FAUNA

THORNY DEVIL The thorny lizard, also known as the thorny devil, or by its evocative Latin name Moloch horridus, is covered in spikes about the size of rose thorns. With the ability to change color in different temperatures or when alarmed, these ant-eating desert-dwellers can be difficult to see, but tracks in the sand can be spotted.

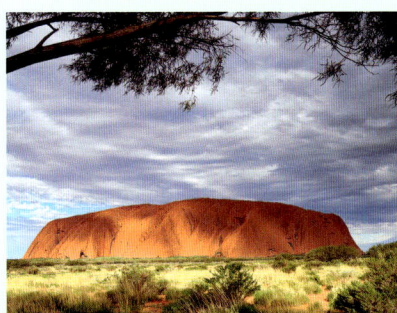

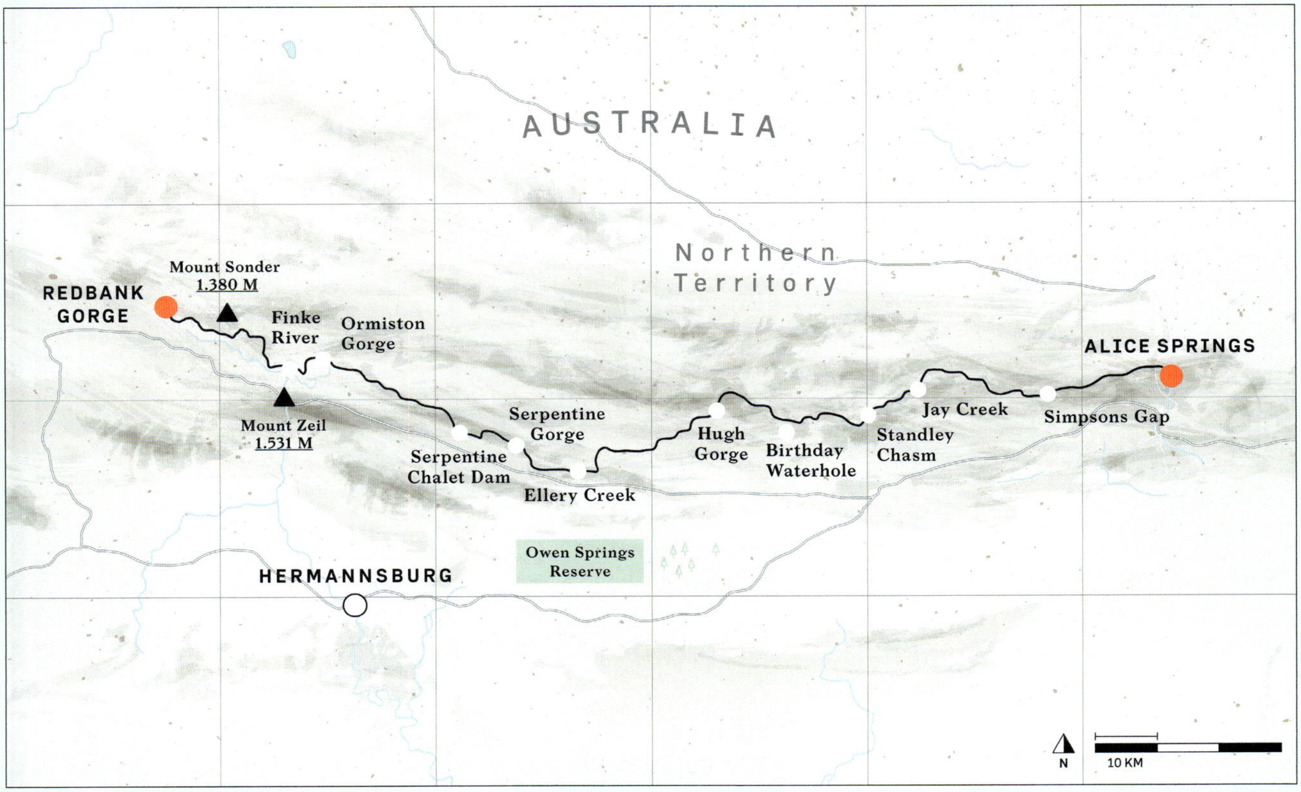

AUSTRALIA

Northern Territory

REDBANK GORGE

Mount Sonder
1.380 M

Finke River

Ormiston Gorge

Mount Zeil
1.531 M

Serpentine Chalet Dam

Serpentine Gorge

Ellery Creek

Hugh Gorge

Birthday Waterhole

Standley Chasm

Jay Creek

Simpsons Gap

ALICE SPRINGS

HERMANNSBURG

Owen Springs Reserve

N

10 KM

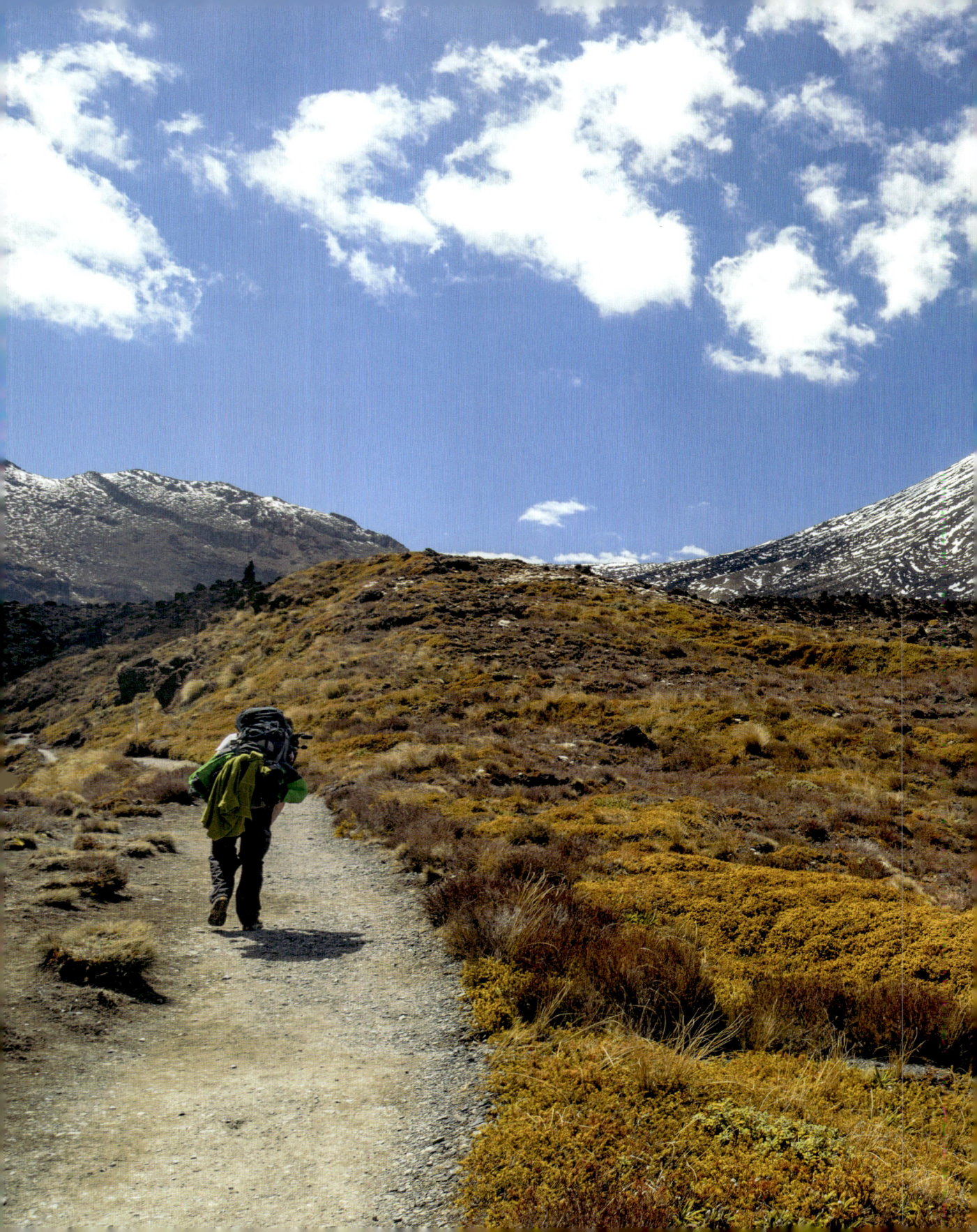

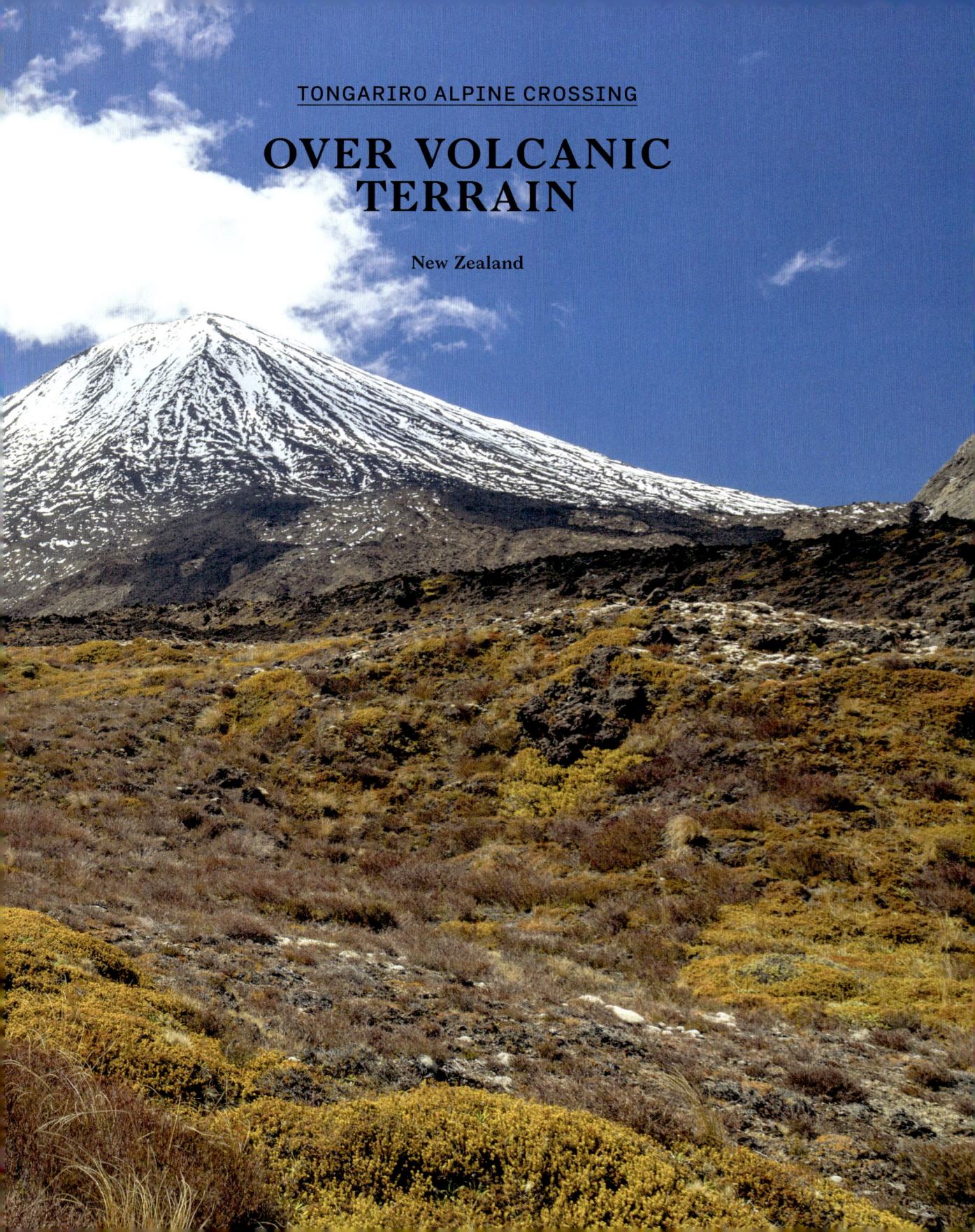

TONGARIRO ALPINE CROSSING

OVER VOLCANIC TERRAIN

New Zealand

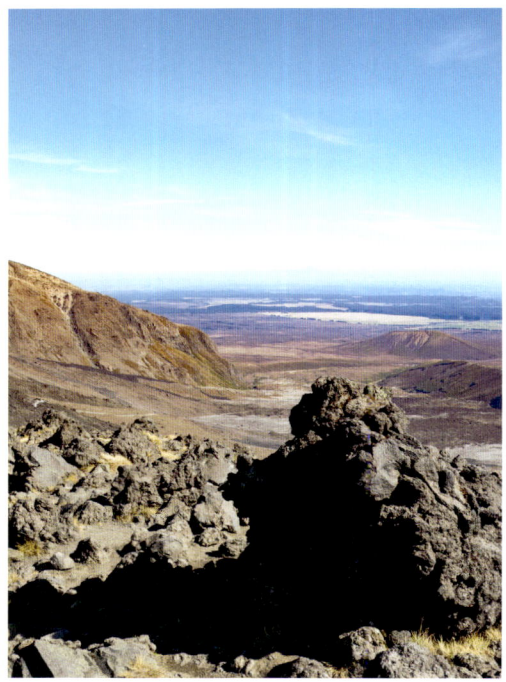

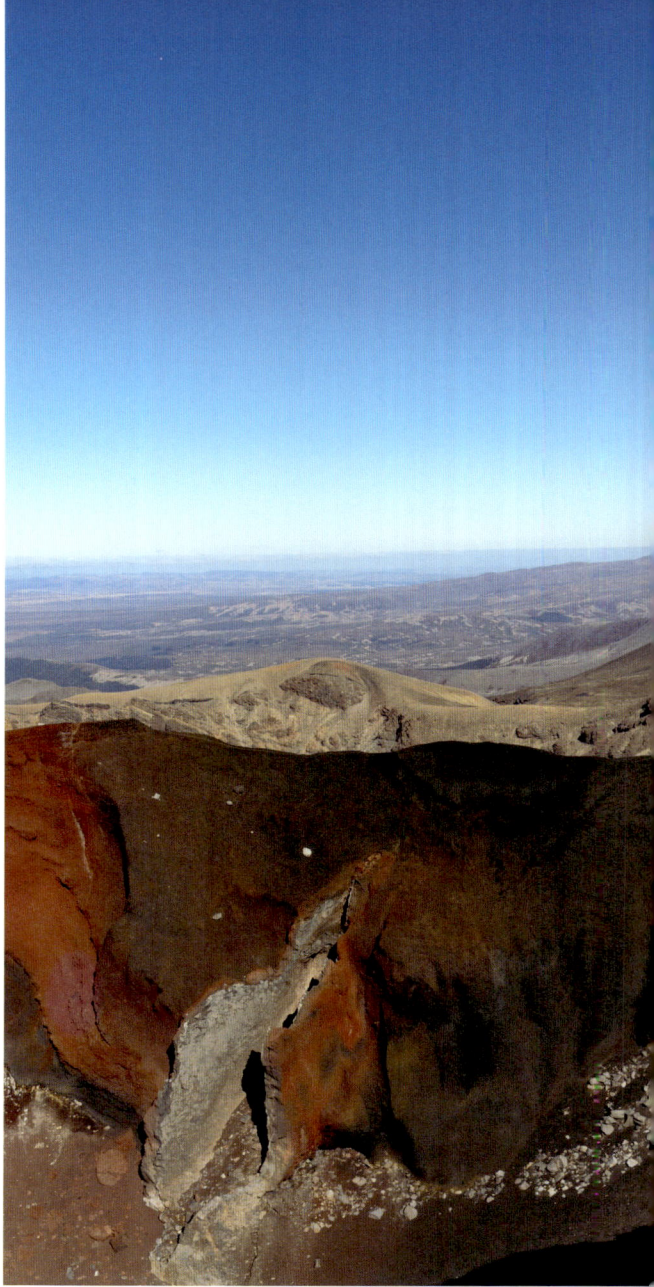

The Tongariro Alpine Crossing on the North Island is commonly referred to as New Zealand's best day hike. Given that the Land of the Long White Cloud (the translation of a Maori name for the country) has a lot of beautiful trails in a diverse range of environments, including coastal paths linking beaches of golden sands, vertiginous climbs, and island circuits, the walk has a great deal to live up to. The reference is wholly justified, though.

During its course, the Crossing traverses a dynamic landscape of old lava flows, whistling fumaroles (vents in the earth that emit steam and volcanic gasses), active volcanoes, and multi-hued lakes. It also passes through alpine tundra—where hikers may see the delicate blooms of mountain daisies and buttercups in the damper areas during the summer months—before finishing in the shady confines of lush native forest. And this is all in the space of just over 19 km (12 mi.).

ABOUT THE TRAIL

→ <u>DISTANCE</u> 19.4 km (12 mi.)
→ <u>DURATION</u> 6 hours (not including side trips)
→ <u>LEVEL</u> Easy to Moderate

The walk is situated entirely within Tongariro National Park. In addition to being New Zealand's first national park, the area is also the fourth oldest of these reserves in the world. Because of its combination of spectacular volcanic terrain and spiritual significance to the Maori people, Tongariro holds both natural and cultural UNESCO World Heritage status, and it was the first location to do this. The Maori people have a strong tie to the land.

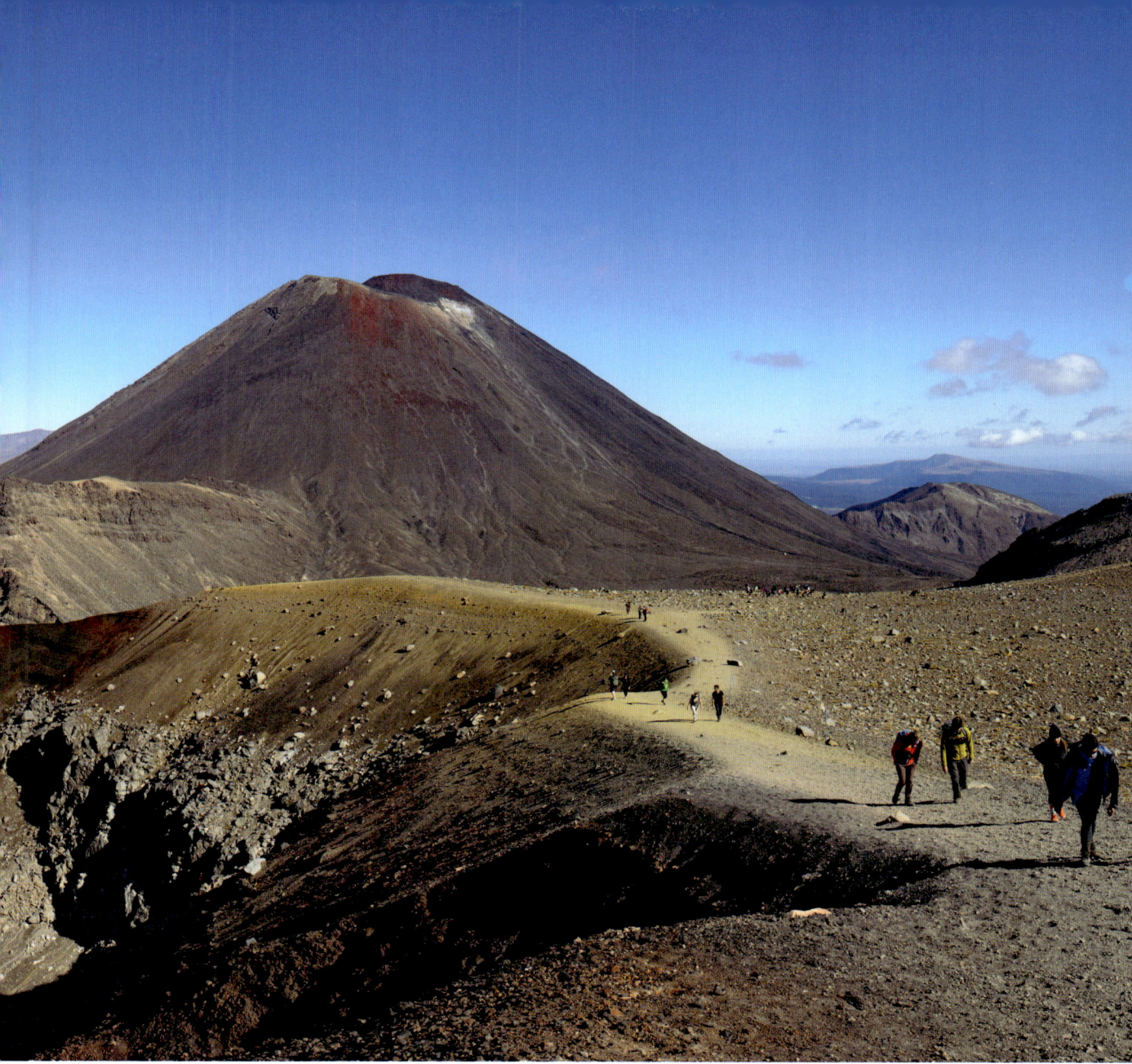

↑ The crater of Mount Ngauruhoe.

They believe that the mountains were once gods and warriors, and that it was a violent battle between six peaks that resulted in the landscape formations in Tongariro.

The Tongariro Crossing is clearly marked with poles and directional signs. However, because of the mostly exposed terrain and often-unpredictable weather—wet, cold, foggy, and windy conditions are common—it is important that hikers come prepared. Walkers should dress in layers, carry a map and navigational instrument, and double check the weather forecast before setting out. Another important consideration is water. There is none available between the start of the hike and Ketetahi hut. It is recommended to bring at least a couple of liters, or double that if trekkers are planning on adding volcano-climbing side trips to their itineraries.

→

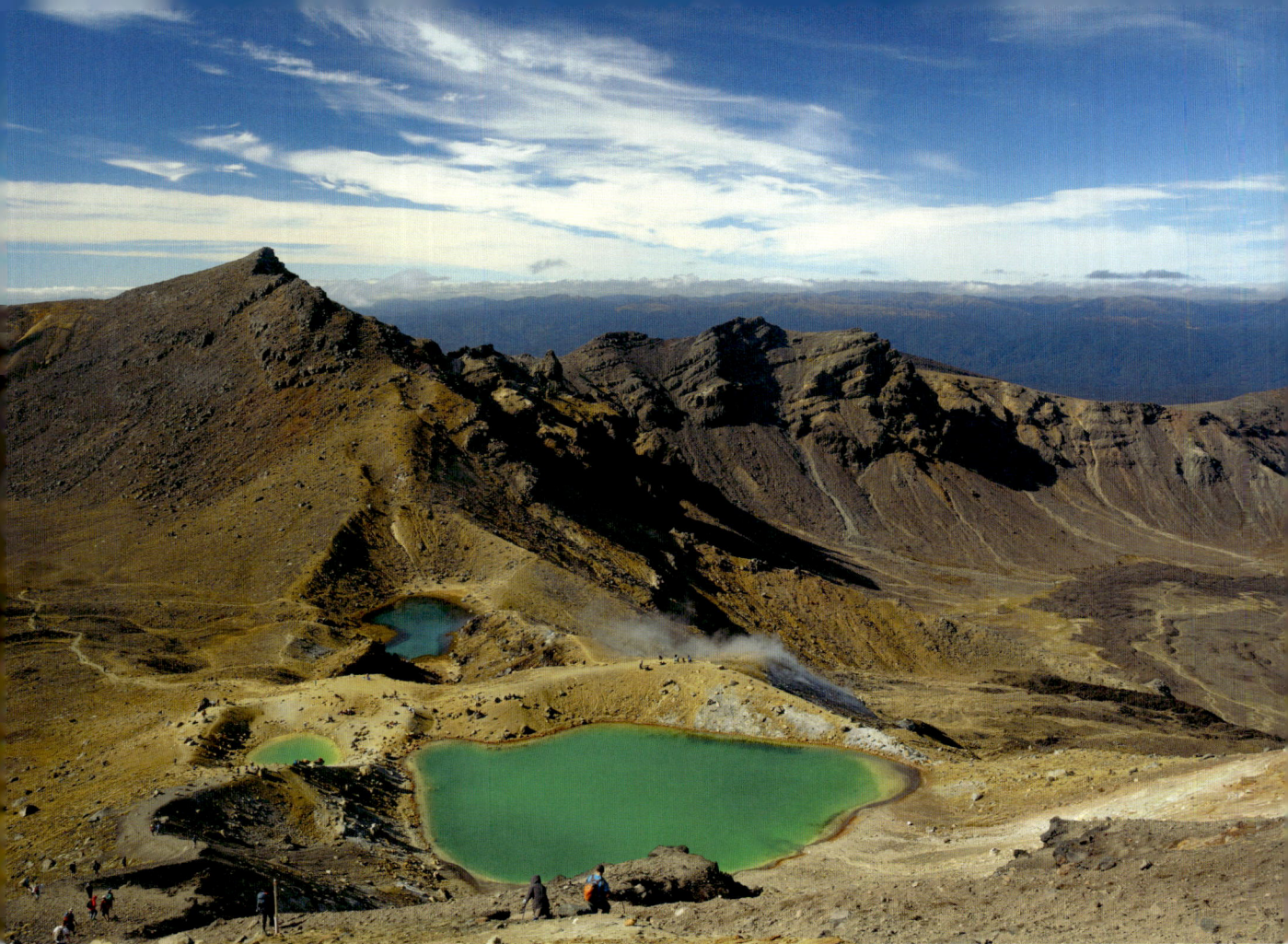

↑ Unearthly features near the summit of the Red Crater.

In fine weather, a not-to-be-missed highlight of the Tongariro Crossing is an ascent of Mount Ngauruhoe. This active volcano—one that has erupted more than 40 times over the past century—doubled as Mount Doom in the final installment of the *The Lord of the Rings* movie trilogy. Though the climb adds on an extra two or three hours to a trip, walkers' efforts are more than rewarded when they reach the top. In addition to taking in the incredible 360-degree panorama, hikers can also walk around the rim and peer into the steaming crater.

With all of the otherworldly beauty on the trail, it is no surprise that the Tongariro Alpine Crossing rates so highly in New Zealand's hiking pantheon. The trek is accessible to hikers of all ages and fitness and experience levels, and it is relatively short and easily reachable by public transport. The barren yet beautiful volcanic terrain is likely the closest that most of us will ever get to walking on the moon—or, of course, venturing into the wastelands of Mordor.

During its course, the Crossing traverses a dynamic landscape of old lava flows, whistling fumaroles, active volcanoes, and multi-hued lakes.

GOOD TO KNOW

START/FINISH
⚑ Mangatepopo car park
⚑ Ketetahi car park

SEASON
October to May

HIGHLIGHTS
Multicolored lakes, moonscape terrain, side trip to the top of Mount Ngauruhoe.

TIP
To avoid the crowds, either trek out of season or start from Mangatepopo at dawn. There is a hut as well as a campsite near the trailhead to make this easier.

HELPFUL HINTS

COLDER CLIMBS A winter crossing is possible. However, in an average year it will require the use of an ice axe and crampons. Current conditions should be checked with the Tongariro National Park Visitor Centre before setting out.

BACKGROUND

MOUNTAIN BATTLES The legends passed down through generations of Maori people tell tales of how they believe the landscape in the central part of the North Island originated. The story of the mountains that stand in the Tongariro National Park is one of warring peaks. Six male mountains were in love with the beautiful Pihanga. However, Pihanga only had eyes for Tongariro. The suitors battled, with eruptions, smoke, fire, lava, and the mountains' rage shaking the ground. Tongariro was the victor and won the right to stand next to Pihanga, while the others—Ruapehu, Ngauruhoe, Taranaki, Putauaki, and Tauhara—moved off to various distances away. The Whanganui River was then formed by the trail of tears shed by Taranaki.

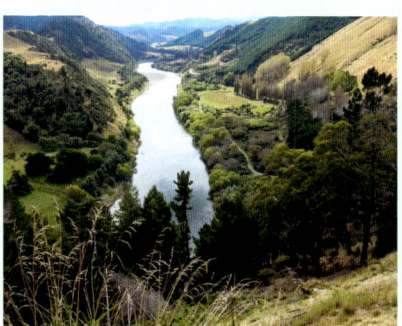

FLORA & FAUNA

INVASIVE SPECIES Tussock grasses in gold and red tones grow in Tongariro National Park. Also present in the western side of the park is heather. Introduced in 1910 as a food source for game birds (that later died out), the vividly colored plant is coarsely beautiful but also invasive, pushing out the tussocks.

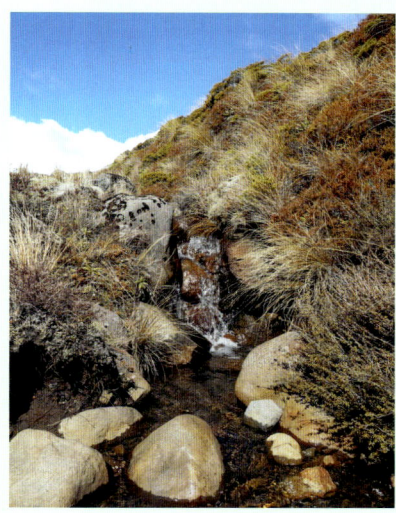

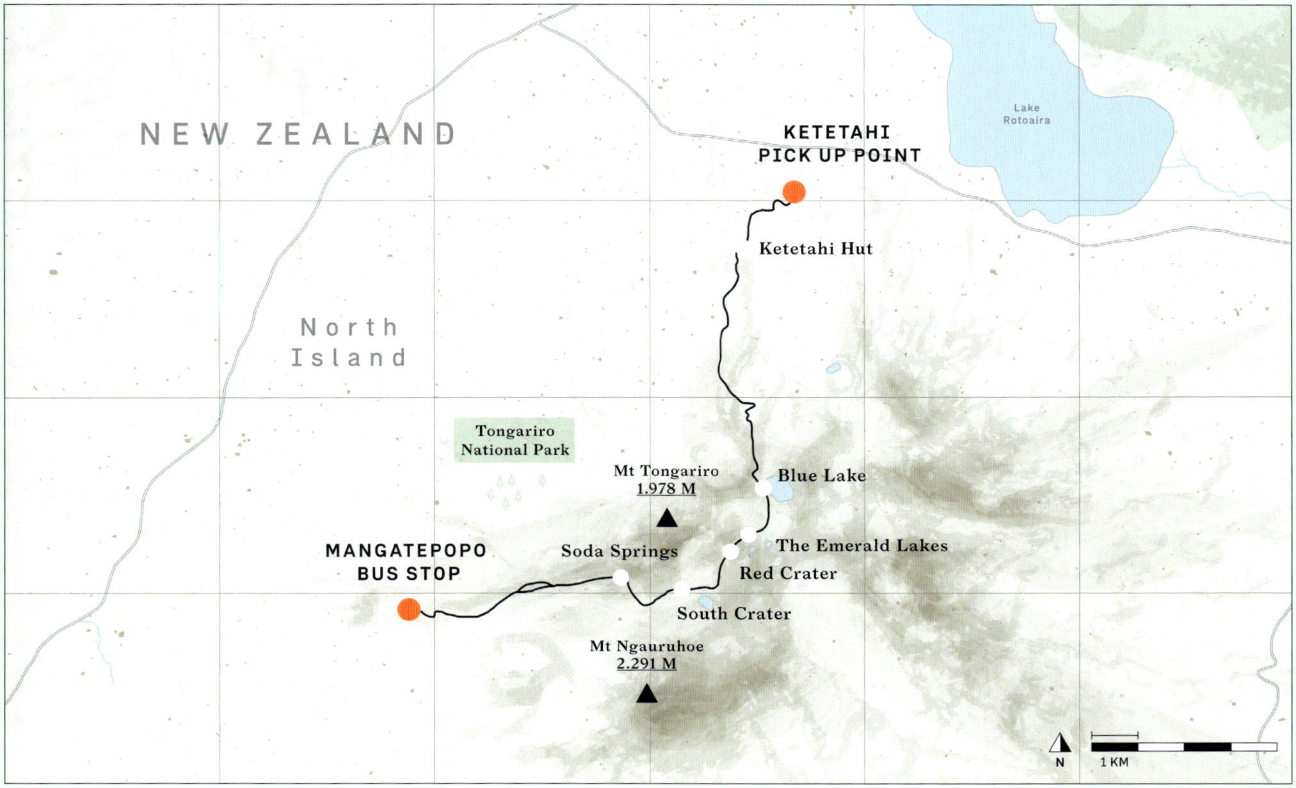

NEW ZEALAND

North Island

Tongariro National Park

KETETAHI PICK UP POINT

Ketetahi Hut

Lake Rotoaira

Mt Tongariro 1,978 M

Blue Lake

MANGATEPOPO BUS STOP

Soda Springs

The Emerald Lakes

Red Crater

South Crater

Mt Ngauruhoe 2,291 M

N

1 KM

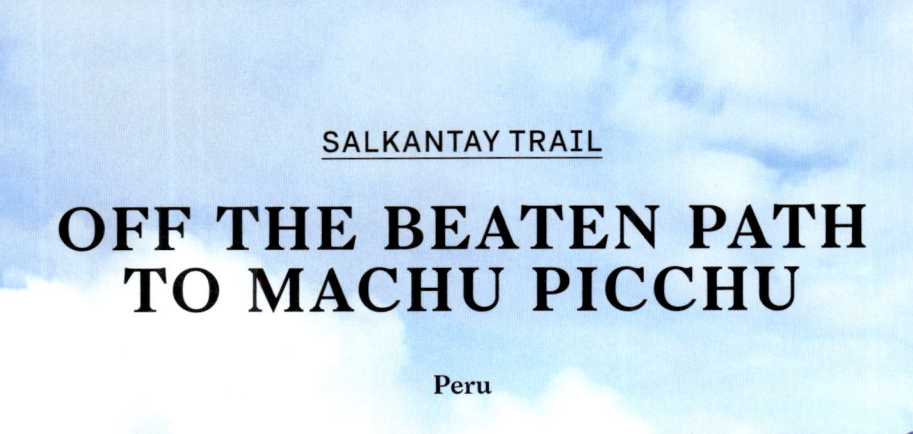

SALKANTAY TRAIL

OFF THE BEATEN PATH TO MACHU PICCHU

Peru

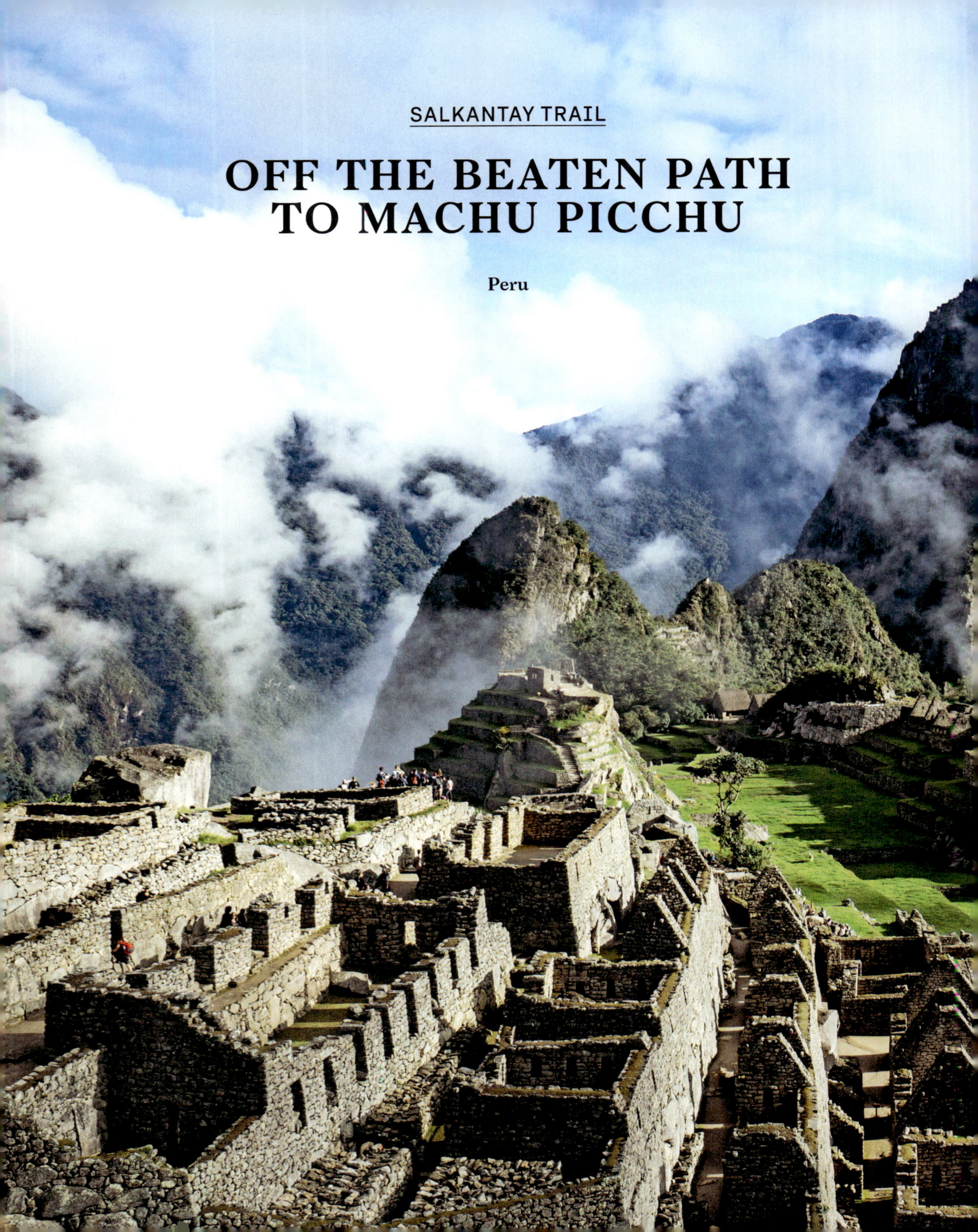

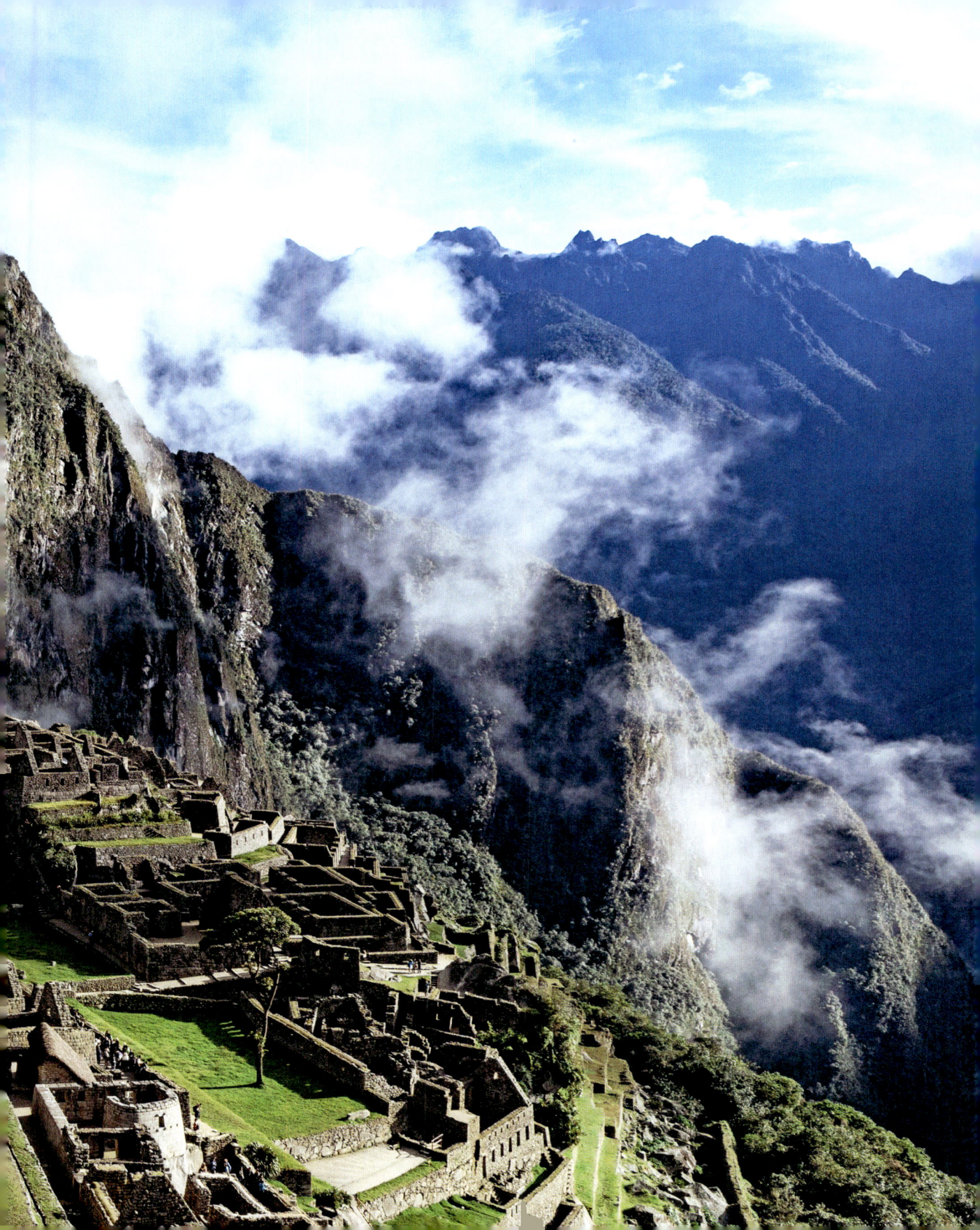

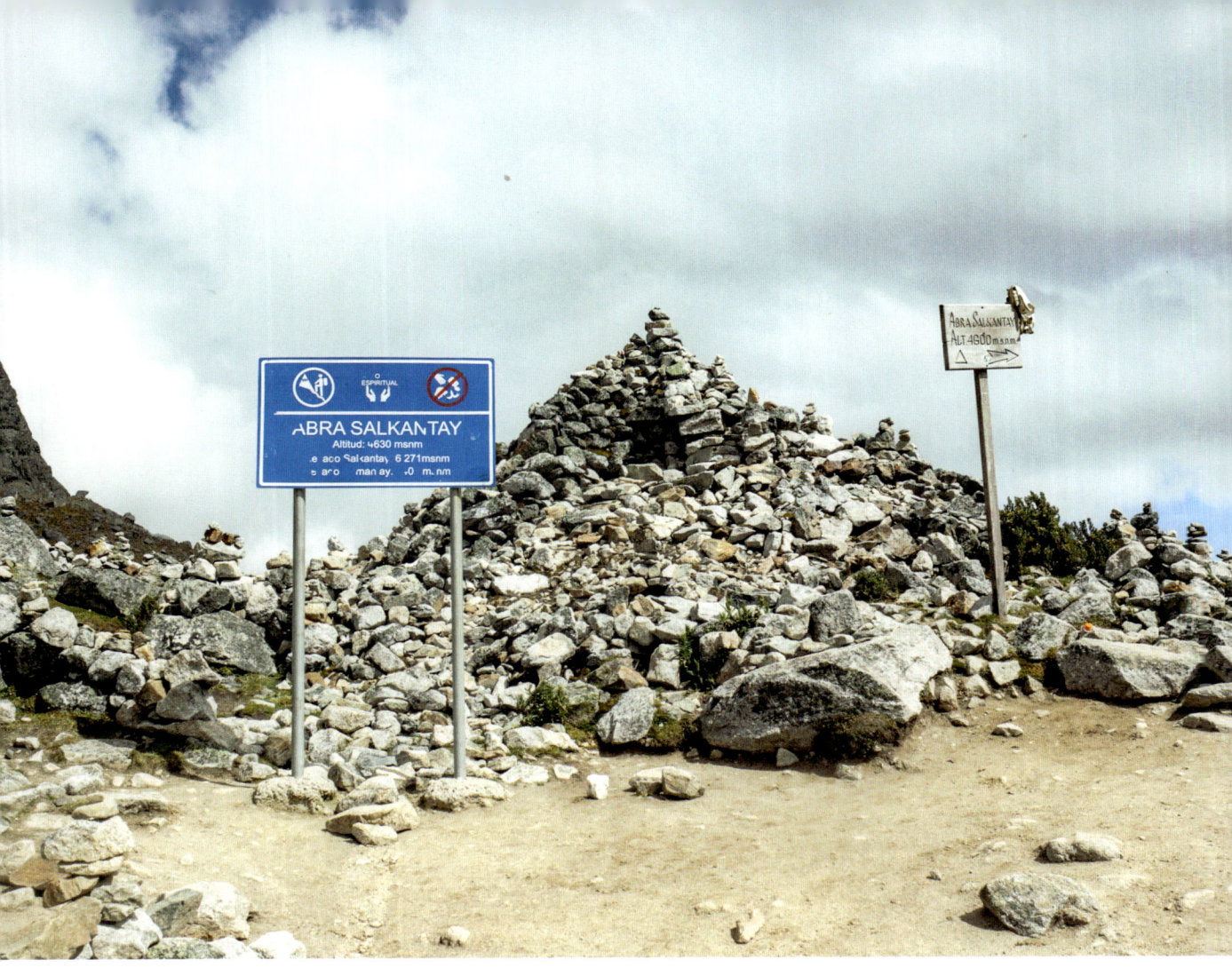

The ancient ruins of an Inca settlement that rest over 2,400 m (7,874 ft.) above sea level on a thin saddle between two Andean peaks, Machu Picchu first became widely known in the West when a Yale history lecturer named Hiram Bingham visited it in 1911. Whether or not it really is the fabled lost city of the Incas that Bingham was hunting, this urban site in the clouds has held a strong fascination for many throughout the years. And not least because the secrets behind the towering structures built by the Incas in the fourteenth and fifteenth centuries are still not fully known.

ABOUT THE TRAIL

→ DISTANCE 84 km (52 mi.)
→ DURATION 4 to 5 days
→ LEVEL Moderate

The most renowned route for anyone wanting to reach these mysterious pre-Columbian ruins on foot is the Inca Trail. As Machu Picchu's fame increased over time, so did the quantity of people wanting to experience this ancient trek and it became overcrowded. In the early 2000s the authorities brought in a much-needed quota to limit the number of walkers—a decision that led to the emergence of the Salkantay Trail on the world's backpacking radar.

The Salkantay should not be considered as a secondary option to the Inca Trail. Its primary focus is on nature, and though it lacks some of the archeological sites of the Inca Trail, it is a less-trodden and more affordable option, whether done independently or with an organized group. The two treks are quite distinct hiking experiences, which both end up at the same magnificent destination.

The Salkantay Trail is characterized by its ecological diversity. The sometimes-rocky path traverses picturesque valleys and alpine meadows, runs up and over a dramatic mountain →

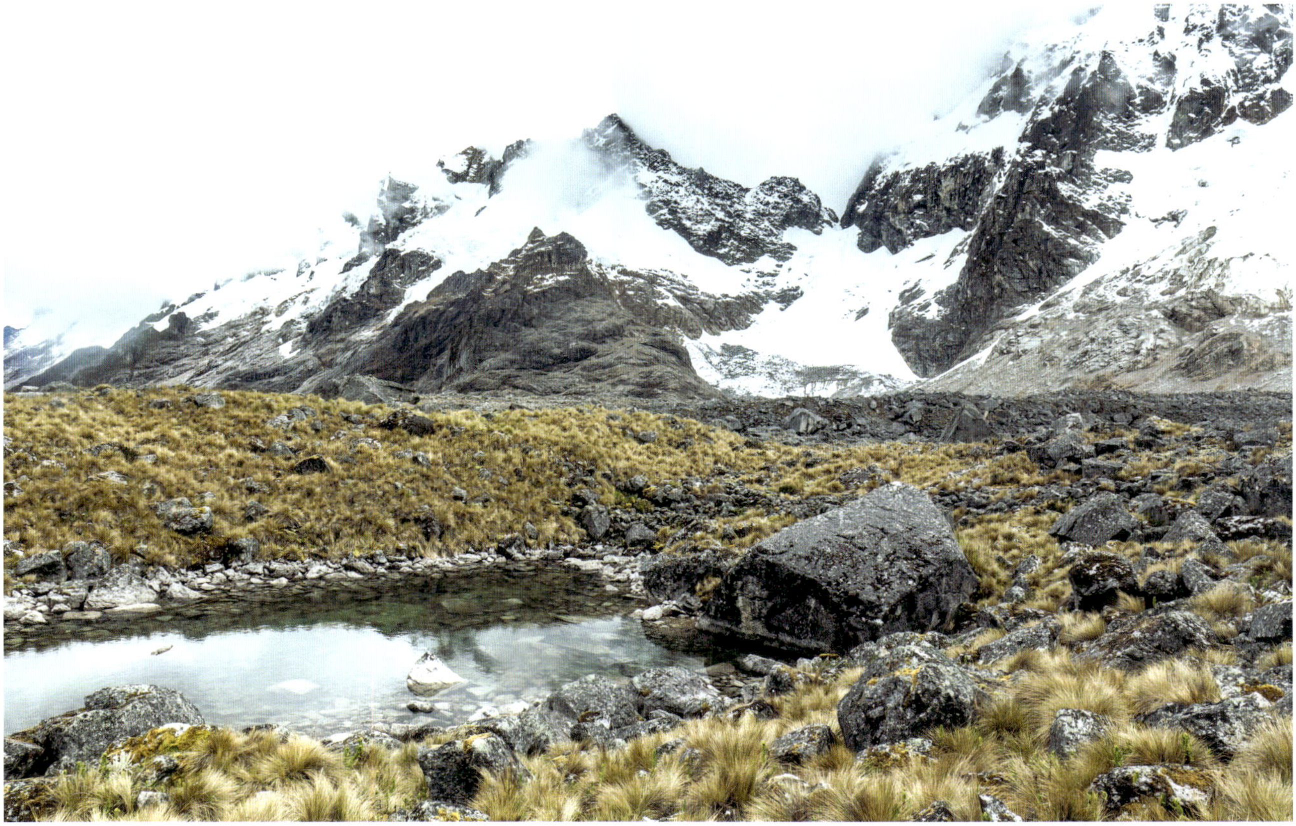

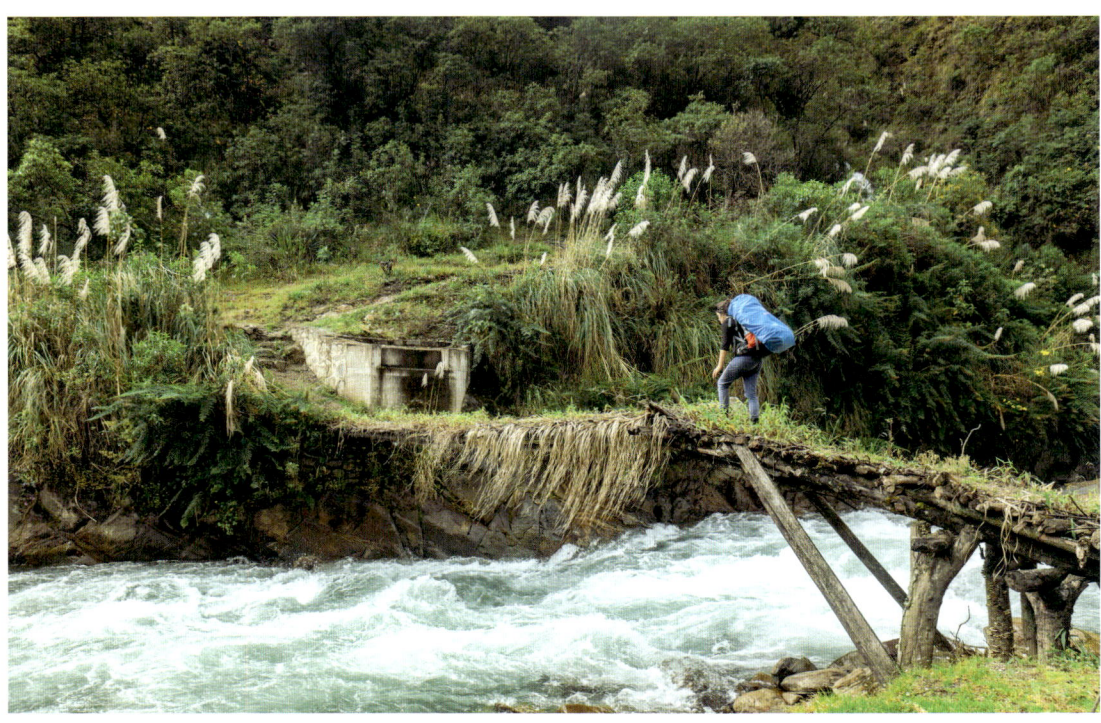

↑ Descending from the Abra Salkantay Pass.
← On the Abra Salkantay at 4,630 m (15,190 ft.).
↓ Passing over choppy waters.

pass, and meanders its way through a lush sub-tropical rainforest. The high point both geographically and scenically is the 4,630-m-high (15,190-ft.) Abra Salkantay, which is some 400 m above the highest point on the Inca Trail. Upon reaching this rocky pass, hikers are afforded unparalleled vistas of Mount Salkantay: a peak that rises to a mighty 6,271 m (20,574 ft.) and one that has long been considered sacred by the inhabitants of the Peruvian Andes. The Incas believed the peak, whose name stems from a Quechua word meaning "wild" or "uncivilized," was a deity that was instrumental in controlling fertility and weather in the region west of Cuzco.

From the pass, the trail descends more than 2,000 m (6,562 ft.) into a beautiful cloud forest, where fog often wraps the vegetation. The change in flora as well as temperature is dramatic. Eventually the pathway links up with an ancient Inca road that leads to the ruins of Llactapata. If possible, travelers should try to camp close to this stepped archeological complex, which is currently thought to have been a ceremonial site that supported Machu Picchu and might have once performed an astronomical function. From it, the views towards the slopes of Machu Picchu are striking—making it the ideal spot to stay on the penultimate night of a trek.

After leaving Llactapata, the route is mostly downhill or flat all the way to Aguas Calientes. Upon reaching this bustling little tourist town, which is bordered with cliffs, lofty cloud →

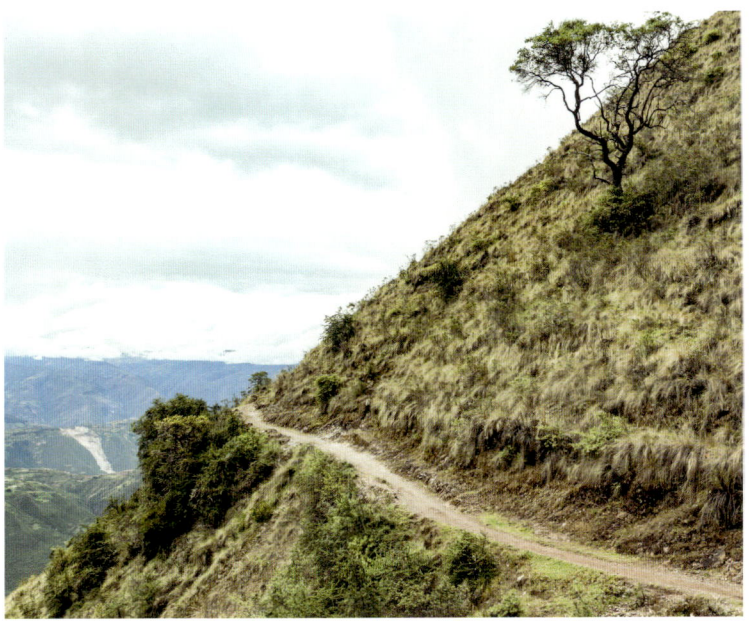

↑ Vegetation at higher levels is not as dense as lower down.
→ Taking in the sights of Machu Picchu.
↓ Along the train tracks to Aguas Calientes.

The trek's focus is on nature, and it is a less-trodden and more affordable alternative to the Inca Trail.

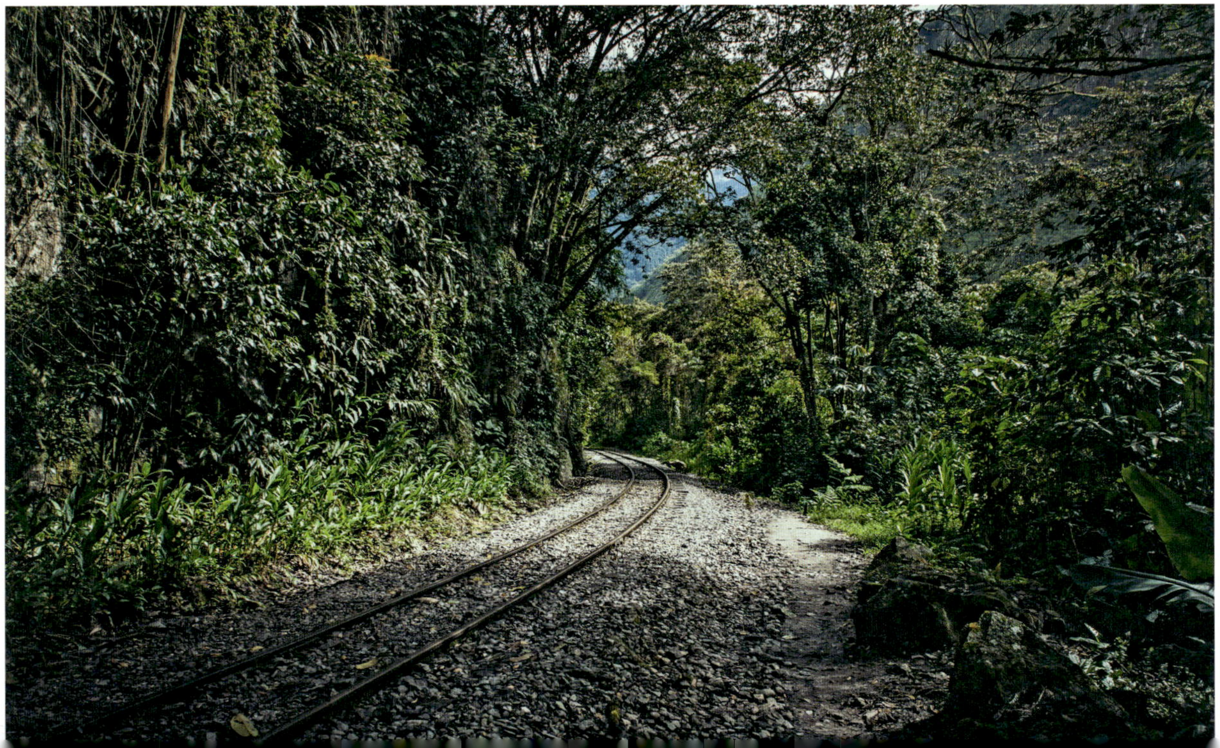

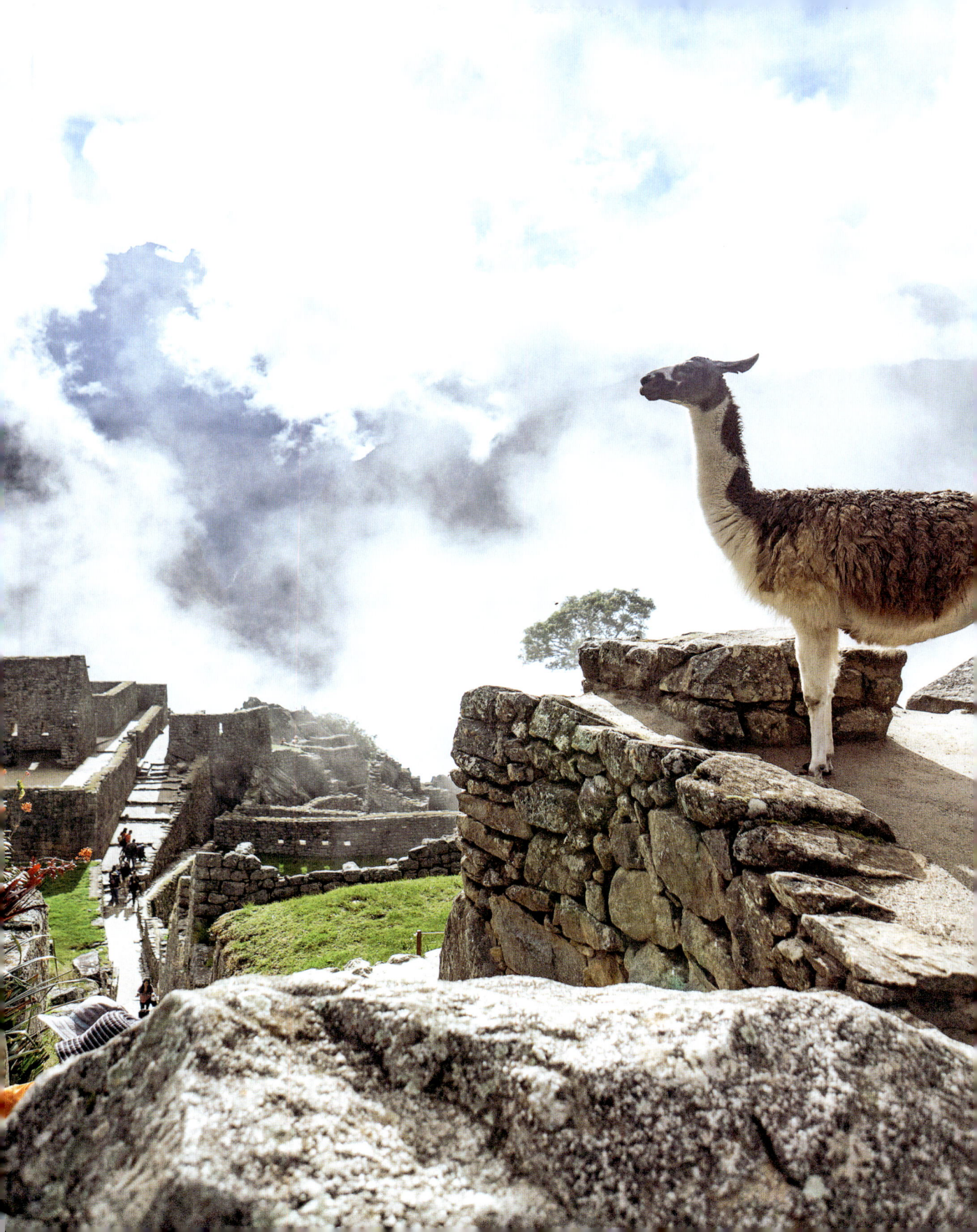

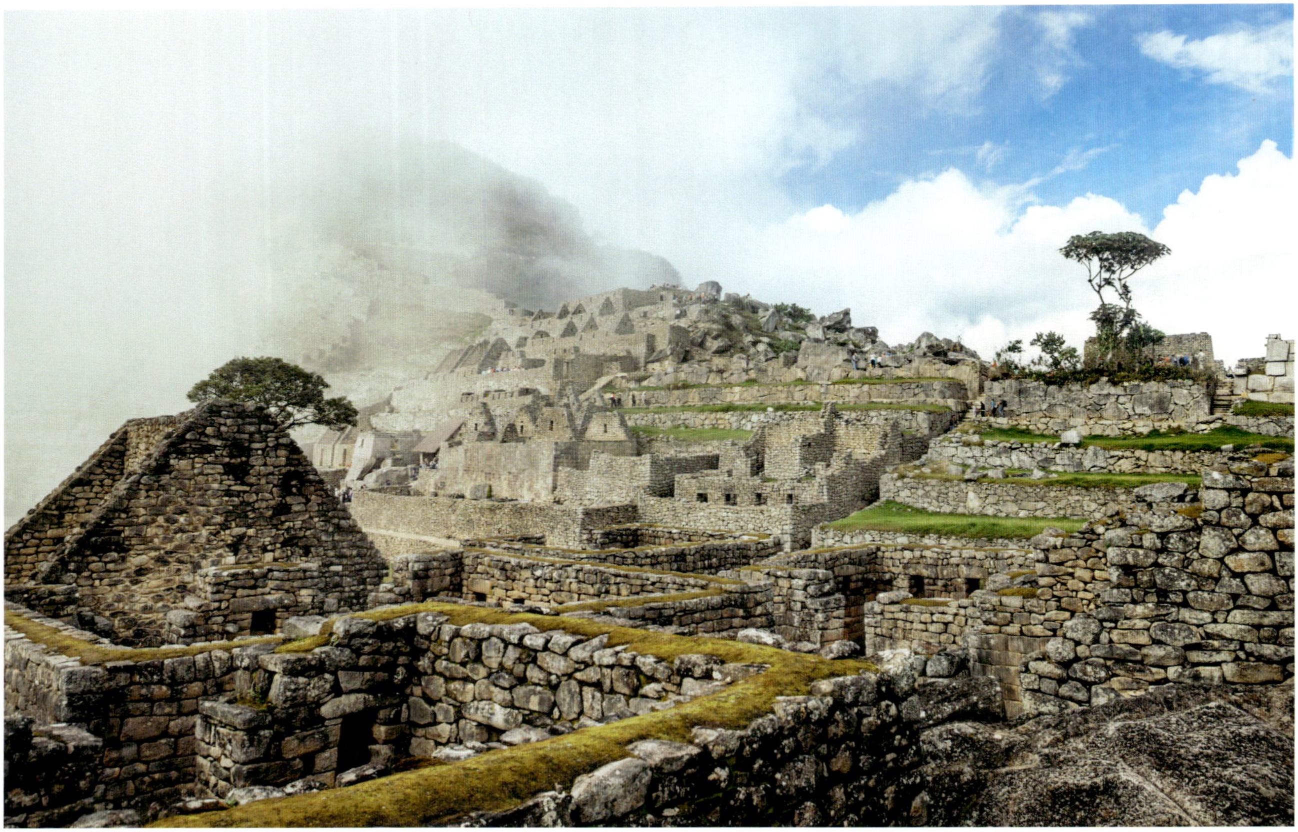

↑ Machu Picchu—as seen in rare good weather.
↘ Taking a break at the village of Chaullay.

forests, and fast-flowing rivers, hikers will find a number of accommodation options on offer. Tired wanderers can have a hot shower, sleep in a real bed, and rest up before the final part of the journey: a steep one to one-and-a-half hour climb to the ancient sanctuary at Machu Picchu.

It almost goes without saying that one should make the effort to arrive at the city at first light. This helps avoid the crowds. Once there, hikers can climb to the summit of Huayna Picchu for early-morning views over the entire site and the surrounding valleys. If it not completely shrouded in mist, Machu Picchu will light up below, and one can really reflect on the Salkantay Trail—the climbs, the descents, the mountains, the forests, the people encountered along the way. And with the journey to the finest remaining achievement of the Incas complete, all that is left to do is to descend and spend the rest of the day exploring it. ————————

It almost goes without saying that one should make the effort to arrive at the city at first light.

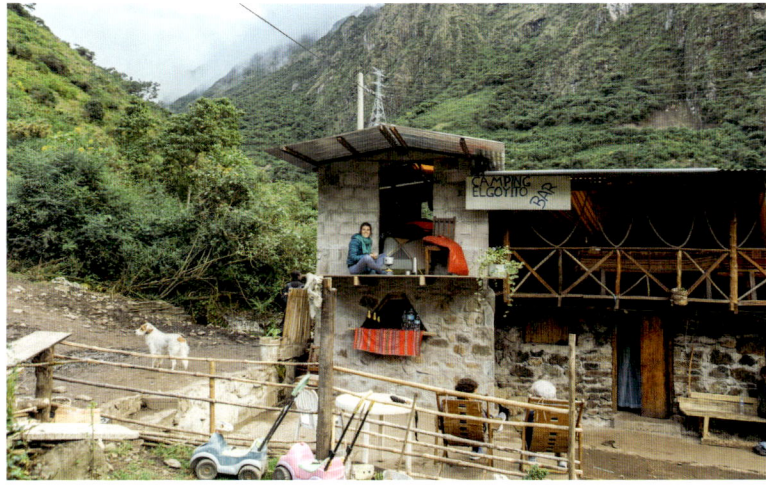

GOOD TO KNOW

START/FINISH
📍 Mollepata
📍 Aguas Calientes (at the base of MP)

SEASON
April to November. The dry season between June and September is ideal.

CONDITIONS
During trekking season, nights can be chilly (0°C [32°F] is common), but days are generally warm and clear. Due to the high altitude reached at Salkantay Pass, hikers should be well acclimatized before beginning this trek.

LOWEST/HIGHEST POINT
1,540 m (5,052 ft.)/4,650 m (15,256 ft.)

TIP
It is possible to rent backpacking equipment in Cuzco, but the quality is not always very high. Hikers are better off bringing everything.

HELPFUL HINTS

OFF ON ONE'S OWN Most people do this trek as part of a guided tour. However, with the necessary gear and a reasonable amount of backpacking experience, the well-signposted hike can be done independently. In that case, supplies should be brought from Cuzco.

BACKGROUND

MACHU PICCHU Called the "Old Peak" in Quechua—the language of the Incas and one that is still spoken in many variants today—Machu Picchu stands next to the "New Peak," Huayna Picchu. The ruins of the settlement that most think of when they hear of the name Machu Picchu sit in the middle of the two mountains on east-facing slopes. The Inca sanctuary is made up of around 200 constructions and appears almost integrated into the steep landscape. Stone walls crisscross the terraced city; irrigation canals, road systems, and evidence of agriculture and domesticated plants and animals make up just some of its sophisticated characteristics. Thought to have been built in the fifteenth or sixteenth century, Machu Picchu was likely constructed when the Inca Empire was at its height. Spanish conquistadors arrived in the 1530s and overthrew the empire within a period of about 40 years; however, it is believed that they never found Machu Picchu.

FLORA & FAUNA

TRAIL BLAZERS Growing in cloud forest habitats in the Peruvian High Andes, the Inca orchid (Sobralia dichotoma) dots hikers' paths with its distinctive purple blooms. Orchids are abundant in Machu Picchu, and evidence exists to imply that the Incas planted them as ceremonial flowers on roadsides.

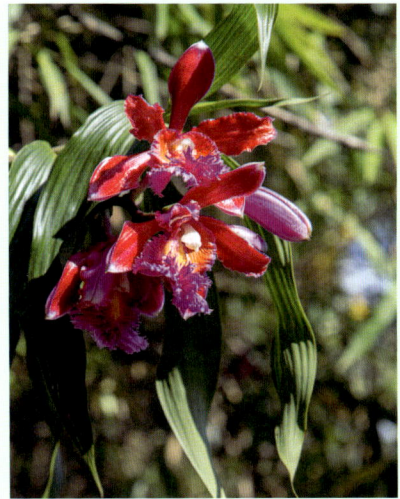

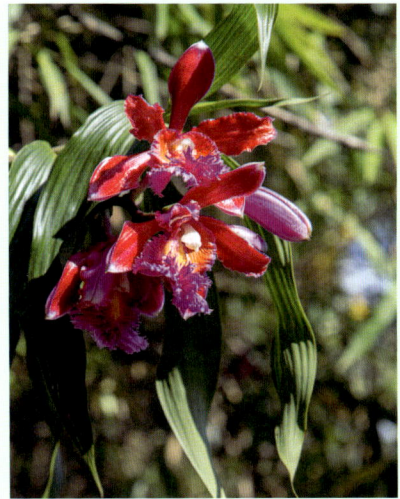

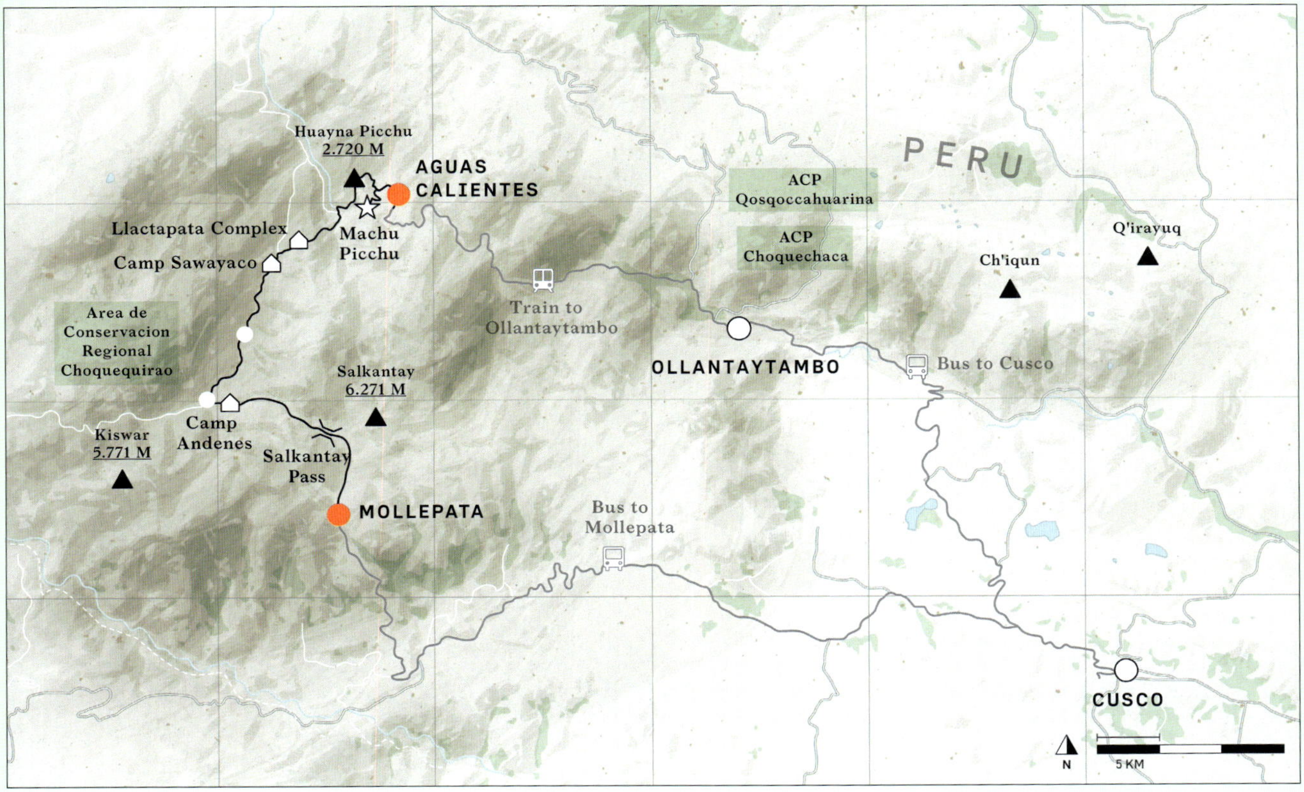

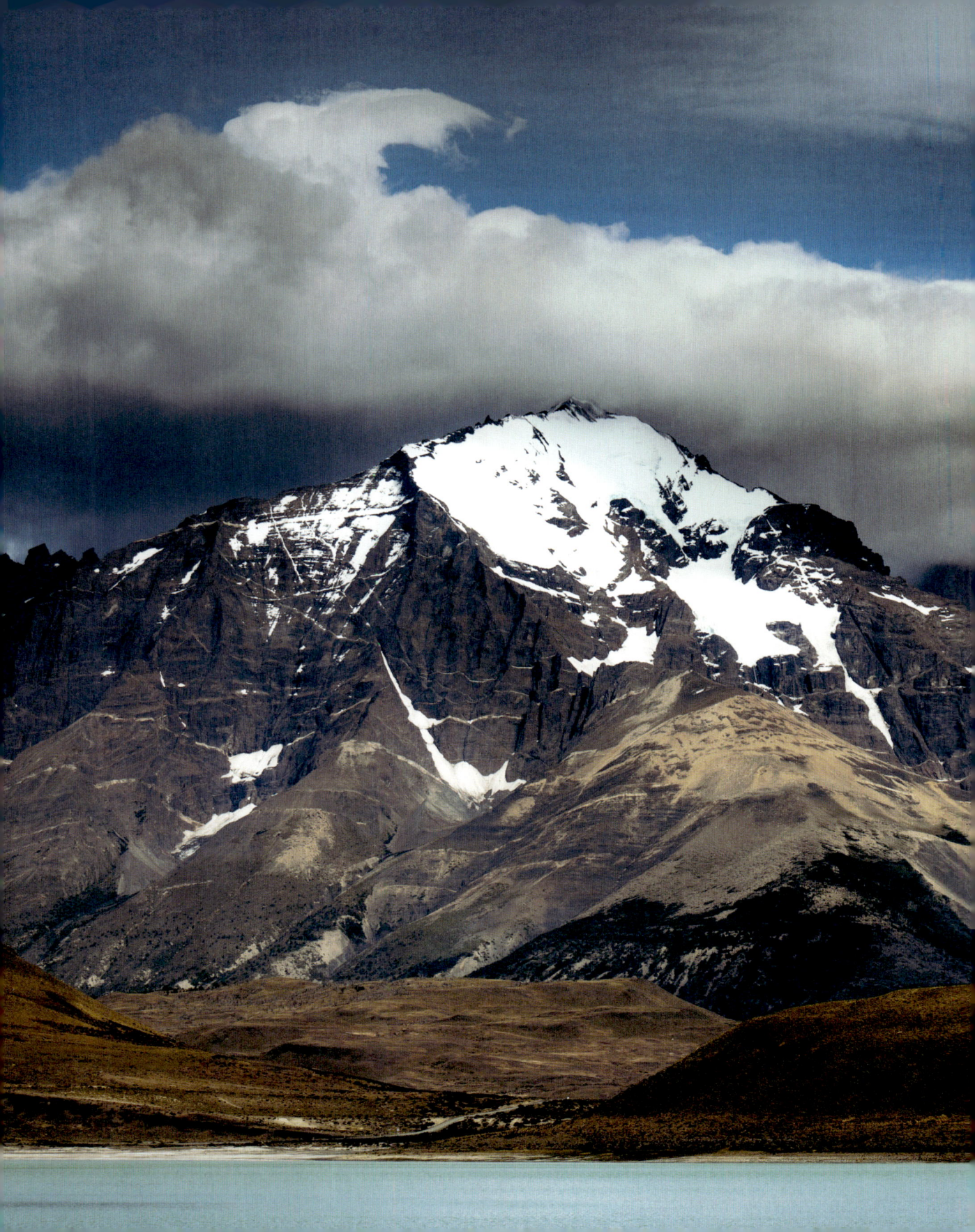

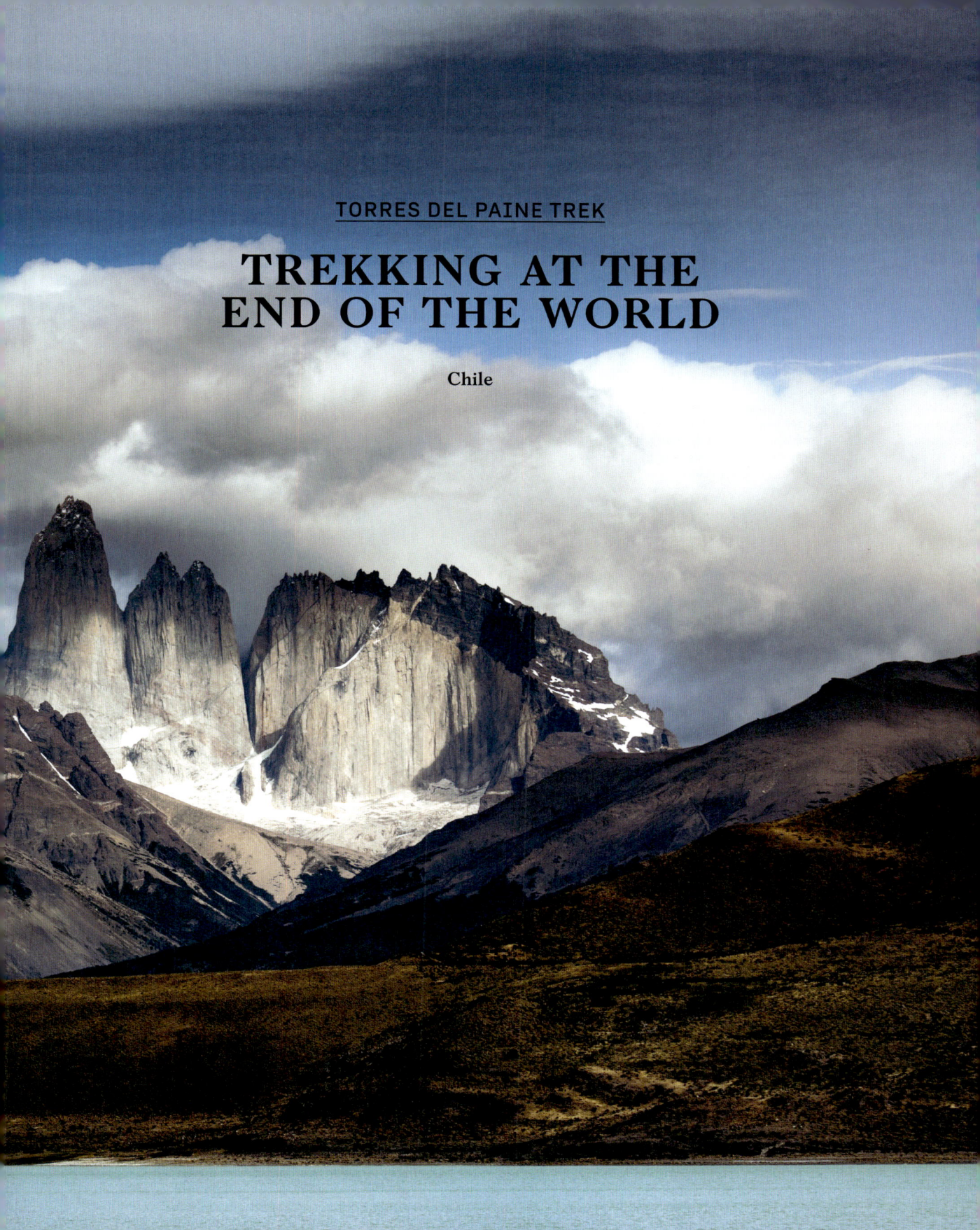

TORRES DEL PAINE TREK

TREKKING AT THE END OF THE WORLD

Chile

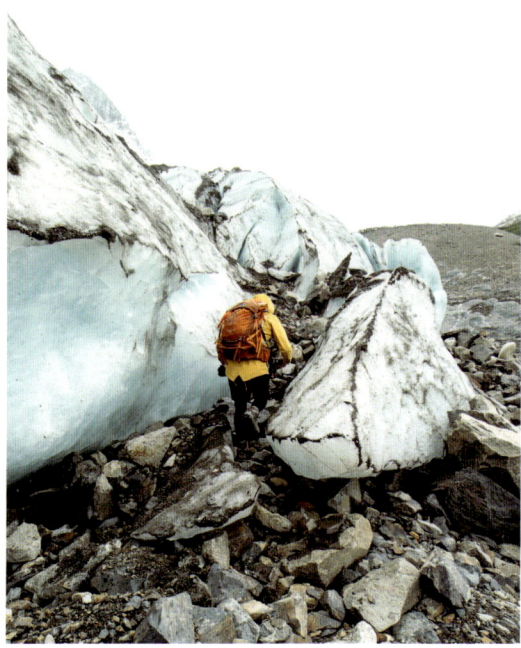

U pon first viewing the Torres del Paine Massif (also known as the Cordillera del Paine) it is hard not to do a double take. The granite spires and mountains of the Massif rise some 3,000 m (9,843 ft.) out of the windswept steppes that surround it. The park takes its name (*torres* being "towers" in Spanish and *paine* the Tehuelche South American Indian word for "blue") from the set of three granite peaks that rise up as one of its main features. With these monoliths, the turquoise waters, and the ridged icebergs, the landscape does not seem quite real—it is almost like something out of Tolkien's Middle Earth. A more breathtaking introduction to a multi-day backpacking trip is hard to imagine.

The Torres del Paine area of southern Chile is an enthralling mixture of jutting mountains, aquamarine waterways, pre-Andean shrubland, and sweeping, jagged glaciers, and so it is unsurprising that the location has long been a mecca for hikers, climbers, and lovers of the outdoors. Granted National →

ABOUT THE TRAIL

→ <u>DISTANCE</u> 130 km (81 mi.)
→ <u>DURATION</u> 6 to 8 days
→ <u>LEVEL</u> Moderate

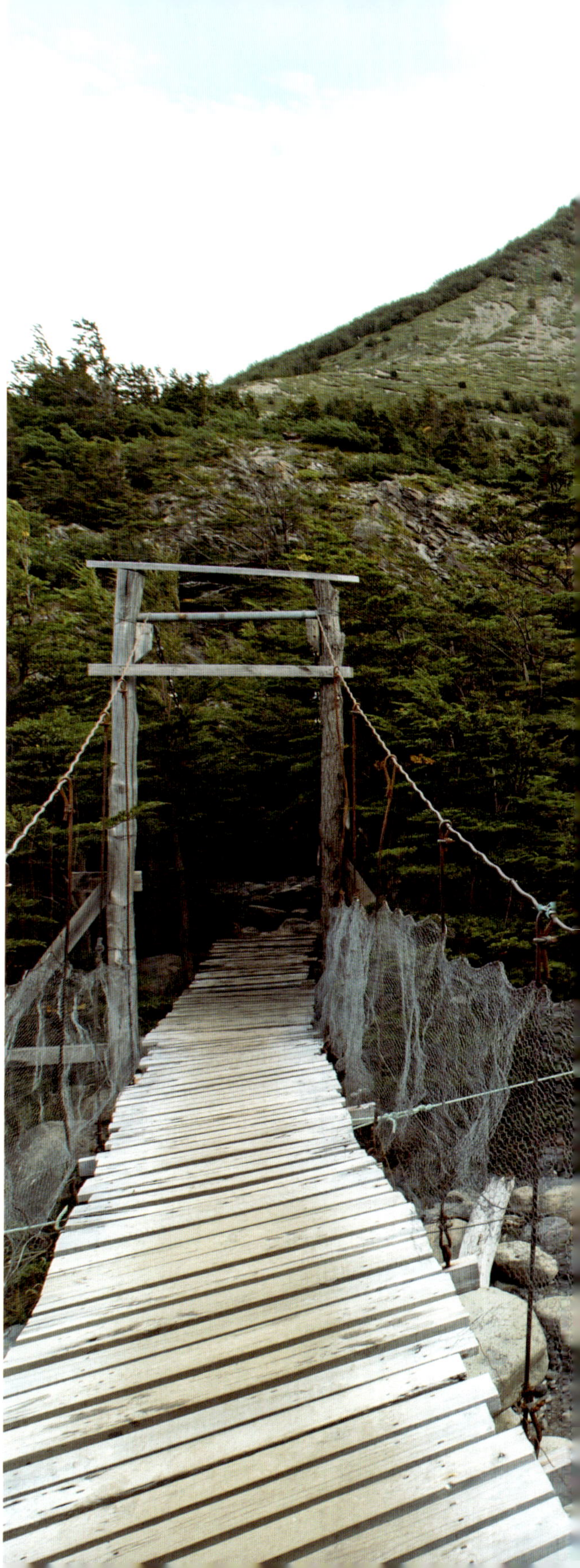

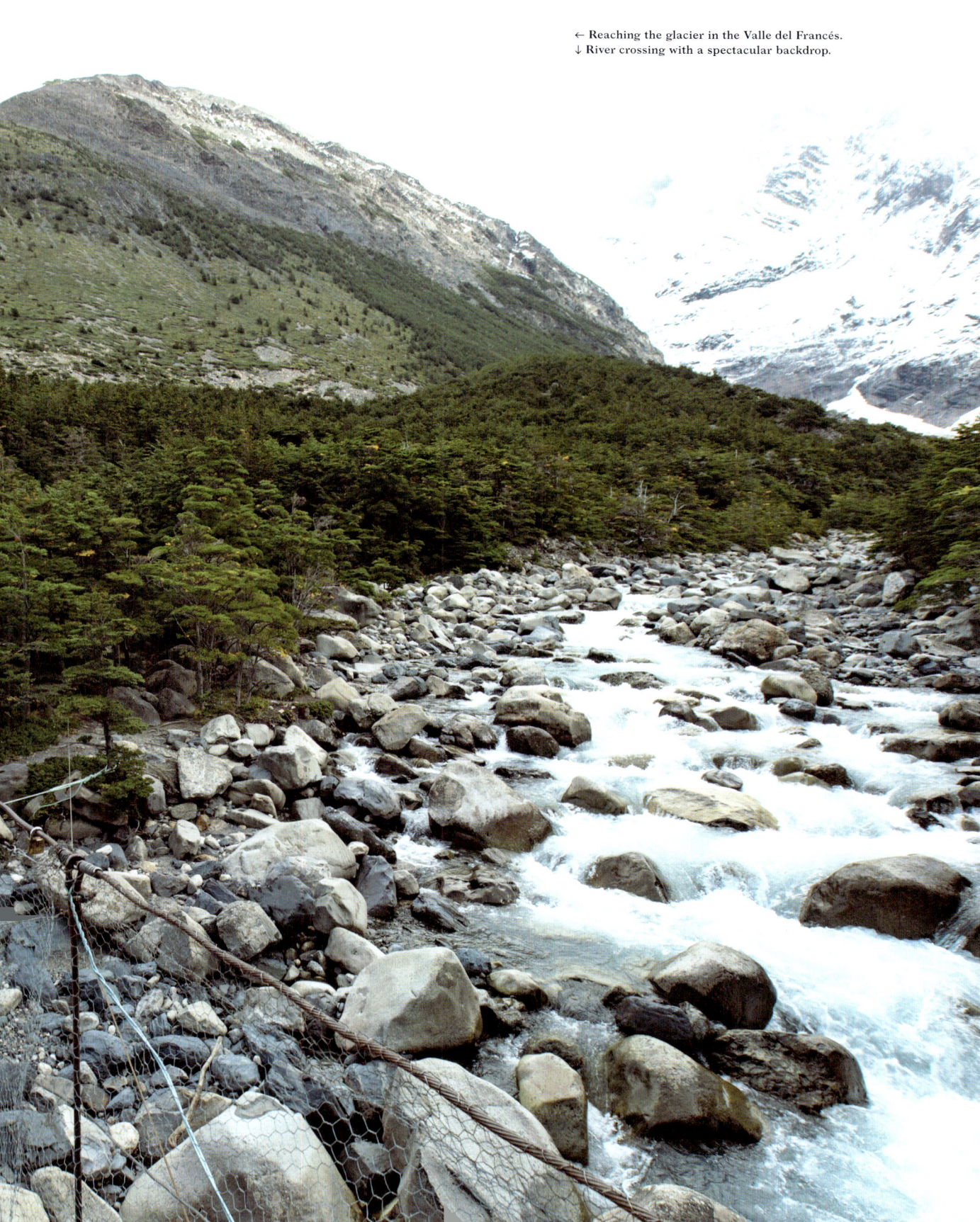

← Reaching the glacier in the Valle del Francés.
↓ River crossing with a spectacular backdrop.

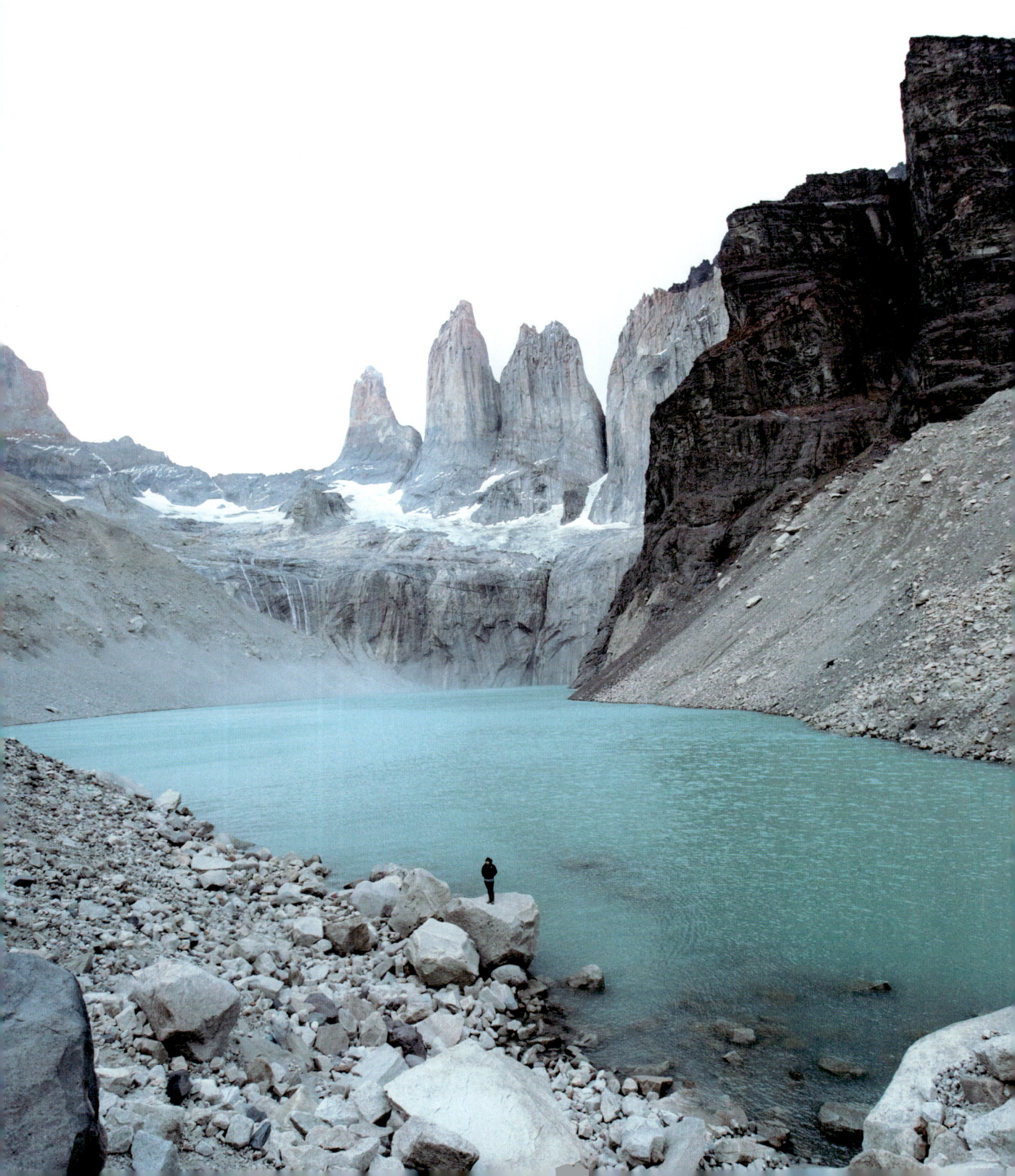

Park status in 1959, the region has an incredible natural beauty, which received international recognition in 1979, when it was designated a UNESCO World Heritage Site. It is even featured on Chile's banknotes.

There are two primary options for long-distance hiking in Torres del Paine: the "W" and "O" circuits. The former is the most popular trip, taking four to six days to complete, and including many of the parks highlights such as Grey Glacier and the Valle del Francés. However, the latter represents a better choice for those looking to experience as many of the region's wonders as possible. A circumnavigation of the entire Paine Massif, the O circuit incorporates all of the W, but also takes hikers around the less-frequented back section of the Park. Peak time for hiking in Torres del Paine is January and February; earlier or later on in the season (November/December or March/April) means fewer people on the trail and not so many issues obtaining hut reservations.

Beginning at Refugio Paine Grande, the O Circuit is approximately 130 km (81 mi.) in length and can be done by the average walker in six to eight days. The trail passes through a myriad of otherworldly landscapes, and also affords hikers the possibility of seeing some of the region's diverse wildlife, including guanacos, grey foxes, condors and the endangered south Andean deer.

In 1880, the three Torres were referred to as "Cleopatra's Needles" by Lady Florence Dixie, who is thought to be one of the first foreign tourists to visit the area.

Accommodation options number three in total: indoor lodgings at the rustic shelters known as *refugios*, free campsites (these are covered by park entrance fee), and private campsites, which have better facilities than the free campgrounds. Many hikers take a hybrid approach by doing a combination of two or three of these alternatives. Supplies can either be purchased beforehand (the option that is the best value for money), or picked up along the way for elevated prices at refugios (the option that means less weight to carry).

There is one very important aspect of hiking the circuit that is not so easy to plan: the weather. Heading into the Patagonian backcountry can be a meteorological roll of the dice at any time of year, so hikers need to pack accordingly. Good wet-weather gear and sufficient layers are a must, and for those planning on camping rather than staying indoors, it is important to have a solid shelter that will hold up well in extreme conditions. The winds in Patagonia can be unforgiving, and a shelter must be storm-worthy, otherwise the best choice is to spend the extra money and opt for indoor accommodation. →

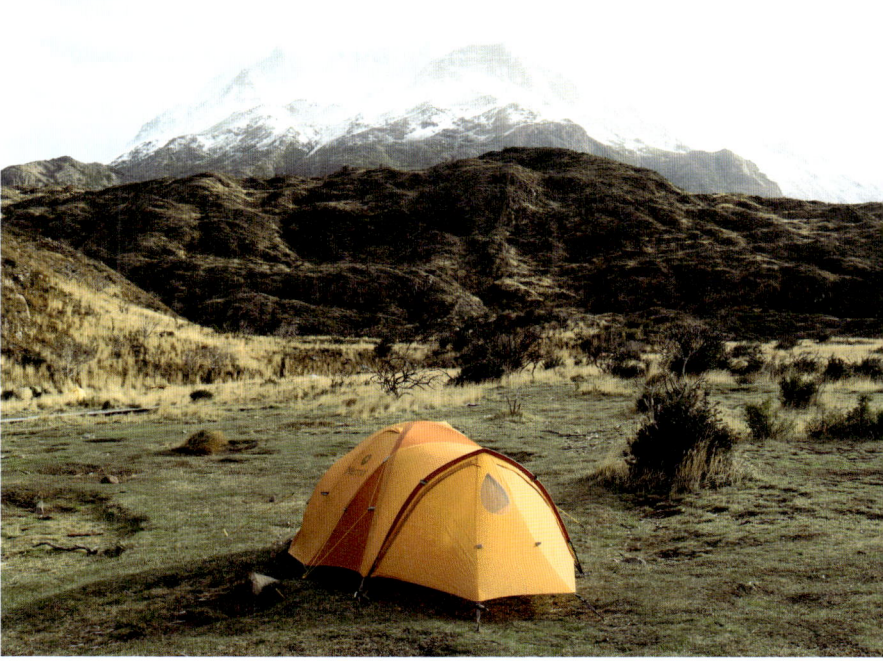

↑ Camping at Paine Grande.
← Early morning at Las Torres.
↓ Clambering through the Valle del Francés.

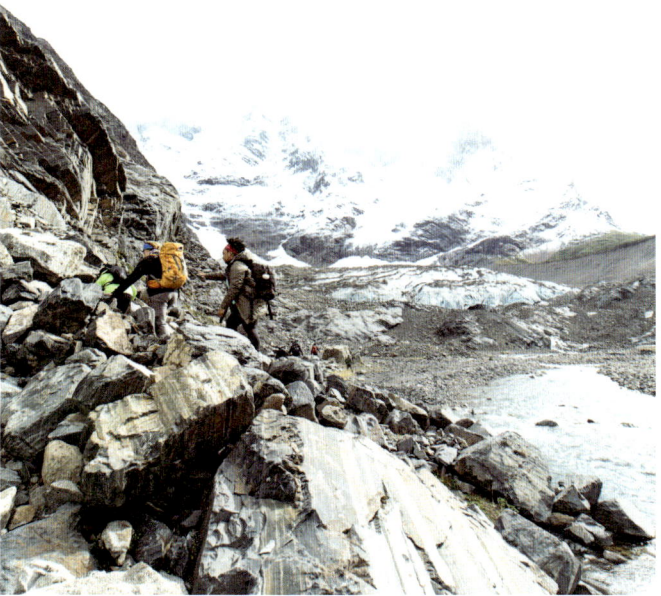

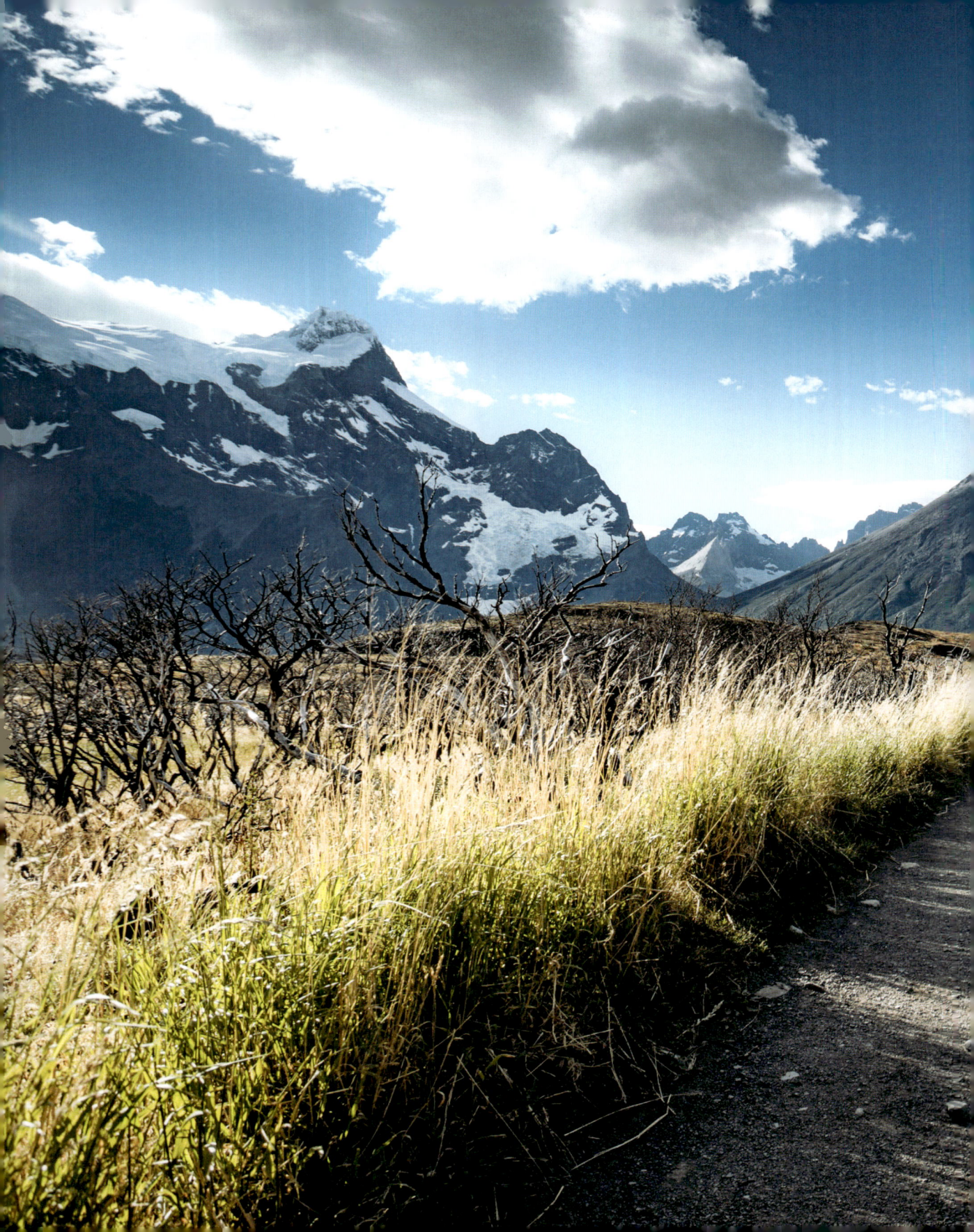

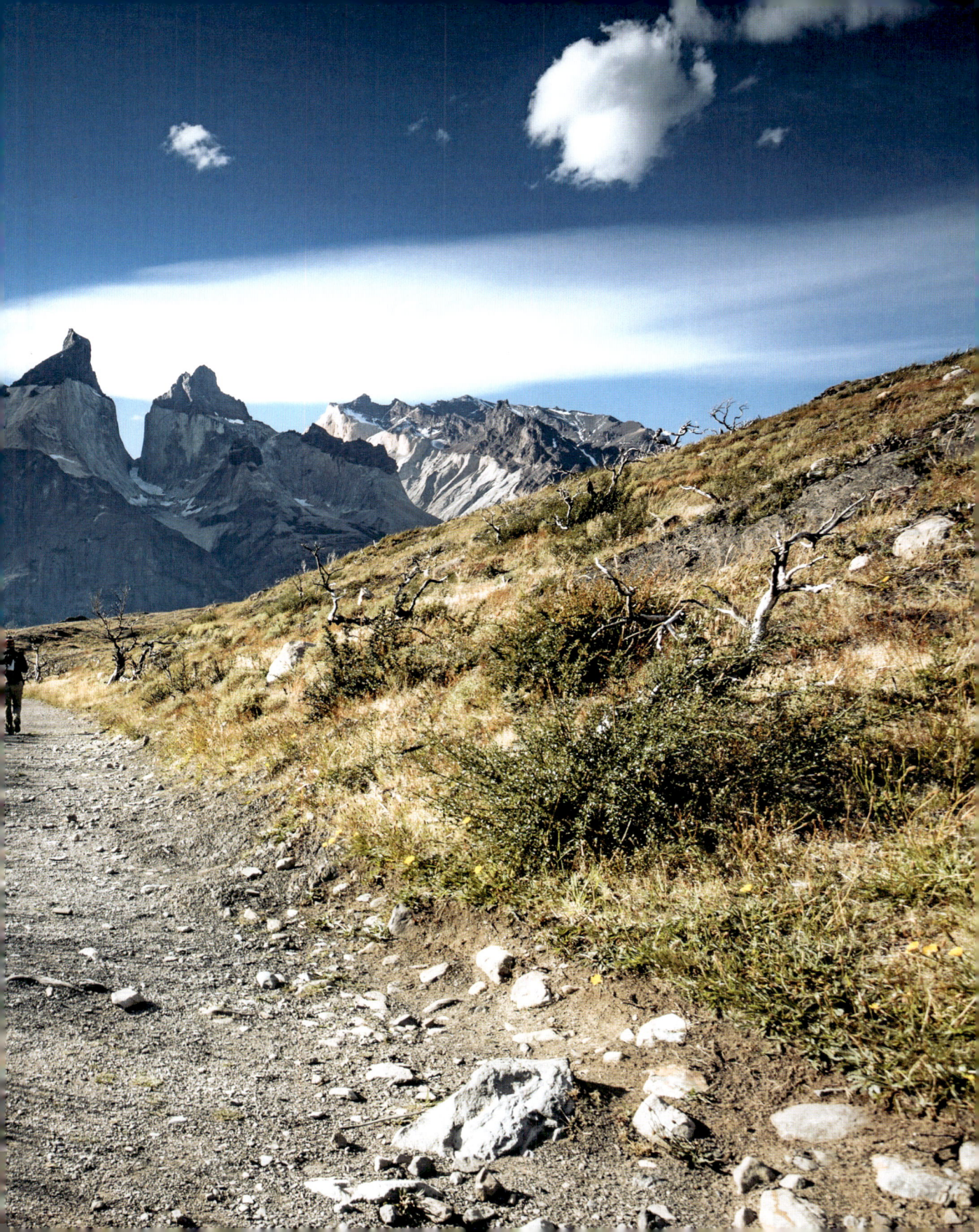

The area is an enthralling mixture of jutting mountains, aquamarine waterways, pre-Andean shrubland, and sweeping, jagged glaciers.

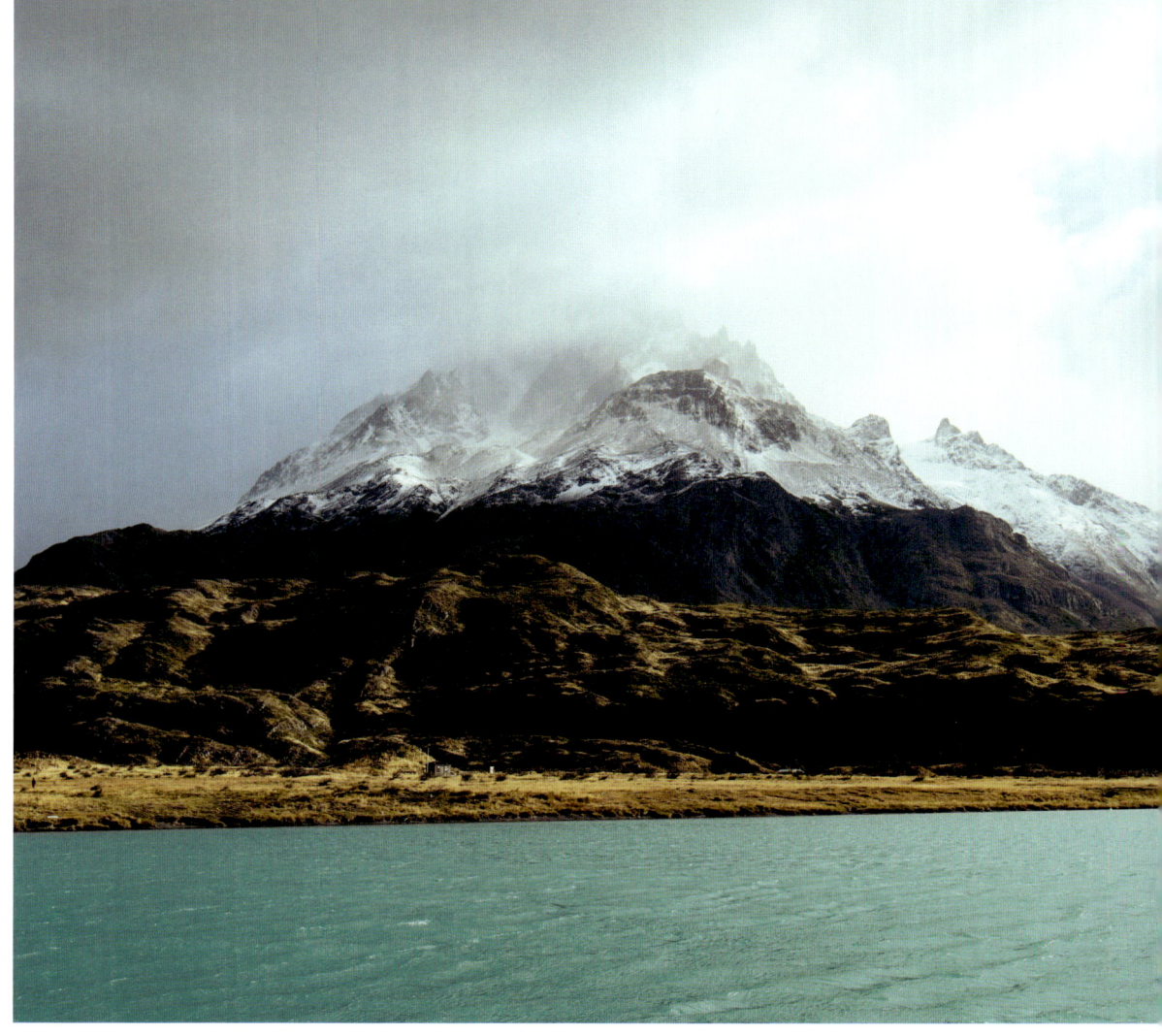

↑ **View from the boat to Paine Grande.**

The most strenuous section of the hike is the climb up and over John Gardner Pass. Sometimes closed because of extreme weather conditions, this high point offers an amazing view over Grey Glacier. Measuring over 30 m (98 ft.) high and 6 km (3.7 mi.) wide, Grey Glacier forms part of the massive Southern Patagonian Ice Field—the second largest non-polar ice field on the planet. Although there still remains 21 km (13 mi.) to the finish, it is on this dramatic windswept pass that hikers are often moved to contemplation—the vast river before them inspiring not only awe, but also a heightened sense of gratitude and appreciation for the natural world. ———————————

GOOD TO KNOW

START/FINISH
🚩 Round trip from Refugio Paine Grande

SEASON
November to April

CONDITIONS
The weather changes quickly, so effective shelters and rain protection are essential if camping.

LOWEST/HIGHEST POINT
Approx. 27 m (98 ft.)/1,200m (3,937 ft.)

ACCOMMODATION
Basic indoor shelters (*refugios*), camping.

WILDLIFE
Andean condors, guanacos, foxes, pumas.

HIGHLIGHTS
Grey Glacier, Valle del Francés, the three *torres*.

TIP
Hike early and late (around 8 a.m. to between 2 and 4 p.m.), as these are the most beautiful times of the day and the trail is relatively people-free.

FLORA & FAUNA

IN SPITTING DISTANCE A frequent sight on the trail is the guanaco. Covered in thick wool and with blood that can carry more oxygen than other mammals, the animals survive well in higher climes. Like their relatives, the camel and the llama, they spit if irritated.

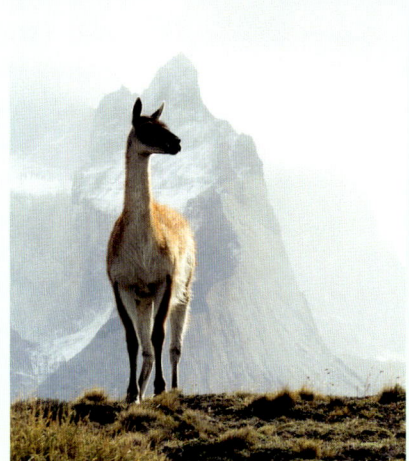

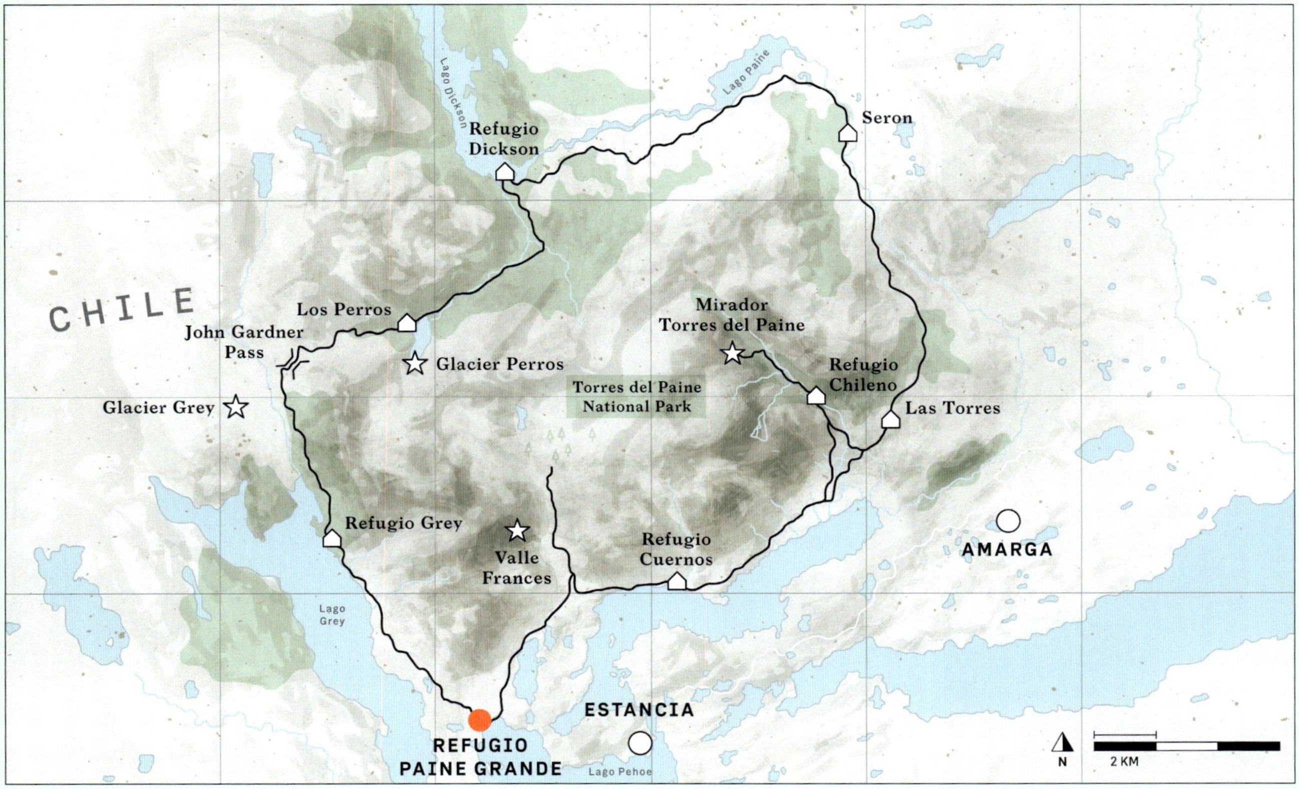

BACKGROUND

THE "W" OR THE "O"? Which is the best circuit to choose? The W Circuit is a shorter trip that incorporates some of the main highlights of the national park, and normally requires four and six days to complete. The O Circuit takes hikers around the less-crowded backside of the park, affords more opportunities to see flora and fauna, and is approximately twice as long.

HELPFUL HINTS

ECOCAMP PATAGONIA At the foot of the *torres* stands the world's first geodesic hotel. Opened in 2001, EcoCamp Patagonia consists of a series of domes, which were inspired by the dwellings of the ancient inhabitants of the site, the Kaweskars. The accommodation is fully sustainable to minimize the footprint of visitors in the national park.

CHILE

Lago Dickson

Lago Paine

Refugio Dickson

Seron

Los Perros

John Gardner Pass

☆ Glacier Perros

Mirador Torres del Paine ☆

Refugio Chileno

☆ Glacier Grey

Torres del Paine National Park

Las Torres

Refugio Grey

☆ Valle Frances

Refugio Cuernos

AMARGA

Lago Grey

ESTANCIA

REFUGIO PAINE GRANDE

Lago Pehoe

N

2 KM

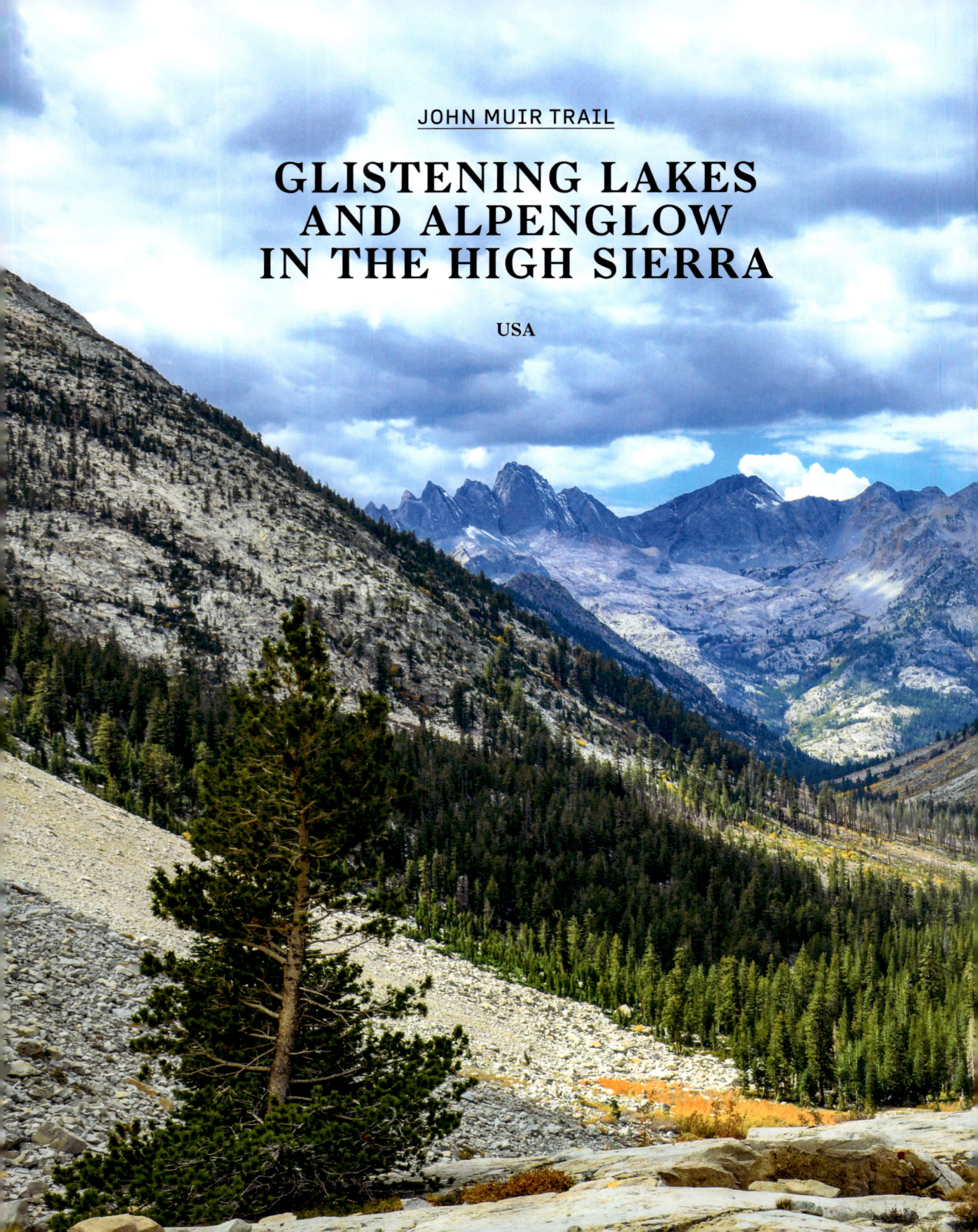

JOHN MUIR TRAIL

GLISTENING LAKES AND ALPENGLOW IN THE HIGH SIERRA

USA

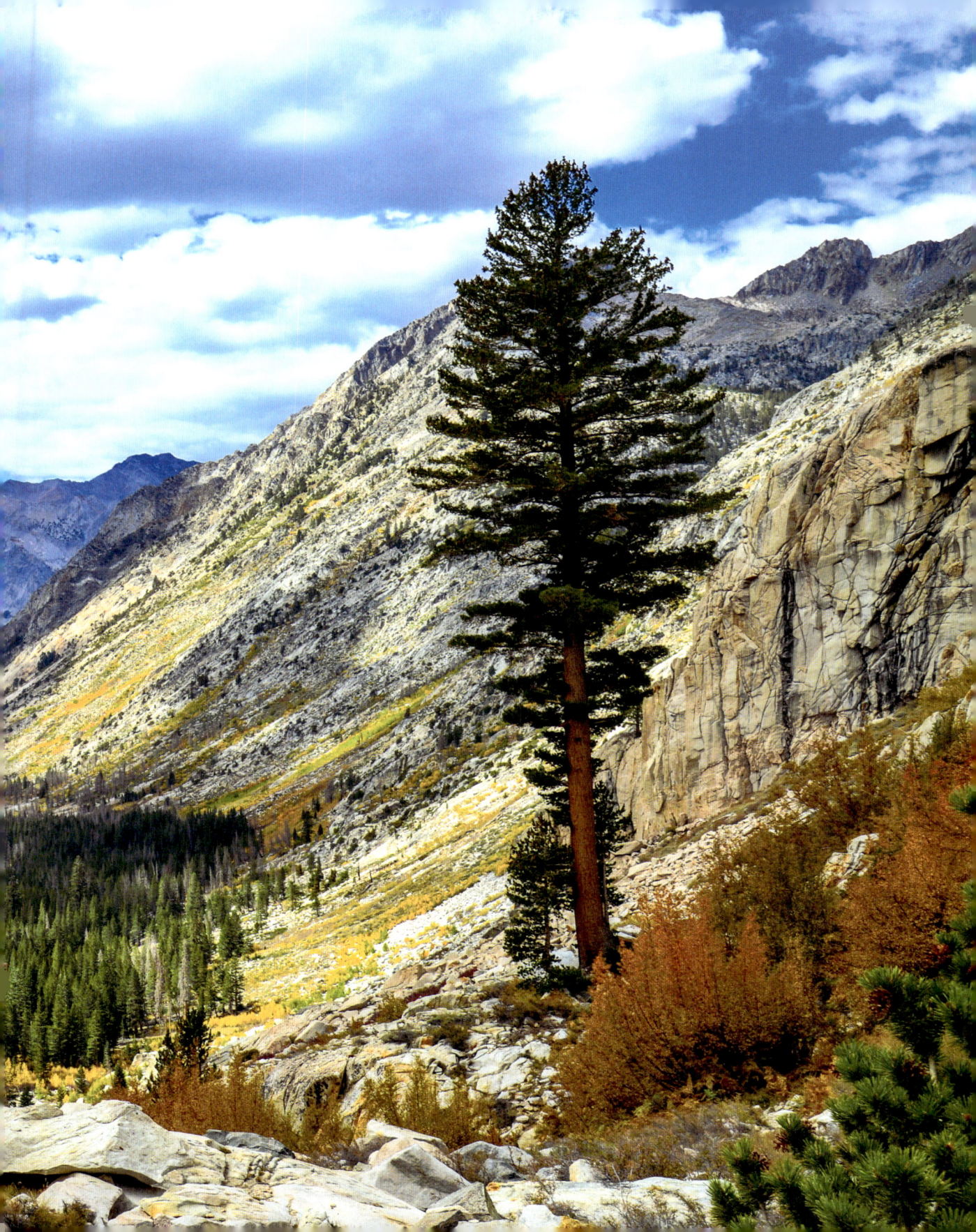

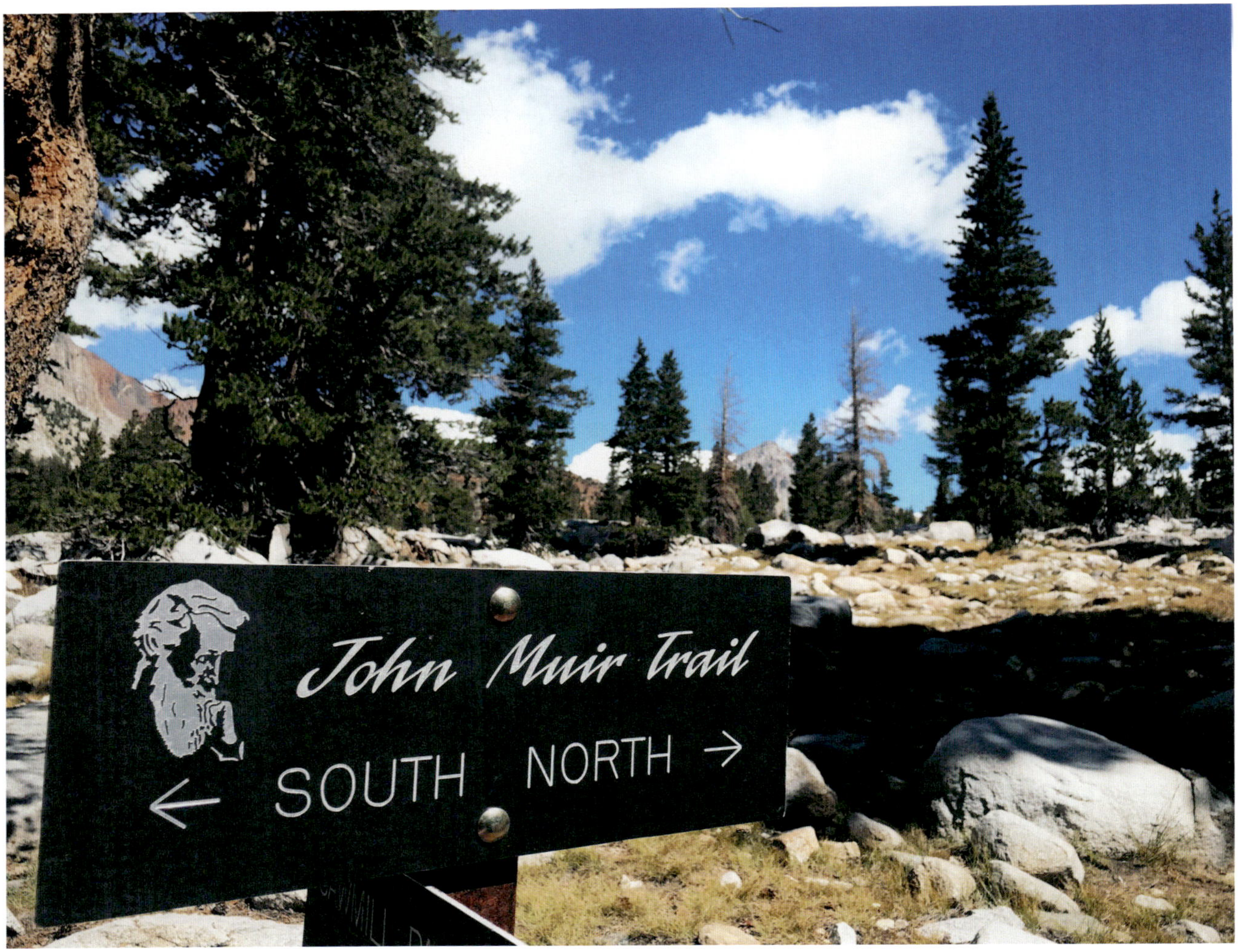

Winding its way through California's High Sierra, the JMT represents an unforgettable combination of jagged granite peaks, thunderous waterfalls, sweeping glacial valleys, and hundreds of alpine lakes.

↑ Decisions to make on the JMT.
↗ The fire-damaged forest around Devils Postpile.
↓ Campsite just north of Lyell Fork Bridge.

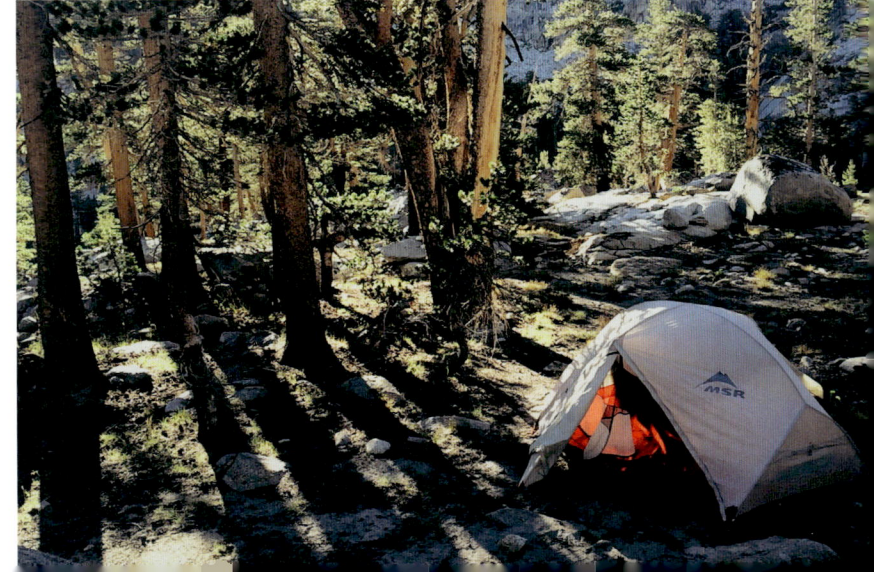

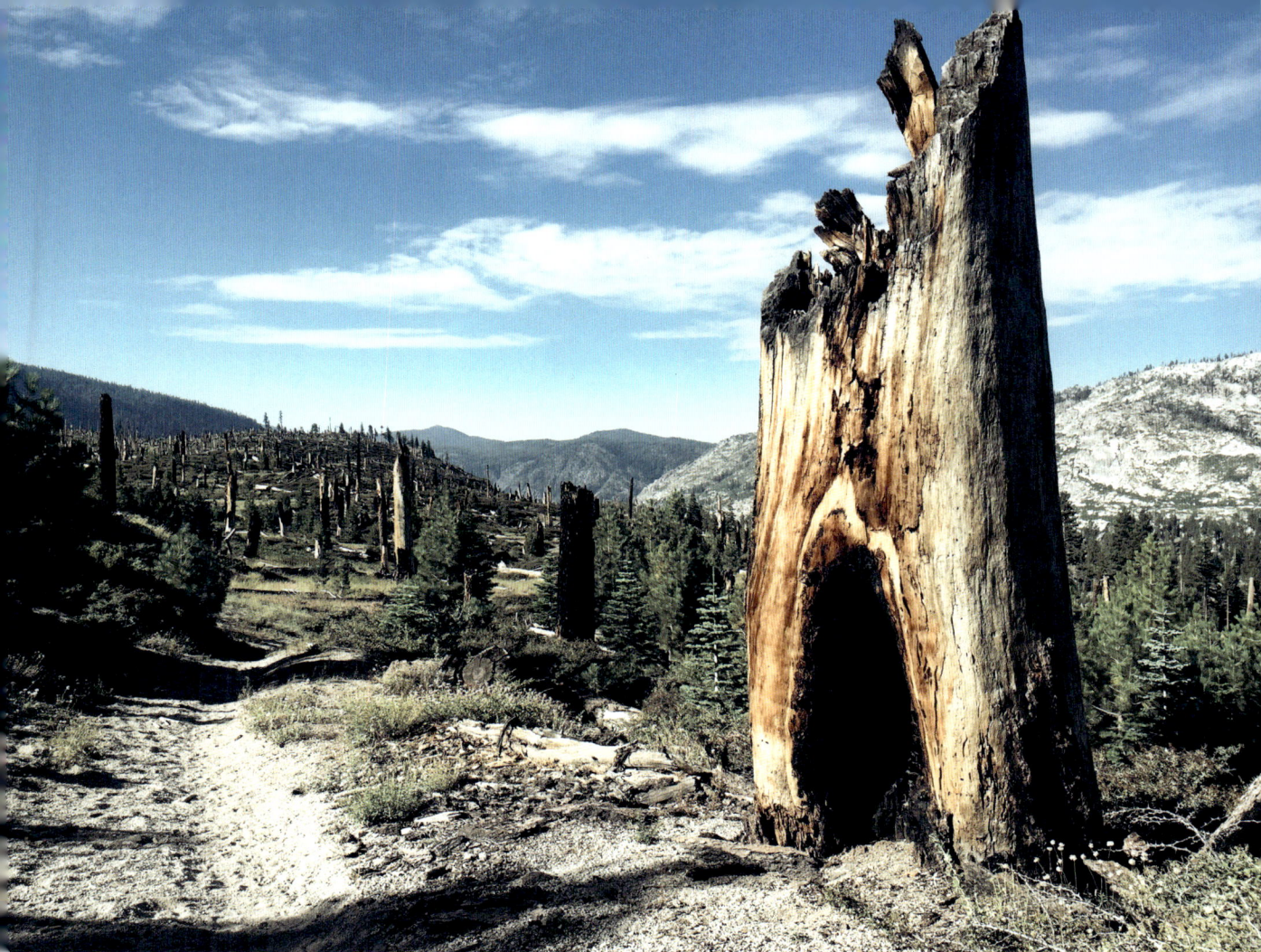

When experienced hikers sit around the campfire and talk about the world's most beautiful pathways, the John Muir Trail is invariably one of the first names mentioned. Winding its way through California's High Sierra, the JMT represents an unforgettable combination of jagged granite peaks, thunderous waterfalls, sweeping glacial valleys, and hundreds of alpine lakes.

The John Muir Trail stretches 340 km (211 mi.) from Yosemite Valley to the top of Mount Whitney, which at 4,421 m (14,500 ft.) is the highest point in the contiguous United States and arguably the most breathtaking finishing point of any long-distance hike in North America. Along the way it passes through three National Parks (Yosemite, Kings Canyon, and Sequoia), two designated wilderness areas (John Muir and Ansel Adams), and some of the most striking mountains on the planet.

As the trail is scenic from start to finish, standout highlights cannot be easily identified. That being said, though, some of the most memorable features include Devils Postpile, a basalt rock formation that was created by lava flow and which resembles a stack of posts on an enormous scale, and Evolution Valley, where picturesque lakes and dramatic mountain vistas can be enjoyed. Rae Lakes and the Muir Pass—the midpoint of the trail and the location of the John Muir Hut built by the Sierra Club (see page 197)—are also worth mentioning. And for approximately 274 of its 340 km (170 of 211 mi.), the John Muir Trail coincides with another of America's most famous long-distance pathways, the Pacific Crest Trail, which runs from Mexico to Canada and is much longer at 4,265 km (2,650 mi.).   →

ABOUT THE TRAIL

→ <u>DISTANCE</u> 340 km (211 mi.)
→ <u>DURATION</u> 17 to 24 days
→ <u>LEVEL</u> Moderate to Difficult

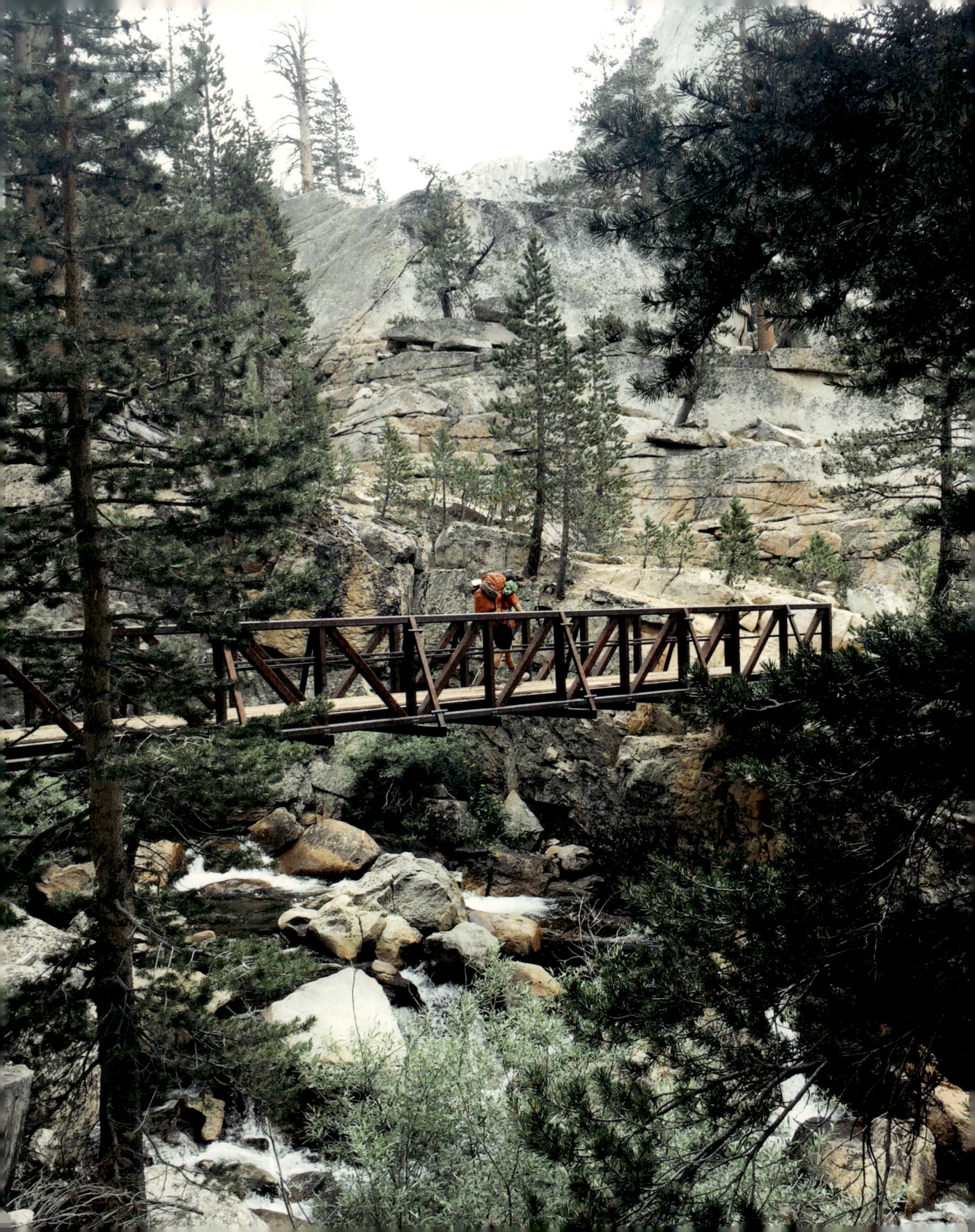

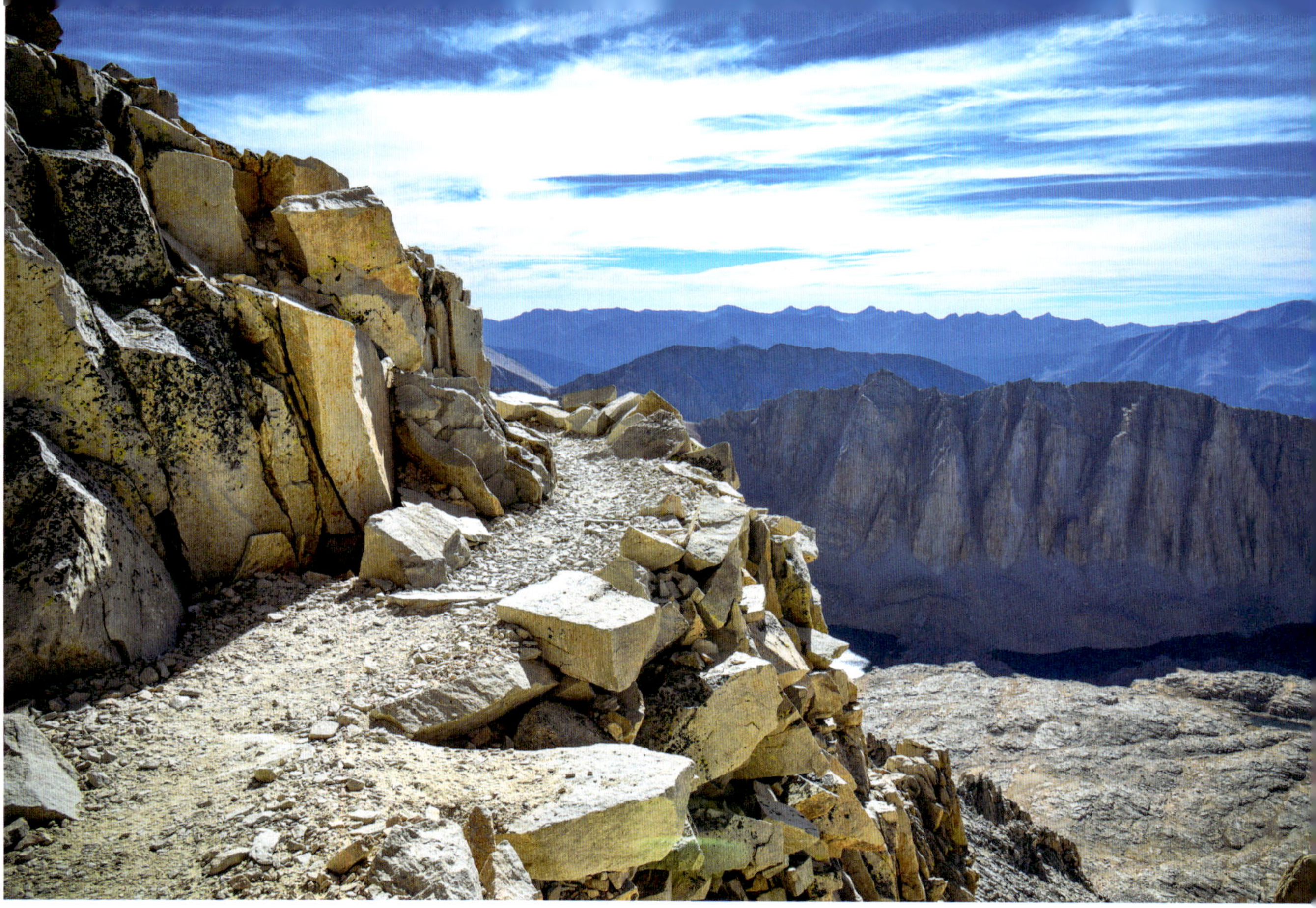

↑ One of the many high rocky passes on the JMT.
↓ Pack adjustments at over 3,350 m (11,000 ft.) on Donohue Pass.

What is perhaps one of the most extraordinary features of the hike is alpenglow. Around sunrise and sunset on an almost daily basis, the granite peaks and turquoise lakes of the High Sierra are illuminated by a crimson glow, which gives the range an almost ethereal quality. In the words of John Muir, the naturalist the trail is named for, in *The Mountains of California* (1894):

"Long, blue, spiky shadows crept out across the snow-fields, while a rosy glow, at first scarce discernible, gradually deepened and suffused every mountain-top, flushing the glaciers and the harsh crags above them. This was the alpenglow, to me one of the most impressive of all the terrestrial manifestations of God."

Although well marked and maintained from start to finish, the JMT is far from an easy trail. Hikers go up and over numerous challenging mountain passes, ford fast flowing streams, and often need to negotiate lingering snowfields. The majority of hikers choose to walk the trail from north to south, as starting at the lowest point and working up to the highest makes acclimatization easier. Altogether there is more than 14,200 m (46,590 ft.) of combined elevation gain, so strong knees and a light pack are highly recommended.

Thru-hiking the JMT requires considerable planning and a good amount of backpacking experience. In regards to the former, permits, resupply drops, bear canisters (containers designed to protect food from bears), and trailhead transport all need to be arranged in advance. This is not a hike where one can simply roll up to the start and hope for the best.   →

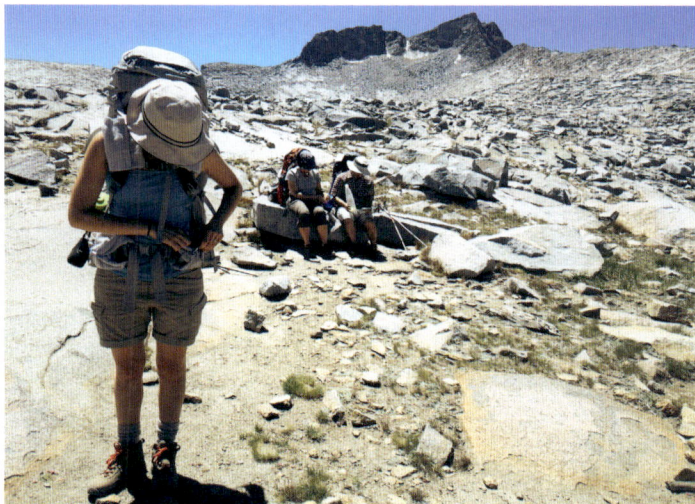

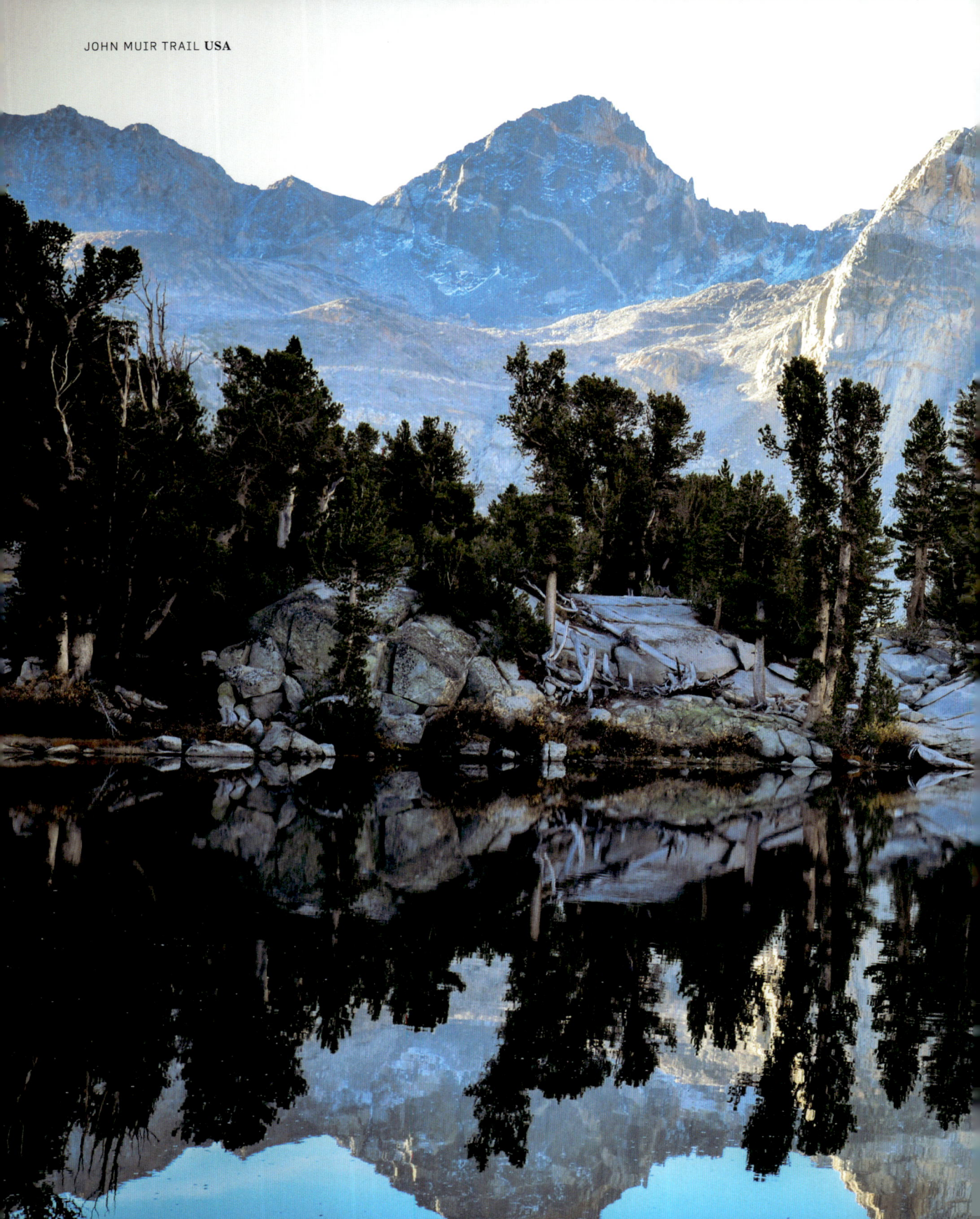

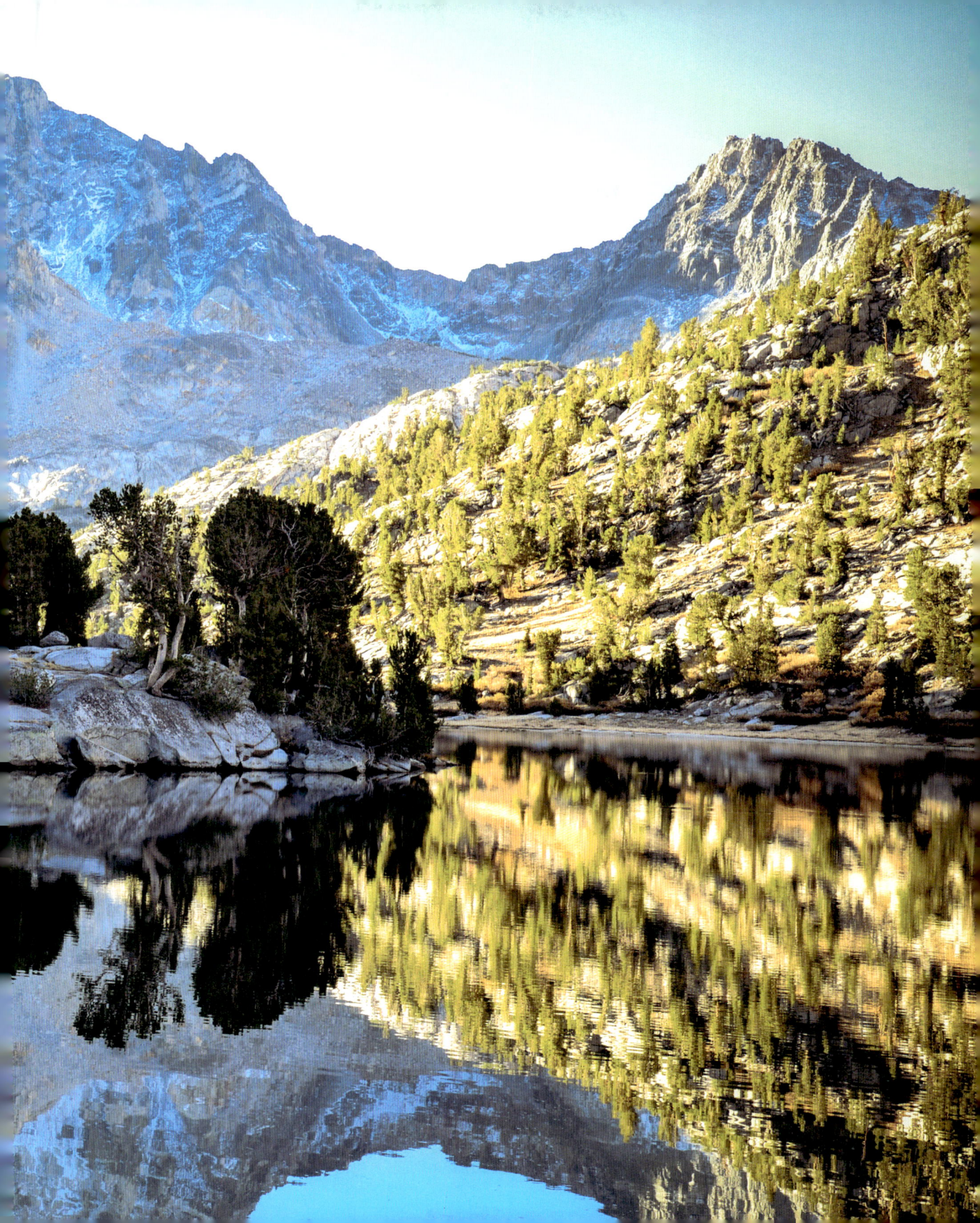

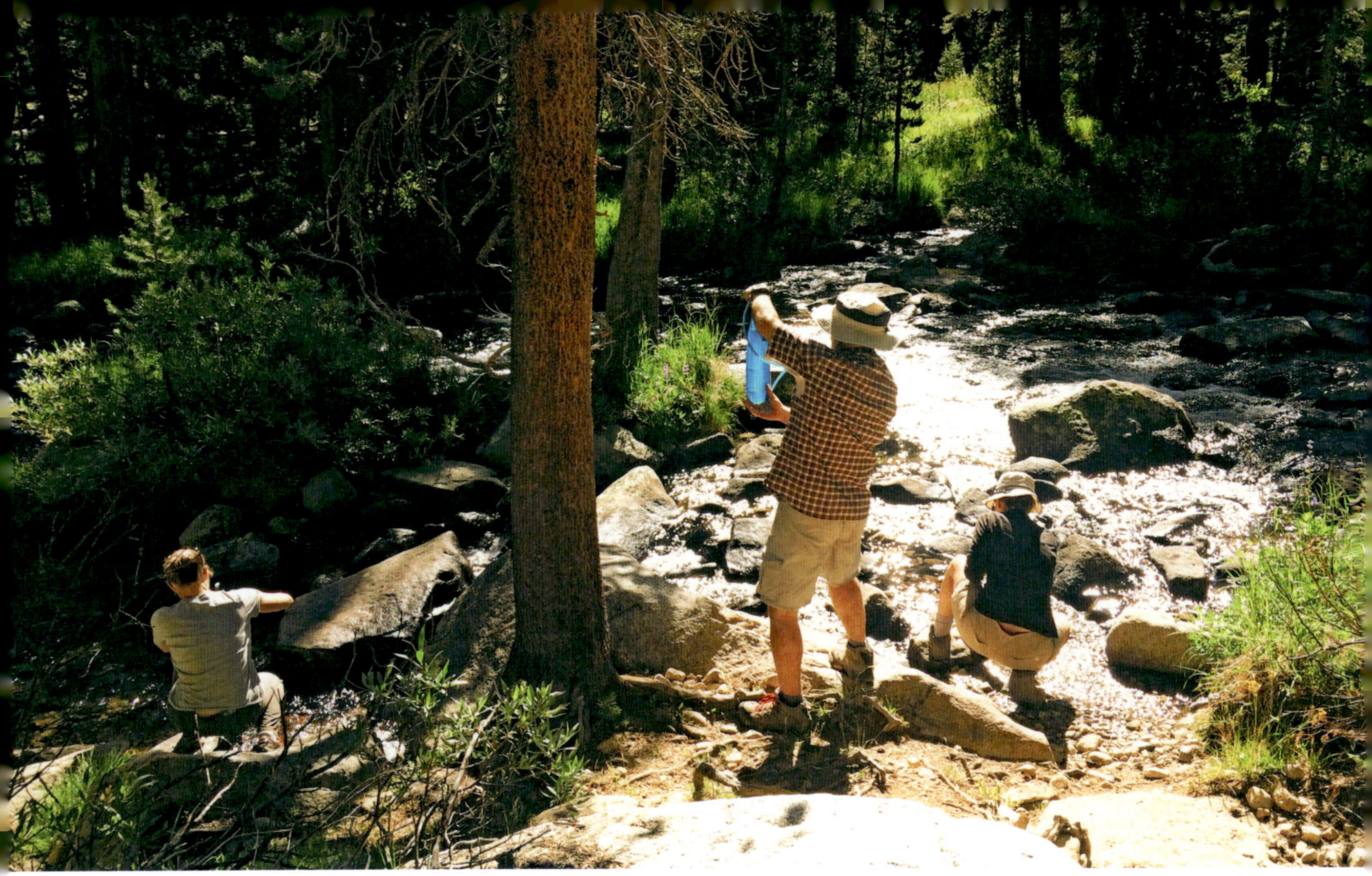

↘ At Devils Postpile National Monument.

It is mandatory to keep your food in "bear canisters," which should be bought or rented in advance.

Even though the John Muir Trail is relatively easy to follow, it is nonetheless a high-altitude wilderness trek that does not cross a single road throughout its course. Most hikers take about three weeks to complete the entire trail, and a lot can happen physically, mentally, and meteorologically during such an extended period of backcountry travel. Therefore, it is strongly suggested that all John Muir Trail aspirants have the requisite skills and equipment before setting out on their journey.

Few hikers that complete the John Muir Trail will return home unmoved by the experience. As with other renowned natural wonders such as the Grand Canyon and Himalaya, it is impossible to overstate the natural beauty of California's High Sierra. The landscape is breathtaking, and it remains affecting, no matter how many photos of it one has seen or how many descriptions of it one has read. On that note, it seems only appropriate to leave the final word to the man after whom the trail is named—the man whose eloquent descriptions of the region have inspired generations of seekers and outdoor enthusiasts. In 1912 in *The Yosemite*, John Muir wrote: "After ten years of wandering and wondering in the heart of it, rejoicing in its glorious floods of light, the white beams of the morning streaming through the passes, the noonday radiance on the crystal rocks, the flush of the alpenglow, and the irised spray of countless waterfalls, it still seems above all others the Range of Light." ——————→

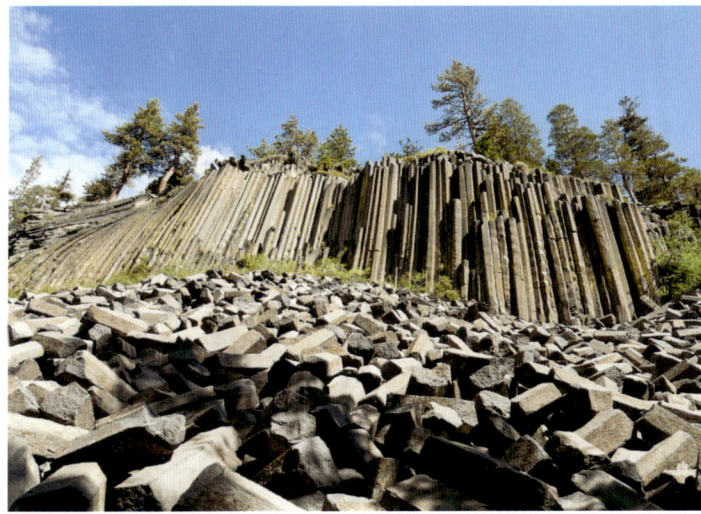

196

GOOD TO KNOW

START/FINISH
⚲ Happy Isles Trailhead, Yosemite NP
⚲ Summit of Mount Whitney

SEASON
Late June to mid-September. Dates can vary according to the snowpack.

LOWEST/HIGHEST POINT
1,220 m (4,421 ft.)/4,421 m (14,496 ft.)

WILDLIFE
Bears, deer, marmots, chipmunks, coyotes, pika, and bighorn sheep. Also a wide variety of birdlife including hawks, falcons, eagles, woodpeckers, and owls.

TIP
Permits are required to hike the John Muir Trail, and need to be applied for well in advance.

BACKGROUND

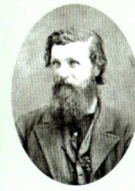

WHO WAS JOHN MUIR?
John Muir was a famous nineteenth-century Scottish-American naturalist and conservationist. Endearingly referred to as John of the Mountains, Muir was one of the leading figures in the fight to preserve America's wilderness, and was instrumental in the establishment of the National Park System. More than a century after his passing, his legacy lives on in the form of the Sierra Club (a grassroots environmental organization that Muir founded in 1892), his much beloved writings, and the famous long-distance pathway that bears his name.

HELPFUL HINTS

TEMPORARY SHELTER At Muir Pass, a high, exposed, and barren point of the JMT, stands the Muir Hut. Made from granite, the memorial shelter was built by the Sierra Club in 1930. Today it provides temporary refuge for hikers who get into difficulties.

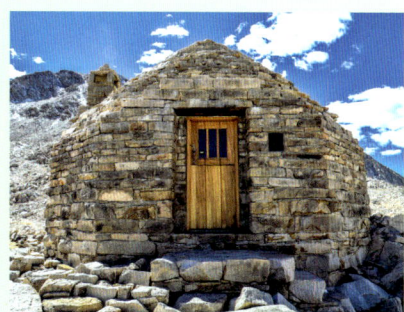

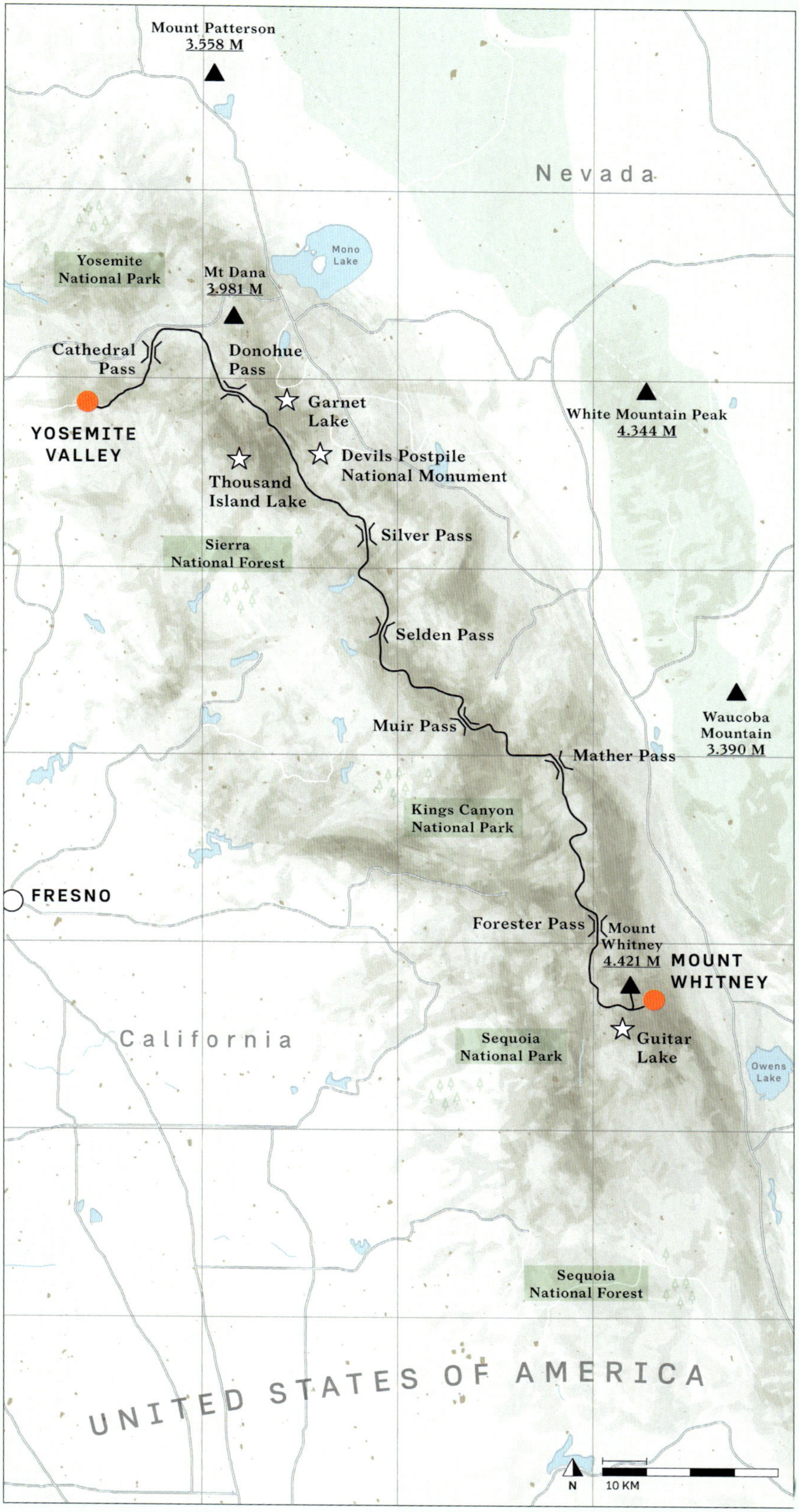

Mount Patterson
3,558 M ▲

Nevada

Mono Lake

Yosemite National Park

Mt Dana
3,981 M ▲

White Mountain Peak
4,344 M ▲

Cathedral Pass

Donohue Pass

☆ Garnet Lake

YOSEMITE VALLEY

☆ Thousand Island Lake

☆ Devils Postpile National Monument

Sierra National Forest

Silver Pass

Selden Pass

Waucoba Mountain
3,390 M ▲

Muir Pass

Mather Pass

FRESNO

Kings Canyon National Park

Forester Pass

Mount Whitney
4,421 M

MOUNT WHITNEY

California

Sequoia National Park

☆ Guitar Lake

Owens Lake

Sequoia National Forest

UNITED STATES OF AMERICA

N
10 KM

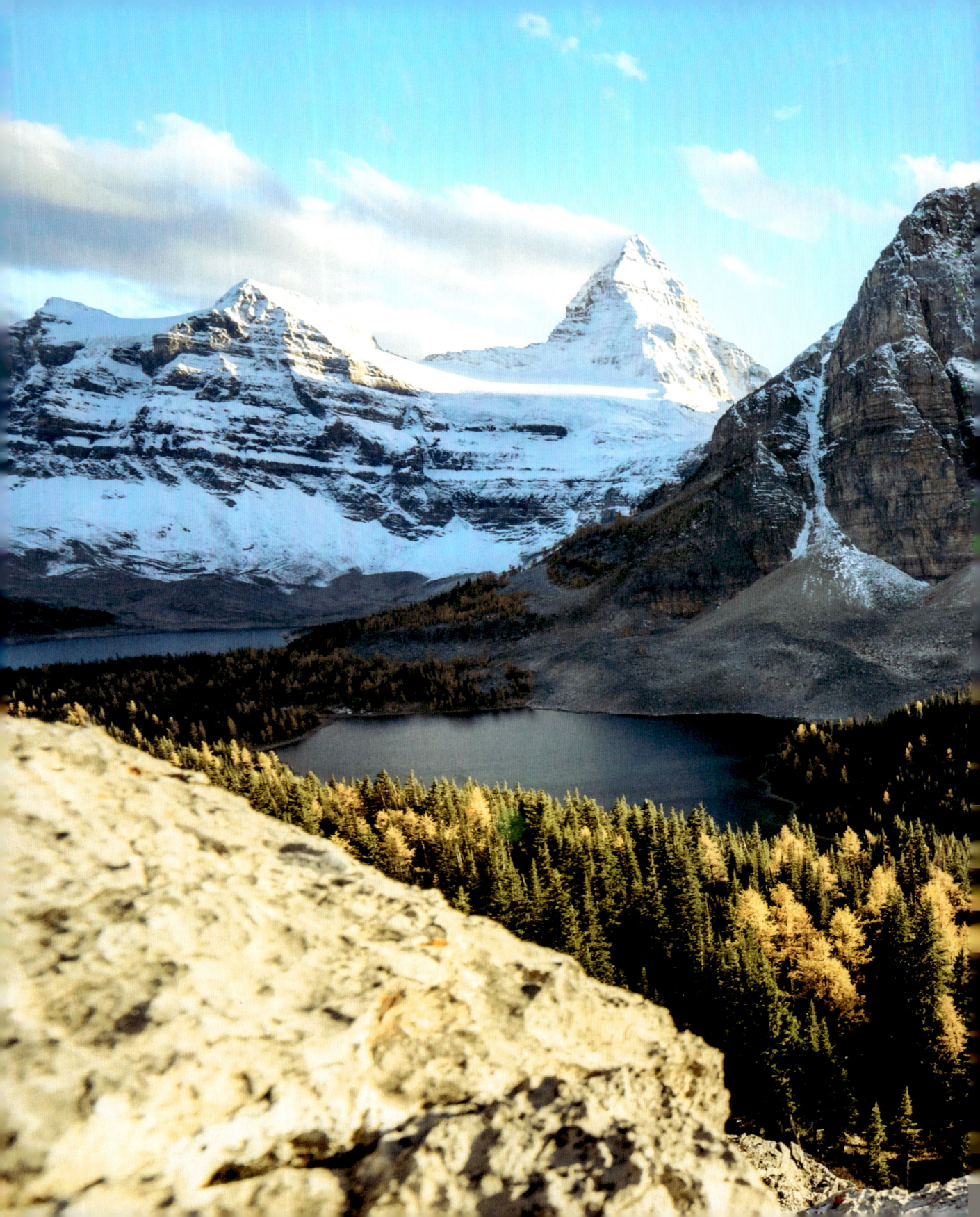

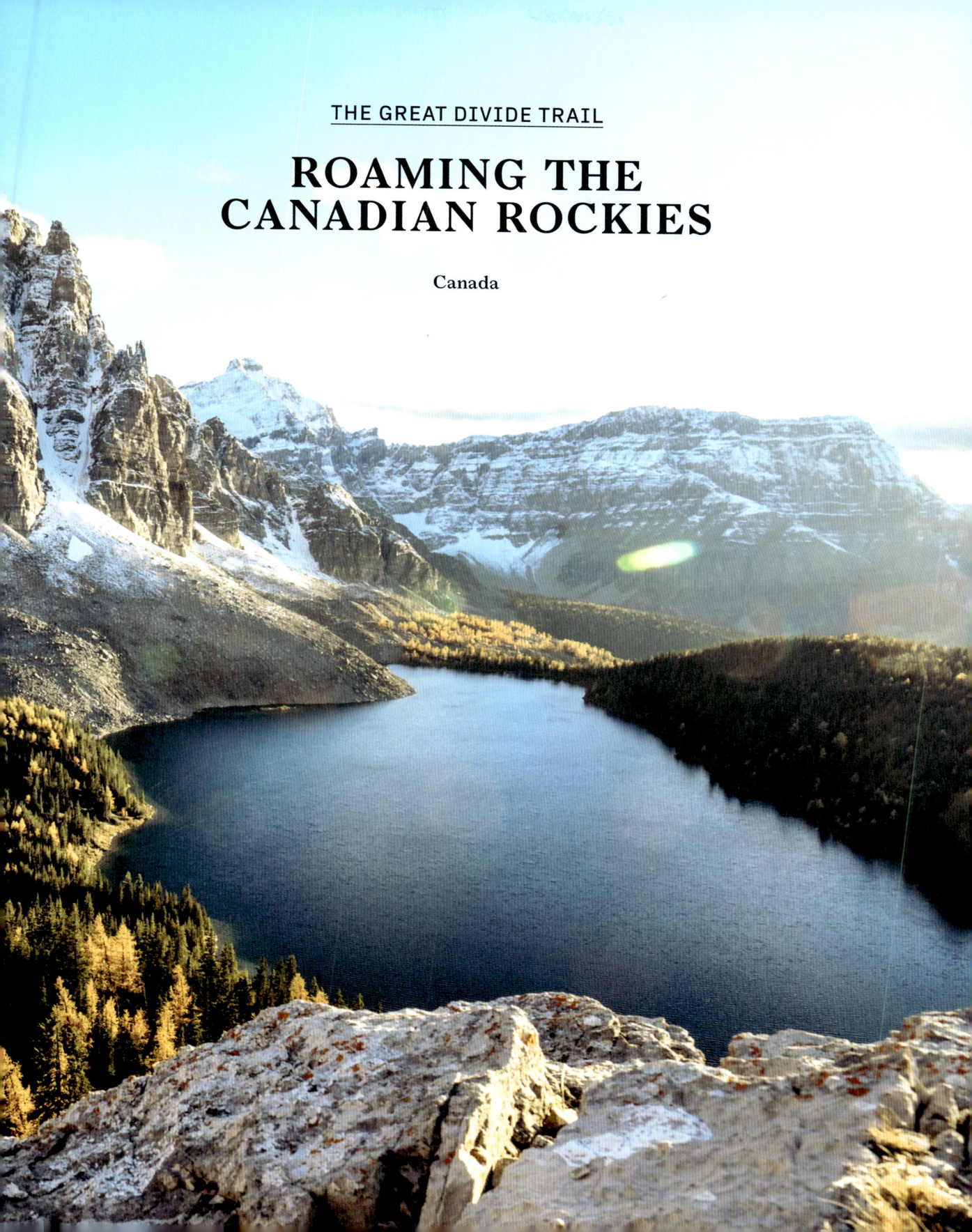

THE GREAT DIVIDE TRAIL

ROAMING THE CANADIAN ROCKIES

Canada

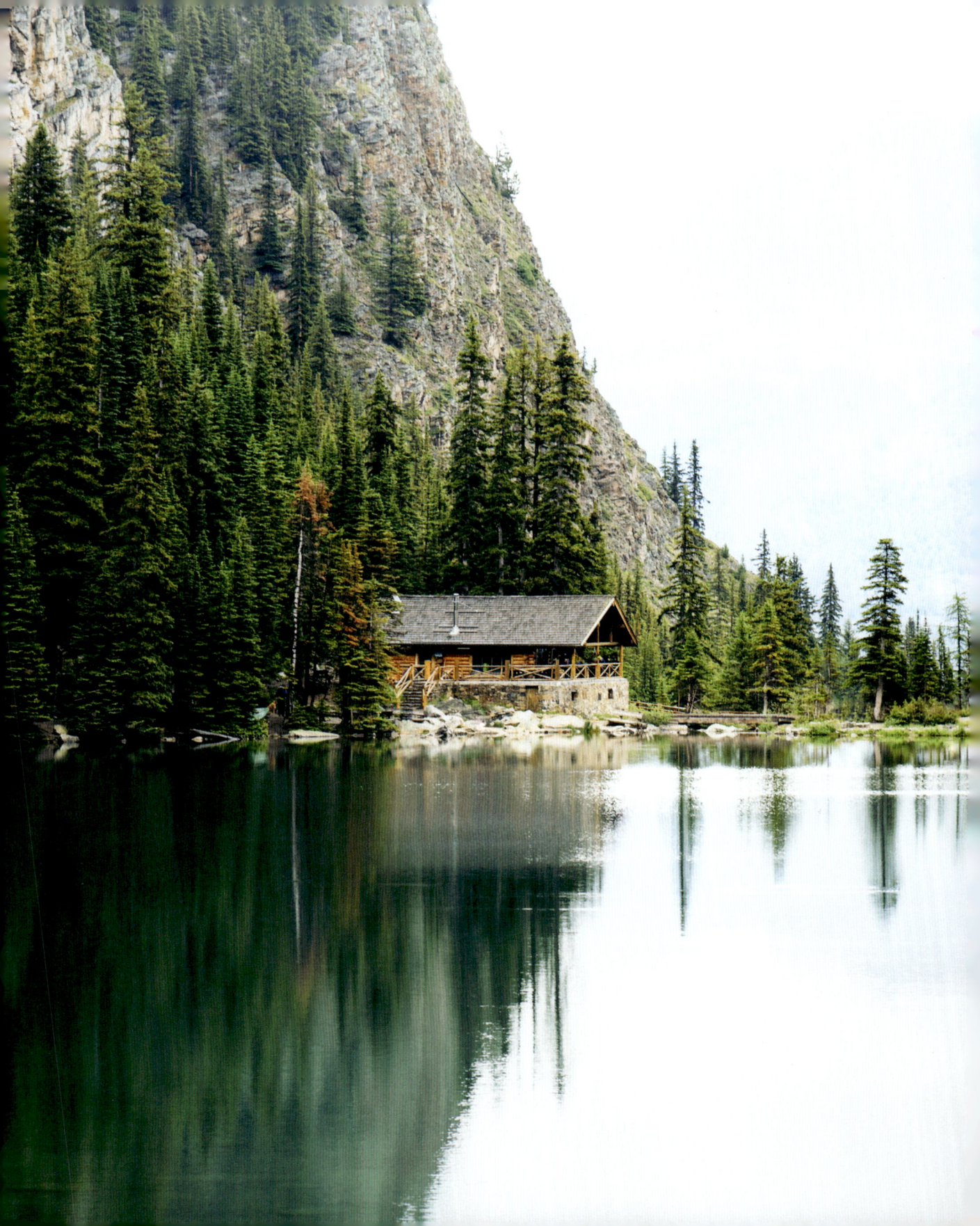

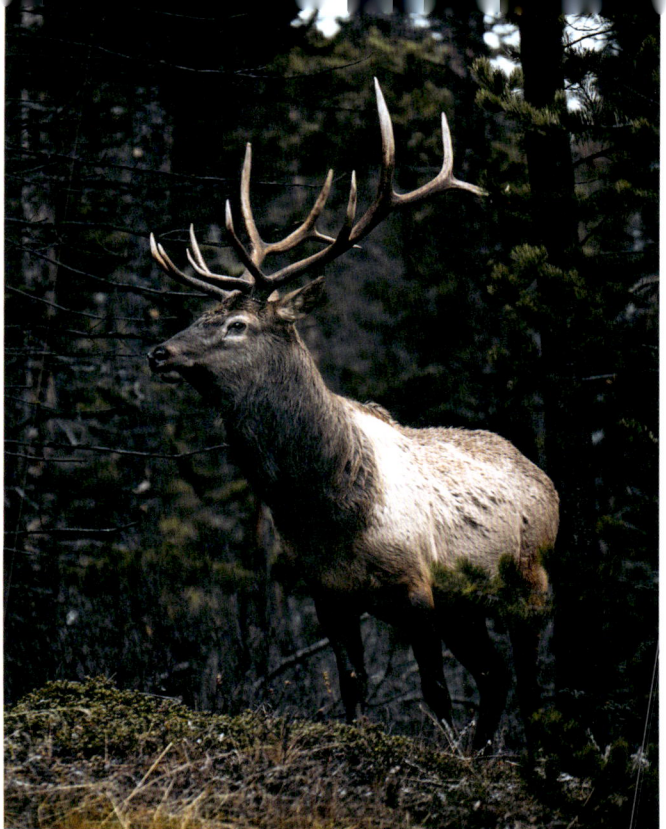

Mount Assiniboine is Canada's answer to the Matterhorn. The tallest mountain in the southern Canadian Rockies, the striking pyramidal peak rises more than 500 m (1,640 ft.) above its immediate neighbors. Viewing Assiniboine's majestic reflection in the crystal clear waters of Lake Magog rates as one of the highlights of a trail that covers some of North America's most pristine wildernesses and includes glaciers, snowcapped mountains, and wildflower meadows.

Beginning at Waterton Lake on the United States–Canada border, the Great Divide Trail (GDT) picks up where the Continental Divide Trail leaves off. It then proceeds to wind its way some 1,200 km (746 mi.) northwest along the Rockies, eventually reaching its northern terminus at Lake Kakwa. During its course it weaves back and forth between the provinces of Alberta and British Columbia, treating the hiker to a continuous course of glacier-carved valleys, glistening mountain lakes, and jagged granite peaks. From start to finish it is an alpine tour de force.

The GDT passes through five national parks and eight provincial parks, and crosses the Continental Divide around 30 times.

Superlatives aside, perhaps the most amazing thing about the GDT is that it is so little known. A large part of the reason behind the hike's relative anonymity can be found in its stop-start history. The idea for a path along Canada's Great Divide was first proposed by the Girl Guides in the 1960s. At the beginning of the following decade, Parks Canada gave the project an official green light, with the goal of completing the trail by 1975. However, more than four decades and quite a few bureaucratic hiccups later, the GDT remains a work in process.

Today the GDT is actually more of a backcountry route than a pathway, consisting of a combination of cross-country travel, pre-existing trails (some maintained, others not so much), and the occasional stretch along remote dirt roads. With the exception of some of the national and provincial park sections, the way is for the most part unmarked. Good navigation and route finding skills are therefore a must.

For seasoned long-distance hikers looking for a new challenge, the GDT represents a wilderness experience par excellence. There are testing river fords, long stretches of overgrown terrain, unpredictable mountain climates, and a diverse range of fauna. Along the path of the GDT, hikers →

↑↓ The wildlife and wild views in Banff National Park.

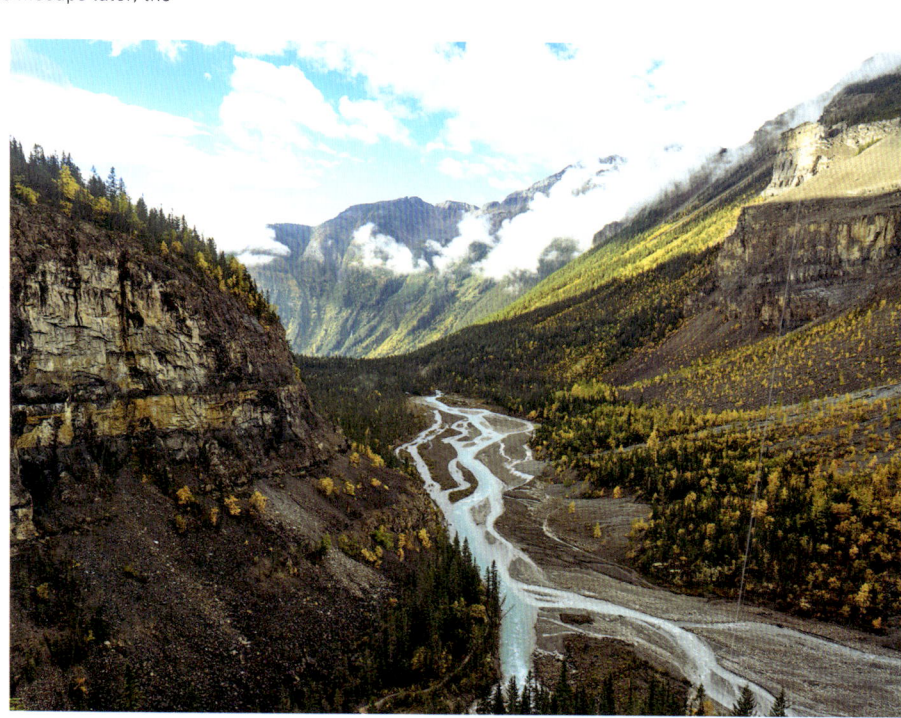

ABOUT THE TRAIL

→ <u>DISTANCE</u> 1,200 km (746 mi.)
→ <u>DURATION</u> 40 to 50 days
→ <u>LEVEL</u> Moderate to Difficult

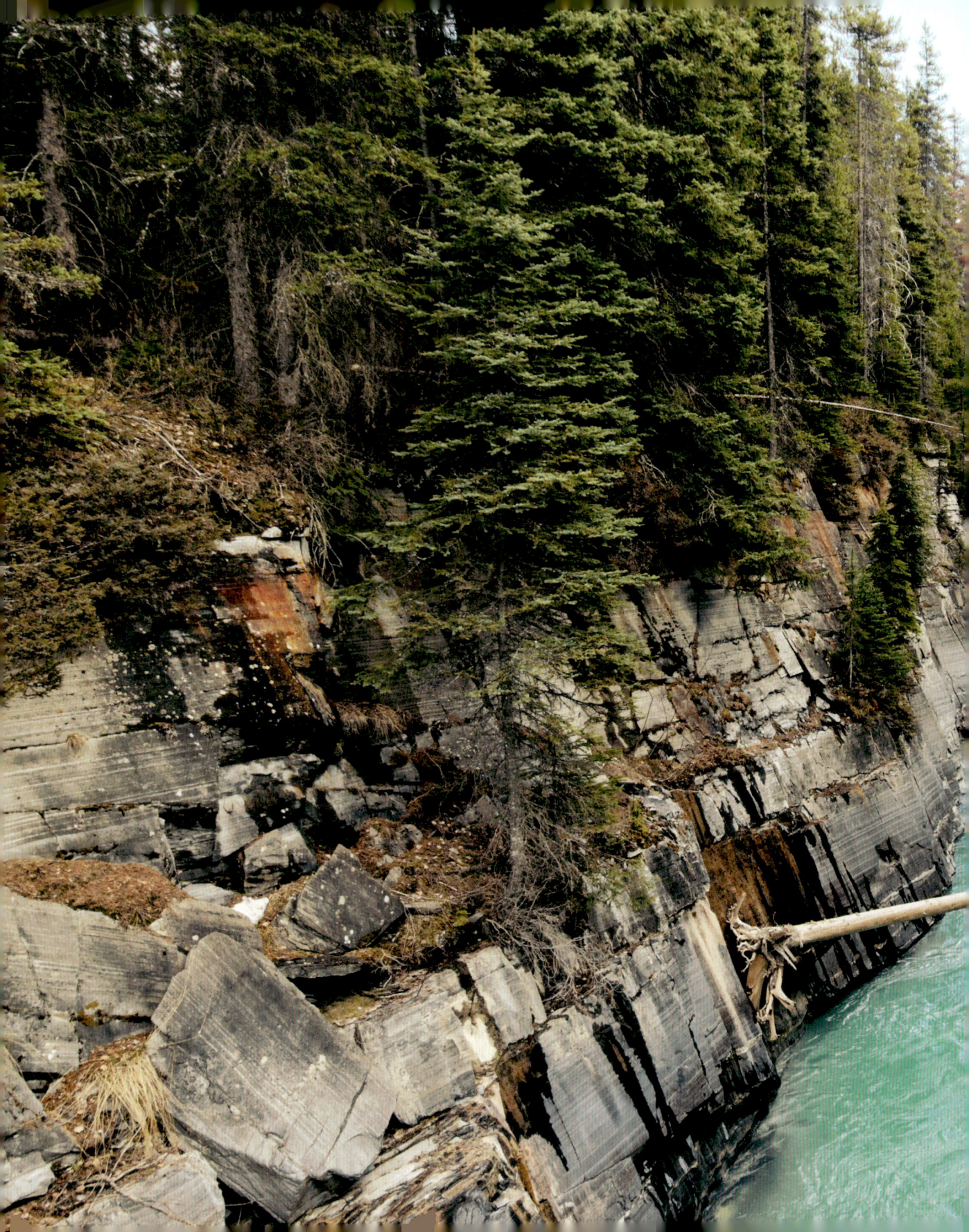

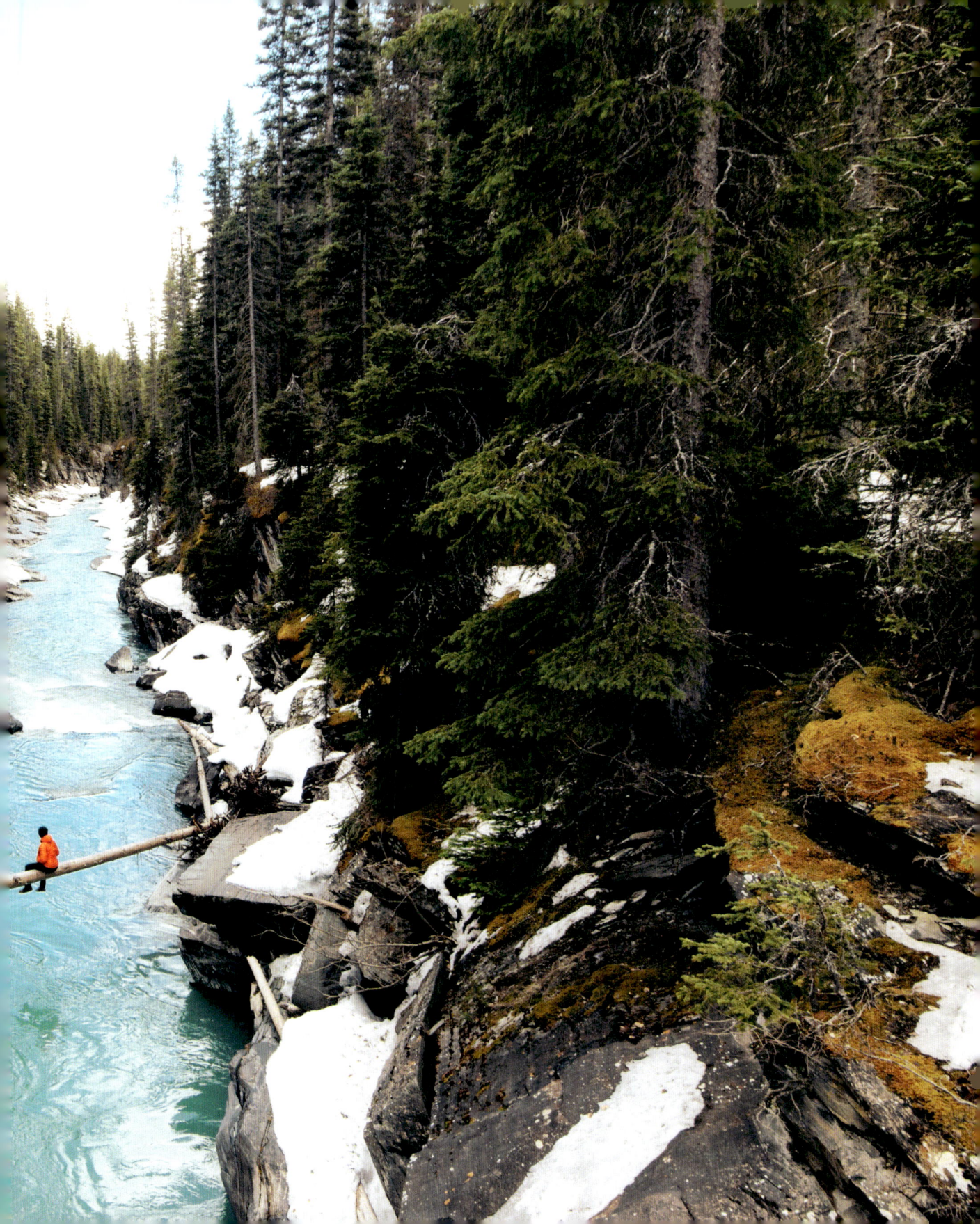

Packages of provisions can be mailed to the resupply points on the trail for pick up along the way.

may encounter moose, elk. bighorn sheep, bobcats, cougars, and, of course, the animals that one both wants to see and does not want to see: grizzly bears and black bears.

The size and potential threat of some of these beautiful creatures means that precautions need to be taken. It is recommended that hikers carry bear spray at all times, and food, cooking gear, toiletries, and basically anything with a scent, should be placed in an Ursack—a bearproof food storage bag widely approved by park authorities in both Canada and the U.S.—while camping. When passing through the National and Provincial Parks sections, walkers can utilize food lockers when available.

If one were to choose a single word to describe Canada's Great Divide Trail, that word might be "big." It has big mountains, big rivers, big distances, big animals, big lakes, and big storms. Hiking the trail may make one feel the exact opposite of that—very tiny—and until recently the number of visitors has also been small. The winds of change have begun to blow, and thru-hiking numbers are gradually increasing. The Great Divide Trail Association, which was reformed in 2013, has been making positive strides towards official recognition from provincial governments, so the GDT's days of relatively anonymity appear to be coming to an end. The time to hike it is now. ————————

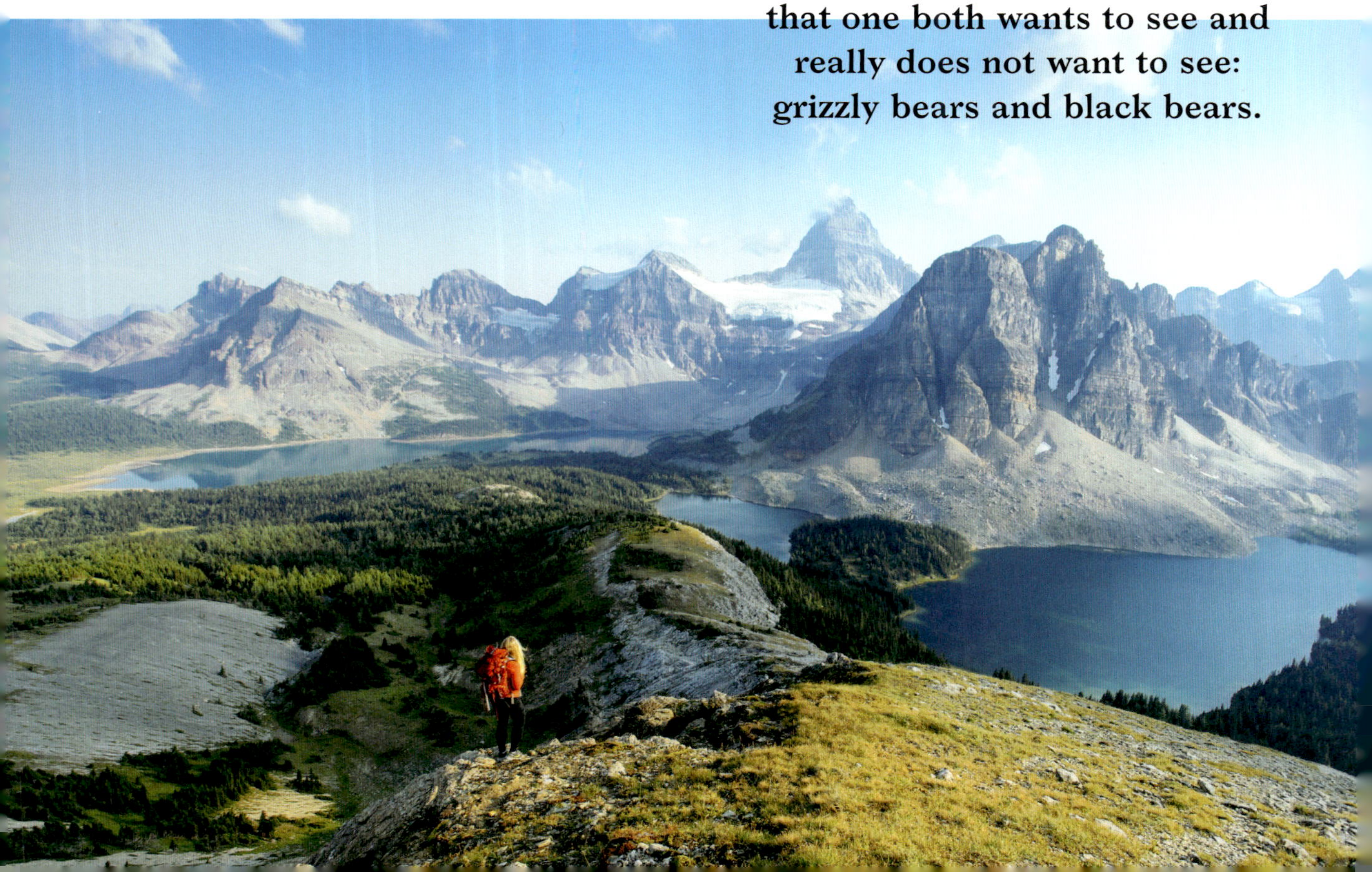

↓↗ **Mount Assiniboine day and night.**

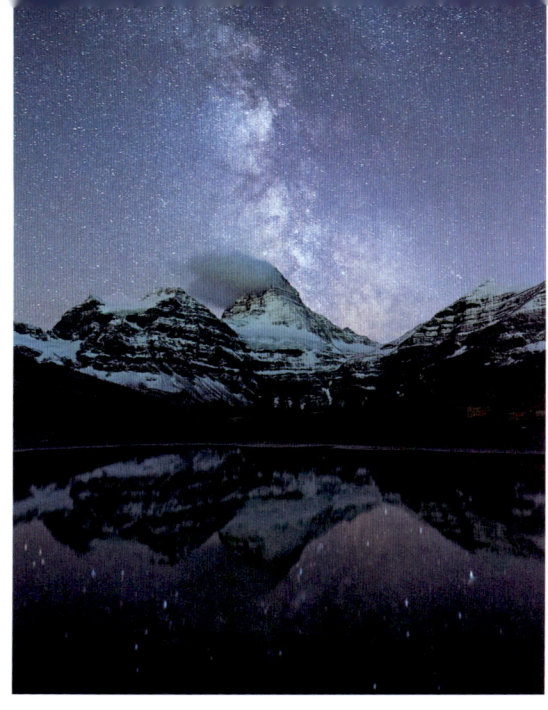

Along the path of the GDT, hikers may encounter the animals that one both wants to see and really does not want to see: grizzly bears and black bears.

GOOD TO KNOW

START/FINISH
⚐ Waterton Lake National Park, Alberta
⚐ Kakwa Lake, British Columbia

SEASON
July to mid-September

CONDITIONS
The trail is an informal route made up of signposted pathways and unmarked sections where navigation skills are required. Conditions can be hazardous in all seasons. This is a trail for experienced hikers only.

LOWEST/HIGHEST POINT
1,055 m (3,461 ft.)/2,590 m (8,497 ft.)

GEAR TIPS
Bear spray, Ursack (bearproof food storage bag), detailed topographic maps, shelter capable of withstanding extreme conditions.

BACKGROUND

THE CANADIAN ROCKIES Stretching from New Mexico in the south to Alberta and British Columbia in the north, the Rocky Mountains is a system of more than 100 interconnected mountain ranges situated in the western part of North America. The Canadian section of the storied mountain range is 1,600 km (1,000 mi.) long, contains four World Heritage Listed National Parks —Banff, Jasper, Kootenay, and Yoho (all of which the GDT passes through)—and boasts a diverse array of landscapes including icefields, glaciers, limestone caves, canyons and wildflower-laden alpine meadows.

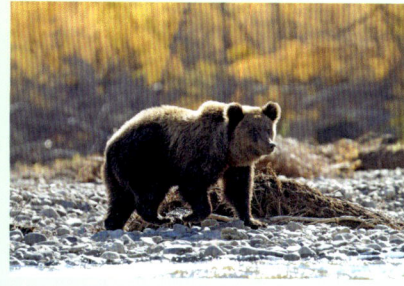

HELPFUL HINTS

LOCATION MATTERS Avoid camping near berry patches or water sources; the latter of which animals tend to frequent at both dawn and dusk. Similarly, it is best not to cook where you camp; a bear's sense of smell is seven times better than a bloodhound and approximately 100 times better than a human. Cooking at a campsite is like ringing a dinner bell for nearby bruins.

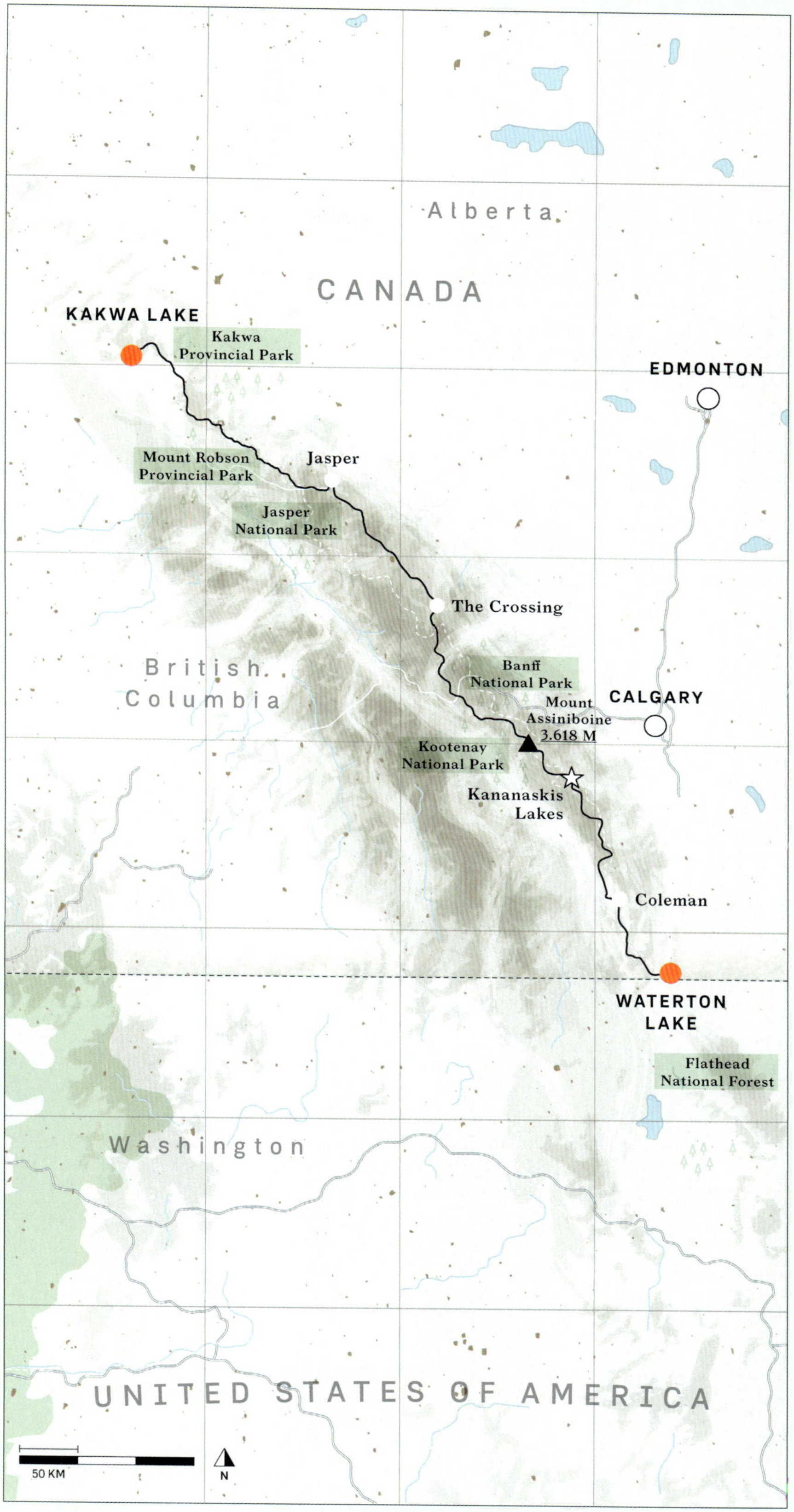

Alberta

CANADA

EDMONTON

KAKWA LAKE

Kakwa
Provincial Park

Mount Robson
Provincial Park   Jasper

Jasper
National Park

The Crossing

Banff
National Park

British
Columbia

Mount
Assiniboine
3.618 M   CALGARY

Kootenay
National Park

Kananaskis
Lakes

Coleman

WATERTON
LAKE

Flathead
National Forest

Washington

UNITED STATES OF AMERICA

50 KM

N

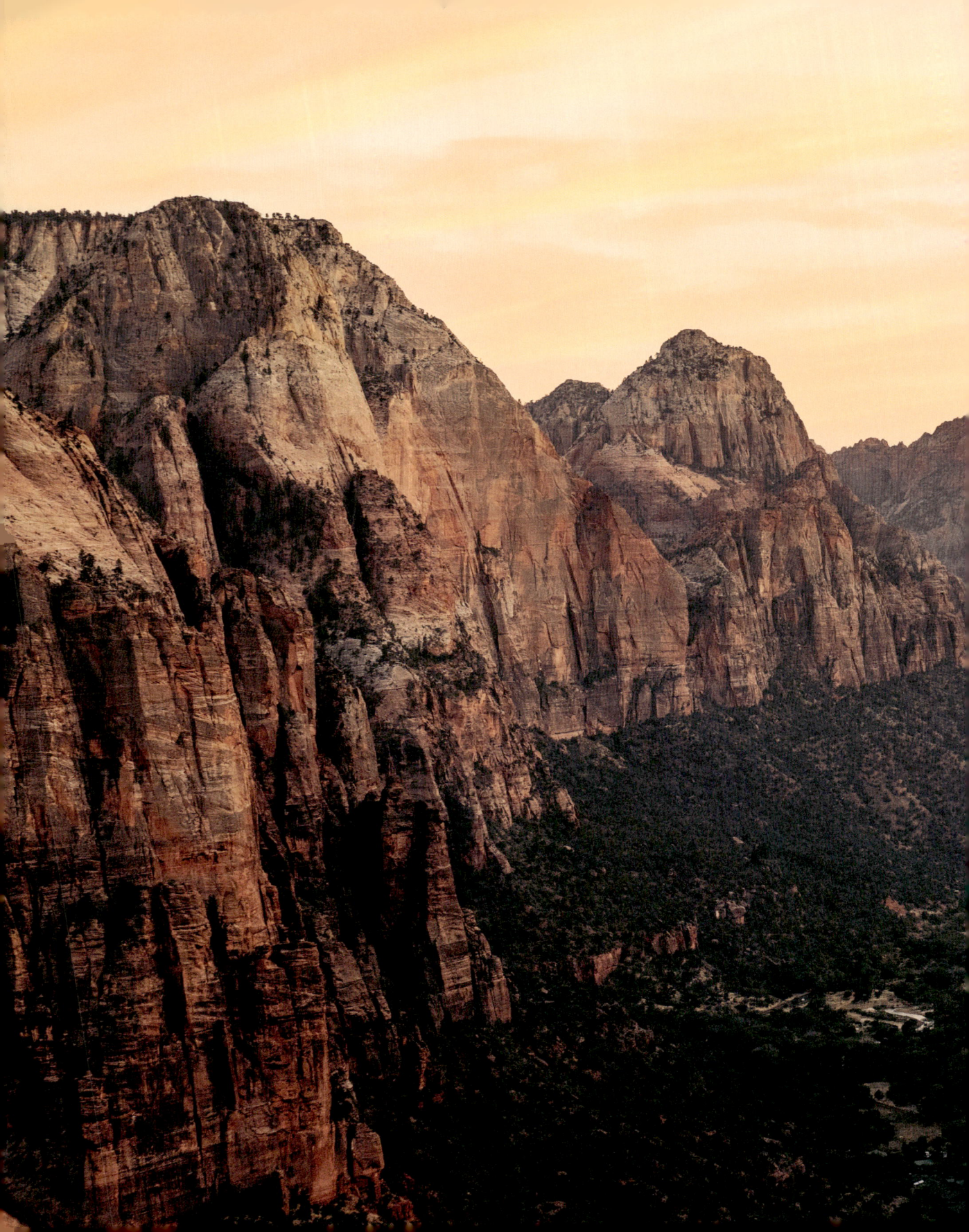

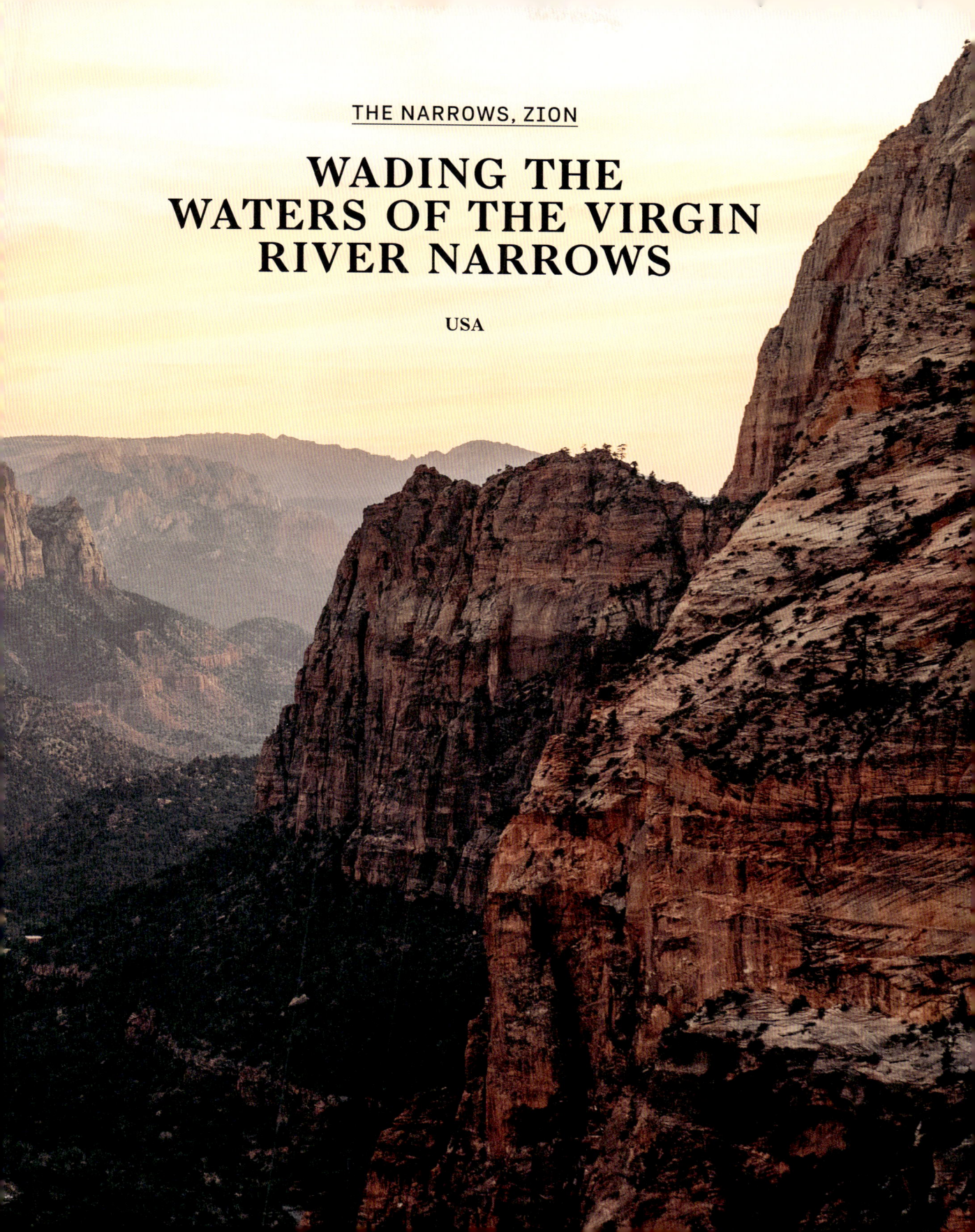

WADING THE WATERS OF THE VIRGIN RIVER NARROWS

USA

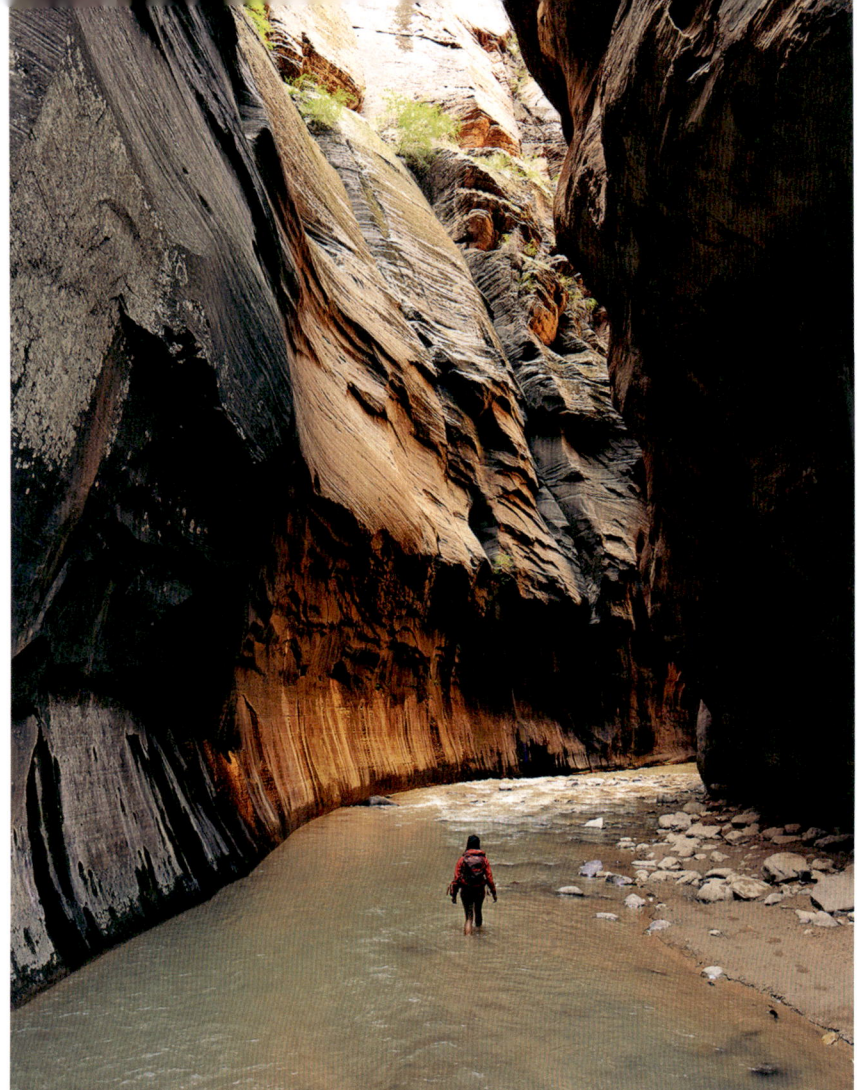

↑ Wading through river waters.
→ Up on Angels Landing.

Shoes with good traction and a tolerance for having wet feet for a day or two are some of the main components for an enjoyable trip.

The 26 km (16.2 mi.) Narrows Top-Down route follows the course of the Virgin River, which has, over millennia, cut a dramatic gorge through the northern reaches of Utah's Zion Canyon. At times the chasm is up to 600 m (1,968 ft.) deep and only 6 m (20 ft.) wide. In times past Native American peoples often avoided the upper parts of the canyon because of its claustrophobic feel and lack of natural light. The first westerner to descend the canyon was geologist and explorer Grove Karl Gilbert in 1872. It is said that Gilbert was the man who coined the term "The Narrows."

The Top-Down route begins at Chamberlain's Ranch, which is situated some 1.5 hours drive from Zion Canyon. The first few miles to Bulloch's Cabin are both easy and dry. Soon after passing this landmark the hiker enters the water for the first time.

Around 10 km (6.2 mi.) of splishing and splashing later, the route reaches North Fork Falls and the confluence with Deep Creek. This marks the beginning of the most spectacular section of the gorge. From here on in, the sometimes-murky waters of the river are a little deeper and the dark terracotta-colored walls, which are broken up by sporadic vegetation, are a lot higher.

The terrain encountered in the Narrows could perhaps best be described as "dampish." Understatements aside, though, more than half of the total distance is spent walking through water. This is not a hike for those who like to keep dry. One of the best tips for hiking the Narrows is not to wear waterproof boots. Boots are heavier and take longer to dry, and as the water is often at shin height or above, feet become soaked regardless of footwear choices. Instead of boots, it is advisable →

ABOUT THE TRAIL

→ DISTANCE 26 km (16.2 mi.)

→ DURATION 10 to 14 hours, or 2 days if camping

→ LEVEL Easy to Moderate

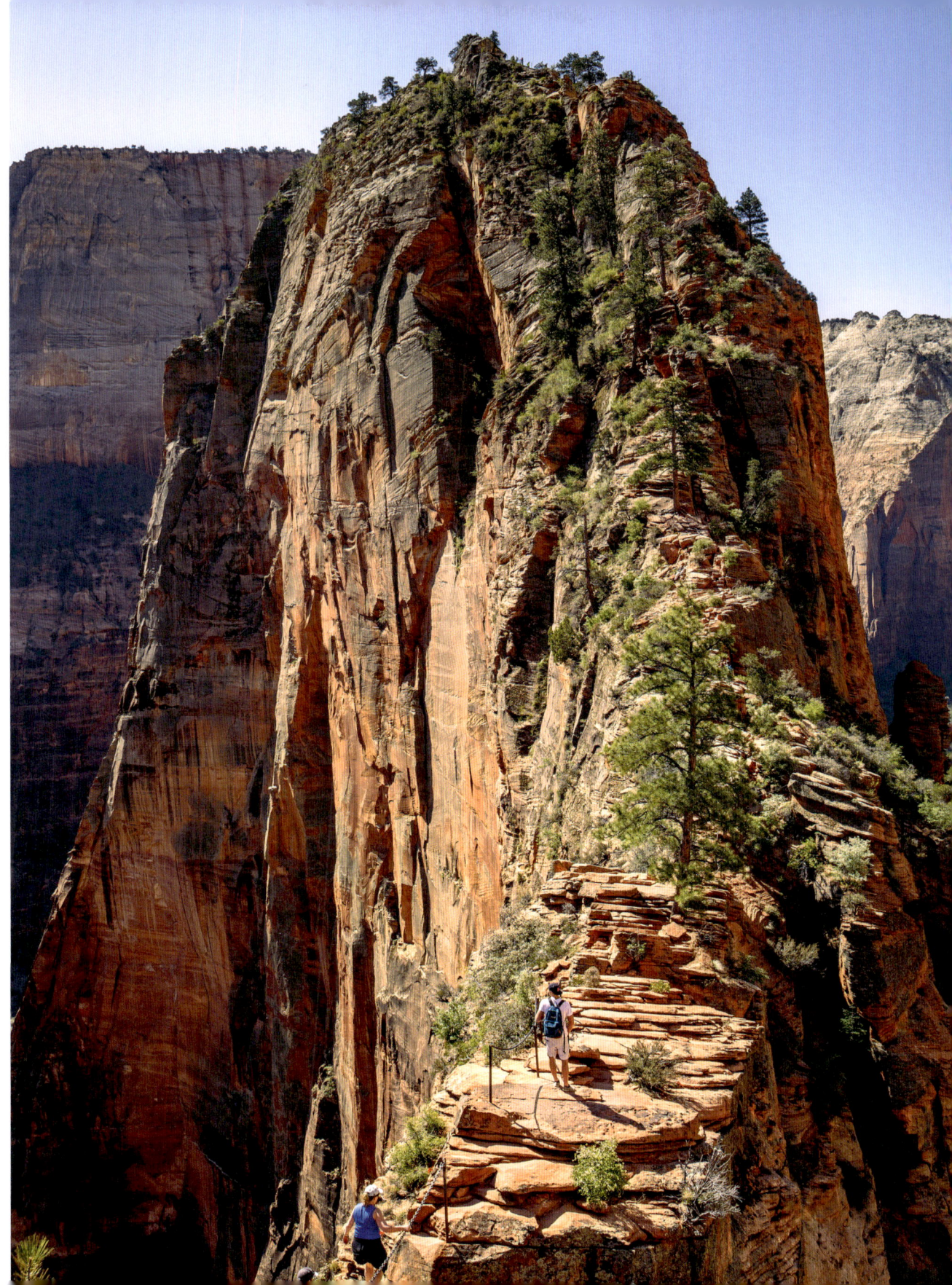

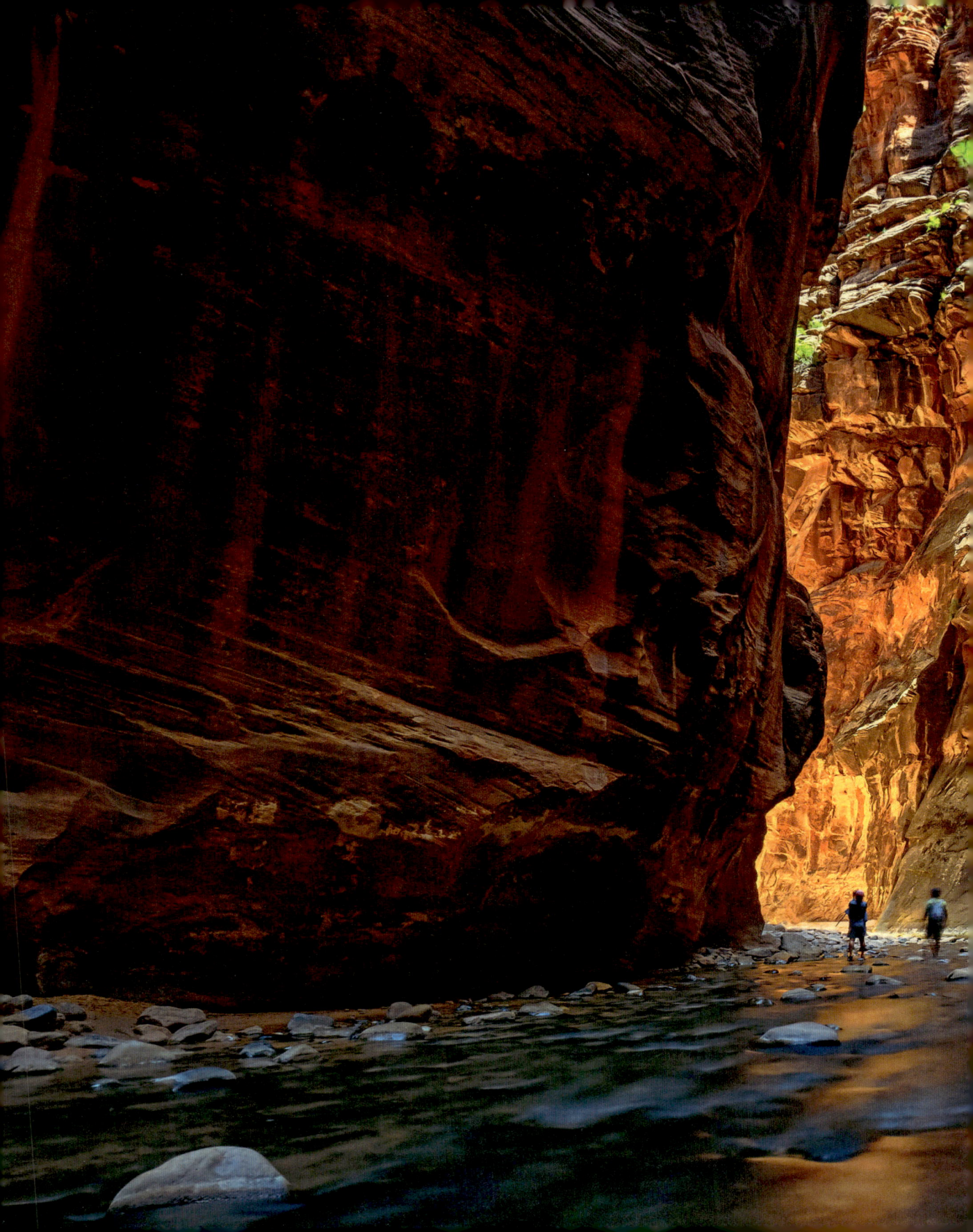

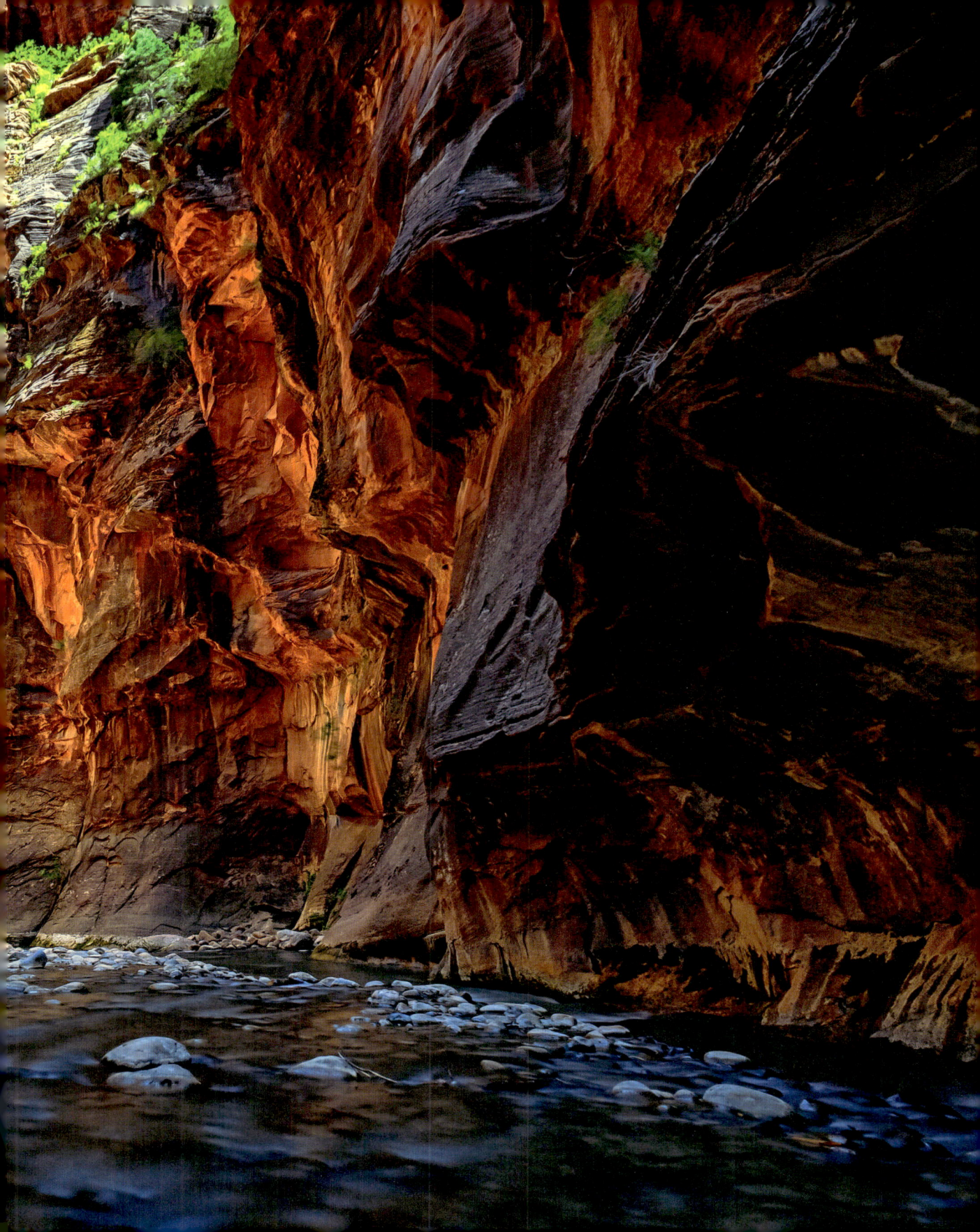

to wear lightweight trail running shoes with good tread and a solid heel counter.

A trekking pole can come in handy for balance purposes, as the rocks underneath the river's surface can sometimes be slippery. As the water in the Narrows is often quite cold, sufficient clothing layers are necessary. This holds true particularly during the early morning hours, when gloves and beanies can make a significant difference to a hiker's comfort level.

The season very much affects this trek. During the winter months water temperatures can be chilly, and a wet- or drysuit might be necessary. Between March and May the hike is frequently closed because of the rising water levels caused by spring snowmelt. Fast-flowing waters or high water levels are the main dangers on this trek, and flash floods are a possibility from mid-summer onwards, so weather reports should be checked before setting out.

The Top-Down route is a spectacular trek that requires no special skills or equipment, and hikers of all ages and experience levels can follow it. Shoes with good traction and a tolerance for having wet feet for a day or two are some of the main components for an enjoyable trip. When combined with the equally impressive day hike to Angels Landing—a steep 454 m (1,488 ft.)

> This marks the beginning of the most spectacular section of the gorge. From here on in, the sometimes-murky waters of the river are a little deeper and the dark terracotta-colored walls, which are broken up by sporadic vegetation, are a lot higher.

climb that is not for those with a fear of heights—the Narrows makes for a great "one-two" combination for hiking enthusiasts visiting Zion National Park. ———

↓ Trekking on uneven and sometimes slippery surfaces.

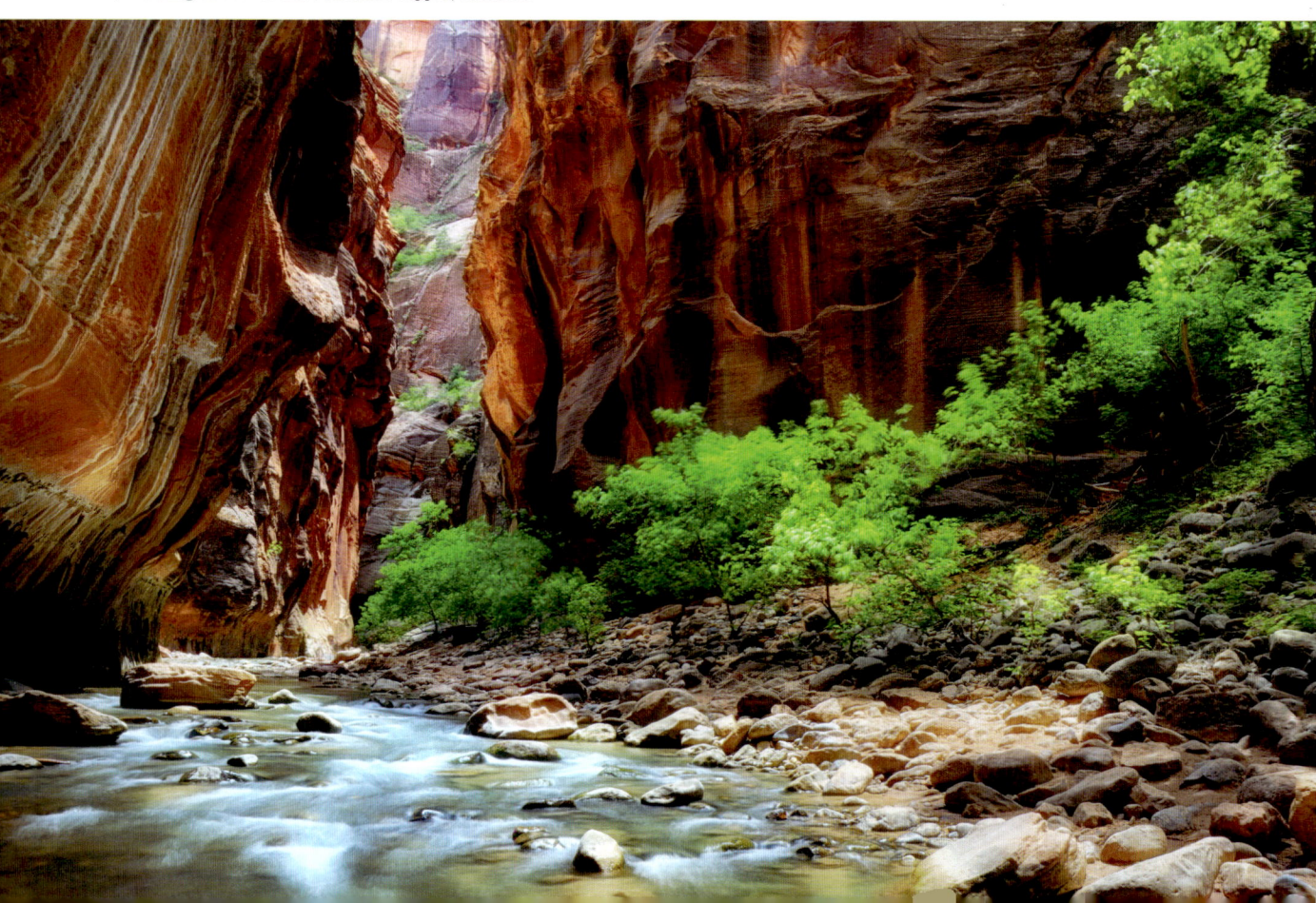

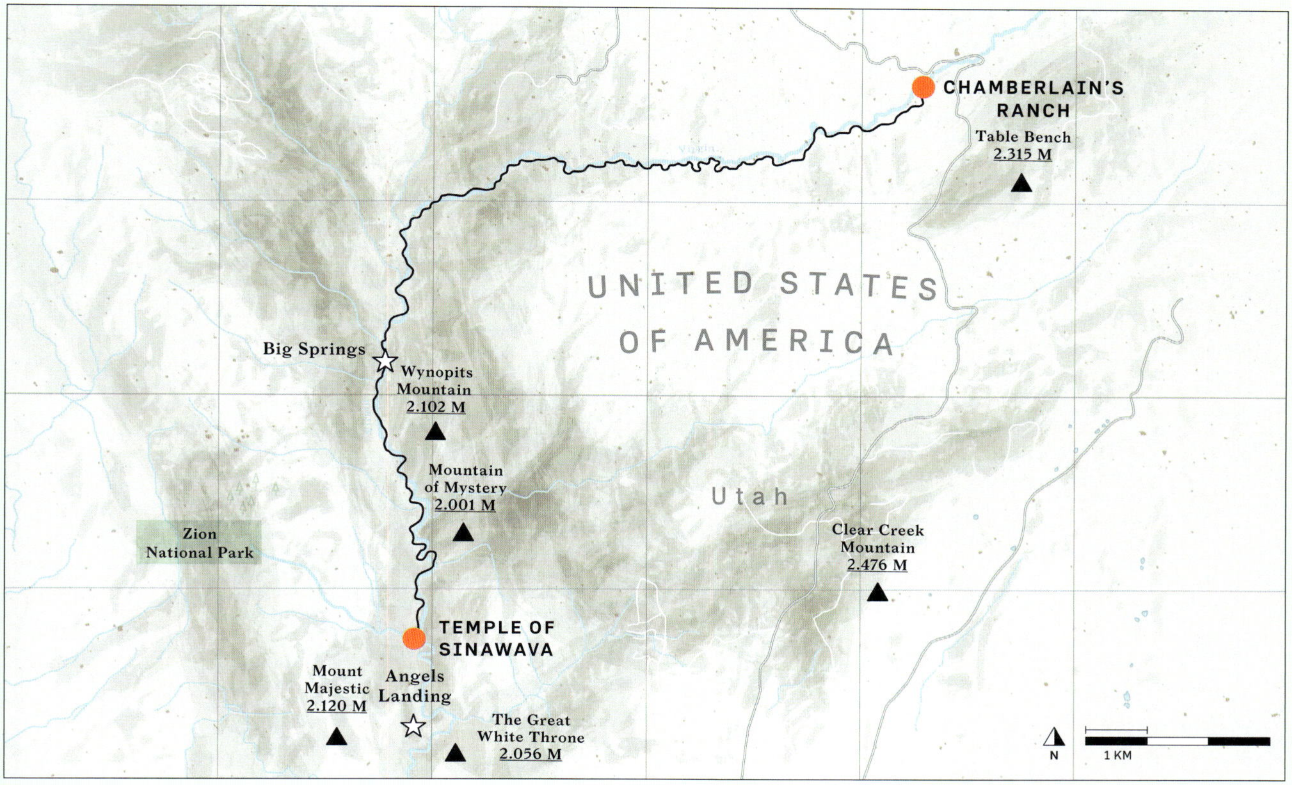

CHAMBERLAIN'S RANCH

Table Bench
2.315 M ▲

UNITED STATES OF AMERICA

Big Springs
☆ Wynopits
Mountain
2.102 M ▲

Mountain
of Mystery
2.001 M ▲

Utah

Clear Creek
Mountain
2.476 M ▲

Zion
National Park

**TEMPLE OF
SINAWAVA**

Mount
Majestic
2.120 M ▲

Angels
Landing ☆

The Great
White Throne
2.056 M ▲

N   1 KM

GOOD TO KNOW

START/FINISH
📍 Chamberlain's Ranch
📍 Temple of Sinawava

SEASON
June to October

CONDITIONS
For the most part, the hike is through water at varying heights. From mid-summer to early fall, there is a higher possibility of flash floods occurring.

TIP
Permits are required, so organize one in advance.

HELPFUL HINTS

OPTIONAL ROUTE A shorter alternative to the full descent from Chamberlain's Ranch is to take a shuttle bus to the Temple of Sinawava and then from there to do an out-and-back hike to Big Spring. The 16 km (10 mi.) round trip includes the most spectacular part of the gorge and no permit is required.

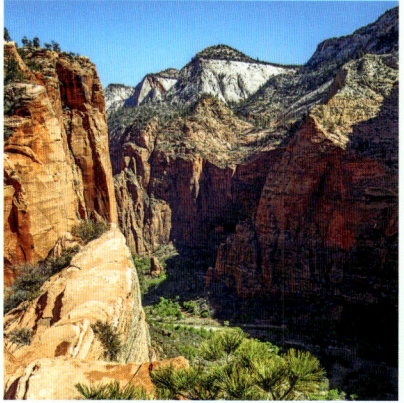

BACKGROUND

CANYON COUNTRY Zion National Park, which spans three counties in Utah, is home to high plateaus, a labyrinth of deep sandstone gorges, and Navajo sandstone cliffs that reveal the traces of ancient sand dunes in their thick layers. Humans have lived in and around the area for approximately 10,000 years, and there are various archaeological sites throughout the park. Wildlife in the reserve includes birds from peregrine falcons to broad-tailed hummingbirds, mammals from the oft-seen mule deer to the elusive mountain lion, and amphibians such as the rock-like woodhouse toad.

FLORA & FAUNA

VERDANT WALLS Zion National Park is renowned for its "hanging gardens," or plants that grow out of the sandstone where water seeps out. These green patches can consist of mosses, ferns, and wildflowers, and tend to stay near the level of the river.

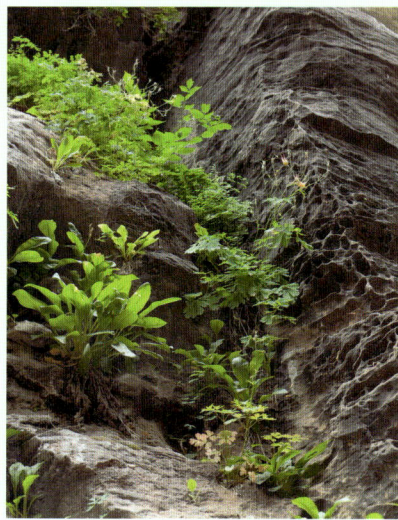

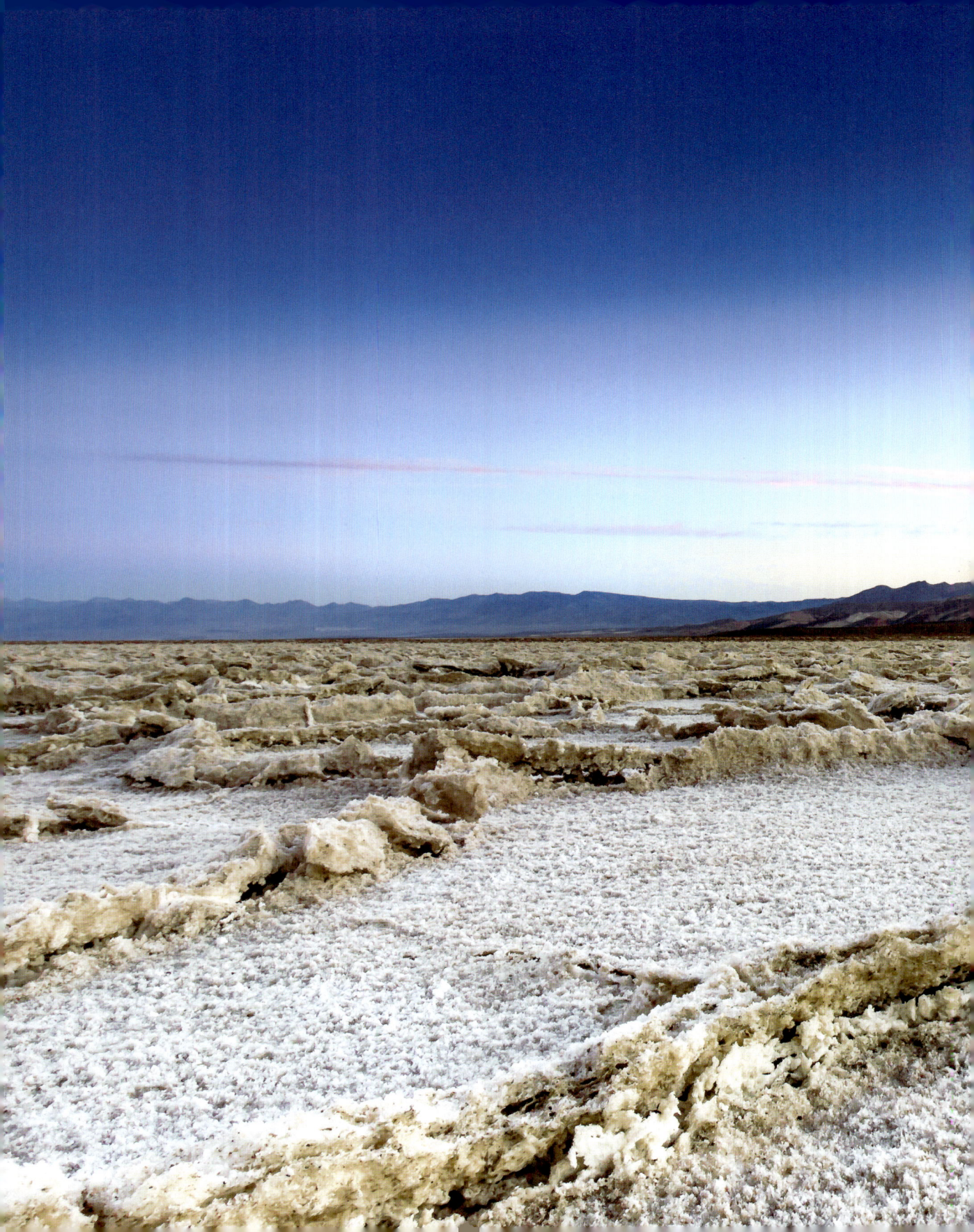

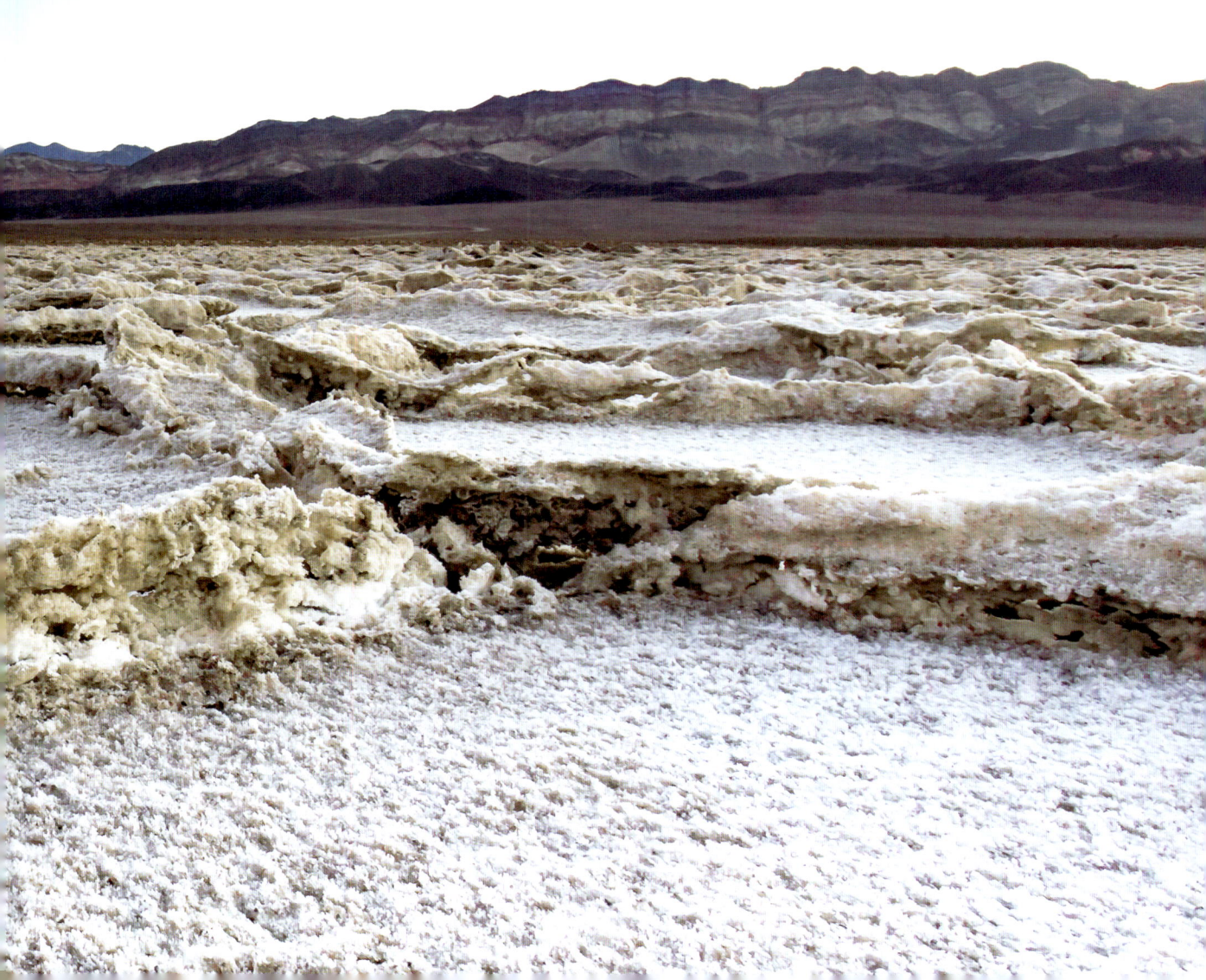

FROM DEATH VALLEY
TO THE SUMMIT
OF MOUNT WHITNEY

USA

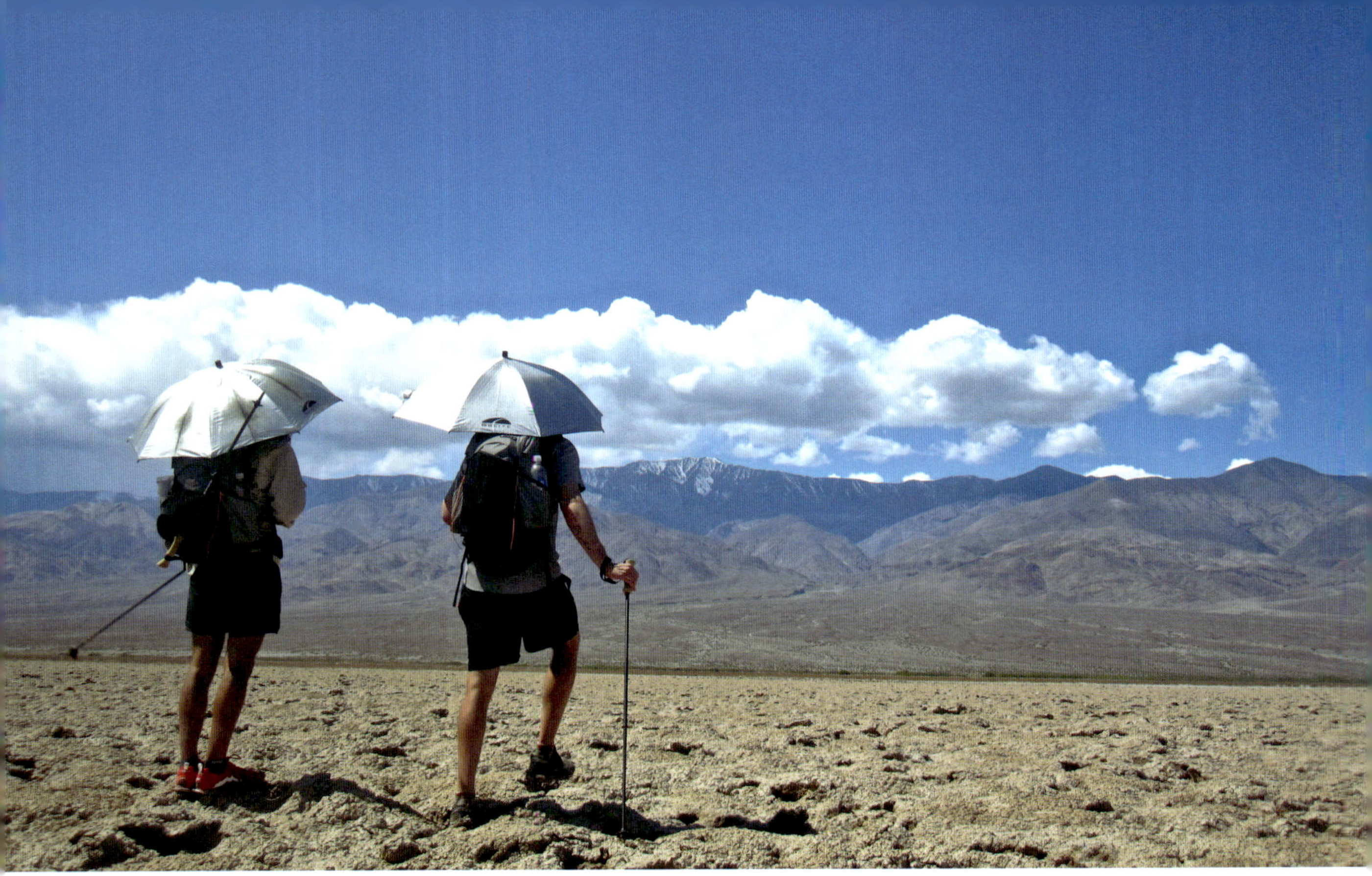

The Lowest to Highest (L2H) is a 217 km (135 mi) backcountry route that takes hikers from salt pans to snowy peaks, via a varied combination of trails, little-used four-wheel-drive tracks, and cross-country terrain. As the name suggests, it passes from the lowest place in North America (Death Valley—85 m [279 ft.] below sea level) to the highest point in the contiguous United States (Mount Whitney—4,418 m [14,495 ft.]) It is a journey marked by extremes rather than trail signs. Whether it be in temperature, elevation, or ecosystem, "change is seemingly the only constant on the Lowest to Highest," according to the route's founder Brett Tucker. He goes on to say, "Perhaps nowhere else on earth can a person so quickly travel on foot between markedly contrasting environments."

The official starting point of the hike is Badwater Basin. It was here that in July 1913 an air temperature of 57°C (134°F) was recorded. More than a century later it remains the hottest on record. Suffice to say, the Lowest to Highest is not a hike you want to be doing in the middle of summer. The optimum time to go is from September to mid-October, when desert temperatures have cooled and the big snows have yet to arrive in the High Sierra.

ABOUT THE TRAIL

→ DISTANCE Approx. 217 km (135 mi.)
→ DURATION 8 days
→ LEVEL Difficult

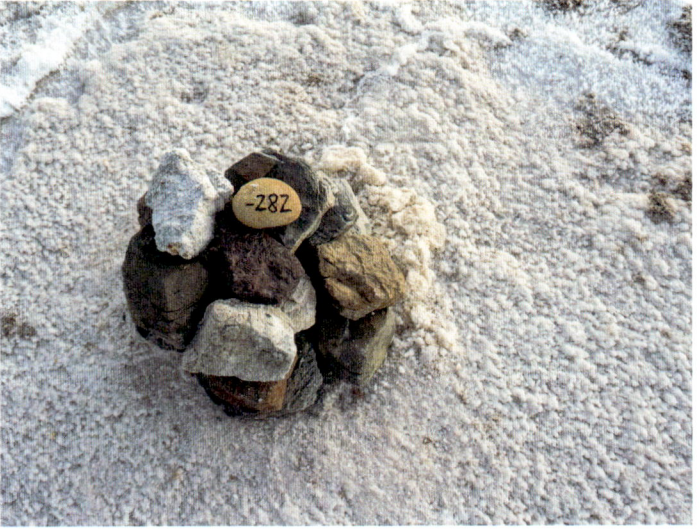

Topographically speaking, the L2H could perhaps best be described as a roller coaster. For the most part, the going is either up or down, with a few much-appreciated flat stretches in between.

From Badwater Basin the route heads west across the sun-beaten salt flats of Death Valley. This ominous-sounding name was given to the area by the pioneer settlers who underwent extreme suffering while crossing it in 1849. When trekking through the scorching heat today, it is advisable to take along a lightweight umbrella to help stave off the harsh rays. The terrain is crumbly and occasionally sharp underfoot, but the severity of the topography is juxtaposed with the striking beauty of the unique landscape in all directions.

The contrasting tone of the journey is established after only a few hours, when the route leaves the salt flats and heads up into the rugged Panamint Mountains. This is the first of three ranges encountered during the hike (later come the Inyos and the High Sierra). Indeed, topographically speaking, the L2H could perhaps best be described as a roller coaster. For the most part, the going is either up or down, with a few much-appreciated flat stretches in between. All told there is 20,000 m (65,617 ft.) of combined elevation gain and loss during the journey.

One of the biggest rewards for all of this exertion comes in the form of sublime ridgetop vistas from the Panamint and Inyo mountain ranges. Gazing out at the horizon, one cannot help but be reminded that the views that must be worked for the hardest are invariably the ones that resonate the most.

In addition to the heat and frequent changes in altitude, the most challenging aspect of the L2H is water. In short, there is not very much. Due to the lack of water sources between China Garden Spring and the town of Lone Pine (a stretch of around 70 to 80 km [44 to 50 mi.]), most hikers choose to cache water along the way. A good location to leave your water drop is Saline Valley Alternate Road, between the 109-km (67.7-mi.) and 121-km (75.2-mi.) marks.

A good general strategy for hiking in any arid environment is to try and cover as much distance as possible during →

↓ The ascent to Mount Whitney.

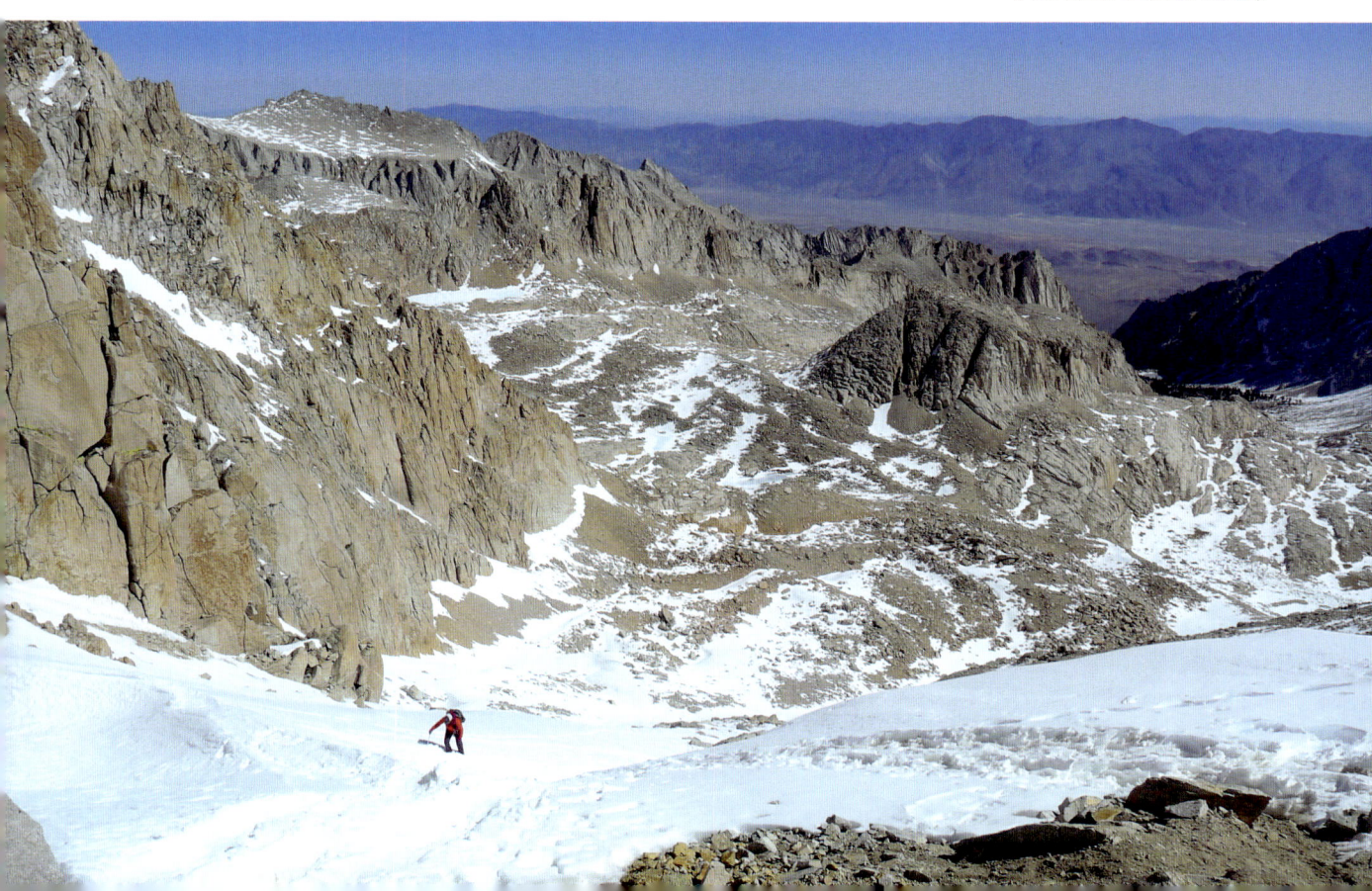

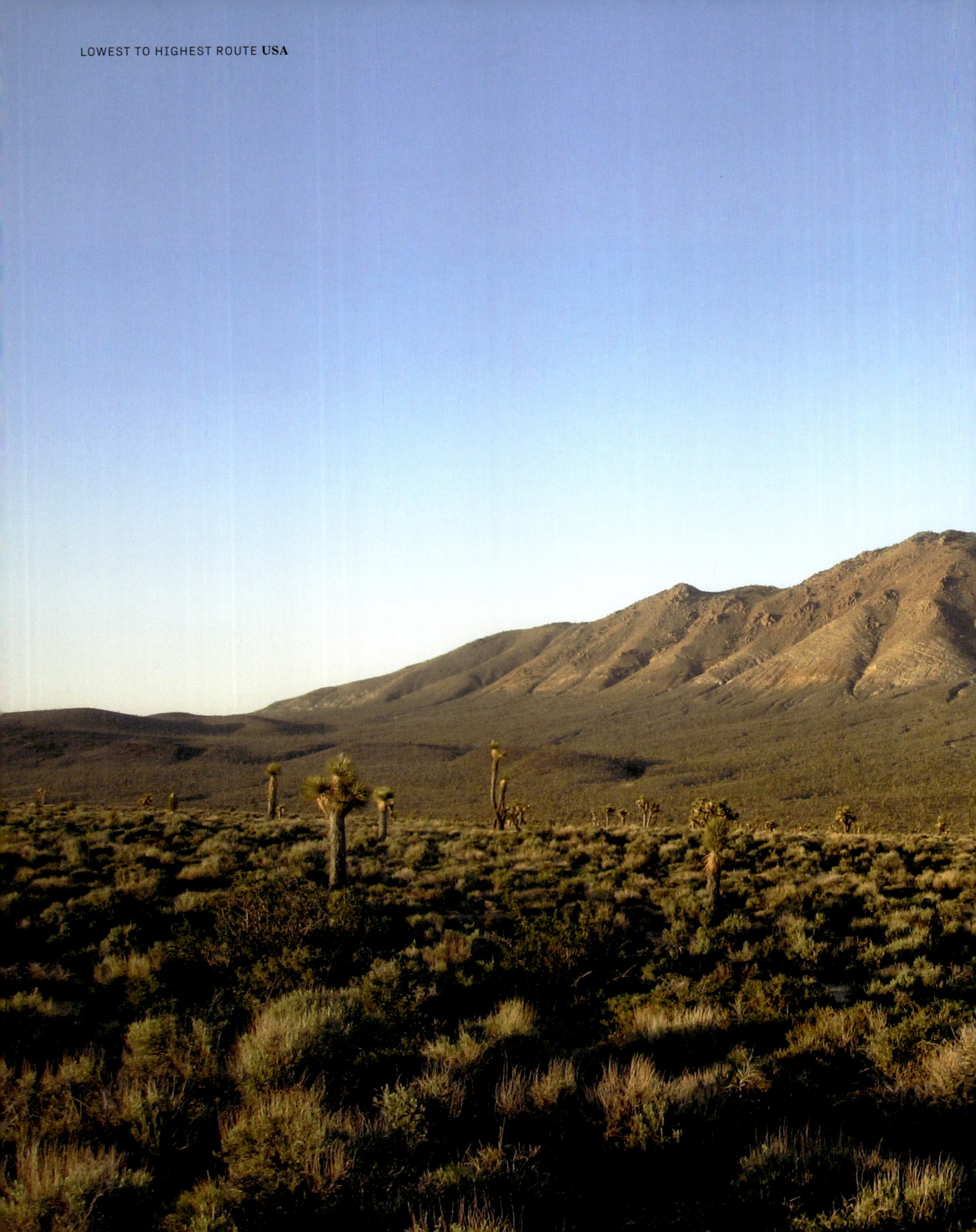

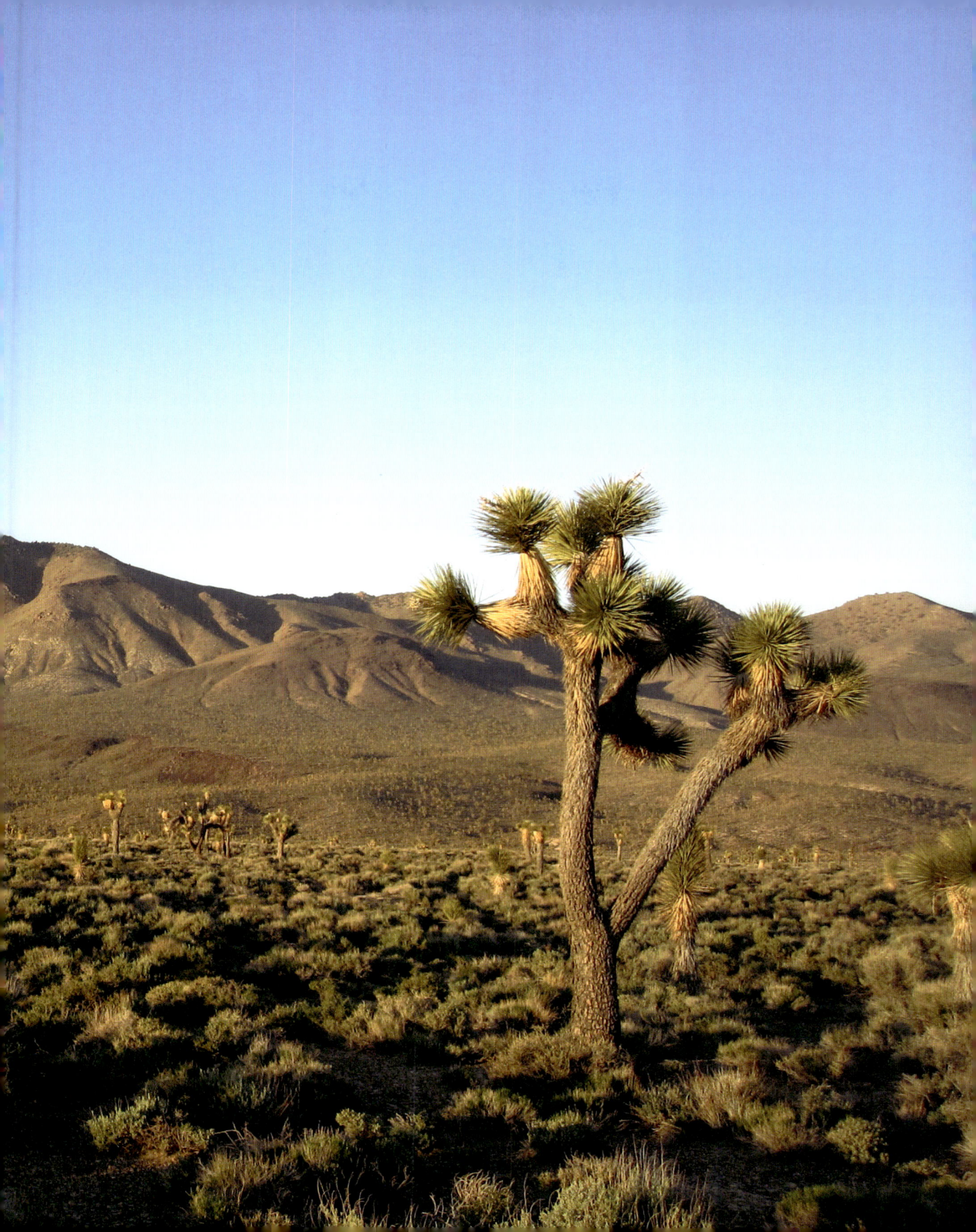

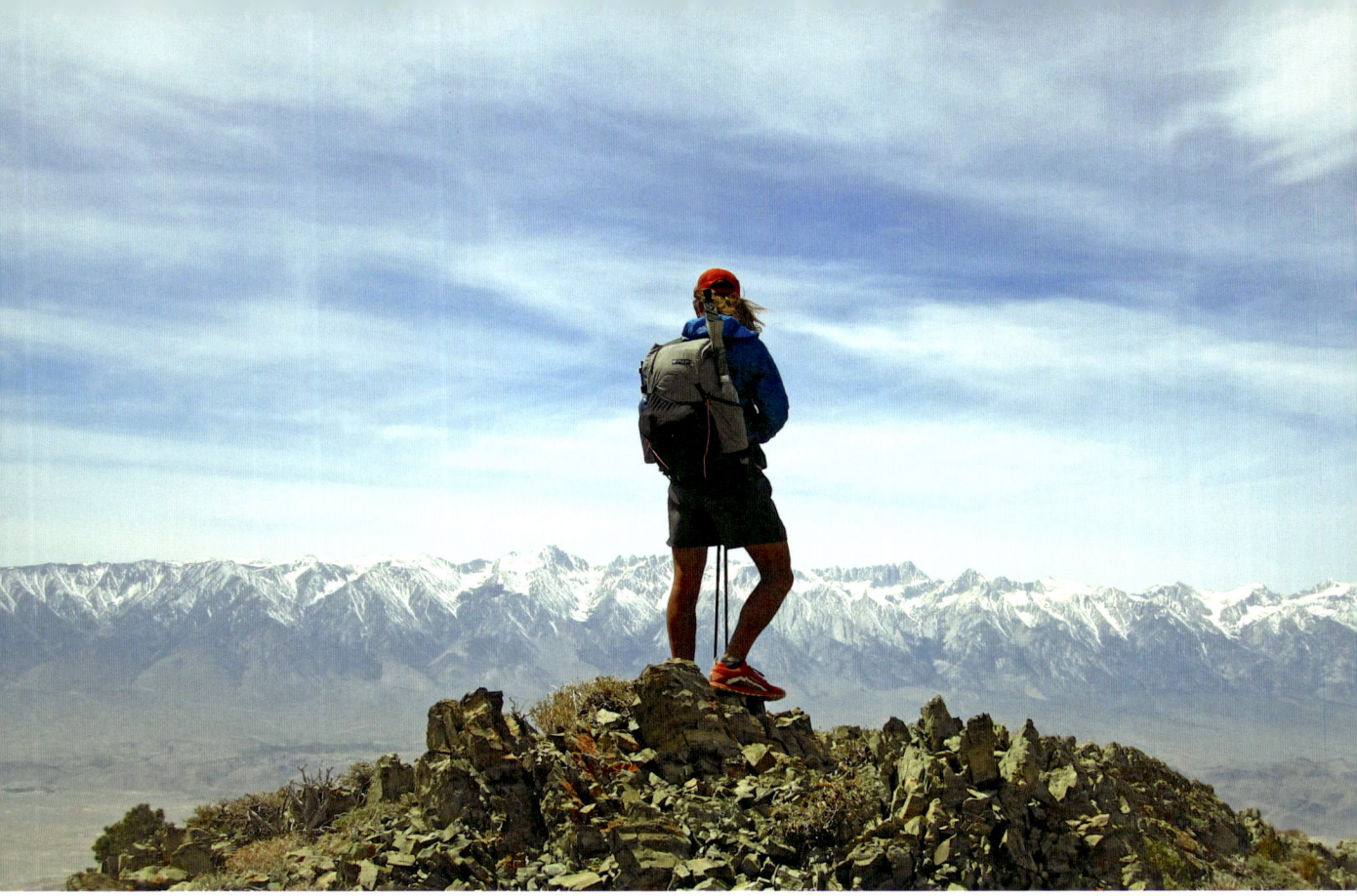

↑ In the Inyos mountains, looking towards the High Sierra.

the early morning and late afternoon hours, and to then take a long break around midday. By doing so, it is possible to make do with less water—and therefore carry less weight—because you are resting rather than exerting during the hottest period of the day.

There are only a handful of water sources that break up the bone-dry conditions of the route. One comes in the form of a waterfall: the beautiful Darwin Falls. With its touches of greenery and refreshingly cool and shady pool, it makes for an idyllic spot to go for a swim. Especially because not long afterwards there begins an 80-km (49.7-mi.) stretch with possibly no water at all.

Alongside the natural wonders of the desert and al-pine zones, the L2H contains many relics of times past. One of these is the Inyo Mountains ghost town of Cerro Gordo. A ma-jor silver-mining center in the late 1800s, Cerro Gordo is today a ramshackle collection of abandoned mines and dilapidated old buildings that boasts a semi-permanent population of one. The L2H passes directly by this fascinating relic of the Old West, and hikers can stop in and explore the area before continuing on with their journeys.

Moving from scorching desert to below-freezing snowcapped peaks, the Lowest to Highest is, by any criteria, a challenge. However, for hikers that possess the requisite experience, plan-ning, and fitness, the payoff comes in the form of one of the most unique and diverse wilderness experiences in North America. ——

Gazing out at the horizon, one cannot help but be reminded that the views that must be worked for the hardest are invariably the ones that resonate the most.

GOOD TO KNOW

START/FINISH
⚐ Badwater Basin, Death Valley
⚐ Summit of Mount Whitney

SEASON
September to mid-October

CONDITIONS
The hike takes place in extreme temperatures and terrain, and there is no ready supply of water. Prior backpacking experience in arid environments is essential.

LOWEST/HIGHEST POINT
-85 m (-279 ft.)/4,418 m (14,495 ft.)

HIGHLIGHTS
Death Valley, Darwin Falls, Cerro Gordo Ghost Town, views from the Panamint and Inyo mountains, the summit of Mount Whitney.

TIP
Water caching—storing water along the way for pick up—is something that should be planned in for safety. An essential source to contact for up-to-date details about available water is Furnace Creek Visitor Center. Every hiker should be sure to do this before setting out. Permits are required only for the Mount Whitney section of the route.

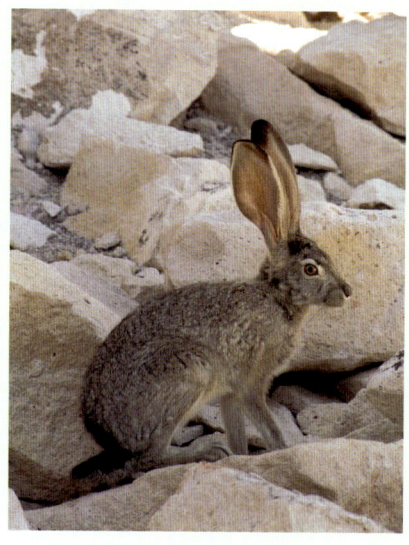

FLORA & FAUNA

DEATH VALLEY WILDLIFE Considering the arid nature of much of its terrain, Death Valley National Park is home to a surprisingly wide array of wildlife. There are desert bighorn sheep, bobcats, coyotes, foxes, jackrabbits, roadrunners, kangaroo rats, desert tortoises, and nearly 400 species of bird.

BACKGROUND

RESEARCH As this is an incredibly demanding route, thorough research, training, and preparation must be done before. Lots of information can be found online: maps, databooks, locations of resupply points, historical water information, and GPS tracks. The route is not signposted, so good navigation skills are a must.

HELPFUL HINTS

GHOST TOWN A former mining town established in the 1860s, Cerro Gordo ("Fat Hill" in English) was once home to around 1,000 people. Nearby mines produced silver, lead, and zinc, but ceased production in the 1950s, leading to the town later being abandoned. Visitors can explore the remains, which include former homes and a hotel.

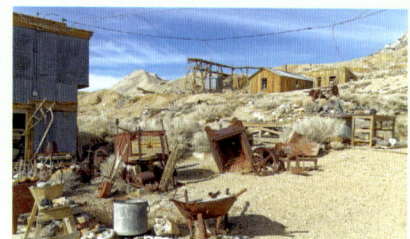

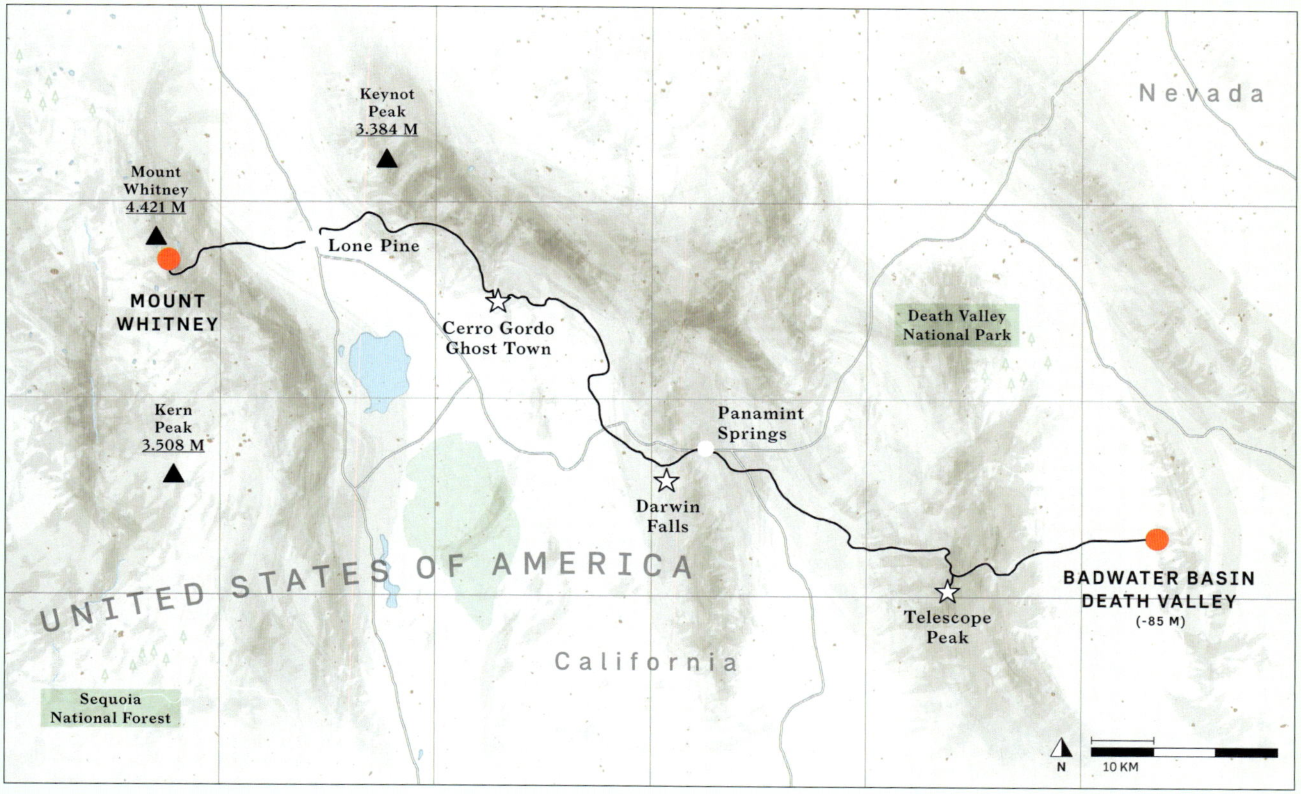

Keynot Peak 3,384 M

Nevada

Mount Whitney 4,421 M

Lone Pine

MOUNT WHITNEY

Cerro Gordo Ghost Town

Death Valley National Park

Kern Peak 3,508 M

Panamint Springs

Darwin Falls

UNITED STATES OF AMERICA

California

Telescope Peak

BADWATER BASIN DEATH VALLEY (-85 M)

Sequoia National Forest

N 10 KM

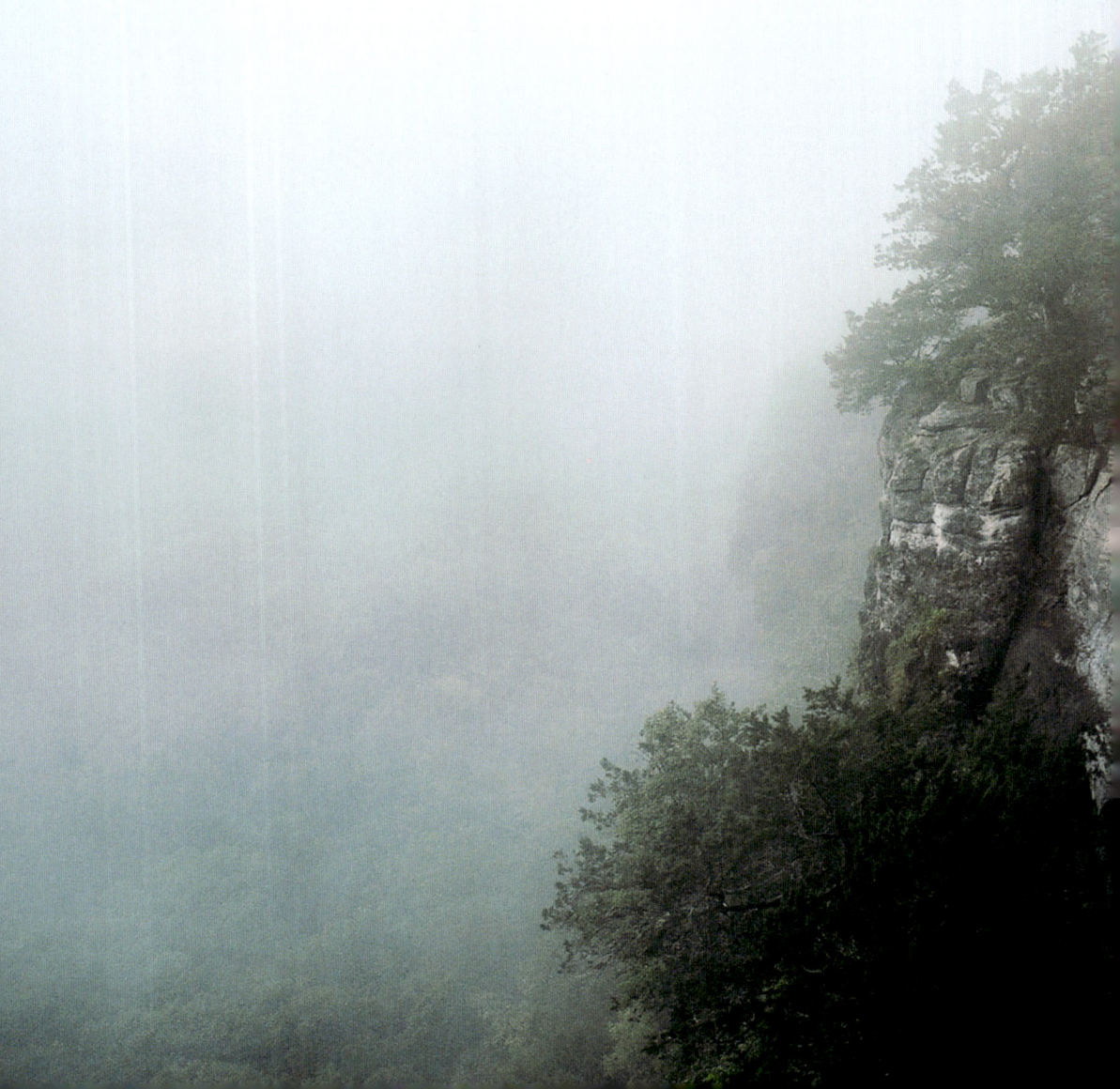

ALONG THE BUFFALO NATIONAL RIVER

USA

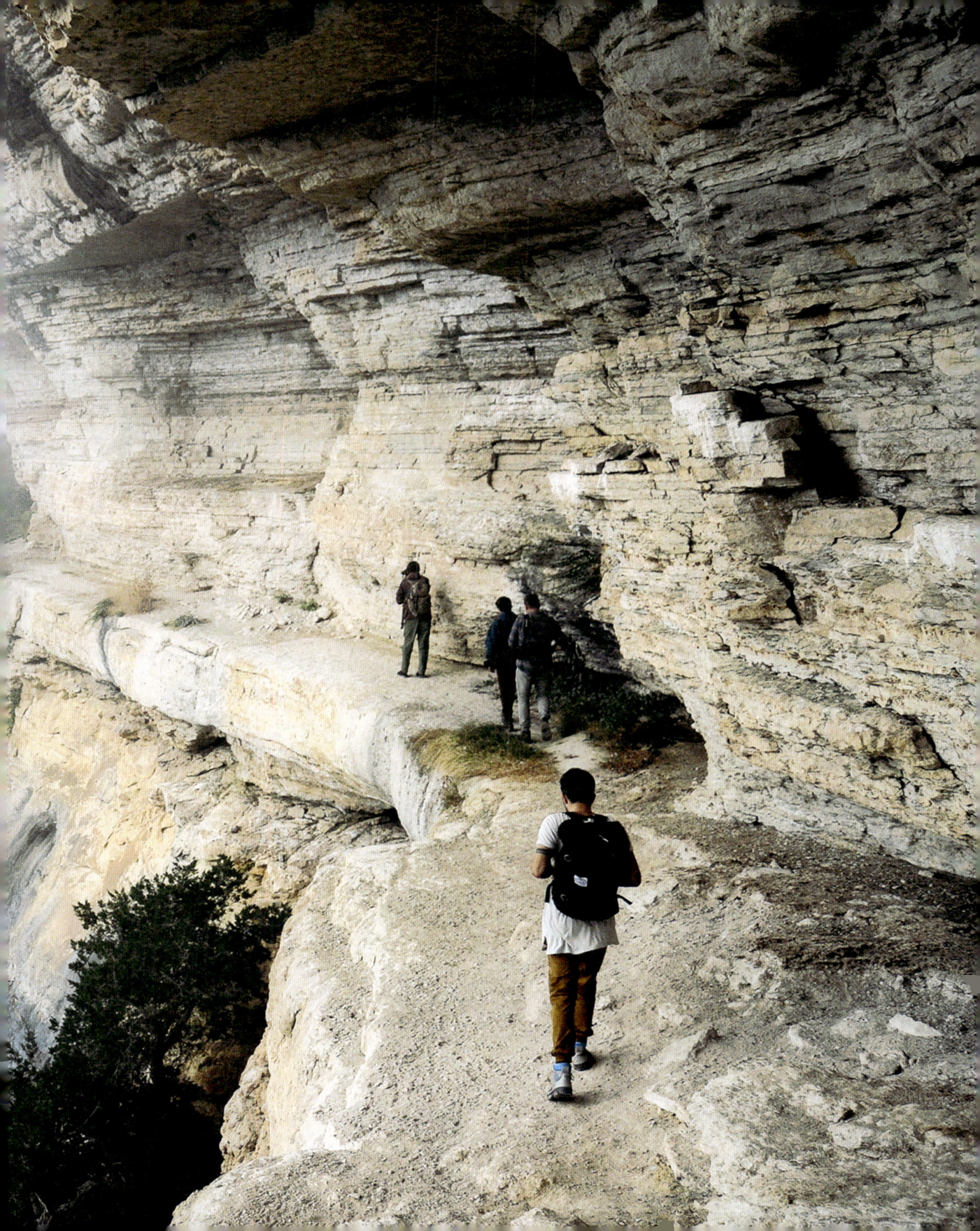

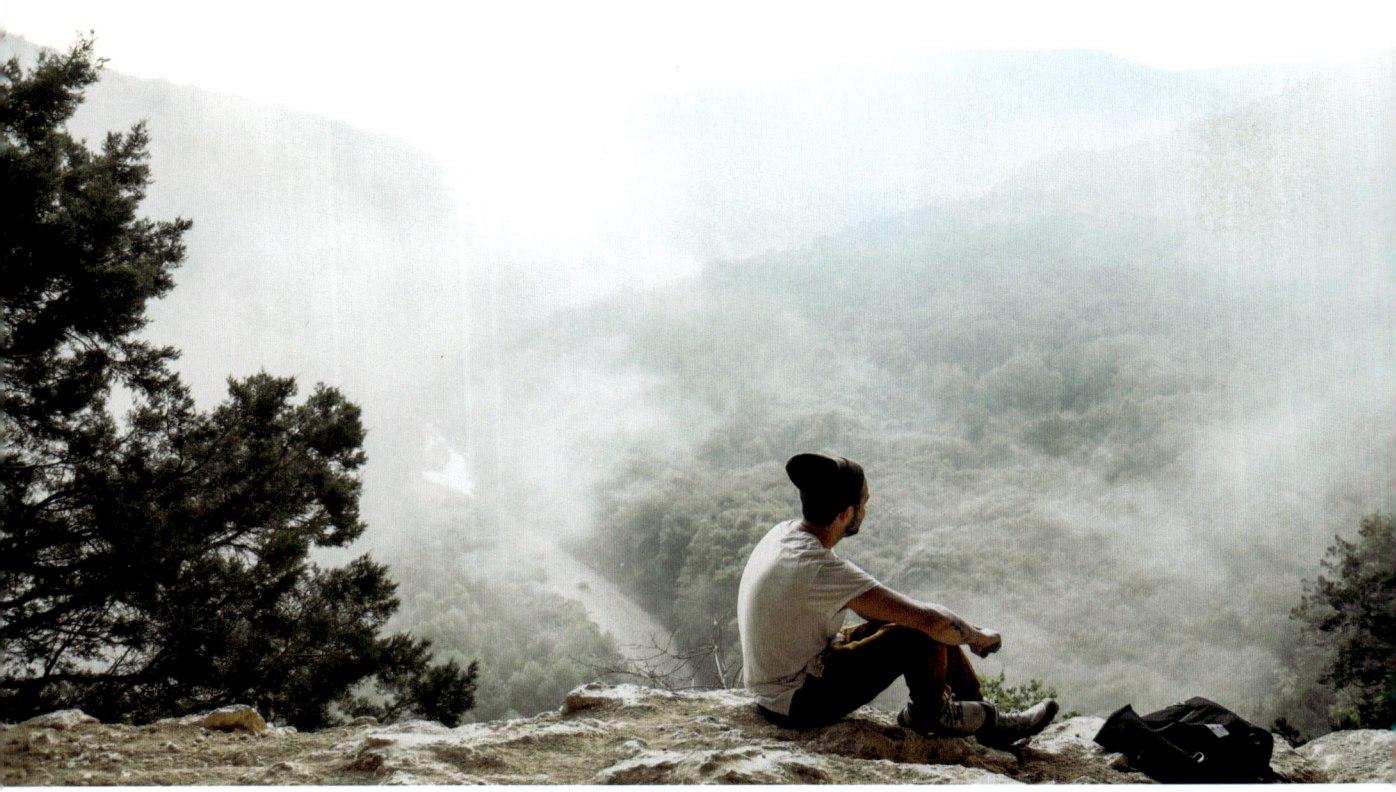

Backpacking trips do not always have to be demanding, multi-day affairs in challenging conditions. Quite often the combination of tranquil surroundings and a picturesque shorter trek can be more than sufficient to satisfy one's hiking needs. The out-and-back journey from the Centerpoint Trailhead to Big Bluff falls into this category. Measuring 10.5 km (6.5 mi.) in total, it can be done as a day hike, a leisurely overnighter, or combined with other pathways to create a longer excursion.

The hike begins in the middle of the Ponca Wilderness in Arkansas's rugged Ozark Mountains. From the Centerpoint Trailhead, hikers descend gradually on a nineteenth-century wagon road that meanders its way through forested environs. The path is easy to follow and occasionally affords impressive views over the surrounding mountains. After 4.3 km (2.7 mi.) of gradual

The irresistible mixture of nature and history leaves hikers in little doubt as to why it is commonly referred to as the jewel of Arkansas's Ozark Mountains.

descent, the Centerpoint Trail reaches a junction with the Goat Trail. At this point, hikers head south towards the turnaround destination of Big Bluff, a narrow ledge overlooking the Buffalo River.

It is said that the Goat Trail derives its name from the domesticated goats that were brought to the area by early settlers. Some of the animals either escaped or were set free, and over the years their feral descendants were regularly spotted out on the bluff, standing like sentinels overlooking the wooded valley below.

More than a century later, it is hikers rather than goats that are drawn to this dramatic location. Situated more than 152 m

---

ABOUT THE TRAIL

- → <u>DISTANCE</u> 10.5 km (6.5 mi.)
- → <u>DURATION</u> 1 day
- → <u>LEVEL</u> Easy to Moderate

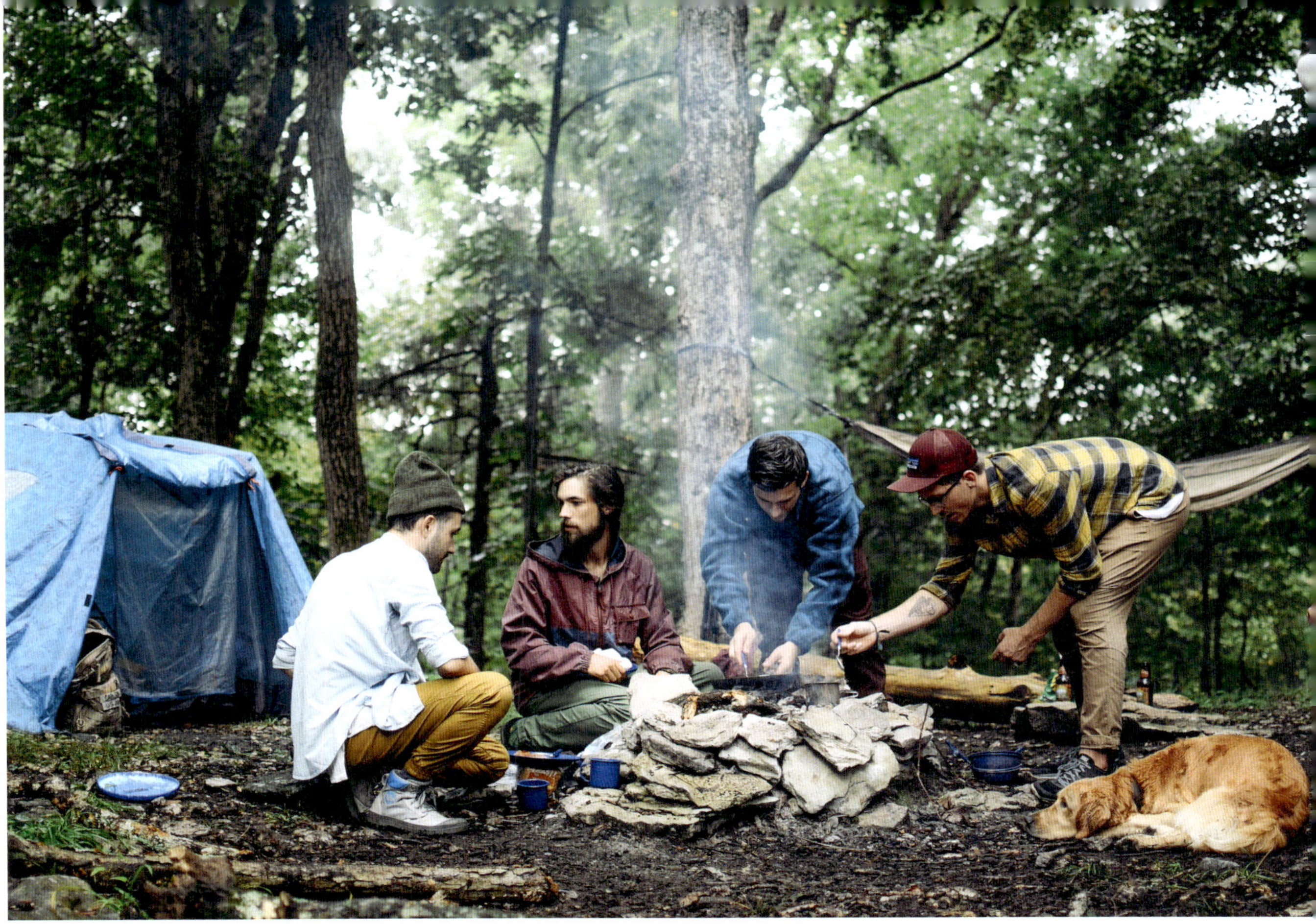

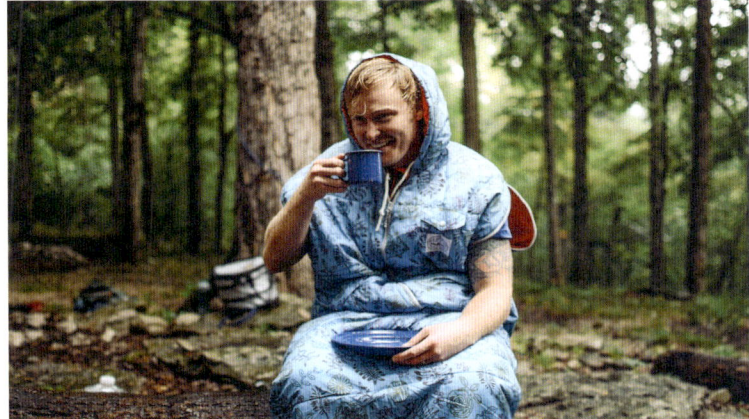

← A break to savor the vista over the Ozarks.
↑↘ Morning rituals in the wild.

(500 ft.) above the Buffalo River, Big Bluff is said to be the highest sheer bluff face between the Rocky and Appalachian Mountains. Although the 180-degree vista of the River Valley is magnificent, extreme care must be taken while traversing the narrow ledge, which at times measures little more than 1 m (3 ft.) wide. Though fatalities are uncommon, over the years there have been several cases of hikers plunging to their deaths.

Because the ledge faces west, one of the optimum times to visit Big Bluff is late afternoon. Watching the sun set over the Ozark Mountains makes for a dreamlike experience—one that can easily be extended into a serene evening of stargazing by hikers who have come equipped for camping. Sites are available back at the trail junction, situated around 800 m (0.5 mi.) from Big Bluff. For walkers planning on visiting the ledge after dark, it is imperative to bring headlamps, and to proceed with even more caution than is necessary during daylight hours.

Once back on the Centerpoint Trail, hikers have two alternatives: either turn west back to the trailhead, or extend their journeys by heading east towards the Buffalo River. If the latter option is chosen, less than half an hour past the junction walkers will reach an abandoned log cabin. This site belonged to one of the area's last permanent residents, the legendary Eva Barnes "Granny" Henderson, who moved in in 1912, and lived there for many years without modern amenities such as electricity, running water, and central heating. She kept animals, worked on the land, and even made it onto the →

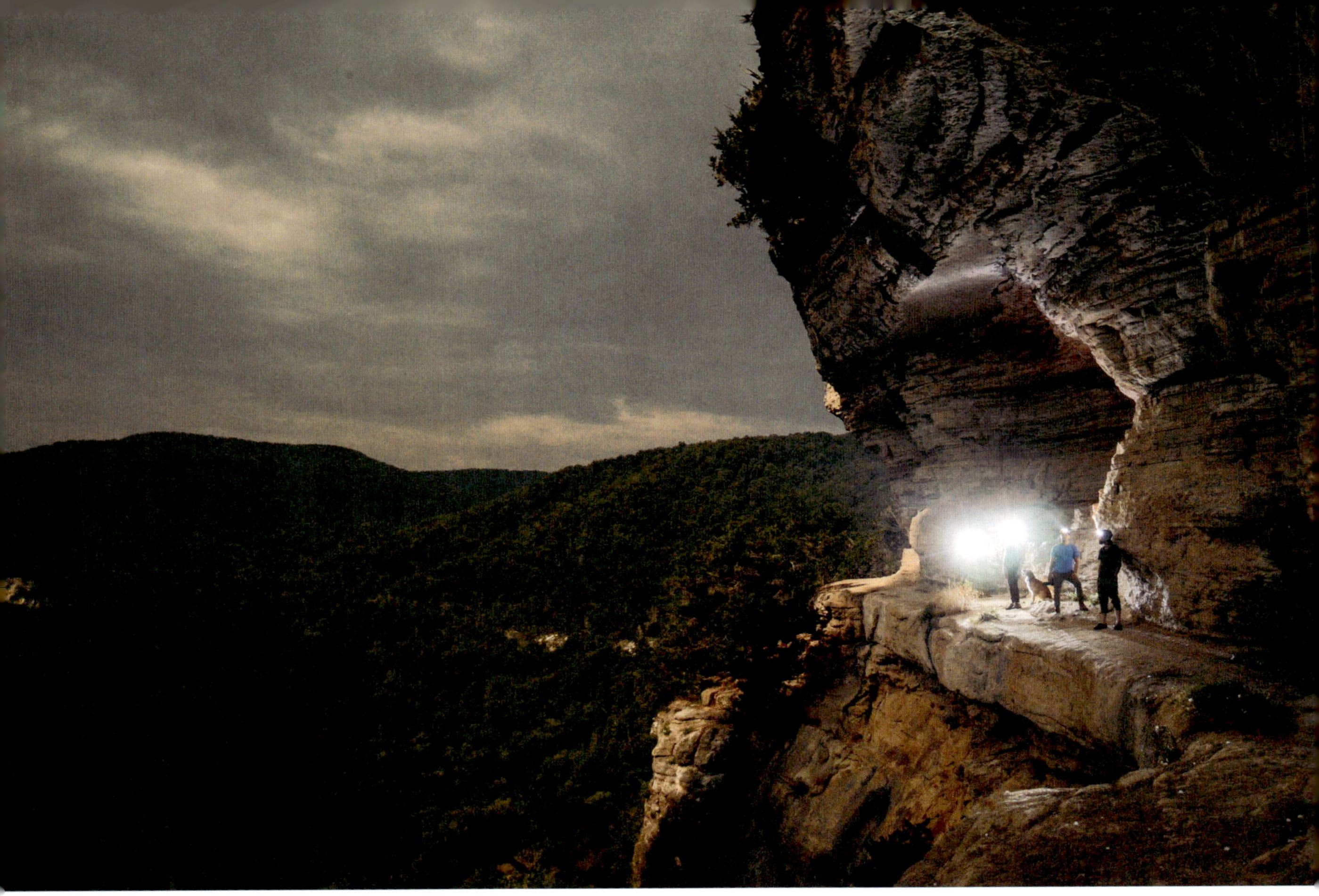

↑ **On the ledges of the Goat Trail.**

pages of *National Geographic.* After the Buffalo was designated the country's first national river in 1978, she was forced to move at the age of 87. Today, visitors can see the dwelling that documents her pioneer lifestyle.

Soon after leaving Granny's cabin, hikers will reach Sneeds Creek, a pleasant open area that boasts excellent camping possibilities. From this point it is possible to intersect with various other pathways in the Ponca Wilderness, including the Old River Trail, Sneeds Creek Trail, and Hemmed-in Hollow Trail. The latter pathway heads north for a couple of kilometers to reach one of the region's most impressive natural wonders, Hemmed-in-Hollow Falls, the tallest cascade in Arkansas (see opposite page).

From the Falls back to the Centerpoint Trailhead is 8.7 km (5.4 mi.), most of which is uphill. However, the challenge of the gradient is mitigated by lingering thoughts of dazzling bluffs, storied homesteads, and plunging waterfalls. Irrespective of the length of one's journey,

Buffalo River country is a place that inspires thoughts of return visits. Its irresistible mixture of nature and history leaves visitors in little doubt as to why it is commonly referred to as the jewel of Arkansas's Ozark Mountains. ───────────────

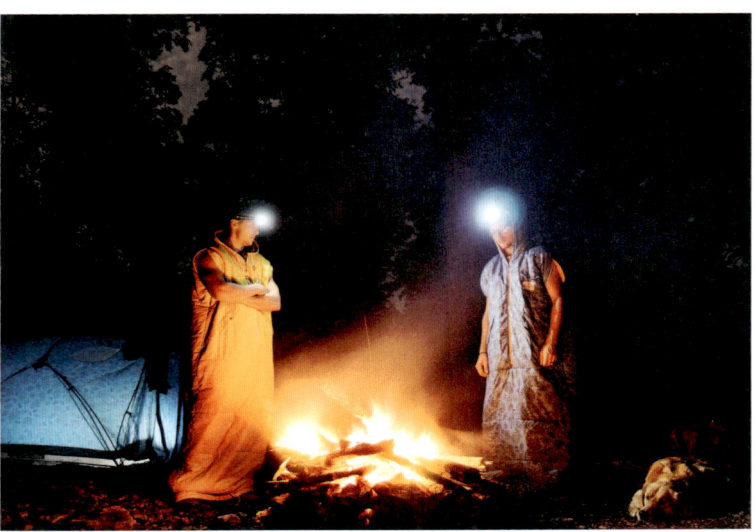

GOOD TO KNOW

START/FINISH
Out-and-back from the Centerpoint Trailhead north of Ponca, Arkansas.

SEASON
Year-round

CONDITIONS
A well maintained, easy-to-follow path, but caution should be exercised when moving along the ledges.

ACCOMMODATION
Camping is possible near the junction of the Centerpoint and Goat Trails. For those that extend their hikes to the Buffalo River, there are also good campsites available near Sneed's Creek.

HELPFUL HINTS

SCENIC CASCADE Further on from Big Bluff is the highest waterfall between the Rocky and the Appalachian mountains, a cascade in the Hemmed-in-Hollow valley. The 64-m-high (209-ft.) falls on the Buffalo National River is best seen at the end of winter or the beginning of spring, when the rainfall is at its highest.

BACKGROUND

RIVER SOURCES The Ozark Mountains run through three U.S. states: Arkansas, Missouri, and Oklahoma. Their name originates from the French term aux arcs, which was used by map makers in the seventeenth and eighteenth centuries to refer to a particular curve in the Arkansas River.

Also running through the Ozarks in north Arkansas is the Buffalo National River. In 1972, the Buffalo was the first waterway to be deemed a national river. This classification forbids the building of dams or other industrial structures throughout the whole length of the 217-km (135-mi.) river to protect its natural character and surrounding flora and fauna.

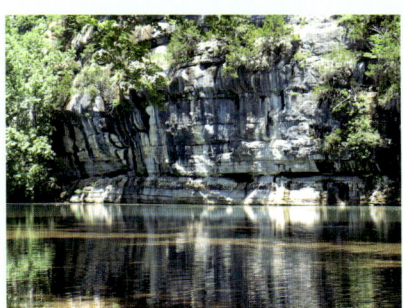

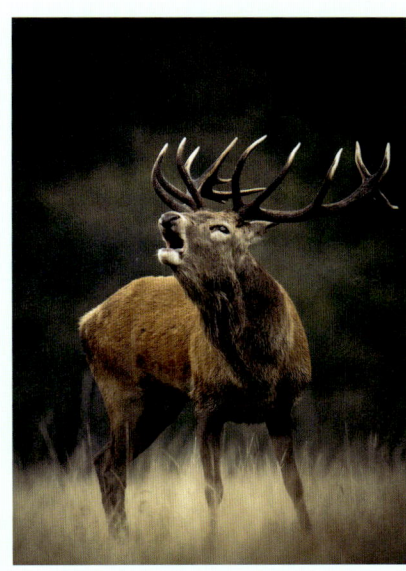

FLORA & FAUNA

WILDLIFE Hunted to extinction in the 19th century, elk were reintroduced to the Ozarks between 1981 and 1985 and their numbers continue to thrive. Elk shed their antlers in later winter or early spring, and within days of dropping, they begin to grow back again.

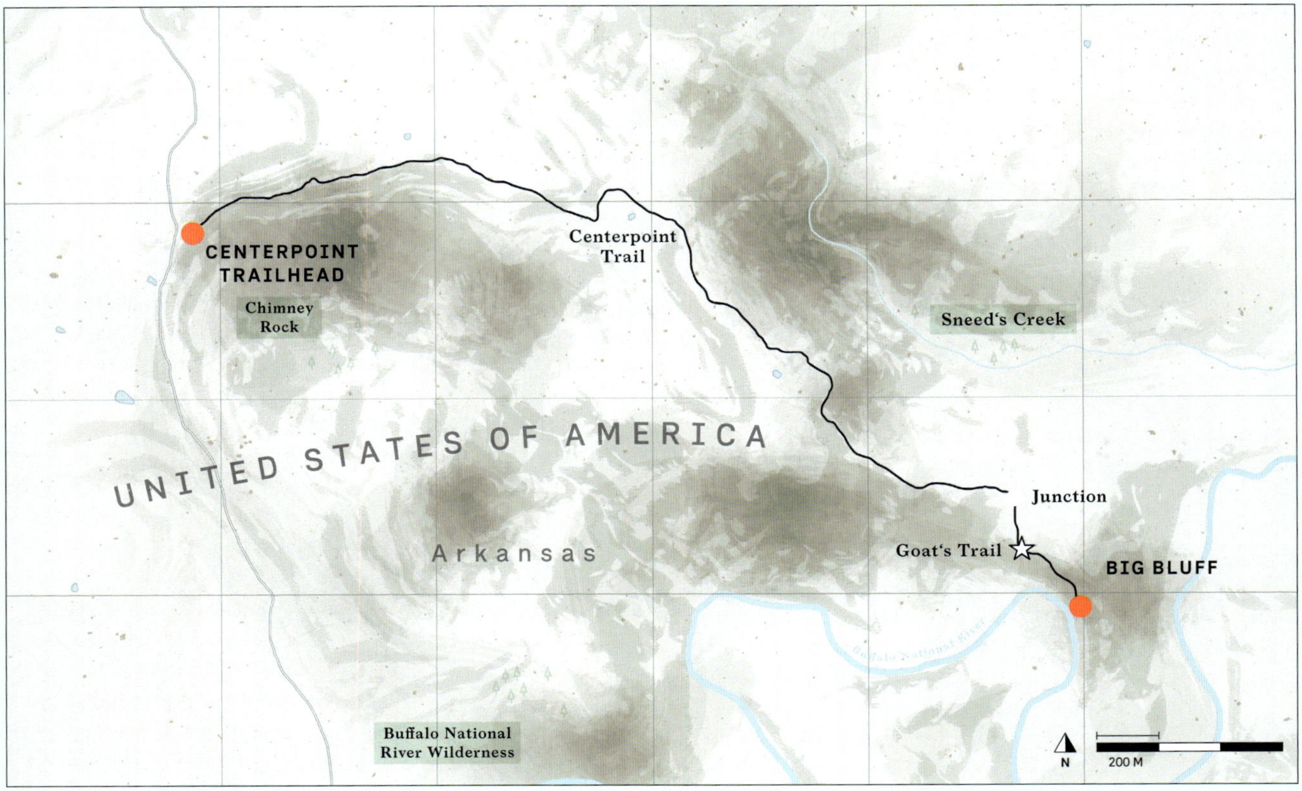

CENTERPOINT
TRAILHEAD

Chimney
Rock

Centerpoint
Trail

Sneed's Creek

UNITED STATES OF AMERICA

Arkansas

Junction

Goat's Trail

BIG BLUFF

Buffalo National
River Wilderness

N

200 M

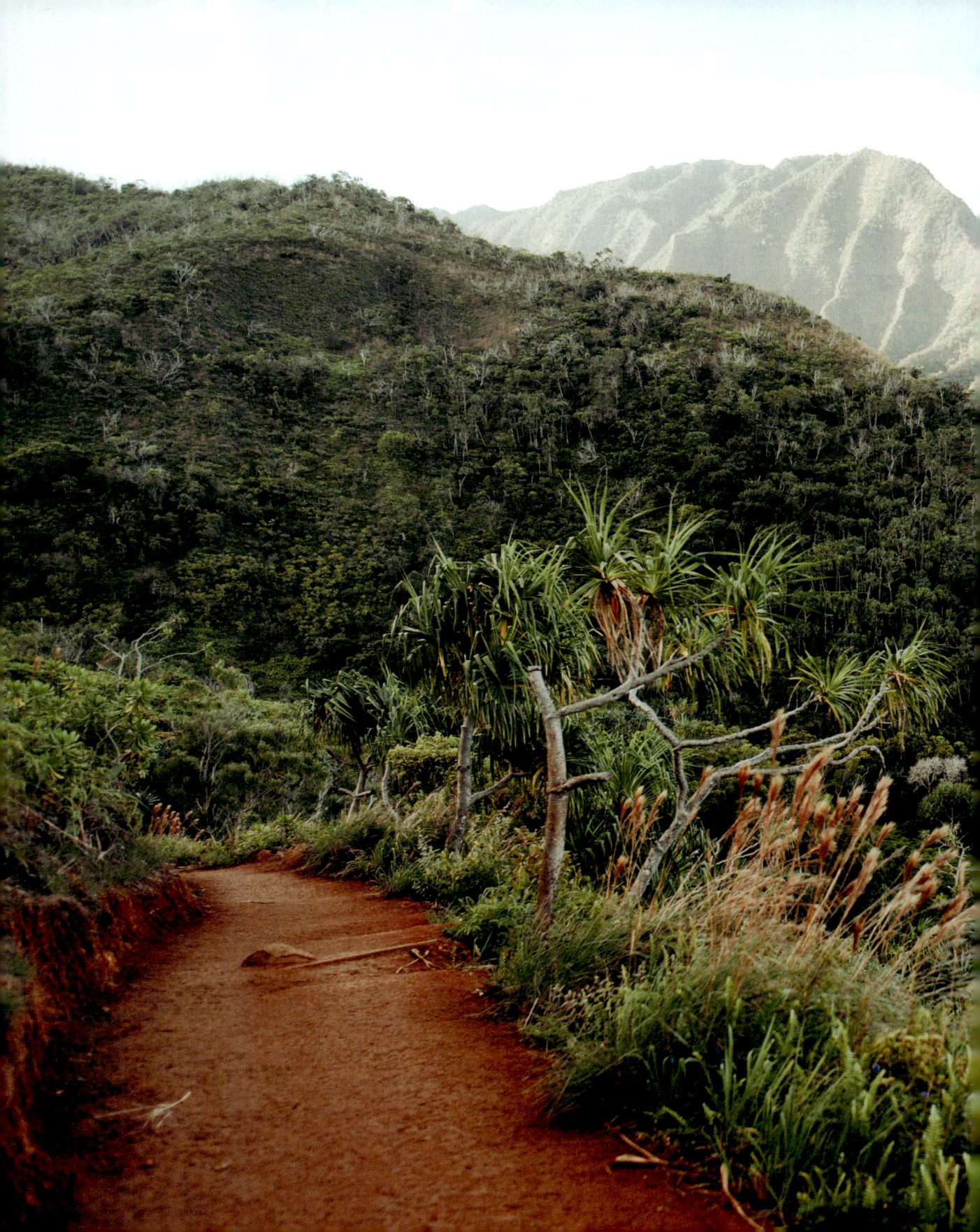

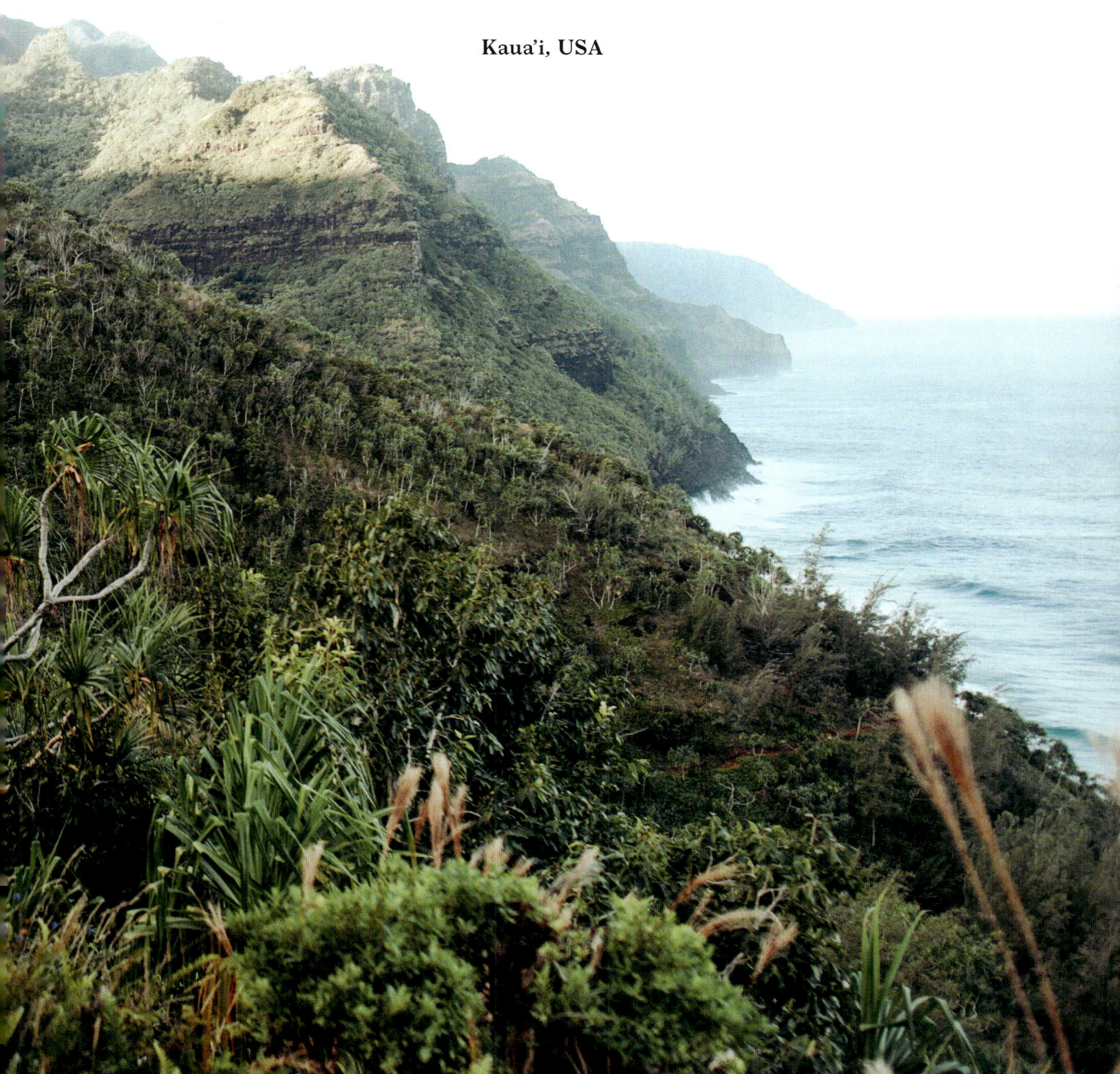

KALALAU TRAIL

A PRECIPITOUS PARADISE ON THE NA PALI COAST

Kaua'i, USA

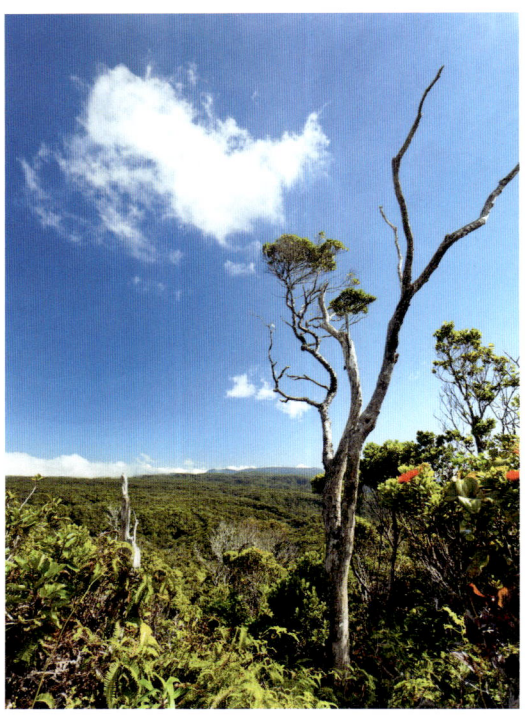

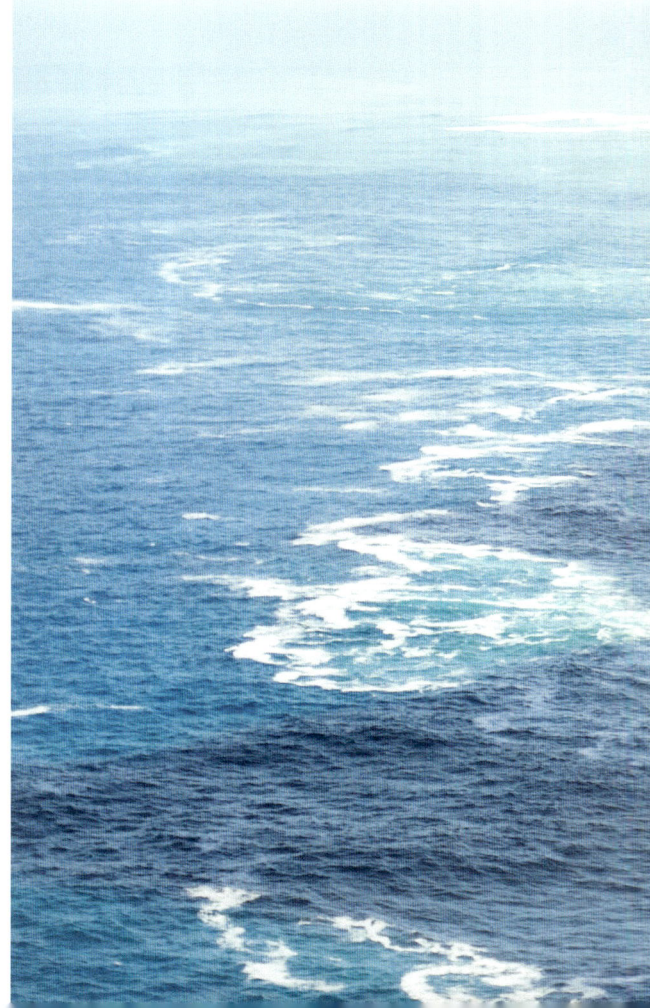

Coastal hiking does not get much better—or much more precarious—than Hawaii's Kalalau Trail. There are pristine beaches, cascading waterfalls, lush valleys, and jaw-dropping 180-degree vistas over the Pacific Ocean. Linking all of these natural wonders together is an often cliff-hugging pathway along one of the world's most dramatic coastlines.

The Na Pali Coast is a jagged range of towering cliffs rising up to a height of 1,200 m (4,000 ft.) over the sea on Kaua'i's north shore. Kaua'i is the oldest inhabited Hawaiian island, and it is known as the Garden Isle. As so often in earth's history, tectonic forces have shaped the dramatic geological formations. These razor-sharp rocks are remnants from a massive ancient volcano that once rose more than 8,000 m (26,250 ft.) from the Pacific seabed.

Over the decades, the Na Pali Coast has acted as a backdrop for dozens of Hollywood movies, including Steven Spielberg's *Jurassic Park* and the legendary original version of →

ABOUT THE TRAIL

→ <u>DISTANCE</u> 35 km (21.7 mi.)

→ <u>DURATION</u> 2 to 3 days

→ <u>LEVEL</u> Moderate

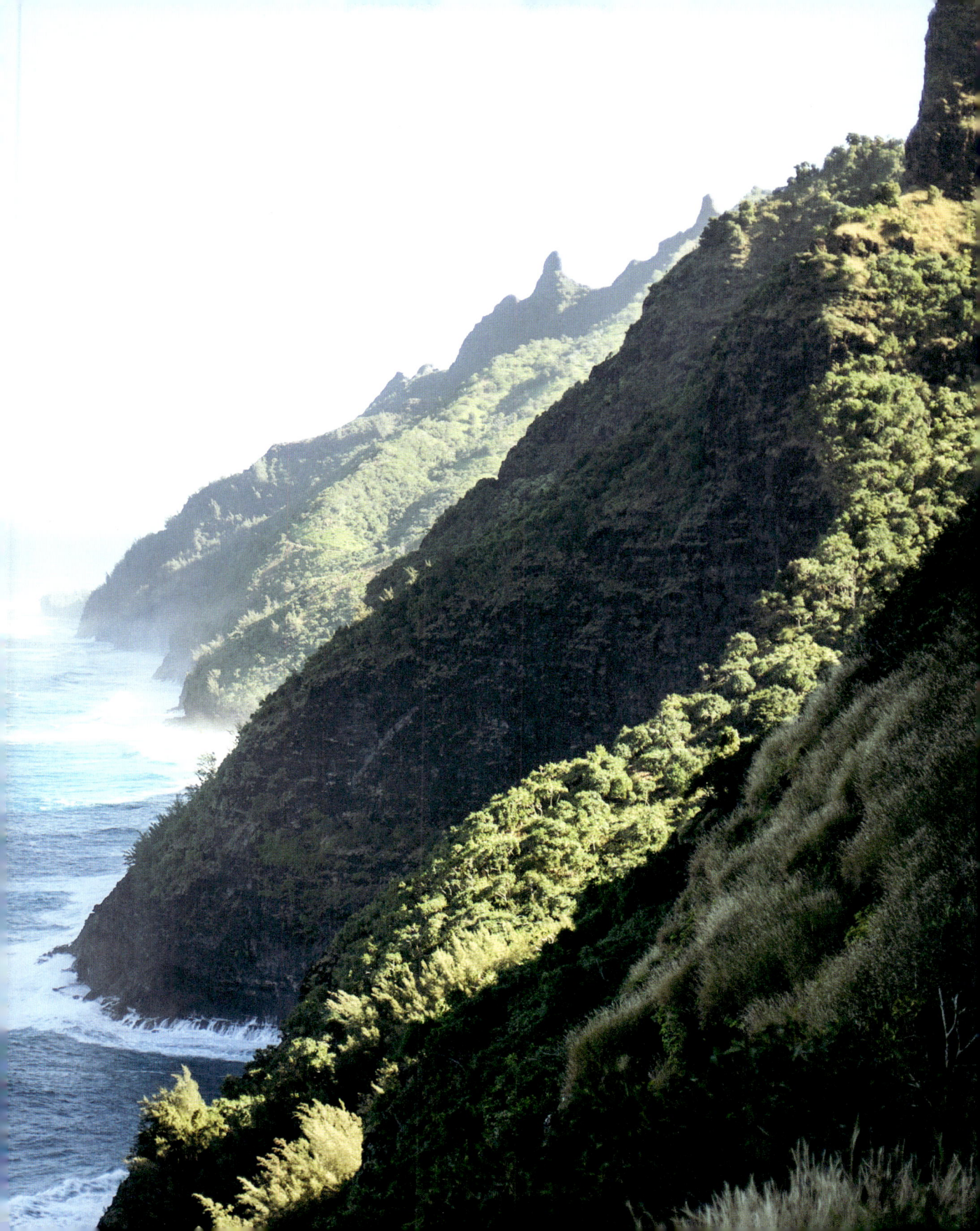

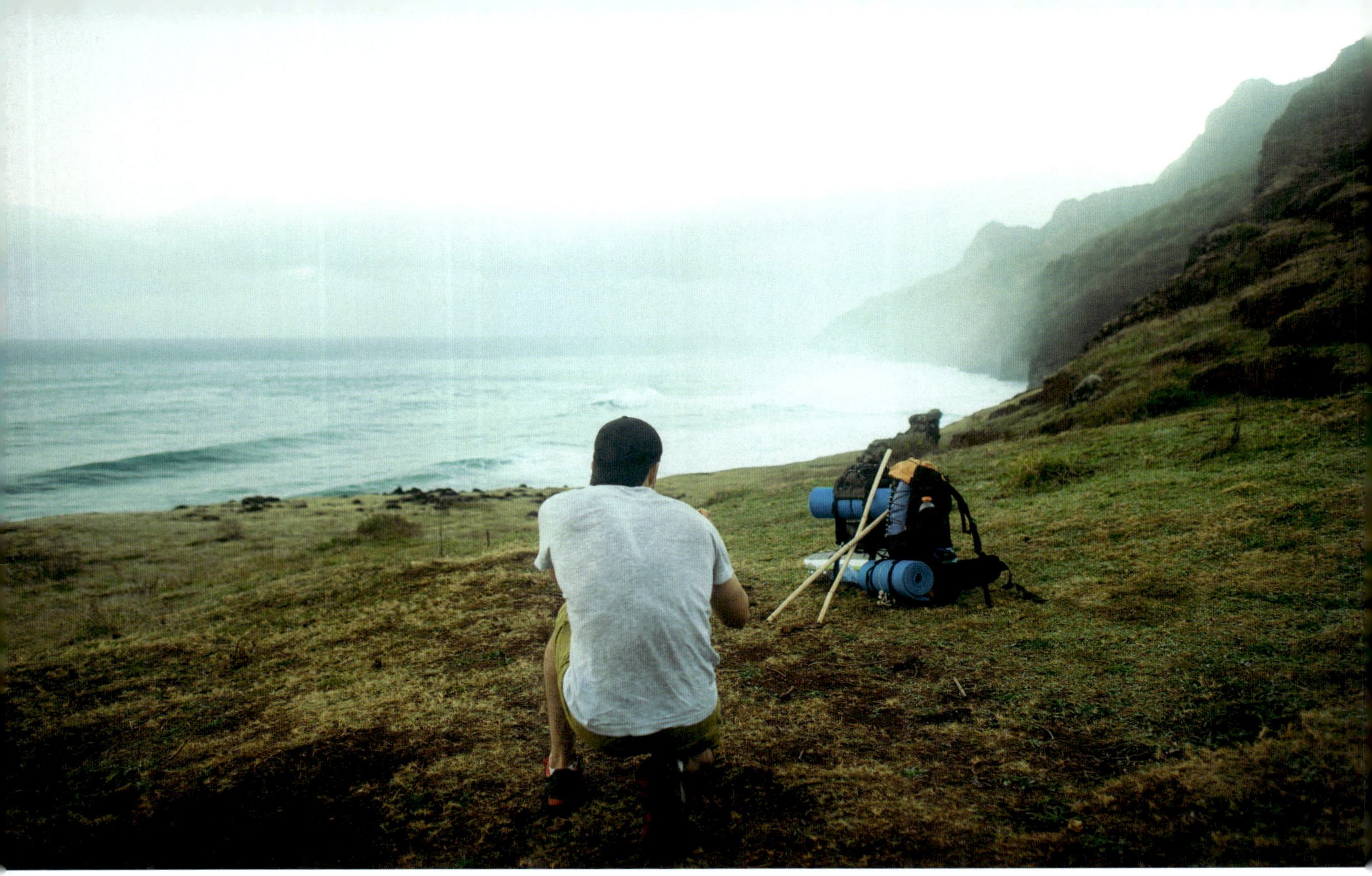

King Kong from 1933. It does not come as a surprise that movie makers have been drawn to Kaua'i to stage these storylines: the island's flora and microclimate do indeed resemble the conditions that prevailed during the periods when dinosaurs and other mighty creatures inhabited the earth.

Apart from serving as a backdrop for science-fiction adventure films, the Na Pali Coast is home to lush vegetation, sparkling springs, and golden beaches. The island is also the place where the majority of American coffee is produced. Were it not for the occasional violent downpour or the subsequent landslides, this corner of the world could easily be considered a sort of paradise on earth. There are no roads that connect the unique ecosystem to civilization. The only way to access it remains reserved for those who are brave enough to venture out and explore it by water or by hiking the Kalalau Trail.

First established in the late 1800s, the Kalalau Trail remains the only way in and out of the Na Pali Coast State Park. During its course, it passes through five lush coastal valleys and negotiates several cliff-hugging sections of narrow pathway. Extreme care should be taken while tiptoeing across these difficult segments as there is not much between you and a sheer 100 m (328 ft.) drop into the Pacific Ocean. →

Despite all the dangers, the area's outstanding natural beauty remains an irresistible draw.

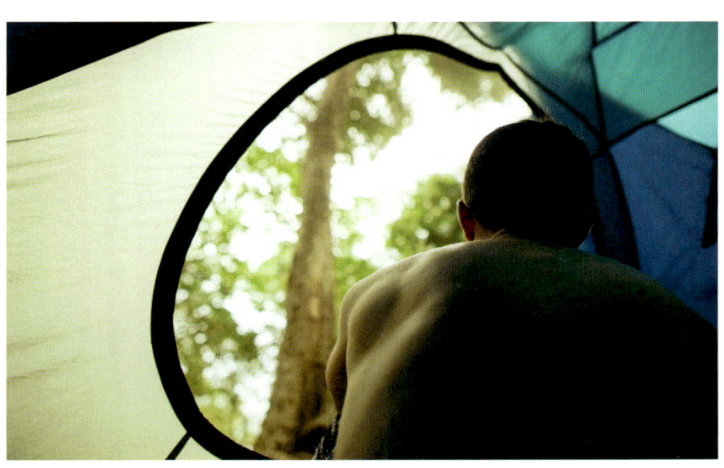

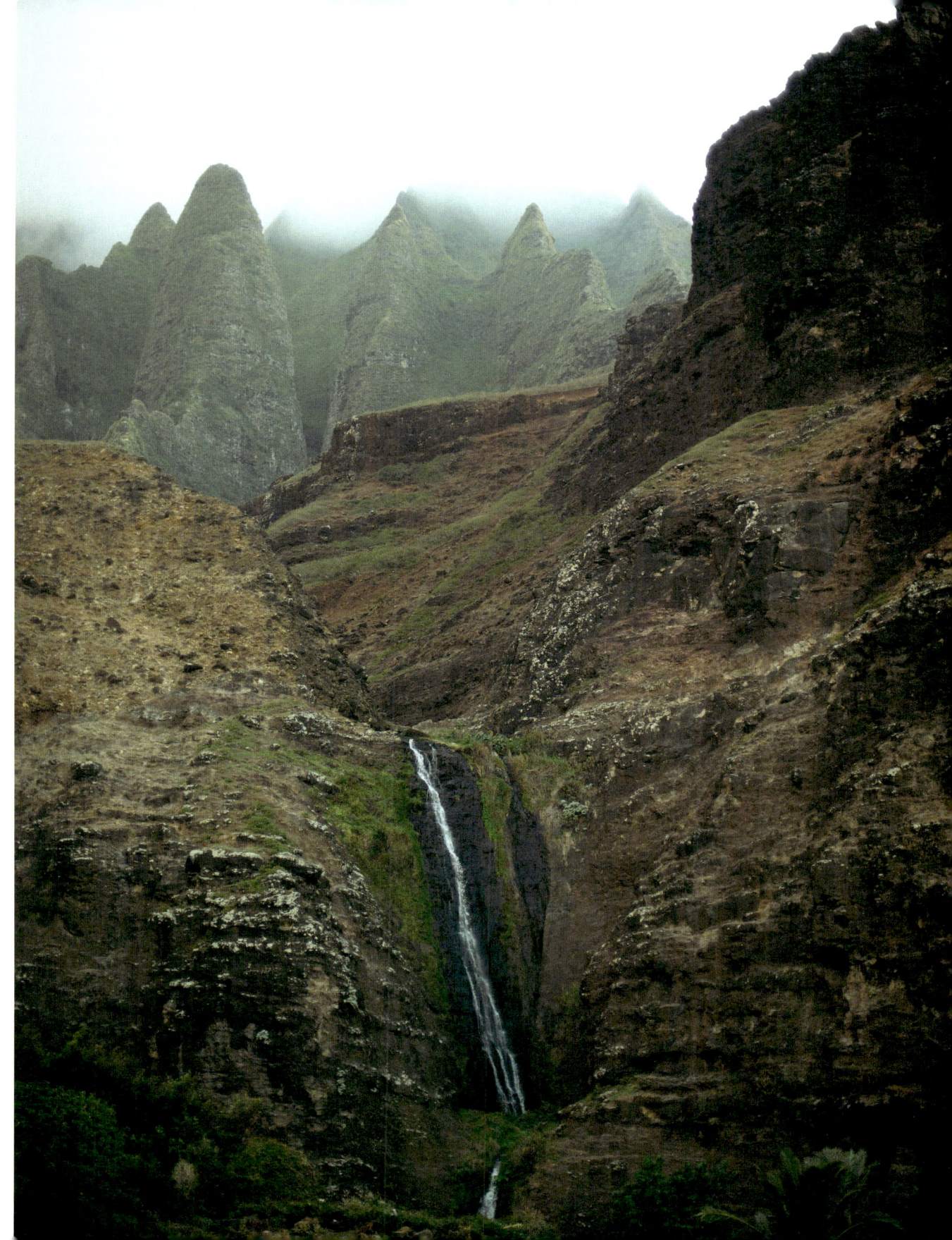

Were it not for the occasional violent downpour or the subsequent landslides, this corner of the world could easily be considered a sort of paradise on earth.

Though the Kalalau is straightforward to follow and the path is well maintained throughout, it can be a challenging hike. Conditions are often hot and humid, and the tread can be muddy and slippery due to the high amount of precipitation. Kaua'i is one of the wettest places on earth, which has an impact on the route. There are numerous streams that need to be forded, and in times of heavy rainfall, these usually mellow crossings can transform into fast-moving torrents. In such situations, hikers should be patient and bide their time. High water levels can drop as quickly as they have risen.

Although it is possible to hike the entire Kalalau Trail in one day, taking two or three days to complete the 35 km (22 mi.) journey is recommended. The Na Pali coast is not easy to reach and so it pays to make the most of any time spent there. There are two out-and-back trips that allow visitors to experience more when venturing off the Kalalau. The first is an unmaintained 7 km (4.3 mi.) trail from Hanakapi'ai Beach up to a glistening waterfall in Hanakapi'ai Valley. The second is a similarly long ascent of Kalalau Valley from the campsite at the trail's end (the Kalalau's turnaround point). These both require permits.

Given all of the above, the Kalalau Trail is regularly described as one of the world's most dangerous pathways. Such descriptions are a little exaggerated, but caution is advised. The weather on the Na Pali Coast changes quickly and can be brutal at times; however, with the suitable preparation and some common sense and patience, the trail is within the capabilities of most hikers. Despite all the environmental challenges, the area's outstanding natural beauty remains an irresistible draw—and the optimal way to experience it is on foot. ———————

↓ Rough winter waves on Kaua'i's north shore.

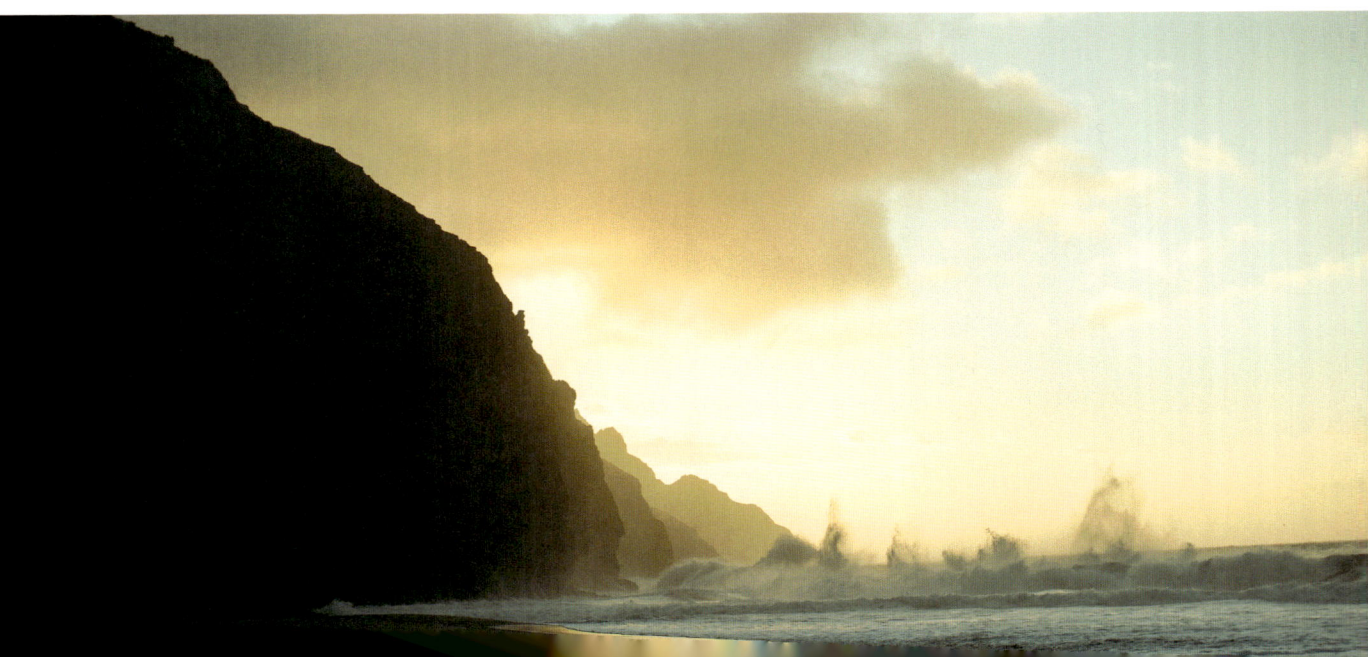

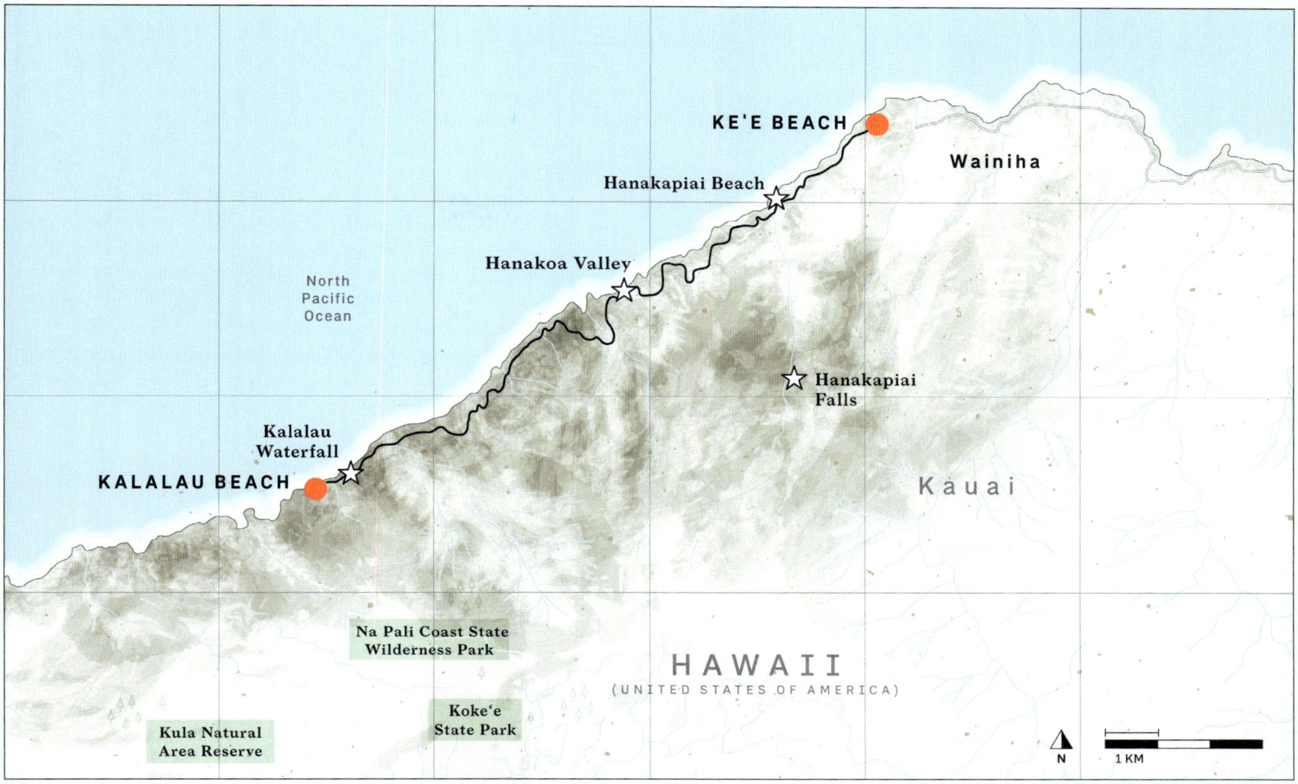

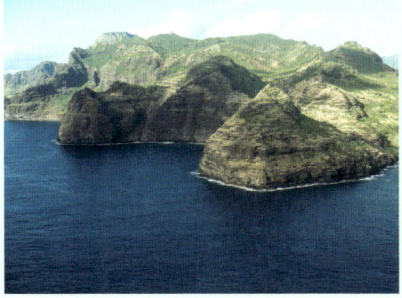

Map labels:
- KE'E BEACH
- Wainiha
- Hanakapiai Beach
- Hanakoa Valley
- North Pacific Ocean
- Hanakapiai Falls
- Kalalau Waterfall
- KALALAU BEACH
- Kauai
- Na Pali Coast State Wilderness Park
- Koke'e State Park
- Kula Natural Area Reserve
- HAWAII
- (UNITED STATES OF AMERICA)
- N
- 1 KM

GOOD TO KNOW

START/FINISH

Out-and-back trip from Ke'e Beach to Kalalau Beach

SEASON

Year round. The weather is usually best from April to October.

CONDITIONS

There is a reason why this trail has been described as one of the world's most treacherous hiking pathways: weather conditions can be unpredictable, rockslides are possible, swimming is definitely not advisable, and steep drops are common.

LOWEST/HIGHEST POINT

0 m (0 ft.)/approx. 244 m (800 ft)

ACCOMMODATION

There are two campsites along the way at Hanakoa and Kalalau Valley, both of which require permits.

TOPOGRAPHY

Kaua'i features dramatic peaks and troughs: from Waimea Canyon, which at 1,087 m (3,567 ft.) deep is known as the Grand Canyon of the Pacific, to the cliffs of the Na Pali Coast, which rise up 914 m (3,000 ft.) from the seabed. It is also the Hawaiian island with the longest length of beaches per coastline: 50 miles in total.

BACKGROUND

ISLAND HOPPING Hawaii—the fiftieth U.S. state and the only one that was formerly an independent country—is made up of eight main volcanic islands: Ni'ihau, Kaho'olawe, Moloka'i, Lana'i, Kaua'i, O'ahu, Maui, and Hawai'i. The first two are inaccessible to visitors (Ni'ihau is privately owned and Kaho'olawe used to be a bombing range), while the last four are the main destinations for tourists. These four islands can be reached by air, and Molokai and Lanai can be accessed by ferry from Maui. Each island has its own quirks: Moloka'i is known as "Friendly Island," Lana'i as the "Pineapple Island" because of its plantations, Kaua'i as the "Garden Island," O'ahu as the "Gathering Place," Maui as the "Valley Isle," and Hawai'i as "Big Island."

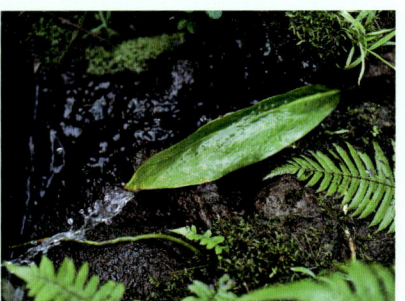

FLORA & FAUNA

THE GARDEN ISLAND Kaua'i takes its nickname from its abundance of lush green vegetation. The island has angular rocky crags, but it is also well populated by plant species, some of which are unique to the state of Hawaii. Here are 120 endangered plant species in the United States and 17 of those are only found on the Hawaiian Islands.

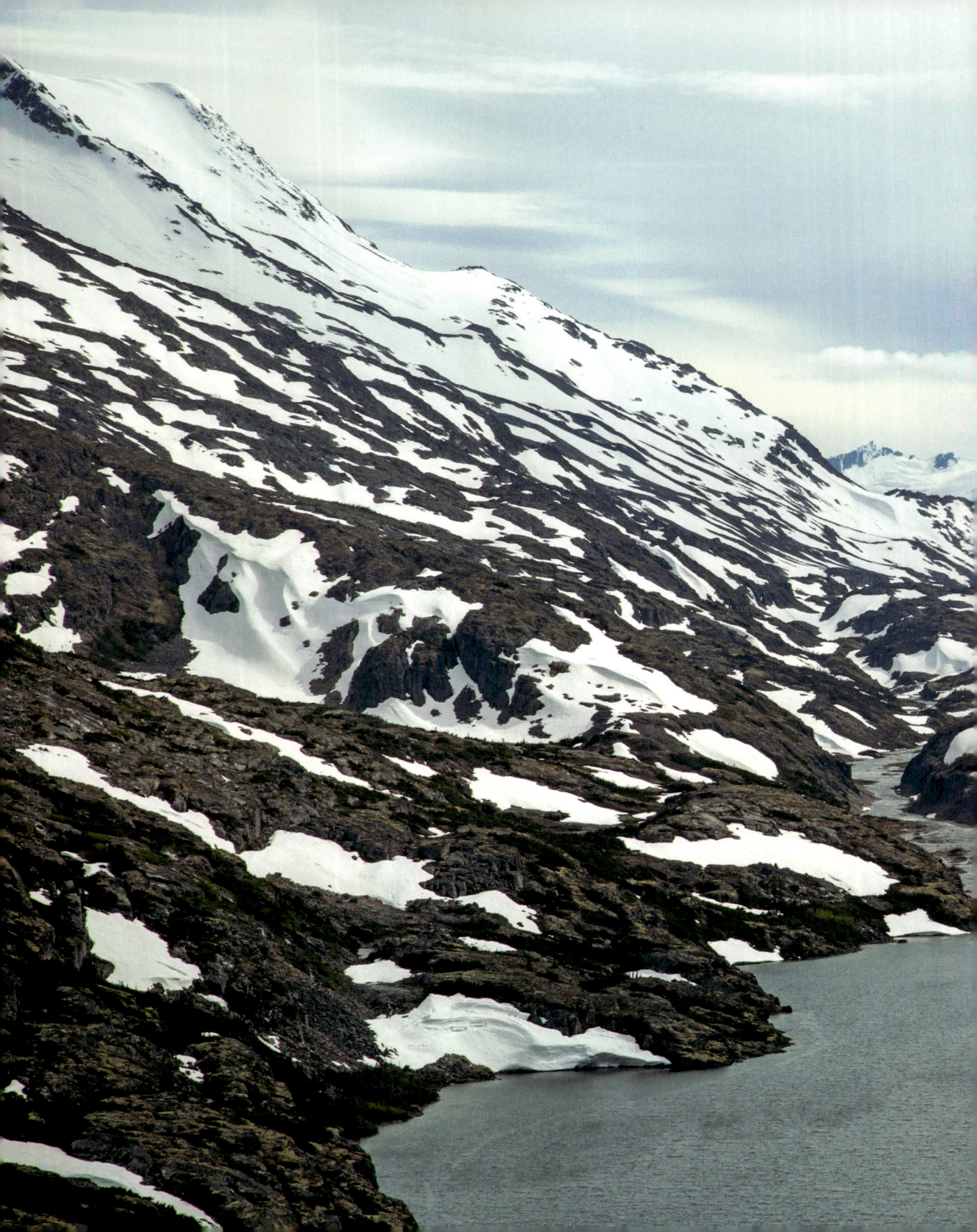

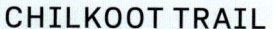

CHASING THE
GOLD RUSH

USA/Canada

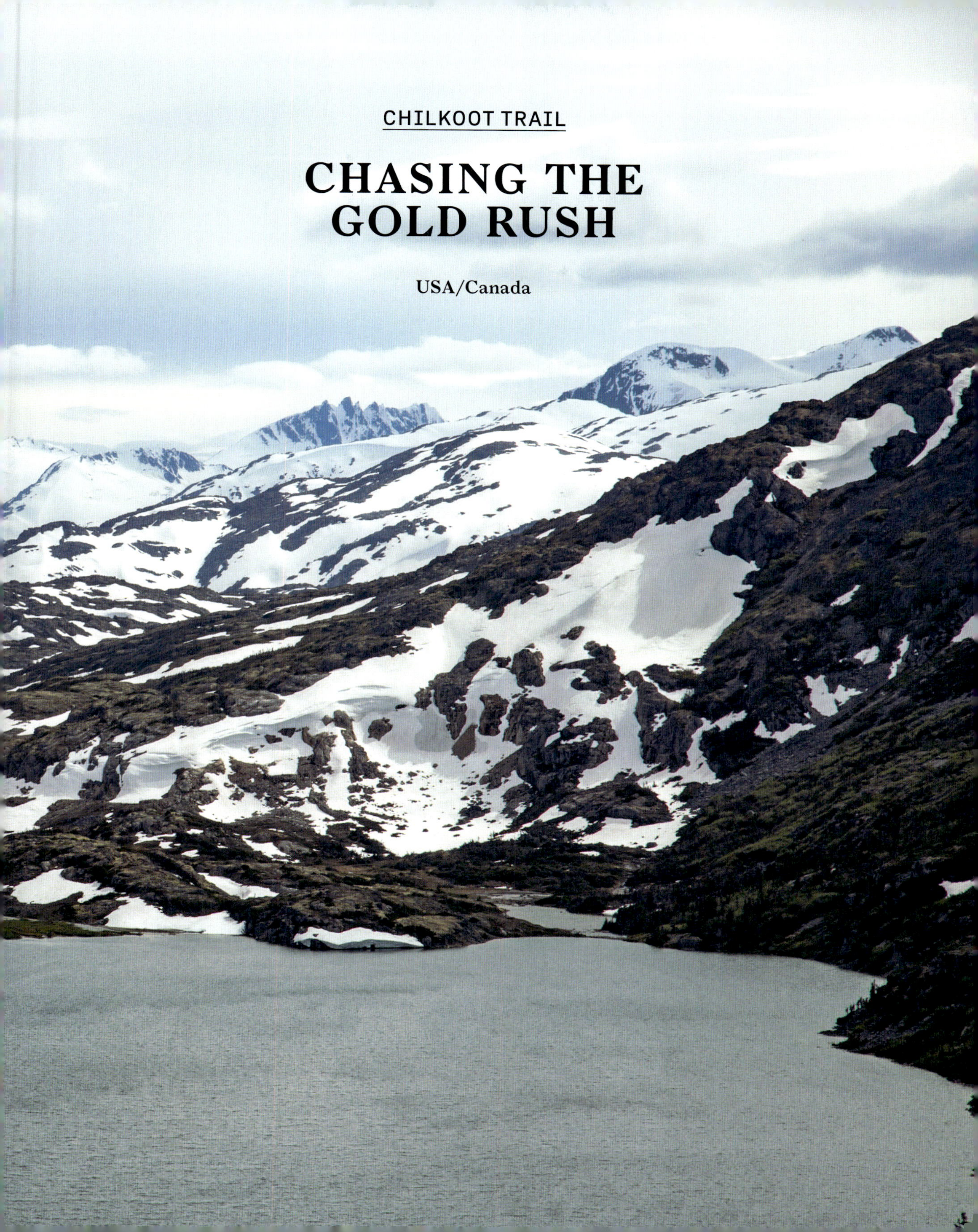

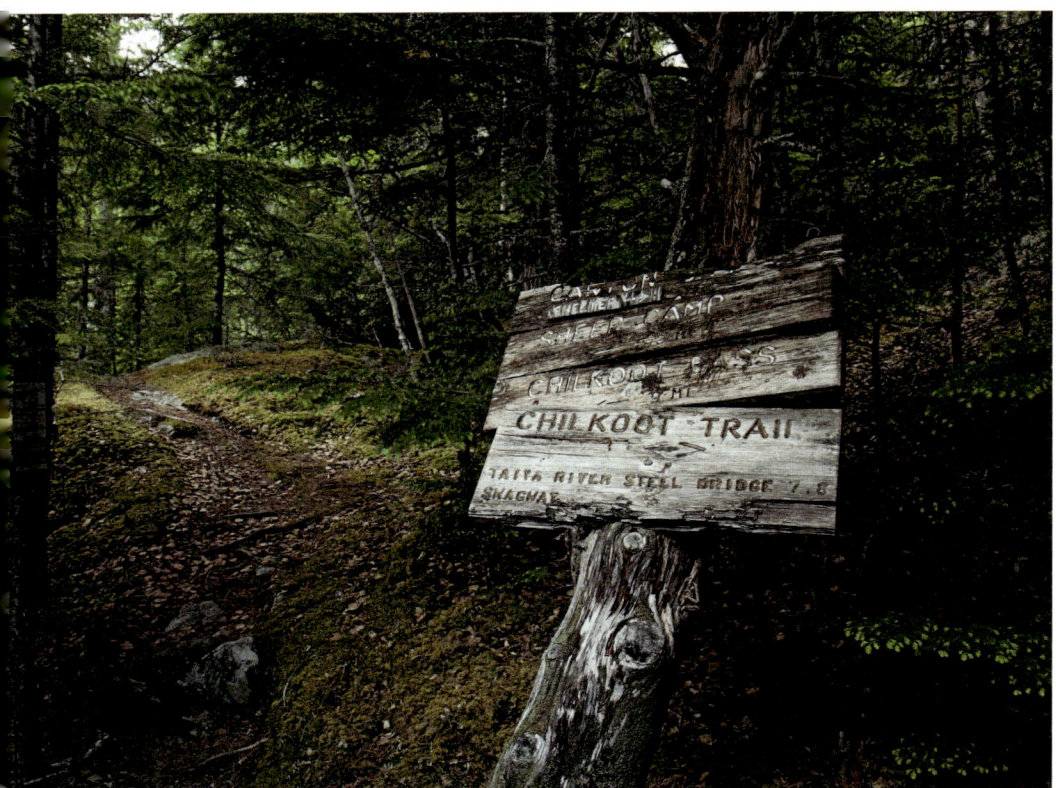

Winding its way through lush coastal rainforest, the pathway follows the Taiya River, regularly passing by Gold Rush-era artifacts, including mining equipment, boilers, and telegraph poles.

The walking is relatively easy for the first 20 km (12.4 mi.) until Sheep Camp. This is the last of the designated campsites on the U.S. side of the trail. It also marks the beginning of the most difficult section of the hike: the fabled climb to Chilkoot Pass. During the Gold Rush, stampeders would often require 40 to 50 separate trips to haul their goods up and over the pass. The location, known as the "Golden Stairs," was, in the winter, a narrow trail of 1,500 steps cut into the ice, which

Originally an important trade route for the Tlingit indigenous people, the Chilkoot Trail became the primary gateway to the Yukon gold fields during the Klondike Gold Rush of 1896–99. Because of its status as the quickest and cheapest route from the Alaskan coast to the Canadian interior, it became a magnet for thousands of "stampeders" looking to strike it rich. Arriving in the port town of Skagway, the fortune seekers would load up with "one ton of goods." This consignment of food and clothing—the Canadian authorities stipulated exactly what was necessary in order to prevent unprepared stampeders from starving in the Yukon—was estimated to be enough supplies for a year and was the minimum amount required for entrance into Canada. After purchasing their provisions, the intrepid travelers would head inland for the next stage of their arduous journey.

Today, backpackers are able to retrace the footsteps of the heavily laden stampeders on a well-marked 53 km (33 mi.) trail that spans two countries, three distinct climatic zones, and hundreds of years of history. Fortunately, the weight regulations that were once strictly enforced by the Canadian Mounted Police no longer apply!

The Chilkoot Trail begins in the ghost town of Dyea, Alaska, which is a scenic 16 km (10 mi.) drive away from Skagway.

had to be tackled in single file. For some, the challenge proved insurmountable. Indeed, it was at the base of the climb's steepest section that many would-be prospectors made the decision to abandon their dreams of riches and return to Skagway.

Comparatively speaking, modern-day adventurers have it much easier. Nonetheless, the 45-degree-gradient climb to the pass is no piece of cake. Loose rocks, large boulders, and unpredictable weather combine to make the exposed 800 m (2,625 ft.) ascent a challenge for even the fittest hikers. The way is well marked with rock cairns and flagpoles, and for those with the energy to look around, Gold Rush-era artifacts are in abundance. Perhaps the most interesting of the relics is a cache of 80 canvas "knockdown boats" situated on the southeastern side of the pass. Each canvas bundle contains wood and hardware, with some more unraveled than others, and the consignment was likely transported there to sell to stampeders. This surreal sight is not something you see everyday on top of a snowy mountain range. →

ABOUT THE TRAIL

→ <u>DISTANCE</u> 53 km (33 mi.)
→ <u>DURATION</u> 3 to 5 days
→ <u>LEVEL</u> Moderate

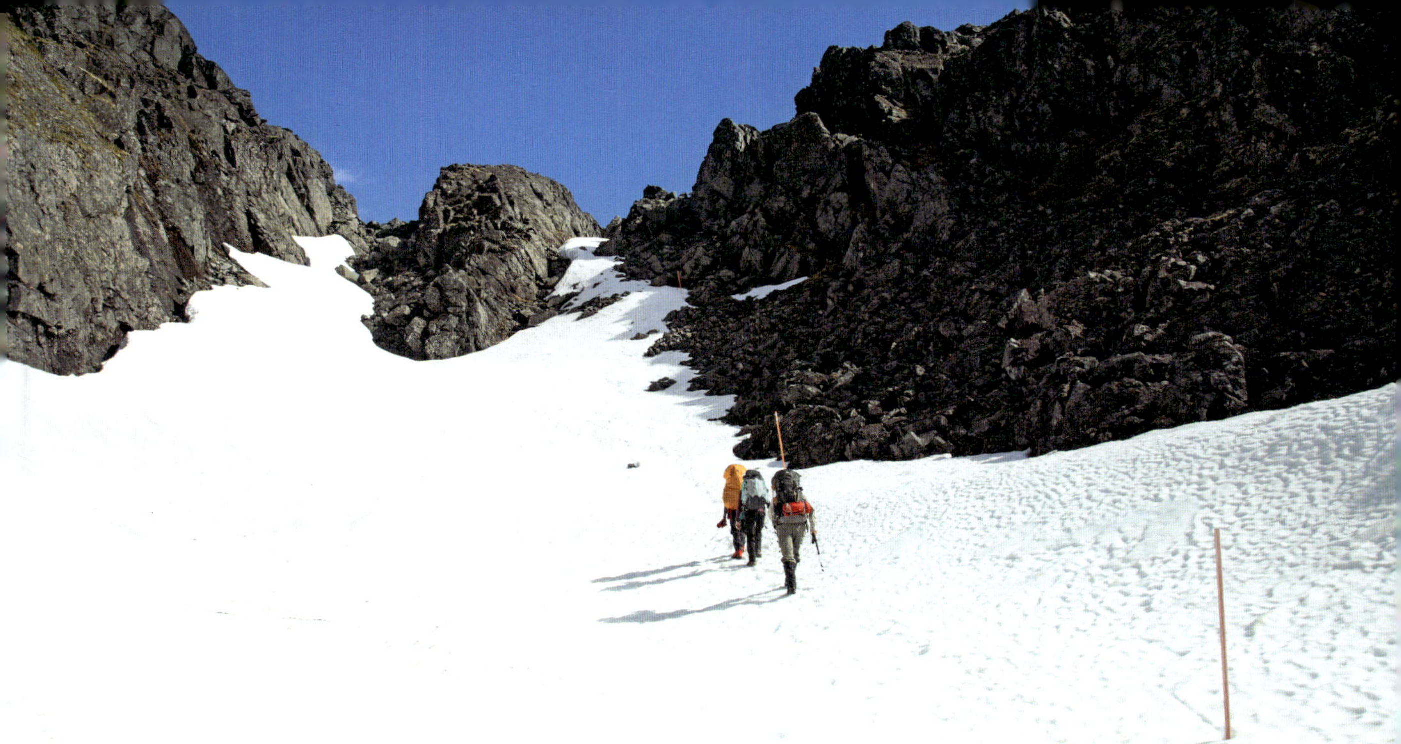

The way is well marked with rock cairns and flagpoles, and for those with the energy to look around, Gold Rush-era artifacts are in abundance.

↑ The final snowy slope up to Chilkoot Pass.
← Pointing the way near Canyon City.
↓ Bennett Church near the northern terminus of the trail.

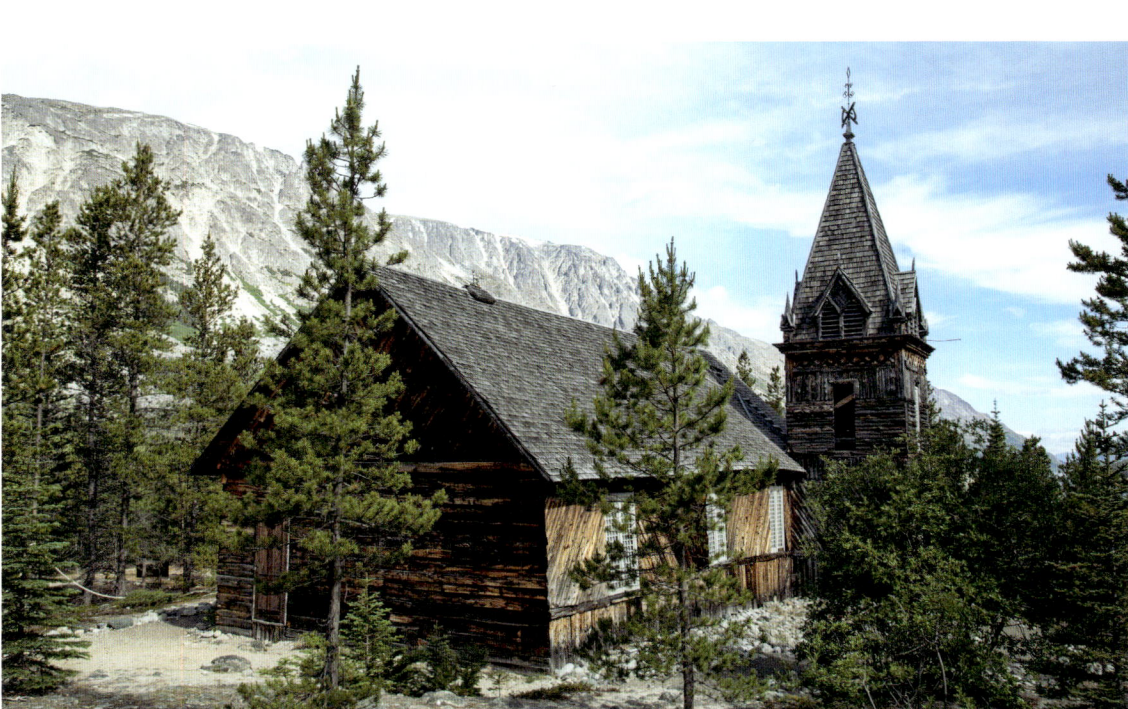

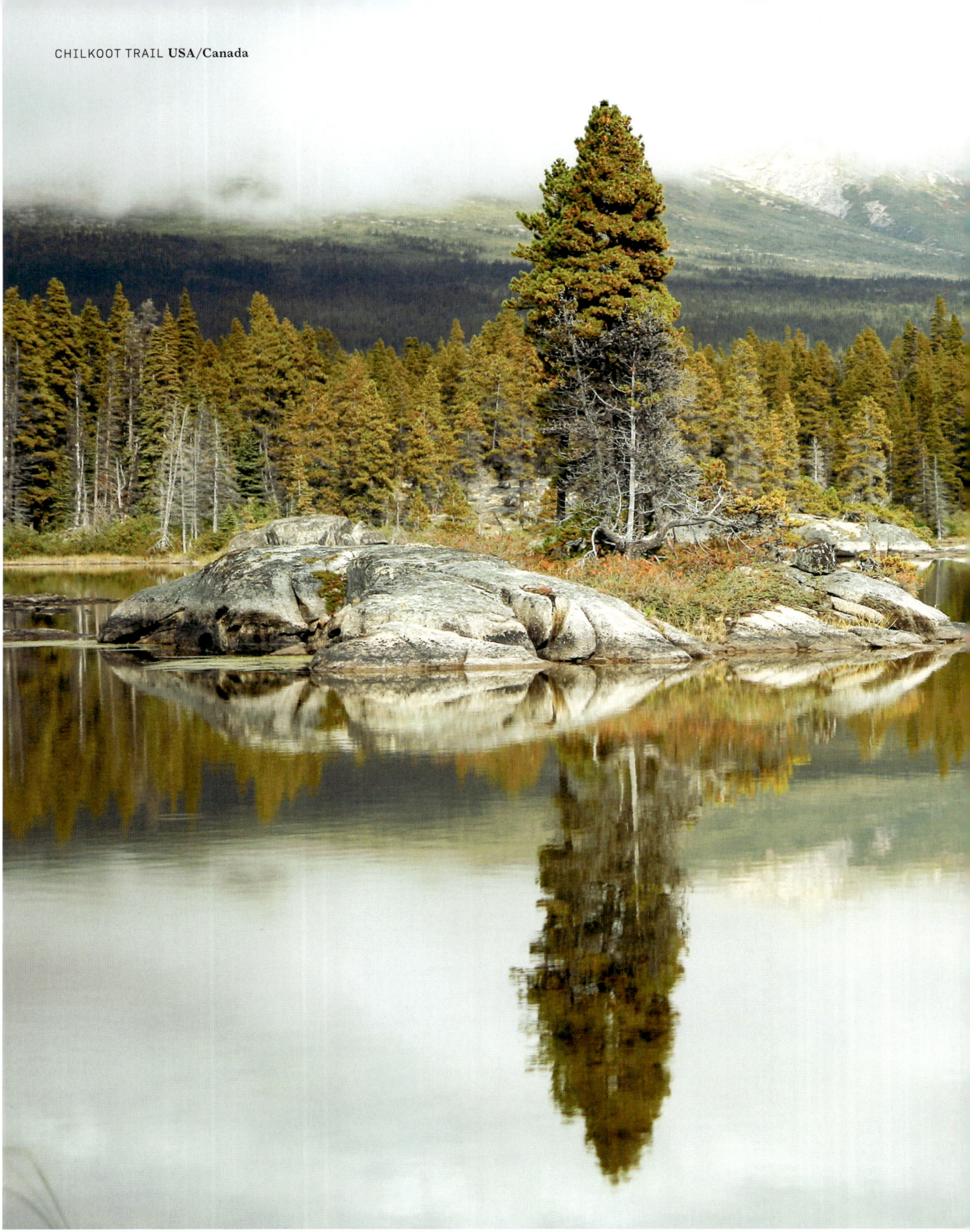

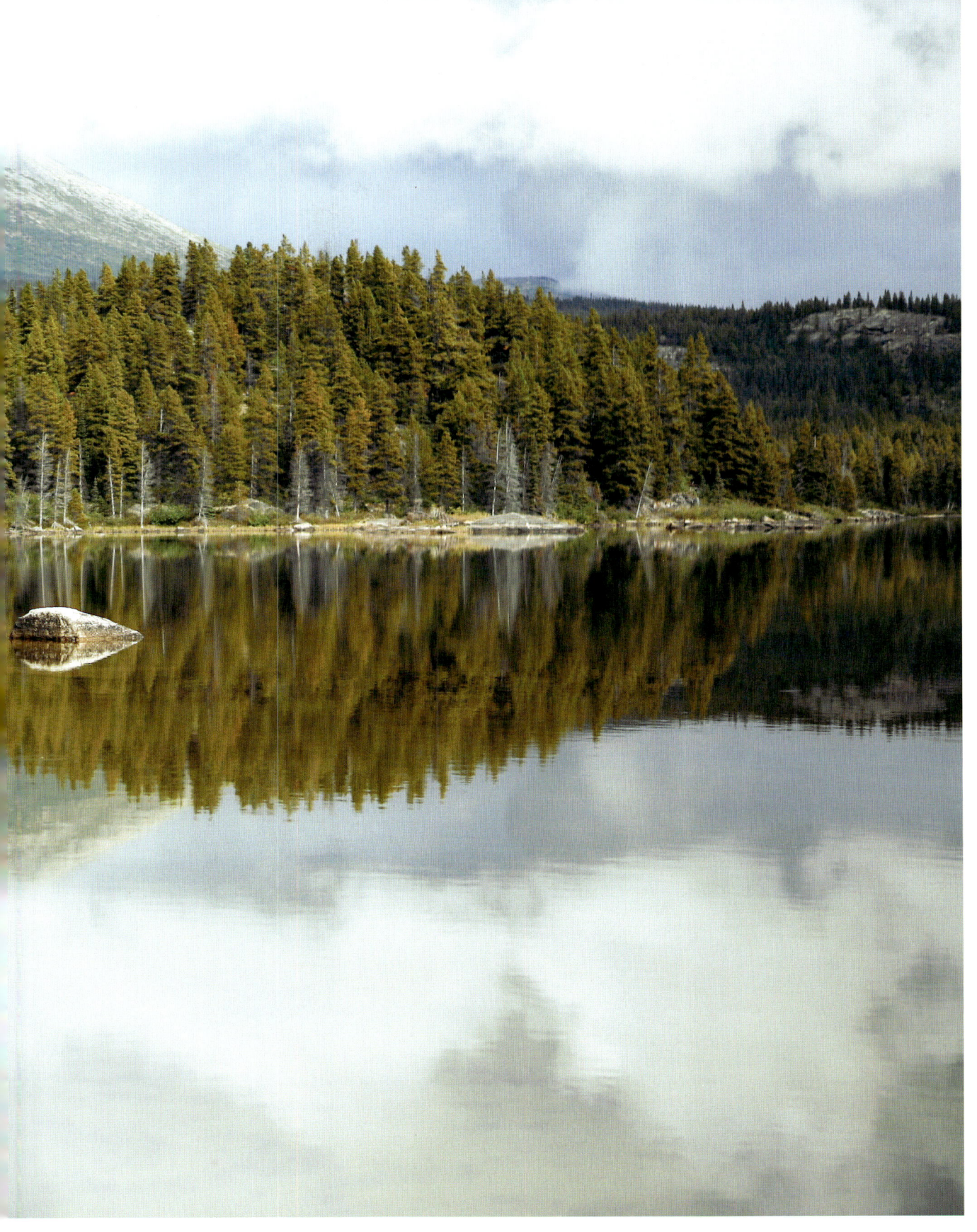

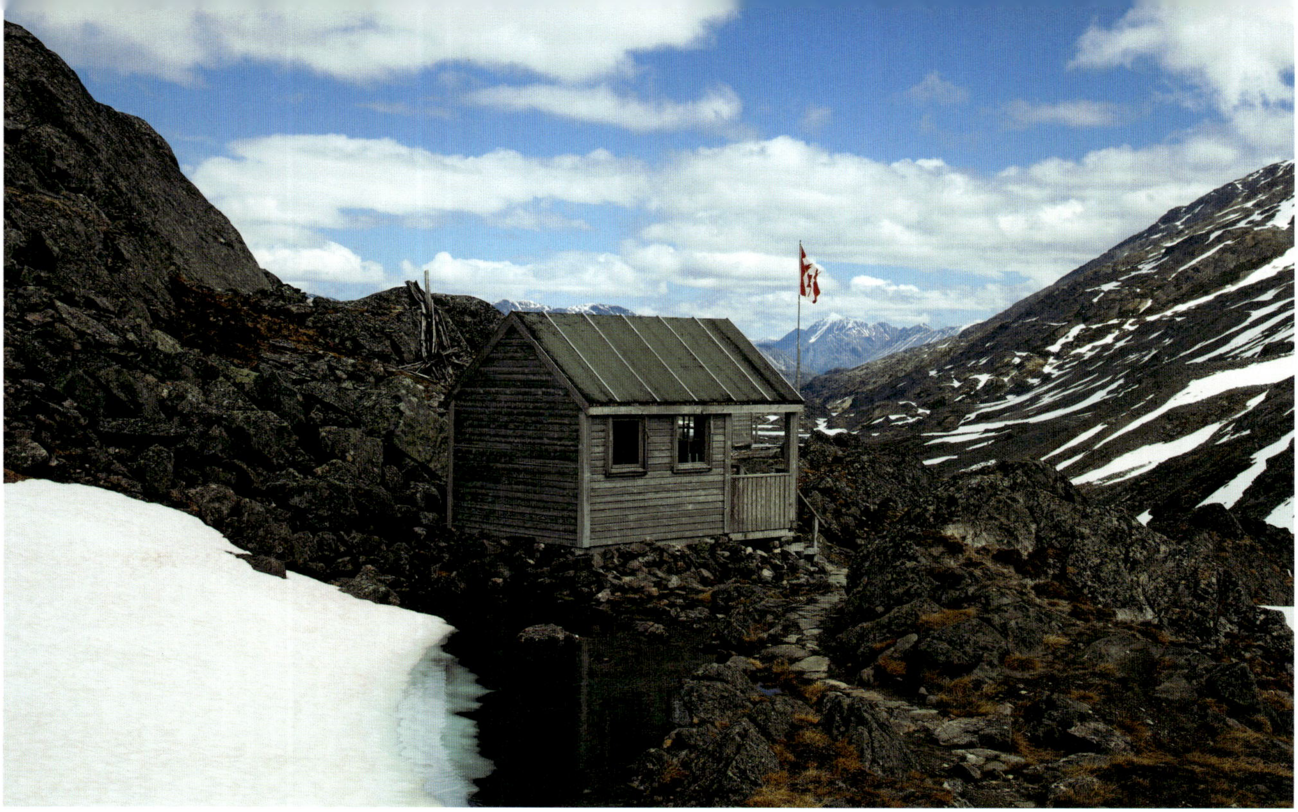

↑ **Warden cabin at the summit of Chilkoot Pass.**
↘ **The White Pass and Yukon Route Railroad.**

Chilkoot Pass represents the trail's geographical high point, the border with Canada, and, perhaps most importantly for hikers that have ascended in freezing rain and fog, the location of a much-anticipated warming hut. This small cabin offers a welcome respite from the elements and makes for a great place to have a hot beverage and some lunch before continuing the journey.

From the pass, the trail winds its way northeast through an alpine landscape of boulders and snowfields. It passes a series of azure mountain lakes, and in fine weather the scenery is magnificent. Eventually the alpine terrain is left behind as the path descends into a boreal forest of alder, fir, and lodgepole pines. One stand-out aspect of this particular stretch is how dry it is in comparison to the temperate rainforest of the trail's beginning. Because of the rain-shadow effect of the Coast Mountains, the Canadian side of the range receives considerably less precipitation than the American one.

The final stretch of the Chilkoot Trail passes by more impressive lakes—namely Long, Deep, and Lindeman—before arriving at its northeastern terminus of Lake Bennett. It was here that the stampeders either purchased, built, or assembled their knockdown canvas boats in preparation for the ultimate stage of their quest: a journey down the Yukon River to Dawson City. The gold fields and the promise of riches awaited.

For present-day travelers, a railroad rather than a river is the preferred means of onward transport from Lake Bennett—specifically, the historic White Pass and Yukon Route train. The railroad was a feat of civil engineering begun in 1898, with the tunnels blasted through the mountains over a period of more than two years. The two-and-a-half-hour journey back to Skagway glides by mountains, glaciers, waterfalls, and gorges; it is hard to imagine a more fitting way for hikers to finish their Chilkoot Trail experience. ——

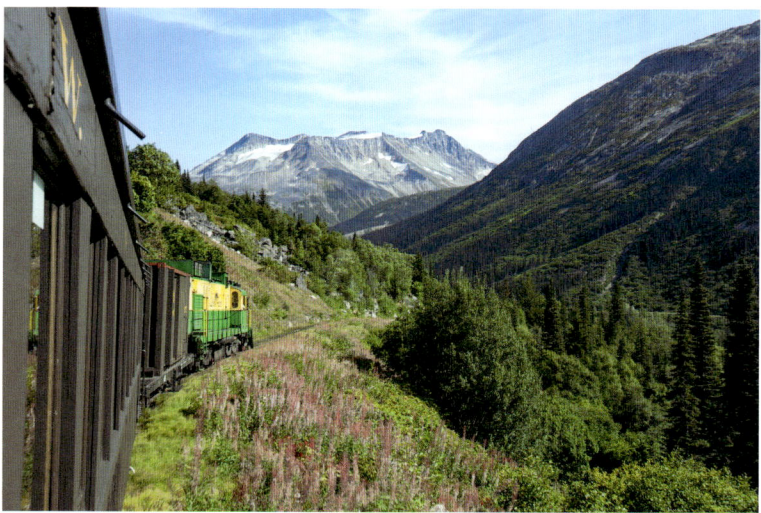

GOOD TO KNOW

START/FINISH
⚐ Dyea, Alaska
⚐ Bennett, British Columbia

SEASON
Late May to early September

CONDITIONS
The trail is well marked and easy to follow
from start to finish.

LOWEST/HIGHEST POINT
0 m (0 ft.)/1,097 m (2,600 ft.)

GEAR TIPS
Passport for crossing U.S.-Canada border,
history guide in ebook or paperback form.

TIP
A permit is required and camping is only
allowed in designated sites.

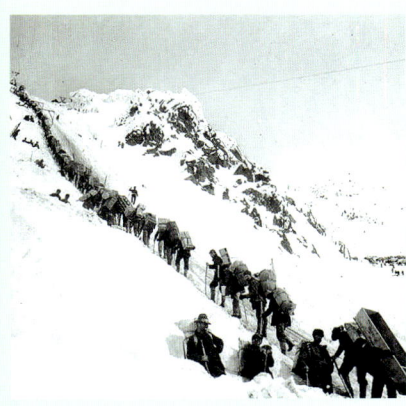

BACKGROUND

THE KLONDIKE GOLD RUSH Between
1896 and 1899, around 100,000 prospectors
migrated from the United States to the smallest of Canada's territories, the Yukon. Gold
was discovered in 1896 in the Klondike region
and a stampede of potential miners headed
to northwest Canada, braving the extreme
climates—hot and dry in the summer, snowy
and extremely cold in the winter—to seek
their fortunes.

The towns of Skagway and Dyea in Alaska quickly became hubs for the prospectors
who were setting out. Dyea, at the beginning
of the Chilkoot, slowly declined from the
1900s onwards, and its ruins are now a historic landmark. Nearby Skagway, however,
flourished—partly because of the White Pass
and Yukon Route Railroad, which brought
people in—and Gold Rush-era buildings can
be seen there today.

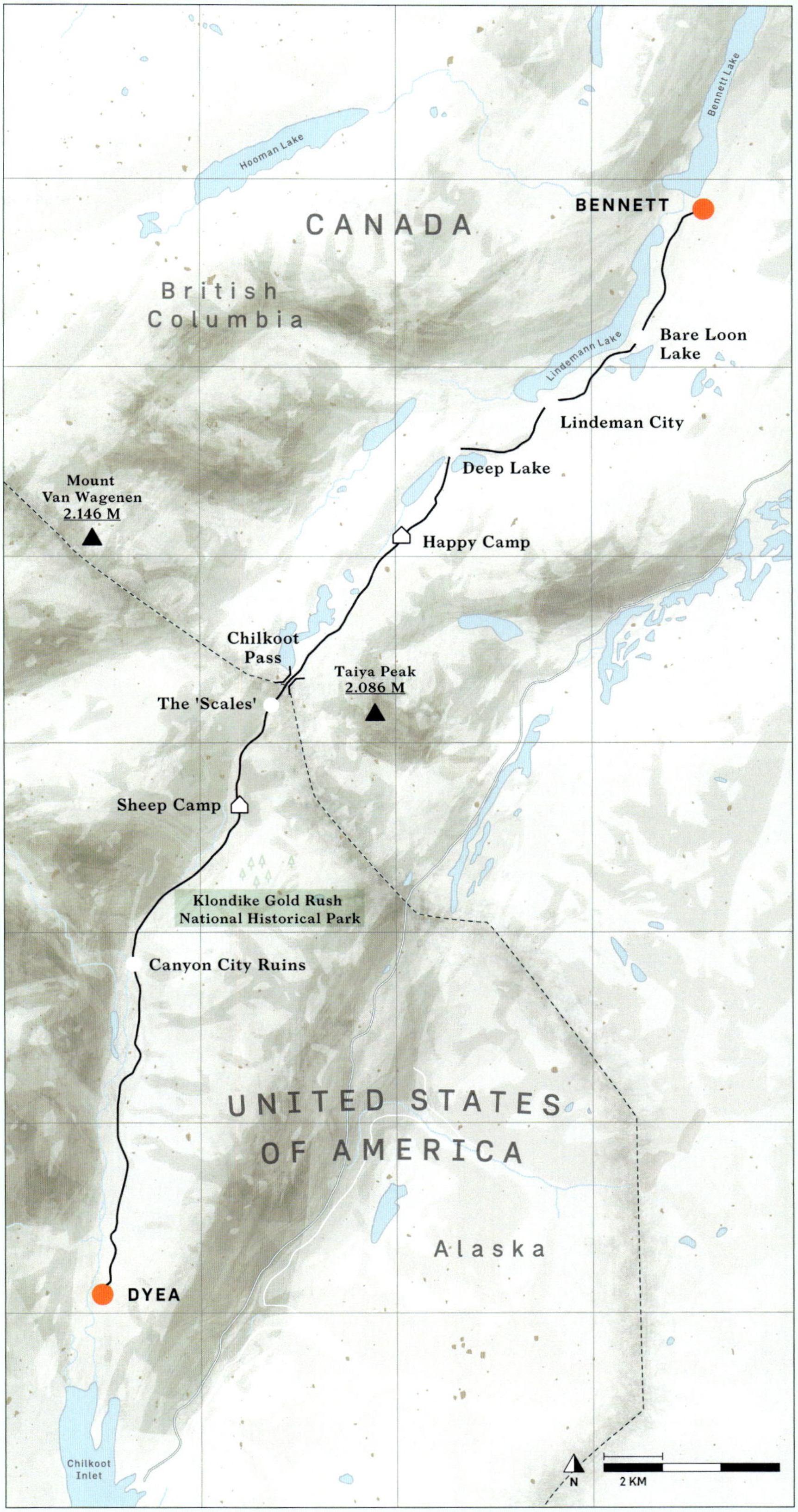

Hooman Lake

Bennett Lake

CANADA

BENNETT ●

British
Columbia

Bare Loon
Lake

Lindemann Lake

Lindeman City

Deep Lake

Mount
Van Wagenen
2.146 M ▲

△ Happy Camp

Chilkoot
Pass

Taiya Peak
2.086 M ▲

The 'Scales'

Sheep Camp △

Klondike Gold Rush
National Historical Park

Canyon City Ruins

UNITED STATES

OF AMERICA

Alaska

DYEA ●

Chilkoot
Inlet

N

2 KM

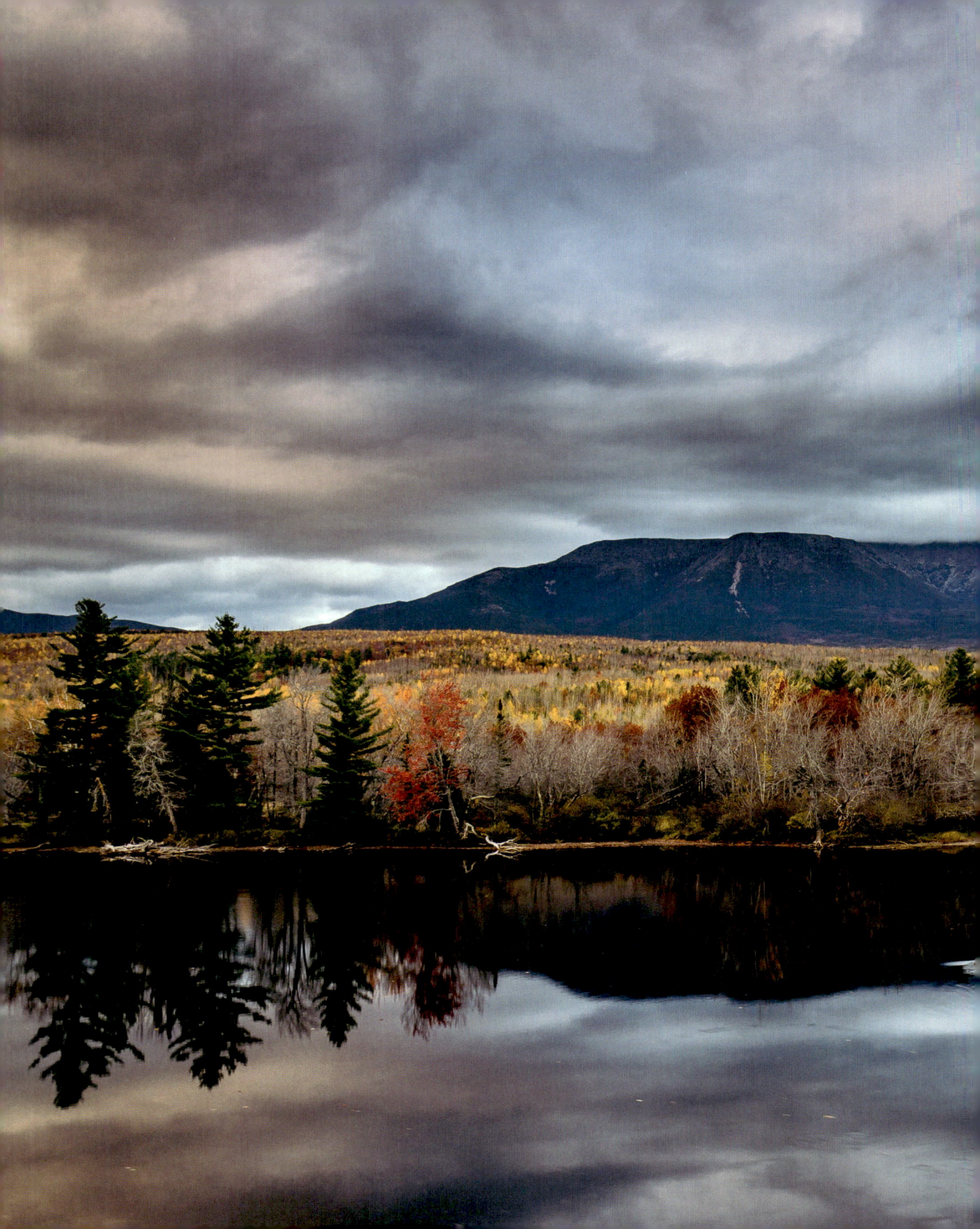

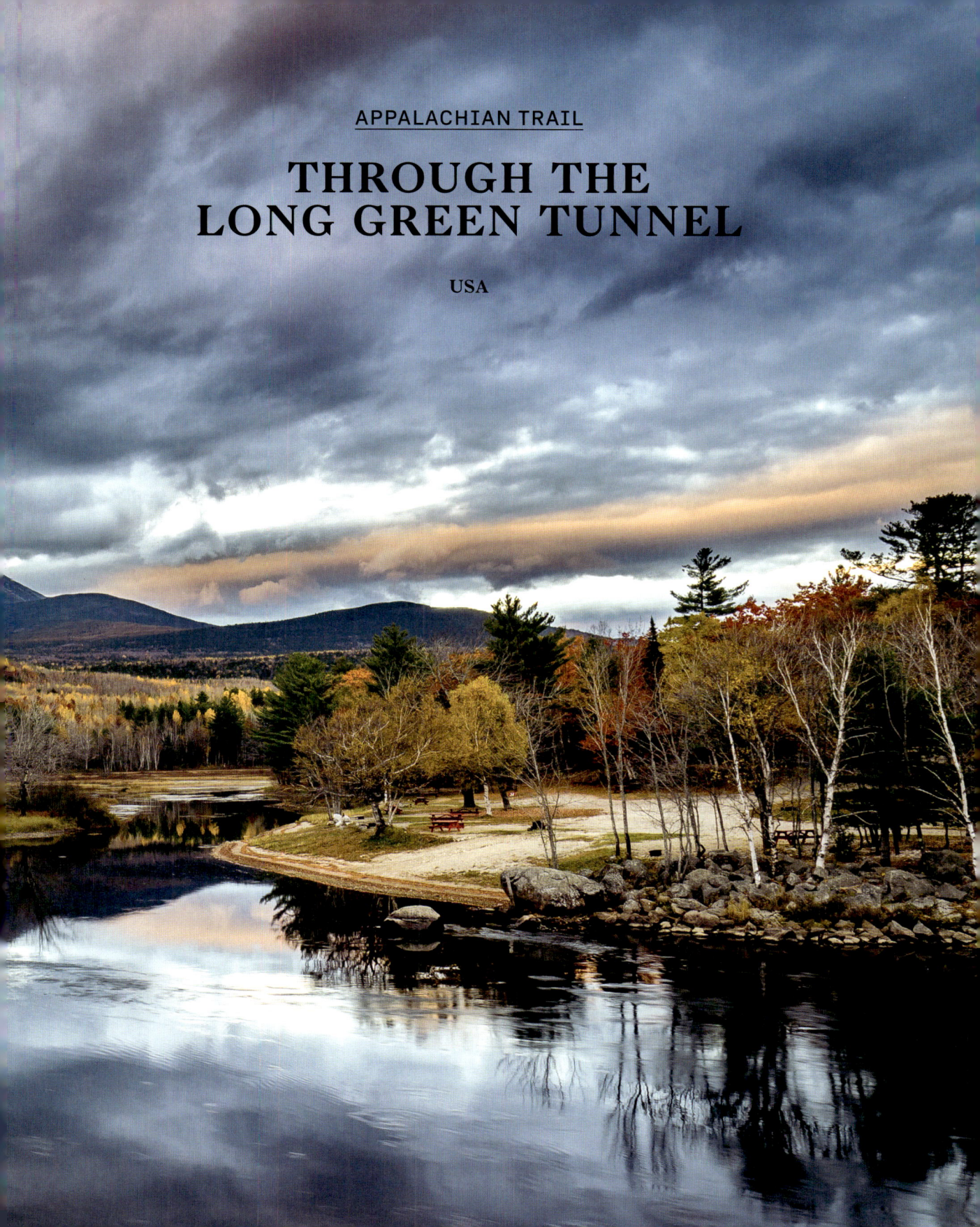

APPALACHIAN TRAIL

THROUGH THE
LONG GREEN TUNNEL

USA

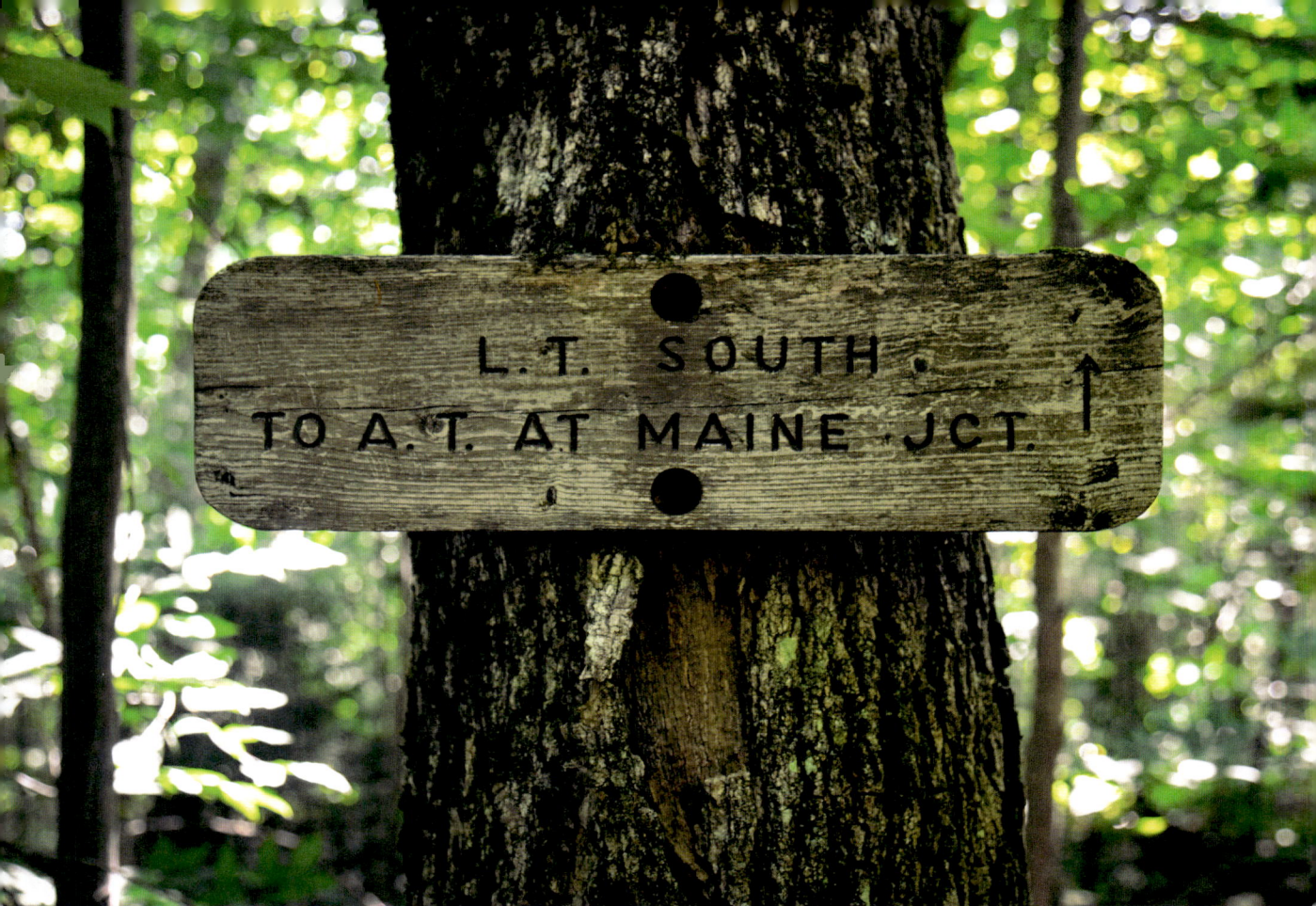

The Appalachian Trail (AT) is the longest hiking-only footpath in the world. Stretching some 3,523 km (2,189 mi.) from Georgia to Maine, it passes through 14 U.S. states as it winds its way along the spine of the Appalachian Mountains. Together with the Pacific Crest and Continental Divide Trails, it forms what is known as the Triple Crown of Hiking.

The majority of the AT takes place in wooded forest (it is commonly referred to as the "long green tunnel"), though small sections also pass through pastoral lands and small towns. Unlike its long trail cousins to the west, the AT does not boast a lot of jaw-dropping vistas. Its beauty is more subtle: the first rays of dawn piercing through the forest canopy, the peaceful melody of a babbling brook, or the gentle sound of leaves rustling in the breeze.

ABOUT THE TRAIL

→ **DISTANCE** 3,523 km (2,189 mi.)
→ **DURATION** 6 months
→ **LEVEL** Moderate to Difficult

The idea for the Appalachian Trail was first conceived by conservationist Benton Mackaye in 1921. The pathway was eventually finished around 16 years later, and in the decades since extensions and improvements have continued to be made. During its evolution, one of the notable aspects of the AT has always been its inclusivity. Thanks to a combination of easy access points, extensive signage, and the tireless efforts of trail-maintenance crews, it is a path that is open to hikers of all levels of fitness and experience. Irrespective of whether one is heading out for a day, a week, or multiple months, the Appalachian Trail has something to offer. Each year approximately 3,000,000 people walk on the AT, making it America's most well-traveled footpath.

Since its establishment, the Appalachian Trail has become best known for its thru-hikers: people who attempt to traverse the whole trail in one calendar year. Among the most notable of these hardy souls are Earl Shaffer, Bill Irwin, and an interesting figure known as Grandma Gatewood.

Shaffer was a Second World War veteran who hiked the trail in 1948. He is credited as being the trail's first thru-hiker. In his own words, Shaffer "wanted to walk the army out of his

> **Over the course of six months, hikers will be forced to deal with conditions ranging from heat waves to blizzards and everything in between.**

system." Irwin was the first blind person to hike the AT. Accompanied only by his German Shepherd guide dog during his thru-hike of 1990, he fell thousands of times, cracked his ribs, and suffered from hypothermia. Nonetheless, after eight long months he achieved his goal and made it to the summit of Mount Katahdin, the highest point in Maine.

The final hiker of the notable trio was Emma Rowena "Grandma" Gatewood. In 1955 she became the first woman to thru-hike the Appalachian Trail. She was 67 years young when she walked the trail, and she enjoyed it so much that she went on to repeat the feat on two other occasions. Gatewood famously eschewed fancy equipment during her thru-hikes, instead preferring to use simple sneakers, an army blanket, and a plastic shower curtain for rain protection. She carried these items not in a backpack, but in a homemade denim duffel bag that she slung over her shoulder.

For aspirants who hope to follow in the footsteps of these legends, the AT is by no means an easy proposition—over 3,500 km (2,175 mi.) is a long way to walk no matter how well marked and maintained the trail might be. Principal among the challenges are the weather and the terrain. Over the course of six months, hikers will be forced to deal with conditions ranging from heat waves to blizzards and everything in between. And the AT could perhaps best be described as a topographical roller coaster. During its course, there is some 141 km (88 mi.) of total elevation gain and loss—the vertical equivalent of hiking to the top of Mount Everest 16 times over.

Despite the physical (and mental) ups and downs, there are plenty of beautiful sections that compensate hikers for their efforts. Highlights of the AT include New Hampshire's White Mountains, which feature majestic alpine terrain and sweeping vistas, and Maine's Hundred-Mile Wilderness, which →

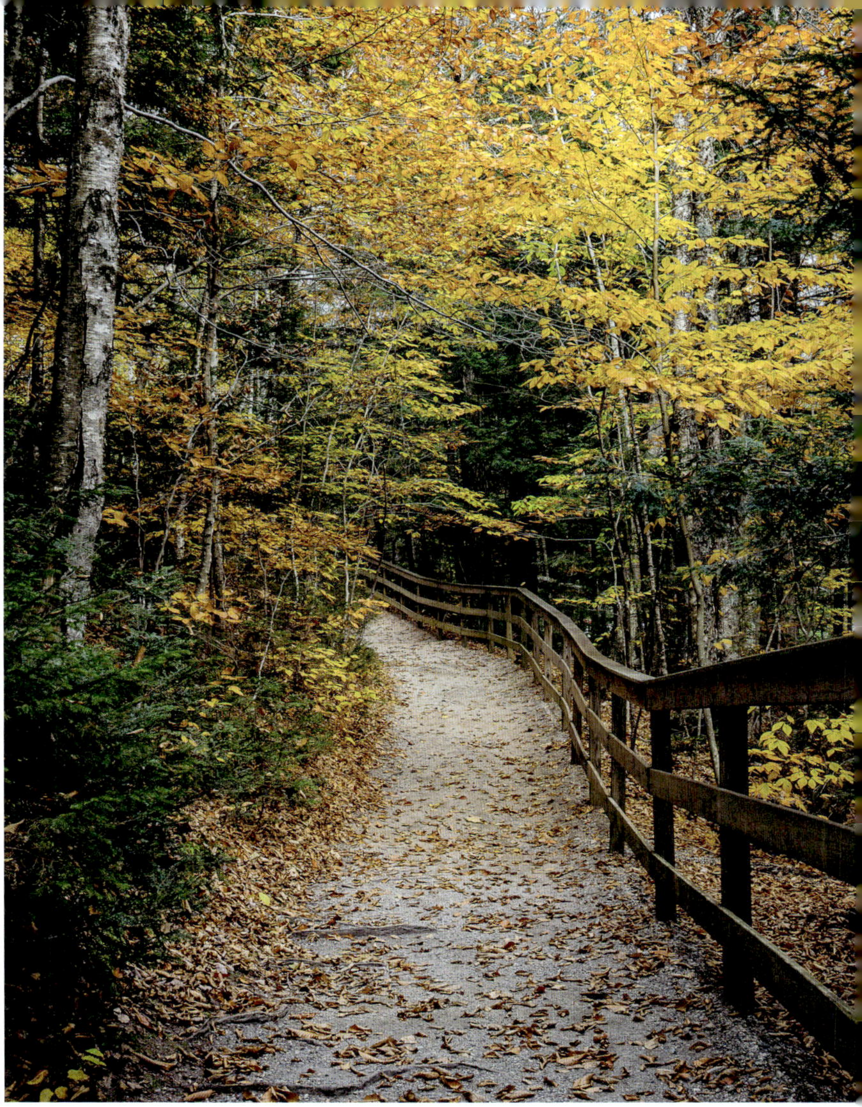

↑ Fall colors in the "long green tunnel."

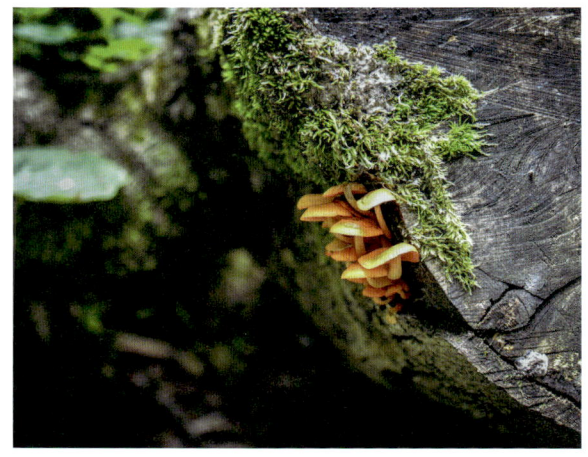

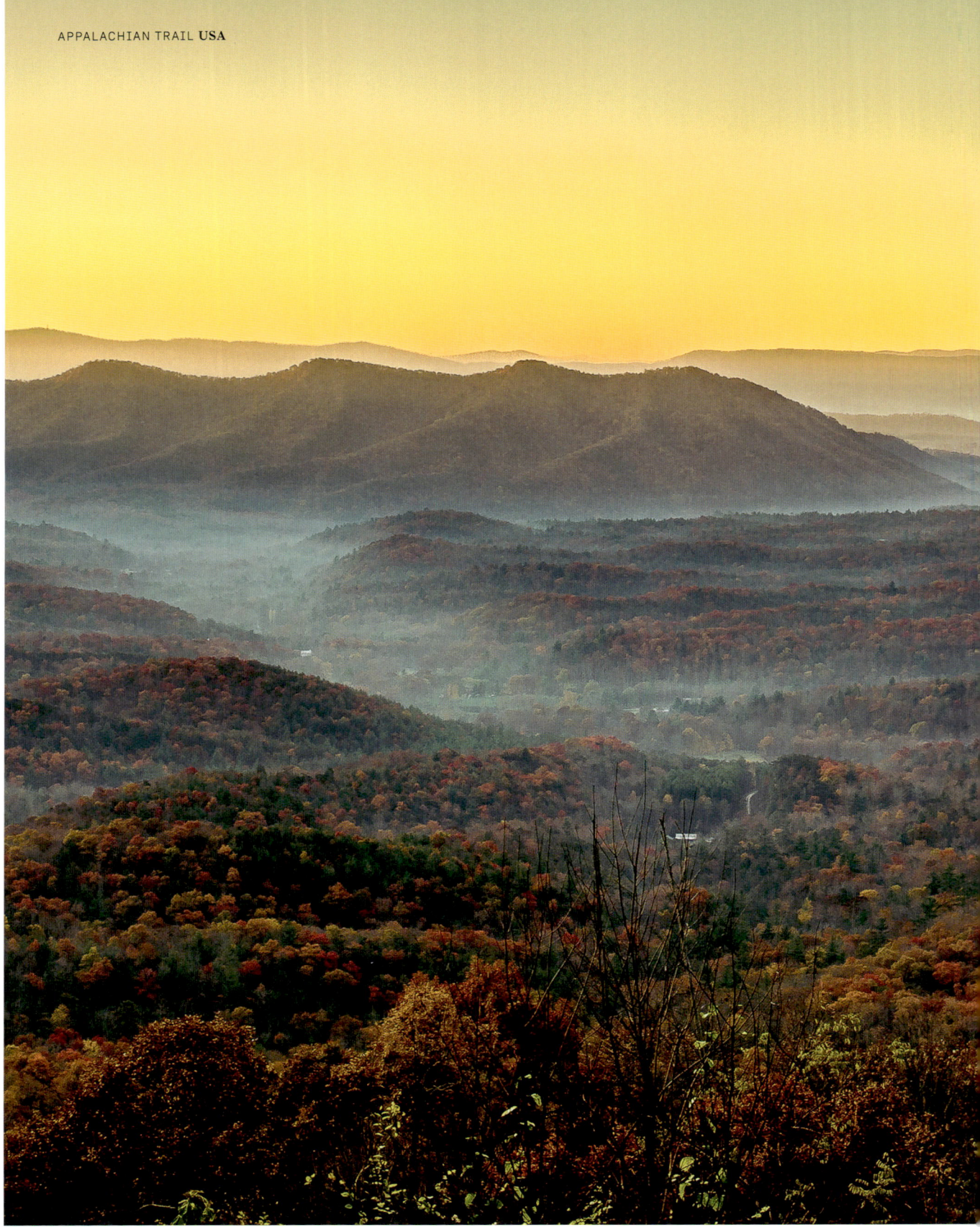

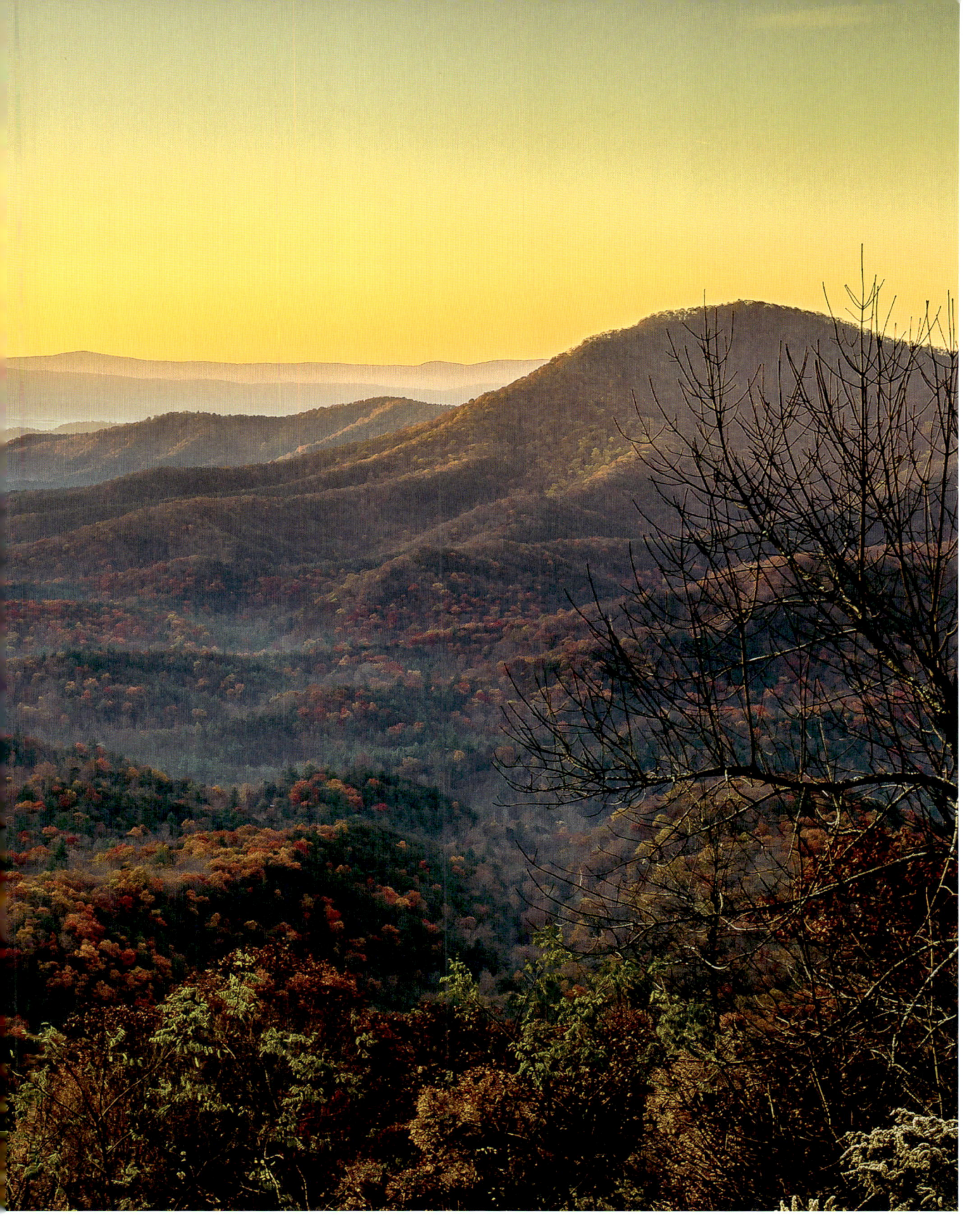

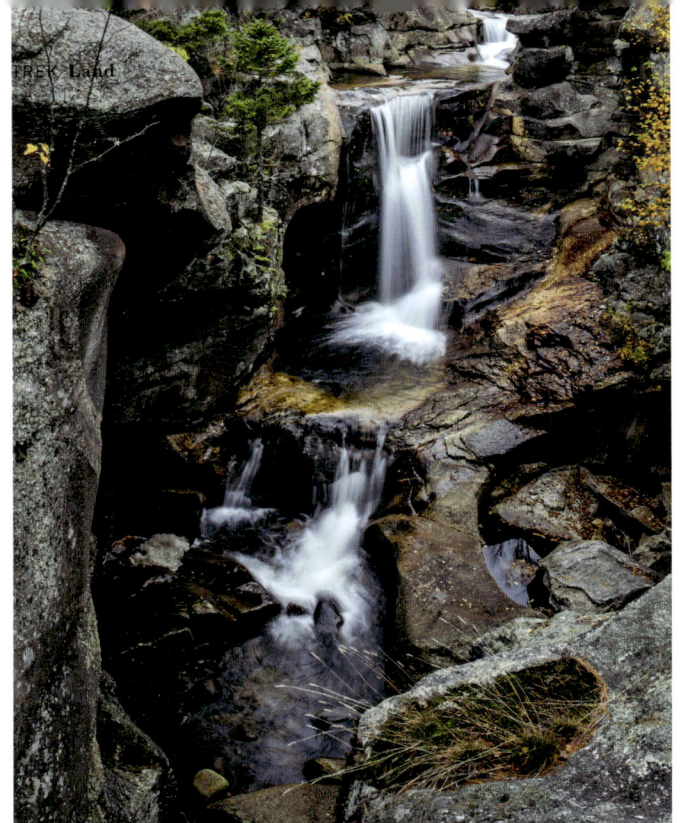
TREK Land

The AT does not boast a lot of jaw-dropping vistas. Its beauty is more subtle: the first rays of dawn piercing through the forest canopy, the peaceful melody of a babbling brook, or the gentle sound of leaves rustling in the breeze.

the highest wind speeds in history—372 km/h (234 mph)—was recorded on top of Mount Washington. The Hundred-Mile Wilderness is almost as challenging, as walkers face fast-flowing rivers, swamps, heavy mud, and more grueling climbs. The toughest of these ascents comes in the form of Mount Katahdin, the AT's fabled northern terminus.

The Appalachian Trail is not the oldest, longest, nor probably even the most scenically beautiful pathway in the United States. What it is, however, is a microcosm of American society—a trail that attracts people of all ages and socio-economic backgrounds. And the best thing about it is that no one really cares where their fellow hikers are from or what they do for a living. On the trail everyone is equal. A bunch of disparate dreamers brought together by the goal of walking between Georgia and Maine. ——————————

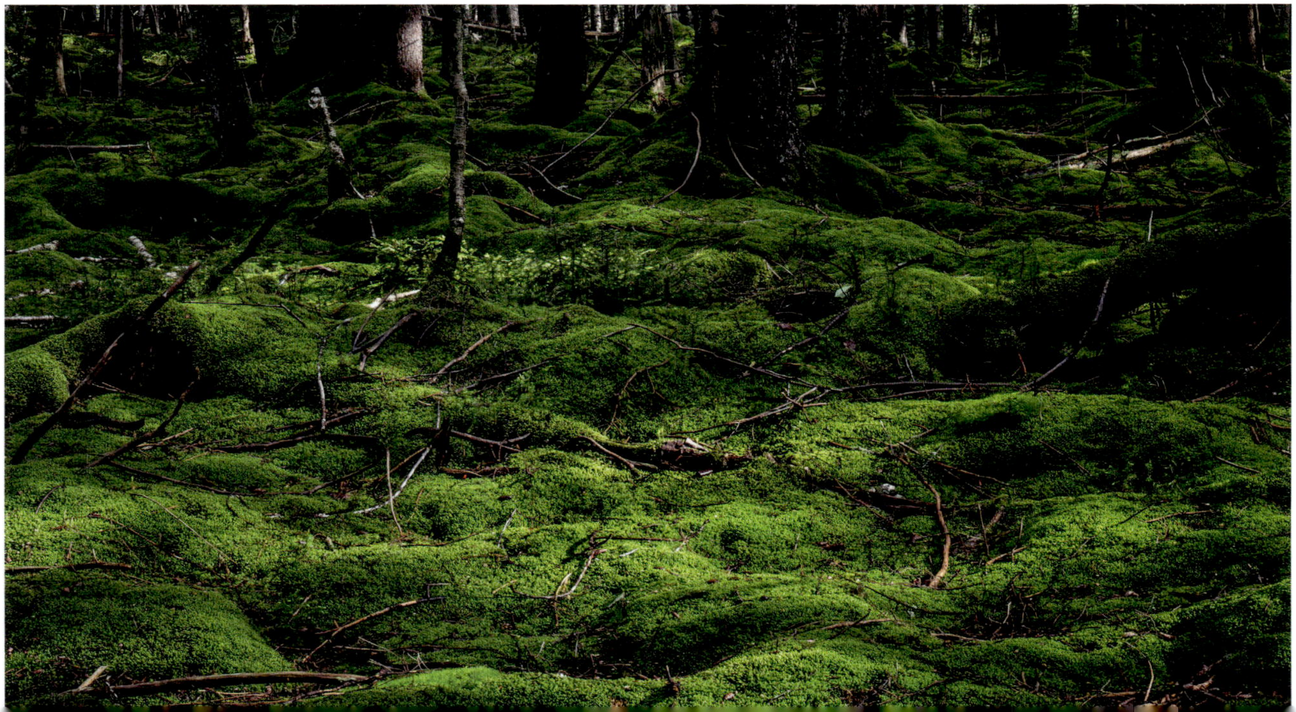

transforms into a kaleidoscope of autumnal shades during fall. Aside from being possibly the most visually impressive sections of the AT, these stretches are also the hardest. In the "Whites," hikers will negotiate steep, rocky climbs and some of the most notoriously inclement weather on the planet. In 1934, one of

GOOD TO KNOW

START/FINISH
🏁 Mount Katahdin, Maine (northern finish)
🏁 Springer Mt., Georgia (southern finish)

SEASON
March to October (northbound),
June to November (southbound)

CONDITIONS
Conditions can vary considerably depending
on start date, direction taken, and pace of
hiker. Over the course of an average five- or
six-month journey, hikers can potentially
face weather ranging from blazing heat and
high humidity to driving rain and blizzards.

LOWEST/HIGHEST POINT
38 m (124 ft.)/2,025 m (6,623 ft)

HIGHLIGHTS
White Mountains, ME; Hundred-Mile Wilderness, NH; sunrise at McAfee Knob, VA; the
summit of Mount Katahdin, ME.

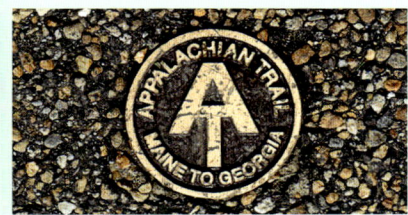

BACKGROUND

THE RIGHT SIGNS Though the scale of
the AT is great—it passes through fourteen
U.S. states and eight national forests—it is
well signed from start to finish with "white
blazes," which are splashes of rectangu-
lar-shaped white paint. These can be seen on
features ranging from tree trunks and rails to
posts and cairns (human-made rock piles).
Where two rectangles are shown one above
the other, this indicates that walkers must be
particularly attentive to direction changes.
Side trails and treks leading to shelters are
marked with blue rectangles. The symbols
are located at varying intervals, but hikers
should check back if they have not seen one
for around 400 m (0.25 mi.). It is said that
there are approximately 165,000 of these
iconic markings between Georgia and Maine.

FLORA & FAUNA

CREATURES GREAT AND SMALL On such
a long and varied trail, the wildlife is diverse:
black bears, deer, moose, porcupines,
and bobcats all feature. Among the smaller
(and, for hikers, probably more annoying)
species there are mosquitos, black flies,
ticks, and mice.

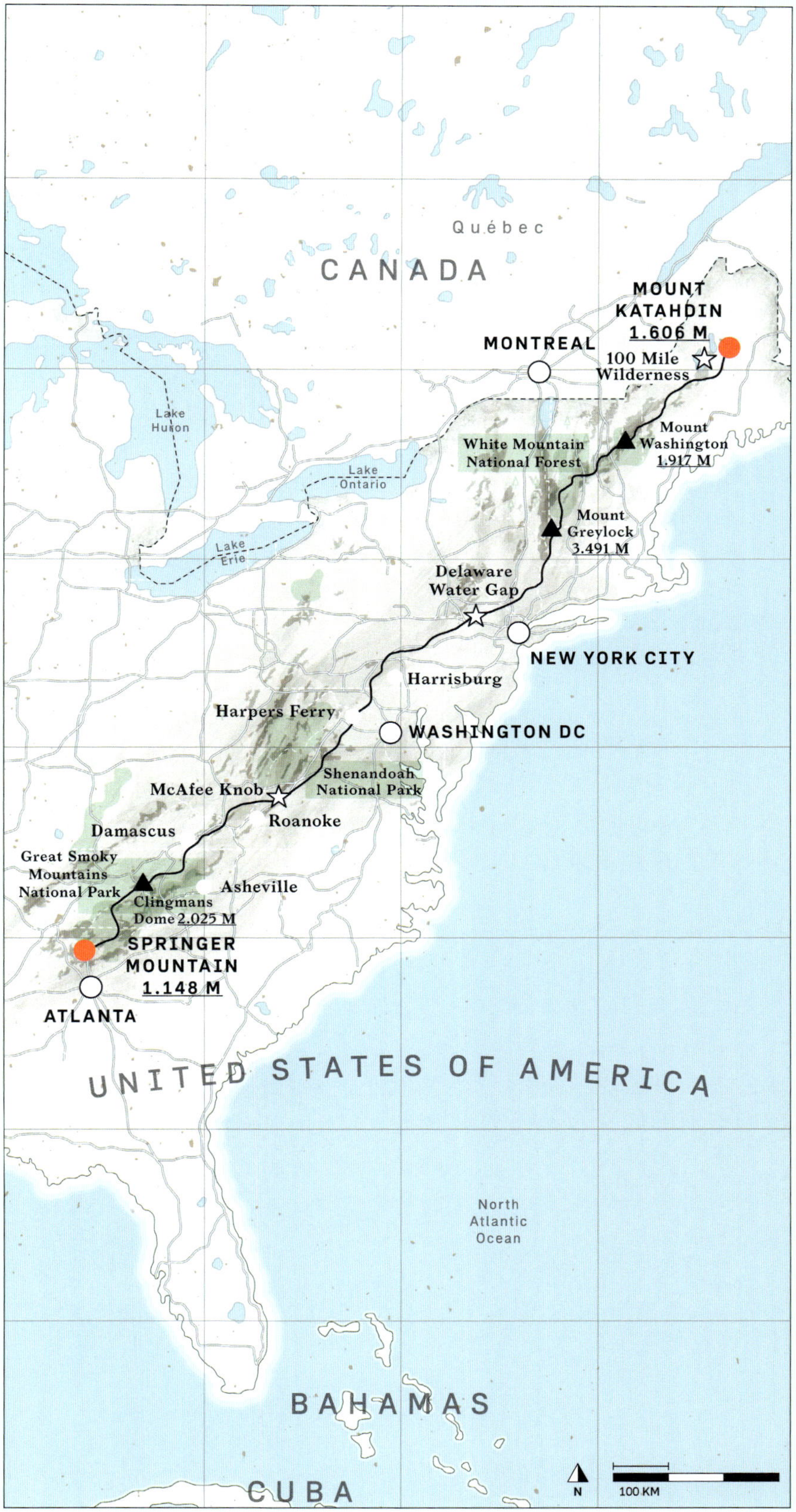

Map labels:

Québec

CANADA

MOUNT KATAHDIN 1.606 M

MONTREAL

100 Mile Wilderness

Mount Washington 1.917 M

White Mountain National Forest

Lake Huron

Lake Ontario

Mount Greylock 3.491 M

Lake Erie

Delaware Water Gap

NEW YORK CITY

Harrisburg

Harpers Ferry

WASHINGTON DC

Shenandoah National Park

McAfee Knob

Roanoke

Damascus

Great Smoky Mountains National Park

Asheville

Clingmans Dome 2.025 M

SPRINGER MOUNTAIN 1.148 M

ATLANTA

UNITED STATES OF AMERICA

North Atlantic Ocean

BAHAMAS

CUBA

N   100 KM

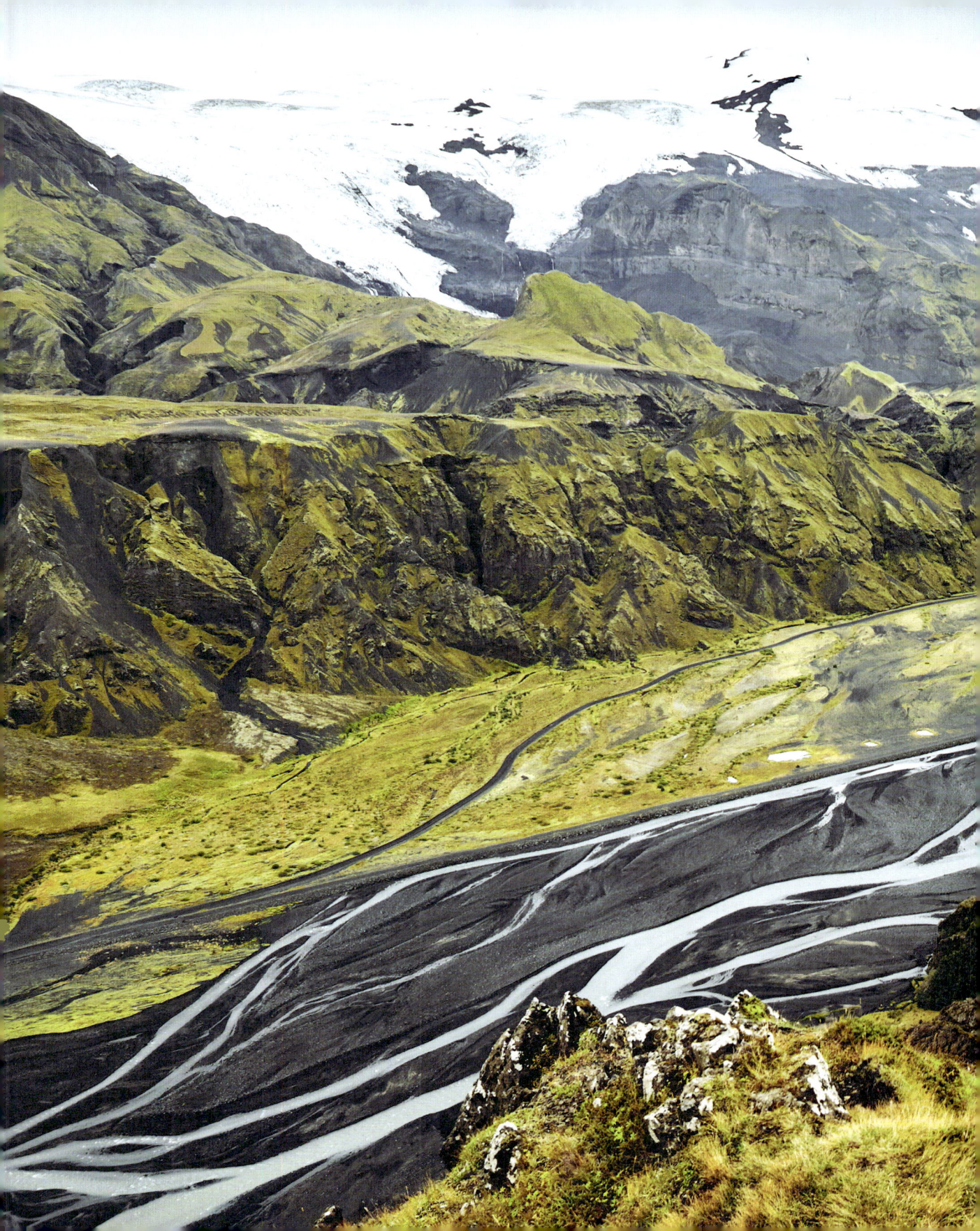

Wanderlust

Hiking on Legendary Trails

This book was conceived, edited, and designed by gestalten.

Edited by **Robert Klanten,** and **Anja Kouznetsova**
With Contributing Editor **Cam Honan**

Introduction by **Robert Moor**
Preface by **Anja Kouznetsova** and **Amy Visram**
Texts by **Cam Honan**
Texts Centerpoint to Big Bluff, South West Coast Path,
Trolltunga as well as fact sheets and captions by
Anja Kouznetsova and **Amy Visram**

Editorial management by **Sina Kernstock**
Copyediting by **Amy Visram**

Design and Layout by **Britta Hinz**
Cover by **Britta Hinz** and **Melanie Ullrich**
Maps by **Bureau Rabensteiner**
Typefaces: Larish Neue by **Radim Peško,**
Zimmer by **Julian Hansen**

Production management by **Vincent Illner**

Cover image by **Daniel Han**
Backcover image by **Jan de Roos**
Flap images by **Stevin Tuchiwsky** (front)
and **Manish Lakhani** (back)

Printed by Printer Trento S.p.A., Trento
Made in Europe

Published by gestalten, Berlin 2026
ISBN 978-3-96704-213-9 New Edition
1st printing, 2026

For more information and to order books, please visit
www.gestalten.com

Die Gestalten Verlag GmbH & Co. KG
Mariannenstrasse 9–10
10999 Berlin, Germany
hello@gestalten.com

Bibliographic information published by the Deutsche
Nationalbibliothek. The Deutsche Nationalbibliothek
lists this publication in the Deutsche Nationalbibliografie;
detailed bibliographic data is available online at
www.dnb.de

This book was printed on paper certified according to the
standards of the FSC®.

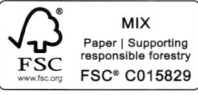

MIX
Paper | Supporting
responsible forestry
FSC® C015829